Learning in Metaverses:

Co-Existing in Real Virtuality

Eliane Schlemmer
UNISINOS – São Leopoldo, Brazil

Luciana Backes
UNILASALLE – Canoas, Brazil

A volume in the Advances in Educational
Technologies and Instructional Design (AETID)
Book Series

Information Science
REFERENCE
An Imprint of IGI Global

Managing Director: Lindsay Johnston
Acquisitions Editor: Kayla Wolfe
Production Editor: Christina Henning
Development Editor: Austin DeMarco
Typesetter: Kaitlyn Kulp
Cover Design: Jason Mull

Published in the United States of America by
    Information Science Reference (an imprint of IGI Global)
    701 E. Chocolate Avenue
    Hershey PA, USA 17033
    Tel: 717-533-8845
    Fax: 717-533-8661
    E-mail: cust@igi-global.com
    Web site: http://www.igi-global.com

                    Library of Congress Cataloging-in-Publication Data

Schlemmer, Eliane.
  Learning in metaverses : co-exisitng in real virtuality / by Eliane Schlemmer and Luciana Backes.
       p. cm.
  Includes bibliographical references and index.
  Summary: "This book discusses a better way to understand this new learning universe, exploring the possibilities of new social organization through the use of avatars in virtual worlds"-- Provided by publisher.
  ISBN 978-1-4666-6351-0 (hardcover) -- ISBN 978-1-4666-6352-7 (ebook) -- ISBN 978-1-4666-6354-1 (print & perpetual access) 1. Information technology--Social aspects. 2. Social networks. 3. Technology and civilization. I. Backes, Luciana, 1971- II. Title.
  HM851.S259 2014
  303.48'3--dc23
                               2014021076

This book is published in the IGI Global book series Advances in Educational Technologies and Instructional Design (AE-TID) (ISSN: 2326-8905; eISSN: 2326-8913).

British Cataloguing in Publication Data
A Cataloguing in Publication record for this book is available from the British Library.

All work contributed to this book is new, previously-unpublished material. The views expressed in this book are those of the authors, but not necessarily of the publisher.

For electronic access to this publication, please contact: eresources@igi-global.com.

Advances in Educational Technologies and Instructional Design (AETID) Book Series

Lawrence A. Tomei
Robert Morris University, USA

ISSN: 2326-8905
EISSN: 2326-8913

MISSION

Education has undergone, and continues to undergo, immense changes in the way it is enacted and distributed to both child and adult learners. From distance education, Massive-Open-Online-Courses (MOOCs), and electronic tablets in the classroom, technology is now an integral part of the educational experience and is also affecting the way educators communicate information to students.

The **Advances in Educational Technologies & Instructional Design (AETID) Book Series** is a resource where researchers, students, administrators, and educators alike can find the most updated research and theories regarding technology's integration within education and its effect on teaching as a practice.

COVERAGE

- Web 2.0 and Education
- Educational Telecommunications
- Game-Based Learning
- Hybrid Learning
- Social Media Effects on Education
- Higher Education Technologies
- Bring-Your-Own-Device
- Curriculum Development
- Online Media in Classrooms
- Virtual School Environments

IGI Global is currently accepting manuscripts for publication within this series. To submit a proposal for a volume in this series, please contact our Acquisition Editors at Acquisitions@igi-global.com or visit: http://www.igi-global.com/publish/.

Titles in this Series

For a list of additional titles in this series, please visit: www.igi-global.com

Intelligent Web-Based English Instruction in Middle Schools
Jiyou Jia (Peking University, China)
Information Science Reference • copyright 2015 • 354pp • H/C (ISBN: 9781466666078) • US $185.00 (our price)

Handbook of Research on Teaching Methods in Language Translation and Interpretation
Ying Cui (Shandong University, Weihai, China) and Wei Zhao (Shandong University, Weihai, China)
Information Science Reference • copyright 2015 • 504pp • H/C (ISBN: 9781466666153) • US $325.00 (our price)

Methodologies for Effective Writing Instruction in EFL and ESL Classrooms
Rahma Al-Mahrooqi (Sultan Qaboos University, Oman) Vijay Singh Thakur (Dhofar University, Oman) and Adrian Roscoe (Sultan Qaboos University, Oman)
Information Science Reference • copyright 2015 • 348pp • H/C (ISBN: 9781466666191) • US $185.00 (our price)

Student-Teacher Interaction in Online Learning Environments
Robert D. Wright (University of North Texas, USA)
Information Science Reference • copyright 2015 • 450pp • H/C (ISBN: 9781466664616) • US $185.00 (our price)

Cases on Technology Integration in Mathematics Education
Drew Polly (University of North Carolina at Charlotte, USA)
Information Science Reference • copyright 2015 • 521pp • H/C (ISBN: 9781466664975) • US $200.00 (our price)

Promoting Global Literacy Skills through Technology-Infused Teaching and Learning
Jared Keengwe (University of North Dakota, USA) Justus G. Mbae (Catholic University of Eastern Africa, Kenya) and Simon K. Ngigi (Catholic University of Eastern Africa, Kenya)
Information Science Reference • copyright 2015 • 347pp • H/C (ISBN: 9781466663473) • US $185.00 (our price)

Learning in Metaverses Co-Existing in Real Virtuality
Eliane Schlemmer (Gpe-dU UNISINOS - CNPq, Brazil) and Luciana Backes (Gpe-dU UNISINOS - CNPq, Brazil)
Information Science Reference • copyright 2015 • 351pp • H/C (ISBN: 9781466663510) • US $180.00 (our price)

Cases on Research-Based Teaching Methods in Science Education
Eugene de Silva (Virginia Research Institute, USA & MRAS - Walters State Community College, USA)
Information Science Reference • copyright 2015 • 425pp • H/C (ISBN: 9781466663756) • US $195.00 (our price)

Tablets in K-12 Education Integrated Experiences and Implications

www.igi-global.com

701 E. Chocolate Ave., Hershey, PA 17033
Order online at www.igi-global.com or call 717-533-8845 x100
To place a standing order for titles released in this series, contact: cust@igi-global.com
Mon-Fri 8:00 am - 5:00 pm (est) or fax 24 hours a day 717-533-8661

We dedicate this work to our fathers: Nilson Luiz Schlemmer and João Frederico Backes.

Nilson Luiz Schlemmer has dedicated his life to education and cooperation. His way of living and sharing and of being in the world have deeply marked him. My father frequently stated, "I am what I am, but I am not always the same," evidencing the importance of having values that steer our lives. At the same time, he reminds us of the timeless time, of the flow of space in which we move on and, therefore, as beings of moving relations, we are constantly in the learning and changing process. He would also say, "the one who cooperates, grows," evidencing that we are stronger and better when we share, recognize the other as legitimate in the interaction, and when we build together.

João Frederico Backes, Geography Teacher, has helped me to understand space as a relational reality, in other words, that everything is related through interaction among men, women, nature, culture, history, society, and work. He saw no difference between the men and women he lived with. He was a man of all times and spaces, my forever inspiration. He was the one who introduced me to Milton Santos. He has always believed in a more human and fair world. Mateus da Rosa, his student at Presidente Castelo Branco State School – in Lajeado, RS, Brazil, had posted on Facebook, "You have thought us not only Geography, but made us know the world...," Carlos Augusto Portela, his student, in the same space had also registered, "Reaching the stars is not easy, but if I ask you, you will teach me the best way!" He was a teacher who had turned his life into a big classroom to all of us. So, having lived with a teacher allows me, today, to identify the complex movements we live in the contemporaneity, called sociality, by Maffesoli (1998).

This way, the fact of having lived values like that, in the complex dynamic of our space of daily living makes us understand, with Nilson Luiz Schlemmer and João Frederico Backes that it is possible to build a society lined by mutual respect, internal solidarity, and cooperation capable of providing everyone's development, and therefore, leading to a more sustainable and supportive growth.

Both are great poets, who recreate life through us and everyone who they live and share with (wives, children, sons-in-law, daughters-in-law, grandchildren, students, work colleagues, friends, neighbors).

But beyond that...

Nilson Luiz Schlemmer and João Frederico Backes, beloved and loving fathers, are among us, lively as ever. People, like them, will never die, they simply change plans, dimension. Their presence is so strong, remarkable, and good that even when physically distant, we are able to feel.

We understand that we are a little or a lot from them: gens, blood, values, principles, and character. This way, their lives live within us and through us, making us think that:

We will always be together!

Table of Contents

Foreword

As a basic element instigator of reflection on learning in virtual worlds one can pose the question: "Why are virtual worlds growing in importance and may these solutions represent a strategy to improve learning quality?"

Starting a reflection on these issues, it is worth analyzing some perceived shortcomings in the educational scenario. A general finding is that one thing missing in education nowadays is the capacity to prepare individuals able to find solutions for faced problems using all the knowledge and technology available today. Even in countries where the use of technology permeates society more intensely, there are concerns of education authorities in preparing the future citizens of the 21st century for the use of computer applications in everyday life, finding and using information necessary to support the most varied decision making processes. The ultimate goal is to enable problem solving situations as they are introduced using the available resources. This involves formulating hypotheses on the basis of the obtained information and experience courses of action that may or may not lead to desired results. This pattern of behavior can and should be encouraged throughout formal education, but unfortunately has been used instead as a more directive approach by educators and a more passive role on the part of students.

When searching for conditions for this more investigative educational approach, based on experimentation, there is a perceived gap recognized in schools and even in universities regarding the lack of laboratories, especially for science learning. This situation severely limits the ability to use a non-directive in place of an overly theoretical approach since the possibility of experimentation is not possible due to lack of conditions. Reason derives from insufficient equipment, materials, and even space for conducting an experiment, even with no specialized features. In some cases, experiments cannot be performed because the risks for students, for the environment, or even in terms of cost of resources. Thus, although there is consensus that the experimental activity is essential to the teaching and learning of science, it seems that in the school environment, this is one of the activities that has little chance of being done. Considering the constructivist learning proposal as the development of knowledge being a result of interaction with the environment, this gap becomes more critical because it implies smaller conditions and opportunities for students to participate in an active learning process.

When analyzing the availability of the computer lab in schools, the situation is slightly more favorable once a good percentage of the schools have some computer infrastructure and Internet access.

On the other hand, it is also widely known that the student population in the country currently has enough level of information literacy. Given the state of the resource availability of computing in schools and the level of information literacy of students, one can see that it has opened a window of opportunity to alleviate the situation of using information technology and communication. Current use of computers by students is mostly dedicated to conducting research, carrying out school homework, answering lessons and exercises proposed by the teacher, play educational games, prepare presentations for colleagues, learning to use the computer and the Internet, and interacting with the teacher. But there is growing realization and demonstration that there is a fairly wide range of new strategies for the use of computers in education, and the virtual world is one alternative, offering a new learning space that starts to become viable.

Technological development and the rapid increase in computer processing power has led to the possibility of deployment of virtual reality based on desktop computers or other devices accessible to students, in school or home. The availability of a high speed Internet connection further increases the use of virtual reality technology enabling user collaboration in an immersive virtual environment. Although virtual environments based on desktop computers failed to provide a totally immersive experience as in more complex environments involving caves and specific hardware for visualization, the quality and realism achieved with the graphical resources available in desktop computing is sufficient to increase student motivation in the educational use of these resources.

The potential of virtual world technologies to improve the quality of teaching and learning has been increasingly recognized by researchers of education. In recent years, there has been a growing number of studies examining the impact of virtual worlds on student learning and achievement in different areas, and the adoption of immersive virtual environments in education grows as a result of these factors. Consequently, the work done by researchers like Eliane Schlemmer and Luciana Backer is especially relevant because they discuss aspects of immersion, telepresence, and interactivity as an educational resource. Their research and the experimentation developed bring new benefits to using virtual worlds as an educational resource and will certainly help to speed up the assimilation of this new technology strategy as an educational resource with qualitative and quantitative benefits in terms of increased learning quality.

Liane Margarida Rockenbach Tarouco
Federal University of Rio Grande do Sul, Brazil

Liane Margarida Rockenbach Tarouco is a Full Professor at Federal University of Rio Grande do Sul in Porto Alegre, Brazil. She is the Director at the Interdisciplinary Center for Studies on Technology in Education / University Federal Rio Grande Sul. She is a researcher at the Graduate Program in Computer Science at and Computers on Education at Federal University of Rio Grande do Sul. She is chairperson of the chapter Brazil-Argentina-Uruguay in Immersive Education Initiative.

Preface

This book represents an intellectual partnership between the authors that began in the year 2000 with the Pilot Projects in the Virtual Learning Environment – AVA-UNISINOS. It was here that Eliane Schlemmer, concept maker of this digital technology, and Luciana Backes, as a participant of the pilot-project, through the postgraduate program in applied social sciences, effectively began an intense interaction process. Their partnership evolved into *"Construção de Mundos Virtuais para a Capacitação a Distância"* (*"Construction of Virtual Worlds for Distance Capacitation"*) and intensified with the creation of the Digital Education Research Group – GPe-dU UNISINOS/CNPq in 2004. It subsequently developed further with Luciana Backes entering the Masters in Education, followed by the Doctorate in Education, both Programs of the Postgraduate in Education at UNISINOS, under Eliane Schlemmer's mentoring. During this period, the authors have taken part in several research projects, which are theoretically systematized in this book and presented in Chapter 15, "Brazilian Experiences in Metaverse."

Within this context, and in the flow of our constitution as professor-researchers, we exchange and share interests, ideas, knowledge, experiences, and construct research practices (in a movement of experiencing the research) related to Education in Digital Culture, more specifically regarding Web 3D technologies – Metaverses, under the perspective of Hybridism and Multimodality. This collaboration between the researchers is based on the perspective of nomadic hybridism and multimodality, in the coexistence of physical face-to-face worlds—analogical and digital virtual worlds—in an extension of culture that reaches Digital Virtual Culture – or even a (meta)culture. From this context emerge actions, relations, and interactions between subjects that share their living and sharing in Metaverses, through the creation of Digital Virtual Worlds in 3D. In this way, more intense theoretical-practical-methodological connections and closeness are translated into a collaborative and cooperative construction, and this work is an example of its results.

This book represents a turning point that consolidates our research in the context of the Digital Education Research Group – GPe-dU UNISINOS/CNPq, which up until the present has mainly been concerned with the theme of "Metaverse Learning" in higher education and postgraduate settings. It is important to note that when developing Metaverse research, especially with Second Life, there are many aspects, regarding the basic educational context, that deserve the attention of researchers. These were not dealt with in this work as they did not match the target group for the research we have been carrying out in the Digital Education Research Group – GPe-dU UNISINOS/CNPq so far. One such aspect refers to the presence of adult content on a different island, which is easily reachable the moment an avatar logs in.

The theme of "Metaverse" arose at the end of the 20th century, at the heart of the movement and of techno-scientific dynamics, with the development and the power of network connection systems, and is therefore associated with a virtualization process. In order to better understand how Metaverses arise, we need to look at history. Metaverse technology currently constitutes new possibilities for the teaching and learning processes, including telepresence and digital virtual presence (through an avatar) of their members in shaped spaces in three dimensions, in a timeless time and in a space of flow of digital virtual nature. This new possibility can configure itself as innovation, linked to pedagogical practices that contribute to the teaching and learning processes.

In this sense, we demonstrate that pedagogical practices based on an epistemological interactionist/constructivist/systemic conception provide experiences in living and collaborating, disturbances and problematization, socialization of representation of perceptions, and the construction of knowledge in a collaborative and cooperative way, fostering the development of a new network learning. Within this movement, we have identified newly emerging paradigms that are coming to the fore. From movement and dynamic perspectives, we have developed an interdisciplinary reflection, based on the theories developed by sociologists such as Castells, Sousa Santos, Maffesoli, Lemos; by biologists in the field of human development, such as Piaget, Maturana, Varela; geography professors, represented by Santos; philosophers, represented by Lévy; educators, such as Freire, Becker, and Moraes; physicists, such as Capra; educators in informatics, like Primo; among many others quoted in this book.

We consider it important to highlight that this interdisciplinary context has been configured because when we started the research in this area there were almost no theories investigating learning in Metaverses using the perspectives of Genetic Epistemology developed by Jean Piaget, the Biology of Learning by Humberto Maturana and Francisco Varela, and the Biology of Love by Humberto Maturana. The use of these epistemologies/theories as our main theoretical grounding is due to their conceptual strength and the fact that they appeared before theories on Metaverse Technology in Education, and therefore need testing in current contexts.

We do not therefore mean to disregard epistemologies/theories so far constructed, but to give them new meaning, through research, aiming to comprehend the changes in learning, when human beings form their thoughts from a new language, the digital language. It is about understanding how living and collaborating take place, including learning, on a daily basis.

More and more often, we understand the movements of humanity from a holistic view, through systemic thinking, from the self-eco-organizing conception, based in the complexity paradigm. As a result, we need to reflect on the educational context embedded in the social context. Castells has contributed to a reflection on currently established relations between people constituted through digital technologies present in the network society.

It is with great satisfaction, then, that we present our book, *Learning in Metaverses: Co-Existing in Real Virtuality*, in which we share our daily living and sharing with some temporary certainty we have been constructing along our path as researcher-professors, and equally some temporary doubts arising from this process. We therefore invite you to join us in this research space, reflecting, dialoguing, along with other researchers we quote throughout the work who have helped us to better understand this new learning universe in Metaverse. We hope your reading will bring you moments of satisfaction, unease, and the desire to know more, opening up the imagination and creating and innovating activity.

To start with, the teaching and learning processes in the Network Society context are approached in Chapter 1, "Teaching and Learning in the Networked Society." We present and discuss subtopics such as: Networked Society; Information and Knowledge; Teaching, Learning, and Development; and the "Homo Zappiens" Generation; with a brief conclusion to the chapter.

In Chapter 2, "Network Learning Culture and the Emerging Paradigm," we approach the need for developing a network learning culture from the perspective of an emerging paradigm in relation to Teaching and Learning in the Network Society. We present and discuss subtopics such as: Emerging Paradigm: Reflections on Reality; Systemic Thinking and Complexity: The Emerging Paradigm; Epistemological Conceptions; The Culture of Network Learning, as well as a brief conclusion to the chapter.

In Chapter 3, "The Metaverse: 3D Digital Virtual Worlds," we approach the arousal of Metaverse technologies in their 3D Digital Virtual World as a possibility that arises in the context of network learning culture, from the perspective of an emerging paradigm, linked to Teaching and Learning in Network Society. We present and discuss subtopics like: Metaverse Technology and the Nature of 3D Digital Virtual Worlds; Second Life Metaverse; Open Source Metaverse; Metaverses on Mobile Devices: Potentials for Mobile Learning; as well as a brief conclusion to the chapter.

In Chapter 4, "Avatar: Building a 'Digital Virtual Self,'" we approach the emergence of the technologicized body, from the perspective of the constitution of a digital virtual identity, the avatar, which appears linked to Metaverse technology, in the construction of 3D Digital Virtual World. We present and discuss subtopics such as: Avatar: A Technologicized Body; The Construction of a Digital Virtual Identity; Avatar: The Representation/Action of the "Digital Virtual Self" through the Technologicized Body; as well as a brief conclusion to the chapter.

In Chapter 5, "Immersion, Telepresence, and Digital Virtual Presence in Metaverses," we approach Immersion, Telepresence, and Digital Virtual Presence in Metaverses (this latest one being a theoretical construction coming from the context of the research developed by GPe-dU UNISINOS/CNPq), possibilities that come from the action and interaction of avatars in 3D Digital Virtual Worlds constructed in Metaverses. We present and discuss subtopics such as: Presence and Proximity; Relational Presence and Social Presence; Telepresence and Digital Virtual Presence; Immersion and Tele-immersion; as well as a brief conclusion to the chapter.

In Chapter 6, "Interaction and Interactivity in Metaverse," we approach the perspective of the interaction potential that appears from the interactivity provided in the Metaverse technology, which is connected to Immersion, Telepresence, and Digital Virtual Presence in Metaverses. We present and discuss subtopics such as: Conceptualizing Interaction and Interactivity; Mutual Interaction and Reactive Interaction; Type of Interaction; Languages and Interaction/Interactivity Forms in Metaverse; as well as a brief conclusion to the chapter.

In Chapter 7, "Autopoietic Machines and Alopoietic Machines: The Structural Coupling," we discuss the context of autopoietic and alopoietic machines, from the perspective of structural coupling that appears in interaction and interactivity in Metaverse. We present and discuss subtopics such as: Autopoietic Machines: Human Beings; Alopoietic Machines: The Nature of the Metaverse; Structural Coupling; Language: The Mode of Speech and Emotion; as well as a brief conclusion to the chapter.

In Chapter 8, "Cognition and Socio-Cognition in Metaverse," we approach different cognitive and socio-cognitive mechanisms that appear in the interaction between subject-avatars and the 3D Digital Virtual World constructed in Metaverses. We present and discuss subtopics such as: Human Cognition; Perception and Representation; Doing, Understanding and Awareness in Metaverse; Collaboration and Cooperation; as well as a brief conclusion to the chapter.

In Chapter 9, "Online Education in Metaverse: Novelty or Innovation?" we approach the perspective of Online Education in Metaverse, from the tensioning between what characterizes a novelty and what characterizes an innovation in education. We present and discuss subtopics such as: Learning Contexts in Metaverse; Methodologies in Metaverse; Pedagogical Intervention in Metaverse; Novelty or Innovation? as well as a brief conclusion to the chapter.

In Chapter 10, "Digital Virtual Communities in Metaverse," we approach the process of constituting Digital Virtual Communities in Metaverse. We present and discuss subtopics such as: Communities: Historical and Conceptual Aspects and Characteristics; Digital Virtual Learning Communities; Digital Virtual Communites of Pratice; Digital Virtual Learning and Practice Communities; Digital Virtual Learning and Practice Communities in Metaverses; as well as a brief conclusion to the chapter.

In Chapter 11, "The Real Virtuality of Metaverses," we approach the Real Virtuality theme that appears in the construction processes of 3D Digital Virtual World in Metaverses. We present and discuss subtopics such as: Virtuality and Reality: Virtual Reality Experiences and Real Virtuality Experiences in Immersive Learning; The Simultaneity of Worlds: Spaces of Digital Virtual Association, Spaces of Association, and Multimodal Hybrids; The Culture of Real Virtuality; as well as a brief conclusion to the chapter.

In Chapter 12, "Digital Virtual Sharing Spaces," we approach the constitution of the Digital Virtual Coexistence Space that happens from the digital technological hybridism and the interaction processes between subject-avatars themselves, and with 3D Digital Virtual Worlds constructed in Metaverses. We present and discuss subtopics such as: Digital Virtual Life? Digital Virtual Space of Sharing and/or Sharing of a Digital Virtual Nature? Configuration of the Digital Virtual Sharing Space: Society Networking in the Era of Avatars; as well as a brief conclusion to the chapter.

In Chapter 13, "Digital Virtual Culture in Metaverse: The Metaculture?" we approach the theme of Culture in Metaverse as a Digital Virtual Culture and as the Metaculture. We present and discuss subtopics such as: Digital Virtual Culture; Digital Virtual Culture in Metaverse; Metaculture Formation in Virtual Digital Coexistence in Metaverse; as well as a brief conclusion to the chapter.

In Chapter 14, "Nomadic Hybridism," we approach the perspective of Nomadic Hybridism that appears from the interaction of subject-avatars as digital technologies, mainly with the Metaverse technology, in a space of flow. We present and discuss subtopics such as: Space of Flows, Nomadism and Interculturalism; Digital Virtual Nomadism or Metanomadism; as well as a brief conclusion to the chapter.

To finish, in Chapter 15, "Brazilian Experiences in Metaverse," we present and discuss some experiences, linked to the research, which were developed in Brazil from the use of different technologies in Metaverses. We present and discuss subtopics such as: AWSINOS: A World of Learning; UNISINOS Island; RICESU Island; as well as a brief conclusion to the chapter.

In this way, we would like to call your attention to the fact that we, professors, constitute our ontogeny from our action and interaction within a physical presential world, analogical, and therefore we are part of the "analogical generation" in a process of naturalization into the digital world. Therefore, it is natural that for us it seems quite strange to create an avatar and with it make part of the 3D Digital Virtual World, acting and interacting with others avatars present in this same world (belonging to the Metaverse domain) and through this discover new forms of social organization. However, for the current digital, hybrid, and nomadic generation, this common practice is part of their routine, where they use different digital technologies, among them several types of Metaverses. In this new possibility, we also discover that it is possible to meet friends, search information, and share interests, ideas, experiences, live challenges, in other words learn and live.

It is also important to reflect on the fact that a little more than two decades ago we could never have imagined what the Internet has become and what it represents to the current society. Today, the Web 3D is already a reality and is becoming an interface as common as the 2D interface was; however, it allows us, among many other things, something that is our main interest: learning experiences and immersive and interactive practice of another nature.

Within this context, you might have thought, What should I do? We understand that observing tendencies, as an augmented reality, a mingled reality, the Internet, experimenting with the Web 3D (both in fixed and mobile devices), participating in meetings and digital virtual events using avatars, is a good initiative for those willing to learn more about these "new worlds." Paraphrasing Maturana and Varela (2002), living is learning and knowing.

We believe that these technologies and the emergent paradigm, being constructed in living through the Web 3D, represent a significant contribution to this generation's education, a generation that is digital, hybrid, nomadic, and that is currently at university, and in a short time will also be in the labor market.

This new reality, which is constituted based on the way of being in this generation's world, its necessities, new ways of learning, building relationships, working, thinking, which develop with and from the use of different digital technologies, represent to us a significant challenge in educating, forming, training, and qualifying, as well as providing new ways of working. This challenge implies combining the archaic and the contemporaneous: for Maffesoli (2012), based on Morin (2007), when they suggest we dialogue about the new and the old without exclusion.

3D Internet is opening doors to a new world of experiences in learning and professional practice, connected to new ways of social organization, possible through living and sharing in digital virtual spaces. Everything is being constructed at this very moment by millions of people spread throughout the world.

Beyond platforms like ActiveWorlds, Second Life, OpenSimulator, OpenWonderland, Could Party, Minecraft, among many others, which are transitory, there are the concepts of Web 3D, Metaverse, 3D Digital Virtual World, Digital Virtual Collaborating Space, Hybrid Living and Sharing Spaces (which integrate different digital technologies, including the Mobile, Wireless, and Analogical ones), and Multimodal (involving the physical presential and digital virtual modalities – mobile learning, ubiquitous learning, immersive learning), Gamification, ARG (Alternate Reality Game), Mixed Reality, and Augmented Reality. These are precisely the concepts we need to dedicate our attention to and from them construct new possibilities for education in this historical time and social space.

Eliane Schlemmer
UNISINOS - São Leopoldo, Brazil

Luciana Backes
UNILASALLE - Canoas, Brazil
São Leopoldo, Brazil, December 30, 2013

REFERENCES

Maffesoli, M. (2012). *O tempo retorna: Formas elementares da pós-modernidade*. Rio de Janeiro, Brazil: Forense Universitária.

Maturana, H. R., & Varela, F. J. (2002). *A árvore do conhecimento: As bases biológicas da compreensão humana*. São Paulo, Brazil: Palas Athena.

Morin, E. (2007). *Introdução ao pensamento complexo*. Porto Alegre, Brazil: Sulina.

Acknowledgment

Firstly, we thank the agencies of research foment in Brazil, especially the National Board of the Scientific and Technological Development, the Coordination and Improvement of Higher Education People, and the Foundation to Research Support of the State Rio Grande do Sul, which, through loans, have supported the development of research that made it possible for us to write and publish this book.

We thank the Universidade do Vale do Rio dos Sinos (UNISINOS), an institution of education and research enabling in all dimensions the accomplishment of the research projects originating this work.

We thank the Centro Universitário La Salle – UNILASALLE and the Catholic Higher Education Institutions Network (*Comitê Gestor da Rede de Instituições Católicas de Ensino Superior* – RICESU) which congregates 13 institutions of the Catholic network of higher education institutions throughout Brazil with whom we have accomplished an important development and research project linked to the theme originating this book.

We would like to thank the whole team of the Digital Education Reseach Group (GPe-dU – UNISINOS/CNPq), coordinated by Professor Eliane Schlemmer, who gathers students from different areas of knowledge who are beginners in the research world, who had important participation in the investigations giving origin to this book, specially to Frederico Andros da Silva, Carine Barcellos Duarte, Deise Tavares Del Sent, Patricia Silva Smurra Frank, Helena Cristina Martelete Soares, Bruno de Faria Bandeira, Luis Fernando Bang dos Santos, Helder Bruno Pinto Ferreira, Felipe Borges de Oliveira, Herbert Spindola Schaefer, Glauco do Amaral Schiefelbein, Christoffer James de Oliveira, Lucas Schlupp, Jonathan Pinto Sperafico, Orlando João Borges Junior Botelho, Pablo Garcia, Jacson Müller Correia, Jodélle Chagas Machado, Lara Cristina Pereira Dourado Laux, Gláucia Silva da Rosa, Wylliam Spindola Hossein, Henrique Fagundes Machado, Marina da Rocha, Norton Neves, Alisson Daniel Gesat Farias, Felipe Marques Berquo Ramos, Daiana Trein, Alessandra J. Marangoni Moita, and Ederson Locatelli, as well as the scholar of Science Initiation Silvana Maria Pferl – UNILASALLE. To all these, we give a sincere thank you.

Finally, we thank everyone who triggered us, guided us, and supported us in the development of this book.

Eliane Schlemmer
UNISINOS - São Leopoldo, Brazil

Luciana Backes
UNILASALLE - Canoas, Brazil
São Leopoldo, Brazil, December 30, 2013

Chapter 1
Teaching and Learning in the Networked Society

ABSTRACT

This chapter presents and discusses some concepts that will contribute to a reflection on how to teach and how to learn in a Networked Digital Virtual Society. The authors present and discuss subtopics like Networked Society; Information and Knowledge; Teaching, Learning, and Development (What is information? What is learning? How do we learn? What is knowledge? How do we know? What is development? How does knowledge differ from learning and from information?); "Homo Zappiens" Generation (Who are they and how does the digital-native "Homo Zappiens" Generation learn? And how can we, teachers and professors from the analogical generation, become "digitally naturalized"?); and a brief conclusion, where the authors present some factors that can contribute to minimizing the "gap" between generations, bringing them together for the construction of a dialogical relationship in education.

INTRODUCTION

Researchers have been investigating social changes and transformations in order to analyze, understand and explain the society we are living in. This scenario has recently brought out various terms such as: "Information Society", "Knowledge Society", "Digital Society" and, "Network Society" among others. Nevertheless the way these designations have been used and understood shows a lack of common sense for it depends on the theoretical construction presented by different authors. When analyzing the terms "information" and "knowledge", for instance, we see that they are attributed a variety of meanings. From our point of view, what best defines the society in which we are currently sharing and living in, would be a "Digital-Virtual Networked Society". But what are the arguments to support this denomination?

Nowadays we are living and acting through different digital-virtual network technologies, meaning that we are living our lives through digital-virtual technologies in a variety of domains linked to work, study, leisure, business or relationships for example. In these different domains we build up networks or take part in virtual communities which connect us to other people. We have virtual friends, virtual work and virtual relationships. We buy, sell, study, research and play in a new context, both analogue and digital.

DOI: 10.4018/978-1-4666-6351-0.ch001

Nevertheless, more important than classifying or attributing a denomination to the type of society we are living in, is to understand the movements and processes it constitutes. In this context we are particularly interested in the movements and processes related to the following questions: What does teaching in a "Digital-Virtual Networked Society" mean? What has changed from the time we were children and adolescents? What implications does living in a growing digital-virtual-technological world bring to parents, teachers and to their own subjects? Why is it that we are observing more and more confused parents not knowing how to educate their children; more unmotivated teachers, with no desire or courage to enter a classroom and children, adolescents and teenagers stating they do not enjoy attending classes? What is this new subject and how do these new learners, these "digital natives", learn? (Prensky, 2002), belonging to the "homo zappiens" generation? (Veen & Vrakking, 2009) How are the concepts of information, knowledge, teaching, learning and development understood nowadays? These issues represent part of the challenges that have presented themselves and what the current reality dictates within educational research, something we will discuss further in this chapter.

Living in a growing "technological" world, where different people live and coexist in a digital-virtual way and are connected by different networks, brings important consequences which represent huge challenges for the teaching and learning processes, both in formal and informal educational contexts. Educating in the current connected, digital networked society where people have easy and quick access to a wide range of information, and also communicate with anyone, anywhere and at any time is significantly different in comparison to the way we were educated; a society in which relationships and interactions were prevailingly established by analogical means; where searching for information could require one to physically go to the nearest library or bookstore to purchase a book, magazine or newspaper and

where communication with physically distant people was done through correspondence or telephone. Digital technology has evolved in such a way that it shortens distances and approaches for people who now live in the instant. Society has changed and it is no longer possible for schools to keep following the industrial society model and inspired by the Fordist model. According to Moraes (2003), this new reality not only plays a part in ways of working in education but it also affects the ways in which a person is enabled to live in this society, in the world of work and within a continuous learning process. Traditional social practices, working relations and professional learning and development have also been rapidly modified.

This new reality within which we are embedded presents new challenges to institutions, parents and teachers – all new, digital immigrants. It demands an approach that makes use of different types of digital technologies so that we are able to understand them regarding their specific nature, their potential, their limits and especially the danger surrounding their use, which it is crucial to understand when raising children's, teenagers' and adolescents' awareness. There is no way to retreat from the evolution of digital technology and there is no way to stop our children using such technologies for they are part of our world, they are part of our lives and interactions. The school we have today is undergoing a structural, organizational, administrative and process-related crisis, including syllabus creation and development. There is unsteadiness in relation to the world and the current speed of society. The paradigm nowadays, basing the methodologies, practices and pedagogical mediation processes we have been building up over time cannot withstand the needs of these new learning subjects. Thus, educating in the networked digital virtual society presents the need to reflect on the changes that are happening in this society's and people's different living situations. To rethink the dominant paradigms, to search for new understanding about how to learn and how to teach in a world where our children, teenagers and adolescents live lives linked by different information and communication networks, in which interaction and interactivity are made more easy. This requires the rethinking of current formal educational systems.

In this chapter we will present and discuss some concepts, which will contribute to the reflection on how to teach and how to learn in a Networked Digital Virtual Society.

NETWORKED SOCIETY

Can we state that the social and cultural changes we are undergoing are derived from the societal-technological movement? And in this sense, isn't it true that technology presents characteristics which depend on technological creation, and does the way it is used trigger the development of a certain culture or society, meaning that this society may need to develop new tools which spread a specific way of thinking?

Starting with the changes in the *"homo socius"* new way of living and to exemplify what we are saying, I invite you to think about what we mean when we refer to society. Before the Internet, having "virtual friends" meant having "imaginary friends", those ones almost every child has at a certain stage during childhood. To follow a person used to mean a physical displacement in time and space to literally follow, or go after, a certain person. To take part in a community meant to participate in a group of people with objectives in common and who, again, physically met at a determined time and in ordinary places. To meet people, to make friends, to date, meaning building up all kinds of relationships, necessarily implied going towards the other through some kind of physical displacement in the geographical space of a physical world.

But what has changed since the dawn of the Internet and its tools, such as instant messaging, social networks, and the metaverse, among oth-

ers? *"Homo socius"* has changed, society has changed, and having "virtual friends" today may mean having friends spread all over the planet, friends who we know only by their texts, voices, photos, videos, and even only by their avatars. We may follow not only one but several people on Twitter. We take part in all kinds of digital-virtual societies, from those concerning relationships, to learning, working, leisure, hobbies, sports or any specific subject in which we may be interested. Therefore, the way we meet people, make friends and maintain relationships as well as the way we study, work, do our shopping or do business - meaning the way we live in different instances - has significantly changed. We are now living within a society interconnected by a telecommunication services infrastructure and by different Digital Technologies, which we come across every day, modifying the way of living in a variety of spaces and societal domains and being modified by them. These Digital Technologies provide communication and interaction between people, enabling access to different means and sources of information, enhancing the exchange of information and experiences, ideas and knowledge. They favor collaborative production and socialization of information almost instantaneously, at any time, in any space, which has significantly contributed to the rise of an ever-growing "technology" and connected society and that has brought about the use of new expressions such as the "Information Society", "Knowledge Society", "Digital Society", "Network Society" and "Cyber Society".

All these changes in the *homo socius'* way of living are made possible through the development of different digital-virtual technologies - the product of this same society - making it easier to aggregate new possibilities, to communicate between different services, to develop new digital technologies and which feed the changes happening in different spaces at a speed hitherto thought inconceivable. In this way we create a constant and growing feedback cycle, encouraging the outbreak of new ways of social organizations and sociability, contributing to the rethinking of paradigms, making room for new ones (such as the complex-systemic paradigm) and new or "fuzzy'" logics. Thus, borders and limits are becoming more permeable which contributes to the rise of new understandings of broader and exponentially enlarged meanings, contributing to the renewed significance of ideas such as community, presence, distance, territory, space, environment, place, real, virtual and living, amongst others.

To help us understand this current society, as well as its social changing processes we are living in, we have looked at arguments by the Spanish sociologist and researcher Manuel Castells. A little over a decade ago the author had already stated that a technological revolution, centered on Information and Communication technologies, was reshaping society's base material at a speed so far unimagined. He mentions the intense and growing movement of interactive computer networks, which favor the creation of new communication channels, designing life whilst also being designed by it. Nevertheless, according to him,

technology does not determine society. It also does not draw up the course of technological changes once many factors, including creativity and entrepreneurial initiatives interfere with the scientific discovery process, technological innovation and social applications in a way that the final result depends on a complex interactive pattern. In fact, the dilemma of technological determinism is probably a baseless problem, since technology is the society, and thus society cannot be understood or represented by technological tools. (Castells, 1999, p.25)

For Castells (1999), the way society takes and controls these technologies is what drives its destiny. Although it may not determine historical evolution and social changes, technology, or the lack of it encourages a society's capacity-changing

ability as well as the uses society decides to give to its technological potential, even in a conflicting process.

According to the author, in this current age, functions and dominating processes are becoming more and more organized as networks. These networks are part of a new social morphology in our society and the propagation of the network logics modifies significantly the operation and the results from the productive processes of experiences, power and culture. A new paradigm of information technology is the base material for the networks to spread throughout the social structure. The power of flows is more important than the flows of power, in a way that the presence or absence of the network and the dynamics of one network in relation to another, are decisive sources of domination and transformation in our society: a networked society. In this networked society the room for flows and an atemporal time are essential bases for a new culture that goes beyond and includes a variety of representation systems, historically transmitted: the culture of real virtuality.

Castells (1999) tells us we are seeing and living the appearance of a new social structure connected to the emergence of a new way of development: informationalism. This informational way of development is constituted by the appearance of a new technological paradigm based on information technology. In an informational way of development, the productivity source relies on the technologies of knowledge generation, information processing and the communication of icons. The search for knowledge and information is what characterizes the function of technological production within informationalism. The specific aspect in the informational way of development is the knowledge of actions upon knowledge itself as the main productivity source. This way, what portrays the current technological revolution is not the centralized knowledge and information but its application in generating new knowledge and the instruments of information processing and communication, thus creating a cumulative feedback cycle between innovation and its use. This feedback cycle between the introduction of a new technology, its uses and development in different domains, takes place at a very fast speed in this new paradigm.

The feedback concept appears as one of the key concepts in the work of Jean Piaget, Edgar Morin and Humberto Maturana. For Maturana, feedback is one of the characteristics of an autopoietic system, being closely connected to a network pattern. For generating feedback, the communication networks may be able to rule and organize themselves. Self organization comes as a central concept in the systemic view, as well as the self-ruling and feedback views which are solely connected to networks.

This way, the technological revolution may be understood in a systemic way:

the diffusion of technology amplifies its power in an indefinite way as long as users take and redefine it. New information technologies are not merely tools to be applied but processes to be developed. Users and creators may become the same thing. In this way users can take control over technology... It follows a very close relation with the social processes of creating and manipulating symbols (the society culture) and its capacity to produce and distribute goods and services (the productive powers). For the first time in history the human mind is the direct productive power and not only a decisive element in the productive system. (Castells, 1999, p.51)

According to Castells (1999), the elite learn by doing and they modify technological applications, whereas most people learn by using, being limited to technology and becoming dependent upon technology. This idea of doing as the object of comprehension and creation is present in the work of the Swiss biologist and epistemologist Jean Piaget, when he highlights the importance of doing in order to understand. The author states that the essence of development is action, or, for the subject to learn and construct knowledge, action is essential. Action constitutes an autonomous knowledge (savoir faire), and its concept is created by afterthought. From a certain level there is an influence resulting from the concept of action, enhancing it in a way which provides higher levels of comprehension and so on.

Castells also argues (1999) that the growing integration between minds and machines has been changing our lives deeply in different dimensions. Because of these changes, machines, as well as knowledge of life, and with help from such machines and knowledge, a "deeper technological change in the categories where we think about all processes" is occurring (Castells, 1999, p.80).

With this in mind, how do we think about the processes of teaching and learning that are establishing themselves in the "Networked Digital-Virtual Society", where the subjects have more and more access, almost instantaneously, to a wide variety of digital virtual networks consisting of information, interaction, communication and the production of knowledge, being independent of time and space? Where sometimes they are user-consumers and sometimes they are author-creators?

The Challenge of Educating in a "Networked Digital-Virtual Society"

With reference to Education in this new society, the "Networked Digital-Virtual Society" brings important implications and consequences and, along with these many challenges for the teaching and learning processes, both in formal and informal educational contexts. We understand that these changes are necessary and they can be achieved if we are able to go from a teaching culture centered on an empiricist conception - in which the core paradigm is the industrial society - to a learning culture, centered on a complex systemic-constructivist-interactionist level of a networked society.

Interactionist in the sense that it recognizes that knowledge is created from a constant and continuous interaction process, of the subject's interaction with physical and social environments. As the subject interacts he starts producing his capacity of knowing and of knowledge itself, in a way that if the interaction between subject and object is changing them, so too the interaction between individual subjects is going to change the subjects in relation to each other.

And constructivist in the sense that knowledge is understood as a permanent construction process that starting from the action upon the knowledge object modifies itself when the subject interacts with the world. It is through the interaction with people and objects, made possible by his action, that the subject constructs his own mind and his own representations of reality.

It is systemic in the sense that the knowledge process is understood as an integrated whole whose core features come from the relations between different parties. Through this, it is constituted of subsystems that interrelate in order to build up a network where they are both interlinked and independent. Under the systemic view and contrary to the idea of knowledge as an edifice built of individual blocks, knowledge is understood as a relationship network. In a systemic conception, the whole structure is seen as a display of subjacent processes in a way that systemic thinking is always process thinking.

It is complex in the sense that the knowledge may be understood either as something intertwined (complexus) or as a combination of meanings that are linked by a common nexus. According to Morin (2007) reality is organized by means of heterogeneous connections that are deeply associated, intertwined, intrinsic and unique whilst being multiple at the same time. Trying a hyper-specialization of knowledge ends up

ruining and taking reality apart, being contrary to a complex-systemic view, where the whole is bigger than the sum of its separate parts because it includes not only those parts but the relationships between them.

Based upon the authors' work cited earlier, this makes us believe that the way to knowledge is not pre-determined, nor is it built around perfectly synchronized universal mechanisms, rather it is a collection of phenomena that "self-eco-organize" to develop autonomy, balance, plurality and disorder.

So, these grounds provide us with elements to rethink the ontological models present in the mechanist paradigm (from which the "teaching culture" originated) and, consequently, build up new epistemological and methodological scenarios that arise from these grounds (allowing us to think about a "learning culture").

But what is this change in reference to a "learning culture"? In a "learning culture" the focus of the educational process relies on interaction, knowledge construction, skills, learning and the development of competencies, which are understood from a complex and systemic 'self-eco-organizing' view. The subject's development pace is respected for it is believed that the learning process is accomplished in a collective context, being individually significant and related to the subject's previous constructions (ontogeny). In this context the educational space is heterarchical, relational, flexible and participative, provoking the subject to interact with the environment and with other subjects, in order to promote the development of autonomic behaviors, collaboration and cooperation, thereby generating mutual respect and internal solidarity. It is an environment in which the rules, direction and activities are drawn up by the group via an agreement between the participant subjects, meaning the students and teachers. The teaching process starts from what the subject already knows and is based upon a discursive process. The learning process happens in an integrated way, based on research, manipulation, exploration, experimentation and discovery through identification and problem solving. The teacher is the mediator and co-participant, playing the roles of the learning facilitator, problem maker, articulator and guide so that the content is constructed upon the creation of information networks which encourage the subject's activity, autonomy and authorship development based on mutual interaction processes, meaning the processes are constantly being constructed by means of negotiations between the interacting agents. In this process of mutual interaction the subjects also act as co-mediators at different moments. Assessment is focused in the learning process follow-up, observing points of view, in order to understand how the subjects are constructing concepts so that is possible to intervene, by doing a pedagogical mediation when necessary in order to trigger and broaden comprehension. Assessment, in this case, uses the subjects' development process, portfolios and projects. It is formative, continual and meta-cognitive, with the objective of correcting routes.

When reflecting on the knowledge constructed in research developed from teaching and learning processes with the use of digital technologies, verified by Schlemmer (2002, 2000-2005, 2005-2007, 2007-2010, 2008-2009, 2009-2011, 2011-2013)[1], we can state that information is the source for building knowledge and for learning, in a way that the use of digital technologies, mainly the Internet, has been revolutionizing teaching and learning methods. Through the Internet, it is possible to access the necessary information at the right moment according to each individual interest. Another possibility concerns the dissemination and socialization of information, which happens in an immediate way and to an unknowable extent. However, the biggest contribution the Internet can make to the educational process is the change of paradigm, pushed forward by the hugely interactive power it offers. It is therefore believed that Web-based computer environments may be a way to share and broaden man's intelligence in a collective way, by means of the constitution of

cooperation nets. These nets are possible due to the creation of virtual communities formed not by the physical proximity but by interest in common topics. All these constitute a new relational space, a new flexible and multi-synchronous impermanence which requires learning to move, self-organize and manage time.

In our research, as previously mentioned, and through the analysis of records from the participating subjects (teachers-to-be) we have evidence that allows us to state the existence of an initial difficulty the subjects had in their organization of digital-virtual space and time. This feeling of "disorganization" is often related to the identification of the need for "a new learning process" and which this context demands. Some subjects claim they believed the fact that knowing how to organize themselves with pencil and paper (analogical resources) would mean they would be equally able to organize in the digital-virtual space, initially unconfirmed, for extremely organized subjects in a physical educational context have shown and claim to be "disorganized" in a digital-virtual educational context. This is causing the subjects to have cognitive disorder, triggering reflection upon the use of digital technologies in Education, bringing them to a process of awareness-building[2] on the fact that the changes in the environment (the technologies, in this case), necessarily imply a personal and collective reorganization. These same subjects have identified a significant differentiation between the way they organize themselves in physical space and time and digital-virtual space and time. They understand that going from one to the other or even being in two simultaneous times and spaces, is not something given and therefore needs to be learned in the process of digital-technological appropriation.

This research, then, corroborates Castells'(1999) statements when he says that time and space reintegrate in functional nets or in image pasting, resulting in a space with flows that replace the space of places. However, based on our research, we understand that these new spaces coexist and present themselves as complementary to the universe of current human relationships. The space of flows and impermanent time are essential foundations of a new culture that goes beyond and includes the diversity of historically transmitted systems: a real virtuality culture. This idea will be developed further in chapter 11 - The Real Virtuality of Metaverses. We have equally shown that identity also builds up the set of fundamental grounds, mentioned by Castells, which will be better developed in chapter 4, Avatar: building a "Digital Virtual Self". This localization model based in the space of flows has as a key element the "innovation model". The capacity of synergy is what defines the specifics of the innovation model, meaning the added value results not from the cumulative effects of elements present in the medium but from its interaction. The new space is then organized around the relationships and the information flows. The emphasis on interactivity between places breaks the special behavior standards in a flowing net of interchanges that form the base for the dawn of the space of flows. The space of flows is a new spatial path originating from the social practices that draw up a networked society. This path, the space of flows "is the material organization of social practices in shared time that work through flows" (Castells, 1999, p. 436).

Time, according to Castells (1999), seems to be specific to a determined context: time is place. Focusing on the emerging social structure, the author says that, "The mind nowadays is the mind which denies time" and that this new "temporal system" is related to the development of communication technologies. Linear, irreversible, measurable and predictable time is being broken up in the networked society.

In our research op. cit., we have evidence that the subject's experience with different digital technologies, the experience within these new spaces and times, provokes this new significance in the way of interacting and communicating, causing an imbalance in the perception of how they learn with and use these technologies and, how they build up their autonomy with these new media. Besides the question related to autonomy, this has resulted in a process of awareness about the place of individual and collective authorship as well as the importance of the possibility of making a construction process visible in this space of flow. This is because anything produced at anytime may be easily recovered, reused, modified, broadened and broken from the linearity many times present in traditional spaces. Other evidence concerns the importance given to comprehending the other in terms of the individual authorship process and in the context of collective authorship. This gives the perception of the other's developmental implications within group development and consequently in the development of the individual self. This movement, responsible for the break in hierarchy, related to someone teaching and someone learning, contributes to the subject's emancipation, the subject who perceives as himself active in the process, and therefore responsible for his own learning process, as stated by Freire (1996) in his research regarding education in physical spaces.

Atemporal time, according to Castells (1999), is only an emerging way of dominating social time within the networked society because the space of flows does not extinguish the existence of places. The real virtuality culture associated with an electronically integrated multimedia system helps to change time in our society in two ways: synchronism and atemporality. In this new context, the organization of significant events loses its internal chronological rhythm and remains organized into temporal sequences conditioned to the social context of its use and viewed this way, it is the culture of the eternal and ephemeral. The eternal-ephemeral time of the new culture goes beyond any specific sequence and adapts to the dynamic, networked society thus allowing individual interactions and collective representations whilst building an atemporal, mental overview.

It is clear then that these new means with which we interact are of a different nature, in the sense that the previously adopted methodologies cannot explore the potential they offer. This is why new methodologies have to arise, taking into account the potentiality of the interaction process enabled by digital technology.

In a Digital-Virtual Networked Society it is no longer possible for schools to follow the industrial, Fordist society model with a series of production lines. With large-scale education, a reformation in the educational system is needed and it has to approach a new way of thinking about how the school builds up its structure, how it organizes itself with and by the use of technology in society, meaning this current social-historical time.

INFORMATION AND KNOWLEDGE: TEACHING, LEARNING, AND DEVELOPMENT

The understanding of how to teach and learn has been constructed throughout time and is one of the researchers' biggest concerns in different areas of knowledge, including not just education but psychology, biology, sociology and philosophy. This understanding is being constructed in different socio-historical-cultural moments and is strongly linked to the understanding of the human being, of society and of development. To understand how to teach and learn necessarily implies a clearer view of concepts such as information, knowledge and development which are implicit in the teaching and learning processes and which are now presented and discussed in sequence.

What is information? Does to have information mean to have knowledge? What does "to know" mean? What is the place of learning in this context? When we learn, might we say we have developed? These are some of the questions we need to constantly ask ourselves as professionals and when working nowadays in the area of human capacity when we have different digital technologies available which can help us in the areas of information, knowledge, learning and development. Although in many situations these

terms have been undiscriminating, without a deeper reflection on their meaning and what they represent in the context of the formation and human capacity building processes, we consider it crucial to clarify them in order to provide more elements to better enable a comprehension of the proximities, distances and balances among them, for these concepts represent beliefs and both formally and informally guide the development of the teaching and learning processes. It is based on this belief that we construct our pedagogical way of acting, that we elect the methodology and practices we are using, as well as the way in which we develop the process of pedagogical mediation and follow up and assessment.

This way, comprehending the information, learning, knowledge and development concepts, as well as establishing the differences among them, is essential for joined-up educational practice. For all and every learning environment, either in the physical or digital-virtual environment (including e-learning[3], m-learning[4], p-learning[5], u-learning[6] or i-learning[7]) has its structure based on this understanding.

What is Information?

The word Information has Latin origins, where *information* means the act of doing, producing, and it is etymologically defined as "the act of giving shape to something".

When we ask a question, we are requesting information, the same as when we read a book, a newspaper, a magazine or an Internet page or when we listen to music or a radio program, watch television or a movie. The content present in these media is information. The same happens when we tell of a situation in which we have lived, tell a story, present a piece of work, or when we talk about something. This though, is not news for us because it was constructed from our own interactive background. Information is something that can be transmitted, used, manipulated and transformed by those watching or listening.

Nowadays the amount of information produced and made available, mainly by digital means, is growing at a fast pace and access to this information is also fast and accurate. For example, in order to check the information I am providing here, one can simply access a search engine such as Google and type something about the information for which you are searching. Within seconds you will have a significant amount of available information, such as web addresses, which you can access to locate the desired information.

So, knowing that the subjects are using Metaverse technology and that they act and interact in different 3D Digital Virtual Worlds, it is possible to ask: what is the "role" of information in the areas of learning? How is this information presented? Is the fact of having information enough to make learning possible in the context of Immersive Learning?

What is Learning? How Do We Learn?

The word "learning" derives from the verb "to learn", which originates from the Latin word *apprehendere* ('understanding'). For a long time, researchers who study the area of human development have been trying to understand how the learning process happens, or, how the subject moves from a stage of less organized knowledge to a more organized one? The main researchers in this area are the biologists Jean Piaget and Humberto Maturana.

For the Swiss biologist Jean Piaget, considered one of the best psychologists in human development, learning in general is provoked by external situations, and occurs only when there is active assimilation from the subject. "All emphasis is placed on the subject's own activity, and I think that, without this activity, there are no possible didactics or pedagogy able to significantly transform the subject" (Piaget, 1972, p. 11). When Piaget made this affirmation he called attention

to the importance of the subject's action in order to accomplish learning, attributing to the subject the responsibility for his own learning process. The author believes that if the educational process context does not provide the space for the subject to act upon the knowledge object in order do understand it, it is unlikely that any learning capable of changing the subject may happen.

For Humberto Maturana, the Chilean biologist, learning is the act of transforming oneself by means of particular recurrent interactions. "Learning happens when the behavior of a life form varies during its ontogeny[8], in a congruent way with variations within the environment, what it does, according to a contingent course in its interactions with it" (Maturana, 1993, p.82).

In simple terms, it means that learning happens when a living being modifies the background of its interactions with the environment. According to Maturana and Rezepka (2000), all human beings, unless under extreme neurological conditions, are equally capable of learning and the way they learn is according to their own human conditions because they are autonomous and autopoietic[9], in harmony with the environment in which they live. This harmony with the environment may cause disturbance in the human beings' structure, which will trigger the learning processes according to what the structure may self-produce to compensate for this disturbance[10].

When we bring the concept of learning into the context of the metaverse we may ask: What is the implication in learning within the metaverse? How does the metaverse form the subject's learning? How does the subject ensure his autonomy and autopoiesis in this context? What is the disturbing element and how is it compensated for? When we learn something, can we say we know it?

In our research, we have discovered that learning within the metaverse initially implies a certain difficulty in the use of this technology. This may be due to its specific characteristics, involving the construction of an avatar and interacting in oral, textual, gestural and graphic ways in 3D graphical environments, which may cause a feeling of "being lost". For the subject to get to know the technology, and to understand its structure, there is the need for effective use and for giving it meaning so that it makes sense for the subject to give himself the option to "dare" and the pleasure of "being in this universe", experiencing both Virtual Reality and Real Virtuality[11]. Living such experiences contributes to provoking a conscious decision-making process about how to learn in these new contexts. In this way, learning within the metaverse implies opening possibilities that arise from the potential that technology offers. It implies sharpening the sense of observation to perceive possibilities, to be autonomous and to be the author of one's own learning process. It even implies exploring, experimenting and relating to the environment and letting one be teased by it, acting and interacting with it and with the other avatar-human-beings, approaching and retreating when necessary, for significance.

In the metaverse some elements are identified as having the potential for learning such as:

- Real virtuality, represented by the creation of 3D Digital Virtual Worlds, dynamic multi-use environments, that can be browsed and that are created on the Net, in which scenarios modify in real time as the avatar-subjects (living there) act and interact with and in that "world";
- Telepresence and digital-virtual[12] presence through an avatar who constructs a digital-virtual identity[13] and can accomplish actions, manipulate tridimensional objects, as well as use different types of communication through oral, textual, gestural or graphic language when interacting with other avatars;
- Graphic representation of the subject (avatar) inside a tridimensional environment, facilitating virtual contact, and allowing the construction of an image with reference to the interlocutors and which contributes to socialization among the participants, "humanizing" the contact and favoring a more effective interaction among the participants in a certain way;
- The possibility of personifying (using an avatar) and contextualizing the study environment (3D Digital Virtual Worlds);
- The autonomy, authorship, mobility and interactive action in a "bi-located" movement (being "here" as the 1st life and "there" as the 2nd life) enabling the connection between worlds (the physical and the digital-virtual);
- Online "face-to-face" interaction, which is possible between avatars at any time, allowing them to see each other even though being physically distant;
- Enrichment of the experience motivated by the feeling of immersion within 3D Digital Virtual Worlds;
- The "feeling" of "being present", minimizing the feeling of physical distance from the online courses and/or classes;
- The presence of the avatar in a 3D Digital Virtual World as an extension of the subjects in a new space;
- The feeling of presence, crucial to establishing places of cohabitation with cooperation and collaborative processes, necessary for building knowledge;
- The understanding that there are many resources, such as text chat - both in public or private - combining voice in a tridimensional space, with the subject present through his avatar. The possibility of simulation, of manipulating objects which allow them to reach a level of interaction and participation not possible by means of other technologies.

Based on Papert (1988), it is possible to say then that the acquisition of any new knowledge may be simple when the subject is able to embody it into his "template arsenal".

Regarding more specifically autonomy and autopoiesis, we may say that human beings are autonomous by their nature and condition of being. However, along their ontogenic history this autonomy may be suppressed or developed through interactions with other human beings and congruent with the environment (physical and digital-virtual space). In this way, the processes of formation and capability may be established as important spaces to overcome self-restraint and to promote the development of autonomy - desirable in this dimension. When we think of the development of autonomy, understood as the objective of the process of formation and capability, the metaverses represent a privileged space for interacting with other human beings, when intentionally used for this purpose.

In the metaverse, the interaction space itself (graphic environments built in 3D) as well as the interactions in this environment, are possible. The construction of an avatar constitutes a disturbing element because the information in this context may be represented in textual, oral, gestural or graphical ways, where the compensation of this disturbance happens in the interaction with the environment and with the other participating subjects. In this way, in the formation and capability processes proposed in the metaverses and in our research we see the development of autonomy in three instances: individual autonomy, autopoiesis and social autonomy. These instances mean: "When we think of individual autonomy, we understand it as inherent to the action of the living being that sets its own rules for this action. It is possible then to verify that the action enables reflection, and that the living being self-produces in the action and in knowledge, creating autopoiesis. In this sense we also verify autonomy towards the group, where the action transforms the relationship

networks, meaning a social autonomy" (Backes, 2007, pp.161-162). We can now say that when we learn something we broaden our significance system, that is, we know.

We can now return to the question presented at the end of the section in which we discussed the concept of information in order to reflect on its "role" in the scope of learning, meeting the subjects that use metaverses, as well as answering the question: Is the fact of having information enough to make learning happen within Immersive Learning contexts?

Information represents one of the necessary elements for learning. Therefore information has the function of disturbing the subject's cognitive structure, but by itself does not constitute learning. This is because subjects need other basic processes such as the action and interaction of subjects upon the information and with the information, in a way that permits them to imbibe, settle and adapt it to construct a new structure or to broaden it, self-producing in order to compensate the disorder caused by information. Let us now move on to the discussion about knowledge.

What is Knowledge? How Do We Know?

The word knowledge comes from the Latin word *cognósco:* 'learning to know, searching to know, recognize'. Jean Piaget was one of the experts who became interested in knowledge as the general coordination of the present (real) or possible (internal) action, meaning general knowledge, not its specific content. Knowledge is a state of balance that tends to keep still or to expand its understanding capacity; if the expansion is small and does not lead to a disturbance of knowledge it is kept still; if, on the other hand if the expansion is more substantial and leads to disturbance of knowledge there is a tendency to compensate this disturbance by means of a reconstruction where recently expanded knowledge returns to its balanced state. If for any reason the reconstruction does not occur then the disturbance of knowledge is suppressed and the previous state of balance is reconstructed.

According to Piaget (1972) knowledge is not a copy of reality, it is not merely looking and producing a mental copy or image of an event. In order to know an object it is necessary to act upon it. "Knowing is to modify, transform the object, to understand this transformation process and consequently, understand the way the object is constructed" (Piaget, 1972, p.1).

According to this conception knowledge is constructed by the subject and acts upon the perceived object by interacting with it, where the social interchanges are demanding conditions for the development of thinking. Human knowledge, in relation to interpersonal relationships (in which it is both a pre-requisite and a component part, when the result is a mutual construction), is something alive that cannot remain still. Therefore, the expansion of knowledge is not something simply added from the outside. In this way, an adult's knowledge objective is not something external and which just happens, it is present inside us and, above all, it is a constructive relation of people's way of thinking, between I and You (singular and plural). It is not the conventional or factual outcome of things that happen in a given situation, but it determines or dictates to its users the necessary universal relations. First and foremost it is not only discovering a subjective reality but the construction, both personal and social, of genuine novelty, which means the construction of a new reality. Piaget is against the idea of an impersonal knowledge, arguing that such knowledge as it is does not exist, meaning that what exists are people in relation to what they know, or rather, that knowledge is personal and depends on the subject who knows it.

For Maturana and Varela (2001) knowledge is something constructed by the living being when interacting in the world. "All knowledge is an action from that which knows", so, cognition is the effective action, it is the structural coupling[14] process in which interactions with the internal and external worlds occur. The cognition process is based on the creation of a field of behaviors within the domain of interaction. What we, as observers, understand by knowledge is what we consider as actions (behaviors, thoughts, reflections…) suitable for that context or domain and validated according to our acceptance criteria.

"Living – unceasing conservation of the creature's structural linkage – is to know in the scope of existing." Maturana and Varela (1997) argue that living is knowing, and knowing is living, in a way that every subject has his own course, translated by the linkages he makes when living and sharing. This is why we can say that knowledge is different from information, because it is related to the intention of those who wish to know. In a very simple way, knowledge is the information meant by the subject.

But how does metaverse knowledge happen? What is the role of social exchange? How do the linkages in these contexts happen?

As we return to the way Piaget (1972) understands knowledge, we may say that knowing in the metaverse occurs from the moment the subject learns, meaning he applies significance to new information (which may be represented in textual, oral, gestural or graphic ways, singularly or combined), starting from the establishment of the relationship with such information in relation to what was previously known, made easy through the speed and facilitated access to either information, the virtual communities or social networks, which may foster social exchanges. Furthermore, in the metaverse context, most significant for knowledge, are the different ways of representing it, especially in the graphical representation that contributes to shifting traditional logics and mobilizes human beings to cooperate for a better representation of their perception and endorsing their connection with the environment (metaverse). The subject may then act, interact or transform and in so doing he may develop his own thoughts when understanding how these processes happen and what their outcomes are and with everything taken into consideration, the characteristics of fluidity, malleability, plasticity in the learning context, that arise in the Metaverse learning environment. Besides this, according to Maturana and Varela (2001) this acting and interacting of the subject with the world occurs by structural assembling, and therefore it is simultaneously an individual and social process, which is connected with the environment (metaverse). The connections also happen in relation to the aspects mentioned above which are created by metaverses.

What is Development?

Development, according to Piaget (1972), explains learning and it is an essential process in which every learning element has a function in total development and therefore learning is subordinated to development. Development, according Piaget, may be seen in two directions. Looking back it is the comprehension of structures of knowledge that are present and felt as inadequate; and looking forward, it is the restructuring of these structures and implies a legitimate element of novelty, of something that was not present before, nor is it pre-programmed in physiological structures.

How Does Knowledge Differ from Learning and from Information?

The knowing and learning process, although different issues, are both complementary poles constituting the whole. Both are continuous and go on throughout the subject's entire life. According to Piaget (1972), while knowledge development is a spontaneous process, related to the embryogenesis process (the development of the body, nervous system and mental functions) that needs to be situated in a general development context, learning, on the contrary, is caused by specific external situations. Learning may be triggered by an educator, for instance, in the development of educational actions or by other subjects in an interactive process.

Regarding the relation between learning and information, Becker (2008) notes that, "Learning passes through a process of reformulating information, reaching comprehension; relying only on memory we cannot reach something new; that is achieved when current knowledge is related with other knowledge" (p. 66).

The fact is that we are used to referring to the means as knowledge carriers, when they are information carriers for those accessing them for the first time. This information will only turn to knowledge within the internal learning process, private from the subject accessing it, and results in a complex process of establishing relationships between new information and the subject's background knowledge and related to his life history. It is through mental action that the subject creates his significance network, allowing him to learn and to know. So, for the information to turn into knowledge it is necessary that the subject knows it, understands it, and gives meaning to this new information.

But what happens inside this establishment of relations, inside this significance? This process is a result of the subject's interaction (existing mental structures) and the knowledge object (information), translated as a mental action derived from the adaptation process (assimilation[15] and accommodation[16]), resulting in learning. In this way, any information present in the environment turns into this subject's knowledge and as a result starts making up a part of his mental structure. It is therefore incorrect to talk about a "knowledge base", similar to that which exists in a computer. What we have is an "information base", because knowledge depends on action, the subject's interaction with information, meaning it is linked with learning, the relationships this subject establishes between the existing knowledge and the new information, in order to give it a meaning and resulting in the expansion of existing knowledge into new knowledge.

The core principle we must rely on is the exchange of information, the sharing of knowledge and ideas with other subjects from different areas and expertise within the field of human knowledge and in different functions. Accepting contradiction, questioning, knowing how to listen and explain a point of view without being too "attached" to "truths" but open enough to what is different in a way that makes it possible to understand the other subject as someone legitimate for interaction, valuing his knowledge and reflecting on the results of the interaction. These are behaviors that enable knowledge. This movement, which relies on diversity, may cause novelty, innovation and creativity.

Knowledge may even be learned as a process or a product. When we refer to the accumulation of theories, ideas and concepts, knowledge is seen as an outcome or product of this learning, but as all products cannot be separated from a process we may then look at knowledge as an intellectual activity in which the subject performs the processes of understanding, accommodation and adaptation, meaning he learns something thus far external to him and making it internal.

Looking back at the different existing digital technologies we can identify technologies which are more suitable for searching and storing information, such as file repositories, links, image and sound libraries, references and texts and learning objects such as simulators, games and teleconferences etc. On the other hand, others such as forums, chats, discussion lists and videoconferences are more adequate for sharing knowledge, ideas and experiences as such tools demand a higher level of interaction. There are others for collaborative and cooperative construction and these tools demand a high level of interaction, for example, they are tools that support project development, case, challenge and problem solving and learning and practicing

in virtual communities. There are also the tools based on "mind maps" and "concept maps", which are a good option for teaching the subject how to organize his thoughts, learning and knowledge. Different technologies with their own particularities may "live together" in the same space, in a way that one environment does not replace the other but instead they complement each other. It is necessary to combine several technologies in order to approach the desirable interaction level, meaning to construct hybrid spaces, blending the digital-virtual (using different digital technologies) and physical (face-to-face).

But how do information, knowledge and learning arise in the context of the metaverse? When we shed light on the teaching and learning contexts in the metaverse we realize that information, knowledge and learning occur with an imbrication, making the subject at times feel uncomfortable for any reason regarding his external search for new information and based on that, when necessary, he rapidly engages with his peers, through the networks in which he participates, in a way which allows him to construct the necessary knowledge according to the situation, meaning that he learns.

THE "HOMO ZAPPIENS" GENERATION

Who is and How Does the Digital-Native "Homo Zappiens" Generation Learn?

What changes in the way in which they learn? How do they develop? In terms of the way we are educating our children, teenagers and adolescents; are the technologies and methodologies we use adequate for the world's reality and for the current society in which they live, thereby contributing to overcoming difficulties they find within this society? Are we, as teachers belonging to the "Homo Zappiens" Generation as digital immigrants, interacting, talking, understanding and making ourselves understandable for the current generation? What is the education offered to those "digital natives" who are taking a university degree in both undergraduate and post-graduate courses (*lato* and *stricto sensu*), in order to be prepared to teach in the field of education as researchers or professors? To what extent do they have contributions which overcome this generation's difficulties? Are we able to provide "Education" in this social-historical time, which necessarily implies the freedom to overcome the challenges they face in their current way of living, or are we still educating subjects for a society that, although it is the core of ontogeny, has been changing in an overwhelming way and at incredible speed?

Since the beginning of the Internet and Digital Technologies, researchers have been using different terms aiming to better characterize the current generation, which lives in a society increasingly affected by the presence of all kinds of digital technologies. Among these researchers there is Topscott, who in 1999, called this the "Net Generation" with reference to the first generation who were born and grew up surrounded by all types of digital technology existing at that time, and for whom, technology is not a threat as it is presented as something naturally integrated to these subjects' day-to-day experiences. In 2001 Mark Prensky introduced the denomination "digital native" when referring to the current students, and who, according to him, are native speakers of the new digital language of computers, videogames and the Internet. The same author coins the expression "digital immigrants" when referring to earlier generations. In 2003 the term "millennials", first introduced by Howe and Strauss (2000) was used to refer to the generation born in the eighties, who have experienced greater comfort, use and empathy with digital media. In 2009 Veen and Vrakking coined the term "homo zappiens generation" in another attempt to describe this current generation.

"Children can easily learn how to use computers and this learning may change the way in which they know other things" (Papert, 1988,

p.21). Furthermore, according to what Seymour Papert stated based on his research developed at the *Massachusetts Institute of Technology* [17], the subjects who were born in the 80s and later have grown up within a society immersed in all types of technology, mainly digital, and they are therefore connected by different types of networks and are considered "digital natives" (Prensky, 2001).

The new learning subjects are people who were born in a hi-tech, network-dynamic world, which is rich in possibilities for accessing information, communication and interaction. For "Digital Natives" digital technologies have always been present, imbricated in their actions, they live and think with such technologies. Technology is present in the way they communicate with and relate to other subjects in the world, and it forms part of their constructed experiences of living and sharing. (Schlemmer, 2006. pp.34 -35)

These subjects belong to the "Homo Zappiens" generation (Veen & Vrakking, 2009),

They are the new generation who has learnt how to deal with new Technologies, who has grown up using a variety of technological resources since their childhood. Such resources allow them to have control of the flow of information, to blend virtual and real life communities, to communicate and cooperate in the network, according to their needs. The Homo Zappien is an active information processor, he easily solves problems using game strategies, and he can communicate very well. His relationship with school has deeply changed... The Homo Zappien is digital and the school is analogical. (Veen & Vrakking, 2009, p.12)

This generation rapidly and easily moves inside this technological world, having access to a wide variety of information, communication and interaction possibilities. This generation has a unique intimacy with these technologies because it has grown up with and is developing amongst computers, cell phones, MP3, MP4, iPod, iPhone, PDAs, Play Station, Play Station Portable – PSP, Wii, Internet, instant communicators, Google and its several services, wikis, blogs, orkut, virtual communities of all kinds, Massive Multiplayer Online Role Play Games, the Metaverse and 3D Digital Virtual Worlds. It is a generation that "thinks with and from the use" of all these technologies with which they live and that they share, thinking of them as part of their world, their culture and therefore, the space where they construct their ontogeny.

The subjects of the "Homo Zappiens" generation, according to (Veen & Vrakking, 2009), aim to be in control of the information flow; they are frequent game players (including many of them who already take part in the so called "Lan Parties[18]"); most of the time they communicate through digital technology (MSN, Skype, Gtalk, chat rooms, cell phones) using their own language; they take part in different social networks (they have virtual friends they interact with despite not physically knowing them, and these virtual friends are often of a much bigger number than their face-to-face friends); they hardly ever read manuals; they create virtual identities to interact in chat rooms and avatars to learn in virtual worlds; they know more URL addresses by heart then irregular verbs; they customize their songs, create texts, images, videos and share them on the Internet, socializing their ideas and ways of thinking; school for them is rather another place to meet friends than a place to learn; they develop iconic competences; they may simultaneously listen to music, interact with different virtual friends through MSN, surf the net and do homework; they process information in a parallel and broken way (zapping is a skill that allows them to construct significant knowledge through broken audio, video and text information flow); they present a non-linear learning approach (non-linear learning strategies demand the content to be reconsidered: learning through action and interaction having different learning objectives available, which may be accessed *just-in-time*);

they create mindmaps as a way of organizing and designing their thoughts. In summary, this generation learns through clicks, touches, screens, icons, sounds, games, intertwining of actions and interactions that involve curiosity, research, discovery, challenge, exploration, experimentation and living in different online conversation networks.

Torres and Vivas (2009), in an extensive review of the literature on this issue, state that:

In all the works already mentioned the concept of generation has become useful when we need to think about the changes in the educational process; we perceive a change in the demographic characteristics of the student, in the technologies and in their behavior related to learning styles. Although there is no standardized terminology to refer to this phenomenon, the use of the idea of a "digital native" embraces other denominations present in literature such as: millennials, net generation or Y generation, screenagers and Google generation, among others. (Ojala, 2008 apud Torres & Vivas, 2009, p.324)

According to Torres and Vivas (2009) the common characteristics presented by the authors refer to their preference for these new learning subjects because they learn in a team and they learn through experimental activities and using technologies. Among the main advantages this generation has is the accomplishment of multiple simultaneous tasks, goal driven tasks, a positive attitude and strong cooperation and collaborative styles. So, the common element according to the presented authors' view is the change regarding the cognitive differences presented by this "new generation", in their social behavior and in the way they learn and communicate.

For Torres and Vivas (2009) however, the dawn of these terms may trigger a debate that reveals the need to gather evidence that justifies the presence of a new generation with attributes that distinguish them, although according to them, we must be careful of falling for stereotypes because,

Besides the enthusiasm and the concern regarding these studies about the new generation, we need to move forward from the personal observation by an expert in computer games to a research agenda, that can support a broader comprehension of the myths and realities of the digital native phenomenon, this expression being the one better accepted by authors from different subjects. (Torres & Vivas, 2009, p.324)

Based on the analysis of this study, Torres and Vivas (2009) state that the previous definitions originating from other works on this issue, present a general description of the "digital native", without going deeply into the factors which could explain the differences between generations, such as context, history, culture, economy and politics. Such factors are implicit in each generation's life course and as "niches" of individual and social developments, they cannot be suppressed when analyzing several generations.

As a result, when Torres and Vivas (2009) analyzed the existing discussion context about the "digital natives", they verified some problematic questions that have to be taken into consideration, including the lack of empirical data that better evidences the statements and also the limitations of the methodological focuses and approaches.

Another piece of research we found was developed by Gary Small and Gigi Vorgan (2008), both neuroscientists from the Semel Institute for Neuroscience and Human Behavior at UCLA, and it is called "iBrain: Surviving the Technological Alteration of the Modern Mind." It discusses the idea that teenagers are growing up immersed in different digital technologies and their brains are becoming more malleable, with a higher plasticity, showing more activity in areas affecting decision-making and complex thinking. According to the researchers, using the Web changes the way the brain processes this data, thus modifying our neural tissue. The research also states that our brains are evolving at an unimaginable speed, meaning that

interaction with different digital technologies is enhancing our mental acuity, cognitive skills and intelligence.

Although the research developed so far has limitations, it is easy to come to the conclusion that this generation, born in and since the eighties, represents a large proportion of our students at different educational levels, including those on higher level and post-graduate courses, and therefore they are "native" speakers of the digital language of computers, video games and the Internet (Veen & Vrakking 2009). This digital-technological context may be influencing the way they develop, perceive and represent the world because they have learned through clicks, touches, screens, icons, sounds, games and in a mixture of actions and interactions involving curiosity, research, discovery, challenge, exploration and experimentation, living in different online conversation networks. This new reality brings new significant challenges for the current Educational field, demanding a constant and continuous training process so that teachers can assume new developments and learning theories that arise, at the same time as they "naturalize" themselves (Schlemmer, 2010) in this digital world, understand it and develop digital technological fluency that allow them to interact with and educate the current generation. This generation establishes configurations of sharing with other subjects, in its own and particular way, linked to digital-virtual spaces and causing what Castells (1999) has defined as "real virtuality Culture".

How Can We, Teachers and Professors from the Analogical Generation, Become "Digitally Naturalized"?

We, the professors and teachers, are learning a new language, we are acquiring new codes, and according to Prensky (2001) we are "digital immigrants". Like when learning a foreign language, we use digital technologies with a certain "accent", we apply old methods to new possibilities that allow us to give new meaning to the analogical as digital, and the digital as analogical. We in the process of building up schemes[19] and cognitive structures[20] which allow us to use and make a better use of technology, meaning we are "naturalizing" ourselves into this new world, the digital virtual world.

Naturalization, from the biological point of view is a process in which a determined species establishes itself in a different territory to that from which it arises. Naturalization is also understood as the subject's action of acquiring, by his own will, a nationality different from his own and given at birth. The naturalization appears almost always linked to subjects who have emigrated, establishing himself in a different territory from the one he was born in and therefore opting to acquire a new nationality, connected with the new territory into which he has been welcomed. Nationality, in this context, is understood from sociology, referring to a nation or ethnic group (subjects with the same characteristics: language, religion, uses, etc.).

We are, therefore, "analogical natives" and "digital immigrants" in the process of naturalizing because we are entering and getting to know, of our own will, the digital world that is welcoming us. This new world has certain characteristics that define it as being digital. However, it is worth remembering that even being digitally naturalized we will always have double citizenship, because we were born in an analogical world, but we live and share in two co-existing worlds, the analogical and the digital.

Although we are undergoing a "naturalization" process, educating the digital native represents a big challenge to our professional practice. Even when trying hard to learn how to be in this new world, we still speak in an analogical language from the pre-digital age, which makes communication difficult in certain circumstances and also causes a "gap" between generations.

What Factors Can Contribute to Minimizing the "Gap" between Generations, Bringing Them Together for the Construction of a Dialogical Relationship in Education?

According to Prensky (2001) the digital native speaks a completely different language and often, they do not understand the way we think, making us totally incomprehensible to them. Whilst we, digital immigrants, process information in a linear, sequential, step-by-step way, from the easiest to the most difficult; they multi-skill and process information in a non-linear, broken way, with no care for pre-requirements, which they only look out for when they need them (*just-in-time learning*) and when they face information they do not understand. We prefer texts and they prefer graphics or maps, while they learn better and more when interconnected with networks. They prefer "serious" work games and often we, as digital immigrants, are not able to understand this world, this new way of organization, of structuring our thoughts and of learning. We have difficulty recognizing the new skills and competencies the digital native acquires and improves by interaction and practice. For instance, we do not understand how our students are able to learn successfully whilst watching TV, listening to music, communicating through MSN, Skype, Gtalk ... . This difficulty is due to the fact that we did not develop these skills and competences when we were students and that the means by which we interacted were entirely different.

Our digital native students have grown up with the Internet and at speed, with the immediacy of hypertext, chats and online messages. They carry cell phones in their pockets and a library in their laptop computers. Most of the time they are plugged into the net, defining the information they are interested in and searching for new ways of getting it fast. They have little patience for long and explanatory classes, for the step-by-step logic, programmed instruction, repetition exercises, tests and exams, or for following a methodology that we submit to and believe to be the only way they are going to learn. But are they really learning this way? Often, we teachers - digital immigrants - assume that methodologies and practices previously used, including from the time we were students, and those which have brought "good results" can continue to be successful.

So, what should be done about the "gap" existing between teachers and students? Will digitally native people need to learn through the old ways or will digital immigrant educators become "digitally naturalized"? Regardless of how much we wish it were so, it is impossible to stop or go back developmentally. The current generation is developing from action and interaction with totally different means from those we have developed ourselves. Children who were born into a new culture easily learn a new language and have strong resistance to using old forms. Some digital immigrants accept their lack of understanding of this new world and try to learn from their children, this way "naturalizing" and integrating themselves into this world. Others are not as tolerant and spend much of their time bemoaning that things were better in the past. Unless we deliberately forget the idea of educating Digital Natives, we need to face these challenges and, when doing so, we need to reconsider the content to be worked with, as well as the methodology to be adopted, pedagogical practices and the way to carry out pedagogical mediation.

In this context, we learn that some factors may contribute to minimizing the "gap" between teachers and students, bringing them closer to the construction of a dialogical relationship in Education, such as:

- The creation of policies and economical actions that enable the teacher to have access to different digital technological me-

dia, including connectivity, in the way that he can have minimum material conditions to be inserted into cyberculture;
- The creation of public policies and related actions to the teacher's digital emancipation as a citizen;
- The creation of public policies connected to and including digital technology at different educational levels;
- The creation of policies and actions for teachers' education and capacity building (from different educational levels) in the use of digital technology, in a way that they are capable of developing pedagogical-didactical-technical fluency, and mainly;
- The organization of hybrid spaces (physical and digital-virtual) for living and sharing, where the teacher can meet the "digital native" and learn with and about him in this new world and where the "digital native" can also learn with the teacher, enabling both to experiment with "living together in the digital-virtual way".

From an educational point of view it is necessary to consider that we teachers belong to an analogical generation ("digital immigrants"). It is unlikely that many of us have experienced a distance learning formation and capacitation process, using different digital technology. We have never been in the distance learning student's "place", so that we could have "lived" the situation, reflected upon how we feel when learning through this method. This means creating and testing hypotheses, thinking about them and carrying out awareness-building procedures, and thinking about the process of learning by having lived with these digital- technologies. Many teachers have arrived late in this world and have not learned how to "think with" these technologies and this is causing suffering and a lack of self-confidence in many cases.

And what of the students? Many of them are undergraduates belonging to a digital generation (being "digital natives") and, certainly will have as students, subjects immersed in this digital technological world. What does this represent in terms of possibilities and limitations? This reality requires the teacher to have a combined development of current ground competences. They go beyond those in their area of specific knowledge, for they include pedagogical-didactical competences allied with digital-technological competencies to assist the current generation in the construction of knowledge and learning.

So how do we think about the teachers' formation and capacitation processes? What model should we use? And what if instead of "models" we could think about "relational dynamics"? About a movement happening inside relationships, in a context including subjects with different knowledge, interests and expectations; in a space of flow, where they are linked with the environment and together they are constantly changing, according to the plasticity of interactions in living and sharing within the group, space and socio-historical time and space. These subjects gather with a common objective: learning. And therefore they "exchange information", "share knowledge, experiences, ideas…", they build up an interaction network, constructing real learning contexts, that allow the subjects to have social autonomy and creative authorship. This occurs within a dialogical, co-operative space, intertwined with mutual respect and internal solidarity. A space where the other subject is recognized as a legitimate being within the interaction and therefore someone with whom it is possible to establish a relationship in which, at different moments, both are co-teachers and co-learners, in a mediation and intermediation process of multiple and relational pedagogy.

Informatics and Telematics can help to enrich the learning environments, to broaden the classroom spaces, to overcome the barriers of time, to serve as cognitive "prosthesis", to help broaden socio-affective and awareness processes, to help understand learners as real subjects of their own learning, to assure collective intercommunication, to help create learning and development communities. All of this, we underline, is possible. But how can it be done? …The majority of educational methodologies and their technologies currently taught in teacher training courses have shown themselves to be inefficient … . We do not know how to help them to achieve the power of thought, of reflection, of creating for themselves the solutions to the problems they face … .The required leap means moving away from an empiricist view of training and practice – control and manipulation of the learner's behaviour changes - that has been guiding pedagogical practices according to a constructivist view of problem solving – to favoring interactivity, autonomy in formulating questions, in searching for contextualized information, experimental proving and critical analysis". (Fagundes, Sato, & Maçada, 1999, p.14)

Analyzing what we have presented and discussed so far it is possible to perceive that, nowadays, instigating the subject's learning, working with human formation and capacitation, involves a high level of complexity and Educational Institutions are on an increasing search for how different technologies, especially digital-virtual ones may help them. Therefore, one of the current challenges leading us towards the future consists of promoting the citizen's digital emancipation and developing methodologies and processes of pedagogical mediation able to take advantage of the possibilities that these new media can offer to both the teaching and learning processes.

By a Citizen's Digital Emancipation we mean a certain level of appropriation of digital-technological fluency, in a way that allows the subject to become a citizen at the time, empowering him to practice social autonomy[21] and creative authorship[22], in a cooperative and dialogical space, passing through mutual respect and internal solidarity. A space where the other being is recognized as a legitimate interacting being and, therefore someone with whom it is possible to establish relations where, in different moments, both will be co-teachers and co-learners, in a mediating process and multiple and relational pedagogical intermediation. This allows subjects to be released from power relationships, in a space where everybody mutually changes each other through digital-virtual living and sharing by the interactions leading to authentic dialogues (Schlemmer, 2010).

Human formation is related to the subject's development as a co-creating subject with others, in a desirable and social, living together space. As for capacity building, it is related to the acquisition of skills and capabilities of acting in the world we live in, with the operational resources to make whatever we wish to live (Maturana & Rezepka, 2000). According to this view, human formation is the basis for any educational process and capacity building is an instrument for educational task accomplishment. The pedagogical mediation is the educational task's movement, towards human formation and capacity, which arise in the interaction process.

When we refer to the formation and capacity processes that happen through digital networks, Okada (2007) introduces the concept of "multiple pedagogical intermediation". In the "multiple pedagogical intermediation", the student also becomes a pedagogical mediator next to the teachers, their assistants and internal (colleagues) and external collaborators (consulted authors and invited lecturers) and he is no longer the only one mediated. Multiple pedagogical intermediation provides learning mediated by everyone. Everybody learns with everybody else (teachers, monitors, tutors and students). All participants are co-responsible for and co-authors of the collective production of knowledge. And everyone helps each other in their individual production (own authorship) (Okada & Okada, 2007 p. 725). However, in order to have effective mediation and intermediation, in the sense of provoking collaboration and cooperative

processes to knowledge building, it is necessary to recognize the other as a legitimate one interacting with the whole, and for Maturana (1997), this is only possible through love.

According to Maturana (2004), we are creatures driven by feelings and these feelings define the course of what we do and how we live and share. For Maturana and Rezepka (2000) love is "having control of the relationship behavior through someone who is considered as a legitimate being living together with someone else" (p.29). Maturana (1997) says that rational decisions are, above all, emotional decisions, "all human behavior, as a way of interaction, comes from and occurs from an emotion which characterizes the action, and this also applies to thinking" (Maturana & Rezepka, 2000, p.30).

According to Trein and Backes (2009), the nature of the spaces dedicated for living and developing teaching and learning processes is historically and culturally physical. It is in the school or university classroom with the presence of both the teacher and the student that these processes occur. However we currently know that this living and sharing may occur in face-to-face physical contexts as well as in digital-virtual contexts, with an imbrication of the "analogical-physical world" with the "digital virtual world". In both of them it is crucial for teachers and students to set their common educational space together, by sharing their ideas in an environment ruled by mutual respect, internal solidarity, collaboration and cooperation. Taking into consideration what Maturana (1999) has stated, the grounds of teaching and learning relies on love, and we understand it is present no matter the nature of the space the subjects live and share in.

To conclude, we understand that we need to be careful with conclusions asserting that the current generation learns more and/or better than the previous ones due to their interaction with digital technologies. We understand that making such a statement requires inter- and trans-disciplinary, and longitudinally compared research, involving researchers from different areas of knowledge such as neuroscience, psychology, education, sociology, anthropology, computer science and communication. Some of the conclusions may be superficial, mainly when the object in question is analyzed only from the angle of one determined field of knowledge. What we do understand as a possible assertion with research developed so far is that the subject's interaction with the current social and physical world is becoming increasingly intense, mediated by different digital technologies, meaning that the current generation's subject develops himself by interacting through social and physical means and more recently, by digital means. As a result we understand that the means with which the subject interacts, as well as the way in which he interacts, may vary and this provides different constructions. This fact needs to be taken into consideration in the educational context and it needs to be thoroughly investigated.

REFERENCES

Backes, L. (2007). *A Formação do Educador em Mundos Virtuais: Uma investigação sobre os processos de autonomia e de autoria.* (Unpublished master's dissertation). Universidade do Vale do Rio dos Sinos, São Leopoldo, Brazil.

Becker, F. (2008). Aprendizagem – concepções contraditórias. *Schème: Revista Eletrônica de Psicologia e Epistemologia Genéticas, 1* (1), 53-73. Retrieved from http://www2.marilia.unesp.br/revistas/index.php/scheme/article/view/552

Castells, M. (1999). A sociedade em rede. São Paulo, Brazil: Paz e Terra.

Fagundes, L. da C., Sato, L. S., & Maçada, D. L. (1999). Projeto? O que é? Como se faz? In L. da C. Fagundes (Eds.), *Aprendizes do Futuro: As inovações começaram!* (pp. 15-26). Brasília, Brazil: MEC. Retrieved from http://www.dominiopublico.gov.br/download/texto/me003153.pdf

Freire, P. (1996). Pedagogia da autonomia: Saberes necessários à prática educativa. São Paulo, Brazil: Paz e Terra.

Howe, N., & Strauss, W. (2000). *Millennials Rising: The Next Great Generation*. New York, NY: Vintage Books.

Maturana, H. R., & Varela, F. J. (2001). A árvore do conhecimento: As bases biológicas da compreensão humana. São Paulo, Brazil: Palas Athena.

Maturana, H. R. (1993). As bases biológicas do aprendizado. Belo Horizonte, Brazil: Ed. Primavera.

Maturana, H. R. (1999). *Transformación en la Convivencia*. Santiago, Chile: Dolmen Ediciones.

Maturana, H. R., & de Rezepka, S. N. (2000). Formação Humana e Capacitação. Petrópolis, Brazil: Vozes.

Maturana, H. R., & Varela, F. J. (1997). De máquina e seres vivos: Autopoiese - a organização do vivo. Porto Alegre, Brazil: Artes Médicas.

Maturana, R. M., & Verden-Zöller, G. (2004). Amar e brincar – Fundamentos esquecidos do humano. São Paulo, Brazil: Palas Athena.

Moraes, M. C. (2003). Educar na Biologia do Amor e da Solidariedade. Petrópolis, Brazil: Vozes.

Morin, E. (2007). Introdução ao Pensamento Complexo. Porto Alegre, Brazil: Sulina.

Okada, A., & Okada, S. (2007). Novos Paradigmas na Educação online com a aprendizagem aberta. In *Proceedings of V Conferência Internacional de Tecnologias de Informação e Comunicação na Educação - Challenges* (pp. 1-12). Braga, Portugal: Universidade do Minho. Retrieved from http://people.kmi.open.ac.uk/ale/papers/a10challenges2007.pdf

Papert, S. (1988). Logo: Computador e educação. São Paulo, Brazil: Editora Brasiliense S.A.

Piaget, J. (1972). Development and learning. In C. S. Lavatelly & F. Stendler (Eds.), *Reading in child behavior and development* (pp. 7–20). New York, NY: Hartcourt Brace Janovich.

Piaget, J. (1987). *O Nascimento da Inteligência na Criança*. Suiça: Editora Guanabara.

Piaget, J., & Inhelder, B. (1968). A psicologia da criança. Rio de Janeiro, Brazil: Difel.

Prensky, M. (2001). Digital Natives, Digital Immigrants. *Horizon*, *9*(5), 1–6. doi:10.1108/10748120110424816

Schlemmer, E. (2002). *AVA: Um ambiente de convivência interacionista sistêmico para comunidades virtuais na cultura da aprendizagem.* (Unpublished doctoral thesis). Universidade Federal do Rio Grande do Sul, Porto Alegre, Brazil.

Schlemmer, E. (2006). O trabalho do professor e as novas tecnologias. *Textual*, *1*(8), 33–42.

Schlemmer, E. (2010). Formação de professores na modalidade online: Experiências e reflexões sobre a criação de Espaços de Convivência Digitais Virtuais ECODIs. *Em Aberto*, *23*, 99–122.

Small, G., & Vorgan, G. (2008). iBrain: Surviving the technological alteration of the modern mind. New York, NY: HarperCollins Publishers.

Torres, F. C., & Vivas, G. P. M. (2009). Mitos, realidades y preguntas de investigación sobre los 'nativos digitales': Una revision. *Universitas Psychologica, 8* (2), 323-338. Retrieved from http://revistas.javeriana.edu.co/index.php/revPsycho/article/view/476/355

Trein, D., & Backes, L. (2009). A Biologia do Amor para uma Educação sem Distâncias. In Proceedings of 15° Congresso Internacional ABED de Educação a Distância (pp. 1-10), Fortaleza, Brazil: ABED.

Veen, W., & Vrakking, B. (2009). *Homo Zappiens: Educando na era digital*. Porto Alegre, Brazil: *The Art of Medication*.

KEY TERMS AND DEFINITIONS

Development: It is an essential process where every learning element has a function in total development and therefore learning is subordinated to development (Piaget, 1972).

Digitally Naturalized: It is a process in which a certain species settles in a territory, being that territory different from the one it comes from. Naturalization is also understood as the subject's action of acquiring, by his own will, a nationality, different from his own one. We are, therefore, "analogical native" and "digital immigrants" in the process of naturalizing, because we are entering and getting to know, by our own will, the digital world which is welcoming us.

Homo Zappiens: They are the new generation, who has learnt how to deal with new Technologies, who has grown up using a variety of technological resources since their childhood (VEEN & VRAKKING, 2009, p. 12).

Information: Information is something that can be transmitted, used, manipulated and transformed by those watching or listening.

Knowledge: Is not a copy of reality; it is not merely looking and producing a mental copy or image of an event. In order to know an object it is necessary to act upon it. "Knowing is to modify, transform the object, understand this transformation process and consequently, understand the way the object is constructed" (Piaget, 1972, p. 1).

Learning: Learning in general is provoked by external situations and occurs only when there is active assimilation from the subject (Piaget, 1972, p.11); Learning happens when the behavior of a life form varies during its ontogeny, in a congruent way with variations within the environment, what it does, according to a contingent course in its interactions with it (Maturana, 1993, p. 82).

Networked Society: This current society, functions and dominating processes are becoming more and more organized as networks. These networks are part of a new social morphology in our society and the propagation of the network logics modifies significantly the operation and the results from the productive processes of experiences, power and culture (Castells, 1999).

ENDNOTES

[1] Presented more specifically over the following chapters and in Chapter 15 – Brazilian Experiences in Metaverse.

[2] Awareness is a Piagetian concept. According to Piaget (1978), "awareness" is a behavior interacting with all other conducts, "it is a real construction, consisting in creating not "the" awareness as a whole, but its different levels as more or less integrated systems" (p. 9) Nevertheless, Piaget has limited himself to study "awareness" under the behavior point of view, from material actions to operations. The problem consists in establishing what the subject is aware of, regarding his own actions, especially towards what he observes from the surrounding rules. This concept is better developed in Chapter 8 - Cognition and Socio-Cognition in Metaverse.

[3] Electronic learning is a distance education modality offered exclusively through a computer.

[4] *Mobile learning* is a distance education modality in which participants interact through mobile devices such as laptop computers, tablets, and smart phones, among other in wireless communication networks.

[5] Pervasive learning is a distance education modality in which the information meets the subject. It follows him through GPS-based finding systems, and it is the subject's responsibility to filter it.

[6] Ubiquitous learning is a distance learning modality which allows learning and teaching processes to take place anywhere at any time with any device in a continuous and integrated way.

[7] Immersive learning is a distance learning modality comprehending learning processes in 3D immersive environments, created from different digital technologies capable of providing immersive learning. This concept is also approached in Chapter 11 - The Real Virtuality of Metaverses.

[8] Ontogeny is the living being's history, from birth to death, or "the history of changes of a certain unit, as a result of interactions on its initial structure" (Maturana e Varela, 2001, p. 277).

[9] Autopoiesis is a concept developed by Maturana and Varela (1997; 2001). It means the action of self-generation. This concept is approached in Chapter 7 - Autopoietic machines and alopoietic machines: the structural coupling.

[10] It is an external factor causing the subjects signification system to unsettle and unbalance.

[11] For Schlemmer and Marson (2013), while the first perspective of virtual reality deals with "virtualization" of an existing reality (simulation), the second one, the real virtuality, deals with "realization" of a virtuality (what is in evidence – idea, imagination, etc.) constructed in the digital world. These concepts are approached in Chapter 11- The Real Virtuality of Metaverses.

[12] Telepresença is the presence through text, voice or image, as a secondary presence;

digital virtual presence is the presence through an avatar, as a primary presence. These concepts are approached in Chapter 5 – Immersion, Telepresence, and Digital Virtual Presence in Metaverses.

13   It refers to an identity constructed in different digital virtual spaces. In the Metaverse such identity happens through the creation of an avatar. This concept is approached in Chapter 4 - Avatar: Building a "Digital Virtual Self".

14   Structural coupling is the capacity the systems have to use elements from other systems to enable their own internal operations. Through the structural coupling a system "borrows" from another, seen as part of the first one, the necessary structures to carry out their own operations. This concept is approached in Chapter 7- Autopoietic Machines and Alopoietic Machines: The Structural Coupling.

15   Assimilation is a Piagetian concept representing the subject's action upon the learning object in order to understand it with the pre-existing cognitive structures.

16   Accommodation is a Piagetian concept representing the action of the object upon the subject, in other words, the outcome of the pressures forced by the environment.

17   http://www.media.mit.edu/people/papert

18   Parties where the subjects meet in the same physical space.

19   The 'scheme' is the core idea in 'Genetic Epistemology' by Jean Piaget and it has been progressively used in all levels of development and in several behavior records. For Piaget the scheme works as an organizer of cognitive behavior and addresses what may be generalized within a certain activity. It is an assimilation tool with the function of disclosing experiences data. According to Piaget (1968) the concept of scheme makes a very tight synthesis between the structural and functional aspects of knowledge: a scheme is an organized whole, in which internal elements imply one another, a group structure is susceptible to being inserted in bigger structures, and an assimilation tool that exists only by its own working. It is, then, simultaneously, an internal organization and the behavior's dynamic. Also, according to Piaget (1987), the scheme operates a functional interaction between the cognoscente and the real subjects. So, the notion of scheme carries out another synthesis, the subjective aspects and knowledge's objective. It approaches the subject's own structures that give the experience data a sense, but these structures also partially depend on their content and are a "synthesis of experiences". For the author, knowing consists of acting upon the real, transforming it, incorporating it to the subject's schemes. The scheme is the basic unit of the cognitive functioning. It is the combination and the coordination of schemes in structures that characterizes the level of the subject's cognitive development. Each of these structures enables a way of relating to and understanding reality.

20   The idea of structure is also vital in 'Genetic Epistemology' by Jean Piaget and we may understand it as the way knowledge constitutes a balance totality. The structure concept is the core of the organization that establishes relations between the subject's parts and whole, and not in the core of adaptation, that rules the relations between the subject and the environment. From a certain development level, the subject's behavior is guided by subjacent structures resulting from his mental activities coordination. According to Piaget there is no global structure, but structures capable of organizing themselves in a certain knowledge domain. This way every structure is structured by something. For Piaget every structure has a genesis and every genesis comes from a certain structure in order to lead it to a more

evolved type of structure. The construction of a mental structure requires a process of reflexive abstraction, because the elements of the structure are taken from structures in an inferior level and afterwards reorganized into a new plan.

21   Besides being a characteristic of the living being, autonomy is also a process constructed throughout life, interacting with others in spotting differences, conflicts and disturbances. The living being, to compensate such disturbances towards others, transforms the action responsible for giving the network a new shape. In this way, in a third degree autopoiesis, we perceive the solution to a problem in the living being's action to transform the group. We therefore experience a social autonomy. In other words, the social system transforms itself through its members' autopoiesis (Backes, 2007, p.121).

22   The authorship rises in the production of differences, in the displacement, in inversion, in the modification able to create novelty in digital virtual spaces (Backes, 2007, p.163).

Chapter 2
Network Learning Culture and the Emerging Paradigm

ABSTRACT

This chapter presents and discusses the Network Learning culture and the emerging paradigm. The authors approach the need for developing a network learning culture, under the perspective of an emerging paradigm, in the context of Teaching and Learning in the Network Society. They present and discuss a subtopic, "Emerging Paradigm: Reflections about Reality," to characterize this paradigm that is under construction. The subtopic, "Systemic Thinking and Complexity: The Emerging Paradigm," cites examples of theories that are being developed in this emerging perspective. "Epistemological Conceptions" is a subtopic where the authors discuss the epistemological, ontological, and methodological foundations of some contemporary theories. The last subtopic, "The Culture of Network Learning," covers the concepts that are involved in the formation of the network society. The conclusion is the emerging paradigm as concepts which are constructed in the everyday life of men and women.

INTRODUCTION

The humankind organization in contemporaneity, which constitutes a society that increasingly organizes itself through different digital virtual media like the network, can be called the "Network Digital-Virtual Society", which represents the ontological construction of a certain group which lives and collaborates, builds knowledge and creates reality in different spaces and dimensions. Every human being, through his ontogeny[1] (the historical construction of interactions carried out from birth to current times), contributes in a singular way to the constitution of this "Network

Digital-Virtual Society", either being a digital immigrant or a digital native[2], as discussed in chapter 1, Teaching and Learning in the Network Society.

We found ourselves in a particularly dynamic time, characterized by the permeability and plasticity of the contours and edges, among different generations and spaces, which were previously defined by Cartesian patterns. In the research developed by Backes (2011), participants from different generations, both from Brazil and France, were engaged and showed particular characteristics from the different generations such as familiarity or not with digital technologies and ease or difficulty in communicating using

DOI: 10.4018/978-1-4666-6351-0.ch002

different languages, as well as characteristics typical of the different spaces, such as Brazilians immediately adhering to digital technologies, and French participants being strongly critical of digital technologies. The ecological disasters, the economic crisis, globalization, individual and social pathologies and the development of digital technologies, empowers us to reframe our relations and rebuild the world in which we live. So, we build up new knowledge, based on different logics of thinking, past and future meet in a present under transformation, according to Maffesoli (2012), a "dynamic rooting", where the archaic (past/origin) is in synergy with the technological development (future/perspective).

When considering contemporary dynamics, so that we can evidence emergent ones, we seek an interactionist understanding – constructive – systemic – complex, which obviously consists of an emerging paradigm. According to Pérez Goméz (2001), a paradigmatic conception implies:

The basic system of beliefs, of principles, of the general view of reality and of knowledge, that guide, condition and empower the work of researchers, intellectuals, politicians and doers was subverted in a deeply radical way which directly affects not only the choice of production methods and diffusion of knowledge, but specifically and clearly, the very concept of knowledge itself, (epistemology) and the consideration of reality (ontology). (p.61)

Given this reality we build and which builds us at the same time, we need to think about our way of thinking, to look inside ourselves in order to raise awareness of our living and sharing. In this way, we can go forward, not through transforming reality but above all, through knowing our intentions, which define the paths we choose. With that said, we do not dominate reality nor do we steer it, rather we are part of it.

In this chapter we firstly describe the paradigmatic trends that contributed to the ontological construction of the reality in which we live, so as to approach the epistemological choice that supports our thinking in a swirl by the converging of divergent flows, as well as with congruent methodologies. By the end it will be possible to demonstrate the ideas about culture and network learning, constituting digital virtual living and collaborating[3].

EMERGING PARADIGM: REFLECTIONS ABOUT REALITY

When we think about human relations, in a current context, based on structured theoretical assumptions from the past, or even, when we think about human relations from the past based on structured theoretical assumptions in contemporaneity, we accept the challenge of breaking the notions of time and space to understand that men and women build their relationships in spaces of flow in a timeless time. Physical mobility also brings digital-virtual mobility as people travel to other countries and start instant communication with people who are encouraged to use digital-virtual spaces, even when there is no technological fluency. So, digital-virtual mobility also brings physical mobility when we want to know our "virtual friend" in a physical way.

Living and sharing structures, especially the cognitive ones, are modified through collaboration. This dialectic can be seen when we read a hypertext through links, modifying the way we use post-its to indicate the links we wish to make in a book.

According to Sousa Santos (2004) we live between two situations:

On the one hand the potential of the technological translation of the accumulated knowledge makes us believe in a threshold of an interactive communication society free from the needs and insecurities that still preoccupy many of us today: The 21st century has begun before beginning. On the other hand an even deeper reflection about the limits of scientific rigor combined with the increasing dangers of ecological catastrophe or nuclear war make us fear that the 21st century ends before it has begun. (p.14)

This day by day living, marked above all by differences, crises and doubts may stress the relationship between men and women, triggering transformations, giving rise to a living that manages time, which is timeless, and a space, which is constituted of flows. Such transformations occur in their own way, affecting social relations, professionals, politicians, religions and educators, forming distinct identities in men and women who coexist in other realities in a single world (physical and digital-virtual), that we still do not know if we are building, destroying or rebuilding.

Under this perspective, science explores new reorganizations and concepts. According to Sousa Santos (2004), this process can be evidenced in breaking the dominant paradigm that emerges so that we can become conscious of our making. The linearity of thinking is tensioned by the dialectic, which is increasingly evident in simple interactions between different generations, in the dynamic of immersion in 3D digital virtual worlds and in the complexity of ubiquity given by digital technologies.

In this context, the Dominant Paradigm characterized by linearity, a single objective truth does not find justification for its comprehensions, when in the network context. This paradigm, driving and being driven by the natural sciences, working with the possibility of a single way of true knowledge, is forming the distinction between scientific knowledge and common sense.

To know means to quantify, divide and classify, in order to determine systematic relations about the object of knowledge. What is not systematically measured is irrelevant. These conceptions that derive from scientific revolution became the model of rationality for modern society, and were based on the domain of natural science and also on social sciences.

Science, in the dominant paradigm, is a total and global model. All knowledge ways that are not guided by the epistemological principles and their methodological rules are uncharacterized as rational and credible. Therefore, emphasis and priority lie in formal logic, in generalizations and in permanent structures - independent of time and space.

In attempting to overcome crisis, humanity, through relations of conjunction and/or disjunction, is to build a group of concepts that emerge in human beings' living and collaborating.

We emphasize that a paradigm is not something given, but something emerging from constructed contexts lived by people, within a certain time and space. We have no intention of proposing a new paradigm, but instead aim to point out elements contributing to the establishment of a new paradigm. As the name suggests, "Emergent" is not something readily provided, but something dynamic, coming from a continuous movement of constructions in all domains.

So, the emerging paradigm, as the name suggests, is not yet a reality, but an emergency in an attempt to overcome a strong characteristic nowadays evidenced. Nevertheless, it announces many intentions that have already been modifying our way of living, to overcome conflicts and crisis.

The knowledge of the emergent paradigm tends to be not a dualistic knowledge, a knowledge that is based on overcoming familiar and obvious distinctions, which we recently considered irreplaceable, such as nature/culture, natural/artificial, living/inanimate, mind/material, observer/observed, subjective/objective, collective/individual, animal/person. (Sousa Santos, 2004, p. 64)

Under this perspective, knowledge is built through overcoming and emancipation based on complementarity, in coexistence and in multidimensionality, which means, in transiting within dichotomies. There are, then, four main theses constituting the emergent paradigm: all natural-scientific knowledge is social-scientific; all knowledge is local and total; all knowledge is self-knowledge; all scientific knowledge aims to constitute a common sense.

In this context, comprehension of what knowledge is presents particular characteristics. The dichotomy between natural science and social science is overcome in its different instances such as: subject/object; subjective/objective; individual/collective; physical/virtual, and so on, because they are inserted in a history and its development process, pertinent to the way men and women live and how they establish coexisting relations. "In short, as natural science approaches social science, they approach humanities" (Sousa Santos, 2004, p.69). So, in the dominant paradigm, the world that today is natural is not social, and the one that is social is not natural, but in the emerging paradigm, with the overcoming of the dichotomies, the world will be both of them (natural and social; physical and virtual).

In the perspective of emergency, the relation between subject and object of knowledge is understanding dialectics, formed in the interactions of living and not only surviving. "Each one is the translation of the other, both text writers, written in distinct languages, both known and required to learn how to like the words and the world" (Sousa Santos, 2004, p.87) so knowledge is what enables the understanding of a world to be contemplated, transformed and not dominated by human beings.

Knowledge also comes to be understood in its universal totality and as life projects of a particular individual or social group, forming through themes that meet each other, interrelation, and that are amplified as a huge network. The post modern knowledge, being total, is not deterministic, being local, it is not descriptive. It is knowledge about

the conditions of possibility. "The conditions of human being possibilities projected in a world from a local space-time" (Sousa Santos, 2004, p.77).

In the emerging paradigm, scientific knowledge will have sense and greater value when transformed into common sense, as a result it will orient actions and will transform life, through assimilation and use. "Post modern science, when taking on common sense, does not disregard the knowledge that produces technology, but understands that like knowledge, technological development must translate into wisdom of life" (Sousa Santos, 2004, p.91). So, it is in this context of an emerging paradigm, that we can comprehend digital technologies, their potentialities and limitations, and make it a space to live and for living with others, so that both can transform in congruence with this digital-virtual media that presents its own characteristics and that perfectly coexists with other physical spaces in the perspective of complementarity.

SYSTEMIC THINKING AND COMPLEXITY: THE EMERGING PARADIGM

In the context of emerging paradigms we can highlight the theory of complexity, the systemic thinking and the conception of auto-eco organized which, although treated separately in this text, are dialectically related in the living and co-living of human beings. The human being, in its relations, is contradictory through interactions with the others they transform the living and co-living and they auto-produce continually in congruence with the environment. These theories take on a proper configuration when inserted in the context of digital technologies, especially in the use of metaverses, which enable the construction of the 3D digital virtual world, a living space for the human being, who in this case, is represented by avatars[4]. The metaverses are formed in the relations and interactions of human beings, who revealed this perspective of world, through graphic representation in 3D that is instantly updated. In this sense we can promote, through the 3D digital virtual world, the intersections of different perspectives, in a dialectical combination of several world representations, belonging to every human being, through their avatar, in the active search for a construction in another world.

The construction of the world occurs in the complexity of interactions between inhabitants and e-inhabitants[5]. According to Morin (2006), complexity "is a problem-word and not a solution-word" (p.6). The term disconnects from its common usage (complication, confusion) and it brings order, disorder and contradiction. In this process there is organization of the use and of the multiple notions that influence one another and simultaneously complement antagonistically. According to the author "complexity is a fabric (complexus: a combined fabric) of heterogeneous constituents inseparably linked: it sets up the paradox of the one and the multiple… complexity is effectively the fabric of happenings, actions, interactions, retroactions, determinations, that constitute our phenomenal world" (p.13).

The ambition of complex thinking is to realize the link between the disciplinary fields that are dismembered by disjunctive thinking (one of the main aspects of simplifying thinking), this isolates what separates and hides everything that reconnects, interacts and interferes. In this sense, complex thinking aspires to multidimensional knowledge… . It implies the recognition of a principle of incompleteness and uncertainty. It also brings in this principle the recognition of linking among the entities that our thinking must necessarily distinguish, but without isolating one from the other… . Complex thinking is also animated by a permanent tension between the aspiration to a knowledge that is not fragmented, not compart-

mentalized, not redactor, and the recognition of the unfinished nature and incompleteness of any knowledge. (Morin, 2006, p.6)

In complexity, according to Morin (2006), it is not possible for absolute and isolated knowledge to exist because the complex thinking is, by definition, relative and contextual; it implies unity with multiplicity and unity in diversity. It refers to the capacity of dealing with the uncertain and the possibility of auto-organization.

So, the theory of complexity is characterized by non-linear thinking, the scientific explanations are built on dynamics and relations. Therefore, the attention of the researcher lies not only in the structures of human beings but also in the process of relations between human beings through these structures.

Once most scientists are used to working with linear models, they are often reluctant to adopt non-linear structures of theory of complexity and it is difficult for them to understand all implications of non-linear dynamics. This is specifically applied to the phenomenon of spontaneous emergence. The way in which conscious experience can emerge from neurophysiological processes can be highly mysterious. However its appearance is a typical phenomenon of emergence. The spontaneous emergence results in the creation of novelties and such novelties are often qualitatively different from the phenomena originating them. (Capra, 2002, p.47)

In this sense, the complexity theory consists of "…having a way of thinking capable of thinking contradictions, of analyzing and synthesizing, of constructing, deconstructing and reconstructing something new" (Moraes, 2003, p.199). With this in mind, digital technologies are able to provide important movements for complexity theory to develop in a consistent way. The use of metaverses in living and sharing inverts the logic of representation of perception in a predominant way, either oral or textual, to the combination of different languages in using graphic representation, metaphoric, through dynamic interactions in a network. So, when different human beings meet inside this large network, through their interaction processes, they establish different disturbances in congruence with the environment. The necessity to compensate for such disturbances is the reason for different social networks.

Social networks are also non-linear organizational patterns, so the concepts to develop them using the theory of complexity, like feedback or spontaneous emergence, probably find their application here. However, network links are not simply biochemical. Networks are, first of all, communication networks involving symbolic language limited by culture, relations of power and so on. (Capra, 2002, p.85)

So, the complexity theory is effective and increases as human beings constitute dialogical relations that consist of the possibility of every human being representing their perspective and condition, with others, transforming the reality in which they live, without being exclusionary.

Dialogue is the moment when human beings meet to reflect on their reality such as they do and undo it. In addition: as communicative human beings who communicate with each other we become more capable of transforming our reality, we are capable of knowing that we know, which is something that goes beyond merely knowing. (Freire, 1992, p.123)

In summary, human relations, by their contradictory nature, allow the breaking down of dichotomies in a complementary sense, through dialogic relations, so that the interaction flow

is kept among human beings that e-live in a 3D digital virtual world, in coexistence with other worlds. This movement enables other forms of understanding and reality, and explains knowledge, consisting of a fertile space for knowledge development of systemic thinking. More and more human beings can meet each other through technologies and build interesting cross-relations of different knowledge, built from everyone's reality.

Thinking systematically consists of alternating the logic perception of the knowledge object through the parts and dichotomizing the whole and the parts, for the comprehension of the logic of everything through the parts and parts through the whole. So, there exists the possibility of alternating the look of one part for another and realizing the different existence levels and the complexity of each level. For Capra (2004, p.46), "the properties of the parts are not intrinsic properties, but they can also be understood in the context as a whole". So, the systemic thinking is to think the context, the environment and the human relations between men and women that give sense to living. Under this perspective the observation is not the object but the relations and interactions that are present in an interconnected network. "This relation web is described through a correspondent network of concepts and models, where everything is equally important". (p.49) The way of observing is realized by the disturbance of the observed. "So, the systemic thinking involves a move from objective science to epistemic science, to a framework in which epistemology – questioning method – becomes an integral part of scientific theories" (p.49).

For Maturana (1997) the systemic phenomenon is characterized "as the result of the action of the components of a system as they realize the relations that define the system as it is, and yet, none of them alone even determines when its presence is strictly needed". (p.24) In the development of biological theories of knowledge, biology of love and cultural biology, systemic thinking is in the comprehension between subject and object "in this line of explanation even the cognoscente and cognoscible are seen as presenting intrinsic properties and are unchangeable, with the proper existence independent of the interaction or inter-relation between them during the knowledge act" (Maturana, 2002, p.22). Knowledge is present in the breaking of dichotomy between subject and object, through relations and articulations, present in a determined context, that refer to other comprehensions constituting the dynamic network of living. In a Metaverse, the systemic thinking effects accordingly to what e-inhabitants establish in dialogic relations to the construction of world (3D digital virtual world) they intend to represent. The possibility of graphic representation implies the use of metaphors that need to be significant to the cognitive context and interpreted in the social context. The relation and established interactions constitute a significant expansion for building knowledge, not only in the conceptual sense, but in the epistemic sense of construction.

For Maturana (1999) network configures itself through a community, in its process, actions, meeting, emotions… defining a proper way to relate and interact, building forms of living between men and women of community and defining the way of living. In the interlacement of doing and emotional, men and women constitute the conversation network, defining everyday what is wished and unwished, the legitimate and the illegitimate, the acceptable and the unacceptable, that are incorporated by the members.

However, the network is dynamic and as it moulds living, it defines the mould. Education then consists of the transformation process in the intimacy, which is present in every dimension: family, school, work, communication means… .

Through this living, every human being is transformed in a continuous process of auto-production, that results in an expansion of his perspective as a legitimate, intelligent, loving, world building human being. To use the 3D digital virtual world to its full potential, e-inhabitants must keep these characteristics, which will allow the construc-

tion of a world that is not only a representation of the physical world, and not a world that is not understandable by others, but a world that can be a space of digital virtual collaboration.

The auto-eco-organizer concept brings us the conception of a human being who is fully capable of generating his own learning and his independent, dynamic and unpredictable development. In discussing the concept of the auto-eco-organizer, Soares (2010) says:

According to Morin (2007, apud Moraes, 2008) all living creatures are capable of organizing themselves through links or processes with their environment. This action explains the intrinsic condition between autonomy and dependence. Dependence is explained through the observation that, for a subject to become autonomous, he needs (and depends on) his relations with the environment, and his constructive capacity. According to Moraes (2008, p.103), 'auto-organization presupposes the ability of auto-production of self, of auto-creation of one's structures, using one's components'. (p.96)

Therefore, the 3D digital virtual world will be constituted as an autopoietic environment when the interaction process between the e-inhabitants, and the e-inhabitants with their environment enables the conservation of organization of every e-inhabitant based on their structural transformations. In the research developed by Backes (2007) we found that students in an interaction process in 3D Digital Virtual Worlds showed significant difficulty in representing knowledge about "Innatism", through a metaphor and/or 3D graphic. In many cases, they looked to their colleagues for alternatives in compensating for their difficulties discussing the knowledge in question (Innatism), as well as paradigmatic knowledge of ways of constructing knowledge itself (metaphoric and 3D graphic representation). The construction of knowledge has changed both students' comprehension (their structure) and the space's "scenario"

(3D digital virtual world). The possibility of structural transformations, through interactions also modifies in a recursive way, the interaction processes, promoting structural couplings[6] in the configuration of a 3D digital virtual world.

EPISTEMOLOGICAL CONCEPTIONS

We can demonstrate the new orientations and significations that are being built in everyday living, as this is necessary for the comprehension of the facts regarding context and the history of a reflexive way. According to Pérez Goméz (2001, p.62)

As a consequence of flexibility, human phenomena are characterized by the singularity and plasticity that give them their learning capacity as well as their emerging character, and by their permanent openness to new forms or ways of being that assume the reconstruction of their previous formulations.

Reality is built in dialectic relations between human beings who live in a construction of new knowledge, and in this way, the shared living generates the necessary movements for a transformation of reality. To further explore the process of reflection, we will focus on ontological particularities, which are epistemological and methodological and are based on systemic thinking, complexity and the concept of auto-eco-organizer.

Ontological Characteristics

Humanity is experiencing a historical and rich moment where huge knowledge can be constructed with the meeting of analogical (or digital immigrant) and digital generations (or digital native). The reframing of notions of space, time and identity of contemporary human beings, contributes to the permeability and the plasticity of edges (territorial, cultural, social, economic), and to the reconstruction of the world. To distinguish something in the world we define edges that configure

the way in which we realize reality, the definitions of the edge are in a distinctions process in relation to what is in the context, especially in terms of interactions and relations to the other.

...that is why, in the cosmos that is emerging with our operation, everything takes place in local interactions that show us a dynamic architecture that occurs as a changing present that only shows itself to us as understandable thanks to the invention of time, allowing us the invention of memory as an aspect of this changing present in non-time. (Maturana & Yáñez, 2009, p.304)

However, the edges with the reframed notions of time and space are becoming more and more imperceptible through the capacity of plasticity that human beings are developing for digital technologies. Paradoxically we close and distance the coexisting worlds.

We are, then, human beings in constant action, as the authors of the world we create, and we are responsible for living and establishing permanent relations that allow us to know other worlds. This knowledge occurs in the interaction process with the other, this other being someone legitimate with whom we can learn.

Within this dynamic we begin to form ourselves as human beings and to participate in this social system. The changes from every individual produce other changes, opening and closing possibilities of articulation in the composition of social system. The social systems are formed by human beings who constitute the same relation constructed by the system. So, each social system is unique and particular, because every individual constituting it establishes their relation and interaction from their ontogeny. This raises a dynamic of transformation, mainly when structured in a 3D digital virtual world.

The possibility of approaching people who are constituted by completely different ontogeny in a representation through an avatar, who are materialized in a metaphoric representation, and who will be interpreted by the other, in the interaction process, certainly constitutes a totally different social system, that can be innovative for humanity. "... the innovation emerges as a network conversation that mixing relations and operations that occur in disconnected domains, is at the origin of a new relational and operational domain that is surprising and desirable at the same time" (Maturana & Yáñez, 2009, p.313).

The processes of relations and interactions, established in a 3D digital virtual world are done so by authors (human beings) who make their world emerge so that they are fixed to the world of other, through operational recursive coherences, that bring the intentions of those they represent, but that is not controlled or predictable. In this sense, new ways of living emerge, influencing and being constantly constructed by the new generations.

For Soares (2010) these transformations indicate the perception that the way of knowledge is not defined by the perfectly synchronized universal mechanisms, but in phenomenon that auto-eco-organizes to produce autonomy balance, plurality and disorder.

We constitute and are constituted by multiple realities that can be different segments and different dimensions. Sometimes these realities meet, blend, other times they are parallels, distant and imperceptible. But at all times these different worlds are constructed in a relational and articulated way. Even without establishing a relation in a 3D digital virtual world, a human being can configure livings with others that can be constructed in the 3D digital virtual world and the 3D digital virtual world will be present in their ontogeny construction.

This movement, resulting in a continuous transformation of humanity, takes place due to the unfinished characteristic of human beings, to produce themselves in relation to other human beings, in congruence with the environment. Secondly, it is due to the creative dimension of each moment in which the human being assumes the role of author of the world in which he lives,

and, thirdly and most importantly, the capacity of intentional change when they are capable of reflecting on their autonomous actions in making their choice.

Epistemological Characteristics

Digital technologies are providing new ways of constituting social systems, so that the process of relations and interaction also passes through these transformations that enable other ways of constructing knowledge. The construction of knowledge happens in the effective action of human beings, the structural coupling with the other where the interactions emerge with the internal and external world, in the living, in congruence with the environment.

So, if the 3D digital virtual world provides the potential for new ways of interaction, relation and representation of perception, and represents a different potentiality of the physical world, that it is very familiar, how can we epistemologically understand the construction of knowledge of a human being who is in congruence with the 3D digital virtual world?

To Maturana (1999, p.79), the construction of knowledge occurs according to the following:

Everyone listens from their own perspective, and listens to what comes from their inside. Everyone who listens, reveals themselves; this must be understood because it is related to the phenomenon of knowing, and to a broader aspect, which is the multiplicity of the cognitive domains in which we exist, each one of us determined by a way of listening, which is also a way of determining what is acceptable and what is not part of this domain.

The novelty the 3D digital virtual world represents to the lives of human beings who e-inhabit it, is a disturbing element, altering the way of seeing phenomena. In the effort to overcome this disturbance, the human being observes the possibilities and limitations of this new space, as well as making use of the autonomy that is inherent to the human being, discovering how to live and survive in 3D digital virtual world, and the authorship, that permits us to give rise to the world we live in, in a graphic representation of perception. 3D digital virtual worlds do not exist, nor are they pre-existing, they are constructed according to their e-inhabitants interaction and constructions, in the recursive relation with the other through their ontogeny. In this way, we are in the coexistence between different worlds.

Knowledge, in this context, is represented in a complex, systemic and auto-eco-organizer way. The logic of representing knowledge by textual or oral language is complemented by the possibility of representing knowledge through metaphors which implies in the comprehension of knowledge, meaning in relation to something metaphorical and in the reconstruction of each interpretation of other e-inhabitants with the constructed graphic representation. In this sense, knowledge only makes sense when interpreted by the other who gives sense to what was constructed. The knowledge comprehension is not only in the representation but also in interactions that representations potentiate. In this way, the e-inhabitants maximize the knowledge construction, resulting in a learning process that drives the development of new learning.

In this context, we constitute ourselves through exploring, experimenting, acting and interacting with other e-inhabitants and with the 3D Digital Virtual World itself, carrying out similarities and differences needed for the signification and re-signification of the real virtuality, represented by the creation of the 3D digital virtual world, in a dynamic environment that modifies in real time and of multiusers that act and interact through an avatar, creating networks.

Action and interaction through an avatar (which can construct a digital-virtual identity) consists of the telepresence of a human being in the 3D Digital Virtual World, such as the presence in digital-virtual, to make actions, construct tridimensional objects and communicate through oral, textual, gestural and graphic languages in the interaction with other avatars. The graphic representation of an human being (avatar) in a 3D digital virtual world enhances the presence in virtual contact (different from other digital technologies where the presence is accomplished by a text or voice) and, in a certain way, it humanizes the contact between human beings through the impression of the physical appearance, mainly when it is possible to personalize the avatar.

Different from other digital technologies, the 3D Digital Virtual World enables a living and co-living that enhances the sensation of being present through immersion and representation via avatar, such as the feeling of belonging to this space that is cooperatively and collaboratively constructed. In this sense, 3D digital virtual worlds are more appropriate for the construction of knowledge in situations of physical distance than other technologies. One of the biggest problems of online education is the student's drop out rate.

Within this context, thinking about knowledge construction becomes a significant challenge. Metaverses can be seen as an important and challenging space for living among human beings that e-live. This shared living space facilitates the construction of new cognitive structures, as it challenges the following: learning how to construct in a 3D digital virtual world; creating the most appropriate metaphor for the representation of knowledge; establishing interaction process using different methods of communication; changing the point of view of knowledge objects, with the simple flight of an avatar; living with others in a cooperative and collaborative way in the construction of living spaces; understanding the presence of the other (who may be physically distant) through immersion via avatar and one's actions and understanding the other as someone legitimate, with whom one can learn. However the interest every e-inhabitant has defines the way we configure relationships and interactions with the other. These interests promote or reduce potential.

Methodological Characteristics

The methodological proposals guide e-inhabitants' actions in the 3D digital virtual world, empowering or replacing them. Just as the methodological proposals do, 3D digital virtual worlds also scale e-inhabitants' actions, because they are in congruence. Coherent with the ontological and epistemological characteristics, the methodological proposals that can meet the characteristics of the complexity theory, of the systemic thinking and the concept of eco-auto-organizer, are focused around dialogic relations so that through mediation interaction processes can be configured, through procedures that develop learning projects based on problems, for a metaphoric representation of knowledge.

The development of digital technologies is characterized by the diversity of the ways of communication, in a textual, oral, graphic or gestural way, or as synchronous or asynchronous interactions. So, when we use digital technologies to their full potential, we need methodological proposals, which contemplate the dialogical relations, as it can involve a great number of e-inhabitants in a continuous and heterarchical flow.

The word dialogue comes from the Greek, *logos* – sense, word; *dia* – through. As a result, dialogue consists of giving meaning to words when pervaded by a group of people. In the pedagogical context the dialogue was widely discussed by Freire (1992, p.123) conceptualizing it as follows:

The dialogue is the moment in which human beings meet to reflect about their reality, the way they do and re-do it. In addition: considering we are communicative beings, communicating with the other, as we are able to transform our reality, we are able to know that we know, which is something other than just knowing.

So, in a pedagogical context the concept of the word dialogue is broadened in the sense that we assign a meaning that is originated from a reflexive and conscious process of a determined group. The dialogic relation, possible in a 3D digital virtual world, consists of the representation of the different worlds brought by every e-inhabitant, in the reflection on different realities in a reframing for the solutions to difficulties, aiming for the group's welfare. There are two extremely relevant aspects: the legitimization of reality brought by the other and the awareness of the reframing process. The 3D digital virtual world enables a cross meaning of different cultures, mainly because they are symbolically represented in graphic constructions, by the objects of by the avatar. In this context, to establish a dialogic relation there cannot be a better reality than the other or the superior, and the reframing of these realities must follow the perspective of overcoming, for the emancipation of the group, not the selection of one reality at the expense of another.

Mediations are established in dialogic relations, that consist of the complex movement there is in the living among men and women. The complex movement that characterizes the mediation, according to Morin (apud Moraes, 2003), consists of articulating the object of knowledge in a contradictory and dual way, understanding the dynamics between the antagonistic and the complementary, understanding the multiple realities in which we live, being human beings in action, interaction and retroaction, of living under the perspective of coexistence, and of being in a constant process of reflection. This reflection consists of the action of making that which is not made by others with whom we live.

Reflection is a process of knowing how we know, an act of turning back to ourselves, the only opportunity we have to find out our blindness and recognize that the certainties and the knowledge of others are, respectively as distressing and as tenuous as ours. (Maturana & Varela, 2002, pp.29-30)

So, to think about mediation as a complex movement of dialogic relations, which results in the reflection of human beings in interaction, consists of:

a communicational and conversational process of conveying meaning, with the objective of opening and facilitating dialogue and developing significant negotiation and content processes to be carried out in educational environments, as well as to incentivize the construction of a relational and contextual knowledge, generated in the teacher/student interaction. (Moraes, 2003, p.210)

In this sense we broaden the comprehension for pedagogical mediation, which occurs when men and women, in the interaction process, establish dialogue for the construction of knowledge, through mutual respect and legitimacy to the other. This relation exists between co-teachers and co-learners who are in the flow of living and sharing. The pedagogical mediation is what happens among human beings regardless of their position in the interaction process to the construction of knowledge (whether educator or learner), because the relations are heterarchies.

The teacher and the learner, when in pedagogical mediation, have their aims and objectives. The teacher is responsible for the teaching process, and is the authority of knowledge, but this is different from the comprehension of authoritarianism. The learner is responsible for his learning, knows what he still does not know and what he would like to know. But in this process, everyone is the learner and the teacher, if they are in a pedagogical mediation. The teacher learns by teaching and the learner teaches when learning.

The participants are also pedagogical mediators when they are more open in the learning process. Students share not only their background knowledge and opinions about the subject but also

critical reflections through multiple feedbacks to all colleagues, who also become co-authors of the production of the course or from their community. (Okada & Okada, 2007, p.725)

Using this perspective it is possible to conceive of pedagogical mediation using the structural coupling that implies in living and sharing with the other, and in congruence with the environment, keeping a dynamic flow of interactions.

Living together for human beings takes place in an environment that is in congruence in a complementary perspective. Human beings interact with each other, placing disturbances, reciprocally performing the role of compensatory disturbances. This way, when two or more autopoietic unities (in this case, the human being) are in the interaction process, one of the unities realizes the other unity through its structure, constructed by the ontogeny, which is unique and particular. Realizing the other unity, distinguishing everything that is different, contradictory or similar, will construct elements of disturbance and structure that will start the process of adaptation and will constitute the conception of auto-eco-organizer.

Adaptation always results from a sequence of interactions of a plastic system in its environment that triggers structural changes or state changes, that at any moment, select a structure from the environment in which it works in (interacts or behave) as a system, or it disintegrates. (Maturana, 2002, p. 137)

"This means that two or more autopoietic unities can be coupled in ontogeny, when their interaction takes on a recurrent character or it becomes very stable" (Maturana & Varela, 2002, p.87). Therefore, recurrence implies in reciprocity, and as they are unique and particular structures, they reveal disturbances among unities and the environment in congruence. The compensation for such disturbances, in which everyone undergoes transformation (human beings and environment), consists of structural coupling.

As a result, all mediation thought by structural coupling, presents characteristics of establishing heterarchical relations, creating the profile of co-learner and co-teacher, proposing the development of the reflection and considering the transformation of everyone who is in interaction.

The meaning and the purpose of pedagogical mediations consist of "(…) maintenance of the interaction flow, in the conversations established, or, in the dialogue and in the living of the process itself…" (Moraes, 2003, p. 212).

In the coexisting perspective, when we approach a 3D digital virtual world, we think about pedagogical mediation to configure the digital-virtual collaborating space, because we are in congruence with the environment (the digital-virtual space, in this case). Digital-virtual living and collaborating have started to become organized through the studies carried out by Backes and Schlemmer (2006) – when they describe the Digital Virtual Living Space [7] interface. Following this, Backes (2007) argues that for the configuring of the digital-virtual space, the human being, represented by his avatar, lives in a 3D digital virtual world in a constant process of interaction. The disturbance resulting from this interaction and the congruence of digital-virtual environments are compensated in mediation among e-inhabitants, so that they can build other knowledge.

it is necessary that the units of living systems in interaction in a determined digital-virtual living space, act in a dynamic way through the context. So that the reciprocal disturbances are effective in the interactions, this dynamic system allows the configuring of a new space, representing the dominium of relations and interactions of the live system with totality. (Backes, 2007, p.70)

So, we are talking about a relational and contextual knowledge, which is

generated in an ecology of thoughts and actions that emerge due to the circumstances created in learning environments, in the ecology of meanings that arise from the dialogue, from living and sharing, where they are mutually being transformed while simultaneously, they transform themselves. (Moraes, 2003, pp.213-214)

Pedagogic mediation takes place when, from this living, men and women transform themselves through a transformation process, by way of which they also modify the dynamic space of relation (physical or digital-virtual). As a result of the pedagogical mediation, it is desirable that, within this transformation, other knowledge is constructed. And, besides that, this knowledge can induce the structure of the human being, and that this human being can accomplish their condition, and can have more power when deciding their living, in an autonomous way, they can transform a better living, focusing on the group's welfare.

In summary, pedagogical mediation is found in the principle of the theory of complexity and of systemic thinking, where we aim to break the dichotomies in the sense of being complementary, through dialogic relations, so that the flow of interactions between human beings is maintained. Pedagogical mediation is not at a defined point, but it is present along the whole interaction process and affects the structure of every human being involved, therefore it is not possible to impose a mediation situation for it implies being co-authors, co-teachers and co-learners, and we must therefore turn to an auto-eco-organizer conception.

In order to be able to actually establish the dialogic relations in a mediation process, our actions must transit between individual and social dimensions. This transit can be enhanced through the methodology of learning projects based on problems. The methodology of learning projects based on problems adapted to universities, according to Schlemmer (1999, 2001, 2005) and Trein and Schlemmer (2009), is based on presupposition of cooperative activity, it allows for interaction and enables a process of action-reflection of human beings who are in a learning process, in the case of metaverse technology, the e-inhabitants who develop the project in a 3D digital virtual world. The presupposition of cooperative activity includes and encourages autonomy through intellectual, social, cultural and political changes, favoring metacognition and awareness.

Methodology using learning projects based on problems considers the relation of dialogue, with the objective of drawing out the potential of creativity and ruptures, according to Freire (1992), bringing illumination to both parts (teachers and learners), through the mediation process. According to Schlemmer (2005), the development of the methodology consists itself, of a learning project that pre-supposes methodological experiences in those who wish to use it. This means that there is not a defined path to follow, but there is an epistemological conceptual base sustaining it.

The methodology can be developed from a thematic or a free platform. Both processes come from a collective decision among teachers and learners from an initial discussion that considers desires, necessities, actualities and characteristics from their area of knowledge, and the purposes of the e-inhabitants. The decisions are heterarchical and the work is developed in an environment of cooperation and mutual respect, in the search for autonomy, cooperation and solidarity.

In the 3D digital virtual world the development of the project and the learning construction coming from the problems treated by the e-inhabitants, are materialized by the construction of the world in graphic representations that can be metaphorical.

Metaphors are considered as:

expressions of life that enrich our meanings and interpretations and that will be an encouragement for the production and the diffusion of knowledge, whenever they are considered as attempts at approaches, as relatively risky hypothesis that evoke reflection and searching. (Pérez Goméz, 2001, p.71)

In this way, e-inhabitants' actions in a 3D digital virtual world, graphically represented by metaphors, imply in movement, transformation and creativity, and represent an innovation in the way of living. The graphic representation of thinking seems to be an entertaining activity, though not very well recognized. However, in the development process of e-inhabitants, it can be understood as a possibility of construction of new cognitive structures, because it gives the representation of knowledge in a different way, by instigating creativity. It contributes in a way to e-inhabitants have a better understanding of knowledge, because the creation of a metaphor implies knowing what they know and do not know, indentify the characteristics of knowledge, the elements which compose their contextualization in collaboration with the other.

The graphic representation of knowledge is understood in its complexity and in systemic relations. When we represent knowledge in a graphical way we need to identify what it means for us, establishing relation with symbols and objects and giving it a sense in the context which is in congruence. Such relations and reflections contribute to the e-inhabitants evidencing what is not understood about the knowledge to be represented, and it also enables self-production to compensate for the cognitive conflict, the disturbance of knowledge.

To understand reality or social reality in the life of any organization, and to rationally intervene in it requires facing complexity, diversity, singularity and the evolutionary feature of such reality, even when this pretension complicates the process of searching for relations and meanings. (Pérez Goméz, 2001, p.72)

We build meanings that are apparently contradictory, we make unpredictable and surprising events, but these are inserted in a context, in the ontological and ontogenic construction.

THE CULTURE OF NETWORK LEARNING

When reflecting about what we do in our daily lives we understand how we process what we do and transform the actions into concepts, systematizing theses processes we make. When we systematize what we do and transform them into concepts and theories, we are also defining such actions of future generations, who will, through their reflexive and conscious actions, construct new a systematization, broadening knowledge. As we configure this new ontological, epistemological and methodological scenario, we can also think of a learning culture which develops within a highly technologicized context, and so, why not consider a culture of network learning?

The concept of culture presents several faces, which remain or change according to how humanity develops, which is initially constituted by communities and then by societies. We can then take a look into our lives and notice that there are many ways to live and share, that are different perceptions and representations about what builds such living and sharing.

The comprehension of culture, while under construction, has passed through many changes. As a result, different theoretical authors, from different areas of knowledge have defined culture as a social heir that determines the individual and the group he belongs to. It has also been understood as a group of knowledge and values of common sense and as a result of human interaction influenced by politics, economic and social levels that acquire meanings.

Pérez-Goméz (2001) considers culture as being:

A set of meanings, expectations and behaviors shared by a given social group, which who facilitates and demands, limits and enhances social interchanges, symbolic productions and materials,

and the individual and collective accomplishments inside a determined spatial and temporal mark. (p.17)

It is therefore possible to understand culture as a configuration of a new living and sharing space, considering its material, social and emotional conditions, represented through values, symbols, feelings, rituals and customs that surround social and individual lives. Living in a certain culture consists of interpreting, reproducing, and transforming it, in other words, the culture both enhances and limits the development of human beings. "The nature of each culture determines the possibilities of creation and internal development, of evolution or stagnation, of autonomy or individual dependence" (Pérez Goméz, 2001, p.17).

When we configure living in an ecological space where different cultural crossings take place, it can represent a space of promotion and autonomy, of identity construction and reflective criticism, for the formation of a new generation. Both in the physical and the digital-virtual space, we search the configuration of ecological spaces, taking into account the particularities and differences in each space.

We can then characterize cultures as:

closed conversation networks, which means closed networks of recursive coordinations of actions and emotions. Nevertheless this emotional configuration that occurs within the closed conversation networks constitutes culture, giving them their own characteristics, different from the individual ones carried out by their members. (Maturana, 1999, p.51)

In digital virtual collaboration, we establish unique and particular relations of a determined group, which, with the plasticity and permeability of edges articulates with other groups through co-participation of human beings in different groups. When we think about the configuration of a digital-virtual living, where different cultures emerge, we are not referring to cyber culture, that Lemos (2007, p.72) understands as:

a social technical configuration where there will be tribal models associated with digital technologies, as opposed to the individualism of the printed, modern and technocratic culture. With cyber culture we are facing a process of acceleration, abolishing the homogeneous space, defined by geopolitical boundaries and chronological and linear time; the two pillars of western modernity. However this general connectivity is not free of criticism.

In this way we can think about digital virtual collaborating and sharing, using the perspective of coexistence of different spaces and times, constituting human beings' identity and identification. In coexisting we enable emergence through overcoming difficulties. So, a culture is considered as emergent because it is under construction and it is still not part of different generations' living and sharing. It is a form of construction of this generation, which is defined by some researchers like Veen and Vrakking (2009), as the "Homo Zappiens", and which constructs and is constructed through the multiplicity of contemporaneous society.

This continuous construction is effected through learning, which in this context involves aspects such as becoming familiar with a new digital-virtual space that implies graphic representation and immersion, acquiring the technological knowledge of how to build the world and an avatar, the different possibilities of interacting orally, textually, through gestures and graphically in a graphic 3D environment, and articulating these different ways to identify when it is most appropriate to use one or another. It is therefore necessary that in its living, every e-inhabitant can convey meaning to its own making and to the making of the other in relation to the social. Only through

this can he constitute himself as an autonomous subject and author of the world in which he lives, conscious of his actions and choices. In this way, learning within the 3D digital virtual world context contributes to developing the author's senses of observation, of carrying out the possibilities, of being autonomous and of his learning process. It also implies exploring, experimenting, connecting, being teased by the environment, accepting and interacting in congruence with 3D digital virtual world and with other e-inhabitants, finding the necessary approach and distance for signification.

In this action among e-inhabitants, we build up networks.

Every community exists as a network of processes, acts, meetings, behaviors, technical emotions, … which configure a system of living relations that penetrates all aspects of living of boys and girls who grow in the course of becoming adults in all dimensions of their doing and feeling. (Maturana, 1999, p.10)

The network configurations are exclusive and particular to each formation, for it is sustained, it organizes and self-organizes through autopoiesis of the human beings composing it. The network configuration defines the behavior that is appropriate or not appropriate to their components, taking into account legitimacy, and therefore the relations are not of a submissive nature.

Considering a certain culture occurs as a closed conversational network, when members from two cultures meet they can live a total cultural disagreement if they do not declare their condition of reflexive human beings and do not listen to one another because they do not want to be together; or their meeting can originate a creative meeting if they listen to each other because they want to be together, and a new culture arises, in the art of conversation. (Maturana & Yáñez, 2009, pp.312-313)

In these digital-virtual spaces the configurations of networks are extended through the constitution of spaces of flow and of timeless time, and empowered through living and sharing of e-inhabitants who have different identities constituted from different cultures. Therefore the relations of legitimacy constituted through feeling are fundamental for the establishment of dialogue between e-inhabitants and they can together configure new living and sharing, and consequently, new cultures.

The emergent culture refers to the spaces of digital-virtual living that coexist with other living spaces that are part of the life of a human being. The way of living, a general way, is characterized through transformation of human beings and the environment. For Lévy (1999, p.127),

A virtual community is constructed on the affinities of interests, of knowledge and mutual projects, in a cooperation process or an interchange one, through everything that is independent of geographical proximities and institutional filiations.

Thinking about a learning culture in a network implies, in thinking about the configuring of spaces where there is affective involvement of human beings. In this sense it is possible to establish relations in order to formulate new opinions, in which human beings can 'self-produce' in a continuous movement of living and knowing, which is often fed by conflicts, differences and contradictions.

CONCLUSION

When we reflect on the important historical moment in which we are living, characterized as complex, plural, systemic, self-eco-organizing, innovative, emergent, we need to raise our awareness of the choices we make, the new worlds we create and everything we are leaving for future generations. In this process of reflection and awareness, we intend to overcome difficulties so that the knowledge we have built can contribute to the emancipation of men and women.

Human beings live and coexist in a highly technologicized society, and it is obvious that such technologization is not available to everyone, and nor is this possible. Many instances of crossing and crisscrossing are established and are important for the dynamic movement that configures the spaces. However, the same network approaching different human beings, and approaching different realities, globalizes identities, diluting the local, the regional and the national. This will bring about new ontological, epistemological and methodological configurations through emerging paradigms like the complexity theory, systemic thinking and the concept of self-eco-organization.

We can also highlight richness and diversity in cultural propositions that we can encounter through digital technologies, but we must not lose sight of anchors of traditions that define our individual and social identities. In this sense, it is important to think about coexistence to avoid influx, as in "dynamic rooting" as proposed by Maffesoli (2012).

The construction and instantaneous socialization of new knowledge, can promote an emancipatory development, if knowledge is not treated as provisory, simple, fragile and partial. It means we can use digital-virtual spaces for the construction of consistent and thorough knowledge. Complexity in an incomprehensible context can constitute passive human beings in their living and sharing, individualized and fragmented beings when not understood in a systemic way and reproducers of a rigid and stagnant reality, when they are not conceived as self-eco-organizers.

Therefore, when approaching network learning culture, under the emergent paradigm perspective, we have the intention of comprehending a reality based on research with a consistent theoretical basis, making use of a network learning model or a paradigmatic matrix incoherent.

The emerging paradigm does not intend to build up models or work with the idea of construction blocks, but with conceptions constructed in men and women's daily lives. Thus, such concepts are then found in something yet to come. We do not have the intention of discussing the Cartesian view as opposite to the ecological view, but we do intent to establish a dialogue between the "old" (origin) and the "new" (future), in a continuous deconstruction-reconstruction process.

REFERENCES

Backes, L. (2007). *A formação do educador em mundos virtuais: Uma investigação sobre os processos de autonomia e de autoria.* (Unpublished master's dissertation). Universidade do Vale do Rio dos Sinos, São Leopoldo, Brazil.

Backes, L. (2011). *A configuração do espaço de convivência digital virtual: A cultura emergente no processo de formação do educador.* (Unpublished doctoral thesis). Universidade do Vale do Rio dos Sinos, São Leopoldo, Brazil and Université Lumière Lyon 2, Lyon, France.

Backes, L., & Schlemmer, E. (2006). Aprendizagem em mundos virtuais: Espaço deconvivência na formação do educador. In *Proceedings of VI Seminário de Pesquisa em Educação da Região Sul – ANPEDSul* (pp. 1-6). Santa Maria, Brazil: ANPEDSul. Retrieved from http://www.portalanpedsul.com.br/admin/uploads/2006/Educacao,_Comunicacao_e_tecnologia/Painel/12_56_53_PA570.pdf

Capra, F. (2002). As conexões ocultas: Ciência para uma vida sustentável. São Paulo, Brazil: Cultrix.

Capra, F. (2004). A teia da vida: Uma nova compreensão científica dos sistemas vivos. São Paulo, Brazil: Cultrix.

Freire, P., & Shor, I. (1992). *Medo e ousadia: Cotidiano do professor.* Rio de Janeiro, Brazil: Paz e Terra.

Lemos, A. (2007). Cibercultura, tecnologia e vida social na cultura contemporânea. Porto Alegre, Brazil: Sulina.

Lévy, P. (1999). Cibercultura. São Paulo, Brazil: Editora 34.

Maffesoli, M. (2012). O tempo retorna: Formas elementares da pós-modernidade. Rio de Janeiro, Brazil: Forense Universitária.

Maturana, H. R., & Varela, F. J. (1997). *De máquina e seres vivos: Autopoiese - a organização do vivo.* Porto Alegre, Brazil: Artes Médicas.

Maturana, H. R. (1999). *Transformación em la convivência.* Santiago, Chile: Dólmen Ediciones.

Maturana, H. R., & Varela, F. J. (2002). *A árvore do conhecimento: As bases biológicas da compreensão humana.* São Paulo, Brazil: Palas Athena.

Maturana, H. R. (2002). A ontologia da realidade. Belo Horizonte, Brazil: Ed. UFMG.

Maturana, H. R., & Dávia, X. Y. (2009). Habitar humano em seis ensaios de biologia-cultural. São Paulo, Brazil: Palas Athena.

Moraes, M. C. (2003). Educar na biologia do amor e da solidariedade. Petrópolis, Brazil: Vozes.

Morin, E. (2007). Introdução ao pensamento complexo. Porto Alegre, Brazil: Sulina.

Okada, A., & Okada, S. (2007). Novos paradigmas na educação online com a aprendizagem aberta. In *Proceedings of V Conferência Internacional de Tecnologias de Informação e Comunicação na Educação - Challenges* (pp. 1-12). Braga, Portugal: Universidade do Minho. Retrieved from http://people.kmi.open.ac.uk/ale/papers/a10challenges2007.pdf

Pérez Goméz, A. I. (2001). A cultura escolar na sociedade neoliberal. Porto Alegre, Brazil: ARTMED.Editora.

Schlemmer, E. (2001). Projetos de aprendizagem baseados em problemas: Uma metodologia interacionista/construtivista para formação de comunidades em ambientes virtuais de aprendizagem. *Colabor, 1*(2), 1–10.

Schlemmer, E. (2005). Metodologias para educação a distância no contexto da formação de comunidades virtuais de aprendizagem. In R. M. Barbosa (Ed.), Ambientes virtuais de aprendizagem (pp. 29-50). Porto Alegre, Brazil: Artmed.

Soares, L. H. (2010). *Complexidade e autopoiese no metaverso - Estratégias e cenários cognitivos* (Unpublished master's dissertation). Universidade Católica de Brasília, Brasília, Brazil.

Sousa Santos, B. (2004). Um discurso sobre as ciências. São Paulo, Brazil: Cortez.

Trein, D., & Schlemmer, E. (2009). Projetos de aprendizagem no contexto da web 2.0: Possibilidades para a prática pedagógica. *Revista E-Curriculum, 4*(2), 1-20. Retrieved from http://revistas.pucsp.br/index.php/curriculum/article/viewFile/3225/2147

Veen, W., & Vrakking, B. (2009). *Homo Zappiens: Educando na era digital.* Porto Alegre, Brazil: *The Art of Medication.*

KEY TERMS AND DEFINITIONS

Emerging Paradigm: Constituting four theses: all natural-scientific knowledge is social-scientific; all knowledge is local and total; all knowledge is self-knowledge; all scientific knowledge aims to constitute a common sense.

Epistemology: Is the science of knowledge, which investigates the nature, sources and validity of knowledge.

Network Learning Culture: The learning culture in a network implies, then, in thinking on the configuring of spaces where there are affective involvement of human beings, for the construction of rules that can comply reciprocity. In this sense it is possible to establish relations in order to formulate new opinions, in which human beings can 'self-produce' in a continuous movement of living, that is also knowing, and many times it is fed by the conflicts, differences and contradictions.

Paradigm: The basic system of beliefs, of principles and of the general view of the reality and the knowledge, that guide condition and empowers the work of researchers, intellectuals, politicians and doers were subverted in a strong radical way which directly affects not only the choice of production methods and diffusion knowledge, but specifically and in a clear way the knowledge itself (epistemology) and the consideration of reality (ontology) (p.61).

Self-Eco-Organized Conception: According to Morin (2007, apud Moraes, 2008) all living creatures are capable of organizing themselves through links or processes with their environment. This action explains the intrinsic condition between autonomy and dependence. The dependence is explained through observation that, for a subject to become autonomous, he needs (and depends on) his relations with the environment and of his constructive capacity. According to Moraes (2008, p. 103), the "self-organization presupposes the ability of self-production, self-creation, his structures and his components" (p. 96).

Systemic Thinking: Consists in alternating the logic perception of the knowledge object through the parts and dichotomize the whole and the parts, to the comprehension of the logic of everything through the parts and parts through the whole.

Theory of Complexity: The term unlinks of the common sense (complication, confusion) and it brings the order the disorder and the contradiction. In this process there is organization of the use and of the multiple notions that influence one another and simultaneously complement antagonistically.

ENDNOTES

[1] The concept of ontogeny is defined by Maturana and Varela (1997), and will be approached in chapter 4 - Avatar: Building a "Digital Virtual Self."

[2] Theme approached under the perspective of digital virtual naturalization, in chapter 4 Avatar: Building a "Digital Virtual Self."

[3] The construction of digital virtual collaboration was investigated by Backes (2011) and is approached in chapter 12 - Digital Virtual Sharing Spaces.

[4] The term avatar has become popular through Web 3D technologies, to designate the human being's representation and immersion into machines and computer screens. Such representation can be created by users, allowing avatars to be "personalized". The theme is thoroughly explored in chapter 4 - Avatar: Building a "Digital Virtual Self."

[5] E-inhabitant is the term used for human beings acting and interacting in digital virtual spaces, as defined in chapter 4 - Avatar: Building a "Digital Virtual Self."

[6] According to Maturana and Varela (2002) structural coupling happens in the interaction process between two or more units, as they establish elements of disturbance with their representation, in congruence with the environment. In this way, by trying to compensate such established disturbance, the units modify and change themselves in their own way, according to their own ontogeny, in a structural coupling. There is, thus, both a transformation of all participants and the environment. This concept is developed in chapter 7 - Autopoietic Machines and Alopoietic Machines: The Structural Coupling.

[7] The digital virtual living space (ECODI) is a concept-technology built from the research developed by the Digital Education Research Group UNISINOS/CNPq. This concept-technology is detailed in chapter 12 - Digital Virtual Sharing Spaces.

Chapter 3
The Metaverse:
3D Digital Virtual Worlds

ABSTRACT

This chapter approaches the rise of Metaverse Technologies in their 3D Digital Virtual Worlds, as a possibility that arises in the context of network learning culture, using the perspective of an emerging paradigm, linked to Teaching and Learning in Networked Society. We will present some of the main existing metaverses and discuss the capabilities and limits of this technology for learning with mobility. We will approach subtopics such as: Metaverse Technology and the nature of 3D Digital Virtual World; Second Life Metaverses; Opensource Metaverses; Metaverses in mobile devices: potentialities for Mobile Learning, as well as a brief conclusion to the chapter.

INTRODUCTION

Metaverse technology is at the core of Web3D with a wide range of possibilities for constructing 3D Digital Virtual Worlds on the internet. This technology may be considered a hybrid of virtual learning environments such as games, instant communication and virtual communities. In one way metaverse technology has launched the popularization of Virtual Reality, which presents itself in a simple and accessible way through software such as Active Worlds, Second Life and more recently, free software platforms such as OpenSimulator and OpenWonderland. This software enables the creation and co-creation, on the net, of Digital Virtual worlds which "materialize" in the collaborative construction of 3D graphic represen-

tations in several ways. These metaverses, which require human action to "become", are viewed by specialists researching different digital technologies and their "impacts" on society as a marker for the internet when compared to the creation of the World Wide Web – WWW.

Rosedale, creator of one of the most used Metaverse Technologies, Second Life, believes that 3D Digital Virtual Worlds may evolve from their biological self-ruled form, because they can be e-inhabited by avatars[1] – Digital Virtual representations of human beings in these worlds and a kind of "digital technological body", through which the subject can act and interact using different textual, oral, gestural and graphic languages, while collaborating in these worlds. In this way, people construct a "digital virtual self",

DOI: 10.4018/978-1-4666-6351-0.ch003

a "digital virtual identity" when interacting with the world and other e-inhabitants – other avatars and through it they also create a " digital virtual life" or, as in the case of Second Life and as the name suggests, a "second life".

It is precisely due to these possibilities that Metaverse Technologies have created interest in different types of organizations trying to understand this "new world" according to their specific interests. Companies like IBM, Nike, Apple, Volkswagen, Philips, Intel, Petrobras and Peugeot have been or are present in this "world" and explore their potential related to e-commerce, publicity, advertising, marketing, people management (recruiting, selection and corporate education) and v-Business. In universities and research centers, in areas such as education, communication, computer science, sociology, psychology, neurosciences and others, driven by the discussion of the man-machine relationship and the interaction between an autopoietic machine (human being) and an alopoietic machine (computer)[2], as well as coupling arising from the interaction, Maturana & Varela, 1997 try to investigate the aspects related to this "real virtuality[3]", this " digital virtual life", in order to comprehend the phenomenon.

According to the creators of the Second Life metaverse, academics are pioneers in the use and research of the metaverse. Researchers and Professors constitute the public who might better take advantage of virtual worlds, according to Cory Ondrejka, one of Linden Lab founders and creator of Second Life. "Professors first construct a virtual campus and usually try to replicate a conventional classroom with desks, chairs, walls, in Second Life…, but after a while they end up perceiving that this world allows different types of movement and communication. They perceive that in a world where one can fly, classrooms are not really that useful. Through this, professors construct new types of online classrooms without roofs, in an explosion of classroom shapes that match with what they are trying to teach" (Ondrejka, 2008). This statement made by Ondrejka (2008) reveals, using

other words, what the learning theories tell us, or alternatively, that this is how the appropriation of new technology occurs. We already use known structures (old forms) when trying to understand the new reality and when trying to replicate it. However, little by little due to this interaction with what is new, in the exploration and experimenting and in collaboration, other perceptions arise and along with them, differentiation schemes, allowing the construction of new structures to assist us in broadening our existing knowledge and/or constructing new knowledge.

In this chapter we will present and discuss concepts and questions involving metaverse technology which allows the construction of 3D digital virtual worlds. We will present some of the main and current metaverses and we will discuss the capabilities and limits of this technology for learning with mobility.

METAVERSE TECHNOLOGY AND THE NATURE OF 3D DIGITAL VIRTUAL WORLDS

The Metaverse: How Does it Exist? What is Its History?

The word metaverse is a compound of the words "meta", meaning "beyond", and "verse" as an abbreviation for "universe", thus constituting a Virtual Reality universe. Virtual Reality appears at the end of the 1970s when military research centers began to construct flight simulators for training pilots (Lévy, 1999). By common logic, Virtual Reality (VR) is known as a simulated environment contrary to what exists in the physical world. However, with the development of digital technologies and human fluency in using them, Virtual Reality has become more than a mere imitation of what is considered "real". "Virtuality always proposes an experience different to the real one" (Domingues, 2003, p.4). Virtual Reality environments provide the subject with the sensation of presence and immersion[4] (Lombard & Ditton, 1997), which means a feeling of belonging allowed by a telepresence and by a digital virtual presence[5]. It is through immersion that we feel part of the Virtual Reality environment.

Virtual Reality may be experienced through different means and may provide, from a technological point of view, a partial immersion, by using specific devices such as gloves, helmets, goggles, outfits or joysticks, or a total immersion, by using Caves (Cave Automatic Virtual Environment) that simulates synthetic 3D worlds and offers the subject the feeling of actually visiting these worlds (Domingues, 2003, p.3) or teleimmersion in metaverses, in 3D digital virtual worlds through the action and interaction with an avatar. However, when discussing the concept of immersion related to teaching and learning processes, and more than simply classifying the immersion according to the technological device used, we are interested in knowing the immersion level of the student's consciousness that can be provided by these different digital technologies.

According to Backes and Schlemmer (2008) the idea of the metaverse, although described in other terms, arose with a variety of names in the genre of cyberpunk fiction[6] as described by the authors Rudy Rucker (1981) and William Gibson, in Neuromancer[7] (1984). However, the term metaverse itself was created by the writer Neal Stephenson, in 1992, in a post modern science fiction novel called Snow Crash and used to refer to a fictional virtual world. Stephenson's book presents a virtual world in which human beings interact with each other through avatars in a tridimensional space (metauniverse).

As in any other place in reality, the Street can be improved. Developers can construct their own paths to enhance the main street. They can construct buildings, parks, signs and everything else that does not exist in Reality, as well as vehicles with light shows and special communities where tridimensional space-time rules are ignored. You put a sign or a building on the Street and a hundred million people, the richest and most important ones on Earth, will see them every day of their lives. The Street does not truly exist. But in this moment, millions of people are walking up and down it. (Stephenson, 1992, pp.22-23)

According to the author, the metaverse is real and has real use, for it is an amplification of the physical world's real space inside an internet-based digital virtual space. The metaverse would then be a kind of "no-space". And so is cyberspace[8], part of which hosts the metaverse, and which is a presence existing in the context of a social/living simulation or a new social experience. In his book, Stephenson describes some of the questions regarding the implementation of such spaces, issues that start being more relevant as these media become more overarching and fundamental in the subjects' lives.

The metaverse itself has, beyond the convergence of different technologies, a strong conceptual and fictional aspect in its conception. It is a term which exists in cyberspace and "materializes" through the creation of 3D Digital Virtual Worlds, with the possibility of immersion and, in which different spaces for collaborating are represented, allowing "parallel worlds" to appear. In this way, Metaverses represent a category of immersive digital virtual environments and establish themselves as platforms in which subjects act and interact, collaborate, live and share, in a representative universe that lets them develop a new social experience, and the configuration of a digital virtual living together.

What Does it Mean for a Student to Collaborate in a Metaverse?

Several theorists, in very different areas of knowledge, have devoted themselves to giving "Life" a concept. The definitions start with the most traditional ones, shedding light on evolutionary biology and carry on up to the most paradigmatic ones emerging from autopoiesis[9] and bio-semiologist theories. Some believe Life is not something exclusive to Planet Earth, others consider the existence of Life based on silicon and not carbon as well as the study on Artificial Life, developed by Computer Science. And what can be said about genetic manipulation and other methods of biotechnology?

According to the Chilean biologists Maturana and Varela (1997) "life is the continuous challenge of facing and learning at every new circumstance. Living is learning. While there is interaction there will be life". Living, and mainly sharing, happens in the relationship and interaction with others. "Human beings are social creatures; we live our lives in continuous imbrications with other human beings" (Maturana, 1999, p.21). From this perspective life is a cognition process and the interactions happening between subjects are always cognitive interactions, constructed while living. It is within this living through our actions and reactions that we create our world and we are created by them and the subject and the world emerge together in congruence. The existence of life presupposes the presence of a network, which involves interactions and inter-relations, so living is sharing. In this sense we can think about how these processes happen in a digital virtual context, meaning, how different technologies allow the living and sharing in a digital–virtual space.

The first digital virtual lives arose on the market by the mid 1970s with the first games characterized by adventures taking place in small "virtual worlds" dominated by theories such as "synthetic worlds". This was the origin of the first multi-user spaces using only text: the M.U.Ds[10], even though we were only at the beginning of the digital age. The first spaces with graphic characters appeared in the 1980s, developed by LucaArts (Castronova, 2005) and in the 1990s the first graphic digital virtual representations of a type of "life" start appearing, for example, with "Tamagochis". These "virtual pets", designed on the screen of a small device and no bigger than the palm of one's

hand, had a kind of " digital virtual life" in them which demanded special care in order to survive. When Tamagochis were launched they caused a certain amount of concern for many parents but mainly for teachers. The discussion split opinion between schools that allowed children to bring their "Tamagochis" into the classroom environment and those strongly against. Some teachers had different thoughts and carried out interesting learning processes in their classrooms, allowing children to learn about human beings' basic needs based on the relationship established with the "Tamagochis'" survival needs and involving children in, rich interdisciplinary work.

The beginning of graphic technologies in 3D also appeared in the 1990s and games with graphics centered on the first person perspective such as Meridian 59, Ultima Online, Lenage, EverQuest and many others. The dissemination of the net-based game – MMORPG (Massive Multiplayer Online RPG), games where different players connect and play simultaneously in the same graphically represented worlds in 2D and 3D, raised the debate around the use of such technologies by children and teenagers. The main concerns of parents and teachers were about the effects such interaction with technology might have on children and teenagers' development as there was a strong belief that such technologies could make them "confuse" the two spaces, the "real physical" world and the " digital virtual" world. In nursery, Elementary and High Schools in Brazil with children and teenagers from 4 to 15 years old, it was possible to see that the reality happening in schools demonstrated a different way in which they were interacting with these technologies. Their attitude towards technological advances showed they knew very well that there were "two worlds", "parallel worlds", with specific properties and rules according to each one's nature.

The history of the Metaverse arises with M.U.Ds, MOOs and with virtual worlds with graphic representations in 2D, such as The Palace[11]

(Figure 1) and, more recently, the ClubPenguim[12] (Figure 2). Among the better known metaverses that enable the construction of 3D digital virtual worlds are Active Worlds[13] (Figure 3), created in 1997, and Second Life[14] (Figure 4), created in 2003. The Open Source *"Metaverse"* Project[15] started to be developed in 2004 in order to supply an important demand from developers for a metaverse server engine, and a client with a flexible and extendable open modular source, that could enable the personalization of one's own world, independent of commercial ones. In 2005, Solipsis[16] started to be developed as a free open code system, with the objective of provid-

ing the infrastructure needed for the creation of the Metaverse. Also at that time there was the *Croquet*[17] Project, open-source software inside a development environment to "create and implement online collaborative multiuser environments with applications in different operational systems and devices. In 2007 there were two free software initiatives in the context of metaverse technology – the *Open Wonderland*[18] Project (Figure 5), currently being developed by the *Open Wonderland Foundation*, and the OpenSimulator[19] Project (Figure 6).

In this way, and with the popularization of the internet and metaverse technology, it is nowadays

Figure 1. The Palace
Source: Author In-Game Screenshot

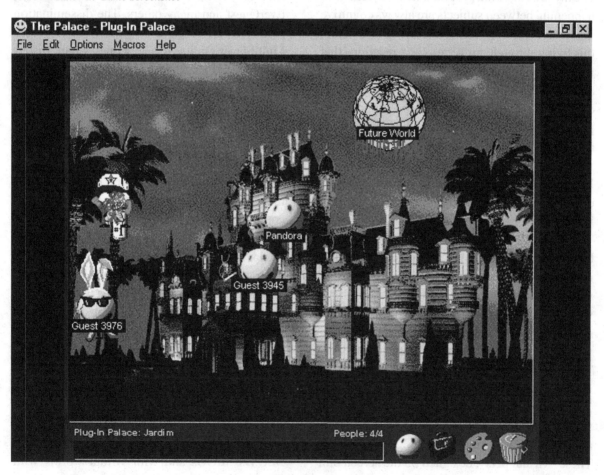

Figure 2. Club Penguin
Source: Author In-Game Screenshot

possible to find many people who are used to creating their " digital virtual SELVES", to live other lives in digital virtual living rooms.

Research in the area of digital virtual worlds, is relatively recent. One of the first studies identified refers to Benford et al. (1993), in which the authors describe the use of metaphors in the creation of spatial models to support communication and mediation of the interactions in a collaborative and cooperative work context. In this investigative process, two key concepts are identified: the "*focus*", (representing the subspace where a person focuses his attention), and the "*nimbus*" (representing a subspace where a person projects his presence).

Today, one of the research groups deserving close attention is *The Immersive Education Technology Group (IETG)*, which links researchers from different institutions with a real collaborative network between universities, schools, research institutes and companies including *Boston College, MIT*[20] *Media Lab and Grid Institute. Immersive Education*, in its online course options, combines the use of interactive virtual reality

Figure 3. Active Worlds – AWSINOS
Source: Authors

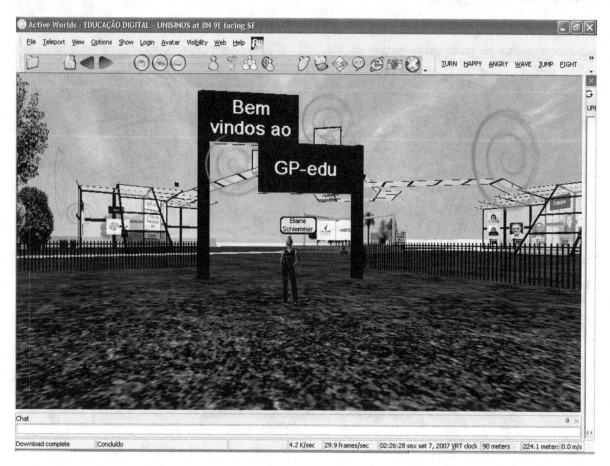

and 3D digital virtual worlds with sophisticated digital technologies (voice chat, modules based on learning through games, audio/video, etc.) and collaborative online environments, aiming to take distance learning to new standards. The *Immersive Education* project was designed to enable the engagement and immersion of students in a similar way to that seen in *videogames*, which are able to attract and maintain a player's attention. Within the main projects developed by the IEGT is the *Wonderland Project,* free *software* that enables the creation of 3D digital virtual worlds. The project is an initiative focused on education, where through immersion subjects can collaborate, simulate real business and learn about immersion technology.

Besides that, the group carries out research on Metaverse Croquet and on Metaverse OpenSim.

There are several universities in the international context with initiatives using and researching Metaverse Technologies, and it is important to mention here the University of Texas and the *Boise State University* (which offer disciplines in Second Life that are part of the *Master of Educational Technology* program), both located in the USA; the University of Aveiro, which built the first Portuguese island in Second Life; the University of Porto and the University of Minho, which staged a recent meeting with the researchers in the area, in Portugal and the *Universität Hamburg*, in Germany, among others.

Figure 4. Second Life –UNISINOS Island
Source: Authors

In the Brazilian context, one of the first pieces of research into digital virtual worlds was carried out in 1998 and refers to a Master's thesis in the Post Graduate Program in Psychology at the Federal University of the State Rio Grande do Sul (UFRGS) entitled "The Child's Representation of Cyberspace when Using a Virtual Environment", in which Schlemmer (1998) investigates cognitive behaviors related to the representation of cyberspace with 8 and 11 years old students using "*The Palace*" software (Figure 1), a 2D networked digital virtual world, in which subjects are represented by *props* (any object used by the subject to represent himself in the graphic 2D environment in order to allow interaction – something similar to the avatar's function) and they can interact with

texts through webchat, while they move in spaces graphically represented in 2D. The theoretical referential supporting this research is mainly based on the theory of The Representation of Space in Children, developed by the Swiss epistemologist Jean Piaget, and on the studies developed by the philosophers Immanuel Kant and Pierre Lévy. The results of this research have shown an acceleration of the subjects' development regarding perceptions and the construction of notional spatial representations when interacting with digital virtual worlds in 2D in cyberspace, when compared to the findings of Piaget and Inhelder (1993), in which the research was done only by experimenting in physical environments. Another result indicated by the research refers to the necessity of adapta-

Figure 5. Wonderland
Source: Authors

tion of the clinical Piaget method when used in an experimentation/exploration context of dynamic digital virtual environments as seen in 2D and 3D digital virtual worlds.

Schlemmer (1998) highlights that the students initially made a transposition, using the properties of physical space to understand cyberspace, making no difference between the properties of either space. Among the interactions it was possible to observe that the students started to include certain judgments in their perceptions, comparing existence in a physical space with cyberspace,

making differentiations between their properties and interpreting logically what was going on. The "*focus*" and the "*nimbus*", concepts used by Benford et al. (1993), were specified according to interest, for example: some subjects presented the environment itself as "*focus*" with the images and graphic representations and the possibilities for exploring places wherein the communication with other subjects who were represented by "*props*" and were were part of the "*nimbus*". For others, it was the opposite, when the "*focus*" was in communication whereas exploring the environ-

Figure 6. OpenSimulator - GPe-dU
Source: Authors

ment was "*nimbus*". We observe that these would vary from student to student according to their age, gender or interests.

Between 1999 and 2002 further important research in this area was carried out and deserves attention: "Cooperative Virtual Reality Learning Environment – ARCA," was developed jointly by the Federal University of Rio Grande do Sul (UFRGS), the Universidade Luterana do Brasil (ULBRA) and the Universidade Católica de Pelotas (UCPEL). The project aims to develop learning and teaching environments that could help in differentiated pedagogical practice, giving conditions for significant learning via a Virtual Reality environment that allows cooperation. For that purpose they used the Metaverse Eduverse[21]. The results achieved show us that:

virtual 3D environments, either immersive or not, can provide a more significant learning experience, facilitating the approach of more complex

themes and assuring the enhancement of social relationships with the use of avatars and other graphic objects. However, in order to construct such learning environments, knowledge and interdisciplinary practices are required. (Arca Project[22], 2002).

Still in the Brazilian context and related to the Metaverse Eduverse, there is "The construction of virtual worlds for distance education", developed by Schlemmer (2000-2005), which originated the AWSINOS – UNISINOS' 3D digital virtual world[23] (Figures 7 and 8) and created in the year 2000, in which the students are authors invited to experiment with the active learning process, constructing knowledge in a collaborative and cooperative way and where autonomy is the background shaping the world's construction. When entering AWSINOS the subject can see a graphical representation of the Research Group and a Teleports Center that gives access to a Central

Figure 7. AWSINOS
Source: Authors

Figure 8. AWSINOS
Source: Authors

Square and also to different "villas" [24] created in AWSINOS, according to the following figures:

The process of bringing students together through AWSINOS drives us to discuss some aspects suggested during the research such as: sensations experienced when interacting in 3D digital virtual worlds; the relationships established in this interaction; the learning provided in the construction of the world; skills and competences needed to interact and the use of 3D digital virtual worlds in didactic pedagogical practices.

In the construction of AWSINOS we perceived that, through active participation, the students can experience the learning process, exchange data and also experiment with telepresence, via an avatar, which allows them to act and cooperate, constructing theoretical and technical resources to understand how this technology can be used in different contexts. This construction happens in a playful way - as an adventure, a game or a "make-believe"- in which adults construct learning when "virtualizing" a world with its intentions and implications, constructing and reconstructing knowledge, interaction and cooperation.

From 1993 to the present day the amount of research related to metaverses and 3D digital virtual worlds has grown significantly and mainly in the last 10 years. However it are still incipient from the point of view of understanding the potential for its use in teaching and learning processes for the development of methodologies and pedagogical mediation processes that support the development of virtual learning and practicing communities (in both formal and informal educational contexts), which could provoke a shift in paradigm regarding teaching and learning even as far as a new level of innovation. One of the research groups that has been thoroughly investigating this theme in the Brazilian context, is the Digital Education Research Group – GPe-dU UNISINOS/CNPq[25] - created in 2004 and linked to UNISINOS' Post-Graduate Program in Education through the development of the following pieces of research: "The construction of virtual worlds for distance education" (2000-2005); "Forming the Educator in the Interaction with AVA in Virtual Worlds: Perceptions and representations" (2005-2007); " Digital Virtual Living and Sharing Space – ECODI" (2007-2010); " Digital Virtual Living and Sharing Space – ECODI RICESU" (2008-2009); Digital Virtual Living and Sharing Space – ECODI UNISINOS VIRTUAL and " Digital Virtual Living and Sharing Space of the Post Graduate Programs (Stricto Sensu) - ECODI-PPGs UNISINOS: a proposal for training researchers" (2009-2011). There are further masters dissertations[26] and doctorate theses within this group.

When we analyze the context of Metaverse research at both a national (Brazilian) and international level, we identify a significant number of initiatives, making clear the researchers' concern in understanding the way this technology works, its limits and its potential for teaching and learning processes. Although this research is still at an early stage, particularly when compared with studies on the use of other technologies in Education such as traditional Virtual Learning Environments – AVAs, individual and/or collective initiatives have shown how rich this research field is, mainly in terms of human learning and contributing significantly to another research universe, *Immersive Learning*.

Metaverse, 3D Digital Virtual Worlds: Fundamentals and Concepts

Metaverse technology enables the creation of 3D digital virtual worlds. Technically speaking, 3D digital virtual worlds are dynamic tridimensional scenarios, which are molded via a computer with graphic computing techniques and that are used to represent the virtual part of a virtual reality system. These environments are designed with the use of special tools such as the programming language VRML (Virtual Reality Molding Language) and Engines 3D[27], and are strengthened using accelerator 3D boards.

There are many concepts within this new technology such as: digital, virtual or real…, making it necessary to bring them into the discussion in order to broaden our understanding and in some cases, even giving them a new meaning.

Let us start with the concept of what is digital, which according to Lévy (1999), means the action of digitalizing. Digitalizing information consists of translating it into binary numbers. According to the author, these digits enable the codified information to flow through electrical wires, inform electronic circuits, polarize magnetic tapes and translate it into sparkles in optical fibers and so on.

Digitally codified information can be transmitted and copied almost indefinitely without any loss of information as it is reconstituted after transmission.

Another equally important idea in this context is the concept of "virtual", which has been extensively studied by Lévy:

The word virtual comes from Medieval Latin virtualis, derived from virtus, meaning strength or power. In scholastic philosophy, virtual is what exists in power but not in act. The virtual tends to update itself without passing through effective or formal concretization. ...Strictly in philosophical terms the virtual does not oppose the real, but the actual: virtuality and actuality are only two different ways of being. ... the virtual is like a problematic complex, the node of trends or strengths following a situation, an event, an object or any entity, calling for a resolution process: the actualization. (Lévy, 1996, apud Schlemmer 1998, p.50)

Looked at in this way, the virtual does not only involve a particular way of being, but also a transformative process from one way of being to another.

What is rigorously defined has only a subtle affinity with what is fake, illusive or imaginary. On the contrary, it has to do with a powerful and fertile way of being, involving the creation process, opening futures, drilling wells of sense under the mediocrity of the immediate physical presence. (Lévy, 1996, apud Schlemmer, 1998, p.50)

The virtual features the selflessness from here and now, the breaking of frontiers, it means "not being present". Something occupies a place in space but does not belong anywhere, characterizing a "virtual occupation in space".

Every life form invents its own world and with this world, a specific space and time. The human beings' cultural universe further extends this variation of space and temporality.

... A situation is then created in which several proximity systems and several practical spaces co-exist. The spaces metamorphose and bifurcate in front of us, forcing us into heterogenesis. (Lévy, 1996, apud Schlemmer, 1998, p.51)

We can then say that we virtualize other worlds through our thoughts and through different languages. 3D digital virtual worlds can be considered as a materialization of this virtualization, meaning they stop existing in the potential sphere and start occupying a space, in this case, in cyberspace.

But then, what is real? There is no single answer for this philosophical question. Among several interpretations, scientific or common logic, real can be understood as something constructed by the subject, in an individual way, and based on these perceptions he constructs his living and sharing in his relationship with the world and other subjects. According to Maturana and Varela (1997, p.156) "reality is a mastery of things, and in this sense, something that can be distinguished from what is real."

In common logic, the term virtual is understood as something that is not real, for it does not exist in the physical field. However this is a mistaken comprehension proving a contradiction. If we do not dedicate ourselves to reflecting about the way we collaborate nowadays we will realize that virtuality is "present" in an intensive way in several day-to-day activities, making up part of our time and existing in reality, but of another nature than the physical one, the digital virtual one.

Using this same logic, there is the discussion about 3D digital virtual worlds. What world is it?

Are there worlds beyond the real physical one we already know, see and collaborate in which we can touch, smell and feel? Is it possible to say that 3D digital virtual worlds are worlds parallel to the physical one or is it better to say that they are representations based on the worlds we know and/or imagine, and therefore are of another nature? This way, 3D digital virtual worlds may constitute a hybrid containing representations of elements in a physical face-to-face world and also representations of elements that come from our imagination, relationships and interaction with avatars through different digital technologies. The action of avatars in a 3D digital virtual world provides results in real time, meaning, in the same instant the student carries out the action through his avatar, the 3D digital virtual world modifies and updates itself. Lévy (1999, p.75) states that,

a virtual world, in its broad sense, is a universe where things are possible and calculable based on a digital model. When interacting with the virtual world, users explore and update it simultaneously. When interactions can enrich or modify the template, the virtual world becomes a vector of intelligence and collective creation. (Lévy, 1999, p.75)

Generally speaking, virtual worlds are multi-user environments where it is possible to browse in space via networks and mediated by a computer. As more and more virtual worlds emerge on the Internet it seems pertinent to consider them a real phenomenon and thus study them as cultural artifacts which provide new ways of esthetics and entertaining experiences. (Klastrup, 2003, p.1)

We can understand the 3D digital virtual world as a hybrid among virtual environments for learning, gaming, instant communication, virtual communities and social networks, meaning the 3D digital virtual worlds have elements from different digital virtual technologies. In the research field we observe that individually, such technologies are at a good level of development although this hybridism represented by 3D digital virtual worlds instigates new research that is not precisely designed. Klastrup (2003) calls attention to the fact that if we understand that such virtual worlds are hybrid, we have to take this perspective when investigating them.

In this context, Klastrup's (2003) concern refers particularly to the creation of an experience and a face-to-face experience in a virtual world. Based on questions such as: "How would you describe the experience of "being there" or the experience of living in a virtual world?", "What creates such an experience?" and "How can we interpret the things happening there?", the author tries to develop a poetics[28] of the virtual worlds, starting from the definition of virtual worlds and the study of the "*worldness*" of such worlds. According to Klastrup (2003), for a poetics of virtual worlds read "a systematic study of virtual worlds as virtual worlds."

For the author, an interesting definition of virtual world relies on the fact that, via simulation derived from a narrative, the virtual world is a new form of cultural text with the characteristic of being "read" (used, accessed) by several users at the same time. And then, since continuous works have necessarily defined the "literacy" of a text it seems logical, in this case, to translate such factors into "worldness", meaning: to look at what makes each virtual world a virtual world. Such a concept is applied on two levels: firstly as an essential aspect of the whole virtual world as a virtual world (as structural property, "ontological") and secondly as defining the characteristics of a specific virtual world (an emerging property, perceived and experimented with by users worldwide).

Given all of the specifics, Klastrup (2003, p.3) proposes that a complete definition of virtual worlds needs to fulfill the following pre-requisites:

- Describe the different genders of virtual worlds (both social worlds and gaming);
- Describe the differences between virtual worlds and virtual environments (not-permanent or of restricted access) and virtual communities (which focus primarily on social interaction);
- Emphasize the interactive aspects: user/user and user/world;
- Describe what differentiates such virtual worlds from other types of imaginary worlds (such as soap operas or films), which are not habitable worlds;
- Emphasize the fact that a virtual world is shared by multiple users (synchronous communication) and therefore other users are also producers in the same world.

Other differences are also relevant, mainly regarding the current MMORPGs and Virtual Learning Environments. In this way, 3D digital virtual worlds differ from MMORPGs by way of the absence of a plot or a pre-defined context for the story to develop. The plot and story are constructed by means of the collaboration between the e-inhabitants. They differ from Virtual Learning Environments because of the graphic 3D environments, with the option of interaction via text, voice gesture or graphic representation. Text can be used in the dialogues between avatars, or to support a discussion or construction, but the subject "sees" what he is doing, creating or developing; he "sees" where he is going; he can handle, hold, manipulate or act upon a certain object. This makes interaction more natural, closer to the actions undertaken in the physical, face-to-face world. And so, from the stated assumptions and according to Klastrup (2003),

A virtual world is a persistent online representation containing the possibility of synchronous interaction between users and between users and the world, within rules of space developed as a browsable universe. "Virtual Worlds" are worlds in which you can move through user representations, contrasting with the worlds represented in traditional fiction, that are worlds presented as inhabited by real people, when they are not exactly habitable. (Klastrup, 2003, p.2)

In this context, the author detects four different but closely related aspects: the experience of the world as fiction, as a space of interpretation and entertainment, for games and finally, as community. The author's proposal is to map what functions are present in the virtual world and in synergy create respectively, the idea of "worldness".

When we talk about metaverse we refer to an immersive environment that allows the construction of a 3D digital virtual world by the subjects e-inhabiting it as "technological bodies" or avatars. According to Schlemmer et al. (2004), a 3D digital virtual world can reproduce a similar or identical form to the physical world or it can be a different creation, developed from imaginary spatial representations, simulating non-physical spaces for the digital virtual living together. These worlds can have their own laws designed by a certain group, in which we can use all our power of invention and creation because we are not attached to physical rules. Another basic characteristic of a 3D digital virtual world is the fact of being a dynamic system, or an environment that modifies itself in real time according to the way users are interacting in it and with it. This interaction can occur to a higher or lower degree, depending on the adopted interface. Virtual worlds can be settled or e-inhabited by human beings, the e-citizens represented by avatars who make actions and communicate, or by "virtual human beings" (Non-player Characters – NPCs) and/or bots and communicative agents.

It is important to consider that while in traditional digital virtual media access to information is possible through a browser, software that enables browsing the internet in an interface based on a dynamic bi-dimensional text environment, without losing access to videos, images, photos, and texts is also important. With this in mind, having understood the virtual as a "problematic complex", according to what was presented by (Lévy, 1999) we need to drive our view of 3D digital virtual worlds as worlds of another different nature, meaning a digital virtual nature and the opposite of what is real, but from the perspective of co-existence. According to Klastrup (2003), in order to study 3D digital virtual worlds, we need to consider them as MDVs and from this perspective we can elaborate questions to understand them better, avoiding comparisons with the physical or real world, and then get to know their real potential.

A metaverse is translated as a cognitive medium, familiar to humans and therefore naturally used in an intuitive way. In this context the possibilities of interaction are broadened in relation to other, already known technologies. In the scope of metaverse technology we will now present Second Life and some free software initiatives.

SECOND LIFE METAVERSE

Second Life is a piece of software designed in 1999 by Philip Rosedale and developed by the North American company *Linden Lab®*[29] in 2003 with the slogan "Your World, Your Imagination". It is technology usually associated with simulators such as SimCity because it is possible to simulate/construct digital virtual cities and program objects within them. Similarly, it is also related to the MMORPG game as well as presenting some of the characteristics of instant communication or social networks. However, Second Life is a metaverse technology that enables the construction of online, 3D digital virtual worlds, currently being the closest to a parallel universe[30] on the internet. In Second Life, a large part of the process of creating objects and the "social" maintenance of the spaces is idealized, constructed and maintained by their resident-avatars (e-residents or e-inhabitants), but

monitored and oriented by *Linden Lab*. According to Soares (2010), *Second Life* is highly complex and takes over a series of social, cultural, economic and emotional situations that interfere with the way your e-resident (avatar) relates to the environment and to other e-residents. In order to provide this interactivity and interaction[31] Second Life provides a sophisticated interface that gathers a series of commands and functions that can be used by the avatar in his routine, or during his collaboration within the 3D digital virtual world. Due to the importance of this interface, which can trigger the student's learning, and taking into account the amount of information implied, we will present, in sequence, some of the basic issues regarding the use of the Second Life metaverse.

Initially, to use Second Life the user needs to enroll on the site www.secondlife.com to create an account. When completing the form it is worth being aware that there are two types of accounts: the basic subscription, allowing access to all resources and to all of the 3D digital virtual worlds in Second Life, and the *Premium* subscription –which, besides the access presented in the basic subscription, allows the purchase of virtual land, allowing the building and maintenance of constructions in Second Life. In the *Premium* subscription there is a monthly fee for the maintenance of the domain. The characteristics of each account are also subject to alteration according to the policies presented by *Linden Lab®*. When creating your account you have to choose a first name, a last name and a standard 3D graphic representation to represent yourself in the Second Life metaverse. *Linden Lab®* will send an e-mail to the registered e-mail address to validate the account, download and install the relevant software. At this moment it is important to note the minimum hardware requirements to make Second Life work properly and which can be checked on the website http://secondlife.com/support/system-requirements/. According to Soares (2010), the high demand for resources required of graphics boards and of the internet connection represents one of the biggest criticisms made by Second Life users.

When running Second Life for the first time, the e-resident (avatar) is welcomed onto a public island called "*Second Life Welcome Island*", where he has access to tutorials about the basic resources for moving, visualizing, communicating – Chat and Instant Messaging – and teletransportation After browsing the tutorials the e-resident is then invited to get to know other islands classified according to their interests (shopping, tourism, entertaining, etc.), and when he leaves the "*Second Life Welcome Island*" this access becomes unavailable.

The e-resident can at any time personalize their 3D graphic representation, which effectively means creating his avatar, his " digital virtual self", his " digital virtual identity". According to Schlemmer, Trein and Oliveira (2008), in the Second Life metaverse the term avatar refers to the graphic representation of e-residents in the 3D digital virtual world. The tools available for creating or personalizing the avatar are simple and user friendly. There is a large variety of tools which when combined, offer even more possibilities, attracting the subjects' attention and making them dedicate a good part of their time to creating and personalizing their avatar.

In Second Life, the avatar can ride, walk, run, sit, fly and teleport to different spaces in a 3D digital virtual world and also go to other islands, by using specific tools in Second Life and keys from the keyboard. The avatar can visualize the 3D digital virtual world and himself in different ways, using a specific tool that modifies the way the camera visualizes, combined with some keys from the keyboard and mouse movements. The avatars can also communicate in different forms, using a textual language (through chat and private instant messages – IM), oral language (through the subject's own voice which the avatar represents in the 3D digital virtual world), gestural language (Second Life has some gesture scripts pre-installed), however many others can be created or acquired for free or are available for purchase) and graphic language through 3D representations that can be created. Besides that, avatars also use facial expressions when communicating with oral language. Communication between avatars can occur both in a synchronous way (when avatars are present in a digital virtual way in the same place and interact using textual, oral, gestural and graphic languages) and also asynchronously (when messages, notes, etc., are left by the avatars for others and in this case the predominant method of communication is by text). Regarding communication in Second Life, we have observed some critics who believe that it is not a suitable technology for the development of Distance Learning. The argument for such a statement relies on the fact that when using Second Life it is necessary to be present in a synchronous way, which means, all avatars necessarily need to be present at the same time – synchronous time – whereas the same critics will argue that one of the main advantages of Distance Learning is the possibility of being asynchronous, which means, every user chooses the time they want to access the environment to develop the activities. This argument, put forward by critics of Second Life, shows a lack of knowledge about collaborating with a Metaverse, for in it the users also decide when they will access the environment and develop the activities, in the same way asynchronous interactions occur when we get in touch with the constructions previously made in Second Life.

The demand for synchronous or asynchronous interaction depends on the proposed activity, which means, whether the activity requires the subjects to meet (for collaborative and cooperative work) or not. For example, in analyzing some Virtual Learning Environments we can observe that the username, when connected and logged into the environment, is visible to other users, regardless of whether he is doing an activity or not, although this does not mean that other online users at that time will necessarily interact with him. The difference is that, in a metaverse such as Second Life, you have a digital virtual presence through an avatar, being significantly different, at least from the "social presence" point of view. This is something that has been stated as a criticism of traditional Virtual Learning Environments and that is considered the main cause for Distance Learning evasion - it is precisely the lack of a social presence, that causes a feeling of loneliness and abandon. And so, what happens is that avatars that are online can see each another, which in a certain way strengthens interaction and communication.

The Second Life metaverse has its own complex geographic system based on the distribution of digital virtual lands. These lands are divided into: lot, region, state, private island, micro continent, main area and continent, related to "e-politics" or "e-territorialized" space. A lot can be from $512m^2$ to $65,536m^2$, and when they reach the maximum size they are then rated as a Region, having a specific name that distinguishes it in search procedures and Second Life mapping tools. A group of lots belonging to a single resident or group is called a State; it also has a specific name and can host thousands of regions in its domain (Tapley, 2008).

A Private Island is approximately $65,536m2$ and has the characteristic of being a land extension ordered by a resident or a group who were virtually located and separated from other Second Life lands. A group of Private Islands form a Micro Continent. This is a frequently used option for commercial entrepreneurships or for building cooperative communities (Tapley, 2008). The places called Main Areas are the oldest regions in Second Life, created and maintained by *Linden Lab®*. These areas expand according to the environment's demand and also describe its own evolution. The Continents consist of large groupings of digital virtual lands, with characteristics very similar to the physical world. They have a mechanic relation that simulates maritime oscillations, climate diversity (from snowy regions to desert extensions) and natural wonders, with canyons and waterfalls (Tapley, 2008).

However, Second Life geography conjures other concepts, such as: "space", "place" and "territory". These concepts are being improved, constructed and reconstructed over the time by different areas of knowledge, like geography, philosophy, sociology, communication, education, computer engineering, among others, which are looking to give them a meaning according to their needs. In the context of our research with Second Life use we try to conceptualize them based on geographer Santos' studies (1980, 2008), linked with the concepts constructed by biologist Maturana (1999, 2002, 2005) and biologists Maturana and Varela (1997, 2002), who underlie the comprehension of human beings' living and knowing, which design the living and sharing spaces. We have made this choice for we consider the Second Life Metaverse a digital virtual space, in which there are living and sharing spaces of a digital virtual nature.

According to Backes (2010), Santos' studies (1980, 2008) present a milestone for geography, which is characterized as "a new geography". The reconstruction of the concept passes through a deep historic-scientific study, in which the author dialogues with studies from the philosophers Gonseth (1948), Hegel (1955), Kant (1929), Durkheim (1895), among others, who have in a one way or another, influenced contemporary thinking. In this historic-scientific path, Santos (1980) describes the proximity of space comprehension related to men and women's action and interaction in the construction of thinking as a social phenomenon[32]. According to Santos' (1980) understanding, space is a group of actions and relationships that can be defined as:

former and recent social relationship representations by a structure represented by social relations that are happening, through processes and functions, before our eyes. Space is then, is a true field of forces where acceleration is uneven. And this is why spatial evolution does not happen in the same way everywhere. (p.122)

For Santos (2008), the definition of space implies complex and dynamic comprehensions, for the concept is formed of two components interacting in a continuous way: the configuration of territory[33], as a group of natural data that can be modified by man, and the social dynamic[34], or a group of social relations, defined by a definite time.

In a systemic conception, complementing the concept structured by geography, space is "the domain of all possible interactions in a collection of units (single or compound units interacting as units) established by these units' properties when specifying their dimensions" (Maturana, 2002, p.130).

Therefore, space is configured through the relationships between men and women and the environment, affected by situations in the past, present and from the perspective of the future. The relationships established between human beings are of different natures, objectives and intentions, favoring different meanings in the concept of space. However, in this context we have the understanding of the relational space, which is understood thus, according to Maturana:

All dimensions of space or relational domain from an organism are lived according to the organism's way of living. So, we, living beings, live when talking, we live all dimensions of our relational space in conversations and with conversations. (Maturana, 2002, p.116)

So, human relationships always occur from an emotional base that defines the scope of collaboration. Therefore people who collaborate yet belong to different social and non-social domains require the establishment of a regulation that operates by defining the collaborative space with a declarative emotional domain which specifies the desires of this living and sharing and the space of actions that make them happen. The construction of a country or nation does that, it bring us together in a national project and, if we generate it as a group, it gathers us in the space of desires and

constitutes a space of mutual acceptance in which living and sharing is possible. It is necessary to understand that: without mutual acceptance there cannot be a coincidence of wishes, and without the coincidence of wishes there is no harmony in living together, neither in action nor in reason, and, therefore, there is no social freedom. (Maturana, 2005, pp.74-75)

Space configures itself in the human way of living through actions, the perspectives of each being, their interactions, acceptance of the other and mutual respect, in order to design possibilities for a common[35] living, proper for each space, for it implies the relationship dynamic which is in agreement with the environment and with digital virtual spaces. The Second Life metaverse and other digital virtual technologies, from this perspective, are not mere tools but they are digital virtual spaces that enable living and sharing and collaboration.

Creation of Spaces/Environments/Objects

To create spaces[36]/environments[37] and objects in Second Life requires a higher familiarity with the metaverse and the possibilities it offers through different tools, that when combined, can result in different constructions. The tools for creation available in Second Life work with two essential objects for 3D molding: the *prims* (primitives) and the textures. The *prims* are virtual masses that can take any format (cube, cone, sphere, etc.) and are used as construction blocks. The textures are images or graphics applied to an object to create visual effects. These textures can be created with other software and copied to Second Life.

The digital virtual spaces/environments in 3D created in Second Life can be either realistic or fantasy depending on the objective or the creator's knowledge, creativity and imagination. However it is important to remember that, besides familiarizing oneself and knowing how to use the creation tools available in Second Life, it is crucial to have a basic knowledge of 3D molding in order to actually produce something. That said, even those who do not have enough knowledge to construct their own spaces/environments/objects and are not willing to learn, can get for free, to rent or to purchase, almost anything they desire from different islands in Second Life including clothing and accessories, apartments, houses or yachts.

The objects constructed in Second Life can be programmed through a proper language for script programming such as the LSL (Linden Script Language) which has syntax similar to Language C. Through the creation of scripts it is possible to establish and control different objects' "behaviors" when constructed in a 3D digital virtual world such as creating animations for avatars or games.

It is also possible to use gadgets in Second Life which interact with sites using XML and "physics engine" to develop simulations and create realistic functionalities for objects.

Economy and Commerce

When Linden Lab created Second Life, they also created an internal currency, the *Linden Dollar* (L$), which is used to buy, sell or rent the wide range of goods (such as real estate, vehicles, all sort of electronic devices, animations, clothing, skin, hair, jewelry, flora, fauna and works of art). Since then, a complex economic system has been created, where all commerce in Second Life is undertaken.

The purchase of L$ usually happens in the *Second Life* viewer called the *Linden Exchange*, where the resident selects a standard form of payment that is always used for future purchases. There are also exchange agencies that specialize in selling L$. The L$ value fluctuates according to the variation of the American dollar. In Brazil and until August 2010, L$1 (one *linden dollar*) could vary between R$0,01 and R$0,0084 (the R$, or Real is the Brazilian currency).

It is important to note that the Second Life economy is established based on commercial transactions between the e-residents and not necessarily on *Linden Lab®'s* actions. The e-resident does not necessarily have to by L$, but may earn them for any work they do on different islands created in Second Life. Among the most common services found are camping, business management, entertaining and the creation of personalized content. This last can be divided into six distinct areas: building creator, texture creator, scripts creator, animation creator, art direction and producer (Rymaszewski et al., 2007, Tapley, 2008). With the exception of camping, the other types of work demand specific knowledge in the areas of creation. Camping is a place where residents can earn L$ by doing activities that increase the search ranking of a store or a place in the environment. The more residents there are in a place, the more publicity it gets. The residents are paid to do simple but repetitive activities such as dancing on stage, appreciating works of art and suchlike. The payment offered is based on the amount of time the resident spends on each activity and each place has its own values and rules (Second Life, 2010). Besides these procedures of buying and selling, the residents can also earn a small compulsory "salary" if they have a Second Life *premium* subscription.

There equivalent to virtual jobs and minimum wages also exists, as well as "charity" organizations that try to introduce new e-residents into the virtual economy. Besides the big currency movement within the environment (*Linden Lab®* announced on its website that between 2008 and 2009 Second Life had moved around $1 billion dollars in business), a large part of the profits gained is used by e-residents to pay for their subscription and land costs in *Second Life* only a relatively small number of users can make big profits in real currency. We can also verify that real estate speculation mobilizes large amounts of assets in business in Second Life and although the virtual land was initially traded by *Linden Lab®*, the property rights are transferred to the e-residents the moment they purchase it and on the premise of renegotiating them in the same way as the real estate market in the physical world. Most Second Life millionaires started their fortune this way (Rymaszewski et al., 2007). In theory and in order to make money in Second Life, all a person has to do is to find someone who wants to pay for a service being offered.

Society

The subject's action and interaction, through his avatar in the Second Life Metaverse, allows him to collaborate in this world along with other avatars – e-residents also present in that world. In this way there is the possibility of constructing social bonds, groups or communities, which organize themselves into societies with common objectives, necessities and laws. But what kind of society is it? What culture is it? What are its main characteristics and how are they constituted?

According to Malizia (2012) this technological transformation has modified social aggregation and this fact is easily noticed when we analyze the beginning of the internet which rapidly triggered the emergence of different virtual communities that organized themselves in cyberspace through textual language. But what can we say if along with textual language it was also possible to communicate through oral language, gestures and graphs and have an avatar representation? What can we say about a community in which there are humanoid avatars, some of whom have themes (cyberpunk, celebrity, erotic, steampunk) and others not; mecha avatars[38]; abstract avatars; furry avatars[39]; non-humanoid avatars?

Malizia (2012) tells us about a multicultural and multiethnic society. Wouldn't this be the real space for expressions of this society, this culture? What are the bonds connecting people, theoretically so different? The Second Life metaverse enables an avatar's action and interaction within the environment and with other avatars, it allows the emergence of a real social context though of a digital virtual nature. This context is formed by expectations when it comes to the way of being in this world, meaning the avatars' behavior, and therefore it is susceptible to social norms, rules, laws and prohibitions, meaning a group of laws that is shared by its e-residents and that rule the action of the avatars in that world. These behavior norms may, however, vary from place to place within the environment. On an education island, for example, shooting the other residents with guns or projectiles (*bump*) is not allowed, nor is walking around as a naked avatar. By contrast, on a war games island the use of guns is expected and desired, and on a virtual nudism beach walking around naked would not be strange. As a result, *Linden Lab®* has given a small number of norms which must be followed or it could lead to a temporary or definite banning from the environment. These norms are known as The Big Six and they establish the following prohibitions (Rymaszewski et al., 2007, Tapley, 2008, Second Life, 2010):

- **Intolerance/Prejudice:** The act of marginalizing or defamation of other residents or groups by the use of words, images, gestures or offensive actions in relation to racial, sexual, religious or ethnic issues.
- **Harassment/Offensive Behavior:** The act of contacting or behaving in an offensive, intimidating or threatening way, whether or not regarding sexual invitations, that may cause misfortune or embarrassment to another resident.
- **Attack:** The act of attacking, shooting, punching or bumping other residents in areas where such actions are not allowed, in a way that impedes the other's entertainment or freedom.
- **Exposure:** The act of disclosing another resident's personal data without authorization, including gender, sexuality, religion, age, marital status or ethnic group, as well

as recording or posting audio or text conversations or exchanging logs from conversations without due consent, and in any way which compromises, at any level, a resident's "first life".

- **Indecency/Vulgarity:** The act of releasing content, communication or behavior of a sexual nature, involving explicit language about sex, violence or material that can be considered offensive in areas where it is prohibited, and that are not defined as being of mature content. (Madura - M).

- **Disturbing the Peace/Perturbing the Order:** The act of interfering in scheduled events, broadcasting content in continuous propaganda format, use of repetitive sounds that disturb the peace in a certain place, use of mechanisms that intentionally make the server work slower, or making another resident's life and freedom impracticable.

These norms are followed by all Second Life media, including sites, forums and *wikis* that are part of the environment. Places in Second Life are distinguished between Mature (M) and Not Mature (PG), and also between Safe or Not Safe, requiring the residents' behavior to be suitable for each category (Second Life, 2010).

In our research we have identified that Second Life is a technology that can integrate the working world, the educational world and the leisure world. The subject-avatars when interacting with 3D digital virtual worlds and with other avatars can experience different types of "Virtual Fictional Experiences – VFE. Often they get into a "flow" state[40] and experience great satisfaction which is shown through records of comments and confirmed by the time they spend on the interaction using this technology.

With regards to the working world, it has mainly been used in the fields of medicine, psychology, army, training and recruiting agencies, publicity agencies, advertising, creation and marketing, e-commerce, e-business, design and architecture and real estate businesses, among others.

When referring to the educational world, it has been used by high schools and universities, as a technology to develop offers online, to make simulations, to create digital virtual laboratories, to create exchange environments or collective and collaborative learning environments, thus offering an alternative to the traditional classroom environment through other environments rich in possibilities for exploration, creation and the construction of knowledge. According to Schlemmer (2008), many universities have been using this technology to develop social simulations, to investigate Second Life residents' social relationships, to investigate history, the theory and practice of representation and architectural production, in order to research issues related to the learning process of subjects with any type of disability, to study skills and competences developed in virtual environments and to study "environments & new digital culture".

However, in relation to the use of the Second Life Metaverse as a Distance Learning technology, another discussion needs to be approached regarding the concept of Distance Learning, for we need to reflect on its meaning and in this case, the use of the term "distance". What kind of "distance" are we talking about since by using metaverse technology, for example, we can have telepresence and digital virtual presence, meaning a "social presence" that makes the "being together digital virtual" and the "relational proximity" possible, minimizing the "lack of presence", understood as physical presence, as well as the feeling of "distance"?

Today, the use of Metaverse Technologies has led to extensive discussion and reflection on the concepts of presence and distance, among others, contributing to the term "Distance Learning" being controversial and triggering researchers to rethink its use and rename the learning experience through this technology. It is important to understand that such traditionally used denominations do not truly represent what is perceived by the students who learn using this technology. Trein and Backes (2009) mean that the use of the term "Distance Learning" assumes that the people involved in the process are distant from each other. But what type of distance are we talking about? The distance between physical bodies? We have been finding in our research that the creation of a Digital Virtual Identity – DVI (avatar)[41] allows the subject to immerse himself in a world where he can act and interact with its e-inhabitants (other avatars), which causes a greater feeling of presence and vivacity. And it is precisely this "social digital virtual presence[42]", which bring subjects together, subjects who can also, thanks to their " digital virtual selves" (avatars), have the feeling of "being there" in the same digital virtual environment yet in a more intense way. So, what are distance and the feeling of absence when we are together in a digital virtual way, acting and interacting in different MDV3D and constructed with Metaverse technology? It seems more appropriate in this case to talk about Online Education, or *Immersive Learning*.

When it comes to leisure, it has been used as a way to make friends, a place to play (in islands where the option "damage" is activated), among others.

According to its creator, Second Life is not merely a game or a toy, but a milestone on the internet that can be compared with the creation of the World Wide Web. Rosedale believes that this world can evolve in a biological way, and be self-ruled. Echoing this perspective, Maia and Mattar state that,

Second Life is a collaborative environment of virtual reality with a 3-D interface, in which it is possible to assemble your avatar, constructs, buy or sell objects (which means an environment that virtually considers the concept of intellectual property) and therefore has its own currency. (Maia & Mattar, 2007, p.80)

Second Life can establish itself as a new collaborative space based on the formation of new social networks for digital virtual learning. In this sense it has structured itself in a way that can significantly contribute to both informing as well as forming or training people, being applied in different domains of society. However, as something new, it needs to go through the investigative processes that help us understand its potential for human development.

OPEN SOURCE METAVERSES

With the arrival of the first property metaverses and the more recent and significant expansion of such technology, we saw the beginning a movement for the creation of the first open source metaverses. In this context we can list: the "Metaverse, the "Solipsis", the Croquet Project, the Wonderland Project, and more recently, the OpenSimulator Project. With reference to the development of such technology we have been observing constant growth and many initiatives make use of these open source metaverses, for the most part since 2009. In this context we can highlight two main open source initiatives, the Open Wonderland and the Open Simulator.

The *Open Wonderland* (http://openwonderland.org/) is an Open Source Metaverse that, in an international context, was developed in the United States through an initiative of the research group *The Immersive Education Technology Group (IETG)[43]*, and is composed of researchers from different institutions such as Amherst College, Boston College, MIT Media Lab and Grid Institute,

The Immersive Education Initiative is an international collaboration of universities, colleges, research institutes, consortia and companies that are working together to define and develop open standards, best practices, platforms, and communities of support for virtual reality and game-based learning and training systems. (Available in http://immersiveeducation.org/)

Immersive Education combines interactive virtual reality 3D digital virtual worlds with sophisticated digital technologies (voice chat, modules based on learning through games, audio/video, etc.) and collaborative online environments in classes and virtual courses, in a way that can take Distance Learning to new a standard. The Immersive Education project was created with the objective of gaining the students' engagement and immersion, in the same way that the best games can attract and keep their players' attention. The IEGT is developing the Open Wonderland Project where free software developed in Java enables the creation of 3D digital virtual worlds. Different from Second Life, the Open Wonderland is an initiative with specifically educational purposes, where through immersion, people can collaborate, simulate real businesses and learn about immersion technology. The main information source on the Open Wonderland is the project's site, where it is possible to find the whole background of the project's development. There are several versions for download, the sources receive weekly updating and are usually stable, and they can be used instead of the preview. The Open Wonderland adopts the modular extension concept, allowing its new features to be constructed without interfering with the code that is part of the system's nucleus (the license for the modules can be different from the platform's license itself). Several modules are available from (http://openwonderland.org/modules/module-warehouse) and even being a platform for the creation of 3D digital virtual worlds, both the preview4 and the sources, available in the repository, come with two configurable pre-defined worlds.

In the Open Wonderland it is also possible to personalize your avatar although the possibilities are fewer than those present in the Second Life Metaverse and they demand a greater level of user knowledge. Oral communication works automatically, capturing sounds on the microphone and transmitting them to the application with no need for a button on the screen. If there is a problem with the sound in startup a message is displayed.

Open Simulator or OpenSim (http://opensimulator.org/) is an Open source Metaverse with great contributions from IBM and based on Linden Labs technology. The Open Simulator is a 3D digital virtual worlds server with a BSD License that can be used to create and develop Virtual Environments in 3D. It can be used to create environments similar to those of Second Life ™ and is capable of running in a standalone way or connected to other Open Simulator levels through the embedded grid technology and it can be easily extended to produce more specialized interactive applications in 3D. It can also be used by the same Second Life visualizing clients. It currently uses the 0.7.1 version and it supports most Second Life features although voice communication is primitive. With a large online community It also supports scripts in LSL/OSSL, C#, JScript and VB.NET and supports physics using the ODE.

Grids and Standalones are types of server created by OpensSim. A Standalone server means the whole virtual world and the modules run on a single computer and by a single process. Using the Grid server, the whole process is separated and can run on multiple computers. For this reason the standalones are easier to configure than the Grids, and many Grids are public and easily accessed.

HyperGrid OpenSim also has an architecture called HyperGrid which allows the users to be "teleported" from one Grid to another, thus linking public Grids without having to install new clients.

When we use property metaverses like Second Life, as well as open source metaverses, like Open Simulator and Open Wonderland, it is possible to identify advantages and disadvantages in both (although that is not the objective of this work). Although the research is recent and in need of further development, we will present some of the advantages and disadvantages of these metaverses.

The first of these enables easier access for creating an avatar and it installs the software, making it possible to navigate and visit different islands, worlds, as well as to interact with spaces and avatars present (except in areas built as restricted). This is an interesting possibility, regarding visibility, socialization and even marketing, though it can cause uneasiness about safety, and content exhibition may be inappropriate, among other things. Because it is property software, there is no way to access to the source code to modify it, nor to create an independent server, meaning that all developed material must be placed into the Linden Lab ® server.

In the second, there is more security regarding access because it is open source software. And there is also the possibility of creating an independent server to allow restricted access or control the access to worlds with passwords. As a result, only authorized avatars can browse and visit the different islands and worlds, interacting both with the space and other avatars present at that time. This possibility, although restricting access only to 'known' avatars, is very interesting regarding security, because avatars are not exposed to inappropriate content. Besides that, all content developed remains located in the creator's own server.

METAVERSES ON MOBILE DEVICES: POTENTIALS FOR MOBILE LEARNING

New Online Education processes have recently come up, related to the use of Mobile and Wireless Technologies and 3D Web. In the context of the GPe-dU UNISINOS/CNPq, connected to the Post Graduate Program in Education, we research the cognitive and socio-cognitive processes related to these two digital-technological fields: Mobile and Wireless Technologies and Web 3D. Mobile and Wireless Technologies, such as cell phones, *smartphones*, PDAs, laptops, among others, allied to the increasingly necessity for mobility in people, objects and information (Schlemmer et al., 2007), trigger the emergence of other educational modalities such as: *mobile learning (m-Learning), pervasive learning*44 *(p-Learning)* and *ubiquitous learning*45 (u-Learning), which, according to Schlemmer et al. (2007) cannot be understood based on the Distance Learning we have known so far, because when we use Mobile and Wireless Technologies in a mobility context new issues are presented forming pedagogical, technological and social challenges. It is in this context that the GPe-dU develops a research in partnership with the Post-Graduate Program in Business Administration and the Post Graduate Program in Applied Computing Science at UNISINOS. These pieces of research seek to comprehend how the subjects learn in a mobility context, either in formal or informal educational spaces and this created the Virtual Environment for Mobile Learning – AVAM, COMpetencies in conTEXT – COMTEXT.

According to Saccol, Schlemmer and Barbosa (2010) learning with mobility (while being on the move) or in a ubiquitous way (anywhere, at anytime, with resources sensitive to the user's context) is not particularly innovative. These learning possibilities have always been researched and strengthened with existing "technologies" such as books, notebooks and other portable instruments, as well as it being common for us to enjoy several contexts and having time to develop activities involving learning. In one way or another, while we live and work, we are always learning, either formally or informally. However, by the end of the 20th century and at the beginning of this one we have been living with a new phenomenon which involves the diffusion of mobility through Mobile and Wireless Technologies and which has enabled communication and the use of computing resources in a variety of places and at any time. Nowadays the popularization of mobile devices such as cell phones, notebooks, palmtops, personal digital assistants (PDAs), *smartphones*, MP3 and MP4, is notable. Similarly, different types of wireless networks, such as cell phones, local wireless networks (Wi-Fi), metropolitan wireless networks (WiMAX), allow us to be connected in different places, such as schools, colleges, universities, cafés, airports, condominiums and hotels and this technology has evolved rapidly. The first mobile telephone systems, for example, started to be seen by the population in general at the beginning of the 1980s (Kadirire, 2009). Since then, these systems have undergone a huge evolution, starting with the first generation (1G) and analogue systems which could only transmit voice, followed by second generation (2G) with limited voice and data transmission, then it reaching 2.5 and 3G generations with data transmission and growing broadband and culminating in the fourth generation (4G), which has a high level of data transmission and accessibility through different devices with high quality voice transmission and multimedia data. As cell phone technology has improved it has developed new resources, such as locating tools (GPS, for example), cameras, recorders and several computing resources. According to Anatel, in 2009 Brazil accounted for more than 160 million cell phones and around the world there are approximately 3.4 billion users of mobile telephones (Ling and Donner, 2009). The diffusion rate of cell phones supersedes most of the previous technologies, including personal computers.

According to Saccol, Schlemmer, and Barbosa (2010), Mobile and Wireless Technologies offer a group of learning possibilities which facilitate, for example, our interactions as teachers or instructors, as well as the interaction with other colleagues and other people with whom we wish to exchange information, share ideas and experiences or solve doubts. In addition that, we can access a wide range

of resources and didactic material, including not only text, but also images, audio, video, and all other multimedia integration possibilities. We can also use the whole range of resources offered on the internet for learning, including e-books, articles, videos, online news, blog content, microblogs and games. Learners then are not limited to a fixed or formal learning space. As they walk around they have access to elements that can enrich their learning in contact with their own world. A wide range of digital resources can be linked to different physical spaces and events (for example, running, galleries, observing nature, doing mobile work, etc.) in a synchronous way and thus enhancing learning. The learners are able to not just access resources or materials but also capture data and make notes, and even generate content in a mobile and ubiquitous way. Everything can be shared in real time (and be made available when necessary) and also stored for further analysis (in a classroom or training place or in the comfort of one's home). There is also a wide range of resources available for doing so. For example, it is possible to take pictures, record audio and video, take short notes, and even access technologies from Web 3D on a cell phone. This generated content can also be shared in real time.

Web 3D comes with infinite possibilities in 3D environments and in networks such as Metaverses (Active World, Second Life, OpenSimulator, Wonderland, etc.) that allow the creation of 3D Digital Virtual Worlds in which avatars live and share; in Massive Multiplay Online Role Play Games that enable the development of strategies for problem solving; augmented reality[46] and mixed reality[47], and also the ECODIs (digital virtual living spaces), that are a techno-digital hybridism where interaction does not only happen textually, as with other technologies, but also in oral, gestural and graphic interactions. These technologies from Web 3D have been contributing to what has been called Immersive *Learning (i-Learning)*.

By using technologies from Web 3D, such as metaverses on mobile devices such as smartphones, the learning processes with mobility are enhanced by the possibility of the subject's immersion via an avatar in a 3D environment. In this context some experiences with the Second Life metaverse are being developed for both Android and iPhone platforms. Two of these main experiences are quoted below:

Mobile Grid Client Second Life and Open Simulator Messaging Client for All Android Powered Devices

Mobile Grid Client is a client for Second Life and for the Open Simulator (OpenSim) for Android cell phones, such as the Motorola Droid, the Samsung Galaxy S (I9000), the Nexus One and other mobile devices using the Android system. It is simple and intuitive in its use and it allows the user to remain connected when answering a phone call or when carrying it in a pocket. It has the following tools: local chat and instant messaging; teleporting to other regions and places where there are other avatars; region maps with the location of other avatars; profiles – for checking one's own profile as well as that of other avatars; complete manipulation of inventory – moving, renaming and excluding items or files. Mobile Grid Client is not a complete Second Life client, and therefore does not share images in 3D nor does it have the facility to personalize an avatar. It is important to highlight that Linden Lab did not develop the Mobile Grid Client and, therefore, the company that created Second Life does not provide any kind of backup related to this tool.

Pocket Metaverse iPhone and iPad Client for Second Life®

The Pocket Metaverse is a client for Second Life, for use with iPhone and iPod Touch. It provides easy access to all of the main Second Life functions allowing the user to keep in touch with his Second Life friends while at work or away from his computer. It has the following tools: chat and

instant messaging; an online friends list; a World Map and Teleporting; a MiniMap showing who is nearby; profiles, groups and a search tool; giving, receiving and managing the inventory; reading notecards and visualizing textures; Uploading and downloading from photo albums and cameras; payments and Installment Media, among others.

CONCLUSION

The possibility of "entering" a graphic environment in 3D, such as a school, a company, a museum, a library, etc., through immersion given to the subject via his avatar's telepresence and the digital virtual presence is an experience totally different to that of accessing a web page or website, because the subject does not browse a page to access forums and chats to collaborate with others. Instead he is "present" in the place where it is happening. It is then possible to understand that a metaverse, a 3D digital virtual world is a more familiar environment, cognitively speaking, to the human being and is therefore, naturally more intuitive to use because the interactions, either those in the 3D space itself or with the other subjects within this space, are possible through representation via an avatar, a "digital virtual body". In this way, as in the physical face-to-face world, in the metaverse, in a 3D digital virtual world, the subjects communicate through a body, which is part of the interaction process with the environment and other subjects represented there.

This subject's immersion through his avatar in a graphic environment in 3D makes the interaction more significant, interesting and encompassing, and the feeling of presence is intensified which has been shown to be essential for the process of distance learning. There are many questions related to presence, presented by the students who participate in the teaching and learning processes in a distance learning modality using the current AVAs. Statements such as "I feel lonely" or "I miss seeing people" enhance the importance of the social presence for the students interacting within these environments. This issue has been mentioned by researchers as a factor in the success of the student's learning and a challenge for current offers in Distance Learning. According to Trein and Backes (2009) however, it is important to remember that both the physical and the digital virtual presence do not configure living and sharing.

We know that migrating from the traditional Virtual Learning Environment paradigms, from environments in 2D and from the predominance of interaction through texts and diagrams, to another that enables the possibility of simulating or emulating the physical world or the representations coming from our imagination, gives us a greater feeling of immersion and "location" (being there). This feeling is important for the student to feel motivated and people present different behaviors according to the place they are in. The Virtual Learning Environments with hyperlink structures do not give the subject the feeling of place, in the sense of this term in daily life.

The degree the of students' involvement and immersion within the content of the courses, the colleagues and the teacher in a virtual reality 3D environment like Second Life cannot easily be reproduced in the traditional learning environments, such as Blackboard, Teleduc, Moodle, etc. (Mattar, 2008, p.88)

It is then easy to perceive that Mobile and Wireless Technologies and the different technologies in Web 3D, with which we interact nowadays are of another nature, which means the previously adopted methodologies are no longer usable as they cannot fully extract the potential these new media offer. New technologies must emerge, taking into account the potential of the interaction process, enabled through these different digital technologies.

Furthermore we understand that educating in this historical-social time and space implies using this society's technologies. This expresses an ecological vision which recognizes the fundamental interdependency of phenomena, in a way that we, as students and society, are part of the processes in the cycles of nature.

REFERENCES

Backes, L. (2010). A cultura emergente na convivência em MDV3D. *Conjectura: Filosofia e Educação (UCS)*, *15*, 99-117.

Backes, L., & Schlemmer, E. (2008). A configuração do espaço digital virtual de convivência na formação do educador em mundos virtuais. In Proceedings of 14° Congresso Internacional ABED de Educação a Distância (vol. 1, pp. 1-11). São Paulo, Brazil: ABED.

Benford, S., et al. (1993). From rooms to cyberspace: models of interaction in large virtual computer spaces. Nottingham, UK: University Park Nottingham.

Castronova, E. (2005). *Synthetic worlds*. Chicago, IL: University of Chicago Press.

Domingues, D. (2003). Arte, vida, ciência e criatividade com as tecnologias numéricas. In D. Domingues (Ed.), *Arte e vida no século XXI: Tecnologia, ciência e criatividade* (pp. 11-14). São Paulo, Brazil: Editora UNESP. Retrieved from http://artecno.ucs.br/livros_textos/textos_site_artecno/3_capitulo_livros/diana2003_arte-vidaxxi_cap.rtf

Durkheim, E. (1895). *The rules of sociological method*. New York: The Free Press.

Gibson, W. (1984). Neuromancer. New York, NY: Ace.

Gonseth, F. (1948): Les conceptions mathématiques et le réel. In *Proceedings of Symposium de l'Institut International des Sciences théoriques*. Bruxelles: Les sciences et leréel.

Hegel, G. W. (1955). *Lectures on the history of philosophy*. Humanities.

Kadirire, J. (2009). Mobile learning demystified. In *R. Guy (Ed.), The evolution of mobile teaching and learning* (pp. 103–118). Santa Rosa, CA: Informing Science Press.

Klastrup, L. (2003). A poetics of virtual worlds. In *Proceedings of Melbourne DAC2003* (pp. 100-109). Melbourne, Australia: DIAC. Retrieved from http://hypertext.rmit.edu.au/dac/papers/

Lévy, P. (1999). Cibercultura. Rio de Janeiro, Brazil: Editora 34.

Lombard, M., & Ditton, T. (1997). At the heart of it all: The concept of presence. *Journal of Computer Mediated-Communication, 3*(2). Retrieved from http://www.ascusc.org/jcmc/vol3/issue2/lombard.html

Maia, C., & Mattar, J. (2007). ABC da EaD. São Paulo, Brazil: Pearson Prentice.

Malizia, P. (2012). Comunidades virtuais de aprendizagem e de prática. In E. Schlemmer et al. (Eds.), Comunidades de aprendizagem e de prática em metaverso (pp. 25-60). São Paulo, Brazil: Editora Cortez.

Mattar, J. (2008). O uso do Second Life como ambiente virtual de aprendizagem. *Revista Fonte, 5*(8), 88-95. Retrieved from http://www.prodemge.gov.br/images/stories/volumes/volume8/ucp_joaomattar.pdf

Maturana, H. R., & Varela, F. J. (2001). A árvore do conhecimento: As bases biológicas da compreensão humana. São Paulo, Brazil: Palas Athena.

Maturana, H. R. (1999). *Transformación en la convivencia*. Santiago, Chile: Dolmen Ediciones.

Maturana, H. R. (2002). A ontologia da realidade. Belo Horizonte, Brazil: Ed. UFMG.

Maturana, H. R. (2005). Emoções e linguagem na educação e na política. Belo Horizonte, Brazil: Ed. UFMG.

Maturana, H. R., & Varela, F. J. (1997). De máquina e seres vivos: Autopoiese - a organização do vivo. Porto Alegre, Brazil: Artes Médicas.

Ondrejka, C. (2008). Education unleashed: Participatory culture, education, and innovation in Second Life. In K. Salen (Ed.), *The ecology of games: Connecting youth, games, and learning* (pp. 229–252). Cambridge, MA: MIT Press.

Piaget, J., & Inhelder, B. (1993). A representação do espaço na criança. Porto Alegre, Brazil: Artes Médicas.

Rymaszewski, M., et al. (2007). Second Life: O guia oficial. Rio de Janeiro, Brazil: Ediouro.

Saccol, A. Z., Schlemmer, E., & Barbosa, J. L. V. (2010). M-learning e u-learning: Novas perspectivas da aprendizagem móvel e ubíqua. São Paulo, Brazil: Pearson Education.

Santos, M. (1980). Por uma geografia nova: Da crítica da geografia a uma geografia crítica. São Paulo, Brazil: Editora HUCITEC.

Santos, M. (2008). Metarmofoses do espaço habitado: Fundamentos teóricos e metodológicos da geografia. São Paulo, Brazil: Edusp.

Schlemmer, E. (1998). *A representação do espaço cibernético pela criança, na utilização de um ambiente virtual*. (Unpublished master's dissertation). Universidade Federal do Rio Grande do Sul, Porto Alegre, Brazil.

Schlemmer, E. (2010). ECODI-RICESU formação/capacitação/ação pedagógica em rede utilizando a tecnologia de metaverso. In Proceedings of XV ENDIPE Encontro Nacional de Didática e Prática de Ensino (pp. 1-13). Belo Horizonte, Brazil: Editora da Universidade Federal de Minas Gerais.

Schlemmer, E., et al. (2004). AWSINOS: Construção de um mundo virtual. In *Proceedings of VIII Congresso Ibero-Americano de Gráfica Digital: SIGRADI* (pp. 110-113). São Leopoldo, Brazil: Anais.

Schlemmer, E., Saccol, A. Z., Barbosa, J., & Reinhard, N. (2007). M-learning ou aprendizagem com mobilidade: Casos no contexto brasileiro. In Proceedings of 13o. Congresso Internacional da ABED (pp. 1-10). São Paulo, Brazil: ABED.

Schlemmer, E., Trein, D., & Oliveira, C. (2008). Metaverso: A telepresença em mundos digitais virtuais 3D por meio do uso de avatares. In Proceedings of XIX Simpósio Brasileiro de Informática Educativa (pp. 441 - 450). Fortaleza, Brazil: Anais.

Soares, L. H. (2010). *Complexidade e autopoiese no metaverso - Estratégias e cenários cognitivos.* (Unpublished master's dissertation). Universidade Católica de Brasília, Brasília, Brazil.

Stephenson, N. (1992). *Snow crash.* New York: Bantam.

Tapley, R. (2008) Construindo o seu Second Life. Rio de Janeiro, Brazil: Alta Books.

Trein, D., & Backes, L. (2009). A biologia do amor para uma educação sem distâncias. In Proceedings of 15° Congresso Internacional ABED de Educação a Distância (pp. 1-10). São Paulo, Brazil: ABED.

KEY TERMS AND DEFINITIONS

3D Digital Virtual World: 3D digital virtual worlds are dynamic 3D scenarios, which are molded throughout a computer, with graphic computing techniques and used to represent the virtual part of a virtual reality system. These environments are designed with use of special tools, such as programming language VRML (Virtual Reality Molding Language) and Engines 3D, and strengthen with the use of accelerator 3D boards.

Digital: According to Lévy (1999) it means the action of digitalizing. Digitalizing information consists in translating it into numbers. The digits enable the information codified in numbers to flow through electrical wires, inform electronic circuits, polarize magnetic tapes, translates into sparkles in optical fibers and so on. The information digitally codified can be transmitted and copied almost indefinitely without loss of information for they are reconstituted after the transmission.

Life: It is a cognition process and the interactions happening between subjects are always cognitive interactions, constructed while living. It is within living through our actions and reactions that we create our world and we are created by them, this way the subject and the world emerge together in congruency.

Metaverse: It represents a category of immersive digital virtual environments, and establishes itself as a platform in which subjects act and interact, live and share, in a representation universe that let them develop a new social experience, configuring a digital virtual living together. The metaverse technology enables the creation of 3D digital virtual worlds.

Reality: "Reality is the domain of things, and in this sense, something that can be distinguished from what, is real" Maturana and Varela (1997, p. 156).

Space: The definition of space implies complex and dynamic comprehensions, because the concept is formed by two components interacting in a continuous way: the configuration of territory, as a group of natural data that can be modified by man, and the social dynamic, or a group of social relations, defined by a definite time, Santos (2008). Space is "the domain of all possible interactions in a collection of units (single or compound units interacting as units) established by these units' properties when specifying their dimensions" (Maturana, 2002, p. 130).

Virtual: Virtual is what exists in power but not in act. The virtual tends to update itself without passing through effective or formal concretization. … Strictly in philosophical terms, the virtual does not oppose to the real, but to the actual: virtuality and actuality are only two different ways of being. (Lévy, 1996).

ENDNOTES

[1] Concept approached in Chapter 4 - Avatar: Building a "Digital Virtual Self."

[2] Concepts approached in Chapter 7 - Autopoietic Machines and Alopoietic Machines: The Structural Coupling.

[3] Concept approached in detail in Chapter 11- The Real Virtuality of Metaverses.

[4] Concept approached in Chapter 5- Immersion, Telepresence, and Digital Virtual Presence in Metaverses.

[5] Concepts approached in Chapter 5- Immersion, Telepresence, and Digital Virtual Presence in Metaverses.

[6] According to McCallum (2000) "Cyberpunk fiction works with technological innovations that cause significant changes in the way human beings orient themselves in relation to the world – or even in the world they inhabit, either virtual or real. Although science fiction is commonly understood as being the exploration of outer space and other planets, cyberpunk alters this theme in favor of the imagination of a "faux" space of networks and databases – information, communication and media systems – in our world." (p.349-350). Cyberpunk fiction is, at the same time, science fiction presenting broad questioning about the meanings of science and human "being."

[7] Cyberpunk romance has brought to literature ideas such as highly developed artificial intelligence and virtual spaces with physical characteristics very similar to the "real" space. The concept of cyberspace itself also appears in this work, defined by Gibson (1984) as a "consensual hallucination, every day being experimented by billions of people."

[8] Cyberspace starts more effectively to develop in the 80s, with very few independent computers linked in a network. The World Wide Web, for instance, started in the beginning of the 90s. At that time the subjects more acquainted with computer culture were able to forecast new interaction possibilities in a new environment, the "no-place" in cyberspace.

[9] Concept approached in Chapter 7 - Autopoietic Machines and Alopoietic Machines: The Structural Coupling.

[10] Multiuser Dungeons, were the first games in the pre-Web age, which used text interface and afterwards, the 2D graphic to create stories to be played by several users, in the Role Playing Games style.

[11] http://www.thepalace.com

[12] http://www.clubpenguin.com

[13] http://www.activeworlds.com

[14] http://www.secondlife.com

[15] http://metaverse.sourceforge.net/

[16] http://www.solipsis.org/

[17] http://www.opencroquet.org

[18] http://www.openwonderland.org/

[19] http://opensimulator.org

[20] Massachusetts Institute of Technology – MIT located in Cambridge – Massachusetts, USA, is one of the most important university institutions in the United States of America - USA and one of the most famous research and teaching centers in the world. http://web.mit.edu/

[21] Eduverse, *software* Active Worlds, retrieved from http://www.activeworlds.com/edu/awedu.asp

[22] Retrieved from http://www.pgie.ufrgs.br/projetos/arca/

[23] Considered to be the Brazilian university that stands out most in this research field, for it was the first university in Brazil to have a Galaxy in Eduverse Metaverse (educational version of the Active World), where they created 3D Digital Virtual Worlds AWSINOS, in the year 2000 and an Island in Second Life, the UNISINOS Island, created in 2006.

[24] The citizens in the users' community Active Worlds have named villa a space existing inside the world, but that is distant or in another dimension.

[25] Research can be found in http://www.unisinos.br/pesquisa/educacao-digital:

[26] "Virtual Worlds in the Educator's Formation: research on autonomy and authorship processes" – Masters thesis in Education, defended by Luciana Backes in February 2007, available at http://www.unisinos.br/pesquisa/educacao-digital. "The Interaction in Digital Virtual 3D Worlds: a research on representation of emotions in learning" - Masters thesis in Education defended by Rosmeri Ceconi da Costa in August 2008, available at http://www.unisinos.br/pesquisa/educacao-digital; "*Online* Education in Metaverse: the pedagogical mediation through telepresence and digital virtual presence via avatar in Digital Virtual Worlds in 3 Dimensions" – Masters thesis in Education, defended by Daiana Trein in March 2010.

[27] 3D Engines are specialized softwares with the objective of treating 3D elements in an interactive way in real time. Such 3D Engines enable the creation of very sophisticated environments and objects with a high level of realism.

[28] Poetics is the systematic study of literature as literature. It deals with the following issue: "What is literature?" and with all possible questions developed from this question, such as: What is art in this language? What are the forms and types of literature? What is the nature of a literary genre? What is the system of an art or language? (Rimmon-Kenan (1983) apud Klastrup (2003)).

[29] *Linden Lab*® was founded in 1999 by Philip Rosedale and its headquarters are located in *San Francisco*. It has a workforce of 250 people, skilled in physics, 3D graphics and networks. Most part of the team comes from companies working with the technology Web 2.0, such as *Electronic Arts, Apple, Midway, Disney* among others. (Second Life Wiki, 2010).

[30] Another world where reality and fiction are mixed up.

[31] Concepts approached in Chapter 6 - Interaction and Interactivity in Metaverse.

[32] The space is a social fact in the sense in which Kosik (1967, p.61) defines social phenomena: a historical fact, as we recognized as an element from a group and so assuming a double function that effectively assures it the condition of historical fact: on one hand it is defined by the group, which also defines it; it is simultaneously producer and product; determining and determined; a revealer who allows decoding by those who decode it; and on the other, at the same time it acquires an authentic meaning, it gives meaning to other things. (Santos, 1980, p.130).

[33] Territorial configuration is the territory plus the group of objects in it; natural and artificial objects that define it. ...Whatever the country and its development stage, there is always a territorial configuration formed by a constellation of natural resources: lakes, rivers, lowlands, mountains and forests, and there are also created resources: railways, roads, all kinds of ducts, dykes, artificial lakes, cities, and so on. It is this union of everything, arranged into a system, that forms the territorial configuration in which reality and extension are mixed up with the own country's territory. (Santos, 2008, pp.83-84).

[34] The social dynamic is set by a group of economic, cultural, political variables that, at every historical moment give specific meaning and value to the technical environment created by man, meaning the territorial configuration. (Santos, 2008, p.120).

[35] Common in the sense of community, which means, the co-inspiration that constitutes a

community makes sense towards its members' desires and wishes, when doing their tasks.

36 Creating spaces implies establishing relationship dynamics between e-inhabitants, giving them a meaning and modifying the environment they live in, in a congruent way.

37 Environment – the Word is connected to INTERRELATION - RELATION (with the ENVIRONMENT (physics-nature, socio-cultural environment), established BETWEEN the environment and human action (anthropic action), both individual and collective, within a dynamic process – always moving on; it interacts within itself by exchanging data. According to Maturana the environment is defined by the classes of interaction, in which the observer* can enter, subscribe to, and which is something he treats as a context for his interaction with the observed organism. "... furthermore, I call environment the middle part of what the observer sees around a system, while he is observing his niche" (Ontology of Reality, 1997, p.86).

38 Mecha is an abbreviation for mechanical. A mecha avatar is an avatar represented by a giant robot (usually biped) controlled by a pilot or controller, that is very common in some science fiction works. A mecha is usually a war machine with legs. They are usually built in an anthropomorphic format (human being) or in animal format.

39 Furries are anthropomorphic animal characters with human characteristics and personality. In Second Life, they are those "hairy" beings similar to a certain animal or mythical creature, thus keeping a basic humanoid frame.

40 The concept of state of flow was developed in 1975 by the Hungarian Psychologist and Professor Mihály Csíkszentmihályi. For Csíkszentmihályi (1990) being in flow means "being completely involved within an activity, where you let your ego fall. Time flies. Every action, movement and thought invariably develops from a previous state; it is like playing jazz". Flow is translated in a mental state, in which the subject finds himself totally immersed in, characterized by a feeling of involvement, focused attention, complete engagement in the task, where all his energy is applied.

41 Concept approached in Chapter 4 - Avatar: Building a "Digital Virtual Self."

42 Concept approached in Chapter 5 - Immersion, Telepresence, and Digital Virtual Presence in Metaverses.

43 The IETG also carries out research in the Croquet Metaverse and OpenSim, and keeps a discussion group in Second Life where it organizes meetings to discuss issues about the research. The IEGT has recently received an innovation award for presenting a promising technology that will considerably affect society in the near future.

44 Educational modality in which information meets the subject. It follows him through localization systems, based in GPS, where the subject's role is to filter it.

45 This modality promises to allow teaching and learning processes to take place anywhere, at anytime, with any device, in a continuous way, contextualized and integrated to the learner's daily routines.

46 Augmented reality consists of the superposition of 3D virtual objects, generated by a computer in a real environment, through a technological device. However, this definition is only complete with the definition of mixed reality.

47 Mixed reality is the interaction between the physical face-to-face world and the digital virtual world, including two possibilities: Augmented Reality, in which the predominant environment is the physical face-to-face

world and the Augmented Virtuality, in which the predominant environment is the virtual one. It is possible to say, the, that the Augmented Reality is a particularization of the Mixed Reality that consists of the enrichment of the physical face-to-face environment with virtual objects, through a technological device working in real time, thus enhancing a human's perception by the addition of information that is not directly perceived by natural senses. The coexistence of the physical and virtual environments has to be balanced in such a way that the user cannot distinguish them.

Chapter 4
Avatar:
Building a "Digital Virtual Self"

ABSTRACT

This chapter presents and discusses the avatar. The authors approach the breakthrough of the technologicized body, under the perspective of creating a digital virtual identity, the avatar, which appears linked to the metaverse technology in the construction of 3D Digital Virtual Worlds. They present and discuss subtopics like: "Avatar: A Technologicized Body," "The Construction of a Digital Virtual Identity," and "Avatar: The Representation/Action of the 'Digital Virtual Self' through the Technologicized Body." In a brief conclusion about the chapter, the authors highlight the multiple identities that constitute us, through the self-consciousness of "self," the body to perform actions, and reflections to assign meaning, and the technologicized body through the avatar. Therefore, the authors have shown the co-existence and the multiple and different dimensions.

INTRODUCTION

In his book, "The Digital Life" (1st edition, 1995), Negroponte reflected in the 90s on this "new way" of life that basically implies the interaction of man and machine. In this context, the concern about developing a digital technology relied on creating friendly systems, perfecting the man-machine interface, making it more familiar and being able to reproduce the physical space reality as Digital Virtual spaces. However, in this work he calls our attention to something that goes beyond this interaction, for he argues that, "we eagerly talk about man-machine interactions and

dialogic systems, whilst we are able to leave one of the participants of this dialogue in complete darkness" (2006, p.124).

After 16 years and since the dawn of metaverse technology that enables the construction of 3D Digital Virtual Worlds, we return to the reflections of Negroponte (2006), broadening them to discuss the interaction process between human beings, who at this time begin to be represented by their avatars and who are in congruence with the environment (relations established in a Digital Virtual space), and in this case, it being a Digital Virtual World in 3D. We can see that increasingly, metaverse technology is being used to its

DOI: 10.4018/978-1-4666-6351-0.ch004

full potential, and not only with the "intention" of merely substituting the physical space or promoting only a man-machine interaction. Human beings can establish interaction processes through telepresence and a Digital Virtual presence with other human beings who are in conditions that would not otherwise be geographically possible.

Another significant aspect is that of the representation of human perception. In this case it is broadened with the possibility of a metaphorical representation in graphic 3D construction that we do not normally use in geographically based interactions. The 3D Digital Virtual Worlds are then tridimensional graphical representations, constructed with metaverse technology through the action of avatars. The avatars are also 3D graphic representations of human beings e-inhabiting these 3D Digital Virtual Worlds. This e-inhabiting, or e-living, consists of being, living, inhabiting, and moreover of living and sharing a 3D Digital Virtual World with other e-inhabitants who are also represented by avatars, and enabling a kind of "Digital Virtual" life. This new way of living and sharing significantly increases the understanding of the relationship and the interaction between human beings and digital technologies as they are in congruence with each other. In this way, when interacting in the 3D Digital Virtual World, human beings establish another relationship with information, metaphorically enabling new ways of constructing knowledge by representing theoretical concepts in graphs. The concepts are usually represented in an oral or textual way, so we are familiarized to maintain a dialogue or to write about a particular theoretical referential using the same words the author refers to: we think in synonyms and/or reproduce their ideas. When we metaphorically represent a concept, however, we need to understand it in order to establish relationships with objects or schemes and we also need someone's validation, through their interpretation, to validate the metaphor. The metaphor only makes sense when it can be interpreted.

The point from which the object of knowledge is viewed can also be considered significant. The possibilities are broadened by the angle of vision upon the object, which itself can be approached from different angles when we move the avatar, when we change the way we look at the object, when we fly, teleport or even when we are in other dimensions in the 3D Digital Virtual World.

Therefore, the avatars' "Digital Virtual lives" are being built symbiotically with human beings' "physical life", through the similarities, differences, contradictions, synergies and triumphs the human establishes when using his avatar representation. The human has a "Digital Virtual life" when he establishes living and sharing relationships or develops interaction processes with other e-inhabitants of the 3D Digital Virtual Worlds through a "Digital Virtual self" represented by a "technologicized body" (Lévy, 1999). In this way, it is through living and sharing that he establishes friendship, organizes communities in cyberspace and builds up Digital Virtual social networks, forming and being formed by this culture that emerges from living and sharing within a Digital Virtual environment.

But who is this human being that lives and shares in 3D Digital Virtual Worlds represented by an avatar and what do we understand by human being? We are initially approaching the understanding of the living being and the human being, who is represented by an avatar when telepresent in a 3D Digital Virtual World. After a thorough examination of the avatar as a technologicized body, in the coupling between human being and avatar, we will discuss the construction of the Digital Virtual identity and the constitution of the "Digital Virtual self". Using this perspective we can reflect on and broaden the different ways of living and sharing in 3D Digital Virtual Worlds and so use this Digital Virtual space to its full potential.

Human beings are living beings understood as units or systems, exchanging energy and having unique organization and structure. So "a unit" (entity, object) is defined by a distinct act. Every time we make reference to a unit in our descriptions we make it implicit or explicit, for both involve distinguishing what defines it and makes it possible" (Maturana & Varela, 2002, p.47).

The units are characterized by their independence i.e. their ability to act, and by autonomy - their ability to define their actions in a responsible way. Through this, such characteristics enable humans to self-produce (when amplifying their capabilities) through their living dynamically with others in congruence with the environment, which consists of an articulated, relational and dialectic way of living. Therefore human beings are the result of their species' history - phylogenesis[1] - and overlapped with the individual's own history - ontogenesis. Living beings grow, develop and modify themselves following a flexible but unpredictable and undetermined evolutionary line, depending on their action and interaction with the environment and other living beings. In this sense, can an avatar evolve? Or does the evolution of an avatar occur through the development of the living being representing it? Can we think of the avatar's development from the living being's development, as is the case in the social networks or communities in which they are considered alive? When there is no development and/or self-production by living beings, both avatars and networks or communities cease to exist or disintegrate.

Every living being knows when they are living, and lives when they are knowing, so we consider the fact that knowing is a particular being's 'living'. This knowing is supported by an organization and a structure that constitutes the living being.

The organization refers to the relationships between the components that make the attributes designed for the unit, meaning, they are relations established within the circuit and which therefore define the unit as something.

This situation – in which we recognize, implicit or explicit, the organization of an object when indicating it or distinguishing it -, is universal in the sense that it is something we constantly do as a basic cognitive act. ... we understand as organization the relations occurring between the components of something, so that it is possible to recognize them as members of a specific class. (Maturana & Varela, 2002, pp.50-54)

This is what makes it possible for him to produce himself in a continuous way whilst remaining in the class to which he belongs.

According to Maturana and Varela (2002) the structure is the group of components and the relationships constituting a particular unit and designing its organization. The structure is variable and particular, but the organization is invariable and common. "We understand as something's structure the components and the relations that concretely constitute a particular unit and designs its organization" (p.54).

The living being, while living with other living beings and with the environment, starts to modify its structure during its ontogeny, making it unique and different from other living beings. This way, "… all knowledge, for that which knows is doing, depending on the structure he knows" (Maturana & Varela, p.40). However, organization is always maintained, and this is what makes him a being from a certain class otherwise he would not exist.

The distinction between organizations and defining attributes is made by the living beings, in the same way that particularities from several units' structures are equally specified. This way the living being is responsible for the articulation between phylogeny and ontogeny, a route taken in the living beings' interactions in their environment. Using this perspective we can move forward to reflections raised by Negroponte (2006) regarding the interaction process with the development of digital technologies. Nowadays human beings, through their avatars, can be immersed in a 3D Digital Virtual World and this represents different forms (textual, oral, metaphorical, gestural). Their phylogenic and ontogenic perspectives to other human beings are equally represented by their respective avatars in an environment where they also have specific characteristics. However, when human beings use their avatars they create a phylogeny (determining a class of avatar, either humanoid or abstract, and an ontogeny that represents their actions related to their history and interactions, which directly or indirectly are related to their lives.

With this in mind, according to Maturana and Varela's (1997) proposal, it is possible to establish the relationship between living beings and machines[2], because both living beings and machines operate through certain properties which allow the accomplishment of certain actions. Could we say the avatar is a machine? Can we predict the actions of the avatars? "We could add however, that due to the relational determinations between the parts of a machine, such a system cannot adapt to situations for which they have not been prepared" (Primo, 2000, p. 78). This way we evince the distinction between machines, being: autopoietic machines and alopoietic machines[3]. The understanding of autopoietic machines consists of the development of non-predictable processes that pushes for adaptation to new and unexpected situations, for they are the results of a history of transformations in harmony with the environment.

In this sense, as living beings we exist in continuous self-production (through autopoiesis) in the dynamic configuration of the relations (through living and sharing spaces) in the same way that we exist in the conservation of our living in a transgerational way, giving us the condition to be human beings. The existence of the human being is marked by language and emotion, which means we exist when we talk[4], through conversational networks. For Maturana (2002) the comprehension of the existence of what is human and the relationship humans establish with others who support this existence, passes through comprehension "...of language and emotions that, in day-to-day life, we refer to the word talking" (p.167). This way, language and emotion are approached in

their relation and articulation, configuring living and sharing spaces through interaction processes in human beings' day-to-day living and sharing. Both concepts will be individually approached in chapter 7 - Autopoietic Machines and Alopoietic machines: the structural coupling.

The origin of humanity, for Maturana and Verden-Zöller (2008), arises through evolutionary history with the origin of the family, more than three million years ago, when humans established emotional relationships with their peers. They then constituted small groups of adults and children, where living and sharing occur for the pleasure of physical proximity and the pleasure of living together. Living and sharing among human beings occur through two characteristics particular to the progeny: neoteny and epigenesis[5].

The possibility for humans to constitute family is characterized by their neotenic capacity, so we can evidence the expansion and conservation of actions verified in their childhood, and which are also verified in adult life. This condition contributes to our ability to constitute ourselves as cooperative, co-dependent beings able to express loving relationships across all age groups.

We propose that we, human beings, are the present of a progeny that has emerged defined by the conservation of the maternal-infant bonding and the mutual acceptance of trust and body proximity in a way that has extended beyond the reproduction age, in a neotenic evolutionary process. (Maturana & Verden-Zöller, 2008, p.62)

Another condition that constitutes human beings is demonstrated in their capacity to construct a history, through language, in the flow of interactions with other human beings and thus transforming living into congruence with the environment. Therefore our sharing behavior is moulded culturally and is effective because the sharing condition is also in our biological base. What we can see is a certain systemic dynamic between the social relationship and the biological condition. "But nothing can happen in our epigenesis that our genetic constitution does not permit" (Maturana & Verden-Zöller, 2008, p.65).

In summary, language and its emotion satisfy the configuration of living and sharing among human beings, and, in this sense, start the coordination of consensual behavior alongside coexistence in a permanent or extended relational basis. Such human characteristics can be seen when they are represented by their avatars in a 3D Digital Virtual world. For example: some participants choose to enter a 3D Digital Virtual world with a high number of avatars; other participants immediately activate a mechanism to identify whether there are "friends" nearby; dialogs are promptly initiated when entering a Digital Virtual world.

In this way, humans develop individually and are simultaneously pushed by social relationships and emotions or, according to Maturana and Verden Zöller (2008), the love that is based in "… accepting the other as a legitimate other in coexistence with somebody" (p.60). Therefore the relationships are constituted through "… mutual trust and absence of manipulation or instrumentalization of relations" (p.60), as well as the mutual respect in cooperative actions.

Cooperative actions are enabled by the biological condition of humans for the organization of consensual coordination in their existence within a recurrent and appropriate dynamic for behavioral coordination. Therefore, in the human condition language and emotions are needed so that there are recurrent interactions in this relational domain – being either permanent or prolonged. The permanence of emotions enables the continuity of living and sharing, constructing a way of living through language continued from one generation to another in the teenagers' learning. From this perspective the human being develops himself and his social relationships, congruent with the environment, in a dynamic with his organizational and individual structures.

Every human being then constructs a particular way of living in relation to others, configuring different living and sharing patterns and constituting cultures that pass from one generation to another. The conservation of a particular way of living and the emotional and rational intertwining therein express our ability to solve the differences between human beings so that we modify ourselves through talking.

Living, for Maturana and Varela (1997), is constituted in the continuous challenge of overcoming difficulties and learning from every new circumstance. Therefore living is learning through interactive processes that enable disturbances, reflections and the compensation of the disturbances resulting in change. So, if there is interaction there is life, as according to Maturana (1999), human beings are social beings, living their daily lives in a continuous interaction with other human beings.

From this perspective the human being's life is a process of continuous cognition, the social relations are interactions that happen between the human beings characterized as cognitive interactions, that are built in their living and sharing. It is in this living and sharing and through our actions and reactions that we create our world and are created by it, and so human beings and the world emerge together in an interactive and inter-relational network.

But how does this happen when we talk about the metaverse, in 3D Digital Virtual Worlds, where human beings as avatars are telepresent in cyberspace configuring a Digital Virtual presence? Can we say that they live through language, by talking in relationships that are configured through emotions?

AVATAR: A TECHNOLOGICIZED BODY

The term "avatar" comes from the Sanskrit avatāra, a concept developed within Hindu mythology that means 'the representation of God in the moment He leaves Paradise towards the Earth' and refers particularly to the representation of Vishnu.

This way, avatar, in Hinduism is considered the mortal manifestation of an immortal being. The ten representations of Vishnu through His avatars symbolize every stage in the biological evolution of life on Earth.

In a fictional context the term avatar was first used by Stephenson (1992) to refer to the representation of humans in cyberspace. In 2009 the term became popular with the movie "Avatar" by James Cameron who had the idea 14 years previously when there were no technological means to make his ideas concrete in a movie. The movie approaches the avatar as a revolutionary technology created to enable life in another world (Pandora), using a technologicized body (avatar) from a human body. The story consists of presenting richness in the biodiversity present in Pandora, the way they live and share with humanoids called "Navi" and who have a particular language and culture. The movie marks the differences in human existence and the world on Earth. Within a Cartesian perspective there is no possibility of coexistence between the two worlds. Some aspects presented in the movie are part of virtual reality as a particular way of living and sharing in the 3D Digital Virtual World such as the different languages. Others are distant from virtual reality, regarding the physical embodiment of the human being in the avatar and the difficulty of the coexistence between the Pandora World and the Earth.

So the term avatar gained ground and evidence in the means of communication both in cinema production and in the new Web 3D technologies, mainly due to the fast and intense dissemination of the use of metaverse, including the Massively Multiplayer Online Role-Playing Game (MMOR-PG)[6], which use avatars as a representation and immersion of what is human in 3D Digital Virtual Worlds. These representations may be created by the users allowing their "personalization" inside

the machines and on the computer screen. Such creation consists of transcending the human image into a Digital Virtual body which allows him to live and share in other worlds.

With the development of the metaverse technologies, which enable the creation of Digital Virtual Worlds both in 2D and 3D, the representations of human beings in Digital Virtual underwent a significant evolution process concerning their appearance and the possibility of actions and interactions was introduced. According to the available metaverse technology, representation can vary from a simple image named "prop", a bi-dimensional model or even a sophisticated 3D model which is pre-defined or totally customized/created by the human being and called an "avatar". The avatar can be a simulation of the physical body or a completely different representation based on the creator's imagination and creativity.

The process of creating an avatar usually starts from the choice of a "standard avatar", with the use of different tools available in the metaverse that allows the editing of several parts of the avatar, up to the point where it gets closest to the appearance desired by the e-resident.

In some cases the choice is a very simple selection from the available commands or characteristics desired for the Digital Virtual appearance such as gender, model, shape, color and size. This process is illustrated in Figure 1, with reference to the Eduverse metaverse – educational version of the Active Worlds software:

In other metaverses creation can be more complex, with a very sophisticated level of detail as in the case of the Second Life metaverse, where the avatars are personalized through scrollbars varying from 0% to 100%. These bars move the polygon frames which modify the avatar model, working as measurers to determine the minimum or maximum capacity of a certain Digital Virtual body characteristic. For example the shoe size:

Figure 1. Creation of the avatar from the standard model
Source: Authors

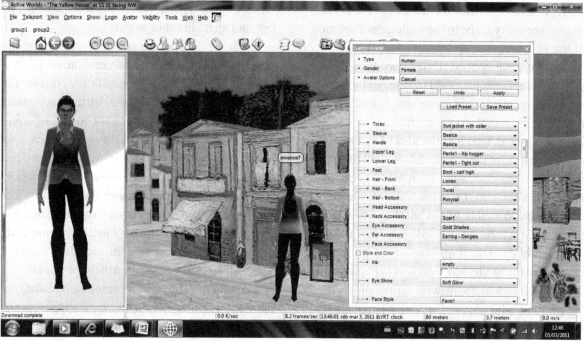

if the bar is at 20% it means the avatar has small feet; if it is at 100% they will be bigger, as can be observed in Figure 2:

The avatars are constructed in layers, having a basic form called a frame. In Second Life, both for creating and modeling the avatar and other objects in 3D, there are two essential tools: the prims (primitives) which are virtual masses that can take any format (cubes, cones, spheres, etc.) which are used as construction blocks; and the textures, which are images or graphs created and/or imported into Second Life and are applied to an object to create visual effects. They can imitate the colors and textures of different fabrics, objects, hair, etc. and can be applied on the prims already created.

So, as the avatars are constructed in layers it is possible to create different objects, such as clothing, accessories, hair or tattoos which can dress or be attached to the avatars as adornments. These objects can be seen in the following images. The moulding of the different Digital Virtual body parts is achieved with the tools available in Second Life. In this way and if they wish, it is possible for the e-residents to dress their avatars in the same way they dress in the physical world. Clothing can also be created in image editing programs such as Gimp or Photoshop which can then be imported into Second Life.

If an e-resident wants to increase the sensation of "realism", Second Life enables the creation of physical effects on objects (clothing, bags, hair, wings, tails, ears, etc.) simulating their movements, for example, when the avatar walks, runs or flies in 3D Digital Virtual Worlds (Schlemmer, Trein & Oliveira, 2008).

Avatar movements are another important characteristic that can be edited in Second Life, meaning every avatar movement and the way he uses this to interact in and with the world, can

Figure 2. Moving the polygon's frame to modify the avatar
Source: Authors

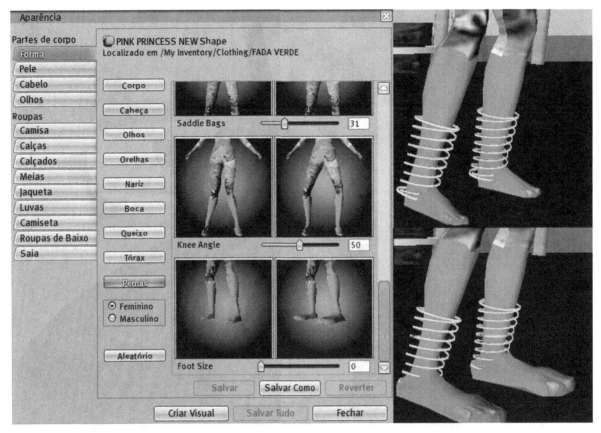

be personalized. Movement and gesture editing occurs outside the Second Life metaverse using specific software such as Poser. The process is as follows: after editing, gestures or movements are imported into Second Life, and this file contains the specific data about the avatar's actions and movements.

The construction/personalization of the avatar is a process of virtualizing the physical body either as a similar or imagined representation and we pick names as well as gender, skin color and height. We can choose to be human, animal, half human, half animal or not human etc. In 3D Digital Virtual Worlds the rules, standards, shapes and parameters are defined by the subject who lives and shares in these spaces and who interacts with other subjects (Schlemmer et al., 2008).

As well as the possibility of creation, e-residents always have the opportunity to acquire new bodies, clothing and accessories, both for free or by paying for them, depending on the level of detail they desire. This way and over time technologicized bodies can pass through a developmental or total transformation process with more sophisticated details.

It is necessary however to observe that when using a form with many prims, there can be differences on the screen due to the interaction of the prims with textures and other objects in the environment. As a consequence, application can be significantly slow - presenting lag - and the images can present sequence failures.

It is important to consider that although many can understand the avatar as a character and use it

Figure 3. Violet Ladybird avatar dressed as a fairy, using the characteristics available in the SL metaverse
Source: Authors

Figure 4. Avatar with attached wings
Source: Authors

Figure 5. Avatar with attached tattoo
Source: Authors

Figure 6. Avatar with attached hair
Source: Authors

- **Humanoids:** Human-like avatars which can also have different themes (cyberpunk, celebrity, erotic, steampunk);
- **Mecha:** Robot avatars;
- **Abstract:** Avatars in shapes that could not possibly exist in the physical world;
- **Furry:** Humanoid avatars with animal features;
- **Non-Humanoids:** Avatars who are completely animal or who do not present any humanoid characteristics.

this way, by creating a character with a personality and interacting through it in the different 3D Digital Virtual Worlds they may enter, we have observed in our research (Trein, 2010) that a large part of our subjects view the avatar as an extension of themselves, another face they have or as an extension of their identity in a Digital Virtual world and co-existing in real life.

In this sense there are almost literal representations of the human beings' physical appearance in the physical world; representations that are totally different to the physical aspect or even representations blending human beings' physical aspects with imagined ones such as with animal-like characteristics, fantastical beings, fictional creatures and hybrid beings. Today, avatar types can be classified as follows:

We believe that the choice of avatar, his characteristics, details and actions are related to the human emotions that are represented involving his history of interaction with other avatars living and sharing in 3D Digital Virtual Worlds and the technical knowledge these humans have. This way we can think of the avatar as a transcendence of the human being because he can materialize situations, movements, actions and interactions in 3D Digital Virtual Worlds which his organism, while human, does not allow.

THE CONSTRUCTION OF A DIGITAL VIRTUAL IDENTITY

The transcendences evidenced in the avatar's technologicized body, in relation to each human who constructs it, can also be perceived in the identity manifestations. It is important to stress, however, that whether similar or contradictory, the identity begins in the human's identity construction which is transcended in the avatar. This way it is important to reflect on the understanding of human identity that results from a complex social construction in order to move forward in the comprehension of how a human constructs his Digital Virtual identity.

The studies about identity emerge at the same time as studies about culture. We can think of the identity as an ontogenic construction and the culture as an ontological construction. So, as humanity has developed through different cultures, those differences make it possible to identify the individual aspects of human beings who belonged to a certain group, meaning, an identity with this group. In every cultural transformation there are also transformations in the human beings' identity. This fact has been strongly characterized ever since human migration began in the world, and with that the differences have become elements of perturbation and ideas about identity have broadened studies in the areas of Anthropology, Social Sciences and Psychology.

In this context Brazil is an interesting country to be taken as an example. The Brazilian identity is strongly characterized in different parts of the world such as the physical appearance of people of mixed race and a communicative, creative and sympathetic personality among others. Nevertheless, each Brazilian region has its own identity too, equally characterized due to the different colonization processes that took place in the country and also due to climatic and geographical differences. For example, the State of Rio Grande do Sul in the far South of Brazil has been colonized by German (1824) and Italian (1875) immigrants.

It borders Argentina and Uruguay and its history was marked by a separatist movement called the "*Farroupilha* Revolution" (1835-1845). These aspects build up the *gaúcho* and *gaúcha* [7]'s own and particular identity. The habits and customs brought by the immigrants blend with the habits and customs of the people who lived in the border regions and created the linguistic representations, traditions, food, clothing and folklore of the region. However every gaucho has his or her own individual characteristics, influenced by other groups they belong to such as a particular soccer team, religion or occupation.

So, according to Cuche (1999), we may say that:

identity is an instrument that allows thinking about the articulation of the psychological and social elements in a subject. It expresses the result of the several interactions between the subject and his social environment, either close or distant. The subject's social identity is characterized by the grouping of his links within a social system: links with a social class, age, nation, etc. The identity allows the subject to find his place within a social system and be socially located. (p.177)

At the present time, humanity is living other transformations that result in new disruptions within the construction of the identity and the interactions in living and sharing, mainly with the development of digital technology and particularly 3D Digital Virtual Worlds. The concept of immigration takes on a new meaning as the Digital Virtual collaborating is configured in this space. Immigration is not only territorial but also Digital Virtual and between the different generations. The subjects taking part in a Digital Virtual collaborating form this group which, through interaction processes, reconstructs a new identity for themselves and for the group. Using the same perspective we find, in the Digital Virtual spaces, a sub division of groups which also construct different sub identities within the larger identity context (or Digital Virtual identity).

So, for Cuche (1999) as we construct different identities within social groups we also develop concurrent inclusion and exclusion processes. The identity identifies the group (according to the members taking part in the group who present identical characteristics from a certain point of view) and this differentiates it from the other groups whose members present different characteristics from the first group yet from the same point of view. When we establish living and sharing in a Digital Virtual space, we also establish ways of building relationships and interactions. We represent our perception through the different digital technological resources and by building references that characterize this group and its way of living and sharing. Other people who do not belong to this Digital Virtual space are therefore characterized as another group which may result in an exclusion process when the first group becomes autonomous or legitimizes the living together. However, as we broaden our awareness through language and in the interaction processes with the different groups (in this case characterized as digital immigrants and digital natives) we can critically reconstruct this from the viewpoint of overcoming the difficulties and limitations of each group and transform ourselves.

In this transformation process, quite normal in human beings, identity is not considered as definite or determined, especially as we are autonomous and autopoietic human beings. Humanity transforms through the autopoiesis of human beings who are in congruence with the environment, and within this context we call attention to the fact that this "environment" where humans interact is not only physical but also Digital Virtual. It is made of different digital technologies, implicit in the relationships constructed in an action/interaction process and making the living and sharing forms, which when passed from one generation to another, are also cultural constructions.

For Lemos (2007), the cultural constructions from Digital Virtual space can also be called cyberculture, so:

Cyberculture forming before our eyes shows, for better or for worse, how new technologies are effectively being used as tools of a social effervescence (sharing emotions, friendliness and community formation). Cyberculture is sociability as technological practice. (p.72)

The digital native generation - nowadays configuring living and sharing in Digital Virtual spaces - is identified by the ease by which they communicate and establish interaction processes, by their fast access to globalized information (even when sometimes they ignore local information) and by simultaneity, amongst other things. This generation is used to multimedia, virtual reality and telematic networks. The feeling of being connected or the identification to a certain collectivity, to a higher or lower degree, gives due importance and meaning to the representations the subjects make in social reality, which in this case is also a Digital Virtual reality. Taking Facebook as an example[8], in which active participants give meaning and importance to the perceptions presented on this social network in a particular way, this is proportional to his identification with the group interacting in this space and defines this Digital Virtual reality.

It is important to stress that a subjectivist approach of identity "… has the merit of considering the variable character of identity and also the tendency to excessively emphasize the ephemeral aspect of identity" (Cuche, 1999, p.181). Under this same approach, identity is considered a social construction and is constructed within social contexts. So we can see in contemporaneity that contexts can be physical or Digital Virtual; that they are constructed and defined by components (human beings) through appropriate behavior for this group and by this can guide every component's representations and choices. This means the human being constructs behaviors that will guide his actions and will redesign adequate behaviors in whatever way actions may demand.

This identity is constructed from the similarities between human beings belonging to the same group and the differences between other groups. Identity is, at the same time, an individual, social and global subject, according to Trukle (1999). Every human being in his interaction history (that we believe can occur both in physical spaces and in Digital Virtual ones) shows different aspects of himself, in professional, personal or social contexts. Nevertheless, when living in the same Digital Virtual spaces people are more and more aware of the multiplicity of their own "unit". This way we can better understand the identity construction as a result of the synthesis between the individual as a social and global object.

We can then consider identity as a result of the interaction processes that trigger transformations in the subject and in the group, and human beings attribute meanings that construct and reconstruct identity inside these social exchanges. "Identity always exists in relation to others, with this other being considered legitimate. This means that identity and otherness are related and are simultaneously dialectic. The identity follows differentiation" (Cuche, 1999, p.183).

In our research we have seen that the construction of a Digital Virtual identity with an avatar representation occurs in the immersion of the subject in a world where he can act and interact with other e-inhabitants, other avatars; establish Digital Virtual living networks; create virtual communities, structure habits and attitudes and define appropriate behavior for this living and sharing in the determined group. We also hope that this Digital Virtual identity is constructed through meaningful relationships in a free way when we consider mutual respect as a primary and basic characteristic.

The construction of the Digital Virtual identity is only possible when one gets in touch with the other and in an expanded vision the "Other" represents the different subjects within a society or group living together on a daily basis. This way the avatar's existence, transcending that of the human being, is realized via another avatar and from the vision of this other avatar. This also allows us to understand the 3D Digital Virtual Worlds from a different view, relating the different points of view and enabling the decentralization of the "self avatar". In this sense we see that the avatars' actions in the 3D Digital Virtual Worlds value the potential of technology and that there is congruence between 3D Digital Virtual Worlds, the avatar and the human being who also inhabits different physical spaces.

In this sense, the subject and social relationship is dialectic and causes a larger sense of presence and vivacity precisely because this "social Digital Virtual presence" brings together human beings who, as their "Digital Virtual selves" or avatars, can have the feeling of "being there" and "being together" in the same Digital Virtual environment yet in a more intense and significant way.

In this way, the feelings of distance and absence, often present in Digital Virtual relationships due to the physical distance, are overcome when we live and share in a Digital Virtual way, acting and interacting in different 3D Digital Virtual Worlds through the "Digital Virtual self" and thus enabling the construction of cognitive structures that transform the human being in an autopoietic way.

AVATAR: THE REPRESENTATION/ ACTION OF THE "DIGITAL VIRTUAL SELF" THROUGH THE TECHNOLOGICIZED BODY

But what exactly motivates us as human beings to live and share via an avatar in a 3D Digital Virtual World? We can think of a "congestion" of physical relations; the need to search for other possibilities that break the limits that physical presence imposes; the desire of "being together" with a group of friends whilst physically living in another place; the active participation within different groups or activities such as work, study, research or offering support and of the sharing of experiences and the human being's constant search for something.

However, as an ontogenic human being we have our own particular way of living and sharing. The human "self" is not defined by the body it inhabits, although it is evident that the "self" materializes through the actions and operations this body carries out and it is through the body that the "self" can speak and therefore exist. We can then say that the "self" and the 'body' are distinct but closely related, or, according to Capra (2002), they are "embodied" in a way that makes their existences subordinated between themselves, and the "self" is constituted through physical nature and physical experiences. However, for Lakoff and Johnsons (as cited in Capra, 2002), human beings have a cognitive unconscious composed of automatic cognitive operations, beliefs and a tacit knowledge that moulds the conscious thinking. This "moulding of the conscious thinking" happens implicitly, such as reading between lines or in metaphoric expression. When we establish distinctions in our living and sharing we create a world which is embodied in the articulation of the conscious and unconscious and we express our abstract thinking in a concrete way. In this moment the human being can think and reflect on how the cognitive unconscious develops the self conscious.

For Maturana (2001) reflection on self-conscience, or reflection of the "self" happens through the following aspects:

Firstly, the author considers that the human condition occurs in the domain of the organism's relationships with others through language and resulting in structural changes. "The dynamic involvement of the *Homo Sapiens'* corporality and way of living is what constitutes the human being" (p.236). However we are not always aware of the changes we go through whilst living. Awareness consists of making the changes in our living and sharing and emerges as one of the multiple reali-

ties that coexist and this reality is coherent with what we do. "And it is as result of awareness that we live in a world with many possible realities arising from what we do, and that we can choose the reality we want to live in according to what we want to keep in our life" (Maturana & Dávila, 2009, p.242). Through this, we can have an awareness of the "self" which happens dynamically as we share these living and sharing exchanges in the flow of language with the other.

Secondly, "the self" materializes within living and sharing, so it cannot be decontextualized from the environment in which it is situated and the relationships it establishes with "other selves". The human being is ontogenic and this ontogeny is constructed via the history of interactions throughout life.

The third aspect consists of understanding that the emergence of the "self" occurs when talking and involves language and emotions. As a result, the "talks that constitute all relationships and entities have to occur, because they only exist in the relational dynamic in the lives of animals who use language" (Maturana, 2002, p.237).

In summary, corporality and the "self" are dynamically related in a life that is possible with the other. Corporality and the "self" are different but inseparable and incarnate and therefore it is in this dynamic that we give meanings to living and sharing through language, and which represents the relationship between thought, concept, body and brain. Can we then think of the avatar in this same domain of relationships? Or can we think of the avatar as another corporality that is in a dialectic relationship with the physical corporality? What are the frontiers between a physical corporality and a technologicized corporality? Is it really necessary to establish frontiers? Do they exist? Can the constitution of the "self" be considered unique?

When we reflect on the frontier between corporality and the self, between the physical and the virtual, human being and avatar, we perceive that it is both subtle and permeable. "While specialists keep talking about real and virtual, people construct a life in which frontiers are more permeable. (...) In the future, permeable frontiers will be the most interesting ones to study and understand" (Turkle, 1999, p.118). According to Turkle (1999), we live the moment of co-existence, that is, there is life in its different dimensions and importance. For the author,

real relationships are those in which people feel sufficiently connected to give them real importance. These are the relationships that determine the way in which everyone perceives oneself (...) or the way in which they see their own capacity for relating with others. (...) In an online life situation, people find themselves in a situation of being able to perform different roles and adopting different personalities in different places within the Network. They see and experience several aspects of themselves. They live such multiplicity intensively (...) In this sense life online approaches an aspect of day-to-day life to take them to a higher level. (...) For many people the virtual community allows a free expression of the countless aspects of themselves. But it is also something that they live alongside in the "rest of their lives". (...) As things get closer and the space is reduced, cyberspace proposes something akin to the game-space: a chance of experimenting with something that does not exist in the rest of life but in Virtual Reality (...) I want to stress that the best possibilities for the development of communities are in the places in which virtual experiences cross and converge with the rest of life. (Turkle, 1999, pp.119- 121)

So, when e-inhabiting or e-living in 3D Digital Virtual Worlds we can give the avatar the technologicized corporality we wish and obviously this corporality is represented by the degree to which the human "self" determines for his "Digital Virtual self" thus defining and revealing himself in a recursive relationship. The similarities or differences of the physical corporality the avatar

assumes are closely related to the "Digital Virtual self" and allows him to distinguish himself from the other "Digital Virtual selves" that are in the relationship.

We therefore believe that there is plasticity in the relationship between physical corporality and Digital Virtual corporality and that both are dialectically related to the "self" (whether Digital Virtual or not). When we create an avatar as an animal, monster or character representation, we reveal the intention of being completely different to our physical corporality in the particular way we see ourselves or our creative desire of being something different, letting the "Digital Virtual self" arise. The similarities and differences relate to these embodiments in the same way that they relate to "the selves" that arise and take part in a certain group. We are then presented with the possibility of having similar or different "selves" that materialize in a single human being, with whom we wish to have understanding of his actions and operations and an awareness of his self.

This way, e-inhabiting 3D Digital Virtual Worlds implies the bringing of the "self" in the dynamic of living and sharing with the other (the avatar) in congruence with the environment (3D Digital Virtual Worlds). In this dynamic of interactions there is the transformation of the self and the environment consisting of a structural coupling and this allows the dawn of a world we desire. So, to be considered an e-inhabitant or an e-resident the avatar interacts with other avatars through text communication, chat or private message; oral communication and gestural or metaphoric communication. In this interaction process there is the "self" that can also be the "Digital Virtual self"; there is a transformation of the living space (the relationship between the avatar's and/or the world's landscape) which constitutes Digital Virtual living and sharing.

This e-inhabitant or e-resident, however, can be construed as an e-citizen. The word citizen derives from the word *civita*, the Latin for city, which correlates with the Greek word *politikos*, meaning the one inhabiting a city. When we think about citizenship in its etymological sense it intends it to be the condition of someone living in a city, and at the same time it approaches the human condition as a member of a group that has its own companionship rules, knows his rights and duties and establishes respectful relationships for himself and for others. In this sense it implies a significant and committed interaction with the group to which he belongs.

In order for the avatar be built as an e-citizen it is necessary that the representation of the "Digital Virtual self" happens through the establishment of living and sharing rules with other "selves" who emerge in a dynamic relationship when living and sharing in harmony with the Digital Virtual space and configuring a Digital Virtual companionship. It is important to understand these companionship rules and to consider the other as a legitimate "self" for the interaction processes and the use of Digital Virtual space to its full potential for the emancipation of the "self" and of everyone living and sharing that Digital Virtual space.

We also use the term e-tourist, explicitly expressed in some metaverses as in the Active World, to communicate with an avatar that has limited permission to do things in the 3D Digital Virtual World. The limits of the action rely on the impossibility of constructing graphic representations. The avatar simply operates through communication with other avatars, establishing the interaction processes and thus representing through language his "Digital Virtual self". The action of the e-tourist may or may not transform the dynamics of the relationships within the group to which he belongs at a certain moment and in a certain way he can materialize his "self".

We return then to the last question asked at the beginning of the discussion. Can the constitution of the "self" be unique? For Maturana (2002, p.181), the constitution of the self happens in two dimensions: in responsibility and in freedom:

a) we are responsible from the moment when we, in our reflection, realize whether we want the consequences of our actions or not;

b) we are free at the moment when we, reflecting on our actions, realize whether we want our will and its consequences, and we also realize that our will or the lack thereof and the consequences of our actions, can change our desires.

Everything is possible and desirable in the constitution of the "digital virtual self" but it does not always happen, being the same process as the constitution of the physical "self". We can perceive that in certain moral, ethical and cognitive aspects, the constitution of the "self" is unique. We also notice that in relation to the aesthetic, communicative and interpersonal aspects the constitution of the "self" can be different or even contradictory. However, in every moment there is an intimate, subtle and embodied relationship between the "self" and the "digital virtual self".

CONCLUSION

When we think of the relationships between human and avatar; the corporal and technologicized body; identity and Digital Virtual identity; self and Digital Virtual self, we need to reflect in a dialectical way and through the perspective of transcendence. There is no way to define the beginning, middle and end, or even to organize thoughts within a hierarchical and linear logic.

The relationships are established through intersection points, through permeable or porous lines that can disappear as limits in a conclusion, resulting in new questions. It might be possible to create a diagrammatic representation to illustrate this, as follows:

In Figure 7 we can see a unit (human being) constituted by the "Self", "Identity", "Body" and "Avatar", interacting with other units (hu-

Figure 7. The frontiers of the constitution of the human being represented by an avatar
Source: Authors

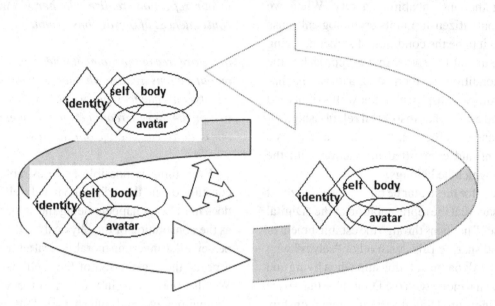

man beings). The elements constituting the unit cross, intersect and mingle according to the unit's dynamic and the dynamic generated in the intersection with other units, and also in congruence with their environment.

But we still do not know if this diagram represents the complexity of this discussion. Thinking about the multiple identities that constitute ourselves when contemplating the "self" in the body that allows the carrying out of actions and reflections as a unit, it becomes more real in the sense of giving meaning, when we live and share in 3D Digital Virtual Worlds via an avatar. In this context we construct elements that enable the understanding of co-existence, of multiplicity and of different dimensions.

Instead of ending here, some of the considerations coming from research contribute towards broadening this reflection.

Living and sharing in 3D Digital Virtual Worlds makes the human being understand the avatar as a transcendence, an embodied and complementary "self", that can be different in many aspects from his "physical self". So, the creation of the avatar that enables communication, relationships and interaction in 3D Digital Virtual Worlds, for most human beings, happens by maintaining a certain correspondence with gender, and most of them also maintaining their appearance with similar characteristics. Research carried out by Schlemmer, Trein, and Oliveira (2008) and Trein (2010) clearly reveals that the avatar allows the participant-subjects the sensation of telepresence and the feeling of being immersed, made possible by the interaction through a technologicized body and allowing a higher involvement in the interaction process with other avatars.

In this sense we can say that the transcendence of the avatar develops a level of action and interaction by the human being in Digital Virtual spaces. According to research also carried out by Schlemmer, Trein and Oliveira (2008) and Trein (2010) the difference between an image representation (avatar in 3D Digital Virtual Worlds) and a textual representation (in virtual learning environments or web 2.0) and in other fora, gives the avatar a greater possibility of representing desired expressions such as gestures, movements, talking and appearance (the graphic representation of his self). It is noticed that such multiple ways of expression increase feelings and perceptions due to the fact that it is possible to "see" the other and his representation. We can then say that what happens is a transformation in the structure of the human being which the avatar represents. The actions of the avatars, however, are limited to his programming and are subordinated to the human's actions.

Human beings are then represented by their avatars when immersed in 3D Digital Virtual Worlds and establish companionship with the intention of developing social systems whilst keeping the human characteristic. The possibility of different interactions, of talking to many people at the same time and through any identity allows proximity and different communication, thus enriching the interactions in this newly constituted social system. The participant-subjects in the research carried out by Schlemmer, Trein and Oliveira (2008) and Trein (2010) recount that the interactions are not "boring and tiring" and that it is more interactive than many interactions offered in physical spaces, as it is possible to see, talk and make gestures. The connection of the telepresence feeling in meetings, and talking in 3D Digital Virtual Worlds with the sensation of not having the usual borders of time and space, makes it simultaneously possible to "be there", discussing and interacting through an avatar. In this sense, we can also claim that the continuity of emotion allows the continuity of companionship, thus constructing a way of living in language.

So, we can understand the avatar as being an extension of oneself as a human being, another side of the self, an extension, a Digital Virtual embodiment or a transcendent identity in a world that is of a Digital Virtual nature and co-exists in the universe of contemporary human relationships.

REFERENCES

Capra, F. (2002). As conexões ocultas: Ciência para uma vida sustentável. São Paulo, Brazil: Cultrix.

Cuche, D. (1999). A noção de cultura nas ciências sociais. Bauru, Brazil: EDUSC.

Lemos, A. (2007). Cibercultura, tecnologia e vida social na cultura contemporânea. Porto Alegre, Brazil: Sulina.

Lévy, P. (1999). Cibercultura. Rio de Janeiro, Brazil: Editora 34.

Maturana, H. R. (1999). *Transformación en la convivencia.* Santiago, Chile: Dolmen Ediciones.

Maturana, H. R. (2001). Cognição, ciência e vida cotidiana. Belo Horizonte, Brazil: Ed. UFMG.

Maturana, H. R. (2002). A ontologia da realidade. Belo Horizonte, Brazil: Ed: UFMG.

Maturana, H. R., & Dávila, X. Y. (2009). Habitar humano em seis ensaios de biologia-cultural. São Paulo, Brazil: Palas Athena.

Maturana, H. R., & Varela, F. J. (1997). De máquina e seres vivos: Autopoiese - a organização do vivo. Porto Alegre, Brazil: Artes Médicas.

Maturana, H. R., & Varela, F. J. (2002). A árvore do conhecimento: As bases biológicas da compreensão humana. São Paulo, Brazil: Palas Athena.

Maturana, H. R., & Verden-Zöller, G. (2008). A origem do humano. In H. R. Maturana, & S. N. Rezepka (Eds.), Formação humana e capacitação (pp. 59-75). Petrópolis, Brazil: Vozes.

Negroponte, N. (2006). A vida digital. São Paulo, Brazil: Companhia das Letras.

Primo, A. (2000). Uma análise sistêmica da interação mediada por computador. *Informática na Educação: Teoria & Prática/Programa de Pós-Graduação em Informática na Educação, 3*(1), 73-84.

Schlemmer, E., Trein, D., & Oliveira, C. (2008). Metaverso: A telepresença em mundos digitais virtuais 3D por meio do uso de avatares. In *Proceedings of XIX Simpósio Brasileiro de Informática Educativa* (pp. 441-450). Fortaleza, Brazil: SBIE. Retrieved from http://www.br-ie. org/pub/index.php/sbie/article/view/735

Stephenson, N. (1992). *Snow Crash*. San Jose, CA: Bantam Spectra Book.

Trein, D. (2010). *Educação online em metaverso: A mediação pedagógica por meio da telepresença e da presença digital virtual via avatar em mundos digitais virtuais em 3 dimensões*. (Unpublished master's dissertation). Universidade do Vale do Rio dos Sinos, São Leopoldo, Brazil.

Turkle, S. (1999). Fronteiras do real e do virtual: Entrevista concedida a Federico Casalegno. *Revista Famecos*, (11), 117-123. Retrieved from http://revistaseletronicas.pucrs.br/ojs/index.php/ revistafamecos/article/viewFile/3057/2335

KEY TERMS AND DEFINITIONS

Avatar: Avatars are representations and immersion of what is human into the 3D digital virtual world. These representations may be created by the users allowing their "personalization" inside the machines and the computer screen. Such creation consists in transcending the human image to a digital-virtual body which allows him to live and share in other worlds.

Digital Virtual Identity: The construction of a digital-virtual identity (with an avatar representation) occurs in the immersion of the subject in a world where he can act and interact with other e-inhabitants (other avatars); establish digital-virtual living networks; create virtual communities, structure habits and attitudes and define the adequate behavior for this living and sharing in this determined group.

Digital Virtual Self: It is the set of actions, interactions, communications and buildings that the technologicized body (avatar) performs in the 3D digital virtual world.

E-Citizen: For an avatar to be built as an e-citizen it is necessary that the representation of the "digital-virtual self" happens through: establishment of living and sharing rules with the other "selves" who emerge in a dynamic of relations when living and sharing in congruence with the digital-virtual space – configuring a digital-virtual companionship; comprehension of these companionship rules, considering the other as a legitimate "self" for the interaction processes; the use of digital-virtual space in its full potential for the emancipation of the "self" and of everyone living and sharing the digital-virtual space.

E-Resident: Or e-inhabitant is the avatar that interacts with other avatars through: text communication, chat or intimate message; oral communication, by speaking; gestural communication, with the avatar's gestures and/or by the graphic communication, or metaphoric. In this interaction process there is the "self" that can also be the "digital-virtual self"; there is a transformation of the living space (dynamic of relations between the avatars and/or the world's landscape) and configures the digital-virtual living and sharing.

Organization: The organization refers to the relations between the components that make that the attributes designed to the unit are in fact what they are, meaning, they are relations established within the circuit and that defines the unit as something.

Structure: Is the group of components and the relations constituting a particular unit and designing its organization.

Technologicized Body: Representation of the "digital virtual self", the 3D digital virtual world, which allows living and coexisting with other avatars. The technologicized body is the structural coupling between human and avatar.

ENDNOTES

[1] "It is a succession of organic shapes that are sequentially being generated through reproductive relations". (Maturana, Varela, 2002, p.117).

[2] In the context of the research developed by the Digital Education Research Group UNISINOS/CNPq we understand machines as digital technology making possible the creation of living and sharing spaces for relations and interactions.

[3] The alopoietic machines will be approached in Chapter 7 - Autopoietic Machines and Alopoietic Machines: The Structural Coupling.

[4] "The word *talk*, in Portuguese "conversar" comes from the junction of two latin roods: *cum*, meaning 'com' ('with'), and *versare* meaning 'going around with' the other" (Maturana 2002, p.167).

[5] Refers to new characters as time goes by (Matturana, Verden-Zoller, 2008, p.65).

[6] Computer game and/or videogame allowing thousands of players to create their characters in a dynamic virtual world at the same time on the Internet.

[7] Denomination attributed to a person born in the State of Rio Grande do Sul (BR).

[8] Facebook is a social network launched on February 4th, 2004. It was founded by Mark Zuckerberg, Dustin Moskovitz, Eduardo Saverin and Chris Hughes, former Harvard students. Facebook is currently in first place, with 590 million visits and a global reach of 38.1%, according to "AdPlanner Top 1000", a website that records the most accessed websites around the world, thorough a Google search tool, as for February 2011. http://facebook.com/

Chapter 5
Immersion, Telepresence, and Digital Virtual Presence in Metaverses

ABSTRACT

This chapter presents and discusses themes such as Immersion, Telepresence, and Digital Virtual Presence in Metaverses (this latest one being a theoretical construction coming from the context of the research developed by GPe-dU UNISINOS/CNPq) and the possibilities that arise from the action and interaction of an avatar in a 3D Digital Virtual World constructed in metaverses. We present some of the concepts that contribute to a reflection on social presence and the sense of proximity in metaverses, and the importance of immersion and relational social presence for the learning process. Both are enabled through interaction via avatar, in a combination of telepresence and digital virtual presence. Some of the subtopics presented are: Presence and Proximity; Relational Presence and Social Presence; Telepresence and Digital Virtual Presence; Immersion and Tele-immersion, as well as a brief conclusion to the chapter.

INTRODUCTION

With the advent of the new digital technologies, mainly those related to the 3D Web such as metaverses, new worlds are created; digital virtual worlds are formed by graphic environments, in three dimensions and are programmable. They can be e-inhabited by different subjects through a graphic representation – the avatar[1]. Moreover, through the avatar, the e-resident can have a telepresence in a digital virtual presence, allowing him, with a certain degree of immersion, to live and share with other e-residents within a certain 3D digital virtual world. This broadens the possibilities of action, communication and interaction between subjects that happen not only through textual language as found in other digital technologies, mainly to those linked to Web 1.0 and Web 2.0, but they are extended and complemented by the use of oral, gestural and graphic languages in a combined way.

We know, due to research developed in the Research Group on Digital Education GPe-dU UNISINOS/CNPq that when using technologies such as the metaverse the subjects may feel initially lost and often demonstrate signals related to

DOI: 10.4018/978-1-4666-6351-0.ch005

losing their references constituted by the meaning of "being present", "being close". This is because they experience another type of presence, a telepresence and a digital virtual presence that also enable a digital virtual presence understood as "digital virtual being together".

Today, "being present", "being close", "being together" are not limited to the physical presence imposed by the condition of the physical body. By means of different digital technology, mainly those related to the 3D Web, we are able to have new "bodies", "technological bodies", "digital virtual bodies" that enable us to be here and there at the same time, or be represented by a physical body in a face to face physical world and be simultaneously represented by a "digital virtual body" in the digital virtual world. We can then live new experiences (Virtual Fictional Experiences–EFV and Real Virtuality Experiences - EVR), have new sensations, virtualize realities and build new ones, many of which would not ne feasible without the use of 3D Web technologies. Such experiences can significantly contribute to the subject's learning.

Thus, this new digital technological context has contributed to concepts such as presence, proximity, relational presence, social presence, telepresence, distance and immersion which are revisited, broadened, redefined, and even created, as in the case of the concept of "digital virtual presence" and "tele-immersion". These concepts are essential nowadays when we approach the teaching and learning processes.

In this chapter, we present and discuss some of the concepts that will contribute to the reflection on social presence and the sense of proximity in metaverses, and the reflection on the importance of immersion and relational social presence for the learning process, both enabled through the interaction via avatar, in a combination of telepresence and digital virtual presence.

PRESENCE AND PROXIMITY

We cannot talk about presence and proximity without addressing the mental models we have built throughout our lives. We immediately think of being together as physically beside someone present, in the same time and space. There is then a direct association to the physical body, and the notion of "being present" and "being near". Notwithstanding Trein (2010), notes that the feelings of presence and proximity, even when strongly associated to the physical body, may also occurs in other ways. For example, when we are physically distant from those we love, we can feel closer to them when we look at a photo, listen to a certain song or touch a specific object related to the absent person, meaning we can bring the beloved person's presence to us. When we receive a letter from someone we care for we can feel and wonder how they would be reading those words to us, and the same happens when we perceive scents, listen to certain music, we somehow remember and can even feel a presence, or someone's proximity. This feeling of having another person there through our memories, feelings or imagination is considered to be the first type of virtual presence we know, because "virtual is what potentially exists, not in action" (Lévy, 1996, p.15). In this way we virtualize people we love, with their bodies, voices, meaning their presence.

"Presence" has been widely investigated by Lombard and Ditton (1997), who understand it as a perceptive illusion, not a mediation one. In their studies, the authors carried out a vast revision of the production of knowledge under presence and came up with six intertwined but distinct conceptualizations:

- **Presence as Social Enrichment:** Related to the socialization amongst subjects;

- **Presence as Realism:** Related to the feeling of "reality" which the subject experiments; feeling the "thing" as "real";
- **Presence as Transportation:** Related to the subject's virtual displacement, that can have the following variations:
  - "You Are There": The subject is transported to another place; this concept is often used in virtual reality discussions;
  - "There and Here": The other place and its objects are transported to the subject;
  - "We Are Together": When two or more subjects are transported together to a place they share. There is no physical presence, but the subjects share the same virtual space;
  - "You Are Around": Represents the oldest version of presence, related to the oral tradition from the first human beings involving a story teller, enabling the subject to be transported to another time and place where the events occurred (Biocca & Levy, 1995 apud Lombard & Ditton, 1997). According to Gerrig (1993) and Radway (1991, apud Lombard & Ditton, 1997), the narrative may have the same effect.
- **Presence as Immersion:** For Heeter (1995, apud Lombard & Ditton,1997) immersion is related to the concepts of intensity, fun, competition, use and excitement. Presence as immersion bears the idea of psychological and perceptive immersion (Biocca & Levy, 1995 apud Lombard & Ditton, 1997), such as in VR, IMAX[2] cinema, planetarium and simulations, where experiences and feelings are immersed in a digital virtual world. Perceptive immersion consists of the "degree to which the

virtual environment submerges the user's perceptual system" (Biocca & Delaney, 1995, p.57 apud Lombard & Ditton, 1997). Presence as immersion also includes a psychological dimension. When the subjects feel they are involved (Palmer, 1995 apud Lombard & Ditton, 1997), absorbed (Quarrick, 1989 apud Lombard & Ditton, 1997), striving and engaged;

- **Presence as a Social Actor in the Environment:** It allows the subject to be involved in a VR experience, making it also possible to act/interact with the environment and experience the situation;
- Presence of the environment as social actor involves the return of the interaction provided by the environment itself, the use of computer programs to perform social roles such as with Agents and robots.

It is possible to understand that the concepts of presence and proximity when associated with the use of technologies, mainly digital virtual ones as well as telecommunication services, need to be (re)defined, broadened and changed, contributing to the emergence of terms such as telepresence and digital virtual presence, among others. In this way, the Emerging Digital Virtual Technologies, including Virtual Reality and Metaverses (that enable the construction of 3D Digital Virtual Worlds, Simulation, Massive Multiplayer Online Role Play Games, Videoconferences, among others) provide the subjects with a higher level of presence, or a kind of mediated experience that results in a strong sense of presence, that according to Lombard and Ditton (1997), can be perceived as "natural", "immediate", "direct" and "real" – whilst other traditional communication means provide a lower level of presence.

Within this context, we can question how presence is conceived of and the feeling of proximity when subjects use a metaverse. Can "presence" and the feeling of "proximity" vary? What are the variables that may contribute to a greater feeling of presence and proximity for the subjects?

When subjects use a metaverse, their presence and feeling of proximity occur in relation to their graphic 3D representation, which means, the 3D digital virtual world, created in the metaverse and, the graphic 3D representation of the subject (avatar) in a created world. Subjects feel they are represented through their avatar, meaning the avatar is the subject in those worlds (and in this case there is a symbiosis between the construction of the subject's identity in both worlds – physical and digital virtual) and this also implies a high level of technological appropriation by the subjects. They can produce their avatar after "their own" image and be present through the possible imbrication between the graphic language (avatar), textual, oral or gestural languages; and, the more the world presents itself as a digital virtual sharing space for the subjects, getting them involved, greater are their feelings of presence and proximity.

Therefore, the "presence" and the feeling of "proximity" may vary according to:

- The digital virtual world created in 3D;
- The avatar representation, including here the digital technological domain so that the subject can make the avatar be whatever the subject wants is to be;
- The possibilities of the use of the 3D digital virtual world, or, how it incites the subject to be present and interact;
- The possibility that the 3D digital virtual world can be constituted as a digital virtual space for living and sharing;
- The use, necessity and/or desire the subject has to be there, together with other subjects in a digital virtual way.

Thus, the 3D digital virtual world representation, the avatar representation, the digital technological domain, the use of the 3D digital virtual world, the configuration or not of the digital virtual

space for living, the establishment or not of a digital virtual living and sharing and the utility, necessity and desires the subject has are the variables that may contribute to a stronger feeling of presence and proximity amongst subjects.

The concepts of presence and proximity are closely related to the concepts of relational presence and social presence, which are presented and discussed as follows.

RELATIONAL PRESENCE AND SOCIAL PRESENCE

When approaching relational presence it is initially necessary to elucidate what we understand as relation, within this context. The word relation is used in this context, as a synonym for linking or an existing connection between two or more greatnesses, between two or more phenomena. Using this concept relational presence is that which is "in between", that necessarily demands action and interaction between the subjects and with the world.

In an educational context, involving teaching and learning processes, it is not enough for the subject merely to be present, as often happens in face-to-face classes, where the subject is physically present, and therefore has his presence represented by a physical body, in a determined time and space. This means that he is there, even if he is not developing any activity, even if not interacting, the student is present. This mere corporeal presence is not enough for the subject to learn, because he needs to act and interact upon the learning objects, being either physical, digital and/or social, in order to convey them with a meaning and consequently learning. This way, what we seek in the educational context is relational presence, which means the one that establishes a relation in "between", and demands action and interaction among the subjects upon the learning object.

Relational presence implies a presence that goes beyond a physical and corporeal one for it essentially cares for the relational aspect imbricated within this presence, that happens with the presence, being either in a physical or digital virtual way, using textual, oral, gestural and graphic languages, individual or combined. The relational aspect of the presence involves more than being in contact, it involves "being in the world", which necessarily implies two closely imbricated contexts: being with the world and with others. We are a "being" in relation to the world and to other subjects in it, which makes the relational presence essential for the teaching and learning processes.

By stating we are a being in relation to other subjects in the world, we emphasize the social aspect of this relation, which is essential for human development. This way, when we approach the presence issue we can talk of a social presence, but what does it mean?

Let us refer back to the situation of a face-to-face physical class. When we are physically present in a classroom context, we have a social presence represented by physical bodies, meaning that the other subjects can see us, greet us, talk to us about a variety of matters that are not necessarily linked to the objective of the class and this enhances the feeling of proximity, of "being with", for in this case it is related to corporeal presence.

Now let us reflect on what happens when we use, for example, digital virtual classrooms, such as those created in Virtual Learning Environments. In such spaces, presence is identified when the subject logs in to the environment and enters the digital virtual classroom. This presence can be represented merely by the login or along with a 2D image. Although it is possible for everyone to see who is online, it is not enough for the subject to have a feeling of proximity, of "being with" (except for in chat, where place and time are determined), on the contrary, we often observe statements of feeling distant, lonely, isolated. It is difficult to have a synchronous interaction between those who are present unless it is a scheduled activity, as in the case of a chat. This means there is not a "meeting"; the social presence is missing which in

the case of a face-to-face classroom is represented by the physical or corporeal presence. *In addition, in the case of using metaverses, how do we have a relational presence and social presence? Is it possible to have this "meeting"? And if so, how?*

In a metaverse, presence is identified in the moment the subject logs into a certain 3D digital virtual world. From this moment on, he enters the 3D digital virtual world and makes himself present under a name and a 3D graphic representation – the avatar – that "materializes" in a digital virtual way in a world, and through this subject, besides interacting by text; can interact by voice and gestures. In this way, all the other subjects online, who are present in the 3D digital virtual world, represented by their avatars can see other subjects' avatars. According to the outcome of our research, the possibility of "being" in a world through an avatar, and being able to see other avatars within that world with him maximizes the feeling of proximity, of "being with", thus minimizing the feeling of distance, loneliness and isolation. This means the social presence of the avatar favors the synchronous interaction and enables the "meeting" – relational presence – essential for learning. It seems that without "meeting" another it is not possible to talk about dialogic Education. In this sense, social presence and relational presence are intertwined.

Thus, when referring to relational presence it is also essential that the designed 3D digital virtual world, as well as the other methodologies and the process of pedagogical mediation created, are enough to provoke the action and interaction of the avatar-subject in the world, with the world and with other avatars, mediated by the 3D digital virtual world. The more this combination of MDV3D image, methodologies and pedagogical mediation are stimulating for the avatar-subject, the more relational presence is enhanced.

Concepts of relational presence and social presence in metaverses are closely related to the concepts of telepresence and digital virtual presence, which are presented below.

TELEPRESENCE AND DIGITAL VIRTUAL PRESENCE

The presence associated with the use of technologies, mainly with information, communication and interaction, as well as telecommunication services has acquired new outlines, originating the term "telepresence". Etiologically speaking the word "tele" in Greek means distance, and therefore the term has been used to designate presence "in distance", meaning a way of non-physical presence, giving the subject the possibility of "being present" even when physically distant in the geographical space. In this case, presence is not connected to matter, to the physical body, but to the communication, either by means of the written, oral, gestural and/or graphic language.

Marvin Minsky firstly used the term telepresence in 1980, in a tele-operation system, which involved the remote manipulation of objects. According to the author, telepresence is the "feeling of being there in the remote site of the operation", whilst virtual presence is "feeling as if present in a computer generated environment" (Misky, 1980, p.120). It is possible to note that Minsky (1980), had established a difference between telepresence and virtual presence.

According to Walker and Sheppard apud Tsan Hu (2006), telepresence is a way of communication that enables the subject to act and interact from a distance with other subjects and objects, and to have the feeling of "being there", "being here and there", and "being together". It is used to describe one or more subjects' digital virtual presence in another place that can be distant or physically unachievable.

In this way, telepresence is connected to a media or technology that is able to provide the subject with a feeling of being physically in a space or time that can be the simulation of a physical space or a very different space, coming from one's imagination. To be telepresent means that the subject can take the image of his own body to another world, not a physical body (matter built

of atoms), but a technologicized body (built with parts), and that its existence in cyberspace can act and interact with others through different ways of communication.

The possibility of being simultaneously in two places distant in geographical space, and being able to "be together" even when distant has formed part of the human being's imagination and desire for a long time. Telepresence is not something new, if we understand it as presence at distance, we perceive that several media/technologies are able to give such an experience, however, levels of interactivity and vividness (how alive the subject perceives himself within that environment) are different according to the media/technology they use.

For Steuer (1992), telepresence is defined as the level of presence a subject feels within a mediated environment, other than the immediate physical one. He takes into account interactivity and vividness as the two biggest dimensions of telepresence in mediated environments. According to the author, the interactivity level a certain mediated environment provides is represented by the degree of influence the user has in the way or in the content of this environment. The vividness represents the capacity the technology has to generate an enriching sensorial experience within a mediated environment.

According to Cantoni (2001), one can be telepresent in a virtual environment, in a physical environment or in a hybrid environment. So, the technologies that enable telepresence are seen as an independent system and a more radical one when compared to VR technology. For the author the main issue of such approaches "is not where you are telepresent, but what you can do being telepresent". The technologies that make telepresence possible allow control, in real time and through an image, the physical reality. "Technology transforms objects in signs and through the signs you transform objects. It is a tele-action upon physical objects" (Cantoni, 2001. p.146).

Lévy (1996), says that the projection of the body image is usually associated to the notion of telepresence, but the telepresence is more than a mere projection of images, for it is not only associated to the digital technologies nor to digital virtual 3D technologies. For Lévy (1996), we can experience telepresence with a phone call. The voice goes through electromagnetic waves and makes us feel the speaker's presence. In Levy's words

The telephone, for example, already works as a telepresence device, for it takes not only an image or the representation of the voice: it transports the voice itself... In addition, the speaker's own sound body is equally affected by the same unfold. So we are both respectively here and there, but with a crossing in the distribution of tangible bodies. (p.29)

Minsky (1980), Lévy (1996), Walker and Sheppard apud Tsan Hu (2006) refer to telepresence as a "sensation" or a "feeling" of being or belonging to some place, independent from the physical body. The sensation or feeling of belonging has a variation of degree, depending on the media used, and this way the telepresence depends directly on the possibilities technology offers the subject in terms of representation, communication, interaction and interactivity.

Nevertheless, telepresence has gained new capabilities and has been empowered with the evolution of telecommunication services (broadcasted via satellites and communication networks) and digital technologies), especially those related to Virtual Reality and 3D Web. Hardware has evolved and today other softwares have been developed initially in VRML (Virtual Reality Mark-up Language) bringing new possibilities with the use of 3D Engines[3], and 3D accelerator boards (devices specialized in treating 3D graphics), inserted in computers and even in certain cell phones such as the iPhone. This is an indication that we are well prepared for 3D technology, regarding hardware, software and connection.

Therefore, with the use of different media/technologies it is possible to simultaneously be present at the same time in two different spaces, allowing us to have two different existences, one of a physical nature and other of a digital virtual nature. Such telepresence and digital virtual presence may be observed in the technologies presented in Figures 1, 2, 3, 4, and 5.

According to the figures above, in telepresence and/or in digital virtual presence, the subject can be represented by himself, which means by the graphic representation of his physical body, by the oral representation of his own voice, by textual representation and by a "prop[4]", a character, an avatar, among others. In this way, telepresence and/or digital virtual presence are possible through the use of different ways of communication, isolated or combined, that are spread by the use of telecommunication resources connected to different types of media and digital technologies such as TV, telephone, radio, cinema, audio, video, teleconference, computer, Virtual Learning Environments, Digital Virtual Worlds in 2D and 3D Digital Virtual Worlds, Massively Multiplayer Online Role-Play Games, Virtual Reality – VR, or even by hybrid systems that include different technologies (Schlemmer, 2008).

Interaction via telepresence and/or digital virtual presence may then vary according to the media/technology used, which enables different ways of communication that allow human expressions using different languages. From the evidence of our researches, developed in the context of the Digital Education Research Group – GPe-dU UNISINOS/CNPq, articulated with the theoretical knowledge available, it was possible to construct the table below, which represents the technology, the prevailing type of language, enabled communication, representation type, level of interaction/interactivity, level of telepresence and digital virtual presence and level of immersion, where applicable.

Figure 1. The Palace – software in 2D, online, and that enables digital virtual presence by the use of PROPs. It allows written communication.
Source: Author in The Palace

Table 1 demonstrates that higher levels of telepresence and digital virtual presence are found in digital technologies using a group of characteristics that simultaneously support: different languages to enable interaction, multidirectional communication, and tridimensional environments where the subject can be represented by an avatar, maximizing the feeling of immersion in the environment generated in the computer.

In this context we can question how telepresence is possible, specifically in relation to Metaverse technology, given that from the research we carried out in the Digital Education Research Group – GPe-dU UNISINOS/CNPq, we identified another concept, that of digital virtual presence,

which in the specific case of this technology can be associated with telepresence. How do these presences occur in the Metaverse technology context?

In the scope of interactions in metaverses such as in Second Life, telepresence enables the own subject's voice to be telepresent in the 3D digital virtual world. When he speaks or talks it is his own voice that will be there, transmitted via digital means, making it possible for him to talk to other avatars; while digital virtual presence refers to a representation of the subject in the 3D digital virtual world, meaning not through the subject's own image that is telepresent in a 3D digital virtual world (like in the videoconferences, where the camera captures the image and "takes"

Figure 2. Club Penguin – software in 2D, online, and that enables digital virtual presence by means of representation of a penguin image that can be customized by the child. It allows written communication.
Source: Author in Club Penguin

it to another geographical place) but in another representation of this subject, and therefore not a telepresence but a different kind of presence, a digital virtual presence through an avatar.

As a result, we name "digital virtual presence" the presence linked to a representation through an avatar – the creation of a graphic "digital virtual identity[6]" that can be customized by the subject, allowing a "face to face", and "eye to eye" between avatars. My digital virtual self (my digital virtual identity) can then "see" the other (the digital virtual identities of others) and the other (avatar) can see me (my avatar). We establish a differentiation in the telepresence concept, that is connected to the use of technologies able to "take", "displace" part of the subject to another "place", "context", that can inclusively be considered a

"space of flow", as in the case of the telephone, where our voice is transported to another place; in the videoconference, where our voice and image can also be transmitted or even in an Virtual Learning Environment, when we are telepresent by means of textual interaction.

Therefore, what the metaverse technology allows is a combination of the digital virtual presence with different types of telepresence. In the case of the Second Life Metaverse, the subject has a digital virtual presence through the creation of an avatar to represent him in this world, which can make gestures and simultaneously have a telepresence by means of the transportation of his own voice to this world, as well as his textual interaction. What these hybrid environments allow is a combination of digital virtual presence

Figure 3. Active World – software in 3D, online, and that enables telepresence and digital virtual presence by choosing pre-defined avatars. It allows written, oral, gestural and graphic communication.
Source: Authors

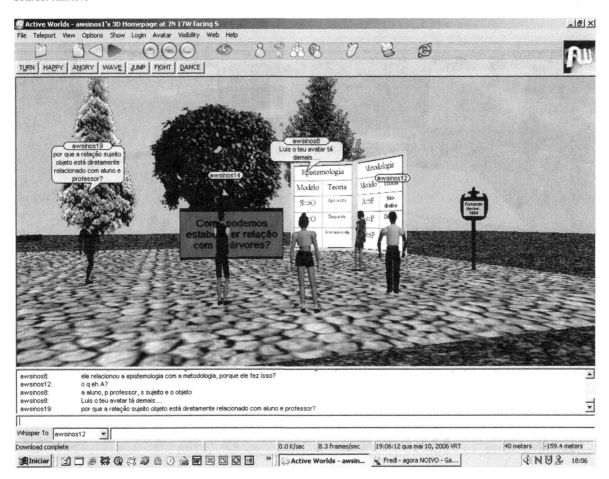

with different types of presence. This possibility in metaverses, causes different sensations when compared to other technologies that allow only telepresence by voice or text, for in the metaverses this is a social presence, evident through the "technologicized bodies" present and that interact in a virtual world. Such bodies can move, speak, and run, jump, fly, visit places that only exist in the digital virtual context and/or that could never be experienced in the physical world. In addition, it is possible for the avatar to show feelings and sensations by textual, oral, gestural or graphic languages.

However, the study of such possibilities of presence that arise with new Web 3D technologies, as well as what they represent in the context of human interaction, of social relations, of human living and sharing, of human learning, are still facing an exploratory phase. We know little about how "meeting" through synchronicity broadens the perception and feeling of presence, possible via avatar in 3D digital virtual world, for example, and how crucial that is for the subjects' learning. What we do know is that 3D Web technologies offer a new paradigm of online learning environment designs, thus contributing to traditional teacher-

Figure 4. Second Life – software in 3D, online, and that enables telepresence and digital virtual presence by the creation of avatars that can be customized by the user. It allows written, oral, gestural and graphic communication.
Source: Authors

Figure 5. Videoconference – technology that enables telepresence through physical representation. It allows oral and gestural communication.
Source: Author in Videoconference - Adobe Connect

Table 1. Technologies, language, communication, type of representation, level of interaction/interactivity, level of telepresence and digital virtual presence and, level of immersion

Technology	Prevailing Language	Communication	Representation Type	Level of Interaction/ Interactivity	Level of Telepresence/ Digital Virtual Presence	Level of Immersion
Metaverse -MDV3D, MMORPG	Graphic, gestural, oral and textual	Multidirectional	Dynamic - avatar in 3D that can be modified in the interaction	High	Telepresence – high Digital Virtual Presence – high	High
Virtual Reality	Graphic, gestural	Multidirectional	One's own physical body (voice, gestures)	High	Telepresence - high	High
MDV2D	Graphic and textual	Multidirectional	Static – image in 2D - prop	High	Telepresence – medium Digital Virtual Presence - medium	Medium
Vídeoconference	Graphic, gestural and oral	Multidirectional	One's own physical body (voice, gestures)	High	Telepresence - high	Medium
AVAs, Blogs, Wikipedia, Orkut	Textual	Multidirectional	Static – image in 2D - prop (when existent)	High /Medium	Telepresence - medium	Low
Simulators	Graphic, textual and oral	Multidirectional/ Bidirectional	Avatar in 3D or physical body (gestures, voice etc.)[5]	High / Medium	Telepresence - high/medium Digital Virtual Presence - medium	High
Telephone	Oral	Bidirectional	Voice	Medium	Telepresence – medium	Low
Instant Communicators	Oral, textual and graphic	Bidirectional	Static – image in 2D - prop (when existent)	Medium	Telepresence– high/medium	Medium
Television, Video, Cinema	Graphic, oral, gestural	Unidirectional	-	Low	Telepresence - low	Medium / Low
Radio	Oral	Unidirectional	-	Low	Telepresence - low	-
Press, Post	Textual	Unidirectional	-	Low	Telepresence - low	-
Web browsing	Textual	Unidirectional	-	Low	Telepresence - low	Low

Source: Adapted from Schlemmer, Trein and Oliveira, 2008c, p.6, Schlemmer 2009, p.58 e Trein 2010

centered practices or the paradigm of delivering information (unidirectional) being tensioned and reconstructed.

The emergence of this new paradigm emphasizes the creation of the 3D digital virtual world, which makes the sharing of learning possible through avatars that are telepresent and present in a digital virtual way. Telepresence, digital virtual presence and the shared space are essential for promoting "meeting" and, therefore, the dialogicity - enabling the construction of active virtual learning communities and enhancing the development of a unique collaborative/cooperative learning experience for the appendix. A new paradigm capitalizes on the 3D digital virtual world's strengths: representation, communication through the combination of telepresence and digital virtual presence, immediate visual feedback, interaction and interactivity, immersion and emotion.

Consequently, the concepts of relational presence, social presence, telepresence and digital virtual presence, possible through metaverses can enhance the feeling of immersion and tele-immersion, as follows.

IMMERSION AND TELE-IMMERSION

The study of the so-called immersion and tele-immersion has been the subject of research in different areas, such as Computer Science, Communication, Psychology, Education, Art, among others. It is by means of immersion and tele-immersion that we feel part of an environment as if we were "in it", "submerged", "inserted" in that universe, having feeling of belonging to a reality. According to Murray (2003), immersive experiences may occur in different frameworks, from literature books to new media. She gives as an example the work of Don Quixote de la Mancha, saying that after wishing to have experienced the adventures described in the book, her mind has been so impregnated with imaginary facts that she now believes they are true. "The experience of being transported to a carefully simulated place is joyful itself ... We refer to such experience as immersion" (Murray, 2003, p.102).

Immersion is a metaphoric term derived from the physical experience of being submerged in water. We look for, in a psychological immersive experience, the same impression that we have when diving into an ocean or swimming pool, the feeling of being involved by a very odd reality, as different as water and air, which captures all our attention, all our sensorial system. We would like

to exit our familiar world, from the surveillance sense caused by being in this new place, and from the rejoicing of learning how to move within it. Immersion may require a single flooding of the mind with sensations ... . Many people listen to music in such way, as a pleasant flooding of the brain's verbal areas.

Murray (2003), when studying immersion, uses the term agency (role of an agent) to express the sensation experienced by a subject when one of his choices or decisions becomes a more significant action. When we consider immersion in the context of the so-called "traditional media", for instance, when we read a book, a newspaper, watch a movie or TV show, etc., there is no possibility our actions interfere in the plot or program. We cannot help the characters to change their course, which has been pre-defined, which means we are not able to act in a significant way and see the results of our decisions and options. In the "traditional media" context, even when we have identified the plot, and want to act upon it, there is nothing we can do, because this media is limited from the point of view of interactivity, in the interaction with the subject, meaning there is no authorship and/or co-authorship from this subject within that context. However, when we think about immersion in the context of "new media" and digital technologies, the subject's action and interaction with the environment and with other subjects is possible, both to a higher or lower degree. This depends on how digital technology used, the subject's fluency in technology, in his relation with the predominant language type, with the communication offered, with a type of representation, with the level of telepresence and digital virtual presence, and, mainly, how this combination of things is "felt" by the subject, capable of submerging his own mind inside this specific context. This combination of these elements is what will offer a higher or lower degree of immersion. Within this context we highlight the 3D digital virtual world, in which there is both telepresence and digital virtual presence by means of an avatar, a "digital virtual identity", which can move and fly toward different directions, it can also interact through textual, oral, gestural and graphic languages and build a world with tridimensional graphic representations. This gives us possibility of acting in a significant way and following up the results of our actions, and in one sense the world can be constantly and dynamically modified by subject's actions/interactions. He is the one to decide how to explore it, experience it, there is no predefined unwinding. It is then that an interaction possibility exclusive to this type of technology arises. The subject's action, interaction/interactivity creates the way to be followed.

Brown and Cairns (2004), indicate that the concept of immersion is related to the level of the subject's involvement within the virtual environment. Philippe Quéau (1993), refers to the existence of an "immersion in image", possible by the current 3D digital virtual world, where the image acquires a status of exploitable "place", being the object of the experience itself, in its own tissue and exactly defined. The consequences of the evolution in the image rules are radical. Corrêa (2009) adds that the sociability that may occur within digital networks is an important component of immersion, as according to her, it demands both an intellectual and practical immersion to the participants. According to the author, "the intellectual immersion imposes on the subjects the construction of new knowledge; and immersion in applications, in the use of devices and in the exercising hypermediatic exchanges, naturally reflect the living" (Corrêa, 2009 p.47).

The concept of immersion is also closely related to the concept of state of flow, developed in 1975 by the Hungarian Psychologist and Professor Mihály Csíkszentmihályi. For Csíkszentmihályi (1990) to be in flow means: "being totally involved in an activity in which the ego is gone. Time flies. Every action, movement and thought is inevitably developed from a previous state, it is like playing jazz" (p.13). The flow can be

translated as a mental state in which the subject is deeply found immersed in the action, characterized as a feeling of total involvement, focused attention, thoroughly participating in the activity and where all his energy is captured. For the flow experience to succeed, provoking the subjects' active involvement, it is necessary to find a balance point between the challenge levels offered and the level of the subjects' competencies and skills, in synchrony with feelings of pleasure.

Csíkszentmihályi (1990), identifies some factors that accompany a flow experience, clear objects (expectations and rules need to be perceptible and the objects reachable and aligned with a set of competencies and skills needed to reach them – the challenge level and the competency and skills level must be in compliance); a high level of concentration in a certain attention field (a person who engages with a certain activity must have the opportunity to concentrate and submerge within it); loss of self-conscious feeling, the fusion of action and awareness; distorted sense of time; direct and immediate feedback (successes and failures along the activity are evident, so that behavior can be adjusted when needed); balance between competency level, skills and challenges (the activity to be developed cannot be too easy nor too difficult); sense of self-control in the situation or activity; activity intrinsically rewarding to trigger an effort towards the action; total absorption in the activity, and focus of the directed conscious for the activity itself.

However, the author calls our attention to the fact that such factors do not necessarily need to be present for the subject to experience the flow state. Csíkszentmihályi (1990) highlights how emotion, pleasure, and fun can evoke "great" conditions for the human beings to enable the state of flow and how it can empower learning.

Thus, through the research we develop in the context of the Digital Education Research Group – GPe-dU UNISINOS/CNPq, we understand that some aspects are essential to empowering immersion and tele-immersion, such as triggering an environment (2D or 3D) that provokes the subjects' emotion and that enables the subject to feel the environment as reality. Language (graphic, gestural, oral or textual); enabled communication (unidirectional, bidirectional and multidirectional); the subject's representation (voice, image (through webcam), graphic in 2D (prop), graphic in 3D (avatar); the level of telepresence and digital virtual presence; the subject's action and interaction with the environment (making authorship possible) and with the other subjects (relational and social presence – the living). Despite this, the main aspect is linked to the psychological subject, because it is concerned with "submerging the mind", pervading it within a specific context – the subject feels he is involved, absorbed, engaged. This may be even more intense when related to the subjects feeling emotions. Therefore, we talk about an individual perspective that occurs in a distinct way for every subject.

This leads us to understand as immersion the feeling of being "inside", plunged into, involved in a universe that takes control of our attention, our mind, in a way that makes us feel part of it. That is, a relation of belonging to that reality, that enables us to "live an experience".

Tele-immersion, thus, would be the immersion in distance. Tele-immersion is enabled by /the combination of physical objects (from the physical face-to-face world) with digital virtual objects (from the digital world, also known as synthetic – computer made). However, sometimes, when we talk about immersion it sounds controversial to discuss distance, for immersion presupposes being "inside", plunged within a reality, reinforcing the perspective that immersion is mainly related to "submerging the mind" and, under such aspect, distance is relative.

Nevertheless, if we take the differentiation previously established between the concepts of presence and telepresence, we identify that tele-immersion, like telepresence, is used when combined with the use of technologies, mainly those of information, communication and interaction,

as well as telecommunication services. This way, for digital technologies "being there" means to cross the edge between physical and digital virtual, entering the universe created in the computer screen in a world that is permeable to the subject, where he can be the protagonist, being completely submerged within a certain context, from his interaction and interactivity. "In a collaborative environment, immersion implies learning how to swim, how to do the things the new environment makes possible" (Murray, 2003, p.102).

Within this context, we focus the discussion of immersion specifically linked to the theory of the Eduverse and Second Life Metaverses and, focus on the graphic representation of the psychological subject in the 3D digital virtual world, so we may question: *How does immersion occur for subjects in the MDV3D? What differences can be present when the subject "takes over a pre-defined character" and when he has the possibility of creating a "digital virtual identity", a "digital virtual self"? What does it represent in terms of immersion for the subjects that take part in a 3D digital virtual world?* We are not neglecting other essential variables such as: the tridimensional representation of the world itself, but deepening issues coming from the research we develop in the context of the Digital Education Research Group – GPe-dU UNISINOS/CNPq, and that seem to be very significant within the context of the discussion about immersion.

In the Eduverse Metaverse, the subject chooses a pre-defined graphic representation, which will be used to represent himself in the 3D digital virtual world and through which he acts and interacts with the world. However, this graphic representation differs from the perspective of available "character", for example, in MMORPG, which associate the graphic representation to a pre-defined "personality", so that the subject, when choosing a certain character, takes over certain previously defined characteristics (usually related to health, power, strength, agility, among others) and starts acting and interacting within the game and the other players from this pre-definition. In the Eduverse, the subject takes over a pre-defined graphic representation only concerning the avatar appearance, being free to act and interact under his own perspective, meaning he does not takes on a "character", there is no pre-defined "role" to be represented and/or previously defined characteristics that may influence the process of action and interaction in the environments, as it happens in the case of games. In the Second Life Metaverse, it is also necessary to choose a pre-defined graphic representation, similar to what happens in the Eduverse Metaverse, however, it is possible to totally transform it through available options in the software. This enables the subject to construct a "digital virtual self", a "digital virtual identity" – an avatar – in a way he can be who or what he really wants to be in that world.

We are not reducing the "self" or the "identity" to a graphic representation, but we are calling the attention to how this possibility offered by the software enhances the subject's feeling of immersion in the world for being connected to the subjects' emotions, which means he can construct the appearance he wants to have.

The avatar, in this sense, is the extension of the "self" in the 3D digital virtual world. The subject feels immersed in an environment that can be perceived in the interaction/interactivity when using the visualization in first person – that one that makes the action, referring to the avatar action. In this extension of the self within the world, by the use of cameras, the subject can follow up the action from an external point of view, as an observer, when "steering" the avatar that represents him in the world (figure 6), and can even

Figure 6. Subject immersed in MDV3D seeing his own avatar
Source: Authors

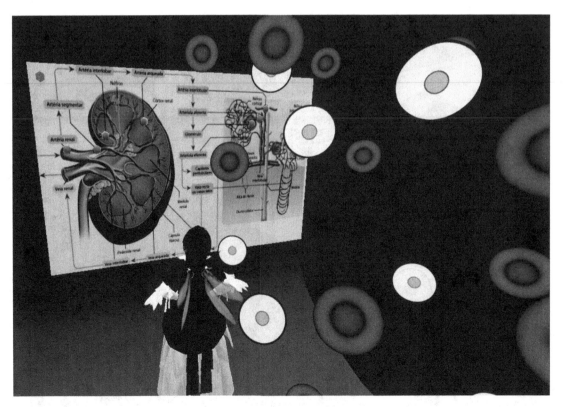

visualize the action of an internal point of view, from his point of view, meaning in first person (figure 7), giving a broader sense of immersion.

In the context of immersive experiences, we can highlight *Virtual Fictional Experiences* (EFV) and *Real Virtuality Experiences* (EVR)[7]. *Virtual Fictional Experiences* are characterized by immersion through characters (as in the MMORPG, for example). It happens in a previously "controlled" context from the point of view of the subject's freedom to act and interact within the world, where such actions and interactions are only possible depending on that character's characteristics towards the tridimensional environment created, and the rules established for the game in question. *Real Virtuality Experiences* are characterized by the immersion of avatars (as in Metaverses like Second Life) and therefore it happens within a context

where the subject-avatar is free to act and interact following his own intentions, within a world in which he can be author and/or co-author along with other subject-avatars, being even capable of modifying his own avatar, the tridimensional environments and rules of creation. Consequently, it is not the character that has the experience, but the subject himself.

However, in both situations, we are transported to other worlds without the need of physically moving. The desire of living a fantasy in a certain fictional universe steers our brain to tune in to what is happening there, temporarily "canceling" the physical world around us. It is the feeling of taking part of another dimension that leads us to enter "a state of deep trance" (Murray, 2003, p.63), which means, it takes us to a new world in which we can take on different identities to those

Figure 7. Subject immersed in MDV3D in first person
Source: Authors

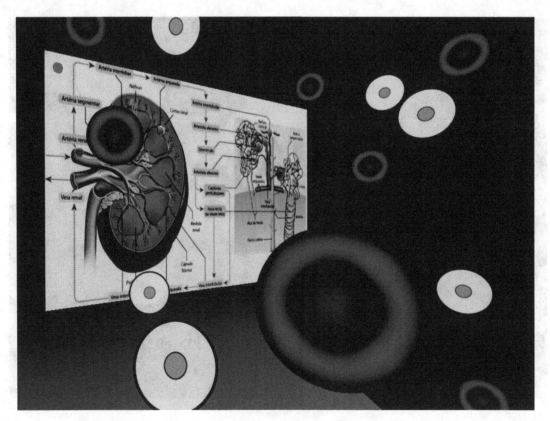

we have in the real world, and that are now always in compliance to our behavior outside that world.

By entering a fictional world we do more than merely "suspend" a critical faculty; we also exert a creative faculty. We do not suspend our doubts when actively creating a belief. Due to our desire of living the immersion, we concentrate our attention on the world that involves us and we use our intelligence more to strengthen than to question the veracity of our experience. (Murray, 2003, p.111)

Such plunging in search for an immersive experience, not reliant on the virtual world we are being transported to, has as its main characteristic the pleasure of experiencing the situation. The 3D digital virtual world urges us to act, to interact, to participate, to do the things it is offering which are not possible outside this world. To learn and to turn this immersion into a participatory activity, on needs to be open.

In this way, the 3D digital virtual worlds constructed, for example, in Second Life are immersive participatory environments, which allow the subject-avatars to have multidirectional communication by using different languages (gestural, textual, oral and graphic), as well as a high level of interaction and interactivity where the subject-avatar's actions modify the environment, other subject-avatars and themselves. The high level of telepresence and digital virtual presence enabled by the use of 3D digital virtual world is directly connected to the subject's possibility of being represented by an avatar. In the 3D digital virtual world the subjects create their own avatars to explore the world where "the cameras represent the gazing look" (Domingues, 2003), and, besides that,

the virtual immersive generates worlds constructed to be experienced, controlled, inhabited, touched through actions. We can also create an identity from the avatars we embody and live in a 3D space, experiencing other parallel realities in worlds with multiple users connected online. (p.3)

Mattar (2008) explains that the level of the students' involvement and immersion with the content as well as with the classmates and the teachers within a 3D digital virtual world created in the Second Life, may not seemingly be easily reproduced in traditional virtual learning environments such as the Blackboard, Teleduc, Moodle, etc. This may be confirmed in different reports from users of the 3D digital virtual world. "The feeling I had from the first synchronous meeting – in May – is of total immersion inside that virtual world. As a professor used to the traditional distance education tools such as the virtual learning environment XXX from YYY…, I could see that the possibility of an avatar's action and interaction brings the classroom to the house, which is feeling the XXX docs not allow. The interaction with the environment opens up a range of possibilities, from feeling really inside the classroom, watching the Power Point presentation, to visiting a medieval city, perceiving the richness of its urban space defined by the buildings, or experimenting the feelings of a schizophrenic patient through sound and images – Virtual Hallucinations"[8]. Therefore, by establishing a comparison between the Metaverse Second Life with the traditional Virtual Learning Environment, Mattar (2008) presents two important and crucial questions, that is, the level of involvement and the immersion that enriches the experience.

The students stop being passive consumers of knowledge, or even mere creators of their own knowledge, they get involved in the creation of their own activities, experiences and own learning environments. Second Life allows the teachers and the students to customize their own environment, allowing them to build up personal learning environments to suit different learning styles. (Mattar, 2008b, p.90)

Trein (2010) when writing her Masters thesis "Online Education in Metaverse: pedagogical mediation by means of telepresence and digital virtual presence via avatar in Digital Virtual Worlds in 3 Dimensions"[9], states that, by starting a participatory observation, during a learning process carried out with teachers from 13 Catholic graduating institutions, in Brazil from RICESU – Catholic Higher Education Institutions Network, in the RICESU Island created in Second Life by the Digital Education Research Group – GPe-dU UNISINOS/CNPq, her researcher view was addressing the issue of telepresence in the Metaverse –SL, and that in a certain way this telepresence could minimize the problem raised in distance in Distance Education. In order to comprehend what the telepresence in the Metaverse-SL meant to the members of the learning process, she developed the following question, from one of the synchronous meetings: "What possibilities can you perceive with telepresence through avatars in digital virtual worlds in 3D within the teaching and learning processes?" The author comments that the answers given were food for thought, triggering further curiosity…, she states that:

It was during my living and sharing in the Metaverse-SL, in the situations observed during the learning process in the RICESU Island …, as well as in the answers to the proposed question from the participants that I realized that the relation between immersion and telepresence through avatars within the Metaverse-SL context that may be a consequence of a more complex thing, but what could that be? The answer came at a particular moment during the course, when I became (embodied) my avatar. (Trein, 2010, p.43)

The author means is that when she created her avatar in the Metaverse Second Life she did not have the necessary technological knowledge to customize it in order to reflect exactly what she meant. It was during the learning process, as she was gradually getting used to the technology, that she created her "digital virtual identity" with the characteristics she wanted (Figure 8). "I am not talking only about physical appearance, but things that reflect my characteristics and that represent me" (p.43).

Trein (2010) says that she has realized the possibility of the process of constructing digital

Figure 8. Daiana John in different moments of the digital technological appropriation in the customization of the avatar
Source: Trein (2010, p.44)

virtual identities, as crucial issue for the immersion in the 3D digital virtual world, based on the conclusion that, the more intensely represented by the (re)creation of his digital virtual identities[10] the subject feels, by means of his avatar in the 3D digital virtual world, the more intense his perception on immersion will be, and consequently his telepresence and digital virtual presence will be, collaborating to diminish the feeling of lack of physical presence in the Online Education.

Within this living and sharing in the 3D digital virtual world this metamorphosis of identities, representations, constructions, projects, fantasies, desires and other things, in a certain moment, I could feel I was there. By there I mean the RICESU Island, and I am Daiana John. (Trein, 2010, p.44)

The author reports a situation she experienced when submerging in the world, in a moment in which all the participants in the learning process were together within the course area in the RICESU Island.

One of the members of the GP e-du UNISINOS was reporting some news regarding the learning process and all avatars were looking at her while she did the talk. I was at the back only watching and taking pictures. At a certain point, she said the participants: "the one helping you in the pedagogical area is Daiana John; she is there at the back, so in case you have a doubt you may go to her". In the very first moment, she uttered my avatar's name (meaning my name or second name, as you wish) all avatars turned immediately to mine. In addition, I felt embarrassed, shy, and that feeling had impact on my physical body: I immediately blushed, my heartbeat was accelerated and my hands sweat. For an instant, I was speechless and I reacted by writing only "Hello there, ask me if you need help!" From that mo-

ment on, I changed my view as spectator; fell in love with the avatars and the possibility of being myself in another space. (p.44)

In this situation, as it happens in others, for example, when a subject sweats while he is playing an action or adventure game in a situation that seems hostile it is possible to perceive that the immersion was so well "accepted" that the experience becomes too real for the subject to the point of showing it physically. Let us see other situations where we can perceive such level of immersion:

When passing by a building I fell into a lake. That lake should not be there, it does not exist in the physical UNISINOS, but my avatar was then at the bottom of it and I did not know how to take him out of there. I was taken by an unexplainable affliction, I felt breathless because I could not breathe under water! Again, I turned to my assessor who immediately and rapidly took me out of there and in great style: I flew away! Wow! I can fly! I was not in risk of falling into unexpected lakes; I could fly wherever I wanted. Apart from some bumps into trees and branches, flying caused me a good sensation. (speaks of a research subject)

Immersion through avatars in a 3D digital virtual world arouses in the subjects a variety of sensations. According to Trein (2010), this sensation occurs because the subject is in a structural coupling[11] with his avatar, becoming the avatar himself (by embodying it). He then starts feeling emotions related to what he is experiencing as the avatar, in that moment. In the above example, the subject refers to a feeling of "affliction", when his avatar is not able to come out from the bottom of the lake. The subject knows the avatar is not going to "drown", but under the human being ontogeny, he "feels" that it may happen in the first place.

When questioned about the significant experiences they had in the 3D digital virtual world, the subjects often have experienced situations that have triggered sensations in their physical bodies when they were submersed in a virtual environment. (Trein, 2010, p.161)

Regarding immersion, Trein (2010) points out the following main results she obtained in the thesis she developed: a) immersion is perceived by the subjects as an important differential when referring to the possibilities of the 3D digital virtual world used for learning. "We are used to seeing things from the computer screen, but we have never "entered" it before. The immersion the environment provides makes all the difference. Being able to move, to come and go, to make gestures for the others…"; b) the association of the simulation, and the feeling of immersion through an avatar provokes the feeling of "actually being there", meaning, it is a combination that results in the feeling of reality the subjects state; c) when immersed in a 3D digital virtual world concentration and involvement are broadened, mainly when something triggers our curiosity, an investigative spirit… we unplug from the real world and start living in a virtual world, that could make some of the learning concepts easy. "The feeling of reality is so intense in certain moments that I forget I have a physical body, for it seems I am in the virtual environment"[12]; d) the immersion is associated to the increase in the sensation of presence, enabled by the avatar. "The avatar is everything, you don't need to see yourself, but you must see the other avatars. Without that there is no immersivity or relation of presence"[13].

Therefore, it is possible to infer that the structural coupling of the subject with his avatar in the 3D digital virtual world enhances telepresence and digital virtual presence, contributing to the feeling of immersion and consequently belonging to these worlds. Nevertheless, Trein (2010) says that the creation of the digital virtual identities contributes to immersion, but the findings of the research showed that it is not a condition for the immersion to happen.

CONCLUSION

"May I go in the computer?"; "Mom, I'm in the UNISINOS Island"; "I've entered a human body"; "Mom, would you come inside my igloo? I'm throwing a party and all my friends are here." When we reflect about such expressions it is possible to understand that digital technologies nowadays represent being somewhere (a place we go to or are in), and sometimes they are digital virtual territories where we can act, interact, construct, communicate, socialize, in other words, be immersed.

Telecommunication, hardware and software constitute a basic technological infrastructure that enables telepresence and digital virtual presence, immersion and tele-immersion in a way that all sorts of technologies enable the multidirectional, bidirectional and unidirectional communication, approaching people in time and geographical space. They can then act and interact by using oral, textual, gestural and graphic language (depending on the adopted technology). This "being together" in a digital virtual way is then empowered and in this context the time lines, continental distances are not a problem that impede the fast and efficient interaction between people.

Using the metaverse technology perspective, digital virtual presence, different ways of communication, interaction and interactivity that are possible in the living and sharing among avatars in the 3D digital virtual world, is what originates the different levels of presentiality, vividness and feeling of belonging. This makes life in a community also possible in these worlds, in a way that physical distance is only a paradigmatic matter and the high level of immersion of conscience is experimented when subjects, through their avatars, become part of this world, penetrating, being completely absorbed, involved within a learning environment constructed with different multimedia resources.

In these worlds, the notion of belonging has changed, for there are not continuous and contiguous spaces, nor geographical territories, but there is nomadism and transnationalities, vanishing of boarders, in which the relations of the e-inhabitants are part of hybrid thoughts, ideas, languages, knowledge and practices.

"Virtual reality" cannot be treated as exteriority or fiction being accessed through sensitive technological devices, but as "real virtuality" (Castells, 1999), as interiority socially shared and expanded by the variety of electronic devices that support the production and the current social-cultural record. While the first perspective deals with "virtualization" of an existing reality in the physical world, the second approaches the "accomplishment" of virtuality constructed in a digital world. Understanding such changes, how they occur and what causes them is crucial to understand the subject and the current society, in order to produce knowledge that allows rethinking the social cultural context, mainly in the educational institutions, within this context a greater concern regards learning the use of such possibilities in the teaching and learning processes and teacher training for the efficient use and the development of a culture of using them.

REFERENCES

Brown, E., & Cairns, P. (2004). A grounded investigation of game immersion. In Proceedings of CHI 2004 (pp. 1279–1300). New York, NY: ACM Press.

Cantoni, R. C. A. (2001). *Realidade virtual: Uma história de imersão interativa.* (Unpublished master's dissertation). Pontifícia Universidade Católica de São Paulo, São Paulo, Brazil.

Castells, M. (1999). A sociedade em rede. São Paulo, Brazil: Paz e Terra.

Corrêa, E. S. (2009). Cibercultura: Um novo saber ou uma nova vivência? In E. Trivinho, & E. Cazeloto (Eds.), *A cibercultura e seu espelho [recurso eletrônico]: Campo de conhecimento emergente e nova vivência humana na era da imersão interativa* (pp. 47-51). São Paulo, Brazil: ABCiber; Instituto Itaú Cultural. Retrieved from http://abciber.com/publicacoes/livro1/a_cibercultura_e_seu_espelho.pdf

Csíkszentmihályi, M. (1990). *Flow: The psychology of optimal experience.* New York, NY: Harper Perennial.

Domingues, D. (2003). Arte, vida, ciência e criatividade com as tecnologias numéricas. In D. Domingues (Ed.), *Arte e vida no século XXI: Tecnologia, ciência e criatividade* (pp. 11-14). São Paulo, Brazil: Editora UNESP. Retrieved April 20, 2007, from http://artecno.ucs.br/livros_textos/textos_site_artecno/3_capitulo_livros/diana2003_artevidaxxi_cap.rtf

Hu, O. R. Tsan. (2006). *Contribuições ao desenvolvimento de um sistema de telepresença por meio da aquisição, transmissão e projeção em ambientes imersivos de vídeos panorâmicos.* (Unpublished doctoral thesis). Universidade de São Paulo, São Paulo, Brazil. Retrieved from http://www.teses.usp.br/teses/disponiveis/3/3142/tde-19092006-134926/

Lévy, P. (1996). O que é virtual? São Paulo, Brazil: Editora 34.

Lombard, M., & Ditton, T. (1997). At the heart of it all: The concept of presence. *Journal of Computer Mediated-Communication, 3* (2). Retrieved from http://www.ascusc.org/jcmc/vol3/issue2/lombard.html

Mattar, J. (2008). O uso do Second Life como ambiente virtual de aprendizagem. *Revista Fonte, 5,* 88-95. Retrieved from http://www.prodemge.gov.br/images/stories/volumes/volume8/ucp_joao-mattar.pdf

Minsky, M. (1980, June). Telepresence. *Omni,* 45-51.

Murray, J. (1997). *Hamlet on the holodeck: The future of narrative in cyberspace.* Cambridge, MA: The MIT Press.

Murray, J. H. (2003). Hamlet no holodeck. São Paulo, Brazil: Itaú Cultural.

Quéau, P. (1993). O tempo do virtual. In A. Parente (Ed.), Imagem máquina (pp. 91-99). Rio de Janeiro, Brazil: Editora 34.

Schlemmer, E. (2008). ECODI - A criação de espaços de convivência digital virtual no contexto dos processos de ensino e aprendizagem em metaverso. *Caderno IHU Idéias, 6*(103), 1-31.

Schlemmer, E., & Backes, L. (2008). Metaversos: Novos espaços para construção do conhecimento. *Revista Diálogo Educacional, 8,* 519–532.

Schlemmer, E., & Trein, D. (2008). Criação de identidades digitais virtuais para interação em mundos digitais virtuais em 3D. In *Proceedings of Congresso Internacional de EaD – ABED* (pp. 1-11). Retrieved from http://www.abed.org.br/congresso2008/tc/515200815252PM.pdf

Schlemmer, E., & Trein, D. (2009). Espaço de convivência digital virtual (ECODI) ricesu: Uma experiência em rede com a tecnologia de metaverso Second Life. In Proceedings of 15° Congresso Internacional ABED de Educação a Distância (pp. 1-12). Fortaleza, Brazil: Anais.

Schlemmer, E., Trein, D., & Oliveira, C. (2008). Metaverso: A telepresença em mundos digitais virtuais 3D por meio do uso de avatares. In Proceedings of SBIE (pp. 441 - 450). Fortaleza, Brazil: Anais.

Steuer, J. (1992). Defining virtual reality: Dimensions determining telepresence. *Journal of Communication, 42*(4), 73–93. doi:10.1111/j.1460-2466.1992.tb00812.x

Trein, D. (2010). *Educação online em metaverso: A mediação pedagógica por meio da telepresença e da presença digital virtual via avatar em mundos digitais virtuais em 3 dimensões.* (Unpublished master's dissertation). Universidade do Vale do Rio dos Sinos, São Leopoldo, Brazil.

KEY TERMS AND DEFINITIONS

Digital Virtual Presence: Is related the presence connected to a representation by means of an avatar – the creation of a graphic "digital virtual identity" that can be customized by the subject, allowing "face to face", "eye in eye" contact between avatars. My digital virtual self (my digital virtual identity) can then "see" the other (others digital virtual identities) and the other (avatar) can see me (my avatar).

Immersion: Immersion is what makes us feel part of a certain environment as if we were "in it", "submerged", "inserted" in that universe, is a feeling of belonging to a reality. It is related to the level of the subject's involvement within the environment. Immersive experiences may occur in different frameworks, from literature books to new media. (Murray, 2003).

Presence: Presence as a perceptual illusion of non-mediation (Lombard & Ditton, 1997).

Relational Presence: It is related to that presence that is established "between", that necessarily demands action and interaction between the subjects and with the world. The relational presence then implies in a presence that goes beyond the physical and corporeal one, for it essentially cares for the relational aspect imbricated within this presence, possible through presentiality, being either in a physical or digital virtual ways, using textual, oral, gestural and graphic languages, individual or combined. The relational aspect of the presence, this way, involves more that being in contact, it involves "being in the world", that necessarily implies in two closely imbricated contexts: being with the world and with others. We are a "being" in relation to the world and to other subjects in it, which makes the relational presence essential for the teaching and learning processes.

Social Presence: It is related to the presence that promotes the "meeting". In the case of the physical classroom, the presence is represented by the physical body, that allows other subjects to see, great and talk to each other about several things, causing the feeling of closeness, of "being with", being present, related, in this case, to the bodily presence. In the case of metaverses, the presence is represented by the graphical 3D representation - the avatar - that "materializes" in the virtual digital world, and through which the subject, in can interact by text, voice and gestures. Thus, all the other subjects that are online, present in digital virtual world, represented by their avatars, can view each other. This possibility of "living" in a world, through his avatar and being able to view other avatars that are in that world with him, maximizes the feeling of closeness, of "being with", minimizing the sense of distance, of loneliness and isolation. The social presence is promoted by avatars' interaction, providing "meetings."

State Flow: To be on the flow means: "being totally involved in an activity in which the ego is gone. Time flies. Every action, movement and thought is inevitably developed from a previous state, it is like playing jazz" (Csíkszentmihályi, 1990, p. 13). The Flow can be translated as a mental state in which the subject is deeply found immersed in the action, characterized as a feeling of total involvement, focused attention, thoroughly participation in the activity and where all his energy is captured.

Teleimmersion: Is the immersion at distance. Distance, here, in the geographical sense. The teleimmersion is made possible by the mixture of physical objects (the physical world face) with virtual digital objects (the digital world, or also known as synthetic - created by computer).

Telepresence: Is related to the distance presence (geographical distance) mediated by the use of technologies able to "take", "displace" part of the subject to another "place", "context", that can inclusively be considered a "space of flow", as in the case of the telephone, where our voice is transported to another place; in the videoconference, where our voice and image can also be transmitted or even in an Virtual Learning Environment, when we are telepresent by means of textual interaction.

ENDNOTES

[1] According to chapter 4 - Avatar: Building a "Digital Virtual Self."

[2] Image Maximum – IMAX is a format of films created by IMAX Corporation with the ability to show images in high resolution and size. A theater screen for film projection in IMAX format is 22 meters wide and 16.1 meters de high, sometimes being bigger. Half of these theaters are educational ones.

[3] Software specialized in treating 3D elements in an interactive way and in real time. They enable the creation of very sophisticated environments and objects, with a high level of reality.

[4] Prop is any object used by the subjects to represent them in the 2D graphical environment to foster interaction - something similar to the role of the avatar.

[5] It depends on the type of technology used by the simulator.

6   According to what was approached in chapter 4 - Avatar: Building a "Digital Virtual Self."

7   Concepts seen in depth in chapter 11 - The Real Virtuality of Metaverses.

8   Comment stated by one of the participating subjects in Trein's research (2010).

9   Original title: *"Educação Online em Metaverso: a mediação pedagógica por meio da telepresença e da presença digital virtual via avatar em Mundos Digitais Virtuais em 3 Dimensões."*

10   According to what was approached in chapter 4 - Avatar: Building a "Digital Virtual Self."

11   Concept seen in depth in chapter 7 - Autopoietic Machines and Alopoietic Machines: The Structural Coupling.

12   Comment stated by one of the participating subjects in Trein's research (2010).

13   Comment stated by one of the participating subjects in Trein's research (2010).

Chapter 6
Interaction and Interactivity in Metaverse

ABSTRACT

This chapter approaches the Interaction potential that arises from the Interactivity provided in the Metaverse technology, which is connected to Immersion, Telepresence and Digital Virtual Presence in Metaverses. Some of the subtopics presented and discussed are: Concept of Interaction and Interactivity; Mutual Interaction and Reactive Interaction, Types of Interaction, Languages and interaction/interactivity in Metaverse, as well as a brief conclusion to the chapter, demonstrating that the Metaverses presents new elements for the educational context, meaning that the methodologies and the pedagogical practices, so far adopted, are not able to exploit to maximum potential the level of interactivity offered by technology. It is therefore necessary to construct methodologies and practices that take into account such potential and be able to enable mutual interaction between those involved in the educational process.

INTRODUCTION

The terms interaction and interactivity have become widely used in recent decades, being as meaningful and popular as ever. Moreover, that popularity is due to the digital technological evolution, which presents the elements that raise the discussion of such concepts to a different level, taking into account that this technology is capable of broadening the possibilities of action upon and through the environment, in this case, of a digital virtual nature.

Besides the traditional means present in the analogical world, day-to-day life is built through these interactions with different digital technologi-

cal gadgets, like computers, tablets, smartphones, videogame consoles, etc., with apps that allow human-machine interaction and the interaction between humans, mediated by machines.

Therefore, it is common to hear about interactive TV, interactive movie theater, interactive games, interactive learning environments, interactive surfaces, making it seem that everything surrounding us has become interactive.

However, what are the concepts of interaction and interactivity based on? In what aspects are they close and how do they differ? Does interaction refer to the action among/along with itself, whilst interactivity refers to the environment's potential to enable such interaction – action among/along

DOI: 10.4018/978-1-4666-6351-0.ch006

with – which in turn can occur between the human and the machine and between human beings mediated by the machine?

Different areas of human knowledge such as communication, education, psychology, and computer science, among others have developed studies of these terms in order to better explain them. However, as expected, there is a polyphony of meanings attached to the particularities of each of those areas and the epistemological conception from every researcher, relating what is global (area of knowledge) to what is local (researcher).

In this chapter, we will discuss interaction and interactivity, as well as languages and ways of interaction-interactivity enabled in Metaverses.

CONCEPTUALIZING INTERACTION AND INTERACTIVITY

Contrary to what it may seem, the word 'interaction', according to Starobinski's studies of historical linguistics (2002), does not find its background in the classical Latin Language[1]. The author states that 'interaction', as a noun, was first introduced to the Oxford English Dictionary in 1832 (being presented, at that time, as a neologism), and the verb 'to interact', in the sense of acting with reciprocity, in 1839. In France, the word 'interaction' only appeared after another neologism: 'interdependency'. (being in the dictionary only in 1867)

The human being lives in constant and continuous interaction with the environment, being it physical or social and, more recently, digital, in a way that interaction is part of the human development process. Moreover, it has formed as an object of study of different theorists like Jean Piaget and Humberto Maturana, who have investigated interaction from the interrelations between biological bases and the social environment, using the perspective of the physical space.

Jean Piaget, a Swiss epistemologist, investigated human development in search of understanding the origin of knowledge, therefore learning, long

before the emergence of digital technologies. For Piaget, *interaction* is the 'action between/along with', occurring between the subject and the environment, either physical or social, meaning the involvement of two or more elements, which can be of the same nature, different ones or combined. If we signify it for the current time, we could say that such environment, besides being physical, can also be digital and/or hybrid.

From the perspective of Jean Piaget's Genetics Epistemology, interaction is the action between/along with, implying a relation of interdependency and reciprocity between the subject and the environment, as a social environment (between subjects) and/or physical (in the context the subject, or subjects, develop the action), in a way that this action between/along with, carries out changes both in subjects and in the context where interaction is developed, which means for Piaget that interaction necessarily implies action and the subject's activity.

Within this context, Piaget (1987) repositions the intelligence issue, frequently defined as the capacity to solve problems, either innate or acquired, and assuring intelligence as a function. In this way, as in all other functions that enable a human organism's surviving, it is purely justified by interaction. Nevertheless, if intelligence is considered a function, how does it work? It always functions as a service of adapting the subject to the interchanges with its environment.

Understanding that knowledge is a relation of interdependency between the subject and his physical, digital, social, context, historical and cultural environment in a non-exclusive way (Schlemmer, 2002), such 'environment' is, for Piaget (1973), both physical and social, as he states:

In the social life, as well as in the individual life, the thought precedes the action and society is essentially a system with activities, having elementary interactions consisting of their own meaning, in actions that modify each other, according to certain laws of organization or balance... . It is from the analysis of the interactions in behavior where it follows the explanation of collective representations, or interactions modifying the individual's conscience. (p.33)

For Piaget (1973), when there is a subject-object relation, where the subject is 'we' and the object is other objects, the interaction happens in a way that knowledge originates neither from the subject nor from the object, but in the indissociable interaction between them, meaning the inter-individual interactions towards a double direction of an objective externalization and a reflexive interiorization. We then understand that the mental facts are parallel to the social facts, where 'I' is replaced by 'we', and the actions and 'operations' become interactions of ways of 'cooperation'. The collective dimension allows interactions to modify each other in search of a coordinated action.

And so, considering the interaction between the subject and the object that modifies them, each interaction between individual subjects will modify the subjects in relation to the others.

According to Primo (2005), "Piaget (1973, p.167), when studying the construction of intelligence, makes clear that a primitive fact is "neither the individual nor a group of them, but the relation between individuals, and a relation continuously modifying individual consciences themselves [my highlight]" (p.12).

It is also possible to understand interaction through the Biology of Knowing, a theory developed by Humberto Maturana and Francisco Varela. According to the authors, interaction is the living being's action towards another living being, and/or in relation to the environment, in which he is inserted, in a congruent way, happening in his living. The interaction necessarily implies a modification in living beings and the environment in a spontaneous way. Therefore, "if life is a getting-to-know process, living beings build up this process not from a single passive attitude, but through interaction" (2002, p.12).

According to Maturana (1993, 1999), the living being is formed in the construction of his ontogeny, through the conservation of organization and adaptation, thus, being the result of his history and circumstance. In the interaction with the other and in congruence with the environment, the human being preserves his identity and organization, configuring his living space, modifying its structure[2]. Therefore, interaction happens in a living space, where the living being shares their perception[3] and perspective as a living being with the other, constructed along the history of transformation. In this way, it demonstrates the characteristic of collaborating inherent to the living being. The interactions that happen throughout life with other living beings and with the environment as a knowledge object, through the act of emotion, underlie the comprehension of living and knowing. Nevertheless, it is important to reinforce that living is characterized by a constant and dynamic structural change for the living being, through the accomplishment of structural couplings, preserving the organization[4].

Living is a history in which the course of the structural changes we live is contingent to the history of interactions by meeting objects. And in this history of structural change, contingent to the sequence of interactions, the living being and its circumstance walk together'. (Maturana, 1993. p.30)

For Maturana (1999), learning is the structural change[5] that happens in the recurrent interaction between the living being and the living beings in congruence with the environment. However, the interactions are not responsible for learning; they are only responsible for unchaining, disturbances and the structural changes as spontaneous biological phenomena.

We talk about the learning process as a caption of an independent world in an abstract operating that almost does not reach our corporality, but we know that it is not like that. We know that learning has to do with structural changes that happen within us in a contingent way with the history of our interactions. (p.60)

Maturana uses the term structural coupling to designate the interaction between the living being and the environment where both change. 'Structural coupling is the product of continuing interactions of a system in an environment which determines disturbances allowing it to recurrently operate within its environment' (2002, p.133). For the author, both systems can become reciprocating structural coupling through structural changes happening during their interaction history. In this case, the changes of state in a system, become disturbance for the other and vice-versa in a way of establishing a domain of paths from a mutually selective state to one mutually triggering change.

Primo (2005) was also concerned in studying the interaction, based in Piaget, and has defined it as 'an action between' the participants of the meeting (Primo 1997, 1998). This way the focus turns to the relationships established between interactants[6], and not in the parts compounding the global system (p.2).

In addition, what happens when the space the subject interacts with, is a digital machine? Does this stop it being considered an interaction with the physical environment? Is not the machine a physical environment itself? What does the fact of this machine being digital mean? What novelty does the digital add to the context of interaction? Would it be interactivity, understood as the po-

tential of a means or system to enable interaction, which is understood as the effective action between people and/or things?

Lévy (1999) and Lemos (2002), establish levels and divisions in the interaction process, in the case of humans and machines, according to them named 'interactivity'. So, for Lemos (1997), interactivity is only a novelty that depends directly on the interface present in the technology. Interface, according to Lévy (1999), "is all material apparatus enabling interaction between the universe of digital information and the ordinary world" (Trein & Schlemmer, 2008, p.3).

Lemos (2007) classifies interactivity on three levels (Table 1): technical-analogical-mechanics, digital-electronics and social, where one does not exclude the other.

Digital-electronics interactivity, according to Lemos (2007), directly affects contemporary relations between men and machines. We can say that it also affects relations between subjects, mediated by machines, for the digital-electronics interactivity is at the same time a social interaction and a techno-social interactivity.

As a result, when in our living and collaborating, we experience in different moments and situations, ways of interaction that are simultaneously technical and social. For example, according to Lemos (2007), when we interact with and through instant communication tools, such as Skype, Gtalk, MSN; in social media such as Facebook, LinkedIn, and Twitter; and in Metaverses such as the Active Worlds, Second Life, Open Simulator, Open Wonderland, and Cloud Party among others, we have

Table 1. Interactivity levels (Lemos, 2007)

Technical-Analogical-Mechanics Interactivity	Refers to the interaction man-machine, which triggers a response, without modifying the environment.
Digital-Electronics Interactivity	Refers not only to the interaction man-machine, but the interaction man-machine-information, which exerts an action on the object, modifying its content, enabling new information.
Social Interactivity	Refers to the interaction itself – in this case, the action among subjects [our highlight].

techno-social interactivity. However, is there an interaction that is social (among humans), mediated by a physical environment (computer, tablet, and smartphone) and digital (apps), which would allow us to talk about interactive interaction?

Lévy (1999, p.82), states that the bigger the communication channel is, the higher the degree of interactivity with a certain technology will be. According to the author, it is possible to measure interactivity in axis such as:

1. The possibilities of appropriation and personalization of the received messages, regardless their nature;
2. The reciprocity in communication (meaning a communicational gadget 'one-one' or 'all-all');
3. The virtuality, here emphasizing the calculation of the message in real time according to a template and data entrance;
4. The implication of image of the participants in messages;
5. The telepresence.

Alternatively, for Lévy (1999), "the possibility of expropriation and of the material recombination of the message by its receiver is an essential parameter for assessing the interactivity degree of a product" (p.79). For technology (or technological tools, software, etc.) to have a high interactivity degree, they have to enable communication among several subjects within a virtual interface where messages are sent and received in real time (synchronous) and in such a way that the subjects feel part of the same space, through telepresence. Lévy (1999, p.83), also presents a table with the different types of interactivity (see Table 2).

Wagner (1994) proposes a distinction between the terms interaction and interactivity. He understands interaction as the communicative relationship between human beings, and interactivity as the communication between people and machines. Interactivity, this way, seems to be more related to the main characteristics of digital technologies, and the technical term meaning the possibility of a user to interact with a machine. In this case, we do not distinguish the interaction of human beings

Table 2. Different types of interactivity (Lévy, 1999, p.83)

Relationship with the Message Communication Instrument	Linear Message, Not Changeable in Real Time	Interruption and Reorientation of the Informational Flow in Real Time	Implication of the Participant in the Message
Unilateral Diffusion	• Press • Radio • Television • Cinema	• Multimodal data banks • Fixed hyper documents • Simulations without immersion or the possibility of modifying the template	• Videogames with a single player • Simulations with immersion (flight simulator) with no possibility of modifying the template
Reciprocity Dialogue	Mail correspondence between two people	• Telephone • Videophone	Dialogues through virtual worlds, cybersex
Dialogue among several participants	• Mail network • Publication system in a research community • Electronic mail • Electronic conferences	• Teleconference or videoconference with several participants • Open hyper documents accessible online or for a community's reading • Simulations (with the possibility of acting on the templates) as a support and debates for a community	• Multiuser RPG in cyberspace • Videogame in VR with several participants • Communication in Virtual Worlds, continuous negotiation among participants about their images and the image of the common situation

in a geographical space and interaction among human beings in the digital virtual nature space.

Belloni (2009) also refers to interaction and interactivity as terms with different meanings. According to him, interaction is "the reciprocate action between two or more actors where there is intersubjectivity" (p.58), it can be direct or indirect (mediated by an information vehicle), while interactivity is "the possibility of the user to interact with a machine" (p.58). According to the author, the term interactivity has been used with two different meanings: a) as a technical potentiality offered by a certain environment and, b) as a user's activity when acting upon a machine and receiving a retroaction in turn. What Piaget and Maturana have coined as interaction, Silva (2001) understands as the interaction term. According to Silva (2001), the concept of interactivity is attached to communication and not to computing. Therefore, he uses the term interactivity to describe communication between humans, between humans and machines and between users and the service. According to the author, in order to have interactivity it is necessary to guarantee: a) the dialogue that associates the emission and the reception as opposite and complementary poles in co-creating communication, and b) individual intervention in the content of the message or program, open to modifications and manipulations. In the educational context, either face-to-face or online, interactivity has the meaning of co-creation, assuming participation, intervention, cooperation and co-construction between the different actors in the process. Silva (2001) criticizes the trivialization of the term interactivity, which has been used as a sales argument or publicity ideology. According to him, software, TV programs, movie theaters and courses that are presented as interactive are merely computerized, but are not attached to the communicational sense of interactivity, according to his understanding of the term.

As for Primo (2005), he uses the term "interaction mediated by computer" when the context involves a digital machine, or the computer in this case, and not 'interactivity' in order to "stake borders in the communicative context in question and avoid the vulnerable term 'interactivity… when talking about interaction mediated by a computer, it is understood that such interactions can occur with, and/or, through a computer and its networks" (p.2).

In this context, Primo (2005) presents five common approaches attributed to the so-called 'interactivity', with the objective of observing if they value *reciprocate action and interdependency*. With this critique, the author aims to make it clear that "from limited visions for communication, this group of studies proposes problematic concepts for the broader study of interaction mediated by computer" (p.3). The approaches presented by the author are transmissionist, informational, technicist, in the market field and anthropomorphic.

Having presented these approaches, Primo (2005) proposes the *Relational-systemic approach of interaction*. According to the author, while mass communication works under the perspective of 'one-all', digital technologies enable work under the 'one-one' and 'all-all' perspective. However, Primo warns that some models and theories used to study mass communication are used in the discussion of so-called 'interactivity'. So, due to the difficulties emerging from this situation, and acknowledging that the study of interactions mediated by computer demands a certain regard that the theories of mass communication ('one-all') do not take into account, it is in the interpersonal communication[7] where the author looks for his basis. According to the author,

It is not restricted to the interactant's particular characteristics, or to the technical specification of information technology systems. What matters is

investigating what is going on between subjects, between the human interactant and the computer, between two or more machines. This study aims to approach the issue under a relational-systemic perspective, emphasizing the relational aspect of interaction, valuing the complexity of the interactive system. (p.11)

In this case, Primo (2000, p. 7) proposes a vision focused in what is going on between the interactants (not focusing exclusively on production, reception or on the channel), in the established relationship. Within this, he proposes two types of broad groups of interactions mediated by computer – *the mutual interaction and the reactive interaction,* where, 'the first is presented as complete and the second one weak and limited'. The reactive interaction flows a mechanistic and linear paradigm and an epistemological and empirical conception that, according to Becker (2003) attributes to meanings the source of the whole knowledge, considering the interaction only as a process of action and reaction. Mutual interaction refers to an interactionist-constructivist perspective, which will measure the quality of interaction from its *process,* that is, in the relation between interactants.

MUTUAL INTERACTION AND REACTIVE INTERACTION

In order to define whether an interaction is mutual or reactive, according to Primo (2000), it is necessary to analyze the following dimensions:

- **System:** Group of objects or entities that relate to each other building up a whole;
- **Process:** Events that present changes in time;
- **Flow:** The course or sequence of the relationship;

- **Throughput:** What happens between the decodification and the codification, inputs and outputs;
- **Relation:** The meeting, the connection, interchange of elements or sub-systems;
- **Interface:** Contact surface, arrangements of articulation, interpretation and translation.

Based upon these dimensions we can differentiate mutual interactions from the reactive ones (Primo, 2000), using Table 3.

We believe that interaction is a combined action, able to occur between subjects; between subject-machine and between subjects and machines, and that the unchained reaction modifies the other, oneself and the relation itself, and the environment where the interaction occurred.

DTs that only enable *reactive interaction* are environments considered closed, seen as merely an auxiliary instrument – an extra resource. It is linear and mechanic – the computer as a teaching machine. In such environments, questions and answers have already been 'pre-questioned' and 'pre-answered' – or programmed. The built up interface infers that it is only necessary to present the information to the student, and that he will absorb the knowledge. Considering that there are only positive and negative reinforcements missing for the regulation of the content's fixation. The knowledge is ready to be 'transmitted' and, while it happens, it fosters learning in a way that the use of technology is seen as an extra possibility to pass the content on or to reinforce it. In this vein, there are the classic courses mediated by technology, Computer Aided Instruction (CAI), Computer Based Training (CBT), Web Based Training (WBT), Web Based Instruction (WBI) and Distance Learning. Within this context, the paradigm is the transmission of knowledge.

DTs that enable a *mutual interaction* are open environments, seen as a possibility for cognitive

Table 3. Reactive interaction and mutual interaction (Primo, 2000)

Dimensions	Reactive	Mutual
System	Closed – the system does not perceive context, notions of reality, the meaningful or interpretative processes, and therefore, does not react. For not making changes with the environment, the system does not evolve. The reactant has few chances of modifying the agent.	Open – Global, made by interdependent elements. When one is affected, the whole is modified.
Operation	Stimulus-response	Negotiation
Flow	Action and reaction	Interdependent actions, mutually influencing their behavior and having their behavior influenced at every communicative event, enabling the relation to transform.
Throughput	Mere reflex or automatic – mechanics. Decodification processes are programmed and automatic.	Confrontation of the received message with the interactant's cognitive complexity. The throughput affects the input in a way that the output can never be totally foreseen – it takes in to account a global complexity of behaviors. The dialogue between interactants is decoded and interpreted, making it possible to create a new codification.
Relation	Rigidly casual	Negotiated construction
Interface	Potential	Virtual

development that enables new ways of thinking and collaborating - empowerment. It has as basis interaction processes supporting the construction of knowledge. They start from the emerging problematic to creative and temporary actualizations – the solutions cannot be defined beforehand. In those environments, construction, free exploration, discovery and invention are allowed. Any issue may be raised and the answers can be built. The built up interface concerns the "transformation-other", the novelty, the unforeseen, and it acts as a meeting point for dialogues between several interactants who gather in a cooperative work. In this way, Virtual Learning Environments appear, Web 2.0 Technologies, and Metaverses, among others, which favor the constitution of learning communities, collaborating networks. Within this context, the paradigm is the construction of knowledge.

For Primo (2000), interfaces can be potential or virtual. *Potential interfaces* refer to the mechanical system and to an empiric concept, allowing only one type of interaction called reactive interaction, which happens through the stimulus-response,

disregarding the process and not suffering any modification in the environment. In doing so, the technologies that use potential interfaces have pre-programmed questions and answers, not accepting anything different to that which was foreseen. *Virtual interfaces* are related in a constructivist conception and enable mutual interactions, in such a way that the effect of this interaction can result in constructing and directly modifying the environment (in this case the software), as well as the subjects involved in the process.

According to Primo (1999), an interactive system has to give total autonomy to the user. The systems presenting a 'mutual interaction' have a virtual interfacing in a way that the interface that is very interactive is the one that works virtually, enabling the occurrence of the problematic and enabling updating. The more an interface allows interactivity, the more it will contribute to the construction of knowledge.

In summary, reflecting on interaction and interactivity from the point the view of Primo (2000), Lévy (1999) and Lemos (2007), we can perceive that interaction is directly attached to the degree of relation/communication established between the subject(s) participating in the action and in the environment. It is from this relation/communication between interactants and the environment that the interaction will happen, whilst interactivity is connected to the interface's potential for the interaction to happen. In this case, depending on the interface, is it possible to affirm that a certain technology is more or less interactive, from the level of interactivity it offers for the interaction to happen? Communication between the interactants can occur in different ways, meaning, through different languages and ways of thinking representation that enable communication, such as:

- **Textual:** Communication is established through texts;
- **Oral:** Communication is established through voice;
- **Gestural:** Communication is established through gestures;
- **Graphic:** Communication is established through images.

We can take as an example, a traditional digital technology – Virtual Learning Environments, in which the interactivity available is textual. This technology does not contemplate interaction in the different communication languages presented above, so the interactivity level is low. The presence of the other is perceived and represented mainly through textual interaction using tools such as chats, forums, etc., lowering the level of telepresence and digital virtual presence within those environments. In some Virtual Learning Environments, it is possible for the subject to be graphically represented, through a prop or a static image, appearing next to his interactions in forums, chats, etc. As a result, we need to re-think the concept of Online Education, because it is through the interactivity provided by the software that subjects will be able to interact us-

ing (or not) different communication languages, consequently giving them more possibilities to develop themselves.

TYPES OF INTERACTION

The interaction process between subjects enables interchange, collaborating, and exchange of different points of view. It enables knowing and thinking about different questionings, about how the other is thinking, and about his own thinking, and this way he develops new learning. When we talk about social interaction mediated by computers in an interconnected network, we are able to distinguish interaction regarding its temporality as synchronous and asynchronous:

Synchronous interaction is that which happens at the same time, meaning, the subjects are simultaneously connected, happening in the same space or in different spaces, and enables the "meeting", the "being together" in the digital virtual way, either by the telepresence (for videoconference – Figure 1) or through a digital virtual presence (Figure 2).

Asynchronous interaction is that which happens in different time and spaces, the subjects do not need to be simultaneously connected or located in the same geographical space to carry out the interaction.

Both synchronous and asynchronous interactions can vary regarding direction and number of interacting subjects, either being one-to-one (communication between only two subjects), one-to-all (communication from one subject to many subjects), all-to-all (communication between many subjects to many subjects, where everybody interacts with each other).

Interaction can occur from 'one-to-one' (possible through the telephone, e-mail, instant communicators, among others), from 'one-to-many' (mainly possible through mass communication means where the same message is sent to everyone from a distribution source, like TV or radio, chat,

Figure 1. Synchronous interaction carried out through videoconference
Source: Authors

e-mail, forums, among others), and from 'many-to-many' (possible in MMORPG, Metaverses, Videoconferences, chat, among others).

So, the telephone, television, video game, computer (with its different web technologies, games and virtual worlds), have different interfaces enabling interactivity. We can say that all these technologies make interactivity possible, but at different levels that can be measured according to the degree of interaction.

We believe that interaction is a combined action that can occur between subjects, between subject-machine or between subjects and machines, and the unchained reaction modifies the other, the self and the relation itself as well as the environment where the interaction happened. That way, when we consider the authors mentioned above, it is possible to comprehend that it is through interaction with the physical, social and more recently,

digital environments that the subject learns. So, learning is understood as an individual and social mediated process, in which subjects construct their knowledge through their interaction with the environment and other subjects, in a constant interrelation between internal and external factors.

Understanding interaction as one of the key factors for the learning process to happen is fundamental when we think about the use of technologies in the teaching and learning processes, as is identifying the types and levels of interaction each technology enables and, the different forms of language that the subject can use during this process. The greater the possibilities and potential for interaction from the use of different languages, the greater the actions the subject will have to develop.

Thus, in the context of this work, we understand interaction as the action between the subjects and the environment, being it analogical, digital or hybrid; and interactivity (attached to the environment's interface) as the propriety in an environment or system that enables interaction.

LANGUAGES AND INTERACTION/INTERACTIVITY FORMS IN METAVERSE

Based on the conjectures of Jean Piaget's Genetic Epistemology, on the importance of the subject's action and interaction towards learning and the development of human intelligence, we understand that Digital Culture, see chapter 13 - Digital Virtual Culture in Metaverse: The Metaculture?, with its multiple ways of interaction and communication, has allowed new ways of developing intelligence. However, according to Schlemmer & Lopes (in press), it is important to highlight that Piaget carried out his research in physical and natural contexts, at a time there was no digital technology, and children and teenagers had limited access to information, usually circumscribed within a local, or close, context. Means of mass communication

Figure 2. Synchronous interaction carried out in the Second Life Metaverse
Source: Authors

were in their early stages, reading was one of the only ways to broaden the limits of local reality, besides contact with foreigners and people from the community who shared their personal experience. So, when we approach Piaget today, we need to consider the changes (cultural, social, technological, economic), and mainly, the centrality communication acquires in the contemporaneity, for the discussion involving network learning.

Schlemmer & Lopes (in press) call our attention to the fact that, from the epistemological point of view, the theoretical Piagetian conjectures for thinking about the role of action in learning are still fecund, and even more so if we consider that the idea of interaction originates in the idea of action itself. The core difference, in this case, lies in the fact that the Piagetian model deals with the

theme of interaction in the relation subject-object, and always takes notions of logic-mathematics schemes to think about learning according to a representative matrix. Such functioning of intelligence structured by logic-mathematics schemes, as previously explained, regards the subject's need for adaptation, having novelty as the unbalancing element. This way, for Piaget, the search for balance never stops, being a continuous movement in the matrix of the development of humans. Nevertheless, when referring to socialization processes, such logic-mathematics schemes do not always explain the gaps left by the balancing process. In the same sense, it is not possible to think about social development with something that can be carried out or that solves itself from heuristics – which means, by the cause and effect relation.

For the social fact, it is not always that an event leads to another. The idea of operation set out and balanced in the relation between two or more people does not consider that social interaction is a communicational phenomena, and therefore, subject to all kinds of noises and interferences, both internal and external to the subject.

According to Schlemmer & Lopes (2013), another important element to be considered in social interactions regards the social-historic aspect in the core of the human's communication phenomena. The development of human's language, as a social-technical phenomena of the own body, relentlessly carries a heritage that is both biological and social. The change itself, mentioned historically in the systems and means of communication denotes that language and thinking modify according to the time and place one inhabits. In this sense, Piaget has contributed a lot by treating language from the perspective of producing signification systems, allowing us to affirm that, culturally speaking, the more diversified the environment is, the more conditions it will have to borrow from cultural signs.

Here we have an important aspect relating directly to Digital Culture. If we take into account, from Piaget that the child's thinking also develops from the need of formalization and demonstration the theme of communication is emphasized again, because the Digital Culture is also network communication. The 'learning with' and 'by means of' may be an imperative from the Digital Culture, and at the same time is a social-political ideal. In fact, the semiotic universe of the cybernetic space has proved that culture is a network of meanings and significations in which we take part, regardless whether or not we are online. The idea of culture as the manifestation of a collective intelligence reinforces the conception that self-development is above all socializing. In this sense, we are all authors and actors of others, and ourselves as we interact.

It is within the Digital Culture that Metaverses arise, digital technologies (alopoietic machines[8])

having a virtual interface with an elevated interactivity potential, that can strengthen and broaden the action and interaction processes, resulting in new ways of 'learning with', living and collaborating. With that, new meanings of time[9], space[10], presence[11], quick access to information in a desired moment and the creation of communication and information networks can contribute to the (re) signification of the representation ways of the subject's knowledge. The relations, the interactions and existence itself among subjects, either in the educational, professional, social or political context push different transformations forward, both in subjects and in the context.

Alopoietic machines are not living beings, for they are characterized by their non-reproduction and absence of intervention history – except in transformations caused by interaction histories constructed by living beings (autopoietic machines[12]) in interaction or through alopoietic machines. In this way, alopoietic machines are subordinated to living beings, depending on external relations, which means that to carry out a transformation they need somebody else's action (in some cases these are internal reactions, resulting from the programming made by a living being, when using Artificial Intelligence – AI, there is an understanding that they self-reproduce). However, they have their own organization that interferes and determines the interaction among living beings.

So, alopoietic machines can be configured as living and collaborating spaces by means of the interaction flow of autopoietic machines. However, in the same way that the environment has its organization, alopoietic machines also have theirs. Such organization does not determine the structural changes in autopoietic machines, but can constitute disturbing elements, triggering such changes, through an elevated degree of interactivity encouraged by its interface.

It is within this context that we approach Metaverses – a hybrid technology, having characteristics of different digital technologies, such as instant communicators, social media, Virtual Learning Environments, games, etc., and therefore being an alopoietic machine, which presents, through its virtual interface, an elevated interactivity potential, offering the subjects - autopoietic machines, action and interaction through different combined languages (textual, oral, gestural and graphic). It is in this way that a Metaverse enables mutual, techno-social interaction at a high level, when taking in to account the concepts proposed by Primo (2000), Lemos (2007) and Lévy (1999), for it presents a virtual interface made by dynamic scenarios with 3D representation, shaped by computer graphics techniques. A Metaverse makes the construction of 3D digital virtual world possible, being 'materialized' by the creation of graphic representation, in a variety of shapes, and needs human action – the alopoietic machine, to 'become' (Schlemmer & Trein, 2008, p.7). This way, these worlds can be entirely created by their e-inhabitants, the avatars, the digital virtual identities, represented by 'technologized bodies' able to talk to each other, construct new worlds, start business, attend concerts, study, in summary, interacting and 'being together' in a 'digital virtual' way.

From the perspective of the type of interaction in Metaverse, it occurs in a synchronous way (the subjects, represented by their avatars – social presence, interact in the same time and space – 3D digital virtual world, using textual, oral, gestural or graphic language) or in a asynchronous way (the subjects, represented by their avatars, interact at anytime, with the 3D digital virtual world and with other avatars that happen to be in the space at the same time). In this way, the subjects can experiment with telepresence and digital virtual presence, through avatars, and share the same digital virtual space, where their actions, meaning the interactions directly modify the environment and the subject involved in the

action, being only one or many. This all-to-all communication is possible by the combined use of different languages (textual, gestural, oral and graphic), that happens through telepresence and digital virtual presence – avatar, therefore social presence, have been found, in our research, as meaningful for the learning process. Such potential makes Metaverses operate with a virtual interface, and therefore presenting a high interactivity level, making mutual interaction possible.

Metaverses make different ways of participation and involvement possible for subjects, for they can live a situation, experience it and effectively be there, take part, representing their thinking through the combination of the textual, oral, gestural and graphic. This is very different when compared to other digital technologies, through which mostly concerns the visualization of texts, images and videos – information as something located outside the subject.

Like interactivity, founded in the Online Education context, it is possible to say that Metaverses can broaden possibilities while educational spaces, as well as the possibility of construction of digital virtual living spaces, pedagogical mediation and multiple pedagogical intermediation, because the subjects are, by means of their avatars, in a 'digital virtual being together' living and collaborating the educational process and acknowledging themselves in different ways.

For the interaction processes in Metaverse, Backes (2010) has identified three levels of coupling: structural coupling, technological structural coupling and structural coupling of digital virtual nature (such concepts are approached in chapter 7: Autopoietic machines and alopoietic machines: structural coupling), that characterizes how the digital virtual living and collaborating is constituted. In that way, the dialeticity between the configuration of digital virtual spaces of living and collaborating (through autonomy, authorship and digital technologies congruence) and the digital virtual living and collaborating (in emotion, through perturbation and recursion) happens in the construction of emerging cultures (in mutual respect, legitimacy of the other and with elements from culture in education) of students in their formative process. Therefore, the formative process needs to be accomplished in pedagogical practices that approach the problematization and contextualization of knowledge through dialogical relations, where everybody is a co-teacher and a co-learner. In this formative process, human beings, e-inhabitants, are aware of their actions, being author of their choices.

CONCLUSION

Of all digital technologies currently available, Metaverses are those offering the most interactivity, for they enable textual, oral, gestural or graphic communication, in addition to the fact that the subject is able to live an experience. They are able to create mutual interaction processes on a higher level, for the interface of Metaverses works in virtuality, making the occurrence of the problematic possible, and enabling updating. The more an interface allows interactivity, the more it will contribute to mutual interaction, because it allows the subject total autonomy, authorship and co-authorship, key aspects for the perspective of construction of knowledge.

Therefore, according to Schlemmer and Lopes (2013), there is a challenging path to be traced regarding the migration process from the traditional Virtual Learning Environments paradigm – with 2D environments and interaction through texts and schemes – to another one with the domain of imagined worlds - simulating the physical world or valuing a more esthetic experience. Nevertheless, we must also consider that people act in different ways in congruence with the place they

are in, and the Virtual Learning Environments, with their structure of hyperlinks, which do not give the subject the feeling of place, in the sense this term has is the daily life. We understand that the feeling of presence (to be there) is important for people to feel motivated and to stay, and that immersive environments more effectively offer those feelings.

According to Mattar and Valente (2007), the pedagogical experiences developed in 3D digital virtual worlds (constructions possible by the Metaverse technology – my highlight) call our attention to the emergence of the 'learning environment', which, according to the authors, is usually ignored in the literature about interaction and interactivity.

The possibility of creating richer and more playful learning places in this way, in several dimensions, leads the students to a more intense and joyful interaction with their colleagues, with the teacher, with the content and, mainly, with the objects and the environment itself. (Mattar, 2012, p.47)

The level of involvement and immersion of subjects with their own avatar, with other subjects represented by their respective avatars, including the teacher; with the 3D digital virtual world – representations created in 3D – concepts (that represent the content built or under construction); the feeling of social presence and of belonging, does not seem something easily attained in other learning environments. We therefore understand that Metaverses present new elements for educational contexts, meaning that the methodologies and the pedagogical practices so far adopted are not able to explore to a maximum level the potential of interactivity offered by technology. As a result, it is necessary to construct methodologies and practices that take into account such potential, and that can enable mutual interaction between those involved in the educational process.

REFERENCES

Backes, L. (2010). A cultura emergente na convivência em MDV3D. *Conjectura: Filosofia e Educação (UCS)*, *15*, 99-117.

Becker, F. (2003). *A origem do conhecimento e a aprendizagem escolar*. Porto Alegre, Brazil: *The Art of Medication*.

Belloni, M. L. (2009). Educação a distância. Campinas, Brazil: Autores Associados.

Galimberti, C., Ignazi, S., Vercesi, P., & Riva, G. (2001). Communication and cooperation in Networked environments: An experimental analysis. *Cyberpsychology & Behavior*, *4*(1), 131–146. doi:10.1089/10949310151088514 PMID:11709902

Lemos, A. (1997). Anjos interativos e retribalização do mundo: sobre interatividade e interfaces digitais. In *Proceedings of Lisboa: Tendências XXI* (pp. 19-29). Lisboa: Associação Portuguesa para o Desenvolvimento das Comunicações. Retrieved from http://www.facom.ufba.br/ciberpesquisa/lemos/interativo.pdf

Lemos, A. (2002). Cibercultura: Tecnologia e vida social na cultura contemporânea. Porto Alegre, Brazil: Sulina.

Lemos, A. (2007). Cidade digital: Portais, inclusão e redes no Brasil. Salvador, Brazil: Edufba.

Lévy, P. (1999). Cibercultura. Rio de Janeiro, Brazil: Editora 34.

Mattar, J. (2012). Tutoria e interação em educação a distância. São Paulo, Brazil: Cengage Learning.

Maturana, H. R. (1993a). Uma nova concepção de aprendizagem. *Dois Pontos*, *2*(15), 28–35.

Maturana, H. R. (1993b). As bases biológicas do aprendizado. *Dois Pontos*, *2*(16), 64–70.

Maturana, H. R. (1999). *Transformación en la convivencia*. Santiago, Chile: Dolmen Ediciones.

Maturana, H. R. (2002). A ontologia da realidade. Belo Horizonte, Brazil: Ed. UFMG.

Maturana, H. R., & Varela, F. J. (2002). A árvore do conhecimento: As bases biológicas da compreensão humana. São Paulo, Brazil: Palas Athena.

Piaget, J. (1973). Estudos sociológicos. Rio de Janeiro, Brazil: Companhia Editora Forense.

Piaget, J. (1987). O nascimento da inteligência na criança. Rio de Janeiro, Brazil: Guanabara.

Primo, A. F. T. (1998). Interação mútua e interação reativa: Uma proposta de estudo. In *Proceedings of Intercom 1998 - XXI Congresso Brasileiro de Ciências da Comunicação*. Rio de Janeiro, Brazil: Anais.

Primo, A. F. T. (1999). Interfaces potencial e virtual. *Revista da Famecos*, (10), 94-103. Retrieved from http://usr.psico.ufrgs.br/~aprimo/pb/interfa2.htm

Primo, A. F. T. (2000). Interação mútua e reativa: Uma proposta de estudo. Revista da Famecos, (12), 81-92.

Primo, A. F. T. (2000). Uma análise sistêmica da interação mediada por computador. *Teoria e Prática*, *3*(1), 73–84.

Primo, A. F. T. (2005). Seria a multimídia realmente interativa? *Revista da Famecos,* (6), 92-95.

Primo, A. F. T. (2005). Enfoques e desfoques no estudo da interação mediada por computador. In *Proceedings of Intercom 2003 - XXVI Congresso Brasileiro de Ciências da Comunicação*. Retrieved from http://www.facom.ufba.br/ciberpesquisa/404nOtF0und/404_45.htm

Primo, A. F. T., & Cassol, M. B. F. (1999). Explorando o conceito de interatividade: Definições e taxionomias. *Informática na Educação: Teoria e Prática*, 2(2), 65–80.

Schlemmer, E. (2002). *AVA: Um ambiente de convivência interacionista sistêmico para comunidades virtuais na cultura da aprendizagem.* (Unpublished doctoral Thesis). Universidade Federal do Rio Grande do Sul, Porto Alegre, Brazil.

Schlemmer, E., et al. (2002). Princípios e pressupostos norteados para a construção de uma nova graduação. São Leopoldo, Brazil: Universidade do Vale do Rio dos Sinos – UNISINOS.

Schlemmer, E., & Lopes, D. de Q. (in press). Ambientes 3D e educação In Tecnologias e mídias na educação presencial e a distância. Rio de Janeiro, Brazil: Editora LTC.

Schlemmer, E., Trein, D., & Oliveira, C. (2008). Metaverso: A telepresença em mundos digitais virtuais 3D por meio do uso de avatares. In Proceedings of XIX Simpósio Brasileiro de Informática Educativa (pp. 441 - 450). Fortaleza, Brazil: Anais.

Silva, M. (2001). Sala de aula interativa: A educação presencial e a distância em sintonia com a era digital e com a cidadania. *Boletim Técnico do Senac*, 27(2), 1-20. Retrieved from http://www.senac.br/informativo/BTS/272e.htm

Starobinski, J. (2002). Ação e reação: Vida e aventuras de um casal. Rio de Janeiro, Brazil: Civilização Brasileira.

Trivinho, E. (1996). Epistemologia em ruínas: A implosão da teoria da comunicação na experiência do cyberspace. *Revista da Famecos,* (6), 73-81. Retrieved from http://www.pucrs.br/famecos/producao_cientifica/publicacoes_online/revista-famecos/fam5/epistemologia.html

Valente, C., & Mattar, J. (2007). Second life e web 2.0 na educação: O potencial revolucionário das novas tecnologias. São Paulo, Brazil: Novatec Editora.

Wagner, E. D. (1994). In support of a function definition of interaction. *American Journal of Distance Education*, 8(2), 6–29. doi:10.1080/08923649409526852

KEY TERMS AND DEFINITIONS

Interactants: According to Primo (2005, p.3), "interactant" (term commonly found in interpersonal communication research), means the one emanating the idea of interaction. Trivinho (1996), on the other hand, proposes the concept of "cyberspace interactant individual," who, according to him, "presupposes an inventor-participating trace having its completion never verified, as in a mass communication receiver, for example." In this sense, it seems too little to be referred as a merely "receiver."

Interaction: The interaction is directly attached to the degree of relation/communication established between the subject(s) participating in the action and in the environment, because it is from this relation/communication between interactants and the environment that the interaction will happen.

Interactivity: Interactivity is connected to the interface's potential for the interaction to happen.

Mutual Interaction: The mutual interaction refers to an interactionist-constructivist perspective, which will measure the quality of interaction from its process, that is, in the relation between interactants. Digital technologies that enable a mutual interaction are open environments, seen as a possibility for the cognitive development that enables new ways of thinking and collaborating - empowerment. It has as basis interaction processes supporting the construction of knowledge. They start from the emerging problematic to creative and temporary actualizations – the solutions cannot be defined beforehand.

Potential Interfaces: It refers to the mechanical system and to an empiric concept, allowing only one type of interaction, so called reactive interaction, which happens through the stimulus-response, disregarding the process, and not suffering any modification in the environment. In being so, the technologies that use potential interfaces have pre-programmed questions and answers, not admitting anything different from what were foreseen.

Reactive Interaction: The reactive and interaction flows a mechanistic and linear paradigm and an epistemological and empirical conception that, according to Becker (2003) attributes to senses the source of the whole knowledge, considering the interaction only as a process of action and reaction. Digital technologies that only enable reactive interaction are environments considered closed, seen as mere auxiliary instrument – an extra resource. It is linear and mechanic – the computer as a teaching machine. In such environments, questions and answers have already been "pre-questioned" and "pre-answered" – or programmed.

Virtual Interfaces: They are related in a constructivist conception and enable mutual interactions, in a way that the effect of such interaction can result in constructing, and directly modifying the environment (in this case the software), as well as the subjects involved in the process.

ENDNOTES

[1] According to Primo (2005, p.3) and Starobinski (2002, p.205), "We certainly find *interagere* in medieval Latin, but in the precise sense of 'serving as mediator'. The word was strongly supported around Latin, whereas this association also existed in French, without the urge of 'interaction' and 'interact.'

[2] These concepts are detailed in Chapter 7- Autopoietic Machines and Alopoietic Machines: The Structural Coupling.

[3] Perception is always related to the living being that perceives, also referred to as the observer. According to Maturana and Varela (2002), perception is created through the living being's experience (observer), determined by its structure, perception being the result of history and actions – biological and social – of every living being. Therefore "… everything that is said by someone" (p.32).

[4] These concepts are detailed in Chapter 7 - Autopoietic Machines and Alopoietic Machines: The Structural Coupling.

[5] Change without losing the component's identity or the relations between components of a certain structure (Maturana, 2002, p.84).

[6] According to Primo (2005, p.3), 'interactant' (term commonly found in interpersonal communication research), meaning the one emanating the idea of interaction. Trivinho (1996), on the other hand, proposes the concept of a 'cyberspace interactant individual', who, according to him, 'presupposes an inventor-participating trace having its completion never verified, as in a mass communication receiver, for example. In this sense, it seems too little to be referred as a merely 'receiver.'

[7] According to Primo (2005, p.11), as acknowledged by Galimberti et al. (2001, p.131), 'Interpersonal communication does not happen exclusively face-to-face. In work contexts, as in private life, there are more and more situations of mediated communication using new online technology artifacts.'

[8] These concepts are detailed in Chapter 7 - Autopoietic Machines and Alopoietic Machines: The Structural Coupling.

9   A temporal time, that enables interaction and relation in a dynamic, reversible and recursive way.

10   A deterritorialized flowing space, where it is possible to create anything at anytime.

11   A presence can be physical, digital virtual, telepresence or hybrid.

12   These concepts are detailed in Chapter 7- Autopoietic Machines and Alopoietic Machines: The Structural Coupling.

Chapter 7
Autopoietic Machines and Alopoietic Machines:
The Structural Coupling

ABSTRACT

This chapter approaches the issues involving Autopoietic and Alopoietic machines, under the perspective of structural coupling that appears in the interaction and interactivity in Metaverses. The authors present and discuss the subtopic "Autopoietic Machines: The Human Beings." In the subtopic "Alopoietic Machines: The Nature of the Metaverse," the authors explore the concept of alopoietic machines in relation to digital technology. In "Structural Coupling," they define the concept based on the theory of Maturana and Varela (2002). The concept of autopoietic machines is extended through the subtopic "Language: Mode of Speech and Emotion." In as a brief conclusion, the authors describe three different situations that contribute to the broadening of the concept of structural coupling.

INTRODUCTION

When we think about a machine, from a simplicist perspective, our thought usually, turns to the icons representing something mechanical, technical, lifeless, meaning a device, tool or instrument capable of carrying out an action or work. With this in mind, thinking in the relation between the human being and the machine is a paradoxical and complex task. Paradoxical because, from a Cartesian perspective, they seem to be contradictory: human (life) and machine (lifeless); and complex because despite being contradictory we

can establish an intense relation, which allows us to overcome this dichotomy, enabling the task. Maturana and Varela (1997) established an interesting relation between human being and machine, which we will express in the search of (re)signifying it in the metaverses context.

To establish the relation between the human being and the machine we need to re-think some concepts and comprehensions previously addressed such as: living being, human being, structure and organization, ontogeny and phylogeny, and deepen other concepts that were superficially addressed as in the case of autonomy, autopoiesis

DOI: 10.4018/978-1-4666-6351-0.ch007

and structural coupling. In this sense, such concepts may help us broaden our comprehension in relation to machines, understanding them not only as a device, tool or instrument, but also as a system capable of producing a process that allows different actions and the accomplishment of tasks.

According to Maturana and Varela (1997), machines are considered all units made of components characterized by certain properties that enable the establishment of relation and interaction processes, constituted by an organization (variable because it defines the species) and a structure (variable because is the result of the history of interactions).

... it is a system that can materialize through many different structures, and whose defining organization does not depend on the properties of the components. On the contrary, in order to realize a certain concrete machine it is necessary to take into consideration the properties of the real components that, within their interactions, allow us to sense the defining relations of the machine organization. (pp.69-70)

Based on this concept, we can say that machines are units with an objective, a purpose that defines the domain and the process in which they carry out their actions, through the organization defined by the interactions between the components' properties and a variable and changing structure. Maturana and Varela in discussing the unit state that, "… (the possibility of differing from a background and therefore from other units) is the only necessary condition for having an existence in any determined domain" (Maturana & Varela 1997, p.90). The unit differs from the other units through a domain of action determining the unit related to the domain in a conceptual way, when we express it or describe it, or in a material way, in the action of its properties. "Consequently different classes of units necessarily differ in the domain they establish and, in having different

existing domains they may or may not interact, depending on the domains able to intercept them or not" (p.90).

We can then think of human beings, avatars and metaverses as machines that have an objective in the action carried out by processes in a certain domain. Usually, the objectives are not the machine's property, but that which to others assign them. We note in the research presented in Chapter 15 - Brazilian experiences in metaverses, that metaverses are machines whose purpose is to construct a 3D virtual digital world, but this goal was outlined, redefined or expanded by the research participants that not only built the 3D digital virtual world through the representation of the avatar, but knowledge, social networks, interaction among others. Nevertheless, when we talk about human beings our objectives are defined by themselves and not by others, but such objectives can be empowered or limited according to the technologized body representing the 3D Digital Virtual Worlds, meaning the avatar.

In the context described, we can perceive that machines do not belong to the same category or classification. Maturana and Varela (1997) distinguish the different types of machines according the characteristics of their structure and organization, in the domain they work, considered autopoietic machines and alopoietic machines.

In this chapter, we are approaching autopoietic and alopoietic machines by specifying them and describing them in the living and sharing context in order to allow us to think in a systemic and complex way about the possibility of structural coupling between them and the way in which they relate and interact through language in a context of emoting.

Autopoietic machines, meaning living systems are self-governing units with the ability to reproduce and regenerate, for according to the previous chapters, they have an organization that preserves a structure that transforms due to their history of interactions. The living being unit is effective in a dynamic and circular way, in the articulation between the organization and the structure, for its self-production, through autonomy, in which the interpretative capacity comes from its origin. In this chapter, we are reflecting on living beings that originate from humans.

Alopoietic machines, though, are not living beings, for their characteristics are non-reproduction and the absence of interaction histories – except for the transformations caused by the history of interactions constructed by the living systems (autopoietic machines) in interaction through alopoietic machines. As a result, alopoietic machines are subordinated to living beings; they are dependent on the external relations, which means that for there be transformation, an action of autopoietic machines it is necessary. However, they have their own organization that interferes and determines the interaction process among living systems.

AUTOPOIETIC MACHINES: HUMAN BEINGS

Human beings are considered units capable of developing through an evolutionary and natural process, which is not predictable or determined, but flexible, and which is defined by the human being himself and conditioned to his organization. Human beings, have at their origin, the need to share food and proximity of body. They therefore organize themselves into families, thorough language, and build social systems that are characterized by their dynamic of transformation (development, improvement, and change) according to the self-production of human beings they constitute, and who are in relation and interaction among themselves.

Human beings, establish relations and interactions with other human beings and configure living and sharing through their "self-producing" nature, for they are the result of the history of their species – phylogeny – as well as every human be-

ing's individual history – ontogeny. Maturana and Varela (2002) understand phylogeny as the "Sequence of organic bodies sequentially generated by reproductive relations" (p.117) and ontogeny as "History of a unit's transformation, as a result of a history of interactions, starting from their initial structure" (p.277).

In this way, phylogeny and ontogeny are in constant articulation, crossed by the subjects' interactions and by the environment, they are in. Therefore, knowledge is part of the historical, dynamic, contingent and recursive process of the development of human beings throughout their ontogeny, and it refers to the effectiveness of our living in definition and in the establishment of our cognitive domains[1].

The units have unique and particular structures and organizations, which give them the capacity of self-reproduction. Organization is the relation between the components that ensure that the attributes designed for the units are in fact what it is, i.e. they are relations established within what is determined by man as homo sapiens and not as a feline, for example. Therefore, "it is understood by organization the relations that occur between the components of something, so that they can be recognized as a member of a certain class" (Maturana & Varela, 2002, p.54).

According to Maturana and Varela (2002), the structure is the set of components and relations that compound a certain unit, and that configures its organization. The structure is changeable, varied and particular, whilst the organization is constant. The distinction between organizations that define attributes is made in the same way the structures' particularities of the several units are specified. Consequently, from a cyclical perspective, as the units reproduce themselves, there is transformation in the structure that will allow new self-productions of the units. Then, human beings, meaning the units, are considered autopoietic machines. To explain what autopoietic machines are we are structuring our thinking around two basic concepts, previously discussed, and that are now deepened: autonomy and autopoiesis. The concepts are approached from the studies carried out by Maturana and Varela (1997, 2002) about living beings.

The autonomy is a system compounded by other systems, and among them is autopoiesis. For this reason, a didactic issue treats the definitions of autonomy and autopoiesis in an articulated and dynamic way, even separately.

Autonomy is understood as:

... we understand living systems as autonomous units, surprisingly varied, capable of self-reproduction. In these meetings, autonomy is obviously an essential aspect of living beings that is always perceived in something that seems to be autonomous; our spontaneous reaction is to consider it living. Although, even when having the homeostatic ability of living beings to keep their identity through the active compensation of deformation ... (Maturana & Varela, 1997, p.65)

A system is considered autonomous when it is capable of specifying its own laws, establishing rules and leading its actions within a context, as well as identifying the meaning of its living through its own interactions, in relation to its ontogeny and with other systems, transforming its structure. Backes (2007), referring to the formation processes, says this type of autonomy is identified as individual autonomy. Human autonomy is related to its autopoiesis, in the capacity of self-reproduction in action and reflection. This means that, for Backes (2007), in the formation processes, human beings are capable of understanding knowledge, establishing the relation with their living, of positioning towards this knowledge, giving it meanings and therefore self-producing. This self-production implies the construction of new knowledge and the comprehension of the relation of this knowledge with living and sharing.

Therefore, the unit formed by an organization and a structure that "produces itself" is called an autopoietic unit. The term autopoiesis was coined

in the 1970s in discussions of Maturana and Varela (1997, 2002), where the previously used term was 'auto praxis', which was limited and could not comprise all the aspects involving autopoiesis.

Autopoiesis is defined as:

The word autopoiesis comes from the Greek word autos, meaning oneself; and poiesis, meaning to produce. When characterizing living beings as autopoietic systems we are saying that they are continuously producing themselves. In other words, we mean by autopoiesis that living beings are networks of molecular productions where the produced molecules generate their interactions in the same network that produces them. (Maturana, 1999, p.93)

According to Maturana and Varela (1997), there are three types of autopoietic systems. First order systems refer to cells as autopoietic molecular systems. Second order systems are assigned to the organisms that are constituted by a set of cells. Third order systems, which are related to social systems, constituted through a set of organisms – being the systems of second and third order, are the most significant ones for us to discuss within the context of this chapter, as they refer to the human being that establishes relations and interactions with other human beings in congruency with the environment, or in this case, the 3D Digital Virtual Worlds.

We can think of human beings represented by their avatars, self-producing in congruence with 3D Digital Virtual Worlds. In this process of the construction of 3D Digital Virtual Worlds, the human beings transform the 3D Digital Virtual Worlds through the autopoiesis produced in the development of construction, either in relation to the technical knowledge that involves the metaverses or the theoretical knowledge that involves the object to be represented. Therefore, human beings construct social systems in 3D Digital Virtual Worlds, which are characterized by the dynamic of relations of autopoiesis.

... it is indubitable that social systems are autopoietic systems of third order by the fact that they are systems constituted by organisms [human beings]. What defines them as they are, while social systems, is not the autopoiesis of their components, but the relation between the organisms that compose them, and that we can notice in our day-to-day lives in the very moment in which we differ them in their singularity by using the notion of 'social system'. (Maturana & Varela, 1997, p.19)

The human being is not independent of his circumstance (relation/interaction) with the environment[2]. The human being is in congruence through the way he proceeds within this relation, which makes actions comprehensible to the components of this living place, in general aspects, they have common objectives. The interactions the human beings face unchain changes between themselves; however, this is not determined in relation to their actions (physical or cognitive). It is the organism and the structure that specify what the human being admits as a perturbation in the development of an interaction process. Therefore, when we alter the structure of organisms we change their perception, which generates different behaviors about the comprehensions and representations of the environment, obtained towards the capturing of an object external to him.

Changes of state are defined by changes in structure, without losing or altering the organization, as it was previously stated. When this unit disintegrates (in structure and organization), or more specifically, when the human being alters his organization, he stops existing or dies. Living beings are characterized by the equal state of their autopoietic organization and differ between themselves by having their own particular structures (Maturana & Varela, 2002).

Although Maturana and Varela understand autonomy (1997, 2002) as something individualized, it is also effective in the social context in relation to other human beings. This way, "we are autonomous in our deep existence in relation to the environment and to the context in which we are inserted" (Moraes, 2003, p.29).

In the development of the proposed educational processes by Backes (2007), it was evident when participating in the research, that human beings are capable of making shared actions with other human beings. They transform themselves through these actions that are coordinated by a common objective, transforming the social system in congruence with the environment, through a compensation of the human being's perturbations, we denominate as social autonomy.

Therefore, social systems are interaction networks developed by human beings and through their behaviors, in the legitimating of the other, specifying appropriate behaviors. When this social system is able to produce itself through human beings' autopoiesis and proposes other possibilities of autopoiesis to human beings in a dialectic way, we have a process of social autonomy.

In this sense, we can say that:

... An autopoietic machine continuously specifies and produces its own organization through the production of components, under the conditions of continuous perturbation and compensation of such perturbations (production of components). We can then say that an autopoietic machine is a self-homeostatic system that has its own organization as a variable that is constantly maintained. (Maturana & Varela, 1997, p.71)

The autopoietic machine produces itself through the compensation of perturbations in which its organization and structure perceive. In this process, the autopoietic machine will keep its identity as a human being during the continuous structural change, only if it keeps a relational systemic identity in which it constitutes and achieves things. Therefore, autopoietic machines are autonomous and subordinate their structural changes to the conservation of their organization.

This means the human being, when represented by an avatar in the 3D Digital Virtual World, carries out his autopoiesis as he compensates for the perturbations perceived in the processes of interaction with other human beings, who are also represented by their avatars, and with the 3D Digital Virtual Worlds, which configures his living and sharing. The structural changes are subordinated to the human organization. However, this autopoietic machine is coupled to the avatar so that he can exist in digital virtual spaces.

In this sense, they have their individuality by maintaining the organization, and they have an identity that does not depend on their history of interactions with the observer. However, it is necessary to highlight that the human identity is a relational systemic phenomenon, not a genetic one that may get lost when we stop living the biology of love. The human beings´ existence in 3D Digital Virtual Worlds and its immersion is subordinated to an avatar's representation. That means, it is the human being who defines the actions and objectives; and it is their structure that determines the disturbing aspects, but it is the avatar's organization that will enable or limit the human beings´ actions in the 3D Digital Virtual Worlds. The human being can exist in many other spaces without the avatar, but the opposite is not true.

Autopoietic machines are those which can determine their own development through the autopoiesis processes, their development can be expected, but not totally foreseen. Their operations will establish the path to follow. This way each autopoietic machine will develop itself in a particular way.

The autopoietic identity enables evolution through reproductive series [in a recursive way] with structural variation and conservation of identity. The constitution of identity of a subject comes before empirically and logically, the evolution process. (Varela, 1997, p.47)

We can say then, that in autopoietic machines an action does not necessarily result in a certain reaction. Autopoietic machines may be disturbed by different external factors and each autopoietic machine may be disturbed in different ways, because their changes are always internal and individual when compensating every disturbance. For this reason, each autopoietic machine is unique and self produces in a recursive way. For Varela (1997), the interaction process that occurs, is the reference for conveying meaning that allows autopoietic machines to be interpretative.

ALOPOIETIC MACHINES: THE NATURE OF THE METAVERSE

As previously mentioned, when we think of machines our thoughts move to instruments or tools that allow us certain actions. This concept is very close to the real concept of alopoietic machines, though it does not reveal the systemic thought that conceives the real complexity behind it. Alopoietic machines are defined with reference to autopoietic machines in the sense of establishing differences and relations. For example, alopoietic machines are created, operated and identified by autopoietic ones. Both autopoietic and alopoietic machines present an organization, but such organization determines the processes for which it was programmed and these processes do not include its self-production, unless it is by means of other programs that allow an "artificial intelligence".

When operating alopoietic machines, they produce something different from themselves, that is, they *reproduce* a product that is continuously the same, differing from the concept of production of an autopoietic machine. Such operating reproduction is determined by an autopoietic machine and will result in an object, therefore, they are not autonomous, "… they are systems we, human beings elaborate, those who can only make sense through the way the design is related

to a product or something different from them ..."
(Maturana, 1997 p.14). Metaverses are software
that enable the construction of 3D Digital Virtual
Worlds, however, the 3D Digital Virtual Worlds
cannot be self-constructed; they depend on the
actions of human beings, represented by their
avatars. This way, metaverses do not produce other
metaverses (software); they reproduce the creation
of 3D Digital Virtual Worlds that are defined by
autopoiesis and their e-inhabitants.

So, conversely to autopoietic machines,
alopoietic ones have an identity that depends on
the observer (or autopoietic machines), which
means that someone has given them a meaning,
for their operation results in something different
than themselves. The observer, who foresees the
result of his action and determines the functioning
of it, establishes their limits. This way, we find
completely different 3D Digital Virtual Worlds
in the available metaverses, some familiar, interesting, and sometimes ideological, and others at
times, incomprehensible.

They produce something different from themselves
... . These machines are not autonomous, since
the changes they experiment are necessarily sub-
ordinated to the production of a different product.
(Maturana & Varela, 1997, p.73)

The processes of entering and exiting alopoietic
machines is also determined by the observer and
is totally predictable and expected. 3D Digital
Virtual Worlds are constructed according to the
objectives the human beings wish to achieve,
they present characteristics determined by these
objectives and its functioning follows the same
logic. This alopoietic machine, however, presents
an organization that allows or limits certain operations. We can construct a 3D Digital Virtual World
that enables teleporting to another dimension, but
we cannot feel climate sensations, for instance.

When taking the metaverses as an example
we can perceive that their comprehension as an
alopoietic machine can be overtaken when we

design a digital[3] virtual[4] nature space[5] of living
and sharing among e-inhabitants. For Maturana
and Varela (2002), the configuration of the living
spaces occurs in the flow of interactions among
living beings and between the living beings and
the environment, which makes the transformation
of the living beings and the environment possible,
intertwined with emotions, representations, perturbations and compensation of perturbations.

Alopoietic machines can then be configured
as living spaces in the flow of the interactions
of autopoietic machines, represented by their
avatars. Therefore, alopoietic machines have an
organization in the same way the environment
has. Such organization does not determine the
structural changes in the autopoietic machines, but
can represent perturbing elements, which means,
those that can unleash such changes.

In summary, the metaverse can create the 3D
Digital Virtual Worlds through graphic, textual,
oral or gestural representation of its avatars who
are immersed in the 3D Digital Virtual Worlds.
In this sense, the 3D Digital Virtual Worlds can
be understood as an alopoietic machine and/or
a living and sharing digital virtual space among
human beings who have their "digital self" represented by an avatar. So, the alopoietic machine,
meaning, the metaverse reproduces itself in the
self-production of autopoietic machines, resulting
also in a living and sharing space.

Therefore, autopoietic machines unleash structural changes in the autopoietic systems through
a disturbance; they may be coupled to other autopoietic and alopoietic machines, in congruence
with the environment. In this way there will be
a structural coupling that suffers the changes in
their structures and in the environment in which
they are coupled.

STRUCTURAL COUPLING

Human beings' living and sharing is configured
in an environment where they are in congruence.

This living and sharing can be configured in different dimensions, including among the human beings represented by avatars in a digital virtual environment. In this sense, living and sharing imply the comprehension of the coexistence and the complementarity among human beings and the environment, where interactions result in disturbances, reciprocally performing the role of compensatory disturbances. This way, when two or more autopoietic units are in an interaction process, one of the units perceives the other unit through its structure, constructed by the ontogeny, therefore unique and peculiar in the sense of legitimacy of the other in order to search for compensation.

"This means that two (or more) autopoietic units can be coupled in their ontogeny when their interactions become frequent or very stable" (Maturana & Varela, 2002, p.87). Recurrence implies reciprocity, or indeed, as both structures are unique and peculiar they unleash disturbances[6] between the other units, in considering them legitimate in the interaction process, and in the environment with which they are in congruence and vice versa.

Structural coupling therefore consists of the mutual modifications between human beings, or autopoietic units, which are in an interaction process without losing identity. For Maturana and Varela (1997), "when the interacting units lose their identity during the interaction, the consequence may be the generation of a new unit, and no coupling is noticed" (p.103). A unit may lose or modify its identity when it is not considered legitimate in an interaction process, or when others deny it. In this sense, no interaction or coupling is concluded. We usually find such situations in the living and sharing when there is a dominating and/or oppressing unit, when no dialogue is possible and therefore, no coupling. The dialogic relationship is understood based on the conceptions of speech, emote and chat developed by Maturana (2002), as a condition of establishing human relationships and interactions by means of legitimacy and respect. As well as in the design of

dialogue developed by Freire (1992) as "... when humans meet to reflect on their reality as we do and re-do" (p.123). Therefore, we are dealing with a process in which everyone involved has the opportunity to represent their perceptions, establish disturbing aspects, and a ratio of legitimacy and respect on the other, discussing ways to transform the reality in question in living and living together in everyday life.

However, for Maturana and Varela (2002) living and sharing may result in four different domains of changes and constitute different conditions:

- Domain of state exchange: changes the structure without changing the organization, keeping the class identity;
- Domain of destructive changes: a change in the structure that implies the loss of organization, losing the class unit;
- Domain of perturbations: interactions that unchain state change;
- Domain of destructive interactions: perturbations that result in destructive modifications.

When we analyze the four domains evident in living and sharing, we realize that not all living results or configures in a structural coupling between the human beings and the environment. The structural coupling is possible in relations with respect, legitimacy and dialogue.

...Unless a unit is not in a destructive interaction with its environment, we, observers, necessarily see that there is compatibility between the environment and the unit. While commensurable, environment and unit will act as mutual disturbing sources and will unleash mutual changes in state. (Maturana & Varela, 2002, p.112)

Therefore, in order to carry out a structural coupling it is necessary to have an adaptation condition that enables the changes in structure and the maintenance of the organization. Consequently, "the individual's ontogeny is a derivation of structural modifications not changed by the organization and therefore with a conservation in adaptation" (Maturana & Varela, 2002, p.116).

In summary, structural coupling may occur in two ways: coupling between the human being and the environment (including the environment being an alopoietic machine); and coupling between human beings in congruence with the environment (also including it to be an alopoietic machine). The first way implies the establishment of congruence and the second way implies in the establishment of a consensual domain, which means the consensual domain is defined by every human being's structure as they interact with the intention of making compensatory deformations. However, in both cases, for the structural coupling to happen, the human being's structure changes, as well as the environment, because, "... we also see it as endowed of a self-structural dynamic, operationally different from the living being" (Maturana & Varela, 2002, p.107).

The result of the establishment of such structural dynamic correspondence, or structural coupling, is the effective spatial-temporal correspondence between the changes in organisms' state and the changes from the environment state, while the organism remains autopoietic. (Maturana, 2002, p.142)

For example, in an interaction process between human beings represented by their avatars in 3D Digital Virtual Worlds, we know the possibilities offered by the metaverse software and we can list the actions that can be accomplished within this context, the software is not programmed to limit regarding its use. Despite this, we cannot foresee the characteristics of 3D Digital Virtual Worlds when configured as a living space for the construction of human beings' knowledge. Human beings, represented by their avatars will react to structural changes according to their nature and patterns (non-linear). Through this, a living be-

ing will structurally couple to its environment for it is a system that adapts when it learns, and it develops itself in a continuous way. Yet, when producing itself through interaction process with others, the human being may or may not attribute a characteristic of dynamism and "life" to this alopoietic machine (3D Digital Virtual Worlds) which develops itself through self-production of the human beings that make it.

As an example, we can observe the two images below, captured in the metaverse AWEDU (educational version of the Active Worlds software), representing the initial moment of the construction of the Virtual Learning World villa, which is located in a different dimension of the AWSINOS, used as a space to metaphorically represent the knowledge constructed in processes of human learning in Brazil and France, developed in Backes' thesis (2011).

As we can see in the figures of the Virtual Learning Worlds villa, located in the AWSINOS, at an early phase buildings appeared isolated, separated by walls. In the living and coexisting in everyday life, participants neared the buildings through paths. In the end, we can highlight the changes and development of an "inhabited" space that took place in a dynamic way through the action of its e-citizens[7], giving us the impression of life within this space. Other 3D Digital Virtual Worlds may represent other characteristics in this life, because they are built in the configuration of the living of other e-citizens. The structural coupling appears in the relation with the environment and with the other who is inserted in that environment. We can couple with an object of knowledge or with another way of thinking. Each coupling, with knowledge or with others, occurs in a unique and particular way, and is related to everyone's recursion, through common grounds. Therefore, we find totally different 3D Digital Virtual Worlds, for their construction will depend on the objectives the human beings have with their construction, congruence with the technology itself, in the coupling of the human being

Figure 1. Beginning of the construction process of the AWSINOS with students from Brazil and France
Source: Authors

with his avatar, his ontogeny with the network he establishes with the other e-inhabitants in the 3D Digital Virtual Worlds. The e-citizens can find and interact with other e-inhabitants for the MDV3D are online and open for visitation and interaction with other avatars, which are not part of a social system constituted for the construction.

In a system of coupling with the other we constitute the idea of network in which everyone is interconnected, in congruence, where one goes through a cognitive instability and searches for compensatory solutions. This means, according to Maturana and Varela (1997), that some compensatory disturbances may arise in the interaction process between autopoietic units, which couple

to compensate their disturbances through their own autopoiesis that can be specified in the process. The result is the structural change along the interaction history of each autopoietic machine.

Such considerations are also valid for the coupling of autopoietic and non-autopoietic units, with correlations regarding the conservation of their identities by the second one. In general the coupling of autopoietic systems with both, autopoietic or non-autopoietic units, is carried out with their autopoiesis. (Maturana & Varela, 1997, p.104)

This way an autopoietic living system interacts with its environment and with other human beings

Figure 2. The transformations in the construction process of the AWSINOS with students from Brazil and France
Source: Authors

Figure 3. Conclusion of the construction process of the AWSINOS with students from Brazil and France
Source: Authors

through structural coupling, meaning the recurrent interactions that unleash structural changes in the system (Capra, 2004). The environment unleashes structural changes, but it does not specify or guide them. The structural coupling establishes the way in which autopoietic, alopoietic machines interact, and how they change in congruence with their environment.

LANGUAGE: MODE OF SPEECH AND EMOTION

The fact of constructing different 3D Digital Virtual Worlds and configuring a variety of living ways in the digital virtual space is a characteristic of the human being when in autopoiesis. It is not the only characteristic form, when digital technologies are going through a fast development. However, it is evident that the development of such technologies is enabling other ways of living and it allows us to make interesting reflections about living and sharing. The human being, throughout his history, has constituted different social groups, by means of the dynamics of relations established in the interactions of his components, making each social system a unique one.

Every individual is constantly adjusting his position in the network of interactions constituted by the group, according to his own dynamic, resulting in his history of group structural coupling. (Maturana & Varela, 2002, p.213)

So, for Maturana (2002), the interaction process is completed when the human being is able to represent his perception of the other and together, in congruence with the environment, each one in his own way can disturb himself and, when compensating such disturbance, modify his initial perception. This whole process occurs within a linguistic domain, which is also the result of an interaction process. In this way, "anytime two or more units, through reciprocal action, modify their position towards the space they specify, there is an interaction". (p.130) Then, the result of the continuous interaction processes between human beings are the structural couplings.

In this sense, we as human beings exist in a continuous production of ourselves in the dynamic configuration of relations, the same way we exist in the conservation of our living in a transgenerational way, giving ourselves the condition of being human. Ways of living are maintained and at the same time reframed, between the different generations that interact in time (and that can also be timeless) and in space (that can be flow), through language.

According to Maturana and Varela (2002), the history of language is related to the organization of human beings in social systems through affective and close relations within the necessity of collecting and sharing food and in the constitution of family.

Lo central del fenómeno social humano es que se da en el lenguaje y lo central del lenguaje es que sólo en él se dan la reflexión y la autoconciencia. ... Así, el linguaje da al ser humano su dimensión espiritual em la reflexión, tanto de la autoconciencia como de la conciencia del outro. Pero el lenguaje es también la caída del ser humano, al permitir las cegueras frente al ser biológico que traen consigo las ideologias descriptivas de lo que debe ser. (Maturana, 1999, p.35)

The core of the social human phenomenon is that it happens in language, and the core of language is that reflection and self consciousness only happen within it . ... Language gives the human being his spiritual dimension in the reflection, both for this self-awareness and the other's awareness. But language may also mean the human being's fall, when it allows blindness before the biological being who brings along descriptive ideologies about what it should be. (Maturana, 1999, p.35).

As human beings our existence is marked by language, in either action, activity or behavior, meaning, we exist when we chat, through chat networks, with other human beings. For Maturana (2002) the human's comprehension goes through the comprehension "… of language and the emotions, which we perceive as the Word talk in our everyday lives" (p.130). Consequently, in different contexts, when we consider the other as someone legitimate in the interaction process, we try to find out the points we have in common and the diverging ones, so that we can together think of overcoming and transforming.

This comprehension may be empowered when we access 3D Digital Virtual Worlds through an avatar and discuss with other avatars a metaphoric representation of certain built knowledge. In this sense, speech is empowered by the different ways of communication available in the metaverse, provoked by the graphic and metaphoric representations of knowledge in the 3D Digital Virtual Worlds accessed and hosted in the possibility of participation of different avatars for being online.

Chatting is related to the human need to sort themselves by means of social systems. As discussed previously, according to Maturana and Verden-Zöller (2008) the origin of the *homo sapiens* happened in the family, over three million years ago, through the emotional feature between the pairs. They constitute themselves in small groups, formed by adults and children, where the living happens by the pleasure of corporeal proximity and of sharing together. The coexistence among human beings happens by two principles: neoteny, and epigenesis.

The possibility of constituting family is characterized by human beings' neotonic capacity, and we can therefore see the expansion and conservation of actions verified in both childhood and in adult life, as well as the reproduction of such actions with the new generations. This condition contributes to constituting us as cooperative and dependent beings in loving relations at all ages. In this sense, we understand that the human being's

nature is love. Such capacity is also revealed in digital virtual coexistence. When we interact with someone who is beginning his interaction history within this space, we try to carry out actions similar to those that other people made when we started our interaction history in digital virtual spaces. In the research developed by Backes (2011), with French students in 3D digital virtual chats, during classes, certain phrases appeared, such as: "I still don't understand the graphic representation we are doing", "I will help you", "follow the path to the *Maison Multiculturelle* sign", "look at the images we posted", "there are many doors", "what do you think about that", "yes, the different doors show the cultural differences and similarities", "now I understand and I have ideas to contribute with". The organization of the 3D Digital Virtual Worlds forming processes says a lot about the history of the constructor in this digital virtual space.

There is something in the condition of being human that allows the condition of building a history in the flow of interactions with other human beings, and then transforming the living in congruence with the environment. However, even though the nature of human beings is to love, the history of all human beings is not always built on this dimension. Consequently, we can say that we have our behavior culturally molded, influenced by the history of interactions. What we can see is a systemic dynamic between social relation and biological condition. "But nothing can occur in our epigenesis without the permission of our genetics" (Maturana & Verden-Zöller, 2008, p.65).

Social relations between human beings occur by means of emotions, which means, in the love that is based on the "… acceptance of the other as a legitimate other in coexistence with someone else" (p.60). Therefore the relations are constituted by means of the "… mutual trust and the absence of influence or instrumentalization of relations" (p.60), as well as mutual respect in cooperation actions.

In this sense, language has the role of enabling the coexistence between human beings, and unleashing the coordination of consensual behavior coordination in the proximity of coexistence in a permanent or extended relational base.

Human beings, even when represented by their avatars, have biological conditions for coordinating consensual coordination that enable an existence in a recurrent and appropriate dynamic for behavior coordination. In order to emotionally move someone, it is necessary to have recurrent interactions in the relational domain – either permanent or extended. The permanence of emotion allows the continuity of existence by constructing a way of living in the conserved mode of speech from generations to generations in the learning of the youth. Nowadays, however, it is difficult to establish a mode of speech between the different generations. The use of devices[8] (meaning the technology, in this context), according to Rabardel (1999), contributes to the construction of new cognitive schemes, as long as there is an appropriation and adaptation of the device, which will alter human beings' logic of thinking and acting. The fast creation of new technologies may seduce the youth and push adults away. In some situations, interactions are difficult because of an absence of legitimacy from the other and the perspective of coexistence in the comprehension of some human beings.

The conservation of a particular way of living in the emotional and rational intertwining expresses our ability to solve the differences between human beings so that we can change ourselves through conversation. Under such a perspective we can be living an important moment when there are two generations clearly defined and that have different cognitive structures. That difference can result in important discoveries about the living of human beings in congruence with digital technologies.

We can then think about different structural couplings between the different generations (native and digital immigrants), the human being and the avatar and autopoietic and alopoietic machines.

In these couplings, carried out in the living and sharing in digital virtual spaces, we can perceive how digital virtual existence is constituted, under the perspective of overcoming disturbances, in the co-existence of analogical and digital, and above all, in the emancipation of human beings, represented by avatars.

For Maturana (2004), the terms language and emotion are understood as verbs, because they are neither things nor events. Their meaning is not in the object or in people, but instead in the flow of living in coordinations of coordinations, in action. Therefore their objective is to imply that what they mean happens in the action of flow of human beings' living even when in different spaces. We perceive that 3D Digital Virtual Worlds, for their graphic organization represented in 3D, the immersion by telepresence and digital virtual presence and textual, gestural and oral communication process, empower language and emotion in the interaction processes in digital virtual spaces.

Language consists of a recurrent interaction flow that constitutes in a system of consensual behavior coordination of coordination where no behavior, gesture, sound, attitude or isolated movement constitutes only element of language, but it is part of it (Maturana, 2002). Therefore, language happens when two or more people in recursive interaction operate through these interactions in a network of cross-coordination, consensual coordination of actions.

The disturbing elements of human beings in the search of coordinating their own knowledge with somebody else's knowledge, have the objective of structuring an agreement to be considered as the suitable behavior for the group that interacts in their living and sharing, through language.

The central point of language is the coordination of actions as a result of the recurrent interactions within a reflection space, where we can see what we couldn't, which means, we accept the disturbance established in the relation with the other in search of compensation for the disturbance. In this way, being in the language is a way of operating in coordination with consensual coordination of action.

Therefore, human existence happens in language and in the rational, starting from the emotional, meaning it is a unique phenomenon of existence. Since our conception, we have lived immersed in the mode of speech and emotion, and the flow of these two intertwined aspects, according to Maturana (2002), consists of talking. Human beings, then, talk within the flow of their conversation.

During our education we learn and change within this coordination of behavior with other human beings. I can, eventually, coordinate behaviors and coordinate coordination of behavior with my dog. But my dog does not live in coordination of behavior; he does not live in language; he does not carry out language with other dogs. But I keep on doing that continuously. We all do. We are only human because we participate in this kind of activity. (Vaz, 2008, p.65)

Action and behavior have the same meaning in language and in this way, we can talk about the mode of speech as an operation within a space of consensual coordination of behavior, or with an operation within a consensual coordination of action. Maturana (2001), in order to exemplify such a situation, tells the story of the husband who arrives home tired and stressed out after a day at work and a traffic jam. He kisses his wife, fights with the dog, pushes a chair, he is irritated. In such emotional state, he could not kiss anyone, and therefore the emotions are states delimited by the domains of action. We, human beings, live through emotions and in these coordinations with emotions we continue talking, and structurally coupling.

CONCLUSION

The concept of autopoietic machines and alopoietic machines was designed at a time when digital technologies did not have 3D Digital Virtual Worlds. Some further considerations are therefore necessary at this point. To think about coupling between autopoietic and alopoietic machines within a 3D Digital Virtual Worlds context implies three different situations that contribute to broadening of the concept of structural coupling.

To think about autopoietic machines (human beings) coupled to alopoietic machines (avatars) means to characterize the relation established between the human beings and the avatar (depending on the metaverse, it is his avatar). According to the evidence in research carried out by Backes (2011), structural coupling occurs when the human being: chooses or graphically personalizes his avatar in relation to himself (similarly or completely differently); moves the avatar in a way that his field of view allows better actions of construction in relation to the spatial notion (the digital virtual nature, in this case); establishes relations of the mode of speech with other avatars using the resources of gesture, text and voice in the interaction process; and self-produces in geographically localized and digital virtual contexts, also changing his avatar (through a technologized body) as he broadens his knowledge.

To think about autopoietic machines (human beings), represented by avatars, coupled with alopoietic machines (3D Digital Virtual Worlds), according to the evidence in Backes' (2011) research, consists of attributing the coupling other characteristics. Thus, we can say that there are structural couplings between human beings and 3D Digital Virtual Worlds when the human being is able to use the resources available in this space to represent his perception. He knows the nature of the space to choose and the best resource for carrying out his actions and constructs a dynamic and representative in 3D Digital Virtual Worlds of the living and sharing of these e-citizens, who constitute our social systems.

In both situations, we can see the *technological structural coupling*. For Backes (2011), the technological structural coupling is characterized, in the forming process, when human beings use digital technologies in a congruent way to configure existence in recursive living. In this way they use digital technology to empower the possibilities offered, to understand the limits imposed, to create new possibilities not previously attributed and to identify the best opportunity for the development in the learning processes and in the construction of knowledge. In this coupling, the perspective is to develop interaction processes in congruence with technology.

To think about autopoietic machines (human beings), represented by avatars, coupled with other autopoietic machines, also represented by avatars, in congruence with alopoietic machines (3D Digital Virtual Worlds) can represent the coupling of the coupling and that results in the existence of the digital virtual nature between human beings in digital virtual spaces. The digital virtual living and sharing, according to Backes (2011), can be characterized when human beings represent their perceptions in 3D Digital Virtual Worlds, using the available resources and are able to interpret the representation of other human beings, to establish interaction processes using the means of communication present in the 3D Digital Virtual Worlds, to configure the ways of sharing between human beings and are able to, through their autopoiesis, constitute social systems and continuously transform the 3D Digital Virtual Worlds using their capabilities.

In this situation, we can see the *digital virtual structural coupling*. For Backes (2011) the digital virtual structural coupling, in the process of human education, is characterized when the human beings, by living in social systems define everyone's space and configure the common space, and where everybody is a teacher and learner. Therefore, they establish dialogic relations in digital virtual spaces; configure suitable behaviors, constructing social autopoietic systems by hierarchical relations and act in a dynamic way among themselves through digital technology. In this coupling, the perspective is to develop interaction processes in congruence with the social system that is constituted through technology.

The different coupling situations are not necessarily seen separately from the interaction process. This means that, at certain points, we can see a human being coupled to his avatar in a 3D Digital Virtual World, or also, the human being coupled to his avatar and to other human being, in congruence with the 3D Digital Virtual World. The social systems constituted by human beings are dynamic, dialectic and complex.

Lo significativo de la reflexión en le linguaje es que nos lleva a contemplar neustro mondo y el mondo de outro y a hacer de la descripción de nuestra circunstância y la del outro parte del médio en que conservamos identidad y adaptación. La reflexión en el lenguaje nos lleva a ver el mundo em que vivimos y a aceptarlo o rechazarlo conscientemente. (Maturana, 1999, p.32)

The meaning of the reflection of language is what moves us to contemplate our world and the world of others, and to make the description of our own circumstance and of the other through the environment in which we keep our identity and adaptation. The reflection in language is what makes us see the world we live in and accept or deny it conciously. (Maturana, 1999, p.32)

Thus, the structural coupling happens through language in the interaction processes, whose purpose is the transformation of human beings, as they become more consistent and responsible for the world we have, and the environment, as the environment becomes the world we want. In this way, in different dimensions of structural coupling, we can be emancipated human beings.

REFERENCES

Backes, L. (2007). *A formação do educador em mundos virtuais: Uma investigação sobre os processos de autonomia e de autoria*. (Unpublished master's dissertation). Universidade do Vale do Rio dos Sinos, São Leopoldo, Brazil.

Backes, L. (2011). *A configuração do espaço de convivência digital virtual: A cultura emergente no processo de formação do educador.* (Unpublished doctoral thesis). Universidade do Vale do Rio dos Sinos, São Leopoldo, Brazil and Université Lumière Lyon 2, Lyon, France.

Capra, F. (2004). A teia da vida: Uma nova compreensão científica dos sistemas vivos. São Paulo, Brazil: Cultrix.

Lévy, P. (2010). Cibercultura. Rio de Janeiro, Brazil: Editora 34.

Maturana, H. R., & Varela, F. J. (2002). A árvore do conhecimento: As bases biológicas da compreensão humana. São Paulo, Brazil: Palas Athena.

Maturana, H. R. (1999). *Transformación en la convivencia*. Santiago, Chile: Dolmen Ediciones.

Maturana, H. R. (2002). A ontologia da realidade. Belo Horizonte, Brazil: UFMG, 2002.

Maturana, H. R. (2004). Amar e brincar: Fundamentos esquecidos do humano. São Paulo, Brazil: Palas Athena.

Maturana, H. R., & Varela, F. J. (1997). De máquinas e seres vivos: Autopoiese - a organização do vivo. Porto Alegre, Brazil: Artes Médicas.

Maturana, H. R., & Verden-Zöller, G. (2008). A origem do humano. In H. R. Maturana, & S. N. Rezepka (Eds.), Formação humana e capacitação (pp. 59-75). Petrópolis, Brazil: Vozes.

Moraes, M. C. (2003). Educar na biologia do amor e da solidariedade. Petrópolis, Brazil: Vozes.

Rabardel, P. (1999). Le language comme instrument? Eléments pour une théorie instrumentale élargie. In *Y. Clot (Ed.), Avec Vygotsky* (pp. 241–265). Paris: La Dispute.

Santos, M. (1980). Por uma geografia nova: da crítica da geografia a uma geografia crítica. São Paulo, Brazil: Editora HUCITEC.

Varela, F. J. (1997). Prefácio de Francisco J. García Varela. In H. R. Maturana, & F. J. Varela (Eds.), De máquinas e seres vivos: Autopoiese - a organização do vivo. Porto Alegre, Brazil: Artes Médicas.

Vaz, N. M. (2008). O linguagear é o modo de vida que nos tornou humanos. *Ciencia e Cultura, 60*, 62–67. Retrieved from http://cienciaecultura.bvs. br/pdf/cic/v60nspe1/a1160ns1.pdf

KEY TERMS AND DEFINITIONS

Alopoietic Machines: They are not living beings, for their characteristics, they are the non-reproduction and the absence of interaction histories – except for the transformations caused by the history of interactions constructed by the living systems (autopoietic machines) in interaction through alopoietic machines. This way, alopoietic machines are subordinated to living beings, they are dependent on the external relation, who means that, to have a transformation, it is necessary to have an action of autopoietic machines. However, they have their own organization that interferes and determines the interaction process among living systems.

Autopoiesis: The word autopoiesis comes from the Greek word autos, meaning oneself; and poiesis, meaning to produce. When characterizing living beings as autopoietic systems we are saying that they are continuously producing themselves. In other words, by autopoiesis we mean that living beings are networks of molecular productions where the produced molecules generate their interactions in the same network that produces them (Maturana, 1999, p. 93).

Autopoietic Machines: Meaning the living systems that are self-governing units with the ability to reproduce and regenerate, because, according to the previous chapters, they have an organization that preserves a transforming structure, due to their history of interactions. The living being unit is effective in a dynamic and circular way, in the articulation between the organization and the structure, for its self-production, through the autonomy, in which the interpretative capacity comes from its origin.

Digital Virtual Structural Coupling: For Backes (2011), the digital virtual structural coupling, in the human education process, is characterized when human beings, by living in social systems: define everyone's space and configure the common space, where everybody is teacher and learner. They establish, this way, dialogic relations in digital virtual spaces; configure suitable behaviors, constructing social autopoietic systems by hierarchical relations; act in a dynamic way among themselves through digital technology. In this coupling, the perspective is to develop interaction processes in congruence with the social system, that is constituted through technology.

Emotion: The social relation between human beings occur by means of emotions, which means, in the love based in the "… acceptance of the other as a legitimate other in coexistence with someone else" (Maturana & Verden-Zöller, 2008, p. 60). Therefore, relations are constituted by means of "… mutual trust and absence of influence or instrumentalization of relations" (Maturana & Verden-Zöller, 2008, p. 60), as well as mutual respect in cooperation actions.

Language: Consists in a recurrent interaction flow embedded in a system of consensual behavior, coordination of the coordination where no behavior, gesture, sound, attitude or isolated movement constitutes an only element of language, but as

part of it (Maturana, 2002). Therefore, language happens when two or more people, in recursive interaction, operate through these interactions in a network of cross coordination, consensual coordination of actions.

Structural Coupling: When two or more autopoietic units are in an interaction process, one of the units perceives the other unit through its structure, constructed by the ontogeny, therefore unique and peculiar in the sense of legitimacy of the other in order to search for compensation. Structural coupling consists in the mutual modifications between human beings, or autopoietic units, which are in an interaction process without losing identity.

Technological Structural Coupling: For Backes (2011), the technological structural coupling is characterized, in the forming process, when human beings use digital technologies in a congruent way to configure the existence in the recursive living. This way, they use digital technology in a way to empower the possibilities offered, to understand the limits imposed, to create new possibilities not previously attributed, and to identify the best opportunity for the development in the learning processes, and in the construction of knowledge. In this coupling, the perspective is to develop interaction processes in congruence with technology.

ENDNOTES

[1] According to Maturana (2002), cognitive domains are characterized by the legitimation of knowledge, in the action and interaction, inserted in a social context that implies the acceptance of living beings through established criteria.

[2] Environments are the relations that constitute and configure the space that can be of a physical or digital virtual nature.

[3] To digitalize information consists of translating it into numbers. Almost all informa-

tion can be codified this way. For example, if we make that a number corresponds to every letter in the alphabet, any text can be transformed into a series of numbers (Lévy, 2010, p.52).

4   ... every "placeless" entity, capable of generating several concrete manifestations in different moments and determined locations, without thus being itself attached to a particular place or time. To use an example outside the technical sphere a word is a virtual entity. The word "tree" is always being uttered in one place or another, in a certain day in a certain time. We will refer to the utterance of this lexical element as "updating". But the word itself, the one uttered or used in a certain place, is nowhere and is not linked to any particular moment (even though it has not always existed) (Lévy, 2010, pp.49-50).

5   The concept of space under a geographical perspective consists of ... a set of representative forms of social relations from the past and present and by a structure represented by social relations that are happening before our eyes and that are revealed through processes and functions. The space is then a true field of powers whose acceleration is uneven. This is why the special evolution cannot happen in an identical way all over (Santos, 1980,

p.122). Under a systemic perspective we can say that space is "... the domain of all the possible intentions of a collection of units (single or compound, that interact as units) established by these units' properties when specifying their dimensions" (Maturana 2002, p.130).

6   ... we use the expression *unleash* an effect, and what we mean by that is that changes resulting from the interaction of the living being and the environment are unleashed by the perturbing agent and *determined by the structure of the perturbed system* (Maturana & Varela, 2002, p.108).

7   Brazilian and French students who constructed a digital virtual living when establishing rules with the others; when comprehending the living and sharing rules; when considering the other as a legitimate "self" for the interaction processes; when using the digital virtual space to its full potential for the emancipation of the "self" and of others who live and share within the same digital virtual space.

8   "The concept of artifact is used here to refer to something neutral, finished and made by humans. Artifacts can be both concrete or symbolic" (Rabardel, 1999, p.245).

Chapter 8
Cognition and Socio-Cognition in Metaverse

ABSTRACT

This chapter presents and discusses different cognitive and socio-cognitive mechanisms that appear in the interaction between subject-avatars, and between subject-avatars and the 3D Digital Virtual World, constructed in the Metaverses, based on the results from the Digital Education Research Group GPe-dU UNISINOS/CNPq. In these contexts, the authors analyze how perception and representation occurs, the acts of doing, understanding, and raising awareness, and finally, enabling collaboration and cooperation in individual and social interaction with Metaverses. As the main conclusion, the experience built in the subjects' living and collaborating, represented by their avatars, and with MDV3D, favors learning processes, regarding the technical and didactic-pedagogic ownership of metaverse technology, as well as the execution of awareness processes about how learning occurs in these contexts.

INTRODUCTION

Cognition and sociocognition, as well as many other themes addressed in this book, are the subject of investigation in different knowledge areas aiming to understand how individuals learn and develop.

This learning and development is understood in a historical and socially located context, as the world in which the subjects live and socialize develops, evolves, modifies and transforms itself, in a dialectic movement with different technologies. In this process, what Lévy (1993) calls "intelligence technologies", appears, that is the techniques developed by human beings over time to understand the world. To Lévy (1993), three key technologies of intelligence conditioned the human beings' way of thinking: orality, writing and computers, while the fruit of human intelligence also helps to shape it. The author says this is not the replacement of one technology of intelligence by another, but the complexity of processes and displacements of centers of gravity, as they have always been present in human evolution history, and in each historical moment, some characteristics of these technologies are highlighted more than others.

DOI: 10.4018/978-1-4666-6351-0.ch008

It is also not hieirarchical, as they complement and influence each other, without a well-defined border between them.

By referring to the intelligence of technology - computers, we are talking about different digital technologies and with it the importance of conducting research on cognition and sociocognition in relation to the subjects with these technologies. This research becomes increasingly necessary as children, adolescents, and young adults start to live intensely in a highly technologized world. In this context, both individual action and interaction, as action and social interaction occur "to" and "from" those technologies, which led to changes in life and existence in its various aspects.

In this chapter we will discuss the cognitive and socio-cognitive perspective in metaverse technology, from the research results developed by the *Grupo de Pesquisaem Educação Digital GPe-dU UNISINOS/CNPq*, analyzing how perception and representation occur; the acts of doing, the understanding and awareness, and finally enable collaboration and cooperation in individual and social interaction with Metaverses.

HUMAN CONGNITION

"Mom, I beat the book!"this is the way Emanuele, five years old, expressed her joy in having finished reading her first book in its physical form (paper).This child, long before learning to read and write, used digital games, both on consoles and computers (laptops).In digital games, when players finish all levels of a game, doing all the steps and challenges, they use the expression "beat" in the gamers language. To Emanuele the fact she had finished reading all the pages of the book, completing all the steps, meant to "beat" the book. Thus, it is possible to understand a language that comes from an experience in digital media used to mean another experiment in an analog medium. Thus, a child who interacts from a very early age (about one or two years old) with different digital

technologies does not realize the world without these technologies, and therefore sees no need to establish a separation between what is analog and what is digital as they are intertwined.

Schlemmer and Lopes (2012), emphasize that digital technologies, for this generation, represent a place where you can go, be, enter. "Can I go on the computer?", "Mom, I'm on the Internet, I'm on Minecraft[1]", "Mom, can you come into my house? I'll have a party and all my friends will be here." Thinking about these events it is possible to understand that digital technologies represent a place (where you go or where you are) sometimes territories of virtual digital nature where you can immerse, act, interact, build, communicate and socialize. In these digital territories, the notion of belonging has changed, since it is no longer about continuous and contiguous spaces or geographic territories, but of nomadism and transnationalities. Thus, there is deletion of borders, whose "e-living" relations are constituted from a hybridity of thoughts, ideas, languages, knowledge and practices.

So, what is happening? The current generation, for "living", "enter", can act and interact with different digital technologies from an early age, they think with and from digital, which contributes to assigning meanings to the analog world. These may originate in their actions and interactions with and in the digital world, constituting experiences, turning into hypotheses, also used to understand the analog world in which they live. This interactive relationship with digital interfaces has moved to other analog surfaces. It is as if the entire surface "should" or "could" be "clickable" and "draggable". Looking is not enough anymore. Openness is necessary for interaction and exchange of information, new directions in constant updating.

Seymour Papert (1988, p.21), in his research developed at the Massachusetts Institute of Technology (MIT), said: "Children can learn to use computers expertly and this learning can change the way they know other things."

In this context, new ways of thinking and expressing reveal new meanings and diverse ways of perceiving and feeling the world, they belong to, a world constituted by digital technological hybridity, where digital spaces coexist with analog spaces, integrating living and socializing of this generation.

Analyzing human development, human cognition, we look for support in Jean Piaget's Genetic Epistemology - the Swiss epistemologist who investigated human development in the search for understanding the origin of knowledge, and therefore learning. Piaget held the theoretical construction of cognition and social-cognition in a pre-digital historical and social time, reframed his concepts in the context of action and interaction of the subject with the virtual or digital media with a hybrid medium that is both physical-analog and virtual digital.

Piaget (1987), considers the question of intelligence, often defined as an ability to solve problems, whether innate or acquired, asserting it as a function. Thus, like all other functions that ensure the survival of the human organism it is justified only from interaction. If intelligence is a function, how does it work? It always works in the service of adaptation of the subject to exchanges with their environment, being it physical, social, and recently digital virtual.

According to Schlemmer and Lopes (2013), Piaget studied the development of human intelligence from the systematic observation of babies, from their first months of life up to the age of two, before language development. From the moment the child in the womb assimilates information from external environment, they are already forming mental structures that ensure adaptation to changes in the environment. Part of these structures is completely inherited, another part is acquired, and most of it is built. Breathing is an example of inherited structure by the subject, an innate function, but that needs the interaction with the external environment to work and accommodate itself to a new reality, different from the intrauter-ine. Most reflex behaviors are inherited and have a high degree of dependence on the sense organs, making up with these the organic structures.

These structures develop as the individual interacts with the world, so there is not only reflex activity. Then, by organic maturation and interaction with the environment, the adaptive activity of the subject establishes the first acquired habits. This organizing (adaptive) activity is where logical systems are developed and through its action on the environment, the individual coordinates these structures and assigns characteristics to objects, constantly forming new systems of meanings. Thus, based on inherited structures, most of them formed by nervous system structures, and the need for adaptation, humans develop their intelligence, accommodating the peculiarities and particularities of the medium due to the assimilation of novelty in the form of mental representations. It is this interactive relation between the individual and environment that characterizes intelligence as a function and qualifies Piaget's interactionism and constructivism.

Also according to Schlemmer and Lopes (2013), for Piaget the functions of assimilation and accommodation are key elements to understanding this process. Assimilation is what allows the subject to appropriate novelty, retain learning, whether in the form of concrete thinking or complex logical structures, while accommodation is to adapt and altering mental structures the subject has already built, or construction depending on the novelty that presents itself. It is the accommodation that ensures assimilation, while what has been assimilated ensures accommodation of cognitive structures, that is, its adjustment. This process of assimilation and accommodation epitomizes what is most interactive in Piaget's Genetic Epistemology.

Schlemmer and Lopes (2013) draw attention to the fact that Piaget's theory is mistaken for that of behaviorists, because it identifies its idea of structures with nerve structures, neurons and synapses. However, this is not what it is about.

Piaget confuses organic structures, responsible for life maintenance, with mental structures, responsible for adapting the subject to the environment in which he/she lives. They are distinct and interdependent structures. These structures, referred to by Piaget, are logical, they will be linking and coordinating as subsystems and forming new systems of signification. This systemic view of Piagetian constructivism is one of the most difficult points of understanding and gives rise to many misconceptions.

In practice, this phenomenon of the development of intelligence is revealed when the subject is in a rich new environment in which he feels the need to assimilate the unknown. Assimilation, then, is a natural need to know the unknown in order to adapt. It is in the assimilation of the new, the subject rebuilds his thinking structures in new structures of meaning, the new is absorbed by the existing structure. These structures, logical systems, organize the network of meanings that connect to each other in non-sequential order in nonlinear systems, but as the result of a systemic and dynamic development of intelligence.

Thus, Schlemmer and Lopes (2013) say that from the assumptions of the genetic epistemology of Piaget on the importance of action and interaction of the individual in relation to learning and self-development of human intelligence, we can assume that digital culture, with its multiple modes of communication and interaction, has enabled new ways to develop intelligence. However, it is important to note that Piaget conducted his research at a time when children and adolescents had a more limited access to information, usually confined to the local context, nearby. At that time, the means for mass communication were in their infancy, reading books and printed materials was one of the few ways to expand the boundaries of local reality, as well as contact with foreigners and people from the community whom shared their personal experiences. Therefore, to think of

Piaget today you need to consider such changes and, especially the centrality that communication takes in the discussion of networked learning.

For Schlemmer and Lopes (2013), from the epistemological point of view, the Piagetian theoretical framework for thinking about the role of action in learning remains fruitful, especially considering the idea of interaction of the very idea of action. The fundamental difference in this case lies in the fact that the Piagetian model treats the theme of interaction in the subject-object relationship, often resorting to the notion of logical- mathematical schemes to think about learning according to a representative matrix. This intelligence operation structured by logical-mathematical schemes, as already explained, relates to the need to adapt the subject, with the novelty element unbalancing. Thus, for Piaget, the search for balance never ceases, it is a continuous movement that is the matrix of human development. However, with regard to the processes of socialization, these logical- mathematical schemes are not always able explain the gaps left by the balancing process. If we consider an equation, which accounts for the social phenomena, we see that the gaps, imbalances and random inconsistency set the tone of what would be social. Similarly, you cannot think of a social development as something that causes or resolves only from heuristics - cause and effect. For the social fact, one event does not necessarily lead to another. The idea of addressed and balanced operations in the relationship between two or more people does not consider, mainly that social interaction is a communication phenomenon and therefore subject to all kinds of noise and interference, internal and external to the subject.

Another important element to consider in relation to social interactions, highlighted by Schlemmer and Lopes (2013), concerns the social-historical aspect that is at the heart of the phenomenon of human communication. The development of human language, such as a socio-technical phenomenon of the body itself, inexorably carries a legacy that is both biological and social in time. The transformation itself historically referenced in systems and ways to communicate denotes that language and thought are altered according to the time and place in which you live. In this sense, Piaget contributed to dealing with language in the perspective of the production systems of signification, which enables us to say that, culturally speaking, the more diverse the environment of a child, the more conditions they will have to appropriate the signs of culture.

An important point to consider, according to Piaget, is that the child's thinking develops from the need to formalize and demonstrate the theme of communication, and it becomes very important, because the digital culture is also network communication. Learning "with" seems to be an imperative of digital culture at the same time as a desired socio-political ideal. In fact, the semiotic universe of cyberspace has shown that culture is a network of meanings and signifiers that we all share, regardless of whether we are online. The idea of culture as a manifestation of collective intelligence reinforces the idea that developing is mainly socializing. In this sense, we are all authors and actors of ourselves, and others as we interact.

Maturana and Varela help in understanding human cognition. As presented in Chapter 7 -Autopoietic machines and alopoietic machines: structural coupling, the entire unit or system has an organization, that is, the set of relations that are necessarily present in the system that you define in their existence. The number of effective relationships between the components in a particular machine within a given space constitute its structure.

Every living organism is disturbed (not determined) by the environment, and the disturbances are interpreted and subjected to an internal balancing mechanism. These internal changes are the common thread. A disruption - does not specify the agent, does not take into account its effects on the structure of the unit, and does not take part of the definition of the unit although it can be connected to it. A given disruption can happen in an indefinite number of ways.

In interactions between living organisms and the environment within the structural congruence, the disruption of the environment does not determine what happens to the living being, but rather it is the structure of the living being that determines what should happen to him.... In this sense, we referred to the fact that the changes that result from interaction between living things and their environments are caused by interference agents, but determined by the structure of the perturbed system. (Maturana, 1992, p.96)

The existence of each organism has its origin as a cell, which has certain initial structures, and these are the result of the history of phylogeny. Continuing the historicity of the body, we are building another story through our life experiences, according to the society in which we live. Our human body has the same organization of living beings, but with a different structure acquires originality as it interacts with the environment. The history of changes in the structure of an organism that is in interaction with others and the environment is the ontogeny and this occurs in structural drift.

In this, the structural changes that occur are contingent on interactions with the environment. They are not determined by the circumstances of the medium, but are contingent with them, because the medium only triggers structural changes in the living being. In addition, the environment changes in a contingent way with the interactions with the organism (Maturana, 2001, p.82).

Formed by a molecular dynamic the body arranges and rearranges itself in terms of the provocations from environment, people and society we live with, while being a disruptive agent, modifying them. This circularity between body and world also expands the understanding of cognition, through studies of perception. Maturana and Varela (1997) consider the nervous system as a closed system, i.e., functioning as a closed network of variable activity relations. Thus, the body and nervous system are in different domains, which interact through sensors elements and effectors. Moreover, as the organism interacts with the environment through structural coupling the nervous system generates sense-effector correlations that give rise to behavior. We understand how the interaction between organisms, the environment and culture occurs, which leads us observe that, even though the body is autonomous it maintains dependence on environment.

Thus, with respect to cognition in Metaverses we can say the subject is represented by his avatar, from existing mental structures, arising from his ontogeny (thus, built over his life and living in a world that is currently hybrid - analog and digital). This happens through its action in and on the metaverse (3D digital virtual worlds) and in interaction with other subject-avatars, it processes information from environment, in this case 3D digital virtual worlds accommodating peculiarities and particularities of these worlds as a function of the need to assimilate novelty. This process may involve the modification of existing structures and/or building new structures, which enable it to adapt to the changes of the medium. Thus, the subject coordinates these structures and assigns properties to objects, constantly building new systems of meanings.

According to research conducted by Schlemmer (2005, 2008, 2009, 2013a, 2013b), linked to initial and continuous teacher training, regarding cognition in metaverses, the categories that emerge with the highest incidence are autonomy, disruption, regulation of imbalances, awareness and metacognition. *Autonomy*[2] prevails due to the need for action and interaction with and in 3D digital virtual worlds to build them, which is related to *disruption*[3] and consequently to the *regulation of imbalances*[4], followed by *awareness* and *metacognition*[5], enhancing learning.

PERCEPTION AND REPRESENTATION

Regarding perception and representation, we once more look for theoretical support in Piaget who deals with perception from two major divisions: the theory of perception –which determines a probabilistic model of how perception works from elements, stimuli, and the theory of perception - which is an overview of perception and its development mainly in its relationship with intelligence.

As referenced in earlier chapters, Piaget says knowledge is not a copy of reality, and does not credit the source of intelligence only to perception. It breaks with the empiricist tradition. "Intelligence comes from an action as a whole, as it transforms objects and the real, and ... knowledge... is essentially active and operative assimilation" (Piaget & Inhelder, 1993, p.30). The authors state that besides the existence of sensations, and reason in mental life, the importance of action cannot be neglected, "perception is, in fact, a particular case of sensory-motor activities" (p.30), it is a function, which is related to the subject's activity, thus not a mere portrait of the real as it is guided by intelligence, that is, "perceptive activities develop with age until they bend to policies suggested by intelligence in its operative progress" (p.40).

The content and development of a concept do not come from perception; as empiricism says, and do not necessarily succeed it. The structuring of concept occurs from non-perceptual content, which comes from action or operations. Development cannot overlook these non-perceptual factors, since perception provides only "... snapshots of this or that point of view, which is the subject for the regarded time, while notion presupposes the coordination of all points of view and understanding of transformations that lead from one point of view to another" (p.42). This coordination requires the activity of the subject not due to perceptual data, since perception itself is driven by it.

Piaget tells us that representation is an extension of perception, which includes the sensations arising from the subject-environment interaction, to the conscious constructions these subjects make from their experiences, memories and mental schemes. Thus, perception is not a mixture of sensations, but a composition of sensations, requiring action of the subject on the object, which reacts to the subject. All perception and representation assume an abstraction, which can occur at different levels, that is, both processes may come from empirical abstraction, as well as a process of reflective abstraction. For Piaget (1995) apud Schlemmer (2002), all new knowledge presupposes abstraction. Abstracting, in a broad sense, consists of differentiation. Separating a feature means isolating certain characteristics from others.

According to Piaget (1995), empirical abstraction is purely descriptive, referring to an immediate confirmation, it is everything that the subject takes from that which is directly observable. However, for the subject to abstract the properties of an object the needs the instruments of assimilation, i.e., it must have a meaning to it. The subject needs to establish relationships and these come from sensory-motor or conceptual schemes that the subject built previously and which are not given by the object. These schemes are needed, on an experimental basis, for empirical abstraction; however, it does not refer to them but instead searches the content (exterior data) that was framed in forms (which will enable the capture of content) by schemes. "From certain concepts (which are the product of reflective abstractions of previous levels) and, through a process of empirical abstraction, certain features are identified on which to build new concepts directly applicable to a given domain of reality" (Piaget & Garcia, 1998, p.192-193). Empirical abstraction implies a construction of concepts. This construction is completed with the extension of concepts to other domains of reality.

Reflective abstraction relies on coordination of actions or operations, (therefore on the activity of the subject). Every time the object is modified by actions of the subject, and enriched by property taken from their coordination, the abstraction performed by the subject is called "pseudo-empirical", because it still needs the object as support, where relations are made from actions on the object, i.e., everything the subject removes from the non-observable, which the object informs after the action of the subject, revealing something that did not exist before the action was performed. In other words, the properties do not exist in objects, it is the subject who does the relation and puts it in objects, because even if it is performed on the object and its observable at the time, as empirical abstraction, the coordinating of his actions, therefore, a particular case of reflective abstraction, produces the findings of the subject. Thus, when the result of a reflective abstraction becomes conscious (i.e., there is an awareness of the new instruments of reasoning used); regardless of the level, there is "reflected" abstraction. Reflected abstraction is based on the forms and in the subject's cognitive activities (schemes or coordination's of actions, operations etc.), where something is taken to be used for other purposes (new adaptations, new problems etc.). In other words, reflected abstraction is the result of reflective abstraction, the subject performs the awareness of the relation used; they are, therefore, reflections on reflections. In this case, the reflection is this awareness and a possibility of formalization.

In reflective abstraction reflection and reflectioning are present, which are two inseparable and complementary aspects that go together and appear in all stages of human development. Reflectioning is the projection (such as through a reflector) to a higher level, that what was taken from a lower level (e.g., from action to representation). Reflection is the reconstruction or cognitive reorganization of what was transferred, enabling the enrichment of the extracted knowledge. "... It is necessary that this abstraction is not limited to using a series of hierarchical levels whose formation would be foreign to it: it is what engenders the conversion of alternating interactions and reflections ..."(Piaget, 1985, p.39 apud Schlemmer, 2002, p.55).

When we talk about perception and representation we always do so in relation to the one who perceives and represents, the one Maturana and Varela (1997, 2002) call the observer (not in the sense of someone who watches a phenomenon, but an active observer in action). These theorists conceive that all explanations are made by an observer of the phenomenon, so everything that is said, is said by an observer, with the operation of distinction basic cognitive operation we perform as an observer. The act of description of the phenomenon, i.e. representation creates a new phenomenological domain, the domain of description of the phenomenon. These authors draw our attention to knowledge as action, telling us:

From the perspective of descriptive meta-domain, the distinction between the characterization of a drive and knowledge of the observer that allows you to describe it in context should be clear. Indeed, knowledge always involves a concrete or conceptual action in some domain and recognition of knowledge always involves an observer who contemplates the action of a meta-domain. (Maturana, 1980, p.22)

Maturana and Varela tell us that the nervous system and the brain do not work like a computer, because the nervous system does not "collect" information from the environment and "treats" it. In addition, there is not a representation of the outside world in the animal or human brain. However, the nervous system is an operationally closed system, structurally determined without inputs or outputs, i.e., working as an autonomous and autopoietic system. Thus, the results of operations of the system are its own operations. Each time it

tries to find the source of a perception he is faced with something like "the perception of perception of perception ..." (Varela, 1989, p.29). Perception is a process of compensation the nervous system makes in the course of interaction.

From this perspective, Maturana and Varela (1997) differ from what is recommended by Neurophysiology and Psychology, based on classical postulates, as the phenomenon of perception is connoted as a funding operation of an external reality, through a process of receiving information of reality. For these authors, learning is the transformation occurring in the set of possible states of a nervous system. Thus, learning is not a process of accumulation of representations of the environment; it is an ongoing process of structural transformation, a body suffers due to the conservation of its autopoiesis[6].

Maturana and Varela (1997), when critical to representation as responsible for the cognitive phenomenon also intended to replace the notion of input-output, which makes the body a system of information processing, the basis of traditional thinking. They then propose, through historical reciprocity, a new definition to show the interaction between an autonomous system and its environment, calling it enaction.

Enaction displaces the role of representation in considering that knowledge is embedded, i.e., it refers to the fact that we are the body. Enaction, then, emphasizes the existential dimension of knowing, emerging from corporeality. Cognition depends on the experience that happens in bodily action. This action is linked to the sensory-motor capabilities involved in the biopsychocultural context. The term means that the sensory-motor processes, perception and action are essentially inseparable from cognition.

So, what can we say about perception and representation in the metaverse? From the point of view of the genetic epistemology of Piaget, Schlemmer (2005, 2008) identified in her research with metaverses, linked to initial and continuing teacher education, a higher incidence of representations arising from processes of empirical abstractions, and at first, the representation of subjects was related to the environment as "novelty", and the avatar as "character ... puppets that moved, a puppet in the case represented them" but did not identify a "purpose", failing to understand how it "worked", emphasizing the incompleteness in significance. As interaction intensifies, so do expressions of satisfaction with the ability to "be interacting with colleagues and other people who were online at that moment", and also observe that it is something new, allowing another way to learn. "The experience of learning in interaction in this environment is new, causing multiple sensations, such as the initial distress, but the satisfaction of realizing I am learning and ina method that is completely different from the traditional one in which we are rooted."

This happens because it is an emerging technology, and presents significant cognitive novelty (graphical 3D representation, teleportation, representing the "virtual digital I", different forms of communication and representation - textual, gestural, graphic and oral) to the subject when compared with the history of interactions with digital technologies already known, which, in most cases, have a predominantly textual form of communication, and with which they are more familiar. Thus, there is an initial estrangement due to the complexity of technology, which requires more time for appropriation and familiarity. These representations are manifested mainly by the need to understand the technology and the doubts and difficulties encountered in exploration.

However, considering the concept of enaction of Maturana and Varela (1997), we realized that in the case of metaverse, knowledge is incorporated and cognition depends on the experience that happens in bodily action. So what happens when that experience occurs in digital virtual worlds in 3D, where the subject has a digital virtual body, also in 3D? As the subject understands and becomes aware of living an experience –the act?

DOING, UNDERSTANDING, AND AWARENESS IN METAVERSE

According to Piaget (1978) acting, can be observed as an object of understanding and recreating. The author says the essence of development, that is, the action is fundamental for the subject to learn and build knowledge. The action constitutes an autonomous knowledge *savoir-faire*, and the conceptualization happens through later awareness. Both (action and conceptualization) proceed according to a law of succession that goes from adaptation zones to the object to reach internal coordination of actions, and, from a certain level there is the influence resulting from action conceptualization. The concept provides the action with more coordination power, already immanent to action, and without which the subject establishes boundaries between his practice (what to do to succeed?) and the system of his concepts (why things happen this way?).

According to Piaget (1978), "awareness" is a conduit for interaction with all others, "it is a true construction, which develops, not "the" consciousness as a whole, but different levels as more or less integrated systems" (p.9). However, Piaget was restricted to studying "awareness" from the point of view of the conduits, from material actions to operations. The issue is establishing what the subject is aware of in his own actions, and especially what he observes from manifest regulations. "The awareness of a scheme of action turns it into a concept, being this awareness, therefore, essentially, a conceptualization" (p.197).

From the point of view of Piaget's Genetic Epistemology, Schlemmer (2005, 2008) identified in the Metaverse research linked to initial and continuing education of teachers, that behavior related to doing, understanding and awareness has occurred since the free exploration - familiarization up to the level of construction, of digital virtual worlds in 3D.

In the sphere of the free exploration area and familiarization with Metaverse technology, acting (herein understood as the action in and with Metaverse) occurs, at first, individually, depending on the need of creating the avatar, however, without a higher understanding from the subject of the reasons for this avatar. This understanding only happens when the subject effectively enters the MDV3D, sees himself represented by his avatar and needs to learn how to move around, interacting with and in MDV3D, as well with the other subject-avatars. At this moment, such acting also turns into a social aspect, which happens in the relation with other subject-avatars. In this way the subject, through this MDV3D experience, establishes relations with other known technologies and starts to establish differences and integrations leading to the comprehension, regarding the environment, resulting in an awareness-building process about his limitations and potentialities.

As familiarization unfolds, comprehension enhances action in a way that makes it more effective in the environment, creating a successive cycle, empowering the subject regarding the signification and appropriation of technology, up to the level of building spaces in 3D, in the Metaverse. In this process, ways of awareness-building are seen in the act of doing and understanding, which work as the "engine" of the new act of doing.

In terms of of construction of spaces in 3D the need to organize groups and plan actions arises. At this moment, recognizing the other as a legitimate entity, different from me, in the interaction, starts to be understood as essential for accomplishing the action plan, therefore the constructions, because the legitimacy of the other enables the variety of knowledge. In this way, participants feel the need to make exchanges with other avatars who are not part of the group in the Metaverse they are in (for this technology allows any subject-avatar to enter the worlds under construction), and therefore they are also understood as legitimate in helping them amplify the significance of the environment. It is interesting to observe that in the initial moment in which the group is being organized and planning actions, the subjects report that they feel the need to finding a physical presential way in order to better organize and accomplish the initial planning of their actions.

Subjects' perception of learning in metaverse, as well as how such learning takes place, where it was identified:

- There are different kinds of information representation in the same space (video, audio, text, images, animations, diagrams, charts, 3D objects, etc.);
- The construction of 3D digital virtual worlds in metaverses makes the learning process visible, not only in handling the experience of exchange with the objects but also among subjects which need not be present physically, time and space start to have a different meaning;
- There is a need to develop digital culture and reframe the forms of interaction and knowledge representation, as in the metaverse it is possible to simultaneously use textual, oral, gestural and graphic language to interact and represent knowledge;
- 3D digital virtual worlds are not ready, they are built as they are used as a space for interaction, on the subject of the action;
- The experience with 3D digital virtual worlds contributes to learning about learning, also observing and learning from others mainly through interaction with individuals trained in different fields of knowledge - the importance of differences and contradictions - through them is occurring movement for learning - the interactions with different areas of knowledge are more complex, difficult and rich;
- Spaces are complementary, and each has its own characteristics, different forms of knowledge representation.

Interpersonal relationships and the subjects reportedthat 3D digital virtual worlds changed the way they interact with others in the following aspects:

- **Approximation of Subjects:** A function of social presence through the avatar, there is a greater perception of the other, of his presence, thus resulting in increasing the motivation to know each other, talk, interact;
- **Lighter, Freer and More Imaginative Relationships:** Seem to playfully push the imagination about the "real other" while I know him/her "virtually";
- The interaction between subjects becomes more real, objective - depending on the 3D view of the avatar;
- The interaction becomes more free, peaceful, and facilitated dialogue is open, generating more exchanges, as everything is possible, it is the subject who leads - there is a sense of security in expressing emotions, doubts, concerns depending on the subject feeling protected by their representation via avatar (each is represented by an 'other'), which generates attitude;
- This shows that emotions arise in online interaction, however, are manifested in other ways (image, text, action, and movement). We also observe a relationship between freedom of action, emotions, doubts, concerns and avatar representation, understood as a way of hiding the identity of the subject.

The presence of metaverse technology in educational processes, and the need for professional skills identified as critical, highlighting the importance of teacher training in the experience, for qualified use of this technology.

The following understanding were also established:

- Metaverses give rise to more interest in learning;
- The possibility of working knowledge non-linearly;
- The processes of construction and reconstruction as fundamental to learning;
- The possibility of creativity development;
- The possibility of can acting with greater autonomy, (re)signifying the forms of interaction leads to act more freely, giving forms and giving words to thoughts;
- When media changes, the processes of teaching and learning need to be rethought,due to the emergence of new elements in the virtual digital interactions (3D environments, social presence via an avatar), the issues of time and space, simultaneity of processes, highlighting the need for different new practices and various methodologies that can fully exploit this medium for learning.

Thus, with respect todoing and understanding, as well as awareness in metaverses, we can say that subjects identify the virtual digital space as a space in which they must "learn to organize themselves" and as something that "arouses curiosity" represents "something new, new learning". More frequent interaction determines the extent to which the subjects begin to develop certain confidence and tranquility, starting a process of reflection about their learning process, the possibilities offered by this new space and the importance of teachers appropriating this technology. Learning starts to be understood as something that depends on mutual effort between teacher and student and that occurs through interaction, discussion, analysis, problematizations, sharing the knowledge of each one. Different coordination's of coordination of actions that occur in interactions start to appear, in that the subjects broaden their understanding of other living situations, articulate knowledge, build new knowledge and make their disturbances also start to emerge, transforming their living.

One of the issues highlighted relates to the fact that being in 3D digital virtual worlds impliespresence, in the sense of action, interaction, unlike as often happens in the physical classroom mode, in which presence is frequentlylegitimized simply as a function of the present body. The environment itself favors a broader analysis of what is happening,which may be due to the newness. Another question concerns the perception that relations are not cold, but there are several expressions of emotions during the interaction process. Some subjects expressed the fact that they had difficulty in positioning, and interaction in metaverses via avatar, helped in thinking about this difficulty, as well as overcoming it. The fact that the subject could be "hidden" in an avatar helps them to feel freer to interact, to stand, to position themselves in relation to the processes. The teacher trainers also expressed one of the biggest lessons was to recognize the fear of the new. Another perception is related to the fact that school favors typographic reading, instead of learning to read images and various representations, such as art and graphics and metaverse technology. To act more in terms of graphics, can contribute in this sense.

Having the experience of exploring metaverse technology provides learning in a more interesting way, different to that which we are used to, as all are subjects of their process and developautonomy for exploring what interests them, making decisions, and being active and not passive. This kind of possibility leads to successful learning and not make-believe, as frequently happens in many classrooms.

It is important to highlight, especially during the construction of digital virtual worlds in 3D, that research results indicate a high level of awareness of behaviors arising from making and understanding, linked to autonomy behaviors, mutual respect and cooperation.

COLLABORATION AND COOPERATION

In order to understand the processes of collaboration and cooperation we looked for foundation in the socio-cognitive theory of Jean Piaget and the studies of Maturana and Varela.

To Piaget (1973), when there is a subject-object relationship, where the subject is a "we" and the object is other subjects, the interaction happens in a way that knowledge does not come from the subject neither the object, but the inseparable interaction between them, the interpersonal interactions, to move in two directions of an objectifying externalization and reflexive internalization. Therefore, he understands that mental facts are parallel to social facts, where "I" is replaced by "we" and "actions" and "operations" become "interactions" or forms of "cooperation".The collective dimension allows modifying interactions aiming a coordinated action, through cooperation. Thus, cooperation is identified as a process in action. According to Piaget (1973, p. 105) "to cooperate in action is to operate in common, to adjust through new matching operations (qualitative or metric), reciprocity and complementarity, the actions performed by each of the partners."

Cooperation is characterized bycoordination of different views; through correspondence, reciprocity and complementarity operations, and the existence of autonomous rules and behaviors based on mutual respect. According Schlemmer (2001), when subjects have a common system of hypotheses or conventions, which can be the basis for other reconstructions, there is a convergence in communication and correspondence between operations. Thus, the balance conquered by the cooperative exchanges takes the form of a system of reciprocal operations. Thus, for real cooperation, Piaget (1973) states the following conditions are necessary: the existence of a common value scale, this scale conservation and reciprocity in the interaction. These three conditions of balance are not facilitating, in relationships that present egocentrism or coercion.

Also according to Schlemmer (2001), awareness of own thinking is stimulated by cooperation. Cooperation implies the autonomy of individuals, i.e., freedom of thought, moral liberty, being required to drive the individual to objectivity, which assumes the coordination of perspectives, while in himself the self remains a prisoner of his private perspective. However, you must understand that "freedom, arising from cooperation is not anarchy or anomie: it is autonomy, i.e. the submission of the individual to a discipline which he chooses and for the establishment of which he collaborates with all its personality" (Parrat & Tryphon, 1998, p.154).

Thus, one can say that cooperation is indeed creative, and when developed the rules become internalized, individuals truly collaborate and leaders only continue being recognized as such, if they incarnate, for their own personal worth, the group ideal. The work is developed not because of external constraints, but intrinsic interests that are the subject of a full internal assent. The members of the group at the same time are units of stimulation and control. Group work has advantages from the point of view of thought formation because personal activity develops freely in an atmosphere of mutual control and reciprocity. Invention and verification are the two poles of this activity.

From the moral point of view cooperation leads to an ethic of solidarity and reciprocity. From an intellectual point of view, that cooperation among individuals leads to mutual criticism and progressive objectivity.

Maturana (2000, 2001) reaffirms that our nature is typically focused on interaction, collaboration, cooperation and legitimacy of the other. The human being is a collaborative and cooperative

quintessential animal; it inhabits a network of cooperative social relationships. This network requires confidence, respect and the absence of domination and manipulation among people. Maturana (1993),

Cooperation only happens with the acceptance of the other. In a relation of domination and submission there is no cooperation, there is obedience, there is submission. Cooperation exists only as a phenomenon in space where the relationship is one in which participants emerge as legitimate in living (p.69).

Therefore, for cooperation to exist it is necessary to legitimate, respect and accept the other equally, and configure a living space. Thus, education means developing in partnership with other beings, that is, our living beings as "linguajantes", cooperative and loving, respecting oneself and the others. In this context, we agree with Maturana and Rezepka (2000):

The task of education is to educate humans for the present, any present, beings in which any human being can trust and respect, being able to think of everything and do whatever it takes, and act responsibly from his social conscience. (p.10)

According to research conducted by Schlemmer (2005, 2008, 2009, 2013a, 2013b), linked to initial teacher training, continuing and graduate level, regarding collaboration and cooperation in metaverse, it was observed that, at first, especially during familiarization with the technology metaverse, collaborative behavior appeared most, which is linked to the need for exchanges of information about what each subject-avatar discovers regarding the exploration of technology, being a process of mutual aid.

Secondly, when it comes to organizing groups and planning of construction in 3D digital virtual worlds collaborative processes slowly start to give way to cooperation processes. These arise mainly during the process of replanning actions and the effective construction of digital virtual worlds in 3D. Thus, we clearly show coordination from different points of view, by correspondence, reciprocity and complementarity operations, the construction of autonomous rules of conduct in interaction, based on mutual respect (considering the fact that the subjects believe that one can learn from the other and in this sense are equal and respect one another) and internal solidarity (they create the laws, so they are internal and subject to continuous review and adjustments).

We can say that there is internal solidarity when a group of individuals are prepared and accept the rule and respect each other. Subjects perceive the need for action and interaction with other subjects as fundamental to the construction of the world, from a common system of hypotheses or conventions, which involves the construction of a 3Ddigital virtual world, and they begin the constructions and reconstructions, causing convergence in communication and correspondence between operations. Thus, the balance achieved by cooperative exchanges takes the form of a system of reciprocal operations.

However, according to the groups, while one unit advances in the construction process new collaboration and cooperation between subject-avatars arises in different groups, which contributes to the formation of a "true virtual learning community". However, it also raises some behaviors of coercion and conformity, mainly due to the anxiety explained by some subjects-avatars, associated with a "certain control" of the construction process of worlds.

It is important to remember that the forms of collaboration and cooperation that we can see in an educational context relate to the belief of the teacher on how the subject knows/learns with the methodology, the pedagogical practices and the means used to develop the process of pedagogical mediation. This set of elements can facilitate or not the development of teamwork, as a proposal for group work, the different individuals that compose it, need to come together around a problem, task, common goal, seeking to share their ideas, experience and knowledge and striving collaboratively and/or cooperatively in order to collectively achieve the goals set.

Thus, if methodology and teaching practice propose, for example, the resolution of challenges or development of learning projects in small groups, involving different themes, it contributes to a more effective process of collaboration and cooperation at the micro level within each group, and a less effective level of cooperation and lack of cooperation by the macro context a group formed by all subjects-avatars. Favouring a micro context, even unintentionally, can set a limit for collaboration and cooperation network at the macro level. This points to the need for a process that is observed in the formative processes, a mediation that encourages interaction between different groups or that the challenges and projects are proposed within the group as a whole, in which more effective interaction between the different groups is necessary.

Group work, through collaboration and cooperation, allows the subjects who integrate it the ability to reflect on the opinions of others and relate to theirs, the opportunity for expression of thoughts in order to make themselves understood by all, and understand all and the ability to learn to deal with the acceptance of criticism, favoring reciprocity, mutual respect and solidarity.

Cooperation assumes the autonomy of individuals. You could say that cooperation is effectively a process of creative character and when it develops the rules it becomes internalized, individuals truly collaborate and leaders only continue to be recognized, if they embody, for their personal worth, the ideal of the group itself. This cooperation of the moral point of view provides an ethic of solidarity and reciprocity, and an intellectual point of view provides mutual criticism and progressive objectivity. Therefore, the ideal of cooperation that aims for education rests on the notions of solidarity and justice.

In the work done in all fields of human knowledge, one must seek an atmosphere of reciprocity and cooperation, both intellectual and moral. It is essential the working group in which subjects are a true society, practices free discussion and objective research. Only then, the ideals of solidarity and justice lived before the object of reflection, may lead to effective learning.

CONCLUSION

The experience built through life and coexistence of subjects, represented by their avatars, and with 3D digital virtual worlds, favors learning processes as regarding technical and didactic-pedagogic ownership of metaverse technology as well as the execution of processes of awareness of how learning occurs in these contexts. Regarding the cognitive mechanisms,disturbance processes are identified, mainly caused by the novelty represented by technology and regulating processes of imbalances driven by autonomy in action and interaction of subjects-avatars with worlds, as well as with other avatars. Doing emerges as crucial to the understanding, yielding processes awareness and metacognition. The emergence of a high level of autonomy can be attributed to the specifics related to the context in the 3D digital virtual worldsdepending on: the need for new ways to understand, communicate and move in this new space; and actions, interventions of other subjects-avatars as a disturbing element that through regulations causes awareness. Regarding sociocognition cooperation appears mainly at the time as organization of the subjects, the planning and distribution of shares as well as the construction of interaction rules among them that arise during the operation and construction of 3D digital virtual worlds processes interdisciplinary interaction, which are based on relationships of mutual respect and internal solidarity.

Regarding the construction of 3D digital virtual worlds it was observed that the learning technology, the construction of the world's important resources occurred to the extent that was necessary, having meaning for the subject (in this case, initial teacher training, continuing and postgraduate level). Thus, the subjects understood that learning occurs because of the need for, at that time, new information that becomes meaningful because of the context and the relationships established. Although the subjects had at their disposal an online tutorial especially designed to support the construction of the world, which was offered in a workshop, this information only made sense, and was only learned, if it was transformed into knowledge, when the subject needed to use it to effect certain action building in the world. This allowed the incorporation of learning in teaching practice. It is also important to consider that for the teacher to develop a teaching practice with the use of this technology means that it is important to experience, to try, to have the ability to move, communicate, act and interact in the world, "to be the subject as a world builder", i.e., being immersed in the training process. Thus, the teacher can realize the potential of these spaces for learning, identifying possibilities and limitations of this technology and develop culture of online work in 3D graphics environments.

Thus, based on research carried out by Schlemmer (2000, 2001, 2002, 2004, 2005, 2008, 2009, 2013a, 2013b), Schlemmer et al. (2006), Schlemmer and Trein(2009), Trein and Schlemmer (2009) for the teacher-researcher in the field of Education develops the skills related to "Digital Education" is fundamental that they may experience a process of "Digital Education". Teacher-researchers may experience, in their formative process using different digital technologies in different modalities, pervaded by the paradigm of learning culture and collaborative and cooperative work, network, based on mutual respect and internal solidarity, in order to foster the development of individual and social autonomy, autopoiesis, manufacturing and creative authorship (Backes, 2007), in an interdisciplinary context (a characteristic digital

Education area) in which couplings occur: structural, structural technological and structural of virtual digital nature (Backes, 2011). However, to make this possible it is necessary to take into account of a deep change in the way teachers are trained/qualified, so that it is possible to signify this new reality within the pedagogical practices using different digital technologies.

This leads us to question the effectiveness of training courses for the teachers to "use", for the "application" of digital technologies as a prerequisite for teaching activities. The research results indicate the fact that teachers are not yet immersed in "digital culture" contributing to further evidence that teacher training needs to occur during the teaching activity and not in a detached way, as a prerequisite, which could lead to frustration and failure when teachers need to incorporate digital technologies to their practice. Training in action allows monitoring of the subject who is starting the use of digital technologies, facilitating the understanding of the theory that is based on situations encountered in his own teaching practice.

REFERENCES

Backes, L. (2007). *A formação do educador em mundos virtuais: Uma investigação sobre os processos de autonomia e de autoria.* (Unpublished master's dissertation). Universidade do Vale do Rio dos Sinos, São Leopoldo, Brazil.

Backes, L. (2011). *A configuração do espaço de convivência digital virtual: A cultura emergente no processo de formação do educador.* (Unpublished doctoral thesis). Universidade do Vale do Rio dos Sinos, São Leopoldo, Brazil and Université Lumière Lyon 2, Lyon, France.

Lévy, P. (1993). As tecnologias da inteligência: O futuro do pensamento na era da informática. Rio de Janeiro, Brazil: Editora 34.

Maturana, H. R. (1980). *Autopoiesi and cognition - The realization of the living.* Boston: D. Reidel Publishing Company. doi:10.1007/978-94-009-8947-4

Maturana, H. R. (1992). Conhecer o conhecer. *Ciência Hoje, 14*(184), 44–49.

Maturana, H. R. (1993). Uma nova concepção de aprendizagem. *Dois Pontos, 2*(15), 28–35.

Maturana, H. R. (2001). Cognição, ciência e vida cotidiana. Belo Horizonte, Brazil: Ed. UFMG.

Maturana, H. R., & de Rezepka, S. N. (2000). Formação humana e capacitação. Petrópolis, Brazil: Vozes.

Maturana, H. R., & Varela, F. J. (1997). De máquinas e seres vivos: Autopoiese - a organização do vivo. Porto Alegre, Brazil: Artes Médicas.

Maturana, H. R., & Varela, F. J. (2002). A árvore do conhecimento: As bases biológicas da compreensão humana. São Paulo, Brazil: Palas Athena.

Papert, S. (1988). Logo: Computadores e educação. São Paulo, Brazil: Brasiliense.

Parrat, S., & Tryphon, A. (1998). Jean Piaget: Sobre a pedagogia: Textos inéditos. São Paulo, Brazil: Casa do Psicólogo.

Piaget, J. (1973). Estudos sociológicos. Rio de Janeiro, Brazil: Companhia Editora Forense.

Piaget, J. (1978). Fazer e compreender. São Paulo, Brazil: Melhoramentos.

Piaget, J. (1987). O nascimento da inteligência na criança (4th ed.). Rio de Janeiro, Brazil: Guanabara.

Piaget, J. (1995). Abstração reflexionante: Relações lógico-aritméticas e ordem das relações espaciais. Porto Alegre, Brazil: Artes Médicas.

Piaget, J., & Garcia, R. (1998). *Psicogênese e história das ciências*. Lisboa: Publicações Dom Quixote.

Piaget, J., & Inhelder, B. (1993). A psicologia da criança. Rio de Janeiro, Brazil: Ed. Bertrand Brasil.

Schlemmer, E. (2001). Projetos de aprendizagem baseados em problemas: Uma metodologia interacionista/construtivista para formação de comunidades em ambientes virtuais de aprendizagem. *Colabor@*, *1*(2), 10-19. Retrieved from http://pead.ucpel.tche.br/revistas/index.php/colabora/article/viewFile/17/15

Schlemmer, E. (2002). *AVA: Um ambiente de convivência interacionista sistêmico para comunidades virtuais na cultura da aprendizagem.* (Unpublished doctoral thesis). Universidade Federal do Rio Grande do Sul, Porto Alegre, Brazil.

Schlemmer, E. (2004). Sócio-cognição em ambientes virtuais de aprendizagem. In Proceedings of XII ENDIPE: Conhecimento local e conhecimento universal. Curitiba, Brazil: Anais.

Schlemmer, E. (2005). Metodologias para educação a distância no contexto da formação de comunidades virtuais de aprendizagem. In R. M. Barbosa (Ed.), Ambientes virtuais de aprendizagem (pp. 29-50). Porto Alegre, Brazil: Artmed Editora.

Schlemmer, E. (2008). ECODI – A criação de espaços de convivência digital virtual no contexto dos processos de ensino e aprendizagem em Metaverso. *IHU Ideias*, *6*, 1–31.

Schlemmer, E. (2009). *Telepresença*. Curitiba, Brazil: IESDE Brasil S.A.

Schlemmer, E. (2013a). *Espaço de convivência digital virtual nos programas de pós-graduação (stricto sensu) ecodi-ppgs unisinos: Uma proposta para a formação de pesquisadores* (Research Report). São Leopoldo: Universidade do Vale do Rio dos Sinos.

Schlemmer, E. (2013b). *Anatomia no metaverso Second Life: Uma proposta em i-Learning* (Research Report). São Leopoldo: Universidade do Vale do Rio dos Sinos.

Schlemmer, E., et al. (2006). ECoDI: A criação de um espaço de convivências digital virtual. In *Proceedings of XVII Simpósio Brasileiro de Informática na Educação* (pp. 467-477). Brasília, Brazil: UNB/UCB. Retrieved from http://br-ie.org/pub/index.php/sbie/article/viewFile/507/493

Schlemmer, E., Mallmann, M. T., & Daudt, S. I. D. (2000). Virtual learning environment: An interdisciplinary experience. In *Proceedings of WEBNET 2000 World Conference on the WWW and Internet* (pp. 134-201). San Antônio, TX: Webnet Journal Internet Tecnologies, Applications & Issues.

Schlemmer, E., Menegotto, D. B., & Backes, L. (2005). Uma nova forma de pensamento na utilização e na construção de mundos virtuais para uma educação on line autônoma e cooperativa. In *Proceedings of IV Congresso Internacional de Educação: A Educação nas Fronteiras do Humano*. São Leopoldo, Brazil: Anais.

Schlemmer, E., & Trein, D. (2009). Web 2.0-context learning projects: Possibilities for the teaching practice. In *Proceedings of World Conference on Educational Multimedia, Hypermedia & Telecommunications*. Honolulu, HI: EDMEDIA. Retrieved from https://www.aace.org/conf/edmedia

Schlemmer, E., & Lopes, D. de Q. (2012b). A tecnologia-conceito ECODI: Uma perspectiva de inovação para as práticas pedagógicas e a formação universitária. In *Proceedings of VII Congresso Iberoamericano de Docência Universitária: Vol 1: Ensino Superior: Inovação e qualidade na docência* (pp. 304-318). Porto: CIIE Centro de Investigação e Intervenção Educativas.

Schlemmer, E., & Lopes, D. de Q. (2013). *Educação e cultura digital*. São Leopoldo, Brazil: Editora UNISINOS.

Trein, D., & Schlemmer, E. (2009). Projetos de aprendizagem no contexto da web 2.0: Possibilidades para a prática pedagógica. *Revista E-Curriculum*, 4(2), 1-20. Retrieved from http://revistas.pucsp.br/index.php/curriculum/article/viewFile/3225/2147

Varela, F. J. (1989). *Autonomie et connaissance - essai sur le vivant*. Paris: Éditions du Seuil.

KEY TERMS AND DEFINITIONS

Accommodation: It is to adapt, to modify mental structures already built by the subject, or because of a novelty, something new.

Adaptation: It is the accommodation that ensures assimilation; whilst what has been assimilated, ensures accommodation of cognitive structures. This process of assimilation and accommodation, that characterizes adaptation, epitomizes what is more interactive in Piaget's Genetic Epistemology.

Assimilation: It is what allows the subject to appropriate novelty, retain learning, whether in the form of concrete thinking or complex logical structures.

Cooperation: It is characterized: by coordination of different views; through correspondence, reciprocity and complementarily operations, and the existence of autonomous rules and behaviors based on mutual respect (Piaget, 1973).

Enaction: It displaces the role of representation, in considering that knowledge is embedded, i.e., it refers to the fact that we are the body. The enaction, then, emphasizes the existential dimension of knowing, emerging from corporeality. Cognition depends on the experience that happens in bodily action. This action is linked to the sensory-motor capabilities involved by the bio-psycho-cultural context. The term means that the sensory-motor processes, perception and action are essentially inseparable from cognition.

Perception: It is a function directly related to the subject's activity, thus not being a mere portrait of the real, since it is guided by intelligence, i.e., "perceptive activities develop with age until they bend to policies suggested by intelligence in its operative progress" (Piaget & Inhelder, 1993, p. 40).

Representation: Is an extension of perception which includes the sensations arising from the subject-environment interaction, to the conscious constructions these subjects do from their experiences, memories and mental schemes.

ENDNOTES

[1] Minccraft is a sandbox-type electronic game, which was created by Markus "Notch" Persson in 2009. This open world allows using building blocks (cubes). Beyond the mechanics of mining and resource gathering building, is in the mixing game of survival and exploration. More information is found at https://minecraft.net/

[2] To be autonomous means to be subjects of their own education. People are autonomous when they are able to specify their own laws, or what is suitable for them. It is said that a subject has more autonomy the more he is able to recognize your study needs, formulate objectives for the study, select content, organize study strategies, seek and use the necessary materials as well as organize, direct, control and evaluate the learning process. Thus, the subject ceases to be the object of driving, inflow, ancestry and educational coercion because it develops a strong inner determination or self-assertion. Autonomy presupposes freedom of thought, moral freedom and political freedom.

3   Disorder occurs when there is an obstacle to the assimilation of the object by the subject. The perturbations may or may not lead to adjustments.

4   Regulation is the reaction from the point of view of the subject to disturbances, imbalances. It is a transformation, modification of the action and does not occur when the disorder leads to the repetition of the action, without any change.

5   *Metcognição* is knowing about knowing.

6   As discussed in Chapter 7 - Autopoietic Machines and Alopoietic Machines: The Structural Coupling.

Chapter 9
Online Education in Metaverse:
Novelty or Innovation?

ABSTRACT

In this chapter, the authors approach the perspective of Online Education in the Metaverse from the tensioning between what characterizes a novelty and what characterizes an innovation in education. They present and discuss the subtopic "Learning Contexts in Metaverse" to draw attention to those aspects that involve the learning process in the context of 3D digital virtual worlds. In the subtopic "Methodologies in Metaverse," they present the methodologies: "Methodology of Learning Projects Based in Problems" and "Problematizing Methodology of Case Study." In the context methodologies, the authors approach the "Pedagogical Intervention in Metaverse." In the subtopic "Novelty or Innovation?" they bring examples of 3D digital virtual worlds that represent a novelty and/or innovation. In conclusion about the chapter, the authors believe that the development of online education in the metaverse can contribute to elevating the quality in education within the world educational scenario through more innovative pedagogical proposals.

INTRODUCTION

In a worldwide scenario, education presents a paradoxical picture characterized by: an alarming index depicting the problem of illiteracy; strategies of actions promoted by different institutions as the United Nations Organization for Education, Science and Culture (UNESCO) and ambitious projects, involving emerging technologies, developed by the world's great reference research centers, such as the Massachusetts Institute of Technology (MIT). Within this paradox, in the last decade it was possible to observe the prog-

ress of different countries, mainly in developing ones such as Brazil, particularly when referring to children's access and inclusion in schools, new policies for the education system and the increase in the number of teenagers in universities. Projects that link different uses of digital technologies in education were created, allowing the teaching and learning process to contribute more and more to the education of men and women at this historical and social time.

In the Brazilian scenario, according to the report from the 2010 census carried out by INEP, some indices may be considered relevant in that

DOI: 10.4018/978-1-4666-6351-0.ch009

there was an increase in the offer of children's education, for those up to 3 years old. The re-organization of pre-school, aimed to children between 4 and 5 years old, and the implementation of elementary school for 9 year olds, started to include children from 6 years old on. This reform implied a decreasing enrollment index, but better profiting and performance of education, making it possible to make suitable adjustments between the age groups and the school year attended.

Another point noticed in the School Census 2010 is the confirmation of the expansion in professional education enrollments, from 780,162 in 2007 to a total of 1,124,388 enrollments in 2010 – a 46% growth in the period. There are 6.5 million university students in Brazil, 6.3 million of them on undergraduate courses and 173,000 on post-graduate programs. Growth in enrollments in 2010 was at 7.1% compared to the year 2009. Such development, though very recent to have its consequences evaluated, shows the changes in a contemporary society.

According to the data presented in the UNESCO Education for All Global Monitoring Report 2011[1], 171 million people could escape poverty, if students from low-income countries had gained basic literacy abilities at school, involving writing and reading. This corresponds to a fall of 12% in the number of people who live with an income lower than US$1.25 a day. However, the report advises that the international efforts that have been made since the beginning of the decade are starting to fade, and the rhythm of progress initially achieved is diminishing. So, the report suggests that governments urgently need to intensify their efforts to achieve the objectives proposed at the World Education Conference in Dakar, Senegal, before 2015.

The paradoxical aspect is that, alongside this critical world situation, there are also societies where modernity is closer, where scenarios are further from lacking welfare. When we are inter-ested in sketching the profile of an educational vision compromised with the current time, these scenarios should be visualized, but without losing awareness of national and international disparities, which are increasingly live and present, and their possible consequences towards countries' economics, politics and social safety. (Moraes, 2004, p.114)

Modernity, equally paradoxical, has been unleashing a process of vast transformations in humanity. "Such a process is conditioned by countless factors, among them the scientific advances that multiply information, distribute knowledge, influence political, economic and social systems, both in the present and in the future" (Moraes, 2004, p.115). Words like globalization, outsourcing, quality, productivity, cost reduction, are part of a day-to-day life, including and excluding human beings in different groups that mingle to construct the so called "global village". And in our intention to go beyond, maybe towards postmodernity, we realize, more and more, the plasticity of different frontiers (geographical, political, economical and cultural).

In the postmodernity context[2], digital technology takes on a dual character role, it either being good or evil. It is sometimes accused of excluding the majority of the population, especially in developing countries, other times used to solve problems in a worldwide political scenario. Actions developed in Brazil such as: the National Program of Educational Technology (ProInfo), whose objective consists on promoting the pedagogical use of informatics in the public sector's basic education, and the One Computer per Student Program – UCA, whose objective consists of promoting digital inclusion through the distribution of one portable computer for every basic education student and teacher in some public schools taking part in the program, represent perspectives to minimize problems in education. The programs bring to schools computers, digital resources and educational content. As a counterpart the States, Federal District and cities must guarantee a suitable structure for the laboratories and train educators to use the technologies.

This way, it would be naive to think of digital technologies as able to cause a world catastrophe, or to think of digital technologies as the salvation for human beings, but it is necessary to perceive that technologies can enable certain actions and limit others. Under this critical perspective it is possible to establish a relation between technology and education in a way where technology, in this case basically digital, can contribute to the development of teaching and learning processes under the perspective of human emancipation, which means, contributing to the accomplishment of the education objective.

Throughout history, technology and education have always followed close paths, mainly after the dawn of the press, and consequently, with the publication and use of books. They represent the lengthening of comprehending time, when registering constructed knowledge, as well as expanding the possibilities of space, as books are published in different countries, modifying relations at school concerning to the cumulative process and the socialization of knowledge.

Nowadays we live the insertion of electronic media in the social context, as was previously discussed, and also in the educational one. "Technical changes caused by those technologies require and produce new ways of representation, origination new ways of knowledge" (Moraes, 2004, p.123). At first, digital technology had the purpose of data processing, meaning its objective was to store and organize large amounts of data, resulting in the possibility of building countless data banks that would organize different information in a way humans are not capable of. Secondly, technologies contributed to the development of business strategies at the front of organizations, directly operated by users who control their ef-

fects upon their own work and directly profit from their benefits, in this case, it was possible to develop different systems that could enable a better management of activities.

In this sense, we are heading towards a third phase, in which we use network digital technologies, improving interaction processes, in a timeless time and in a space of flow, according to Castells (2003)[3]. So, when we talk about the web 2.0 age, this allows, according to Valente and Mattar (2007, p.84), "the user a better navigability, more interactivity and the functionality equivalent to the desktop", and its new stage, the 3D web (Metaverses, virtual reality, among others). With the development of metaverse technology the interaction processes are marked by the different representation possibilities of human beings' perception and their telepresence, represented by the immersion of the avatar in 3D Digital Virtual Worlds, constructed in the metaverse. We then start using metaverses in hybridism with different digital technologies, helping a concept of digital virtual living space to emerge – ECODI (Schlemmer et al., 2006; Schlemmer, 2008).

In this way, digital technologies have been modifying teaching and learning processes, developed in an educational context, at the same time as education has attributed meaning to technologies the same way it contributes to the development of new technologies. We have been currently developing educator training processes, through research carried out within the context of the Digital Education Research Group UNISINOS/ CNPq, in different 3D Digital Virtual Worlds, in countries like Brazil and France, coming up with new possibilities of understanding and representing the construction of knowledge.

What we want to observe is that every type of intellectual technology, being oral, written and informative, which we simultaneously live with, attributes a particular emphasis to certain cog-

nitive dimensions and to certain values, which are recurrent in specific cultural manifestations. (Moraes, 2004, p.123)

Through this, we configure new ways of carrying out actions through other instruments in a certain social context, thus constituting different ways of living, developing other habits and attributing meaning to the accomplished actions. In this sense we have recursively altered humanity's way of doing and living, constructing a new ecologic environment. The ecologic environment, for Lévy (2010), is constructed in the propagation of representations compounded in human minds in technical networks for storing, transforming and transmitting representations.

The human mind, meaning the subject's cognitive equipment, is influenced by culture, collectivity that provides language, by the classifying systems, by concepts, by analogies and metaphors and by images. Therefore, any modification in storing techniques, change in the transmission of information and knowledge representations causes changes in the ecologic environment in which representations are spread, causing changes in culture and knowledge. (Moraes, 2004, p.124)

Let us take the context of France, where Backes carried out her research from 2008 to 2011, as an example. In France, 2008, there were countless critics of Facebook[4], through the means of mass communication, concerning its policies of utilization and the possibilities of leaving a situation that is made in a living space, but a living that is in the "hands" of its creators. In that moment, then, the French searched for an alternative that constituted in a decentralized social network, as is the case of the Diaspora[5].

In 2010 the film "L'autre monde"[6], directed by Gilles Marchand was released in France. The film tells the story of the adolescent Gaspard who passes time with a friend and his girlfriend, in the South of France. By chance, a boy and a girl's (Audrey)

attempt to commit suicide, takes Gaspard to get to know Audrey better, and the reasons for her attempt to commit suicide. Audrey had created an avatar (Sarah) to attract people to the "Plage Noire" and to commit suicide in a "game" carried out in 3D Digital Virtual Worlds. After that, Audrey asked these same people to commit suicide in their physical lives. From that moment on, the life of an adolescent goes through a big change. When interacting in the game, Gaspard gets to know other avatars and he is seduced by Sarah (Audrey) to commit suicide in the "Plage Noire". In this sense the film alters the risk of human beings developing mental pathologies when using metaverses and it gives food for thought about the relations that are established among adolescents through these technologies, which means, another way to look at and understand these technologies that are developed in cyberspace.

In this context, developing an educators' training process, in metaverses, becomes a big challenge. To break the dichotomy between the comprehension that such technologies can save the world or ruin it represents an important construction when opening critical thinking towards their possibilities and limits of use, and, above all, to the comprehension of metaverses while enabling the configuration of digital virtual spaces of living among human beings that co-exist in spaces of other nature and thus constituting digital virtual collaborating[7].

The ecologic perception of the world and of life comprehends the change as an essential component of nature, and nature has flexibility, plasticity, interactivity, creativity, autonomy, integration, cooperation and self-organization. Everything is relative, merely probable, unsure and, at the same time, complementary. (Moraes, 2004, p.136)

So, thinking about the development of online educational proposes, as an innovation in teaching and learning processes is far more complex than thinking only about a novelty for pedagogical practices. In order to comprehend the complexity, the systemic thinking and the self-eco-organizing conception behind the innovation, we need to be clear on how learning in 3D Digital Virtual Worlds is carried out, the methodologies that enhance the characteristics of 3D Digital Virtual Worlds, and the necessary mediation to trigger the development of the learning process. How can we then think about the development of an innovative online education?

LEARNING CONTEXTS IN METAVERSE

An emerging paradigmatic conception demands a coherent epistemological conception, which means, an epistemological conception about how human beings construct knowledge so that we can think about education from the perspective of the emancipation of the human being living in the contemporary life. In this way the epistemological conception, present in the comprehension of both the educator and his students, will define the learning context they are in. However, thinking of education from the perspective of emancipation implies thinking about a certain epistemology. When acknowledging education as "… a process in which the child or adult shares with the other, and lives with the other, changes spontaneously in a way that his mode of living is carried out in progressively greater congruence with the other's way of living in the sharing environment" (Maturana, 2005, p.29); so, education "implies a search that is carried out by a subject, which is the man. The man must be the subject of his own education. He cannot be its object (Freire, 2007, p.28). Therefore it is necessary to build up a learning context featured by: the relations and interactions, flexibility, participation, autonomy and alterity[8], cooperation, among others, in order to think of men and women that respect themselves and others using a sharing perspective.

The context, according to Figueiredo and Afonso (2006), is a combination of significant circumstances that allow the construction of new knowledge by means of action. For Almeida (2009, p.78), the concept of context can be related to the concept of ecology, "Since all elements within a context can be found in an interdependence, all and every change that is processed within this context is systemic, for the change is an element that causes effects in others and in the system as a whole, and this corresponds to the changes and local interventions".

In this sense, we can think of a learning context that is developed with the presence of digital technology, mainly in metaverses, considering: the co-existence of different ways of living (physical and digital virtual natures); the need for exploring this new digital virtual space (where the representation of perception occurs through graphic language, in an imbrication with the textual, oral or gestural languages); and the living and sharing among human beings through new ways of action (that occur in a timeless time, in the space of flow, through the immersion, teleimmersion, telepresence and digital virtual presence[9]).

This way, when considering the learning context in metaverses we need to (re)signify the aspects involved in a learning event, according to Figueiredo and Afonso (2006): apprentice – the ontogenic construction of the human being empowers or limits learning; content – the object of learning, which can be the information, technology, situation and/or the other; context – all relevant situations for the construction of knowledge through digital virtual spaces.

The context is considered in its complexity and multidimensionality as a whole, embodying the subjects' social-historical, cultural, cognitive and affective dimensions, as well as the technologies taking part of it, which characteristics must be understood so that they can be incorporated under a critical perspective. (Almeida, 2009, p.78)

In this way, the interaction process between 3D Digital Virtual Worlds' e-inhabitants can occur in a comprehensive way, between: human beings, the human being and the knowledge, the human being and the digital virtual space, and, in a dynamic way, between: human beings, the knowledge and the digital virtual space, but in all moments this happens through perturbations[10]. Digital spaces enable work in a timeless context and in a space of flow, resulting in different ways of acting for the human being, as well as the possibility of representing the perception from a dialectic perspective. The construction of knowledge is the result of the joint action of all aspects previously mentioned, which means, a social action, when attributing the object a meaning, broadening or constructing a new knowledge.

Within a digital virtual space the construction of knowledge has a social action empowered for being from a deterritorialized space, where the crossing of cultures can broaden reflection and develop awareness in the human beings involved within that construction. In this sense, we think about the construction of knowledge through contradiction, from different points of view, of plural truths, of the legitimacy of the other as someone who I can learn with. According to Maffesoli (2012), this is the metaphor of the conflicting harmony. We can then think of the construction of knowledge in digital virtual spaces as a novelty in education that can be developed in a creative and innovative way.

However, in order to comprehend the construction of knowledge in digital virtual spaces it is necessary to live and share, which means, to configure an existence with others in digital virtual spaces, which allows becoming conscious of how we learn and contribute, to promote new opportunities for the construction of knowledge within this context.

When developing research within the context of the Digital Education Research Group UNISINOS/

CNPq we found that learning within the metaverses context implies the coordination of simultaneity at least in three particular learning processes: learning about metaverses technology; learning about the object of knowledge to be studied; and, in many cases, learning about the methodology used to develop the teaching and learning process in the Metaverse.

Learning about metaverse technology is necessary in this historical time for it is an emerging technology. The metaverse was created in 1995 by Alpha Worlds, but later incorporated to Active Worlds. In 1999 Second Life was created, but only developed in 2003. In this period there were other initiatives such as Lively, from Google, and There, among others which were discontinued. The movement we currently observe, however, refers to the creation of open source metaverses, such as the Open Simulator and the Open Wonderland[11]. In a certain way they follow the same logic observed in Virtual Learning Environments, which initially arose as owners' software and little by little gave space to the open source ones. The dissemination and use of metaverses is also connected to the development of technology in computer network systems. For its technological complexity their use demands a particular configuration in the computer, mainly regarding the graphic board, and a significant network speed. These can be considered as some of the elements that contribute to metaverses that are not as well known as other digital technologies, besides the fact that this technology contributes to breaking a textual culture, so far hegemonic within the educational context.

We believe that, with the development of technology and its use in pedagogical practices, the learning curve needed to use metaverses will be less steep, for its logical structure is internalized in the users' cognitive structure of this technology. We can take as an example instant communicators. Currently their use does not demand learning about its software. For any communicator, its use is carried out in an automatic way, with no need for a lengthy learning curve.

Learning about a knowledge object in a metaverse may occur in a particular way, if we consider learning in a physical context or in other digital virtual spaces, for, contrary to them, the main language in metaverses is graphic, which in a certain way contradicts the current educational culture, in which knowledge is represented in textual and/or oral ways. In this way, the first language we perceive when accessing a metaverse is the graphic language, which combined with the gestural, oral and textual ones, present the communication possibilities available for interaction. Beyond representing knowledge in a textual/oral way, in metaverses we can access or represent the object of knowledge by means of 3D graphic representations. Graphic representations may appear through schemes, reproduction of an object or metaphoric constructions. For Fichtner (2010)

Metaphors, in general, are elements constructed for our conception of reality. We structure our different experience fields (areas) in a systematic way by means of a metaphor. Through them we construct our imagination as "pictures" that create connections between fields, phenomena and very different and contradicting processes, forming a coherent system. (p.37)

Metaphoric construction implies the relation of equality, when saying that an object constructed in the 3D Digital Virtual World represents a theoretical concept, at the same time it implies relations of inequality when keeping their original characteristic, which means the concept is not the constructed object. When there is validation and invalidation of equality, we relate that to a metaphor.

In the research carried out by Backes (2007), the metaphoric representation of knowledge from the students' part demands a complex comprehension about the object of knowledge. When a student

represents knowledge in a metaphoric way it implies comprehending it as a whole, establishing a relation with the objects and characterizing it through these objects in such a way that they are comprehensible by the other, articulating equality and inequality.

Considering what was previously said we can infer that the use of metaverses for the development of learning processes can be considered a real possibility for improving and enhancing actions in online education.

Online Education[12], according to Maturana (1999) consists of a space that enables living and sharing in a conversational way in order to make the existent diversity emerge. Therefore, it involves the construction of common projects between different people, independent of its origin, that validates all participants (students and educator), accepting their cultural history as a legitimate starting point for the development of studies. This also implies considering knowledge already constructed by the students, respecting each student's learning pace and keeping the students legitimacy within a dynamic between the co-learner and the co-teacher.

Distance education, when accepted and welcomed, allows a modification in listening, seeing and doing, in the country's living; that means its physical space, in a way that allows cooperation at any level, since it casts off all cultural, class and economic barriers due to the individual's effective valorization. This means it allows broadening the accomplishment of a democratic living. (Maturana, 1999, p.149)

So that online education, especially in the metaverse context, can be effective under that perspective, the educator is considered a mediator and co-participant in the process, assuming different functions such as: facilitator, problematization, articulator and tutor of the students' learning as they get the complex comprehension about the construction of knowledge. The educator is then also learner, when he comprehends what every student learns, meaning, the educator learns about the students learning.

The one who teaches also learns, transforming his own teaching act in the relation it establishes between the teacher and the student. The apprentice, when learning, also teaches, based in the uni-duality present in the relation teacher-learner and learner-teacher. When talking about the teacher we acknowledge his position as a learner vice-versa. (Moraes, 2004, p.150)

The educator's action can contribute to knowledge being constructed in the creation of information networks, encouraging the action of the participants, the development of autonomy, of authorship, from mutual interaction processes, meaning processes constantly constructed through the negotiations carried out by their interacting agents.

Therefore, the student is understood as:

An individual who presents a particular profile of intelligence from the moment he is born. A unique being in his genetic capital, is perhaps the only one in the entire human species. It is singular in its morphology, anatomy, physiology, behavior, attitude and intelligence. All these aspects are dimensions of a living individuality, from an open system that exists in a phenomenal world. He is a being with quality, a being of existence, in search of his autonomy of being and existing. (Moraes, 2004, p.138)

Through this teacher and this learner, who live and collaborate in a 3D Digital Virtual World, we can develop online education in a way that makes it possible to reach the objectives of education from the perspective of emancipation. "This way, the big challenge for the teacher-learner is to guarantee movement so that the process can be kept, steering changes" (Moraes, 2004, p.149).

METHODOLOGIES IN METAVERSE

As a starting point we take the congruence between human beings, in living and sharing with the environment, and the different possibilities that digital virtual dimensions offer to the development of online education, in order to reflect on pedagogical methodologies in the process for training humans in the Metaverse context (3D Digital Virtual Worlds).

As we discussed in Chapter 2 - Network Learning culture and the emerging paradigm, the methodologies used to enhance the development of the learning and teaching process in Metaverses are based on the theory of complexity, on systemic thinking and on the self-eco-organizing conception. Therefore they are explored in dialogical relations, reflection processes, mediation, as well as in the construction of metaphors.

The methods of dialogical education bring us the intimacy of society, the reason of being for each object of study. Through a critical dialogue about a text or a moment in society, we try to enter it, to reveal it, to see the reasons he is the way he is in a political and historical context they are in. (Freire, 1992, pp.24-25)

So, we consider that the methodology for teaching and learning processes in metaverses needs to differ from the methodologies used in other educational processes, in order to use the metaverse to their full potential, as well as to configure it as living space between human beings. However, in order to understand that metaverses are only tools, the methodology for the development of the training process, the congruence existent between human beings and the environment (digital virtual) must be coherent, as well as the epistemological conception of teaching and learning. We then highlight three important characteristics for methodological construction in the use of metaverses: presentiality, integration of digital technology – hybridism and perturbation.

When thinking about the process of relations between human beings undertaking training, what we expect the active participation of each one in the process of construction of knowledge. For that, the methodology for the pedagogical practice in metaverses must allow every human being to establish his presentiality in living and sharing.

Presentiality is established by the actions, reactions and reflections that are represented in the living with the other. The feeling of belonging to a certain group encourages the human being's participation and responsibility in living and collaborating in harmony. For Maffesoli (2007), the feeling of belonging happens due to the desire of touching the other, of being together. Therefore, the more we are responsible for a group, the more significant our actions are and the feeling of belonging will be part of this relation. In digital virtual spaces, such as 3D Digital Virtual Worlds, presentiality can be intensified by the telepresence and the avatar's digital virtual presence in the 3D environment, which contributes to a greater feeling of immersion, but that necessarily needs this avatar to be in action and interaction with the other avatars.

When we use metaverses in pedagogical practice, in the research carried out within the Digital Education Research Group UNISINOS/CNPq for people's training, we usually use them integrated with other technologies, for the methodological development, in a way that the possibilities of interaction and the representation of knowledge are expanded and diversified to the full. In this hybrid way, we use, for example, the Eduverse metaverse coupled to blogs (Figure 1), Eduverse metaverse sites (Figure 2) or Eduverse metaverse virtual learning environments (Figure 3), as we can see in the images of the AWSINOS, through the frames to the right, as follows.

Or the combination of several technologies using, within the digital technological hybrid context, metaverse, virtual learning environment

Figure 1. AWSINOS coupled to the blog "Analyze du travail et Polyvalence"
Source: Authors

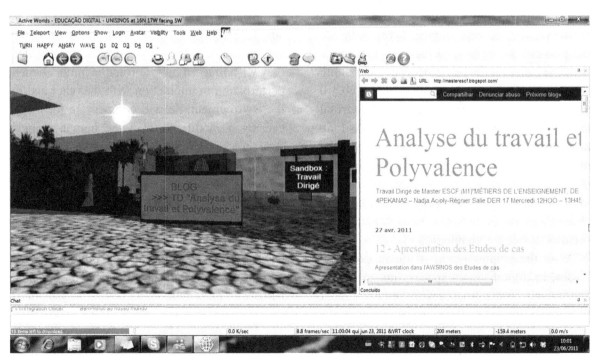

Figure 2. AWSINOS coupled to the site "Alegoria da Caverna" Platão
Source: Authors

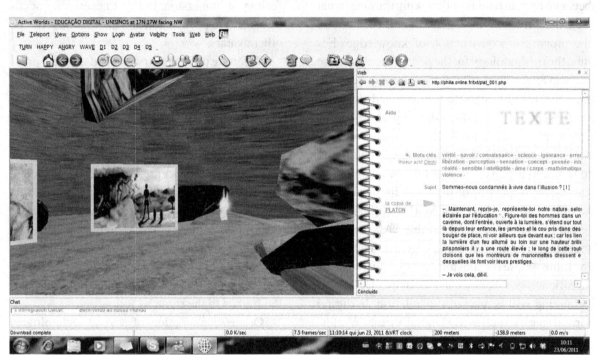

and communicative agent, as in the case of the ECODI[13] Schlemmer et al. (2006) and Schlemmer (2008, 2009, 2010), previously.

In the integration of different technologies within the digital technological hybrid context, the research we developed makes it clear that, in a first instance, the participants in the training process use the technologies related to web 1.0 and web 2.0 more often – for example, virtual learning environments, sites and blogs. As long as the participants familiarize themselves with the metaverse technology, they intensify the interaction process in 3D Digital Virtual Worlds created in these metaverses. We believe that this fact will change with the more frequent development and use of Metaverse technologies.

With the empowerment of interaction processes, in digital virtual spaces, human beings live and share in congruence with the environment which may not be familiar to them, and, therefore, this environment may cause perturbations in human beings' structures. This means that human beings are closed systems because they are the structures that identify the disturbing aspects, the aspects that are strange to them and from which they wish to learn more. From the human being, perturbation in interaction with the other and/or the environment, he will compensate for them, causing a modification in the human beings' structures and/or in the environment.

So, in the interaction between a living system and his environment, although what happens in the system is determined by its structure, and what happens in the environment is determined by the environment's structure, it is a coincidence that these two factors that select the changes of state will occur. The environment selects the structural

Figure 3. AWSINOS coupled to AVA-UNISINOS
Source: Authors

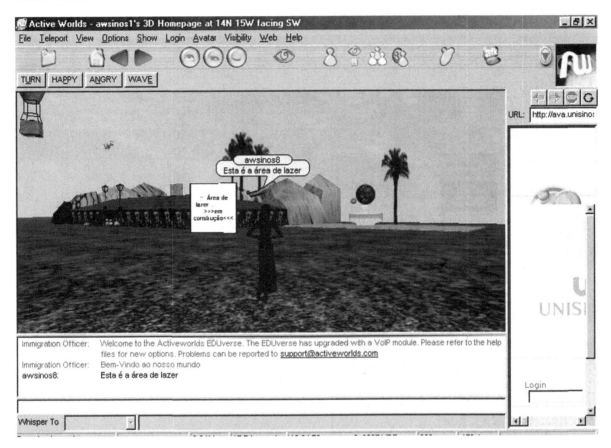

change in the organism, and the organism, through its action, selects the structural change in the environment. (Maturana, 2002, p.62)

Taking into consideration what is mentioned above, we can talk about specific methodologies that can contribute to the constitution of pedagogical practices that empower emancipation, inspired by Freire (1992).

Sometimes I like to talk about parallel pedagogies, when the teacher applies several modalities in class simultaneously. If the dynamic prelation, which is questioning, coexists with the presentations carried out by the students, work groups, individual works, essays, research work outside

the classroom, and so on and so forth, the format of the course itself reduces the risk that the teacher's speech becomes a lecture for the transfer of knowledge. (pp.58-59)

In this context, we understand that problematizing methodologies, such as the methodology of learning projects based on problems, coherent with an ontological and epistemological conception, that are the grounds for this book, can significantly contribute to the teaching and learning processes in metaverses.

The methodology of projects was and is used in different ways and for different purposes within the educational context. It is therefore essential to make clear which conception of project is steering

Figure 4. ECODI-UNISINOS (3D Digital Virtual World AWSINOS+VLE AVA-UNISINOS+ Communicative Agent MARIÁ)
Source: Authors

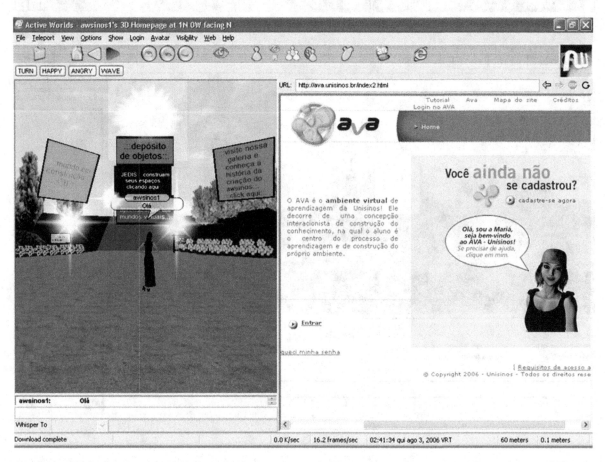

methodology. According to Fagundes, Sato and Maçada (1999): "The activity of making projects is symbolic, intentional and natural to the human being. It is through this that men search for solutions to problems and develop a process of constructing knowledge, generating both arts as well as natural and social sciences" (p.15).

The comprehension of the project guides two distinct ways of using it within the educational context: teaching by projects and learning by projects, according to what is presented in the following table, by Fagundes, Sato and Maçada (1999, p.17).

The methodology used in the proposal for training is guided by the conception of learning by

projects. In this way, the methodology of learning projects based on problems, adapted to graduate studies, according to Schlemmer (2001, 2005), is based in the conjecture of cooperative activities, encourages interaction and enables an action-reflection process in the learning subjects – the members of the project's development community. The conjecture of cooperative activity includes and encourages the interdisciplinary work, because it fosters the development of thinking and autonomy through intellectual, social, cultural and political exchanges, favoring metacognition and raising of awareness.

The methodology by learning projects implies a relation of dialogue, with the objective of bringing

Figure 5. ECODI-EL GATE (UNISINOS – SL Island+ Website)
Source: Authors

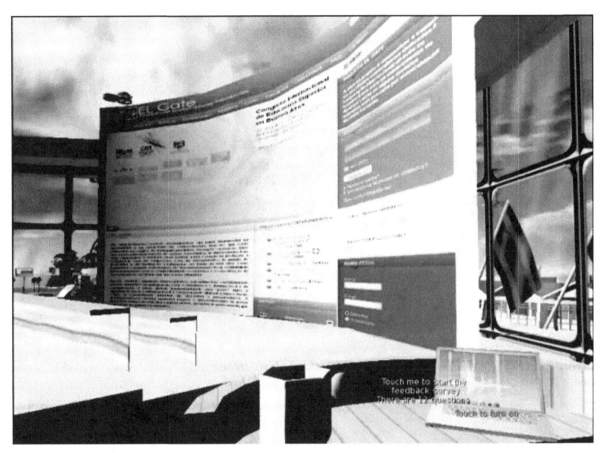

up the creative potential and rupture, according to Freire (1992), bringing clearness to both parts (students and educators). This way, educators become tutors, articulators, problematizing, research and experts in the development of projects.

According to Schlemmer (2005), the methodology by learning projects is based on the epistemological assumption interactionist/constructivist/systemic. The development of the methodology consists, itself, of a learning project that presupposes the methodological experience of the person willing to use it in his teaching practice. That means there are no defined steps to be followed, but an epistemological concept base as a support.

Methodology can be developed from a theme platform or a free issue. Both processes start from the collective decision between students and teachers after an initial discussion pondering wishes, needs, current events, characteristics of the knowledge area and purposes to be pursued. The decisions are heterarchical and the work is developed within a collaborative and mutually respectful environment in search of the development of autonomy, cooperation and solidarity.

The methodology of learning projects based in problems works in five dimensions: temporary convictions; temporary doubts; objectives; development and systematization. According to Trein and Schlemmer (2009) the organization of these five dimensions depends on each group, there is no order or pre-defined rules. The work is developed in a collaborative and cooperative way.

Figure 6. ECODI-UNISINOS (UNISINOS – SL Island+Web 2.0)
Source: Authors

Figure 7. ECODI-UNISINOS (UNISINOS – SL Island+LiveStream
Source: Authors

Table 1. Teaching by projects and learning by projects (Fagundes, Sato & Maçada, 1999, p.17)

	Teaching by Projects	**Learning by Projects**
Authorship. Who picks the theme?	Teachers and pedagogical team	Students and teachers individually and, at the same time in cooperation
Context	Controlled by external and formal criteria	Student's reality
Who does it please?	Control of the consequences of the syllabus content	Curiosity, desire, will to learn
Decisions	Hierarchical	Heterarchical
Rules, directions and activities definition	Imposed by the system; follows determinations without choosing them	Elaborated by a group; there is common agreement between students and teachers
Paradigm	Knowledge is passed on	Knowledge is constructed
Role of the Teacher	Agent	Stimulating/steering
Role of the Student	Receiver	Agent

When we develop learning projects based on a problem in 3D Digital Virtual Worlds, systematization can occur in a graphic and/or metaphoric way, which implies the comprehension of the complexity of the knowledge that involves the problem and how we can make it clear in the image that represents the construction of knowledge made in the learning project: Epistemological conceptions, developed by Backes (2007).

In Figure 8 we see metaphors about epistemological conceptions: innatism, represented by a board that teletransports the avatar to a box located in another dimension within the 3D Digital Virtual World (a metaphor used to represent the human mind); empirism, represented by a borough with marked borders, where streets lead us to buildings, houses, squares, but cannot be visited (metaphor used to represent stimulus and response, without knowing the process); interactionism, represented by a house which can be accessed though different doors and there is no roof (metaphor used to represent the importance of interaction and understanding the knowledge construction process).

In Figure 9, research developed by Locatelli (2010), the letters IHS, identifying the Society of Jesus appear in the center. Besides that, the side boards contain the steps of the Spiritual Exercises and the relationship with society, metaphorically represented by trees, fish and the space, as a whole, inside the globe. Taking into account that the Society of Jesus' pedagogical proposal is grounded in spirituality, participants in the research take part in a spiritual retreat, contributing to the spiritual thread represented in the digital virtual space. Living and collaborating among participants were configured within the space represented by the globe, so that everyone could feel they were living an experience; one of the aspects implied in the Ignatian Pedagogical Paradigm.

We have developed research, in Backes (2011), about human education in metaverses, using the Problematizing Methodology of Case Study, inspired by the Methodology of Case Study Research, which involves the direct observation of contextualized events, theoretically based on documents, artifacts and images.

According to Yin (2005) the case study comprehends the investigation of a phenomenon and its contextualized conditions. However, in the Problematizing Methodology of Case Study the relation between the phenomenon and the context is established in the ecological view, which, according to Capra (2004) consists of:

A holistical view of a bicycle, for instance, means to see the bicycle as its functions and to under-

Figure 8. Epistemological conceptions
Source: Authors

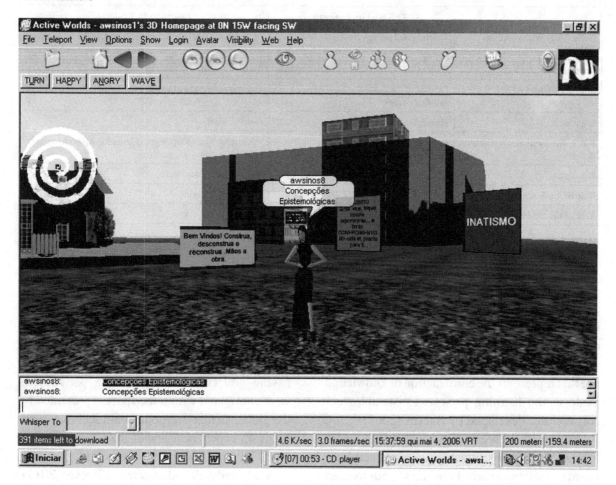

stand, in compliance to that, the interdependences of its parts. The ecological view of a bicycle also includes that, but also includes the perception of how the bicycle fits in its natural and social environment – where its parts come from, how it was manufactured, how its use affects the natural environment and the community by whom it is used and so on and so forth. (p.25)

So, when we develop the training process with the Problematizing Methodology of Case Study, we use cases from two different sources: from the cases described by the students referring to a concrete situation; and from cases described by the educator. The cases described by the students reveal their uneasiness, their way of perceiving the context and the aspects they consider important. In the cases described by the educators they gather specific objectives proposed in the training process, referring to some knowledge that was not approached in the cases described by the students.

In this methodology the students work in big and small groups for solving the cases. All students are invited to discuss and come up with concepts for all the cases. Afterwards the students form small groups and pick up a case to be explored

Figure 9. Ignatian Pedagogical Paradigm (Context-Experience-Reflection-Action-Evaluation), a space constructed by teachers from Jesuit Schools
Source: Authors

and systematized. The students use the theoretical reference available, research, background knowledge and other concrete situations.

Discussions and systematizations can be carried out in spaces in the web 2.0, in chat and graphic representation in the 3D Digital Virtual Worlds and they are followed by everyone involved in a way the discussion about a case can help in the discussion about another one. The representation of the case and concepts used for discussion is made in a graphic and metaphoric way in 3D Digital Virtual Worlds, which is presented and assessed by the big group, with criteria previously defined

by the students. The representation of a Case Study made in the training process developed by Backes (2011) can be seen in the following Figure 10:

Figure 10 represents the different hallways a French student can go through along his school life. The right path represents primary school, as well as the success those students usually find, thanks to the coherent and contextualized pedagogical structure. The corridor to the left of the image represents the professional school, where doors represent the subdivisions of subjects, and a failure in math is represented by a red board indicating danger.

Figure 10. Case study: Lycée Professionnel
Source: Authors

In this methodology the students manage the representation of two aspects: the concrete situation of the case and the concepts used for reflection about the case. As a result, it is necessary to previously present it to the groups so that each one can contribute with the other in order to contemplate both aspects.

What makes the teaching and learning process efficient is the epistemological-didactic-pedagogical supporting the use of certain technology. In our research we identified that the methodologies and the pedagogical mediation developed constitute as ground factors for the learning process to occur in a satisfactory way, both for the student and for the teacher. In this way, teacher education is a priority for being a "good" teacher in the physical face-to-face way is not a guarantee that the teacher will be "good" at developing an online educational process. Therefore an educational process in which the teacher can experience what an online student is, is necessary, so that they can really understand what it means and how it affects the way of promoting learning. (Schlemmer & Backes, 2008 p.530)

The use of metaverses in the educational context is complex and gives a dynamic dimension. We articulate the conceptions of teaching and learning, the potentials of a technology (3D Digital Virtual Worlds, in this case) and the interaction with other available ones, the pedagogical methodology and the particularities of every participant, which make the educational process dynamic and unique. So, how does the pedagogical mediation process happen within this context?

PEDAGOGICAL INTERVENTION IN METAVERSE

The word mediation has its meaning defined as a relation that is established between two people, two objects or two concepts. When we talk about mediation we refer to the relation "between", which means, what is within the environment. However, if we understand mediation based on the theory of complexity what is "between" or in the environment is the contradiction, the different, the multiple between two people, the two objects or the two concepts.

When we establish mediation in the process of teaching and learning, we refer to pedagogical mediation, which will have its concept and its effects in congruence with the epistemological conception of the person making the mediation. At this moment, we will specifically address pedagogical mediation. Chapter 2 - Network Learning culture and the emerging paradigm, has already discussed the process of pedagogical mediation, the interactions carried out in living and sharing, dialogical relations, reflection, perturbation and structural coupling. We then configure our living spaces so that we are able to transform.

Under the perspective of complexity it is possible to think of pedagogical mediation in a dialectic way. The dialectic roots can be found in Heraclitos' words: "The contrary is converging, and the diverging originates the most beautiful harmony, and everything follows the dispute" (Fragment 8 in Franco, 1999, p.13). Following Heraclitos' ideas, according to Franco (1999), Hegel describes the dialectic with the triad thesis, antithesis and synthesis. Having a thesis as starting point, it originates the antithesis which then originates the synthesis. The synthesis is not the thesis, nor the antithesis, neither the combination of the two. The synthesis consists in some aspects of the thesis related to some aspects of the antithesis, overcoming both as a final result. So, the overcoming is the denial of aspects of a certain reality, the conservation of something that is essential existing within this denied reality and the transformation into something better.

So, the construction of knowledge through pedagogical mediation, in a dialectic way, for Piaget (apud Franco, 1999) happens when the subject interacts with the object in a dyad dialectic. "That means we can understand the construction of knowledge when we think about the subject and the object as the two faces of a same coin, or as two extremes within the same shade" (p.15).

For human beings to meet in a pedagogical mediation within the same shade they have to be considered as a legitimate being, which means, they have to establish emotional relationship based in love. For Maturana (2005) feelings are dynamic body devices that define the different domains of action we move by. So, when we change emotions, we change our domain of action.

The emotion that allows us to mediate is love. Love is the emotion that allows us to be in recurrent interaction with the other for love is the only thing we have with which to make the other someone legitimate to live with.

Love is the essence of humans' lives, but it is nothing special. Love is the base of social life, but not all living together is social. Love is the emotion that constitutes the domain of behaviors making it possible to operate acceptance of others as legitimate in living and sharing, and it is this way of living we refer as to social. (Maturana, 2005, p.23)

Accepting the other as someone legitimate to live with, enhances the pedagogical mediation and contributes to the configuration of the living space. So, how can we understand the pedagogical mediation in 3D Digital Virtual Worlds? What are the poles we find in this totality?

According to Trein (2010) pedagogical mediation in educational online contexts is related to the techno-didactic-pedagogical fluency of the users and the possibilities the technology offers. In CAI, CBT and WBT, for instance, pedagogical mediation is limited because the possibility of interaction is only between the human being and the information being transmitted, according to Schlemmer (2005).

In the web 2.0, which enables authorship, pedagogical mediation is empowered with the broadening of the interaction process between human beings and the human beings with technology, also encouraging processes of multiple pedagogical intermediations, defined by Okada (2004). Multiple pedagogical intermediations happen when we go beyond the limits between educator and student relations, and we invite everyone involved in the educational context for a dialogical relation side by side with educators and students, building up a community. According to Backes (2013, p.200), "Under the collaborating perspective, when we approach MDV3D, we think of pedagogical mediation to configure the digital virtual collaborating space, because we are in congruence with the environment (being a digital virtual space, in this case)".

In the 3D web, however, we use digital virtual spaces as spaces to be constructed in the flow of interaction between human beings, pedagogical mediation and the multiple pedagogical intermediation which can encourage learning process resulting in the construction of new knowledge.

Pedagogical mediation in 3D Digital Virtual Worlds happens in three different contexts: in the relation between the human and the metaverse; in the relation between the human being and the object of knowledge, in congruence with the metaverse and in the interaction between human beings, inserted in the metaverse. These contexts are not separated and they are constantly crossing each other.

The relation between the human and the metaverse, has the pedagogical mediation unleashed by the legitimacy the human being gives the metaverse, the perturbation in using the metaverse, the coupling between the human being and the metaverse as the human being uses the metaverse to represent his perception and the adaptation in the moment the human being identifies other possibilities in the metaverse. In this case, according to Backes (2011) what happens is a technological structural coupling.

In the relation between the human being and the object of knowledge, the pedagogical mediation happens due to the necessity of learning the object of knowledge, and the different possibilities of representing that object in 3D Digital Virtual Worlds cause perturbation. The coupling between the human being and the object of knowledge happens as the human being gives the object of knowledge a meaning, representing it in 3D Digital Virtual Worlds in congruence with the technology and identifies other situations in which he can learn other objects of knowledge.

As for the interaction between human beings who are in pedagogical mediation within a metaverse, the legitimacy with the other is necessary, through the coordination of coordination, establishing perturbation, in order to compensate the perturbations through structural coupling, and thus construct a new knowledge in the relation. In the last two contexts of pedagogical mediation, for Backes (2011), the structural coupling occurs in a digital virtual nature.

NOVELTY OR INNOVATION?

Metaverse technology, with the possibility of creating different 3D Digital Virtual Worlds, certainly represents a novelty in the social context, in a broad sense and in an educational context, in a more restrict way, which is attracting even more men and women who live and share in a contemporary society, triggering creativity and innovation in the construction of representations of other worlds. As we can see in the following images, 3D Digital Virtual Worlds represented in different metaverses, show those characteristics of creativity and innovation, in some cases, which are in congruence with the level of familiarization of the creators of 3D Digital Virtual Worlds and the knowledge about their potential with the technology.

In some images it is easy to identify the physical world simulated in 3D Digital Virtual Worlds, as in the case of the Brasil Rio Surf world (Figure 15), Paris 1900 (Figure 16) and Amsterdam (Figure 17), showing concrete and representative icons, such as the Moulin Rouge from Paris, for instance. However there are 3D Digital Virtual Worlds constructed from metaphoric and abstract representations of a non geographical or territorial world, but they are the representation of a conceptual world (as in the case of the Van Gogh world – Figure 13, that represents the impressionist movement in the context of Arts) or an experience (as in the case of the Gay Pride Month world @ L-Word Island, which represents the homosexual expression). The Gay Pride Month world @ L-World Island, which deals with adult content, is not made accessible

without submitting a subscription and having it accepted. The Figures were found through Google images on a blog about a variety of subjects, with no access restriction. The mechanist adopted by the Month group world @ L-Word Island in the 3D digital virtual world is the correct and legal attitude to be taken, because even though under 18s are forbidden to subscribe in 3D digital virtual worlds, many children and teenagers have their avatar and may enter worlds with inappropriate content.

As e-citizens in different metaverses, we face many 3D digital virtual worlds built for publicizing and/or exploring adult content. Each avatar, however, may pre-define in his preferences, to have adult content excluded. If you then try to enter a 3D digital virtual world, you'll be sent a warning message in case the area you're about to visit contains adult content. Nevertheless there is no control on adult content for the avatars interacting with other avatars in 3D digital virtual worlds. Restrictions on

Figure 11. Greece (AWedu)
Source: Authors

Figure 12. Egypt (AWedu)
Source: Authors

Figure 13. VanGogh (AWedu)
Source: Authors

Figure 14. Medieval (AWedu)
Source: Authors

Figure 15. Brasil Rio Surf (Second Life)
Source: Authors

Figure 16. Paris 1900 (Second Life)
Source: Authors

Figure 17. Amsterdam (Second Life)
Source: Authors

avatar actions regard movement commands such as: bumping, flying, object-building, protected lots where avatars cannot be seen or heard by other avatars located in a different lot.

We understand the internet, being a vast net, works in a way enabling both positive and negative aspects, for good or for evil. There are countless cases of pedophilia, homophilia, pornography, frauds and crimes broadcasted in the media. Education professionals must approach the issue in a critical way, making students aware of the different faces of the internet, as well as 3D digital virtual worlds.

In the educational context, the use of 3D Digital Virtual Worlds represents a novelty, though often misused, reinforcing the misuse of the internet in digital virtual worlds, putting it too far from educational purposes. The 3D Digital Virtual Worlds are real advertisements for educational institutions. In 3D Digital Virtual Worlds we can find a variety of different representations of

educational institutions and pedagogical proposes. As we can see in the following images, we identify representations that are reproductions of the geographically located space of the educational context, as in Figure 20 from Class 3D and in Figure 23 from Universidad a Distancia de Madrid, UDIMA. We can also see icons of epistemological conceptions, as in Figure 20 Ilha do Empreendedor SEBRAE (Entrepreneurship Island), where rooms have restrict and limited access, regardless atemporality and flow. We can also observe the graphic representations of objects of knowledge in Figure 19 Chemeet, in congruence with the metaverse's technology, with the movements involving objects, 3D perspectives, problematizing questions enabling interaction.

From observing the figures we know, without a doubt, that metaverse is a novelty; but how can we know if this novelty is also an innovation?

Moving forward in this reflection about innovation, when we look at the figures, can we

Figure 18. Class3D (AWedu)
Source: Authors

Figure 19. Chemeet (AWedu)
Source: Authors

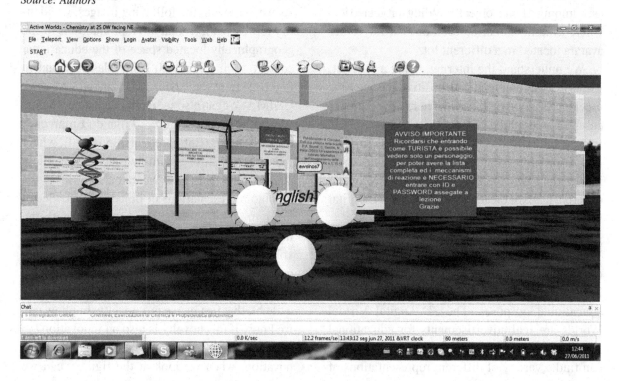

Figure 20. SEBRAE's Entrepreneur Island (Second Life)
Source: Authors

Figure 21. Universidad a Distancia de Madrid, UDIMA – Madrid's Distance Learning University (Second Life)
Source: Authors

identify what is being represented in 3D Digital Virtual Worlds? What we can see is another way of representing the physical spaces, or is there a transformation in the way of representing them, which could offer different views of comprehensions within the learning and teaching processes?

We can consider that innovation has two aspects: the individual and the social, which means that something can represent an innovation for the human being, without representing an innovation for the social system to which he belongs. When we think of a family relation, creating an avatar for the father can be an innovation, whereas for the son putting wings onto his avatar can be considered only a novelty. Often people think that what they are proposing is innovative, but little by little they realize that it was innovative only for themselves, and not for the others. So, when we enter into innovation in the social aspect, meaning, innovation

in the context in which we are inserted, it has to be understood and legitimated by the others as an innovation. As in the case of the Van Gogh world, for instance, to discuss knowledge about impressionism, highlighting the characteristics represented in the course of Arts.

To go further in the reflection on innovation we need to broaden the comprehension of the term *innovation*, which is nowadays understood under multiple regards and different definitions, being present in a variety of situations: in ascendant markets, in digital virtual technologies, in pedagogical practices and in the different sectors of economy.

Innovation has been associated, in general, to the act of turning making new, somehow introducing the *novelty* in human beings' actions. Rios (2002) states that, "under the common sense view novelty is associated with progress; furthermore, with improvement" (p.156). However the author also emphasizes her concern about what men and women consider being a novelty: "Does a novelty necessarily imply an improvement? Does it imply transformation that brings benefits? Is it necessarily reinvigorating?"

Based on the reflections proposed in the figures and by Rios (2002), we understand that innovation in education goes beyond presenting something new or a novelty once it consists of a deliberate and conscious change with the objective of improving educational actions, which require paradigm ruptures (Sousa Santos, 2004). To innovate in education is, therefore, a potentially changing action, capable of breaking hegemonic logics by proposing other ways of acting in the world, of establishing relationship and interaction, of being, living and sharing.

We can then say that:

Innovation appears when an observer sees someone doing something that positively surprises him, and that he or she considers that can solve operational difficulties in his living in a suitable way not before perceived. (Maturana & Dávila, 2009, p.313)

In this sense, innovation requires a constant search for autonomy, authorship and emancipation of the human beings involved in the teaching and learning processes. So, in order to innovate in the educational context it is necessary to modify the ways of dealing with the objects of knowledge; the way of establishing relationships between educators and students, from the perspective of pedagogical mediation; the rupture of the dichotomy existing between theory and practice, from the perspective of contextualization; and configuring a living space where living and sharing occur through questioning, reflection, differences and co-existence. In this way we can think that;

the role of education is to create a space of transformation for people's living and sharing. It is not supposed to serve a company or any other task in particular because doing the work is something that comes with the living. (Maturana, 1999, p.140)

So,

the simple fact of using a novelty, such as 3D Digital Virtual Worlds, does not mean an innovation in the Educational context, because, in order to make it possible, teachers/researchers need to get to know this technology in order to comprehend it thoroughly within the context of its specific nature, which demands new methodologies, new practices and processes of pedagogical mediation according to the possibilities offered. We believe it is possible for the teacher/researcher to extract the highest potential from 3D Digital Virtual Worlds in respect to human development. (Schlemmer & Backes, 2008, p.531)

Therefore, it is the role of people situated in cultural contexts and several realities like us to think about innovative educational methodologies, that problematize realities and call for reflection, as well as new technologies that promote democracy and the improvement of the quality of teaching and learning processes, so that men and women can develop themselves in human emancipation. We believe then, that we can think about digital emancipation.

CONCLUSION

We believe that the development of online education in metaverse, based on the complexity theory, on the systemic thinking and on the conception of self-eco-organizing, can contribute to elevating the quality in education within the world educational scenario, through more innovative pedagogical proposals that will contribute to the development of education (both in its physical and digital virtual ways).

With the use of metaverse we are able to develop teaching and learning processes through pedagogical practices involving metaphors for the construction of knowledge, once the metaverse has the interesting possibility of graphic representation. However we can also think about the classes developed in a geographically located context, exploring more metaphors, images and schemes. Within a digital virtual space there is no order of participation, the students do not need the authorization of the educator to express their point of view, and consequently, we can reconsider relations in classes in geographically located contexts, in a more dialogical and less hierarchical way.

Metaverses are digital virtual technologies that can empower relations, interactions and dialogues between the participants in a dynamic and heterarchical way. So, it becomes possible to establish pedagogical mediations that result in reflections, and above all, changes, configuring the living space through the legitimacy of the other, mutual respect, autonomy, authorship and cooperation. In summary, a digital virtual space is constantly under construction while its e-citizens act and interact in a critical and conscious way.

However, 3D Digital Virtual Worlds only represent possibilities. The human beings that e-inhabit the 3D Digital Virtual Worlds are the ones who can transform possibilities in potentials. When making these potentials concrete we can configure livings through the participants' changes in congruence with the environment, aiming for the common good of everyone and therefore emancipating men and women who construct digital virtual living. Under the perspective of this living, we aim to develop online education in Metaverses. An online education in which we can

make a new culture emerge, when we configure digital virtual collaborating and we hope that this emerging culture comes from a perspective of a liberating culture[14].

REFERENCES

Almeida, M. E. B. (2009). Gestão de tecnologias, mídias e recursos na escola: O compartilhar de significados. *Em Aberto*, 22, 75–89.

Backes, L. (2007). *A formação do educador em mundos virtuais: Uma investigação sobre os processos de autonomia e de autoria*. (Unpublished master's dissertation). Universidade do Vale do Rio dos Sinos, São Leopoldo, Brazil.

Backes, L. (2011). *A configuração do espaço de convivência digital virtual: A cultura emergente no processo de formação do educador*. (Unpublished doctoral thesis). Universidade do Vale do Rio dos Sinos, São Leopoldo, Brazil and Université Lumière Lyon 2, Lyon, France.

Backes, L. (2012) Metodologias, práticas e mediação pedagógica em metaverso. In E. Schlemmer, P. Malizia, L. Backes, & G. Moretti (Eds.), Comunidades de aprendizagem e de prática em metaverso (pp. 179-202). São Paulo, Brazil: Editora Cortez.

Capra, F. (2004). A teia da vida: Uma nova compreensão científica dos sistemas vivos. São Paulo, Brazil: Cultrix.

Castells, M. (2003). A sociedade em rede. São Paulo, Brazil: Paz e Terra.

Fagundes, L. da C., Sato, L. S., & Maçada, D. L. (1999). Projeto? O que é? Como se faz? In L. da C. Fagundes (Ed.), *Aprendizes do futuro: As inovações começaram!* (pp. 15-26). Brasília, Brazil: MEC. Retrieved from http://www.dominiopublico.gov.br/download/texto/me003153.pdf

Fichtner, B. (2010). *Introdução na abordagem histórico-cultural de Vygotsky e seus Colaboradores*. São Paulo, Brazil: USP. Retrieved from http://www3.fe.usp.br/secoes/inst/novo/agenda_eventos/docente /PDF_SWF/226Reader%20 Vygotskij.pdf

Figueiredo, A. D., & Afonso, A. P. (2006). *Managing Learning in Virtual Settings: The role of context*. Coimbra: Universidade de Coimbra.

Franco, S. R. K. (1999). Piaget e a dialética. In F. Becker, & S. R. K. Franco (Eds.), Revisitando Piaget (pp. 9-20). Porto Alegre, Brazil: Mediação.

Freire, P. (2007). Educação e mudança. Rio de Janeiro, Brazil: Paz e Terra.

Freire, P., & Shor, I. (1992). Medo e ousadia: Cotidiano do professor. Rio de Janeiro, Brazil: Paz e Terra.

Lévy, P. (2010). A inteligência coletiva: para uma antropologia do ciberespaço. Rio de Janeiro, Brazil: Editora 34.

Locatelli, E. L. (2010). *A construção de redes sociais no processo de formação docente em metaverso, no contexto do programa Loyola*. (Unpublished master's dissertation). Universidade do Vale do Rio dos Sinos, São Leopoldo, Brazil.

Maffesoli, M. (2007). Tribalismo pós-moderno: Da identidade às identificações. *Ciências Sociais*, *43*, 97–102.

Maffesoli, M. (2012). O tempo retorna: Formas elementares da pós-modernidade. Rio de Jenairo, Brazil: Forense Universitária.

Maturana, H. R. (1999). *Transformación en la convivencia*. Santiago, Chile: Dólmen Ediciones.

Maturana, H. R. (2002). A ontologia da realidade. Belo Horizonte, Brazil: Ed. UFMG.

Maturana, H. R. (2005). Emoções e linguagem na educação e na política. Belo Horizonte, Brazil: Ed. UFMG.

Maturana, H. R., & Dávia, X. Y. (2009). Habitar humano em seis ensaios de biologia-cultural. São Paulo, Brazil: Palas Athena.

Moraes, M. C. (2004). O paradigma educacional emergente. Campinas, Brazil: Papirus.

Okada, A. (2004). A mediação pedagógica e tecnologias de comunicação e informação: um caminho para a inclusão digital? *Revista da FAEEBA - Educação e Novas Tecnologias*, *22*(13), 327-341. Retrieved from http://people.kmi.open. ac.uk/ale/journals/r03faeba2004.pdf

Rios, T. A. (2002). Competência ou competências – O novo e o original na formação de professores. In D. E. Rosa, V. C. Sousa, & D. Feldman (Eds.), Didáticas e práticas de ensino: Interfaces com diferentes saberes e lugares formatives (pp. 154-172). Rio de Janeiro, Brazil: DP&A.

Schlemmer, E. (2001). Projetos de aprendizagem baseados em problemas: Uma metodologia interacionista/construtivista para formação de comunidades em ambientes virtuais de aprendizagem. *Colabor*, *1*(2), 1–10.

Schlemmer, E. (2005). Metodologias para educação a distância no contexto da formação de comunidades virtuais de aprendizagem. In R. M. Barbosa (Eds.), Ambientes virtuais de aprendizagem (pp. 29-50). Porto Alegre, Brazil: Artmed.

Schlemmer, E. (2008). ECODI - A criação de espaços de convivência digital virtual no contexto dos processos de ensino e aprendizagem em metaverso. *Cadernos IHU Idéias*, *6*, 1–32.

Schlemmer, E., et al. (2006). ECoDI: A criação de um espaço de convivências digital virtual. In *Proceedings of XVII Simpósio Brasileiro de Informática na Educação* (pp. 467-477). Brasília, Brazil: UNB/UCB. Retrieved from http://br-ie. org/pub/index.php/sbie/article/viewFile/507/493

Schlemmer, E., & Backes, L. (2008). Metaversos: Novos espaços para construção do conhecimento. *Revista Diálogo Educacional (PUCPR)*, *8*, 519-532.

Sousa Santos, B. (2004). Um discurso sobre as ciências. São Paulo, Brazil: Cortez.

Trein, D. (2010). *Educação online em metaverso: A mediação pedagógica por meio da telepresença e da presença digital virtual via avatar em mundos digitais virtuais em 3 dimensões.* (Unpublished master's dissertation). Universidade do Vale do Rio dos Sinos, São Leopoldo, Brazil.

Trein, D., & Backes, L. (2009). A biologia do amor para uma educação sem distância. In Proceedings of 15° Congresso Internacional ABED de Educação a Distância (pp. 1-10). Fortaleza, Brazil: ABED.

Trein, D., & Schlemmer, E. (2009). Projetos de aprendizagem baseados em problema no contexto da web 2.0: Possibilidades para a prática pedagógica. *Revista e-Curriculum (PUCSP)*, *4*, 1-20.

Valente, C., & Mattar, J. (2007). Second Life e web 2.0 na educação: O potencial revolucionário das novas tecnologias. São Paulo, Brazil: Novatec Editora.

Yin, R. K. (2005). *Estudo de caso: Planejamento e métodos.* Porto Alegre, Brazil: *The Bookman*.

KEY TERMS AND DEFINITIONS

Innovation: Innovation appears when an observer sees someone doing something that positively surprises him, and that he considers it can solve operational difficulties in his living in a suitable way not before perceived (Maturana & Dávila, 2009, p.313).

Metaphor: Metaphors are, in general, elements constructed for our conception of reality. We structure our different experience fields (areas) in a systematic way by means of a metaphor. Through them we construct our imagination as "pictures" that create connections between fields, phenomena and very different and contradicting processes, forming a coherent system (Fichtner, 2010, p.37).

Method of Dialogical: The methods of dialogical education bring us the intimacy of society, the reason of being, of each object of study. Through a critical dialogue about a text or a moment in society, we try to enter it, to reveal it, to see the reasons he is, the way he is, in the political and historical context they are in (Freire, 1992, p.24-25).

Methodology of Learning Projects Based in Problems: It is based in the conjecture of cooperative activities. It encourages the interaction and enables an action-reflection process in the learning subjects – the members of the project's development community. The conjecture of the cooperative activity includes and encourages the interdisciplinary work, because it fosters the development of thinking, and the autonomy through intellectual, social, cultural and political exchanges, favoring metacognition and awareness taking.

Online Education: The term online Education is used in the studies developed by Trein and Backes (2009), where the process of education occurs in the active presence of students, regardless of distance, hence the term distance education seems inconsistent.

Pedagogical Mediation: In the process of pedagogical mediation we use, in the interactions carried on living and collaborating, the dialogical relations, the reflection, the perturbation and the structural coupling. We then configure our living spaces, so that we are able to transform it. This way, for human beings to meet in a pedagogical mediation within the same shade, they have to be considered as a legitimate being, which means, they have to establish emotional relationship based in love.

Perturbation: The state of neural activity, carried out by different disturbance, are determined in every person by their individual structure, and not by the characteristics of the disturbing agent (Maturana & Varela, 2002, p. 27).

Problematizing Methodology of Case Study: This methodology is originated from two different sources: from the cases described by the students, referring to concrete situations; and from cases described by the educator. The cases described by the students reveal their uneasiness, their way of perceiving the context and the aspects they consider important. In the cases described by the educators, they gather specific objectives proposed in the training process, referring to some knowledge that was not approached in the cases described by the students.

ENDNOTES

[1] Retrieved from http://unesdoc.unesco.org/images/0019/001911/191186por.pdf

[2] According to Maffesoli (2012) postmodernity is emerging, and therefore we cannot conceptualize it, we only make approaches to contributing to our comprehension. The author states that the pace of life runs from a fixed point, so "Isn't a water spring the origin of rivers? The vital flow does not escape this necessary law. A Law we are discovering. ... Law, in summary, is the "source" of postmodernity, reminding us of the importance of what is complex, the need for roots, deepening the surface. In short, the useful involvementism to all growth. The grain's tegument, the subject's body skin, the body remembering good memories".

(p.13) For Maffesoli (2012) it is essential knowing how to think.

[3] The concept of timeless time and space of flow are approached in Chapter 14. – Nomadic Hybridism.

[4] Previously referred to in Chapter 4 - Avatar: Building a "Digital Virtual Self."

[5] Diaspora is a network distributed in a way separate computers can directly connect to each other, without passing through a central server, as in the case of Facebook. https://joindiaspora.com/.

[6] Translation: Black Heaven.

[7] Concept defined in Chapter 12 - Digital Virtual Sharing Spaces.

[8] When we mention alterity we mean a collective subject, meaning, "myself" and also what others think about me. This concept is approached in Chapter 12 - Digital Virtual Sharing Spaces.

[9] As discussed in Chapter 5 – Immersion, Telepresence, and Digital Virtual Presence in Metaverses.

[10] "The states of neural activity carried out by different disturbances are determined in every person by their individual structure, and not by the characteristics of the disturbing agent" (Maturana & Varela, 2002, p.27).

[11] Metaverses presented in Chapter 3 – The Metaverse: 3D Digital Virtual Worlds.

[12] The term Online Education is used in the research developed by the Digital Education Research Group GPe-dU UNISINOS/CNPq and was coined in the studies developed by Trein and Backes (2009), and Trein (2010), and it is in compliance with the term Distance Education, used by Maturana (1999).

[13] Discussed in Chapter 3 – The Metaverse: 3D Digital Virtual Worlds and Chapter 12 - Digital Virtual Sharing Spaces.

[14] Theme developed in Chapter 13 - Digital Virtual Culture in Metaverse: the Metaculture?

Chapter 10
Digital Virtual Communities in Metaverse

ABSTRACT

This chapter discusses the process of forming Digital Virtual Communities in the Metaverse. The authors present and discuss subtopics like "Communities: Historical and Concept Aspects and Characteristics," "Digital Virtual Learning Communities," "Digital Virtual Learning and Practice Communities," "Digital Virtual Learning and Practice Communities in Metaverses." As a main conclusion, it is possible to say that another perspective and tendency for Digital Virtual Communities of Learning and Practice lies in the nomadic-hybrid-multimodal Digital Virtual Communities of Learning and Practice, which means they use different technologies of any kind, including games and simulations in fixed or mobile devices at any time and space, in coexistence with spaces of action and interaction of the physical world face. Thus, it is possible to say that the current generation lives, collaborates, inhabits, co-inhabits, and inhabits-and-co-inhabits new spaces, made of and in the communities created, not living in one space, in one community, in one world and one universe.

INTRODUCTION

The technological changes, which have been happening for some time, have not only changed ways of learning, but also, and more usually, the ways of social gathering, professionality and work, creating new radical phenomenology. (Malizia, 2012, p.25)

The evolution of digital technological gadgets, mainly mobile ones: the broadening of network connections, mainly wireless; the variety of apps enabling all-to-all communication, related to people's communication needs, interaction, being together, making changes, sharing ideas, knowledge and projects, have contributed to the construction of Digital Virtual Communities[1], of all natures, at any time and space.

This reality is the case both in the formal educational sphere, in socially recognized institutions; as well as in non-formal education, in companies and Non-Governmental Organizations. They arise, mainly due to to the increasing necessity for updating, and training throughout life, as well as the acknowledgment that many of a subject's learning needs are unlikely to be fulfilled through forma-

DOI: 10.4018/978-1-4666-6351-0.ch010

tive processes, offered in the logic of "courses", with a linear and strict organization, previously planned and developed in the same way for everyone, simultaneously.

It is within this context that Digital Virtual Communities of Learning and Practice are constituted as a new way of social organization and they contribute to changing the way in which the subject relates himself to information, learns and generates knowledge, being the object of investigation by several researchers, among them the Spanish sociologist Castells (1999, 2003, 2013). For the author, the informational way of development present in those communities can contribute to the rise of a new economy of knowledge.

In the scope of metaverse technologies, the constitution of Digital Virtual Communities of Learning and Practice is empowered and the feeling of belonging to the community is intensified by the subject's digital virtual presence, through the avatar. Through the avatar he interacts in 3D digital virtual worlds and with the other subjects, also represented by avatars, by the combination of textual, oral, gestural and graphic languages, configuring a social presence, favoring a higher feeling of presentiality and immersion[2].

In this chapter we shed a light on conceptual and historical aspects, as well as on the basic characteristics that make up a community. We conceptualize Digital Virtual Communities, discuss Digital Virtual Communities of Learning and Practice, and finally Learning and Practice Digital Virtual Communities in Metaverses, along with our conclusions.

COMMUNITIES: HISTORICAL AND CONCEPTUAL ASPECTS AND CHARACTERISTICS

Before we begin the discussion of Digital Virtual Communities it is crucial to understand the concept of community. The idea of community leads us to the feeling of belonging, identification, sharing

of common objects, collaboration, cooperation, joined forces, strong bounds that constitute the reciprocity of actions and interactions for a "common good".

According to Schlemmer (2012), the term community originates from the Latin word *communitate*, meaning the quality of that which is common, congregation. This term is used to refer to any type of social gathering or social aggregation, and as a synonym of society, social system, social organization, social group of different natures, such as neighborhood community, religious community, scientific community, indigenous community, afro-descendent community, gamers community, among many others. It is through these that we try to explain phenomena that can be constructed from a geographically marked place, or other elements that refer to common identity from a certain group of people.

So, community is polysemic concept, and has been widely studied by theorists from different areas of knowledge. According to the area in which it is used, it acquires greater accuracy regarding the characteristics of a community; in others it opens spaces for specifications that give the concept a certain plasticity.

In common usage, the term is used to name a group of people that live spatially (geographically) close to each other, have objectives in common and similar and complementary interests, and share the same set of rules, history and culture.

According to Schlemmer (2012), among the most referenced classic authors in conceptualizing the term "community" is the German sociologist Ferninand Tönnies, who published his work "Community and Society" in 1887. The author presents the difference between the concepts of community and society. For him a community is "Everything that is shared, private, lived exclusively together" and society "…the public life – the world itself. … We can, in a certain way, understand the community as a living organism and society as a mechanic and artificial aggregated" (TÖnnies, 1995, pp.231- 232).

The concept of community has also been the subject of investigation by Koenig (1967). For him community is "a group of people occupying a defined territory, with which they identify, and where there is a certain level of solidarity" (p.210). It is a group of people who live together and have a mutual relationship, sharing or not, a group of particular interests, that constitutes a community.

Giddens (1991) states that communities are marked by the physical social presence, where the time is determined and space geographically delimitated and both coincide.

According to Peruzzo (2002 apud Schlemmer, 2012) different classic authors present basic characteristics, needed for a community, such as:

- Locality, in the geographical sense, including nomadic communities, for at a certain time they inhabit a certain common territory, even temporarily;
- Live in common through relationships and intense interaction among their members;
- Self-sufficiency (social relations can be satisfied within the community);
- Common goals;
- Common language;
- Common culture;
- Natural and spontaneous identity between their members' interests;
- Awareness of their identifying singularities; and
- Feeling of belonging, of community, from social cohesion and co-participation.

By analyzing these characteristics presented by classic theorists, in relation to the current context in which subjects live and share - more and more immersed in different digital technologies, we understand that if they were interpreted in a rigid way this might stop us identifying new configurations of communities, that arise from social-historical and techno-scientific changes, causing

resignification of concepts and attributing them a certain movement, plasticity. Even considering the statement, it is necessary to preserve a relationship based in cohesion, convergence of objectives and view of the world, interaction, feeling of belonging, active participation, sharing cultural identities, co-responsibilities and cooperative character, in order to characterize a community.

So, as Malizia (2012) states, in order to understand the changes we are going through we need first to comprehend the genetic mutation of DT, which from being instruments of elaboration and data transmission become instruments of communication and interaction, whose potential has still not been totally explored. According to the author, there are two main factors that characterize this change: the first is related to the definition of the geometry of the communication flows between people; the second is the broadcasting of codified data to multimediality (Malizia, 2006).

As for the first mutation element, it is important to emphasize how mass production has made us accustomed to distinguishing between instruments for interpersonal communication and instruments for mass communication. The network makes this opposition considerably obsolete, through a synthesis that synergically integrates the one-to-one communication modalities and the one-to-many communication functions; besides that, they guarantee functions of dialogues between people and filter standardized information based in parameters and categories specified by the user. The second factor of evolution, the transformation of the network, from codified data vehicle to multimediality, the main effect of which is the valorization of contexts; in the moment that information technologies were exclusive property of big structures, that could economically support the complex codification complex and recontextualization of knowledge, multimediality brought the possibility of publishing contexts and producing them at limited costs. The new network communication and cooperation instruments allow users to exchange different types of messages (text, sound and images), creating a new cooperation environment. New technologies considerably reduce the coordination costs of communication because they limit the use of procedures of knowledge codification. It is in this context of structural modification of technologies where virtual communities arise, as new ways of organizing collective learning processes and the development of shared knowledge, of the "way of working" together, doing business, knowing/learning. (p.26)

Menegotto (2006) suggests that, through the development of Communication and Information Technologies, the concept of communication is associated with a "virtualization" process, where the space is no longer determined by a geographically defined place. For Backes et al. (2006), what happens in this process is nothing more than a "territorial transcendence", making it possible for people to organize through Digital Virtual Communities regardless of time and space.

So, in these intertwined representations about what a community is; of criteria that allows us to identify if a certain social group constitutes a community, of ways of keeping them alive, active, in a process of a vertiginous social transformation, which we are experiencing in a more intense way in recent decades, strongly contributing to certain community types gradually dying out, vanishing, and many others coming to actively constitute themselves; it is when we state the resignification of the concept of community, mainly connected to the technological digital context. It is this social transformation, this digital technological evolution that has triggered the appearance of new ways of social organization and sociality, contributing to paradigms becoming superseded, making space for new paradigms (the systemic-complex paradigm)[3], new logics (fuzzy logic), new comprehension and "broadened" meanings, or even (re)signification of

concepts such as: community, presence, distance, territory, space, environment, place, real, virtual and living, among others.

It is then through different digital technologies that digital virtual social networks are constituted, and with them new types of communities –Digital Virtual Communities, representing new ways of organizing communication processes, sociality, professional interaction, formative and business in the *sensu lato*. These communities are organized from affinities and common interests, in a digital virtual space in which they develop, modifying the way the subject relates to others, works, studies, entertains, teaches and learns, in other words, lives and shares.

DIGITAL VIRTUAL COMMUNITIES

For Castells (2013), subjects create meanings; giving sense, when interacting in their natural and social environment, connecting their neuro-networks with the natural networks and social ones. The constitution of networks is operated by the action of communication, this being understood as the process of sharing meaning in the exchange of information, as for the society in general the main source of social production of meaning is the socialized communication process, which exists for the public domain, beyond interpersonal communication.

The continuous transformation of communication technology in the digital era broadens the reach of communication means for all domains of social life, within a network that is simultaneously global and local, generic and personalized, in a constantly changing standard. The process of construction of meaning characterizes a high volume of diversity. There is, however, a characteristic common to all processes of symbolic construction: they broadly depend on messages and structures created, formatted and broadcast in multimedia communication networks. (p.11)

Although every subject constructs their own meaning from the way they interpret the information communicated regarding their ontogeny, according to Castells (2013), "this mental processing is conditioned by the communication environment. So, the change in the communicational environment directly affects the norms of constructing meaning and, therefore, the production of power relationship" (p.11).

As Schlemmer (2012) suggests, it is at the end of the XX century, in the core of the techno-scientific movement, with the advent of the internet and, therefore, associated with a virtualization process turning into a digital one, that the concept of Digital Virtual Communities is created. Those communities are constituted by telepresence and by digital virtual presence[4], in timeless time and in a space of flow[5], of a digital virtual nature. Nevertheless, in order to better understand them we need to look at history.

According to Castells (2003) online communities have very similar origins to the counterculture movements and the alternative ways of life appearing in the 60s. The first users of computer networks, which were strongly marked in that historical moment by democratic ideas and the desire for freedom, inspired the practice of online interconnection. Furthermore, at the end of the 60s and beginning of the 70s timeshare systems appeared, like the PLATO (Programmed Logic for Automated Teaching Operations)[6], developed by Donald Bitzer7 and, with the first online communities. In 1979 these communities were spread with the creation of the textual RPG "Avatar" and by the appearance of USENET[8]. Rheingold (1993) and Castells (1999) also highlight the appearance, in 1989, of Bulletin Board Systems (BBS), contributing even more for the proliferation of Digital Virtual Communities. However, according to Schlemmer (2012), it was in 1993 with the work entitled, "The Virtual Community" that Howard Rheingold, influenced by the "WELL" (Whole Earth 'Lectronic Link)[9], that the term gained force. According to Rheingold (1993) digital

virtual communities are "… social aggregations that come in the network when a group of people carries on public discussions long enough, and with sufficient human emotion, to build up relationship networks in cyberspace" (p.5).

Lévy (1999) and Palloff, and Prat (1999) define Digital Virtual Communities as electronic networks of interactive communication, formed from affinities of interests, knowledge, mutual projects and exchangeable values, offered in a cooperation process[10], regardless of geographical proximity and institutional filiations. This way, the participants of a virtual community establish relations and mutually interact through the big network, the Internet.

According to Castells (2003) there are two main aspects upon which Digital Virtual Communities work: free and horizontal communication (connected to the practice of free global expression that comes with the creation of Internet) and, shared value (that he referred to as "formation of autonomous networks", meaning that any subject can form a group and spread their own information). So, the development of Digital Virtual Communities is supported in the interconnection, it is constituted through the contacts and interactions of all kinds, involving and integrating different ways of expression, as well as the diversity of interests, values and imagination, including the expression of conflicts.

For Turkle (1999), community is linked to identity, and so the community cannot exist in the transitory. Turkle (1999) is interested in the "identifying" effects of online experiences, which involve the feeling of continuous experimenting when a role is taken, making it part of another's life, typical of the community. "I will not, thus, call communities the non transitory places in the Internet, because I believe that the question is still open. Either way, I address them as they cause the effect of identity. Personal histories are intertwined in them" (p.2).

According to Schlemmer (2012), a Digital Virtual Community is constituted by subjects that share the same interests and objectives, and that interacts, relating in a digital virtual way, using different languages (textual, oral, gestural and graphic), through several digital technologies[11], using the Internet as a platform. In this way, a Digital Virtual Community is a more or less permanent collective, depending on the maintenance of participants' interest, for they are supported from the flow, from interactions and inquietude and from human relations that are deterritorialized in the digital virtual space. According to Malizia (2012), this community not only understands interpersonal aspects in general, but also declines in a diversified way according to functions, logic and learning practices, professionality in the *sensu lato*, organizing, governing and business, learning and of knowledge development (p.36).

In the production of knowledge referring to Digital Virtual Communities, we find derivations such as: virtual learning communities, virtual practice communities, among others, both expressions of a culture of real virtuality, which are presented below.

DIGITAL VIRTUAL LEARNING COMMUNITIES

According to Schlemmer (2012), Digital Virtual Learning Communities can be understood as a group of people that through telepresence and digital virtual presence[12], act and interact, sharing common interests of learning, and together defining learning objectives, strategies and actions to attain them, in a timeless time and in a space of flow, of a digital virtual nature. Learning is the main goal.

Digital Virtual Learning Communities are fed by the actions and interactions among the subjects within them, who can share, discuss and reflect on information, experiences and ideas and produce knowledge in a collaborative and cooperative way. The subjects involved in it are responsible for their process, they are authors and producers,

teaching and learning, enhancing the development of autonomy and authorship. Without interactions, the community simply does not happen.

In this way, the Digital Virtual Learning Communities are constituted as spaces for the socialization of the discoveries that come up during the interactions happening at different levels, generating differentiations, proximity, distance, conflict and contradictions in the ways of thinking, for they interact in the same digital virtual space. Subjects with different ways of perceiving the world, of acting, often from different regions, countries, beliefs, habits, in other words, different cultures, all with the same objective – constructing knowledge, and learning with each other. The conflicts and the contradictions are exactly what trigger the disturbance of the system of subjects' signification, and that can encourage the process of raising subjects' awareness in the teaching and learning processes.

So, for Schlemmer (2012) Digital Virtual Learning Communities are constituted in the interaction practices in the network, implying getting involved in the processes, activities and learning contexts, from the joint elaboration of rules and norms in order to achieve the objectives to which the community has assigned itself.

According to Souza (2000) "…learning happens even apart from programs and formal structures. Even in discussion forums, which have no formal objectives to reach, or in exclusively "social" interactions in DVC, there is a kind of continuous learning which is also very worthy, reaching the participants in an uneven way." This "kind of learning" stated by the author was defined by De Marchi and Costa (2006) as,

a self-guided constructivist learning, based on collaboration and self-organization, counting on the active participation from all participants. Participation through the exchange of contributions starts the dialectic processes of propositions and responses, which enable the construction of knowledge. (p.15)

According to Pallof and Pratt (1999), in self-guided learning, the process is centered on the community members, who follow interactions wherever they may take them, making decisions on the whole process' pace and direction, not depending on a teacher's action. The result of this way of learning is discussed by Jonassen et al. in Pallof and Prat (1999), who comment on the ease provided by learning environments that encourage construction in the personal way, as well as the social construction of knowledge and meaning through interactions with other student communities which is preferable to the teacher's interventions, which control the sequence and the content.

However, according to De Marchi; Costa (2006) for the self-guided learning of the community participants to succeed, actively involving them in the production of knowledge, there are some functions to be performed by them. Such functions were adapted from Pallof and Pratt (1999) for the informal Digital Virtual Learning Communities depicted in Table 1.

Also according to De Marchi and Costa (2006), playing those roles is the minimum requirement for the Digital Virtual Communities participants to enjoy the benefits of the offered learning. However, the environment must have certain characteristics to provide collaboration, which according to Pallof and Pratt (1999) shown in Table 2.

De Marchi and Costa (2006) emphasize that it is not enough for the environment to present all the characteristics for fostering learning if the participants do not play an active role during the

Table 1. Adapted from De Marchi & Costa (2006, p.15 and p.16) apud Schlemmer (2012, p.269)

Knowledge Production	Members are responsible for finding solutions to the problems in each area of knowledge, study focus, and for taking these solutions to a more complex level. It is essential that they analyze the problems and questions from different perspectives, discussing the proposals of other members, in order to create new knowledge and new meanings. In this way, according to Pallof and Pratt (2002) members "learn how to learn, besides acquiring the capacity to research and think critically."
Collaboration	Members need to work together in the production of more complex comprehension levels and in the critical evaluation of the study material. They need to share other, additional material, relevant data, etc. Collaborative work makes it easy for the development of learning in a group and also helps to reach results. According to Pallof and Pratt (2002), when participants work together, they produce deeper knowledge, at the same time "they refrain from being independent to become interdependent."
Process Management	The role of process management is linked to the self-guiding principle. The active participant has to follow elementary rules and interact with others, always giving his opinion about what is happening in the Digital Virtual Communities. This way he is acquiring responsibility and will be directly involved in his learning process.

Table 2. Adapted from De Marchi & Costa (2006, p.16)

Allow the group to come up with an objective for their learning process:	This refers to the proposal to the community, established by negotiations, in order to create rules to be followed.
Encourage members to use problems, interests and personal experiences as motivating tools:	Members are encouraged to include aspects related to their daily routines. Real problems can trigger them, facilitating the construction of meanings, which is part of a constructivist approach that encourages collaboration.
Consider dialogue the essential way of researching:	The dialogue is essential for collaborative learning, being encouraged by online communication means, which make it possible for everyone to take part, including the more introvert ones. Those, according to Pratt (1996 in Pallof and Pratt 2002 p.30), can also have better performance online that in a traditional environment, mainly due to the absence of the social pressure present in face-to-face situations. The dialogue can be stimulated by questions that trigger reflection on the material and the topic being discussed.

whole process. It is not the environment *per se*, but participation of the members that sustains and supports much interaction for the learning to happen. It is during these interaction processes that active participants construct and express competencies.

Pallof & Pratt (1999) present, as essential elements for the students' success, the interactions between the students, between the teacher and the students and the collaboration/cooperation in learning resulting from those interactions. The authors indicate that the subjects acting and interacting in Digital Virtual Learning Communities become more committed to and responsible for their own learning and feel more engaged to contribute to their colleagues' learning. Pallof and Pratt (1999) also present some indicators that can help us identify the formation of Digital Virtual Learning Communities, such as:

- Active interaction, involving both content and personal communication;
- Collaborative and cooperative learning, perceived in the comments addressed from one student to the other, rather than from one student to the teacher;
- Socially constructed meaning, evidenced by agreement or by questioning;
- Sharing of resources among students;
- Expressions of support and encouragement exchanged between students, in addition to the will to critically assess the colleagues' work.

According to Dias (2001, p.27) "the formation of a learning community involves the creation of a collective participation culture in the interactions that support their members' learning activities". So, digital technologies can significantly contribute to the development of formative practices centered on the interaction for a collaborative and cooperative construction of knowledge, in a way that, by sustaining active communication

and an interaction network, the community can learn with their own mistakes, because they will be spread across the network and return to their origin through the feedback loops. It is thanks to this that the community is able to correct their mistakes by regulating and organizing itself.

Lévy (1999) defends the idea that recognition and validation of the subjects' knowledge within virtual communities could be confirmed by the qualification of the subject, because when we use digital technologies in education and formation we need to think about validation mechanisms for learning. They propose a "controlled deregulation" of the current system of knowledge recognition, that would favor the development of an alternative formation, encouraging collective exploration pedagogies and all kinds of initiative that value social experimenting, professional experience and explicit formation. This could incentivize a socialization of the functions of classical schools, in a way that all available forces could participate in following the personalized learning paths, adapted to the different objectives and needs of subjects and communities.

With this in mind, Digital Virtual Learning Communities can be created/constituted both in the formal education sphere, in socially recognized institutions, such as schools, colleges, universities and training institutes, capacitating and training (integrating teachers, students, researchers, as active subjects in the construction of knowledge), and the non-formal (also known as informal Learning Digital Virtual Communities), in companies, Non-Governmental Organizations, (integrating teachers, students, researchers, professionals in different areas of knowledge and other subjects interested in contributing for the construction of knowledge), and whose formation happens due to personal interests in a way to define a self organized relationship network, possible through interactive communication, with common objectives leading them to continuous learning along their lives.

DIGITAL VIRTUAL COMMUNITIES OF PRACTICE

Communities of practice, in a general sense, are defined as a group of people gathered for a common task.

le comunità di pratica si delineano ... como nuove forme organizaative che si affiancano a quelle tradizionali integrandole, con l'objettivo dipromuovere El instillare buone pratiche a supporto dei processi dicondivisione di conoscenza, di apprendimento e di cambiamento/innovazione (Elia, & Murgia, 2008, p. 187 apud Moretii, 2010, p.167)[13]

Practice refers to a group of procedures, routines, common habits, but above all the process of,

Caption, development, sharing, preservation and exploration of knowledge within the community. The group of ideas, tools, information, actions, documents, history, experiences, learning activities, knowledge base that participants share. A successful practice develops knowledge sharing processes tacit and explicit that sustain the community's potential value. (Elia & Murgia, 2008, p.191, apud Moretti (2010, p.168)

According to Wenger (2006), apud Schlemmer (2012) the term "community of practice" has its origin in the theory developed by the Anthropologist Jean Lave. For the author, people are used to think about learning as a relationship between student and teacher, but studies reveal a more complex group of social relations through which learning occurs. The term community of practice was coined to refer to the community that acts as a life circle for the learner. A community of practice is dynamic and involves learning from everyone.

For Wegner (2006), a Community of Practice is a group of people sharing an interest or passion for something they do, and learn how to make it better when they interact regularly (Wenger, 2006, p.1). It is about a community of people sharing ways of working together, experiences, instruments and practices, and they believe that shared learning is a value to be preserved. This sharing happens in an informal and spontaneous way, everyone is continuously learning "he who shares what he does, does it better" According to Wenger (2006) three characteristics are essential for Digital Virtual Communities of Practice (see Table 3).

In this way, Digital Virtual Communities of Practice are built up and grow through the combination of these three elements. Table 4, proposed

Table 3. Adapted from Wenger (2006, p.2)

The Domain	A community of practice has an identity defined by a domain of shared interests. Adhering to it implies a commitment with the domain, and therefore, a shared competency that distinguishes members from other people.
The Community	In keeping their interests in their domain members take part in activities and discussions together, helping themselves, and sharing information. They construct relations that allow them to learn with each other. Similar groups having a common identity, do not necessarily constitute a community of practice, because in order to be a Digital Virtual Community of Practice they need to interact and learn together, however the same members of a community of practice need not necessarily work together every day. Impressionists, for example, used to gather in cafés and studios to discuss painting styles they were creating together. Those interactions were crucial for making them into a community of practice, even though they would often paint alone.
The Practice	A community of practice is not only a community of interests – people who like certain types of films, for example. Members of a community of practice are doers. They develop a shared repertory of resources: experiences, history, instruments, and ways of facing recurrent problems, in practice. This takes time and sustained interaction. The development of a shared practice can be more or less self-conscious, for example, the nurses that get together regularly for lunch in a hospital coffee shop cannot perceive that their discussions over lunch are one of their main sources of knowledge about how to take care of patients. In all these conversations, they develop a group of histories and cases that become a shared repertory for their practice.

Table 4. Wenger (2006, p.2) apud Schlemmer (2012, p.271)

Problem Solving	"Can we work on this design and brainstorm some ideas; I'm stuck."
Request for Information	"Where can I find the code to connect to the server?"
Seeking Experience	"Has anyone dealt with a customer in this situation?"
Reusing Assets	"I have a proposal for a local area network I wrote for a client last year. I can send it to you and you can easily tweak it for this new client."
Coordination and Synergy	"Can we combine our purchases for solvent to achieve bulk discounts?"
Discussing Developments	"What do you think of the new CAD system? Does it really help?"
Documentation Projects	"We have faced this problem five times now. Let's write it down once and for all."
Visits	"Can we come and see your after-school program? We need to establish one in our city."
Mapping Knowledge and Identifying Gaps	"Who knows what, and what are we missing? What other groups should we connect with?"

by Wenger (2006, p.2) gives us some examples of activities developed in a community of practice.

Communities of practice for Elia and Murgia (2008, p.191 apud Moretti, 2010, p.168) can offer the members of an organization the means for coordinating their interactions in a digital virtual universe of knowledge. Organizational learning become a creative process, a co-generation process, where a varied range of new knowledge can open the possibility of new and positive identification, helping to motivate each other to feel gratitude and facilitate interaction with the complex system in which the organization and the individual are immersed. The communities of practice are the meeting point of experiences of different members, resulting in knowledge of the community. And so, knowing a community is continuously enriched by the experiences their members have in different contexts.

The main objective of a Digital Virtual Community of Practice is to exchange information, and generate and share knowledge, mainly linked to professional practice and which can be linked with formal or informal organization. According to Moretti (2009)

generating knowledge for an organization means not only acquiring information and data, but before that, creating a dynamic system in which

data, information and experiences are connected in order to produce a type of global knowledge bigger than the mere addition of preliminary knowledge. To do this, an organization needs to develop a production of knowledge in each element of its part. The basic elements constituting an organization are, according to the thesis of Argyris and Schon (1998), Porter (2003), Nonaka (1998), Wenger (2000, 2006), Davenport and Prusak (2005), the men who act in the organization. That means the main producers of knowledge are the workers, and also the technological artifacts they work with. ... Men who work are, in fact, the only ones capable of producing new knowledge. However, the creation process for new knowledge is not automatic, neither for men. The knowledge produced by an individual is the outcome of the experiences, theoretical knowledge and competencies he has. (pp.5 - 6)

According to Moretti (2009), Wenger's (2009) work about communities of practice describes what happens in a complex organization, where communities are real places for the production of a company's value. A community of practice is, above all, spontaneous and its main objective is the sharing of practices between their members, generally by the use of digital technologies, such as: forums, blogs, chat, wikis, and others. These technologies are also used to make communication possible and to share also in the physical absence of people.

For Moretti (2009), the only weakness of technologies like forums, blogs, chat, wikis, is that they do not allow the primary virtuality – the type of digital virtual presence that is the "primary" presence, though many sensations can be expressed, as well as collaboration and cooperation being developed.

According to Schlemmer (2012) it is common that communities of practice are born, develop and when the project they are working on ends, the life of the community also ends. It serves until the necessity is satisfied, meaning that for every different necessity, another community will be born. However, according to Wenger (2007), some aspects have to be considered regarding Digital Virtual Communities of Practice: the communities of practice cannot be created, they can only be cultured; the most common means for that is the Internet, due to the speed of communications and the ease in finding information – even when the target person is not connected at that time, he can have left the solution to a problem, for example, in a forum and; last but not least, in this type of community the practice is what is shared.

Practice means a methodology of doing things, procedures, work ideas, assuming that between the community members strong bonds are developed, the same level of interest for work, personal connections, among others. This sharing of practices, experiences, is what allows the production of new knowledge. Therefore, the concept of experience is crucial in the construction of practices, on one hand, and for the production of knowledge on the other.

A community of practice, therefore, more than being a community where subjects learn, is a community that learns. The subjects taking part in it are not limited to sharing and benefitting from others' experiences, but are called to develop

"better" practices together; they are, in other words, an absolute possibility of accomplishment of the "knowledge society". (Malizia, 2012, p.45)

Also according to Wenger (2006 apud Schlemmer, 2012), the Community of Practice is not a common denomination for all organizations, which can also be recognized as learning networks, theme groups or technology clubs. They can present different forms: small, large, with a core and many branch members, local, regional, national, international, face-to-face, online and hybrid. They may be inside an organization or include members from different organizations. They can be formally recognized, being sponsored by a budget, or completely informal and even invisible. All of us belong to a community of practice and take part in many of them along our lives.

DIGITAL VIRTUAL COMMUNITIES OF LEARNING AND PRACTICE

According to Moretti (2010 apud Schlemmer, 2012), the concepts of Digital Virtual Learning Communities and Digital Virtual Communities of Practice are deeply linked, and it is very difficult to pull them part and analyze them separately, because working contexts become learning spaces. So, every Digital Virtual Community of Practice enables learning through the sharing of practices. Learning can be the reason the community comes together or an accidental outcome of interactions between its members.

However, according to some authors, Digital Virtual Learning Communities differ from Digital Virtual Communities of Practice. Daniel, Schwier McCalla (2003 apud Moretti, 2010) present Table 5, showing the differences between the two "types" of communities.

Moretti (2010) quotes Daniel, Schwier, and McCalla (2003) who understand that Digital Virtual Learning Communities have a higher emphasis

Table 5. Daniel, Schwier McCalla (2003 p.48) apud Moretti (2010, p.174)

Virtual Learning Communities	Distributed Communities of Practice
• Less stable membership • Low degree of individual awareness • More formalized and more focused learning goals • More diverse language • Low shared understanding • Strong sense of identity • strict distribution of responsibilities • Easily disbanded • Low level of trust • Life span determined by extent to which goals or requirements are satisfied • Pre-planned enterprise and fixed goals • Domain specific/interests	• Reasonably stable membership • High degree of individual awareness • Informal learning goals • Common language • High shared understanding • Loose sense of identity • No formal distribution of responsibilities • Less easily disbanded • Reasonable level of trust • Life span determined by the value the community provides to its members • A joint enterprise as understood and continually renegotiated by its members • Shared practice/profession

in individuality, as their members search, individually, for personal objectives connected to specific learning contents. They develop individual roles within their communities, in a way that the community's identity and the level of participation of their members relies on every member's capacity to reach their personal objectives. So, when a community of practice is learning what it needs, to be balanced and the accomplishment of common objectives with individuals ones, that can coexist, depending on the level and quality of the participation and learning.

However, for Moretti (2010, apud Schlemmer, 2012), it is hard to achieve both types of communities in an independent way. It is more likely that they coexist in a community with characteristics of both, as often practice and learning are very closely related as a community. According to Wenger (2007) apud Moretti (2010), communities can be interpreted in a broader way as social systems of learning, capable of combining individual learning with collective, meaning, the place where every member's individual contribution becomes part of an intellectual asset for the whole community.

Communities of practice have as their main objective finding solutions to problems through the exchange of experiences, divulgation of new instruments or working processes. In the technological

sphere we use data or applications developed to facilitate cooperation and the identification of the best solutions or tests of new procedures.

Communities of learning can be defined as groups of people who share the objective of acquiring certain knowledge and skills. For that purpose there are tutorials and virtual classrooms for transference of knowledge, individual and group exercises and for the assessment of learning and testing for evaluation. (Formez, 2002, p.6 apud Moretti, 2010, pp.174 - 175)

According to Schlemmer (2012), as the main objective of community of practice is solving problems and sharing best practices for doing so, the objective of learning communities is constructing knowledge and developing skills. Even if this is not explicit, in a community of practice, the practice, learning has a strong value. Not all communities of learning can be communities of practice, although it is possible that communities of practice are also communities of learning.

As a result, based on Schlemmer (2012), it is possible to say that a Digital Virtual Community of Learning and Practice is constituted by sharing practices and by the study and discussion of themes of common interest by the community members, and that the rules, the working norms are defined through group negotiation. The content of a Digital Virtual Community of Learning and Practice is produced in the interactions from discussions, reflections and readings that can be suggested by any community member. Knowledge is being constructed and the subject learns in the self-organization process of his own thinking, as he needs to coordinate his point of view, with other points of view, arguments and evidence brought by the community members. So, through the Digital Virtual Communities of Learning and Practice, it is possible to generate knowledge in a dialogical relation, based on collaboration and cooperation, where all members can develop the ability to listen and express, in a process of autonomy (regarding identifying their own learning needs, as well as the ways to develop them) and authorship (regarding the responsibility for the content and its action/interaction, by relations it produces or by the knowledge it presents). Follow-up and assessment are as a process, accomplished by all members continuously.

Therefore, subjects acting and interacting in Digital Virtual Communities of Learning and Practice can become more committed and responsible for their own learning. Feeling more engaged in contributing with their colleagues' learning, it becomes possible for the subjects to establish and strengthen affective bonds, besides providing development of processes and collaboration and cooperation. The success of a Digital Virtual Community of Learning and Practice relies on its members' active contribution over time, in a way that through this collaboration/cooperation can achieve the common objective defined by the community.

Nevertheless, as presented by Lévy (1999), a human group is only interested in forming a Digital Virtual Community in order to get closer to the ideal of the intelligent collective, more imaginative, faster and capable of learning and inventing than a collective intelligently managed.

According to Moretti (2012) we can talk about communities of practice located and distrib-

uted regarding the geographic proximity of their members. The Internet, through different digital technologies, mainly in the Web 2.0 context, has certainly enabled the creation of spread communities, which collaborate almost exclusively online, and that can collect members in different States or Regions. However, with the digital technological evolution there came Web 3D and along with it new possibilities such as Metaverses, and so, next we will present the constitution of Digital Virtual Communities of Learning and Practices in Metaverses.

DIGITAL VIRTUAL COMMUNITIES OF LEARNING AND PRACTICE IN METAVERSES

In order to comprehend the potentiality that Metaverse technology adds to Digital Virtual Communities of Learning and Practice, we have also brought elements from Computer Mediated Communication. According to Malizia (2012) research about the CMC developed at the beginning of the 80s and aimed to both "describe and explain the conditions in which telematics could be efficiently applied in the process of office automation (which were not arising), while describing the characteristics and other intrinsic effects these new communicative technologies bring" (Malizia, 2012, p.29). According to the author, it was an evaluation of socio-psychological aspects of new communication technologies that started being used in work places. One of the questions referred to concerns over "the effect of a communication entirely based in the text, where there are necessarily missing gestures and facial expressions, present in the face-to-face communication along with the words" (Malizia, 2012, p.29).

It is a model inspired in the concepts of social presence and media richness, developed by Short and Williams (1976). Short's idea was that the CMC was "characterized by a very low level of social presence which does not have non-verbal elements characterizing face-to-face communication". With "social presence" Short wanted to express the perception, by the user, for a communication means, the environment's capability of opportunizing the presence of communicating subjects, whist understanding "the media power" as the environment's communication capacity of connecting, among itself, different themes, making them less ambiguous and offering the possibility of learning them in a certain amount of time. Basically from such concepts, ten years later comes the Reduced Social Cues (RSC) model, whose basic thesis is that communication via computer is inherently poor, as it lacks the typical face-to-face metacommunicative communication channels (gestural, voice intonation, etc.).

After that, according to Malizia (2012) there came other interpretative schemes such as the Side model – "Social Identity De-individuation", the SIP model – "Social Information Processing" and the "Context Social Model" or "situate action", which state that the effects of CMC are not univocal and monolithic, nor are they necessary; they depend on the symbolic valence and not the social "environment" generated in a peculiar group of people and in a particular moment (Malizia, 2012, p.31).

According to Schlemmer, Malizia, Backes and Moretti (2012) the constitution of Digital Virtual Communities of Learning and Practice in Metaverse, although recent and with research at an embryonic point, is growing associated with independent groups that are forming from interaction in different 3D digital virtual worlds, constructed in several Metaverse; but it has begun also to be found in the formal education sphere, in socially recognized institutions for this purpose, and also in the non-formal education sphere, in companies and Non-Governmental Organizations. The rise of these communities is based on affinities and interests (when they occur in independent groups)

or because of the increasing need for insertion and professional updating, for training throughout life, or training and reflection in action, in a way that it is meaningful and effective from the perspective of daily problem-solving, changing and transformations needed.

It is in these contexts that Digital Virtual Communities of Learning and Practice in Metaverse represent significant differentials under the cognition and socio-cognition[14] point of view, because they allow us to understand the importance the experience[15] is acquiring and the co-experience for attributing meaning, and therefore signification, that happens through the incorporated knowledge (enaction), offering then learning experiences and immersive and interactive practices of a digital virtual nature.

Moretti (2010), in his doctorate dissertation entitled: "La simulazione come strumento di produzione di conoscenza: comunitá di apprendimento e di pratica nei mondi virtuali", investigates and discusses the creation/implementation of Digital Virtual Communities of Learning and Practice in Metaverses, through the immersion of subjects, represented by their avatars, in 3D Digital Virtual Worlds

According to the author, the development of Digital Virtual Communities of Learning and Practice in Metaverses, through the immersion of subjects represented by their avatars, in 3D Digital Virtual Worlds presents added value regarding those being trained in the use of Web 2.0 technologies. For Moretti (2010), if the Web has allowed the development of collaborative and cooperative learning, the use of Metaverses can develop other dimensions such as: the possibility of constructing new "knowledge objects" in 3D; the concrete visualization of abstract elements; the sharing of experiences and emotions in an informal and highly personalized way. According to Moretti (2010), we can summarize the characteristics indicating the formation of a Digital Virtual Communities of Practice as: informal creation and spontaneous aggregation; sharing of practices; construction and sharing of meanings; sharing of objectives; no need for physical presence but a "common purpose", a "unity of spirits".

So, we need to understand and show how such characteristics are developed through action and interaction in 3D Digital Virtual Worlds. It is possible perceive that despite the differences described between Digital Virtual Communities of Practice and Digital Virtual Learning Communities, a Digital Virtual Community of Practice is automatically a Digital Virtual Learning Community, but the contrary is not necessarily true, because the development and sharing of best practices is not necessarily present in the development of Digital Virtual Learning Communities. When we think of the use of immersive 3D Digital Virtual Worlds in the construction of Digital Virtual Communities of Learning and Practice, the following questions arise: could relations between participants start being built in immersive virtual environments, where their members are graphically represented by an avatar and, through this representation they manifest their personality and identity? Could immersion, telepresence and digital virtual presence support the "virtual" actions in the community, without eliminating the need for physical contact, but increase the number of quantity and quality of digital virtual relations?

According to Schlemmer (2012), impelled by the use of different digital technologies, both those linked to the Web 2.0, and Web 3D, the Digital Virtual Communities of Learning and Practice are constituted and expanded, causing a rethinking about ways of teaching and learning, that can impel paradigmatic ruptures regarding the educational process, in which the constitution of Digital Virtual Communities of Learning and Practice represents the new challenge to be incorporated to Digital Education culture.

Therefore, working with Digital Virtual Communities of Learning and Practice means working under the perspective of "Learning Contexts" which is intertwined (*complexus*) with the action

in the relation and the interrelation subject(we)-object(other subjects). It is through the establishment of connections, interconnections, links between concepts, that knowledge networks are built, being constantly, referred by actions and interactions, making it possible to be self-regulated and self-organized.

According to Schlemmer (2002), thinking of the educational system, and therefore online Education, in a systemic-complex conception implies comprehending the need for a new organizational structure for educational institutions, regarding the way teaching is structured, the conception of the course, the understanding and organization of the syllabus, subjects, content, assessment, development, "promotion of learning". And in addition, of tools and methodologies that support such processes in a systemic-complex conception.

For Moretti (2009), an organization is a complex system, compounded by elements connected to each other and that relates with the external environment (market, other organizations, etc.) in search of a more intense way of "learning to learn". In this way, an organization that learns is a community of people who are constantly sharing information, capacities and competencies with the objective of developing new ideas together (Senge, 1995, Argyris & Schonn, 1998). According to Nonaka and Takeuchi (1997), the production of knowledge is the main objective of all contemporary organizations, despite not always being immediately visible.

So, according to Moretti (2012), thinking the use of Metaverse technology for the constitution and development of Digital Virtual Communities of Learning and Practice presupposes thinking in Digital Virtual Collaborating Spaces[16]. According to the author, one of the main problems related to the implementation of Digital Virtual Communities of Learning and Practice in Metaverses could be related to the "regress" – what is it "left" for the participants? Because, measuring the effects, understanding "what the intervention really served to do" is not an easy element to identify in the case of works achieved entirely through 3D Digital Virtual Worlds. How can we evaluate these phenomena based on a digital virtual experience? A first problem related to the educational processes in Metaverse is the possibility of measuring interventions, whist the second problem is related to the acquisition of competencies that can be used in the physical world – "the real world". The participants learn in 3D Digital Virtual Worlds, but what happens in the physical face-to-face world – "the real world"? How can what was learned be used in the physical world – "the real world"?

Regarding the first problem, the first indicator for measuring the effects of learning can be represented by the returns, given by the subject-avatars, in Metaverses, after and beyond the courses. However, this indicator only verifies the representation of subjects about the experience of the learning lived, which means that, it is not possible to verify the competencies acquired or developed in Metaverse, only the representation the subjects have of them, that way, not evidencing the process per se (unless this is object of following-up and, therefore, continuous assessment).

A second indicator can be the search for subjects, after the meetings carried out in Metaverses, in order to evoke a collective experience, share it and transform it in real applications (in the physical world). This presupposes that participants do not know each other before the course, or that they do not reveal their true identity before being in the *inworld*. This is only possible until certain point, and is hard, for example, in the case of international communities, for it implies gathering people from different parts of the globe. In this case, if the community was created during a course and the participants share emails and online chat contacts, the relation can be extended to the digital virtual, but with traditional tools. This is the case in which we evidence a gradual transition in the knowledge constructed in the digital virtual for the physical face-to-face – "real", going through different technological tools, conceived to gradually bring more participants.

In the case of more local organizations, these methods do not work very well. Members belonging to the same organization gather every day, and it is reasonable that they share ideas and opinions about the activities they are doing, including courses with experience in Metaverse. In such cases, what happens is a superposition of the digital virtual plan with the physical face-to-face one – "real", in a continuous interaction that can contribute to making the Metaverse a daily meeting place (or, a regular base for a certain time), a place where subjects who already know each other in the physical world get together to experiment different ways of learning.

So, by the end of the formative path, they can use the same indicators valid for traditional courses, because the participants who are already in contact with each other in the physical world don't have difficulty in relation the content of the course work in the digital virtual world and daily life. According to what was revealed by the observations made concerning the success cases from the RICESU Island, UNISINOS[17], Indire and Didagroup, the problem of "going back to real life" in Moretti's opinion (2012), becomes a false problem. The Digital Virtual Communities of Learning and Practice created in Metaverses, that work together and that have a good knowledge and comprehension of the technology used, do not consider the digital virtual organization as something completely separate from the physical face-to-face "real". In the words of the members of the Research Group in Digital Education – GPe-dU UNISINOS/CNPq, has been identified as a Metaverse concept as something closely related to the physical life and work – "real".

It is important to note that, for some of the later questions in the interview, focused on the return to "real life" after "the Metaverse work", most of those questioned did not answer, because they did not understand the question. The research team's coordinator, on the contrary, has given an answer that clearly explains how, for the members of the group, the question was not clear because it is not conceivable. For the members of the GPe-dU, who work together every day simultaneously in metaverses and physical spaces, a division between "real" and "virtual" work does not exist: the virtual reality and the real virtuality recursively penetrates the physical face-to-face – "real", in a way there is no other, no replacement, but a congruence, extension from one in other, they complement each other. For the members of the group, the digital virtual experience is also the "real" experience and vice versa. What they learn in Metaverses directly reports to the physical world – "real", without making "conversions" or translation from the physical – "real" to the digital virtual, or vice versa. The members of the Group obviously use metaverses as a technology for specific purposes, in that case, the students' learning and researchers' formation[18]. Where the learning process is understood as a continuous process, none of the experiences compounding it are separable from each other, whether they are "real" or virtual.

According to Moretti (2012) this line of thinking can be useful for exposing what we call "false feedback problem", and it helps to explain that there is no need to state the problem when the mentality involved is a systemic mentality, not an exclusive one, and if the technologies are considered useful for the person's global development, not merely with tools that have a purpose in themselves.

However, Moretti (2012) calls attention to the fact that Metaverses, like Second Life, are custom made for the subject, even when he immediately gets in touch with others and develops relations with them. The only one to decide about his second life is the subject himself, who is given the choice of the name, or appearance to be used, places to visit, friendships to be established, and so on. In this way, the digital virtual is nothing more than an instrument for the individual's affirmation as such, what allows him to create his own world about the social reality around him, considering he does not like interferences. However, instead of a being a cause it is an effect: the success in virtual worlds, even before the MUDs and MMORPGs derives from "hyper affirmation" of individuality, the individualism that characterizes the contemporary society. The individual, increasingly closed in him, looks for an escape route from the alternative reality and technology allows him to "escape" in the virtual. But it is through this that new social interactions arise: the individual recreates in his second life a kind of society, choosing its image and size, establishing and making relations with people, who, like him, have "escaped" reality. Having escaped or not, in any case these people create a "new society", through virtual communities; it is here that, through the exasperated search for individuality, a new way of association is born, one that feeds itself and finds in the Web 2.0, and now 3D Digital Virtual Worlds, its place to develop.

CONCLUSION

The face of living and sharing in an increasingly technologicized world, where different digital technologies proliferate, contributes to communities of all natures being constructed in the digital virtual universe. This is representative of a significant growing tendency in recent times, either regarding a more formal, institutionalized sphere, that constitutes different types of organization, or regarding more informal sphere, that constitutes different contexts mainly connected to the Web environment.

It is important to perceive that in the universe of human relations, all kinds of communities live together, from the more traditional ones, of territorial basis, to those constructed from the social movements and different digital virtual spaces, such as the Digital Virtual Communities of Learning and Practice, enabling the arousal of spaces rich in subjects' action and interaction in the context of sharing practices and in the construction of knowledge as a collaborative and cooperative way.

In this scenario of perspectives and tendencies, we identify the communities of online players; mainly those formed from games like the MMORPG, which in order to respond to the challenges inherent in the game and the constitution of such communities, stimulate collaborative and cooperative competition processes. So, each player competes against all the others to be the best and win the most relevant items. Despite this, competitors often come in groups and the player needs to join a group and establish collaborative and cooperative relations in order to reach a certain common goal. So the players who establish a higher level of cooperation and a higher number of bonds become more evolved. This concept can be applied to different organizations, which they can benefit from.

Another perspective and tendency for Digital Virtual Communities of Learning and Practice consists of the nomadic-hybrid-multimodal Digital Virtual Communities of Learning and Practice, which means they use different technologies from Web 2.0 combined with technologies of Web 3D[19], of all natures, including games and simulations, either in mobile or fixed devices, at any time and space, coexisting with action and interaction spaces in physical face-to-face worlds.

Indeed, it is possible to say that the current generation lives, shares, collaborates, inhabits, co-inhabits, e-inhabits, e-co-inhabits new spaces, made of and in the communities created, not living in one space, in one community, in one world and one universe.

ACKNOWLEDGMENT

Parts of this chapter were originally published in Schlemmer, E. (2012). A aprendizagem por meio de comunidades virtuais na prtica. In F. M. Litto, & M. Formiga, *Educação a distância: o estado da arte* (pp. 265-279). São Paulo, SP: Pearson Educational do Brasil, and Schlemmer, E., Malizia, P., Backes, L., & Moretti, G. (2012). *Comunidades de Aprendizagem e de Prática em Metaverso*. São Paulo, SP: Cortez.

REFERENCES

Argyris, C., & Schön, D. (1996). *A aprendizagem organizacional II: Teoria, método e prática*. Reading, MA: Addison-Wesley.

Backes, L. et al. (2006). As relações dialéticas numa Comunidade Virtual de Aprendizagem. *UNIrevista, 1*, 1–12.

Castells, M. (1999). A sociedade em rede. São Paulo, Brazil: Paz e Terra.

Castells, M. (2003). A galáxia da internet: Reflexões sobre a internet, os negócios e a sociedade. Rio de Janeiro, Brazil: Zahar.

Castells, M. (2013). Redes de indignação e esperança: Movimentos sociais na era da internet. Rio de Janeiro, Brazil: Zahar.

Daniel, B., Schwier, R. A., & Mccalla, G. (2003). Social capital in virtual learning communities and distributed communities of practice. *Canadian Journal of Learning and Technology, 29*(3), 113–139.

De Marchi, A. C. B., & Costa, A. C. da R. (2006). CV-muzar – Um ambiente de suporte a comunidades virtuais para apoio à aprendizagem em museus. *Revista Brasileira de Informática na Educação, 14*(3), 9–26.

Dias, P. (2001). Comunidades de Aprendizagem na Web. *INOVAÇÃO, 14*(3), 27–44.

Giddens, A. (1991). As conseqüências da modernidade. São Paulo, Brazil: Unesp.

Kant, I. (1983). Crítica da razão pura: Os pensadores. São Paulo, Brazil: Abril Cultural.

Koenig, S. (1967). Elementos de sociologia. Rio de Janeiro, Brazil: Zahar.

Lévy, P. (1996). O que é virtual?. São Paulo, Brazil: Editora 34.

Lévy, P. (1999). Cibercultura. Rio de Janeiro, Brazil: Editora 34.

Malizia, P. (2006). Comunic-a-zioni. Roma, Italy: Franco Angeli.

Malizia, P. (2012). Comunidades virtuais de aprendizagem e de prática. In E. Schlemmer et al. (Eds.), Comunidades de aprendizagem e de prática em metaverso (pp. 25-60). São Paulo, Brazil: Editora Cortez.

Menegoto, D. B. (2006). *Práticas pedagógicas on line: Os processos de ensinar e de aprender utilizando o ava-unisinos.* (Unpublished master's dissertation). Universidade do Vale do Rio dos Sinos, São Leopoldo, Brazil.

Moretti, G. (2009). Sistema i impresa. Roma, Italy: Polimata.

Moretti, G. (2009). Mundos digitais virtuais em 3D e aprendizagem organizacional: uma relação possível e produtiva. In *Proceedings of IV Congreso de La CiberSociedad.* Espanha: Crisis Analógica, Futuro Digital. Retrieved from http://www.cibersociedadnet/congres2009/es/coms / mundos-digitais-virtuais-em-3d-e-aprendizagem-organizacional-uma-relasao-possivel-e-produtiva/644

Moretti, G. (2010). *La simulazione come strumento di produzione di conoscenza: Comunità di apprendimento e di pratica nei mondi virtuali.* (Unpublished doctoral thesis). Universidade de LUMSA, Roma, Italy.

Moretti, G. (2012). Comunidades virtuais de aprendizagem e de prática em metaverso. In E. Schlemmer et al. (Eds.), Comunidades de aprendizagem e de prática em metaverso (pp. 127-178). São Paulo, Brazil: Editora Cortez.

Nonaka, I. T. (1998). The knowledge creating company: Creare le dinamiche dell'innovazione. Milano, Italy: Guerini e Associati. doi:10.1016/B978-0-7506-7009-8.50016-1

Paloff, R. M., & Pratt, K. (1999). *Building learning communities in cyberspace – Effective strategies for the online classroom.* São Francisco, CA: Jossey-Bass Publishers.

Rheingold, H. (1993). *The virtual community: Homesteading at the electronic frontier.* Cambridge, MA: Addison-Wesley Publishing Company. Retrieved from http://www.rheingold.com/vc/book

Schlemmer, E. (1998). *A representação do espaço cibernético pela criança, na utilização de um ambiente virtual.* (Unpublished master's dissertation). Universidade Federal do Rio Grande do Sul, Porto Alegre, Brazil.

Schlemmer, E. (2008). ECODI – A criação de espaços de convivência digital virtual no contexto dos processos de ensino e aprendizagem em Metaverso. *IHU Ideias, 6*(103), 1–31.

Schlemmer, E. (2009). *Telepresença.* Curitiba: IESDE Brasil S.A.

Schlemmer, E. (2009). *Espaço de convivência digital virtual – ECODI RICESU* (Research Report). São Leopoldo: Universidade do Vale do Rio dos Sinos.

Schlemmer, E. (2012). A aprendizagem por meio de comunidades virtuais na prática. In F. M. Litto, & M. Formiga (Eds.), Educação a distância: O estado da arte (pp. 265-279). São Paulo, Brazil: Pearson Educational do Brasil.

Schlemmer, E., Malizia, P., Backes, L., & Moretti, G. (2012). Comunidades de aprendizagem e de prática em metaverso. São Paulo, Brazil: Cortez.

Souza, R. R. (2000). *Aprendizagem colaborativa em comunidades virtuais.* (Unpublished master's dissertation). Universidade Federal de Santa Catarina, Florianópolis, Brazil.

Tönnies, F. (1995). Comunidade e sociedade. In F. Tönnies, & O. Miranda (Eds.), Para ler ferdinand tönnies. São Paulo, Brazil: Edusp.

Turkle, S. (1999). Fronteiras do real e do virtual: Entrevista concedida a federico casalegno. *Revista Famecos*, (11), 117-123. Retrieved from http://revistaseletronicas.pucrs.br/ojs/index.php/revistafamecos/article/viewFile/3057/2335

Wenger, E. (2006). Comunità di pratica: Apprendimento, significato, identità. Milano, Italy: Raffaello Cortina.

Wenger, E. (2009). *Communities of practice: A brief introduction.* Portland, OR: CPsquare. Retrieved from http://www.ewenger.com/theory/index.htm

Wenger, E., Mcdermott, R., & Snyder, W. (2007). Coltivare comunità di pratica. Milano, Italy: Guerini e Associati.

KEY TERMS AND DEFINITIONS

Communities: Meaning the quality of what is common, congregation. This term is used to refer to any type of social gathering, social aggregation, including as a synonym of society, social system, social organization, social group from different natures, such as neighborhood community, religious community, scientific community, indigenous community, afro-descendent community, gamers community, among many others. It is through them that we try to explain phenomena that can be constructed from a geographically marked place, or other elements that refer to common identity from a certain group of people.

Community of Practice: It has, as main objective, to solve problems and share better practices for solving them.

Digital Virtual Communities: They are electronic networks of interactive communication, formed from affinities of interests, knowledge, mutual projects and exchangeable values, offered in a cooperation process, regardless geographical proximity and institutional filiations.

Digital Virtual Communities of Learning and Practice: They are constituted by sharing practices, and by the study and discussion of common interest themes and the rules, by the community members. The working norms are defined through group negotiation (Schlemmer, 2012).

Digital Virtual Communities of Learning and Practice in Metaverse: They are constituted through the immersion of subjects, represented by their avatars, in 3D Digital Virtual Worlds. They present an added value, in comparing to those formed from the use of Web 2.0 technologies, representing significant differentials under the cognition and socio-cognition point of view, because they allow us to understand the importance the experience is acquiring and the co-experience for attributing meaning, and therefore signification, that happens through the incorporated knowledge (ennation), offering learning experiences and immersive and interactive practices of a digital virtual nature.

Digital Virtual Communities of Practice: They have the main objective to exchange information, generate and share knowledge, mainly linked to the professional practice. They can be linked with formal or informal organization.

Digital Virtual Learning Communities: They can be understood as a group of people that, through telepresence and digital virtual presence, act and interact, sharing common interests of learning and, together defining learning objectives, strategies and actions to reach them, in a timeless time, and in a digital virtual space of flow. Learning is the main goal (Schlemmer, 2012).

Learning Communities: It has, as main objective, to construct knowledge and develop competencies.

ENDNOTES

1   Although the term Virtual Communities is found in literature to refer to communities built in the internet, we use the term Digital Virtual Communities because we understand that what makes and distinguishes this type of community form the other ones in the analogical space, is the fact that they are built in the digital space. The virtual, as in the concept stated by Lévy (1996), has always existed, and therefore the difference is the digital.

2   As approached in Chapters 4 - Avatar: Building a "Digital Virtual Self" and 5 – Immersion, Telepresence, and Digital Virtual Presence in Metaverses.

3   As approached in Chapter 2 - Network Learning Culture and the Emerging Paradigm.

4   As approached in Chapter 5 - Immersion, Telepresence, and Digital Virtual Presence in Metaverses.

5   As approached in Chapter 1 - Teaching and Learning in the Network Society.

6   PLATO was a system involving the following possibilities: email, newsgroup, chat and online games.

7   Professor and electrical engineer from the University of Illinois.

8   The first big online forum.

9   WELL is one of the oldest Virtual Communities and it is still active and congregating approximately 4 thousand members. Available in http://www.well.com/

10 According to what was discussed in Chapter 8.

11 Virtual Learning Environment (VLE), blogs, fotolog, wikis, Metaverses (Active Worlds, There, Second Life, etc) Massive Multiplayer Online RPG, different social networks, such as: Orkut, MySpace, Facebook, Flickr, among others.

12 According to Chapter 5 - Immersion, Telepresence, and Digital Virtual Presence in Metaverses.

13 Communities of practice are described as ... new organizational ways that happen together with the traditional ones, integrating them with the objective of promoting and fostering good practices to support the process of knowledge sharing, learning and change /innovation (our translation).

14 This theme is discussed in Chapter 8 - Cognition and Socio-Cognition in Metaverse.

15 Living the experience, thus experiencing through simulation of a reality of the physical face-to-face world, in a digital virtual one; as well as by the creation of real virtuality, from the realities imagined.

16 The construction of this concept-technology is better explained in Chapter 12 - Digital Virtual Sharing Space.

17 This research is discussed in more detail in Chapter 15 - Brazilian Experiences in Metaverse.

18 Particularly the project ECODI – STRICTO.

19 Metaverses and Digital Virtual Worlds in 3D of all natures, including games and simulations.

Chapter 11
The Real Virtuality of Metaverses

ABSTRACT

This chapter approaches the Real Virtuality theme that appears in the construction processes of Digital Virtual World in 3D in Metaverses. The authors present and discuss subtopics like "Virtuality and Reality: Virtual Reality Experiences and Real Virtuality Experiences in Immersive Learning," "The Simultaneousness of Worlds: From the Digital Virtual Space of Coexistence to the Space of Hybrid and Multimodal Coexistence," "The Culture of Real Virtuality." The chapter concludes that it is possible to understand that i-Learning, through the Real Virtuality Experiences and Virtual Reality Experiences, may represent an effective possibility to subjects' education nowadays. In this context, the authors believe it is fundamental to (re) think Education for the current generation, the prospect of a Network Society, a Cultural Hybridism and Multimodality.

INTRODUCTION

The students of today are increasingly immersed in different 3D Digital Virtual Worlds, in overlapping analogue spaces that coexist in the world of dialectical relationships. This fact has contributed to (re) signifying the analog world itself in which they live and coexist. These students, while living in their physical bodies and physical spaces - schools or internet cafés, for example, also live through digital representations which may be graphic such as in virtual digital bodies (when, for example, the student assumes a specific character and has a unique personality in a game such as

when you create your own avatar to interact in 3D Digital Virtual Worlds, digital virtual spaces, or simply a simulation of physical reality. Thus, the student can both act and interact in an experience that simulates 3D, a certain physical reality, as in an imaginary fictional context whose situation does not correspond at all to what one knows of the analogue, physical world. This allows him to have experiences in both Virtual Reality (VR) and Real Virtuality (RV), according to Castells (1999). The present generation owns galaxies, islands, clouds, houses, virtual digital castles, and has virtual friends and virtual relationships. In short, a virtual digital life is constituted, enabling

DOI: 10.4018/978-1-4666-6351-0.ch011

countless experiences, and thus showing that an appropriation of the analogue world also happens by means of attributing constructed meaning in the virtual digital world.

In this technical and socio-cultural context, researchers and educators from different areas of knowledge, seek to understand what challenges, changes and transformations this reality brings to education. So, what education is necessary for the student of this historical and social time and how can we maximize the learning process? In order to provide information to answer these questions we will discuss the concept of Virtuality and Reality - Virtual Reality Experiences and Real Virtuality Experiences in Immersive learning; we will discuss the Simultaneousness of Worlds – from Digital Virtual Living Spaces to Hybrids and Multimodal Living Spaces, The Culture of Real Virtuality and finally present some of our conclusions.

VIRTUALITY AND REALITY: VIRTUAL REALITY EXPERIENCES AND REAL VIRTUALITY EXPERIENCES IN IMMERSIVE LEARNING

Virtuality, broadly speaking, is what has quality or virtual character, that is, the potential to accomplish something. The term is commonly used to refer to situations in which the action, communication, interaction does not occur in a physical classroom form in analog spaces but in a digital form, using different digital technologies in a web environment. As discussed in Chapter 3 - Metaverse, 3D Digital Virtual Worlds, the concept of Virtuality is related to the virtual and according to Lévy (1999), can be understood in the sense: *technical* - related to IT; *current* -"virtual" means "unreality" once "reality" presupposes a material realization, a tangible presence - it is believed that something must be either real or virtual, and therefore cannot have both qualities

simultaneously, and; *philosophical* - the virtual is what exists only in capacity and not in fact, the force field that tends to be solved in an update. The virtual is prior to the formal or effective implementation:

The word virtual comes from the Medieval Latin virtualis, derived from virtus, strength, power. ... In strictly philosophical terms, the virtual does not preclude the real, but the current: virtuality and actuality are only two ways to be different. (Lévy, 1996, p.15)

Can we then say that we virtualize different worlds through our thoughts, which in turn can be updated through different languages in the representation?

Thus, based on Lévy (1996), we can say that virtuality refers to everything that characterizes the detachment of time and space, "deterritorialization". Yet, what can we say when this term is associated with the digital? Could we then think of a "territory" of another kind, as digital? In this case, the digital would be a form of accomplishing the virtual – that which is the virtual representation of a pre-known physical classroom space, which is simulated in the digital, is the virtual representation of an unknown imaginary space, which is conceived in digital. In both cases, what happens is an update, that is, the realization of which is in capacity and that in turn is accomplished in digital.

In this context, the creation of 3D Digital Virtual Worlds in Metaverses can be considered as the "digital materialization" of this virtuality, that is, the world ceases to exist in the potential sphere and begins to take its place in space, in this case, of a digital nature.

However, what is it? What is real? There is no single answer to this philosophical question. Among several interpretations the real can be understood as something that is constructed individually by the student from the perceptions that construct their living and coexist in the relationship with the world and other students. According to Maturana (1997, p. 156), "the reality is a domain of things and in that sense, what can be distinguished is real."

This discussion has been also addressed in the film industry, as we see in this dialogue between Morpheus and Neo from The Matrix (1999):

Morpheus: This is the construction. It is our loading program. We load everything, clothing, equipment, weapons, and training simulations, anything we need.

Neo: Are we in a computer program?

Morpheus: Find it hard to believe? Their clothes are different, the plugs are gone from your body, and your hair has changed. This appearance is what we call residual self-image. It is the mental projection of your digital "self".

Neo: Is this not real?

Morpheus: What is "real"? How do you define "real"? If you are talking about what you can feel, smell, taste and see, then "real" is simply electrical signals interpreted by the brain. This is the world you know. The world as it was like in the late 20th century. It only exists now as a neurointeractive simulation that we call the Matrix. You lived in a dream world, Neo. (Wachoeski, A., & Wachowski, L. The Matrix. 199. Dialogue between Morpheus and Neo.)

This dialogue provides a reflection on what we mean by virtual and real today, and brings us to analyze the contribution of the digital and to rethink these concepts. When *Morpheus* shows the simulated world as a construction in which one can upload everything one needs, and *Neo* is startled by the possibility of being inside a computer program, *Morpheus* encourages him, making him reflect on the changes in his representation in this world (his digital virtual self), *Neo*, puzzled, touches objects and asks: "Is this not real?" *Morpheus* then discusses the understanding of what is real, how to define what is real and brings perception to the discussion, the representation resulting from the significance of the conception that real is that to which we attribute meaning.

In the common usage of the term, 'virtual' is often understood as something that is not real because it does not exist in the physical realm. Nevertheless, this understanding is misguided and highlights a contradiction. If we devote ourselves to reflecting on how we live and how we coexist nowadays, we perceive that virtuality is intensively "present" in various activities in our day-to-day, taking up our time and thus having an existence, a reality, but one that is of another nature, not physical but virtual digital.

Along the same lines follows the discussion of 3D Digital Virtual Worlds, after all, what worlds are these? May there be worlds beyond the physical world we know, this world in which we see, we live, we coexist, we can touch, smell and feel? Could we say that 3D Digital Virtual Worlds are parallel to physical worlds or would it be better to say that they are representations of the worlds we know and/or think of as being worlds of another nature? Therefore, 3D Digital Virtual Worlds can constitute elements representing the physical world and representations of elements that are the product of the imagination, relationships and the interaction of avatars with different digital technologies.

The action of avatars in a 3D Digital Virtual World brings real time results, that is, in the instant the student, through his avatar, performs an action, the 3D Digital Virtual World undergoes modification and updates itself.

Thus, understanding the virtual, while a "complex problematic", as presented by Lévy, 1999, we must look at the 3D Digital Virtual Worlds of any other nature, in other words, a virtual digital nature not just opposed to the real, and not as a parallel world, but from the perspective of coexistence and recursiveness.

In this context Moretti (2012), emphasizes the importance in the context of Metaverse technology, of *space*, the *complexity of dynamic simulation; collaboration, and cooperation*. According to the author and regarding - *the space*, the Metaverse allows what she calls the primary potential in presence and in which the students are digitally present through an avatar. They therefore have a social presence, move, act and interact in 3D Digital Virtual Worlds which is only possible because it is a habitable immersive environment where student-avatars can relate to other student-avatars and objects in 3D who occupy their own space, creating a common space of relationships. An environment in this way allows ... *l'inclusione fisica dell'utente, dotato della capacità di interagire con le immagini, consentendone la trasformazione in quello che da più parti è stato definito "spettattore"* (Alinovi, 2000, p.157 apud Moretti, 2012, p.141). Moreover, according to Moretti (2012), immersive 3D Digital Virtual Worlds allow the student to act and interact with objects, and not just with images, thus making a genuine passage from "witness" to "actor". Being immersed in a 3D Digital Virtual World means to see oneself as part of that environment in relation to space, time, one's own bodily coordination and that of others. These relationships are enabled and are given potential in immersive 3D Digital Virtual Worlds.

Again according Moretti (2012) it is because of this, that the 3D element becomes so important. The subject-avatars can experience spatial perceptions that let them see immediate and practical events, and intervene therein, either individually or in groups. The student-avatar is a person who moves on the computer screen via its graphical representation designed in that world (as an avatar) to experience that world itself. The avatar is built ad hoc, often changing some physical or behavioral characteristics, but the student "is always behind the screen", and this has implications for the transposition and (re)creation of the graphical representation on the computer. This transposition and/or (re)creation, this "change of identity" is never complete, especially in structured

communities with the goal of learning. In online communities, for instance in Massively Multiplayer Online Role Play Games, the scope of the presence is quite different, because the scope of activities (i.e. games) is inserted into the game, where each individual represents a character immersed in that world, but for purposes which can be completely different from the physical world presence. In 3D Digital Virtual Worlds the subject enters as an individual who learns and, therefore, takes a good part, if not all, of their "original" personality.

Moretti (2012) also points out that this also happens because of the particular conformation of the so-called "social virtual worlds", of which Second Life can be considered the most representative. In virtual worlds of this kind, where the scope is not defined in principle, but depends on the student who decides, "because being in the world" during and after having explored it, everything is experience:

expertise in virtual worlds such as Second Life is more dispersed, because the range of activities is much greater (encompassing building, playing, scripting, creating machinima or socializing, for instance). Each of these activities would involve particular forms of expertise. (Oliver, 2009, p.446 apud Moretti, 2012, p.143)

All actions and interactions performed in a Metaverse are considered experiences that are related to the ontogeny of students, both built in the present, physical world, as in virtual digital environments, whether or not they are predominantly textual, 2D, or 3D. According to Moretti (2012), the objectives pursued in learning communities in SL do not end in themselves, while it is true that the majority of active users consider Second Life as "real" as much as their "first life." Learning, professional and 'inworld' practice communities, have very real scopes, such as how to develop skills that can be used in the real world, or use

SL as a platform for simulated training activities/ work, the results of which may ultimately be used in real life.

According to the author, with respect to the second aspect of most importance, the dynamic simulation of complexity, Metaverses allow

the reproduction of complexity, not a static reproduction or a copy, but a reproduction of the basics of this complex formation, is therefore a dynamic reproduction, a development of basic mechanisms which, relating to each other generate complex phenomena. It is easy to imagine how these systems are handy in scientific simulation, and even more for the learning of scientists. The same goes for organizational learning. (Moretti, 2012, p.143)

Last, but not least, is the aspect of collaboration and cooperation. This aspect is potentialized by the first two aspects mentioned above, and probably represents the true value of this technology. In Metaverses, collaboration and cooperation can be experienced in practice, allowing immediate visualization of these processes. We can say that in these cases, either Virtual Reality Experience (VRE), as opposed to the Experience of Real Virtuality (ERV), where a group of people working together and doing an experiment (such as exploration, construction or discovery) collaborate and cooperate in building this common experience through which they learn. The key element for this process to be carried out is what we will call virtual digital presence, meaning that virtual digital presence is mediated by an avatar.

Moretti (2012) refers to *telepresence*, meaning that which occurs through text, voice or image as *secondary presence* and, *digital virtual presence* by means of avatar as a *primary presence*. The secondary presence - *telepresence* - is viable in AVA and in Web 2.0 technologies

and does not replace the physical presence, or allow access to the same communication pos-

sibilities offered by meeting face-to-face. Telepresence "infects" all our actions at all times of the day: the phone, the computer, all electronic devices, despite being "old", allow us to increase our physical presence in places physically or geographically distant, through transmission of voice or text. (p.144)

The primary or digital virtual presence by an avatar is viable through the Metaverse.

Embodied as an avatar in a virtual world, people get a sense of physical presence. They feel like they are in the virtual place as opposed to sitting at their computer at their current location. When they meet the other avatars in their group, they get a sense of social presence. They feel like the others are there with them. There is enough willing suspension of disbelief to allow people to have a strong sense of being with the other people allowing them to interact as they would if were in close physical proximity (Molka-Danielsen, & Deutschmann, 2009, p.94 apud Moretti, 2012, p.145). ... where chat and forum cannot offer the "perception of physical presence," or the feeling of interacting personally, the avatar allows, on the contrary, the realization of which, according to Schlemmer et al. (2006), called virtual digital presence. (p.145)

Thus, according to Moretti (2012), talking about "virtual digital life" and "digital-virtual self" means using the two dimensions of digitality and virtuality, combining them to arrive at the dimension that is characteristic of virtual worlds, which is not only telepresence, but a different and more complex type of presence. The size of digitality itself concerns the computerized and technological aspect of the construction of MDV3D and avatars that e-inhabit it; virtuality is understood as the possibility of creating environments, worlds and relationships, alternative to the physical classroom environments, and potentially the follow up[1] within it.

Also according to Moretti (2012), virtual digital presence is the expression of primary virtuality, or virtuality in presence, and allows a high level of development of interactions with other subjects through immersion and personalization, that is, the creation remains the digital virtual self.

It is from the perspective of immersion that we introduce the concept of Immersive Learning (i-learning). According to Laux and Schlemmer (2011), i-Learning is an educational modality, whose processes of teaching and learning occur in graphical 3D environments, created from the use of different digital technologies and the Web3D, in which learners participate in an immersive way. The concept of i-Learning refers to two other concepts: Virtual Reality and Real Virtuality. Virtual Reality (VR) is understood as a set of technologies and methodologies that enable the creation of interactive and immersive 3D graphical environments. Real Virtuality has been used to represent or create worlds mimicking a physical reality; therefore, physical worlds are represented in virtual digital form.

From a different angle, our research, developed within the Digital Education Research Group - GPe-dU UNISINOS/CNPq has shown the construction of a Real Virtuality (Castells, 1999), and with it the creation of fictional worlds, imaginary worlds that have no direct correspondence with the physical world, but that provoked and produced new meanings for physical existence, while that constitutes existence as a virtual digital nature. Thus, in the context of an i-Learning 3D environment, it can promote the development of Real Virtuality Experiences and Virtual Reality Experiences and even a combination of these. For Schlemmer and Marson (2013), while the first perspective is the "virtualization" of an existing reality in the physical world (simulation), the second is the "realization" of a virtuality built in the digital world. Thus, both Real Virtuality and Virtual Reality are constituted as founding elements of i-Learning.

One of the most recent pieces of research conducted by the Digital Education Research Group – GPe-dU UNISINOS/CNPq, into i-Learning refers to the Anatomy Project in Metaverses: a proposal for Immersive Learning which is a project financed by the Research Foundation of the State of Rio Grande do Sul - FAPERGS and developed between 2010 and 2012. The research was carried out in the context of the Network of Catholic Institutions of Higher Education - RICESU by an inter-institutional (UNISINOS UNILASALLE and UCPel) and interdisciplinary (teachers of anatomy, teaching staff and technical staff) group. The research problem was to understand how the processes of teaching and learning the concepts of anatomy could be developed in the context of developing an experience with i-learning, using Metaverse technology.

In the context of the research, one of the modeled systems was the renal system, where the avatar could enter an artery and through the system reach the bladder (an experience that can only be afforded by 3D Web technologies). The following are the different situations of teaching and learning developed with respect to the renal system. The renal system is internally represented in the figure by the human body modeled (Figure 1).

Clicking on the image of the kidneys, the avatar (virtual digital representation of the student) is teleported into the artery and thereafter has the ability to explore each created part of the renal system. As you move in the artery, components such as red blood cells, white blood cells and other substances pass through it. At different points, the avatar can find maps of sensitive locations with textual and graphic information. (Figure 2)

Along the way the avatars come across many questions (Figure 3), which present challenges when clicked on, and any potential problems with the experience, for example: "Challenge 2: What are these particles you are seeing?"

After covering the arteries, the avatars reach the region "Glomerulus", and again meet a map

Figure 1. Laboratory of Anatomy: Transparent human body with sensitive systems developed by the team UNISINOS
Source: Authors

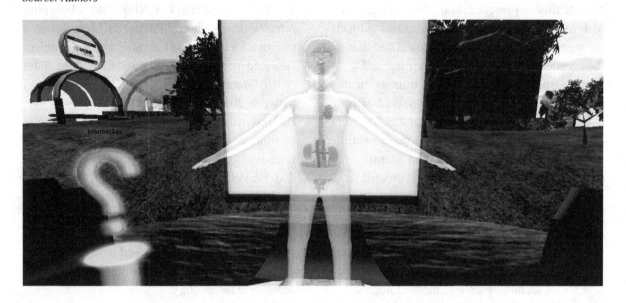

Figure 2. Artery: Internal environment to the renal system and location map with information
Source: Authors

Figure 3. One of the challenges in the course of the experiment within the arcuate artery and the particles to which the question refers in the challenge
Source: Authors

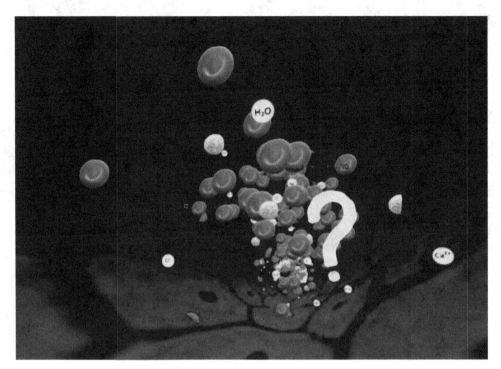

of a sensitive location with textual and graphic information relating to this part of the renal system (Figure 4).

In the sequence of the experiment, they meet a region known as the "Bowman Capsule", where again there is a map of sensitive area with graphic and textual information. (Figure 5)

As a result, we find that the systems modeled in 3D facilitated the attribution of meaning to the concepts and processes related to different systems, especially when there is the possibility of the avatar entering the system being studied (heart, artery, bladder, etc.) and to go through the process as if they are one of the components of the system being studied. This immersion, when associated with challenges and problems, provides a greater involvement for the students with the different concepts. We found that i-Learning experiences could enrich the Anatomy Learning contexts, composing hybrid environments, from the perspective of multimodality.

One of the main advantages of i-Learning is the maximization of the feeling of presence and belonging, through a social presence nurtured by a graphical representation of themselves - the avatar, or in the case of digital games, a character, in a graphically represented environment - 3D Digital Virtual Worlds, favoring immersion and enabling the development of Real Virtuality Experiences and Virtual Reality Experiences.

However, during Real Virtuality Experiences and Virtual Reality Experiences, students mentioned how learning experiences could be enriched if it were possible to mix what they

Figure 4. Image representing the Glomeruli region
Source: Authors

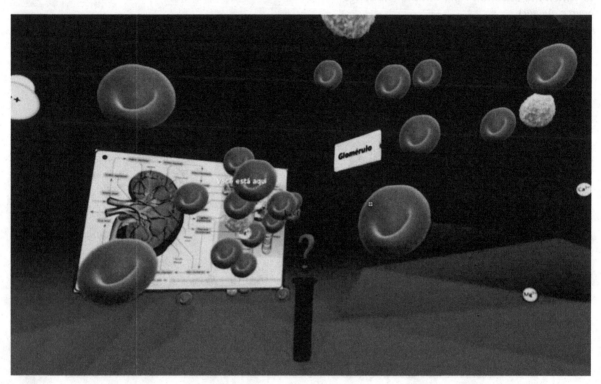

Figure 5. Image representing the region of the Bowman Capsule
Source: Authors

were experiencing in 3D Digital Virtual Worlds with the physical space of the anatomy lab, atlas, videos, and the teacher´s physical presence. Thus, we discuss below, the simultaneity of worlds.

THE SIMULTANEITY OF WORLDS: SPACES OF DIGITAL VIRTUAL ASSOCIATION, SPACES OF ASSOCIATION, AND MULTIMODAL HYBRIDS

We can observe the simultaneity of worlds when we witness the current generation, physically present and simultaneously present in analogue and digital virtual form, through characters and/ or different 3D Digital Virtual Worlds avatars, which allows them to "be" in that (meta) universe, understood as a place where you can go, or be and a place where you can immerse, act, interact, build, talk and learn. In these digital territories, the notion of belonging has changed, since it is no longer about continuous and contiguous spaces, or even geographic territories, but nomadism and transnationalities, deletion of the edges, permeability, whose relationships of "e-inhabitation" are constituted from a hybrid of thoughts, ideas, language, knowledge and practices.

But then, what is happening? The current generation, by "being", "entering", and able to act and interact with different Digital Technologies from an early age, think digital, which contributes to assigning meanings to the analogical world and which may originate from their actions and interactions with and in the digital world, thus becoming experiences that turn into hypotheses which are also used to understand the analogical world in which they live. Thus, new ways of thinking and expressing reveal new meanings and diverse ways of perceiving and feeling the world they belong to, a world constituted by digital technological hybridity in digital spaces that coexists with analog spaces, integrating the living and coexisting with this generation.

From the perspective of the simultaneity of these worlds we can resume the technological concept of a Digital Virtual Living Space as presented in Chapter 12 - Digital Virtual Living Space. According to Schlemmer et al. (2006), Schlemmer (2008, 2009, 2013) a Digital Virtual Living Space comprises:

- Different integrated digital technologies such as virtual learning environments, Digital Virtual Worlds in 3D, Web 2.0 technologies and conversational agents (created and programmed for interaction), among others, to encourage different forms of communication (textual, oral, graphical and gestural);
- Flow of communication and interaction among individuals in this space, and;
- Flow of interaction between individuals and the environment, i.e. the technological space.

A Digital Virtual Living Space assumes, fundamentally, a type of interaction that enables the "e-inhabitants" (according to their ontogeny) of this space, to set it up collaboratively and cooperatively, through "living and coexisting" (Schlemmer, 2010, p.14).

However, during development of the latest research: "Espaço de Convivência Digital Virtual nos Programas de Pós-Graduação (Stricto Sensu) UNISINOS: a proposal for the training of teacher-researchers", linked to the Bolsa Produtividade em Pesquisa do Conselho Nacional de Pesquisa (CNPq)[2], which is in the process of completion; "METARIO - Network Research and Teacher Training in Metaverses: Skills Development for teachers in Management", funded by Coordenação de Aperfeiçoamento de Pessoal de Nível Superior (CAPES)[3], also in the process of completion and, "Anatomy in the Metaverse Second Life: a proposal for i-Learning", Fundação de Amparo à Pesquisa do Estado do Rio Grande do Sul (FAPERGS)[4] funded, completed in June 2013, we observed significant reference by the participants to the importance and the contribution that different integrated digital technologies (mainly Web 2.0 and Web 3D), also used on mobile phones and tablets linked with analogical spaces, can bring to learning and thereby referring to coexistence and the need for an overlapping of the physical and digital virtual worlds.

In addition, search results for "Anatomy in the Metaverse Second Life: a proposal for i –Learning" showed that some students experience Virtual Reality Experiences and Experiences of Real Virtuality, through immersion via 3D in an avatar environment, and mentioned that the systems modeled in 3D facilitated the attribution of meaning to the concepts and processes relating to different systems of the human body, especially when it is possible for the avatar to enter the system being studied and go through the process as if it were a component of the system. It was possible to determine that this immersion, when associated with challenges and problems (elements also present in the mechanics of games), provides greater student involvement with the object being studied and this manifested itself in reports such as: "it looks like a game, we learn by playing, it's fun, we didn't notice the time passing", made at various times. Thus, experiments on i -learning can enhance learning contexts, composing hybrid environments, from the perspective of multimodality.

These indications lead us to consider the possibility of the setting up of social Hybrids and Multimodals, which entails an overlapping of Digital Virtual Living Spaces with other analog spaces, as well as the perspective of multimodality, integrating mobile learning (use of mobile and wireless technologies) and immersive Learning (3D Digital Virtual Worlds) and a physically present mode, as well as investigating in more detail, the contributions of the concept of gamification for the students' learning.

Thus, elements of immersive learning and gamification learning were included as a possibility for innovation within the processes of teaching

and learning at undergraduate level (Figures 1, 2, 3, 4, and 5), as well as an experiment developed using UNITY[5], associated with Kinect[6] SDK technology, which involved the creation of a system where the student, by touching a particular body part, related to such system or organ, the interface caught the gesture and presented information about that system or organ. Situations like this fulfill the proposal, which allows greater interaction between the student and the system modeled in 3D, allowing its action in the physically present environment to take effect in the virtual digital medium. Thus, this technology was used in order to test a more natural and intuitive interface, which allows using the movements of the body's own organs to select and view them in 3D (Figure 6). This initial experiment opens possibilities for the development of other experiences that will broaden the understanding of the use of this technology in education, from the perspective of innovation in teaching and learning not only at undergraduate but also other levels of education.

Thus, the latest research undertaken by the Digital Education Research Group – GPe-dU UNISINOS/CNPq - completed or in the process of completion, as previously mentioned, contributes to the following: deepening of research linked to the technological concept of Digital Virtual Living Spaces associated with the perspective of Gamification in the process of teaching and learning; expanding the understanding of the technical and didactic-pedagogic skills - teacher know-how (understood as the result of the articulation of the specific field of expertise of knowledge, skills for teaching and the pedagogical skills in the field of digital technology); expanding the understanding of the process of teacher education, and the search results that corroborate other studies developed by the Digital Education Research Group – GPe-dU UNISINOS/CNPq which highlight the need for teachers to live the experience as learning students in the teacher training process for Digital Education so that they can effectively assign meaning to the learning process in such a context, through

Figure 6. Experience with UNITY and KINECT
Source: Authors

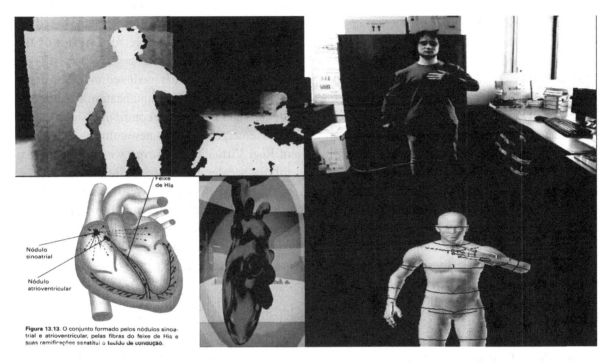

their learning process, and then, from their own learning experience build a didactic- pedagogical perspective, linked to the teaching process. Thus, for technical, didactic and pedagogical skills, a teacher´s expertise can be developed; the training processes need to be thought of from a systemic perspective, that is, not to train a teacher in a fragmented way and in isolation (expertise in the area of knowledge, expertise in the area of teaching and expertise in the digital technology area). It needs a method that arises from the interaction of these three elements, because the processes of teaching and learning are systemic. Thus, it is not possible to want innovation in education if the type of training afforded privileges the "use" of a certain digital technology. The perspective needs to change the "use" for construction of pedagogical-didactic practices for this historical and social time, which necessarily involves digital technologies.

THE CULTURE OF REAL VIRTUALITY

According to Castells (1999) in the networked society, the space of flows and timeless time constitute the fundamental basis of a new culture that transcends and includes the diversity of systems of historically transmitted representation: the culture of real virtuality. According to the author, culture is mediated and determined by communication, and all forms of communication, according to Roland Barthes and Jean Baudrillard apud Castells (1999), are based on the production and consumption of signs. Their own cultures, that is, our belief systems and historically produced codes are substantially transformed by the new technological system and will be even more so over time.

The emergence of a new electronic communication system characterized by its global reach, integration of all media and potential interactivity is changing and will change our culture forever ... a new culture is emerging: the culture of real virtuality. (Castells, 1999, p.355)

Castells (1999) states that it is not about thinking of "virtual reality" merely as superficial, or fiction created and accessed from sensory technological devices, but as "real virtuality" as an inwardness socially shared and extended through many electronic devices that sustain production and the current socio-cultural record. Therefore, there is no separation between "reality" and symbolic representation. In all societies, humanity exists in a symbolic environment and acts through it.

Thus, what is historically specific to the new communication system is the construction of real virtuality and not virtual reality. In other words, reality as it is lived, has always been virtual because it is always perceived through symbols. It is through the ambiguous character of our discourse that the complexity and quality of the contradictory messages of the human brain are manifested. This amount of cultural variation of the meaning of messages is what enables our mutual interaction in a multitude of dimensions: some explicit, some implicit.

According to Castells (1999), all realities are communicated through symbols. In addition and in human interactive communication, regardless of the medium, all symbols are somewhat displaced from the semantic meaning assigned to them. In a way, all reality is perceived in a virtual manner. Thus, a communication system that generates real virtuality,

is a system in which reality itself (that is, the symbolic experience/the material of people) is entirely captured, fully immersed in a composition of images in a virtual world of make-believe, in which appearances are not just a communication screen experience, but become the experience. (Castells, 1999, p.395)

The ability to include comprehensiveness from all cultural expressions is what characterizes the new communication system, based on mainstreaming the multiple scan modes of the communication network.

Then if the culture is mediated and constructed through processes of communication, the different digital technologies have contributed significantly to the emergence of this new culture - the culture of Real Virtuality. However, we understand that this has accelerated the use of digital technologies such as MMORPG, Metaverses and 3D Digital Virtual Worlds which are built through the communication, action and interaction of the students (represented by avatars) between themselves, and with other avatars, and with the environment (the 3D space).

Thus, it is possible to say that beyond the capabilities of 3D Digital Virtual Worlds, living and coexisting in these worlds contributes to the emergence of a new culture, which is based on elements that exist only in the context of these worlds from their specificities. The manifestation of this culture is directly linked with the possibilities of construction and existing symbology in 3D Digital Virtual Worlds, which are loaded with meanings, constructed by the interaction between students - avatars from different cultures. The diversity of symbols and meanings that exists within these worlds makes them true communication systems producing a new culture.

The experience of living and coexisting in 3D Digital Virtual Worlds, where we are involved from the beginning with the very conception of the world, its laws, rules etc., and through our avatars, i.e., through the existence of our technologicized bodies, enables us not just "to walk in many worlds at different points in our lives, but to create different worlds to change our living" (Maturana & Rezepka, 2000, p.35).

Thus, Metaverse technologies can be used as a great social simulator, allowing the creation of a social network where relationships are constituted through "life", setting up a new way of living that relates to virtuality, which we call the Coexistence of a Digital Virtual Nature and leads us to affirm that a *Life* happens in "real virtuality".

Thus, we believe that these worlds have an existence, a reality, but of another nature which relates to virtuality. We cannot have a presence, represented by avatars, through "technologized bodies" which inhabit these worlds, allowing the existence of a virtual digital life as something that is not real, because it is what Castells (1999) called "Real Virtuality".

Living in 3D Digital Virtual Worlds can awaken the avatar's sense of belonging, which is shared by the entire spectrum of regular avatars. The avatars exist in 3D Digital Virtual Worlds, as we exist in the analogical world: they create their own society and their own culture of Real Virtuality.

CONCLUSION

The theoretical construction of this chapter also highlights challenges, changes and transformations that this new reality produces (as experienced by a significant part of the students – born since the 1980s, when making use of digital games and more recently in the Metaverses is commonplace) – and who are now at different levels of education, providing clues so that we can restate the questions presented in the introduction, namely: What education is required for the student of this historical and social time? How can we help them learn? We understand that what was presented as i-Learning through the Real Virtuality Experiences and Virtual Reality Experiences may represent an effective possibility for educating the students today.

In this context, we believe it is fundamental to re-think education for the current generation, with the prospect of a Networked Society, Cultural hybridity and multimodality. This necessarily implies going beyond the didactic - pedagogical knowledge and area of expertise, to knowing who

the student is, what technologies they use and for what purpose they use them. For example, understanding how these technologies are part of their life. It implies knowing the possibilities and limits of digital technologies and their different forms, experiencing them in practice in order to understand the potential for the processes of learning and teaching. It implies analyzing the institution, the school or university, in order to understand if it effectively integrates a Digital Culture. We understand that it is the articulation of such knowledge that may give clues to guiding the construction of education for the student at this unique moment in time.

We understand that these technologies and the paradigm that involves Web 3D, in view of hybridity and multimodality, can become significant for learning in the field of Education and Organizational contributions, and can be designed for this generation that is not only digital, but hybrid multimodal and nomad, and which is now at university and will soon be in the labor market. This new reality which is based on the this new generation's way of being in the world, their needs, their new ways of learning, of relating to each other, of working, and of thinking, that they developed with and based on the use of different digital technologies, represents for us a significant challenge for us to educate, train and qualify new ways of working.

Platforms such as Active World, Second Life, Cloud Party, OpenWonderland and OpenSimulator are transient, but the concept of Web 3D, Metaverses, 3D Digital Virtual Worlds and Digital Virtual Living Spaces or Augmented Reality are definitely not.

It is important to realize that in the field of digital technologies, both in educational institutions and in business, government and non-governmental organizations, the digital technological hybridity and multimodality is a trend.

In this context, the Hybrid and Multimodal Living Spaces, may constitute laboratories for the discovery and development of social and educational experiences, which differ from the related instructional teaching practices of Distance Learning. This approach is seen in children and adolescents with different digital technologies and combined according to the format used. Unlike adults, children discover the limits and potential of these digital technologies, in the same way that you find out about the presence of the physical world through curiosity, conducting trials and experiencing it. They create new forms of representation, rules of interaction, coexistence and use of the properties and potential specific to these new methods.

Meanwhile, our generation uses these new media with a strong "accent" of traditionally known media, that is, we represent these new media "worlds": places, cities, study spaces and work, which are familiar to us, leading our first life to a "second life" and reproducing models of interaction and coexistence which are already consolidated. Our "crystallized" and somewhat distorted view of the new prevents us from exploring the potential and possibilities of the nature of that medium, which could cause us to experience new forms of social organization and new rules of coexistence which is effectively a form of innovation.

Within this context, beyond digital technological hybridism, we could ask: is humanity changing into 'hybrid nomads'? Hybrids, in the sense of having a physical identity and several digital virtual ones / physical existence (physical body) and digital virtual existence (technologicized body – avatar) / living simultaneously in a physical face-to-face geographically located world, and also in a digital virtual one.

Both (digital virtual body-avatar and virtual digital world) are exploitable "spaces" which do not refer to a "pure space" as an a priori condition of the world experience, as found in Kant (1983) apud Schlemmer (1998), but it constitutes the very object of experience, whereby the avatar and the

student lives, creates and recreates his identity; coexisting and creating virtual spaces of digital living, where a world happens.

It seems to us that current generations have their objectivity and subjectivity constituted from that hybridism. They are nomads in function that are constantly changing, ignoring borders, in order to seek new spaces which are able to satisfy their desires and interests. "While experts continue to speak of the real and the virtual, people build a life in which the boundaries are increasingly permeable. ... In the future, permeable boundaries will be the most interesting to study and understand" (Turkle, 1999, p.118). According to Turkle (1999), the defense of the boundary between the virtual and the real, the effort to locate certain types of experience in either dimension is currently more prevalent among specialists than among users, citizens of virtual communities, refuting this boundary and clearly expressing the human desire to have access to both aspects simultaneously. For the author,

real relationships are those in which people feel connected enough to give them real importance. These relationships determine the way in which each is perceived ... or the way you see your own ability to relate to others. ... In life online, people are in a position to play different roles, adopting various personalities in different places on the network. They come and experience numerous aspects of themselves. Intensively live this multiplicity... . In this sense, online life takes on an aspect of everyday life and transports it to a higher level. ... For many people, the virtual community allows a freer expression of numerous aspects of themselves. However, this is something that also lives in the "rest of life". ... To the extent that things are closed and the space is reduced, cyberspace offers something along the order of space-game: a chance to try something which is nonexistent in the rest of life in the R-V. ... I want to highlight that the best possibilities for the development of the communities are in places that intersect virtual experiences and the rest of life (pp.119-121).

We know that the world views we have are the result of interpretations of the reality in which we live, highlighting the epistemological framework that involves these paradigms. Each subject knows, thinks and acts according to the paradigms that pervade their culture. The current generation lives in a culture that is multimodal hybrid, nomadic; inhabits, e-inhabits and co-inhabits in new places and new worlds, using different media or combined technologies and which enable the development of different skills (which further reinforces the importance of coexistence with these media and technologies). They are also students who, through virtual communities, are able to leave one space to experience one community, one world, one universe and are thus able to foster their development and immersive interactive experiences in a richer way, contributing to the construction of new world views, new paradigms.

According to Schlemmer, Malizia, Backes and Moretti (2012), we understand that observing trends such as augmented reality, mixed reality and 3D web experiences on fixed and mobile devices, attending meetings and events in different 3D Digital Virtual Worlds using avatars, is a good initiative for those who want to better understand these "new worlds" in order to identify their strengths and limitations for education as well as understanding the culture of present generations. To paraphrase Maturana and Varela (2002), all living is knowing.

REFERENCES

Castells, M. (1999). A sociedade em rede. São Paulo, Brazil: Paz e Terra.

Laux, L. C. P. D., & Schlemmer, E. (2011). Anatomia no metaverso Second Life: Colaboração e cooperação interdisciplinar e interinstituicional. In *Proceedings of VII Congresso Internacional de Educação* (pp. 1-13). São Leopoldo, Brazil: Casa Leiria.

Lévy, P. (1996). O que é virtual?. São Paulo, Brazil: Editora 34.

Lévy, P. (1999). Cibercultura. Rio de Janeiro, RJ: Editora 34.

Maturana, H. R. (1997). A ontologia da realidade. Belo Horizonte, Brazil: Ed. UFMG.

Maturana, H. R., & de Rezepka, S. N. (2000). Formação humana e capacitação. Petrópolis, Brazil: Vozes.

Maturana, H. R., & Varela, F. J. (2002). A árvore do conhecimento: As bases biológicas da compreensão humana. São Paulo, Brazil: Palas Athena.

Moretti, G. (2012). Comunidades virtuais de aprendizagem e de prática em metaverso. In E. Schlemmer et al. (Eds.), Comunidades de aprendizagem e de prática em metaverso (pp. 127-178). São Paulo, Brazil: Editora Cortez.

Schlemmer, E. (1998). *A representação do espaço cibernético pela criança, na utilização de um ambiente virtual.* (Unpublished master's dissertation). Universidade Federal do Rio Grande do Sul, Porto Alegre, Brazil.

Schlemmer, E. (2008). ECODI - A criação de espaços de convivência digital virtual no contexto dos processos de ensino e aprendizagem em metaverso. *Cadernos IHU Idéias*, *6*, 1–32.

Schlemmer, E. (2009). *Espaço de convivência digital virtual – ECODI RICESU* (Research Report). São Leopoldo: Universidade do Vale do Rio dos Sinos.

Schlemmer, E. (2010). Formação de professores na modalidade online: Experiências e reflexões sobre a criação de Espaços de Convivência Digitais Virtuais ECODIs. *Em Aberto*, *23*(84), 99–122.

Schlemmer, E. (2013). O trabalho do professor e as novas tecnologias. In M. J. Fuhr (Ed.), Sob a espada de dâmocles: Relação dos professores com a docência e ambiente de trabalho no ensino privado (pp. 98-115). Porto Alegre, Brazil: Carta Editora.

Schlemmer, E., et al. (2006). ECoDI: A criação de um espaço de convivências digital virtual. In *Proceedings of XVII Simpósio Brasileiro de Informática na Educação* (pp. 467-477). Brasília, Brazil: UNB/UCB. Retrieved from http://br-ie.org/pub/index.php/sbie/article/viewFile/507/493

Schlemmer, E., & Marson, F. P. (2013). Immersive learning: Metaversos e jogos digitais na educação. In Proceedings of 8ª Conferência Ibérica de Sistemas e Tecnologias de Informação. Lisboa: Anais.

Turkle, S. (1999). Fronteiras do real e do virtual: Entrevista concedida a federico casalegno. *Revista Famecos*, (11), 117-123. Retrieved from http://revistaseletronicas.pucrs.br/ojs/index.php/revistafamecos/article/viewFile/3057/2335

KEY TERMS AND DEFINITIONS

Immersive Learning: It is an educational modality, whose processes of teaching and learning occur in graphical 3D environments, created with the use of different digital technologies, and the 3D Web, in which learners participate in an immersive way. The concept of i-Learning refers to two other concepts: Virtual Reality and Virtuality Real.

Real Virtuality: It is understood as a set of technologies and methodologies that enable the creation of 3D graphical, interactive and immersive environments. RV consists in the representation or creation of fictional worlds, imaginary worlds that have no direct correspondence with the physical world, but that has provoked and produced new meanings to physical existence, while constituting virtual digital existence.

Real Virtuality Experiences: They are understood as experiences enabling "virtualization" of an existing reality in the physical world (simulation).

Reality: "the reality is a domain of things, and in that sense, what can be distinguished is real." Maturana (1997, p. 156).

Virtual Reality: It is understood as a set of technologies and methodologies that enable the creation of 3D graphical, interactive and immersive environments. VR has been used to represent or create worlds mimicking a physical reality; therefore, physical worlds are represented in virtual digital form.

Virtual Reality Experiences: They are understood as experiences enabling the "realization" of a virtuality (which is in capacity- idea, imagination, etc.).

Virtuality: Broadly speaking, it is what has quality, or virtual character, that is, the potentiality to accomplish something. The term is commonly used to refer to situations in which the action, communication, interaction do not occur in a physical classroom form in analog spaces, but in a digital form, using different digital technologies in a web environment.

ENDNOTES

[1] Cfr. Levy, 1999, op.cit.

[2] O Conselho Nacional de Desenvolvimento Científico e Tecnológico (CNPq) is an agency connected to the Ministry of Science, Technology and Innovation (MCTI) to foster research in Brazil. For further information access: http://www.cnpq.br/

[3] Coordenação de Aperfeiçoamento de Pessoal de Nível Superior (CAPES) is a fostering agency for Brazilian research, acting to expand and consolidate post-graduate courses

(Master and Doctorate) all over the country. For further information access: http://www.capes.gov.br/

4   Fundação de Amparo à Pesquisa do Estado do Rio Grande do Sul (FAPERGS) is an institution for research fostering all areas of knowledge. For further information access: http://www.fapergs.rs.gov.br/

5   The software Unity is an integrated development engine that provides a pioneering functionality for creating games and other interactive content. You can use Unity to mount your art and feature scenes and environments; physically adding, editing, and simultaneously testing your game and, when ready, posting it on your chosen platforms, such as fixed computers, the network, iOS, Android, Wii, PS3 and Xbox 360.

6   The Kinect is a device with cameras and microphones that can be connected to the PC using a small adapter with USB output. The Kinect, associated with the Software Development Kit (SDK) allows you to develop and deploy solutions that give you the ability to interact naturally with computers, just talking and gesturing. Using the SDK it is possible to: Map the skeletons of one or two people who are in the preview area of the Kinect, the default camera access beyond the camera returns to the position and distance (XYZ) of an object; access to resources such as suppression microphone, acoustic noise and echo cancellation.

Chapter 12
Digital Virtual Sharing Spaces

ABSTRACT

This chapter deals with ways of living and socializing in the context of digital technological hybridism. The authors begin the discussion with the sub-topic, "Digital Virtual Life?" After that, they deal with living in digital virtual spaces of sharing and/or sharing of a digital virtual nature. Finally, they talk about configuring the digital virtual sharing space: society networking in the era of avatars. The authors conclude the chapter with a view of hybridism, where it is no longer possible to distinguish the individual and the social, the natural, and the technological.

INTRODUCTION

Humanity has developed through the movements of reproduction, (re)signification, transformation and the creation of new concepts, theories, technologies and instruments aiming to improve human being's lives. This has not always been the way though, or it is not totally possible, as we can see in the history of the German physicist Albert Einstein (1879-1955), who developed the theory of Relativity which gained him the Nobel Prize for Physics in 1921. The development of atomic energy was made possible by the theory of Relativity, even though the benefits and drawbacks hadn't been thoroughly contemplated. It is for the same reason that the developments of humanity also happened due to the need to adjust and

modify things along living and sharing lines. Such adjustments and/or modifications regard theories, technologies, human beings and the comprehension of what "living better" is.

The title of this chapter comes from the perspective of a "digital virtual living space", which initially proposes to (re)signify concepts such as space, living and the virtual digital as human beings start to establish relationships and interactions through daily living with different Digital Technologies. Within this context, and through research developed by GPe-dU UNISINOS/CNPq, we reconstruct the understanding of digital virtual living spaces by linking different contexts in different areas of knowledge Backes (2007, 2011), Schlemmer (2005, 2008) and Backes and Schlemmer (2006). We build some ideas about the nature

DOI: 10.4018/978-1-4666-6351-0.ch012

of living in a digital virtual space, Backes (2011) and recreate the conceptual technology of Digital Virtual Sharing Spaces Schlemmer et al. (2006) and Schlemmer (2008, 2009, 2010).

In this reconstruction of the digital virtual living space, different Digital Technologies and human beings' living and sharing mediated by them – as described in Chapter 3 – we have managed to bring together theorists from the areas of geography, Santos (1980, 2008), biology and human development, Maturana (1999, 2002, 2005) and Maturana and Varela (2002), sociology, Cuche (1999), Palloff (2002) and Castells (2003), Psycology, Turkle (1997; 1999), administration and technology, Pratt (2002), philosophy, Lévy (1996, 2010a, 2010b) and Negroponte (2005), who have presented the possibility of thinking the space in contemporary way. We then find new elements and other complexities, without establishing replacements or exclusions, but by constructing the living and sharing among human beings in a digital virtual way.

How should we think of such space? The space can be conceived from two perspectives: space in terms of the space of all time, permanent, topographically limited and specific to each place; or space as it is presented today, our space, the space of our time and as a group of relationships implied within a history of past and present. Therefore, Santos (1980, p.122) states that:

Space defines itself as a group of ways of representing both past and present social relationships and by a structure represented by social relationships that are happening before our eyes and that speak through processes and functions. The space is, then, a real force field with uneven acceleration. That is the reason spatial evolution does not occur equally everywhere.

From Castells' perspective (2003), both time and space suffer modifications through technology's paradigm, causing social changes in congruence with technological changes. This means that theoretical constructions contribute to the creation of new technologies in the same way that such technologies demand new theories that modify human beings' lives. In this "new" life, human beings reconstruct the theories and place new meanings on technologies in a continuously changing movement of humanity. Currently, collaboration is organized and structured in digital networks in which human beings establish relationships through flows. "By flows, I understand the intentional, repetitive and programmable sequences of interchange and interaction between positions physically dissociated, kept by social authors in economic, political and symbolic structures of society" (Castells, 2003, p.501).

The space of flow is the material organization of social practices in a society that establishes relationships and of a digital virtual nature, using digital technology with which different combinations can be structured between human beings and through networks. The key concept of this discussion regards the digital virtual space as initially stated by Backes (2007, p.70):

digital virtual spaces are made of hardware and software, and they can comprehend virtual learning environments, virtual reality environments — virtual worlds, virtual learning and relationship communities, instant communication, weblogs, electronic mail and communicative agents, among others.

From this perspective and for Backes (2011), digital virtual spaces are made only by hardware and software that enable *action* and *interaction* processes between human beings as well as the *sharing* of representations and perceptions, or, when it is possible to configure a relationship space between human beings through digital technology. This relationship space establishes the flow, for Castells (2003), through the network and construction of social systems. Therefore, the configuration of the virtual digital space (relationship space) of every social system presents its own characteristics, because human beings who belong to that social system live together in congruence with digital technology and build up the "scenario" and the dynamic of the space through its actions.

According to Backes (2011, p.76):

Some distinctions have to be pointed out, for not all hardware and software can be characterized as a digital virtual space because they need to provide the possibility of relationships and interaction between human beings. Not all relationships and interactions can be considered as constructors of digital virtual space because that implies the coordination of actions between human beings that take place in a space that is of a different nature, a digital virtual nature.

In order for a space to be considered as a force field of human beings' actions, they have to be able to understand the actions coordinated between the participants and give them a meaning thus making the coordination of the coordinated actions.

The digital virtual space in the Metaverse context can be clearly identified by the way in which the different actions are developed between the e-citizens[1] living in that world according to Figures 1 and 2 taken from the Metaverse AWEdu, in AWSINOS world.

These images reveal the representation of the e-citizens' relationships and interactions as well as the coordination of the actions carried out between e-citizens when acting and collaborating in a process to train educators, in the research developed by Backes (2007, 2011). In the beginning

Figure 1. The beginning of the construction of the Learning Village in Virtual Worlds– 2005
Source: Authors

Figure 2. The Learning Village in Virtual Worlds, present time – 2012
Source: Authors

of the construction, as we can see in the figure, the digital virtual space was incomplete and not understandable for a visitor. As the problematizing pedagogical practice was carried out, the avatars were encouraged to e-inhabit the 3D digital virtual world, and to construct daily collaborating among the e-citizens, thus building a dynamic and understandable environment for a visitor, as we can see through the different buildings, paths and teleporters in each representation. Teleporters are 'links' used to teleport an avatar from one place to another, even to a different dimension.

The comprehension of the digital virtual space in the Metaverse is enhanced by an e-citizen when entering an "empty" space. This "empty" space is the result of the need to act in order to e-inhabit the world. This fact is registered in the Metaverse chat, at the time of its construction by the students who take part in the construction process as: "we need to build to get to the other side", "I'm making a way of letting the e-inhabitants[2] know they can access this building", "this bricklayer life is hard".

However, besides the situation of building a 3D Digital Virtual World, we also find ready-made 3D Digital Virtual Worlds as spaces created to configure living. Regarding such possibilities there are two main aspects to be considered: in the first – 3D Digital Virtual Worlds enable the construction of the digital virtual space through the interaction and representation of voice and text as well as the coordination of actions between human beings represented by their avatars, resulting in the effective construction of a 3D Digital Virtual World; in the second, 3D Digital Virtual Worlds where construction is addressed and imposed by the developer in 3D Digital Virtual Worlds, the developer directs the actions and interactions between human beings through activities, rules, and pre-established behavior, enabling the constitution of this "space" although only a digital virtual one.

The concept of the digital virtual space is then related to the possibility and the power of digital technology to configure living between human beings through relationships and interactions characterized by recursion and the construction of social systems, and in acknowledging mutual respect and the construction of suitable behavior. As seen before, the concept of digital virtual space is still under construction. At every new investigation, the concepts are broadened, redefined and rebuilt. Firmino and Silva (2010, p.1) pondered the complexity of the construction process in the concept of space:

Terms like no-place, cyberspace, virtual space, digital urbanity or deterritorialization should not be considered as contemporary unmitigated facts, but as implosive-concepts that, with the addition of technological, philosophical, geographical, socioeconomic aspects they can be reintroduced to its basic concept (place, territory or site) and extinguish the possibilities of answers to the question "what is the space in contemporaneity?".

Therefore, concepts like: sharing in a digital virtual space, digital virtual living together and Digital Virtual Sharing Spaces are currently in their exploratory phase, combining the original concept (space) with implosive concepts (emerging in the new contemporary scenario). This happens because concepts are conceived from the living and sharing of human beings that are in constant change with different digital technologies and also in constructing a digital virtual life.

DIGITAL VIRTUAL LIFE?

Human beings' daily life is dynamic and changeable as they are able to adapt and change themselves. In different sections, we have witnessed several different transformations. One of the most evident changes in people's lives is related to banking operations. Money, in its physical state, is being used less and less and leads to developments in the fields of security and digital signatures.

"Hackers" are hired to fight other "hackers" in a dimension where the bandit and the hero can be the same characters.

Purchasing a product is also possible through Internet sites and the payment for such purchases is made by credit card. Using the customer's purchase background the credit card companies establish a profile for each client, in case their card is not being used by the real customer. They also immediately block the card when a purchase is identified as "suspicious" and the customer is notified by phone. We could approach other situations in which people's daily lives have been transformed because of advances in technology. That is why, in Negroponte's words (2006, p.159) "The digital life will demand less and less you be in a certain place at a certain time, and the transmission of the place itself will then become reality". What was written about the future in the first edition of his work in 1995, is now the present. Today it is possible to perceive that the boundaries between what is physical (the world constituted by atoms) and the digital virtual (the world made with bits and bytes) are plastic and permeable.

The decision to live overseas means rebuilding new forms of proximity between family members, friends and colleagues who are in the country of origin. Research carried out on studies abroad is connected to research groups based in their country of origin in different ways. The experience of GPe-dU UNISINOS/CNPq can be used as an example, as they use the UNISINOS digital virtual island, constructed in the Second Life Metaverse, as the space for their meetings. At times they may appear to look like magicians; all together discussing the aspects related to the research, sharing feelings of loneliness coming from living abroad and this all goes so fast; at other times they are dramatic, the participants who are physically close overlap each other in the conversation, making the comprehension of communication via Second Life impossible.

In 2011 the mini course "Digital Virtual Living Spaces and 'Real Virtuality' Culture: what are the contributions to *EaD* (Distance Learning)?" was created. It took place at the 8th SENAED – *Seminário Nacional ABED de Educação a Distância* (National ABED Seminar for Distance Education), in Brazil, with the physical presence of Eliane Schlemmer and the digital virtual presence of Luciana Backes in France and Gaia Moretti in Italy. This situation confirms Negroponte's thoughts (2006, p.170) "In a digital world, distances are becoming meaningless". The digital virtual space used for the mini course was the UNISINOS Island (in Second Life) and the AWSINOS world (in AWEdu). According to Turkle (1999, p.118) "… while experts keep talking about the real and the virtual, people are building their lives in which borders are increasingly permeable".

The idea of the course didn't only come about because everyone involved has an avatar in Second Life and/or citizen access to AWEdu. The relationship between the boundaries of both physical and digital virtual worlds has begun now that we understand what real virtuality is. Gaia Moretti got to know Eliane Schlemmer through Internet searches and after that they managed to have a physical meeting in Brazil in order to build on their relationship that started in the digital virtual space and in which the main objective was to investigate digital virtual communities in the Metaverse. In her investigation Gaia Moretti enters GPe-dU digital virtual community, along with Luciana Backes and all other members (students, educators, researchers, technicians, sympathizers). In this way, different activities, research, work and social relations are developed as for Turkle (1999, p.120) "the continuity enables the construction of social rules, rituals, sense".

For Pallof and Pratt (2002), human beings' intention has always been to create communities in order to establish communication, and of course technological development gives us different approaches regarding interactive pos-

sibilities through communication. When creating the community, human beings begin to belong to a group, sharing ideas on their living together and each taking part in the other's life. "I talk about the feeling that in an online discussion group, I can write and immediately afterwards someone may take my idea, develop it, and return something else to me. Such gratification is exciting and generates a feeling of affiliation (Turkle, 1999, p.121).

Family, friends and colleagues can easily communicate amongst themselves, regardless of the time or their geographical location. Communication can be synchronous, immediate or in real time, through instant communication, or it can be asynchronous, through social networks. In this perspective we have the concept of asynchronous, meaning "Not all communication has to be immediate and in real time" (Negroponte, 2006, p.162). This way we can collaborate in different social groups.

There are two relevant aspects regarding this situation: the understanding of who your social group friends are and the type of information you share in this digital virtual space. According to Raleiras (2007) technology and the broadening of our existence in a digital virtual way allows us to observe and be observed. We find children and adolescents in different social networks, and there are cases in which the adolescent knows, or has some sort of reference to only 20% of the friends associated to his or her profile. In this case it is important to explain how this is used to represent, in relation to the content published by him and the relevance of the people to whom he has no reference. This does not mean though that an adolescent cannot take part in social media but it is important to think and encourage them to think about the possible consequences of such interactions.

For Turkle (1997) one of the elements of seduction in digital virtual life is that there is always someone willing to interact with us. As a result, we define our existence in the digital virtual space and are legitimized in the communication processes. In the course *Analyse du travail et Polyvalence*, on the Master in *Métiers de L'enseignement, de la Formation, de la Culture, l'Université Lumière Lyon 2*, research developed by Backes (2011), the students carried out a group assignment of case studies related to the course theme, and afterwards they presented their theoretical and practical considerations in a blog using Pixton software. During a physical meeting it was proposed that the students organize themselves into groups, choose the case to be discussed and begin the organization of their work, the activity was to be carried out face-to-face in the classroom. Everything was under control when the physical space fell silent followed by some giggling. Students were looking at each other but were not talking. I then realized that, when checking the blog to pick up a case to be studied, the students were publishing comments about the different cases, creating a "macro" interaction among the different "small" groups.

In France, it is believed that digital technologies are pulling people apart and making them more individual. However, we are evidencing proximity between students for they were showing interest in each other's studies, in a respectful relationship by contributing with the different cases and in the act of becoming emotional in the sense of legitimizing the other as somebody they can learn from.

In this situation we can say that students established real relationships and they made the boundaries between the physical and the digital virtual spaces that are permeable and plastic.

I call real relations those in which people feel sufficiently connected in order to give them real importance. Such relationships determine the way each one perceives if they have had a good or a bad day, or the way they see their own capacity for having a relationship with others. (Turkle, 1999, p.119)

We can then think about the real relationship between human beings, represented by their avatars, in 3D Digital Virtual Worlds. In this digital virtual life, we find real relationships which are similar to those established in the physical context, and when meeting avatars we know, for example, we greet them and immediately ask how they are doing; and other relationships that are inherent in the digital virtual context. Interestingly, we can think of these relationships from the perspective of educator, student, administrator, mother, friend, colleague, who, regardless of the "personality" used, or the "place" they have in the relationship network, will surround my actions. Such multiplicity can be experienced both in the physical and in the digital virtual contexts of life. For Turkle (1999, p.119) however "online life retakes that and brings it to a superior level". That means that human beings feel freer to express the different aspects of themselves, through their avatars, where they can represent such multiplicity not only through actions but through their bodily representation.

The possibility of a permeability between boundaries, the development of digital technologies, the construction of digital virtual communities, asynchrony and the multiplicity that are experienced in digital life will allow the configuration of a collaborative digital virtual living and sharing space.

DIGITAL VIRTUAL SPACES OF SHARING AND/OR A SHARING OF A DIGITAL VIRTUAL NATURE

The term Digital Virtual Spaces of Living and Sharing is a (re)signification of the concept of Living Space as defined by Maturana and Varela (2002) and Maturana (1999; 2002), because the studies carried out in order to coin such definitions were not developed in digital virtual spaces. This re(signification) is necessary for the configuration of the living space to happen in congruence with human beings and the environment. So when changing the nature of the environment, there are modifications in the configuration of space.

For Maturana and Varela (2002), the configuration of living spaces occurs in the flow of interactions between human beings and between human beings and the environment which enable both human beings and the environment to transform, intertwined with emotions, perceptions, representations, disturbances and an understanding of the disturbances. The configuration of the living space occurs through living and sharing on a daily basis.

As previously discussed, digital virtual spaces which are available through different digital technologies broaden the possibilities of sharing between human beings as there are no impositions on the geographical space or chronological time, besides offering a significant variety of ways of communicating and increasing the possibilities for interaction and representation and thus allowing plurality and dynamism. In this way, the configuration of digital virtual sharing spaces happens when human beings establish their living in interaction with others and in congruence with the environment by means of a digital virtual nature. According to Backes (2007, p.165) "That is the reason why digital technology cannot be understood as a tool or instrument, for it implies that every living being has to represent their own perception and configure the space they find common and desirable."

When configuring the digital virtual living spaces, human beings represent their comprehension and definition, establishing each space within that living together. In such living together, it is through their disturbances and the comprehension of their disturbances that they define the suitable behavior for the group, configuring what is common, from a coexistence perspective and through the relationships in which human beings are authors and coauthors. For Backes (2011), in the dynamic of configuring the digital virtual living space, human beings join forces and develop their own autonomy and autonomy processes, for the social system is constructed according to individual acts.

To make configuration possible it is necessary that the living systems' units, in interaction within a certain digital virtual living space, act in a dynamic way through a context. As reciprocal disturbances are effective in interactions, this dynamic scheme enables the configuration of a new space, representing the domain of relationships and the interactions of the living system as a whole. (Backes, 2007, p.71)

In the 3D Digital Virtual Worlds, the living digital virtual space is configured when human beings (through their avatars) can represent their perception, either through text, voice, gesture, graphic or metaphorical means, within a social system context. When representing their perception, human beings define their space and configure a common space for their group. We need to make it clear that human beings change in the actions they carry out through their avatars, also changing the 3D Digital Virtual Worlds in which they are e-inhabitants.

We take as an example the learning project based on the problem "Interactionism Epistemological Conception", which results in graphic and metaphorical representation, constructed in the training process of educators, in the research developed by Backes (2007).

In Figure 3 we can see a representation of a house similar to the one in the physical context and with which there is little relation to the concepts involving the epistemological conception in question. After several interactive processes between the participants in the group involved in the construction who have approached subjects such as: ways of building their representation, the objects available for construction in the Metaverse, the best understanding of concepts and the combination between epistemology and the possibilities in

Figure 3. Representation of the Epistemological Conception of Interactionism– 09/11/2005
Source: Authors

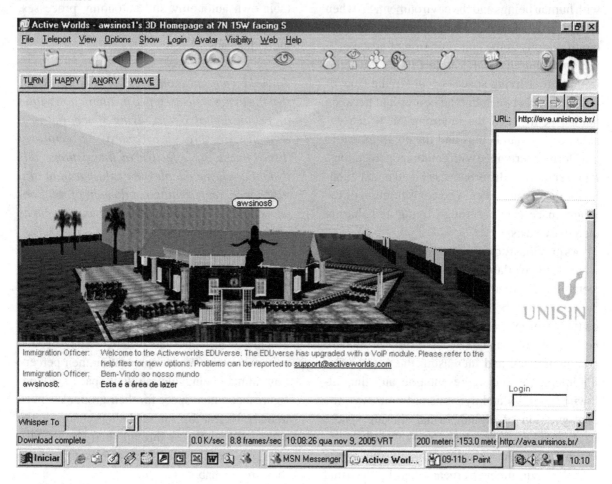

the Metaverse. In Figure 4, the construction has changed, along with the meaning of concepts, related to broadening knowledge on the power of this particular technology, to represent thinking, leading to a very different conception of a house, without a roof, with objects beyond walls and links to other websites. This clearly demonstrates the change of the digital virtual space, carried out by human beings (represented by avatars), in congruence with the environment, when building and re-building significance and resulting in such a representation.

Within this context we can understand the importance of congruence in relation to the digital virtual space because the more congruent this relationship is (between the subject and his/her avatar; between the subject and the environment; between the subject, avatar environment and concepts; between avatars; and between avatars, the concepts and the environment), the more powerful the subjects will be, regarding the representation of constructed knowledge and through other possibilities offered by the Metaverse. According to Backes (2011) in this way, in the configuration of the living digital virtual space, human beings carry out technological structural coupling, "a human being's concern in exploring the digital technology and their capabilities and/or in creating

Figure 4. Representation of the Epistemological Conception of Interactionism– 17/08/2006
Source: Authors

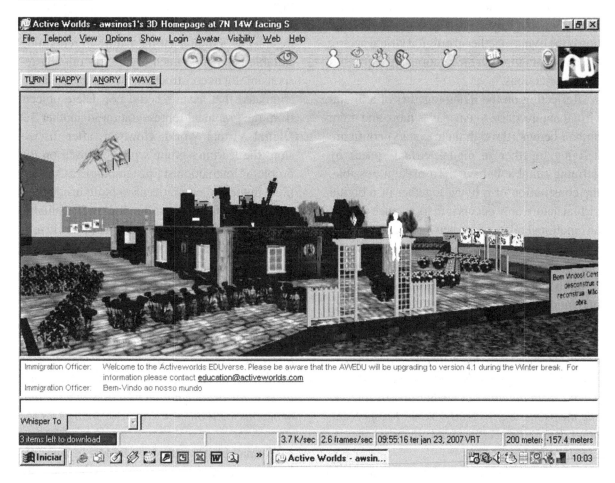

new possibilities for Digital Technology hitherto unthought of" (Backes, 2013, p.350); and on digital virtual structural coupling, "human beings direct their attention to ways of using digital virtual spaces by other human beings, so, the potential of the digital technology or new possibilities is no longer the main issue, nor is it a disturbing element any longer – it is already part of the living and sharing" (Backes, 2013, p.352). This also results, according to Rabardel (1995), in processes of instrumentation and instrumentalization, respectively. From such an understanding, the coupling of different dimensions and the instrumentation and instrumentalization processes can contribute to configuring digital virtual spaces of living together in a complex way.

Digital virtual spaces of living together are configured in the interaction between living beings in the digital virtual space. Such configuration occurs in the relationships between living beings and the environment, in a particular way, through their living together. Therefore, the need for (re) signifying the relationships established there from the current educational context, where educator and students construct in a recursive way, is essential. In this way it is possible to configure digital virtual spaces of living together in digital virtual spaces. (Backes, 2007, p.71)

In the educational context, digital virtual spaces of living together have been effective between human beings who are co-teaching and co-learning, thereby changing the traditional understanding of teaching and learning processes. In this relation, something that may arise in this other configuration is the living together of a digital virtual nature, which occurs through the relationship flows and their interactions.

Reflecting on the living together of a digital virtual nature starts to emerge as more and more human beings (through their avatars) configure a living together in digital virtual spaces by defining suitable behavior. To make it possible, the constitution of a living together of a digital virtual nature only occurs if in its essence there is an emotional relationship between human beings who are e-inhabiting a 3D Digital Virtual World. Emotion, for Maturana (1993, p.34), is the action of not being indifferent to another human being in relation to the other,

The one who accepts the other in his/her space of existence and does not deny its legitimacy. The one who can meet another in his/her dignity, and when I meet the other in his/her dignity and he/she meets me in my dignity. When I respect the other, he/she respects me back.

As previously discussed, the act of emotion is evidenced in the human being's interaction with others. Human beings are constituted in the relational sphere; what we think, our values and our character are related to our living in the community to which we belong. Nevertheless, the constitution of the human being does not happen in any relationship, but in the loving ones, with another in a legitimate living together – in summary, where there is no indifference. "I think that not all human relationships are social ones, it is emotion that sustains a relationship and gives it its character, and I think that the emotion that constitutes and sustains social relationships is love" (Maturana, 1999, p.9). In this sense, the living together of a digital virtual nature can be constituted by heterarchical relationships between human beings, through mutual respect and acceptance.

In this way, the e-inhabitants, in configuring their digital virtual space of living together, in the action of constructing the world, built a living together of a digital virtual nature in redefining suitable behaviors. Each group was initially responsible for its construction; the suitable behavior stipulated that avatars could not delete objects from the graphical representation in another 3D Digital Virtual World. However, after discussion, the learning group's project based on the problem "Interactionist Epistemological Conception" invites other e-citizens to build inside their representation in an autonomous way. Suitable behavior was redefined to consider other citizens as legitimate for such construction, as there was mutual respect and acceptance.

For Costa (2008), the digital virtual space,

is constituted as a space in which emotion is possible when it is considered to be an environment for relationships, where subjects meet, talk or learn together, in the same sense that Maturana gives to the act of emotion as a flow of a domain of actions to the other in a dynamic living. (p.156)

Human beings are social beings because we live in interaction and in relation to the other, so, by the act of having emotion it is possible to define suitable behavior for the social system. Social systems are built on interaction, within the sphere of individual phenomena, as autopoietic beings, and in the sphere of social phenomena, through structural coupling, under a perspective which is not exclusive but dialectic. In this way, the individual and the social are in recursive congruence[3] and for this reason and in the constitution of the living together of a digital virtual nature, the act of having emotion takes a larger part.

Every time the members of a group of living beings constitute their behavior within an interactive network, which operates for them as an environment where they come about as living beings and where they therefore, keep their organization and adaptation, and exist in a co derivation contingent to its participation in such network of interactions, we have a social system. (Maturana, 1999, p.26)

The understanding between the *individual* and the *social* happens through systemic thinking: "In the new paradigm, the relationship between the parties and the whole is inverted. This implies that the properties of the parties can only be understood based on the dynamic of the whole" (Moraes, 2004, p.72). We take as an example the relationships in a working group, like the learning project based on the problem "Interactionist Epistemological Conception". The construction of the representation is peculiar to that group, because it is composed of students coming from philosophy and pedagogy courses. This means the person in the group, taking his/her own defined place, in the same way the group is in the person through the construction carried out using suitable behavior within that group. As a result the whole is more than the sum of its parts, because it evolves beyond the parts, primarily the relationships and interactions that are built between the parts.

So through language people construct collaborative and cooperative behavior for this social construction. The control of emotion is the observation within the interaction space between the person and the group. There are two types of system: a closed system (individuals) and an open system (group). Both systems have a dialectical relationship with each other; the individual influences the group in a recursive way. This is the base for learning (it is closed because it is peculiar to each individual) and for the construction of knowledge (it is open because it happens in the interaction between individuals: the group), which is typical of human beings that have an autopoietic system. Consequently, when dealing with individual phenomena, we broaden our comprehension of social phenomena.

According to Maturana (1999), in order to have a social system it is necessary for there to be recurrence in interactions resulting in the coordination

of behavior and of its members; we can say then that recurrence happens in cooperative interactions[4], and the living together of a digital virtual nature happens in the structuring of autopoietic social systems. If there are cooperative interactions, there is also autopoiesis of the human being.

But even though, as every individual's properties and characteristics are determined by his/her structure, as these structures belonging to a social system change, their property changes and the social system they create with their behavior also changes. (Maturana, 1999, p.27)

Suitable behavior, redefined by e-citizens participating in the Learning Project based on the problem "Interactionist Epistemological Conception", was recurrent to the e-citizens taking part in the learning project based on the "Wonderland" problem (later denominated "Unilínguas English Club"), case study made in Backes's (2007) research. The recurrence can be evidenced in the following figures, where there is a redefinition of behavior and the transformation of the action of e-citizens in the construction of graphical and metaphorical representation in 3D Digital Virtual Worlds.

The representations initially made in the problem-based learning project 'Wonderland' referred to the story of 'Alice in Wonderland', Figure 5. In the living configured between the research participants, it was possible to identify possibilities of 3D digital virtual worlds, thus broadening the story 'Alice in Wonderland' with many other stories, Figure 6. 'Wonderland' has turned into 'Unilinguas English Club', Figure 7. Even at this time, participants have kept many objects and images from the first construction, later replaced with more appropriate and detailed objects, as a consequence of the participants learning how to use the Metaverse technology, in other words, being familiar with digital virtual technology.

Figure 5. Beginning of the construction of the "Wonderland" project
Source: Authors

This recurrence happens because the central focus of the human social phenomenon is language, and the central focus of language is reflection and self-awareness. This makes it possible for e-citizens to build up autopoietic social systems. So, through language (representation) it is possible to access human being's perception that may trigger the other's awareness of talking. Such relationships between human beings happen through a dialogue.

The construction of knowledge also happens through language, for it enables the representation of questioning and problem solving and impels the living being to have a reflective action, revealing their thoughts. The thought has a direct connection, previously mentioned, with the history of the species and the history of the individuals' lives.

Human beings can belong to many social systems both simultaneously or successively. It is only necessary that during our living process we carry out the due behavior of each social system in a proper place. ... If by carrying out the different suitable behavior of the social systems we do not involve our own lives and just intend to do it we do not belong to them nor are immersed in their respective behavior until we are found and expelled as hypocrites or parasites. (Maturana, 1999, p.29)

The living together of a digital virtual nature happens when human beings, through the interaction and structural coupling in the digital virtual spaces, live and share through dialogic relationships, reflecting together about what they

Figure 6. Transition process of the "Wonderland" Project to "Unilínguas English Club"
Source: Authors

know, what they don't know and what they would like to know. These relationships are effective in a heterarchical way of living and of sharing representations in digital virtual spaces. Within this diversity of representations, human beings establish suitable behavior[5] for the social system, that becomes common sense in living together up to the moment it is no longer desirable or it does not correspond to the group's needs. It is therefore through disturbance, that common behaviors are defined and redefined, because they are autopoietic social systems.

In order to define digital virtual living, human beings mobilize within their interaction processes in digital virtual spaces and feel emotion when they share their representations; disturbance, provoked by the other or by the environment, but defined by the structure of the disturbed human being; and recursion, as they construct the relational domain in a responsible way. In this way, when constituting living of a digital virtual nature, human beings, according to Backes (2011), carry out structural couplings of a digital virtual nature, also resulting, according to Rabardel (1995) in the instrumentalization process. In this understanding, coupling of a digital virtual nature and the instrumentalization process, alter human being's structures, broadening the living together.

Figure 7. Final construction of the representation of the "Unilínguas English Club" project
Source: Authors

CONFIGURING THE DIGITAL VIRTUAL SHARING SPACE: SOCIETY NETWORKING IN THE ERA OF AVATARS

The advances and the development of digital technology are mobilized by two aspects that are mutually related: the digital technological creation and its significance for humans. According to Rabardel (1995) the use of an artifact (or digital technology) initially happens from the human being's intention to acquire, which attributes a functional value. Nevertheless, when the human being uses the artifact in the social context, within the group he/she belongs to, other values and meanings are constructed and shared. The artifact has multiple senses which also contribute to the creation of new technologies. Also, for Rabardel (1995), a certain stability can be seen in the senses attributed in the relationships and interactions in different groups.

Some empirical considerations found in the research developed by the GPe-dU UNISINOS/CNPq, carried out within the context of digital technological hybridism show that, at first, the intention of appropriation of the Digital Technology occurs in the reproduction of physical spaces, or, in the possibility of replacement. We have seen some 3D Digital Virtual Worlds which are the exact reproduction of a classroom or the buildings of a university – making it clear that it is a transposition – being the first stage of the signification process. There is also advertising like: "Distance Entrance Examination" and "Freedom to choose how to study: physical site (geographical), via internet or DVD". In these situations there is a choice to be made between the geographically located space and the digital virtual, with no possibility of coexistence.

Secondly, as digital technology is given the meaning of digital virtual spaces between different groups, other meanings are built under the perspective of geographical spaces and/or in the possibility to go beyond geographical spaces. This implies the use of digital technology from the perspective of coexistence, serving the particulars of interaction, representation, signification and creation of human will. Some 3D Digital Virtual Worlds have undergone transformation processes and are having their nature and scenario changed, through the interaction of their e-citizens.

And thirdly, inserted into the educational context, we show that the participants perceive the relationship between digital technology and didactic-pedagogical practice in the processes of teaching and learning. At this point, participants identify the different possibilities Second Life offers to the "class", as well as the ease in understanding the concepts studied and the ludic aspect present in it. In this way, participants understand the software as a potential for the development of different didactic-pedagogical practices. However, facilities problems, mainly related to the processing capacity of computers and the low bandwidth, as well as the time for data collecting, have pointed to the existing limitations.

With this maturity and the development of online education, the use of digital technology in the context of education has been rethought; studies in this area have started to build on new concepts. Among the concepts that have brought great advances to both teaching and learning processes with digital technology is the understanding of digital technological hybridism. With this in mind, Schlemmer et al. (2006), Schlemmer (2008, 2009, 2010) systematized Digital Virtual Sharing Spaces concept-technology, in order to translate the different questions concerning the constitution of the living together of a digital virtual nature.

Digital Virtual Sharing Spaces consist of a digital technological hybridism where the interaction and representation of knowledge happens through a combination of Technologies from web 1.0, web 2.0 and web 3D. This way, human beings can interact and represent their perception through textual, oral, gestural and graphic languages.

According to Schlemmer et at. (2006) and Schlemmer (2008, 2009, 2010) an Digital Virtual Sharing Spaces understandds:

- Different integrated Digital Technologies such as: Virtual Learning Environments, 3D Digital Virtual Worlds, Web 2.0 technologies and communicative agents, among others, that favor different ways of communication (textual, oral, graphic and gestural);
- Communication and interaction flow between the subjects present within this space;
- Interaction flow between the subjects and the environment, meaning the technological space itself.

So, a Digital Virtual Sharing Space implies the possibility of interaction between "e-inhabitants" (considering their ontogeny), in congruence with this space, to reconfigure it in a collaborative and cooperative way through living and sharing. Under this perspective, digital technological hybridism can be thought of as an instrument and is stated by Rabardel (1999, p.248) as:

Une théorie instrumentale étendue doit avoir, à nos yeux, pour objectif de rassembler et d'organiser en un ensemble cohérent (mais pas nécessairement non contradictoire) ce que nous savons aujourd'hui de l'activité humaine, considérée sous l'angle de ses moyens, de quelque nature qu'ils soient, c'est-à-dire des instruments que les sujets s'approprient, élaborent et mobilisent au sein de l'activité, des actions et opérations en tant que médias de leur réalisation.

Digital technological hybridism consists of a coherent group (even when sometimes it seems contradictory) of the possibilities of accomplishment by human action in a digital virtual space. Such integration takes effect when human beings take, create or mobilize the instruments (digital technology) in their interactions. Figures 8 through 12 are some of the possibilities of Digital Virtual Sharing Spaces already used in research.

In Figure 8 Digital Virtual Sharing Spaces are compounded in digital technological hybridism by Metaverse technologies (Eduverse – 3D Digital Virtual World AWSINOS), virtual learning environment (Virtual Learning Environment -UNISINOS) and a communicative agent (Mariá), contemplating the concept of virtual learning communities used by Virtual Learning Environment -UNISINOS. In Figure 9 Digital Virtual Sharing Spaces are compounded in the digital technological hybridism by Metaverse technologies (Eduverse – 3D Digital Virtual World AWSINOS), blog (Analyse du Travail et Polyvalence) and

interactive presentation software (prezi). Digital Virtual Sharing Spaces, using the Eduverse Metaverse, is accessed through a single window, compartmentalized by the frame on the right.

Figure 10 is compounded in the digital technological hybridism by Metaverse Technologies (Second Life – 3D Digital Virtual Worlds (Unisinos Island), a virtual learning environment (Moodle), Twitter (micro blog – Digital Education Research Group UNISINOS), a blog (Digital Education Research Group UNISINOS) and wiki, contemplating the concepts of virtual communities and social networks (Orkut and Twitter). When Digital Virtual Sharing Spaces are accessed in the Second Life Metaverse, it opens a new window for the chosen technology, as seen in Figure 11,

Figure 8. Digital Virtual Sharing Spaces UNISINOS Interface, accessed by Eduverse Metaverse
Source: Authors

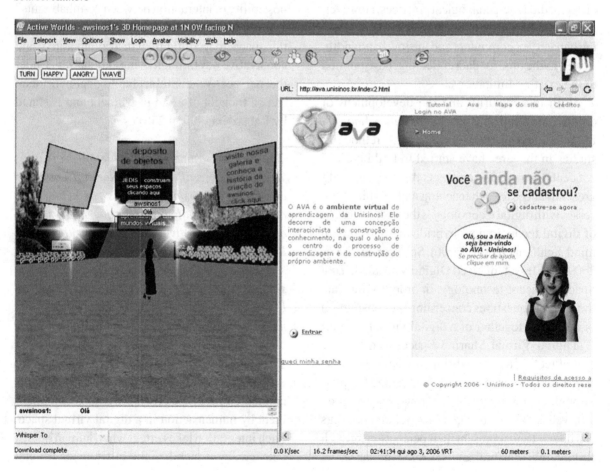

Figure 9.Digital Virtual Sharing Spaces Doctoral Thesis, Backes 2011 Interface, accessed by Eduverse Metaverse
Source: Authors

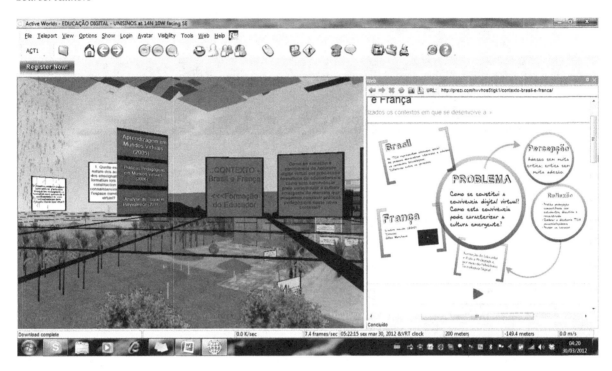

Figure 10. ECODI UNISINOS, accessed by Second Life Metaverse
Source: Authors

Figure 11. Twitter Digital Education Research Group UNISINOS, technology of ECODI UNISINOS
Source: Authors

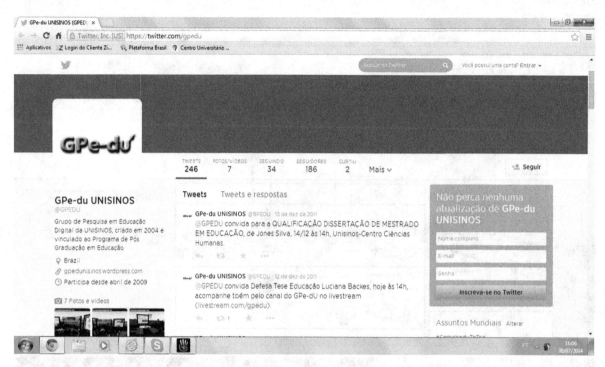

which represents the interface of Twitter Digital Education Research Group UNISINOS. As we can see, there is no single fixed and determined way of compounding the digital technological hybridism in a Digital Virtual Sharing Space. Digital technological hybridism is compounded by the technologies available and which are meaningful to the e-inhabitants and which can change with each new digital technology, signified by the subjects.

Nevertheless, digital technological hybridism itself is not enough to constitute Digital Virtual Sharing Spaces, as it is made up of the following conditions:

- Communication and interaction flow between the subjects present within this space,
- Interaction flow between the subjects and the environment, meaning the technological space itself,

- Interaction between "e-inhabitants", in order to configure space in a collaborative and cooperative way, through living and sharing,
- Innovation in both teaching and learning processes.

Besides this, there is the fact that the constitution of Digital Virtual Sharing Spaces implies the possibility of interaction among the "e-inhabitants" (considering their ontogeny), in congruence with this space, in order to configure it in collaborative and cooperative ways and through living and sharing.

Therefore, in this articulation between digital technologies as digital virtual spaces and human beings (interacting with each other) two processes are developed and defined by Rabardel (1995) as instrumentation and instrumentalization. Instrumentation consists of giving an instrument new property, functions and meaning, which were not foreseen in its creation. The possibility of personalizing your own avatar, of carrying out actions in a Metaverse, as in the case of Second Life, has led to several studies and the construction of new knowledge about identity and digital virtual identity.

In this process there is the improvement of the instrument as other Metaverses develop and improve their technologies. Instrumentalization consists of transforming the human being as he adapts, modifies, updates and creates new mind maps for using the instrument. The possibility of graphical representation provided by Metaverses has brought about the use of metaphors, as well as an understanding of their importance for the construction of knowledge. As a result, pedagogical practices are transformed and/or created. We can also take the example of the avatar, as psychological pathologics arc beginning to be studied from the avatar's interactions. In this process, the human being is enriched.

Both processes contribute to the outbreak and evolution of instruments, although, depending on the situation, one of them can be more developed, dominant, according to the implementation.

Functions, resulting from these processes, are a characteristic of the instrumental entity's property, since, from our perspective, they reflect both the subject and the artifact, functions equally present such mixed character. They are rooted in the artifacts' components and instrument's scheme. (Rabardel, 1995, p.138)

So, to choose the digital technology that will be part of Digital Virtual Sharing Spaces some aspects need to be observed to contribute to the development of both instrumentation and instrumentalization processes, in the configuring of a digital virtual living and sharing space and in the constitution of a digital virtual living

together. In this sense, the digital technology has to be in digital virtual spaces, where personalization by users is possible, and the presentation of characteristics belonging to the group using it; empowering the interaction process and allowing heterarchical relations between all other human beings; to enable different ways of representing knowledge - meaning textual, graphic, gestural, oral or other - that may be created; to allow the construction of virtual communities as well as the formation of social networks to establish dialogical relations, suitable behavior for the group and autopoietic social systems.

The networked society, in a certain way, represents our current living and sharing, when there is a problem on the Internet network, it is almost as serious as a problem in the electricity supply network. However, it is this social dynamic that demands deep reflection. For Castells (2003, p.566)

A social structure based on networks is a highly dynamic open system susceptible to innovation without threatening its balance. Networks are adequate instruments for the capitalist economy based on innovation, globalization and decentralized concentration; for work, workers and companies turn to flexibility and adaptability; for a culture of continuous deconstruction and reconstruction; for a policy that addresses the instant processing of new public values and humor and for a social organization that aims to supplement space and invalidate time. But network morphology is also a drastic source of reorganization for power relationships.

Indeed, reflection happens when we develop instrumentation and instrumentalization processes, which allow us to look at ourselves, through our history, and to try to understand our actions and mistakes, and this results in an understanding of the world we live in, and an evaluation of whether it is the one we want.

CONCLUSION

The digital technologies used in the research developed within the Digital Education Research Group UNISINOS/CNPq, presented in Chapter 15 - Brazilian Experiences, are understood as space. This refers to space as: a representation of territorial relations (nature and matter), and social relations (past, present and future); structure of the current moment lived (processes and functions belonging to 'our' space) and force field of actions (uneven actions). So, according to Backes (2007, 2011), digital technologies can be considered as digital virtual spaces. In other words, spaces that: enable action, relation, interaction and the sharing of human beings' representations; are unique and particular of each social group (being human beings in congruence with the environment) and empower coordination of actions (human beings understand actions and give meanings).

With the development and socialization of digital technologies, we start living and collaborating as a hybrid form of human being, technique, machine, offering a new way of seeing 'reality', which has never been 'pure'. For Santos (2006), it is currently not possible to determine where nature's work ends and where man's work begins, moreover, to indicate where technique ends and where the social starts. Therefore we say that hybridism consists of 'mixing' objects in a way that they cannot be explained separately.

Within the context of hybridism, human beings live with each other, and also in digital virtual spaces, thus configuring digital virtual collaborating spaces. The configuring of digital virtual collaborating spaces can be enhanced, in the digital-technological hybridism, consisting of mixing, crossing, integration and articulation of digital technologies, under the coexisting perspective.

The configuring of digital virtual collaborating spaces, within the digital-technological hybridism context, happens in the definition of everyone's space, suitable behavior and common space. Within this digital space human beings, represented in different ways, coexist when they are authors and co-authors of the actions, and construct knowledge where everyone is co-teacher and co-learner.

As a result, the technology-concept Digital Virtual Sharing Spaces has emerged. Digital Virtual Sharing Spaces are technological-digital hybridism where the flow of interaction and communication between human beings happens in a textual, oral, gestural and/or graphical way and where one digital technology is not understood without another, as they are not seen separately. For Backes (2011), each Digital Virtual Sharing Space is compounded by a certain technological-digital hybridism, considering the participants' congruence with digital technologies. We can therefore say that Digital Virtual Sharing Spaces are recreated in every situation.

The digital technological hybridism that forms different Digital Virtual Sharing Spaces, intends to give an opportunity for new technologies to be used as digital virtual spaces and not just as tools, in order to configure digital virtual spaces of living, with a common space, and to constitute a living of a digital virtual nature that is conscious and desirable. However, Digital Virtual Sharing Spaces is a possibility and not a fact; it creates itself through the autopoiesis of its e-inhabitants.

Through this, they constitute a digital virtual living together using suitable behavior defined within the group and which is redefined at their convenience; in mastering the actions through causing emotion, in legitimacy and in mutual respect and in the way of speaking. For Maturana (2005), the way of speaking is the re-conceptualization of language as action, for reflection and self-conscience; in the heterarchical relationship and through interaction and dialogue; and in the recurrence of such actions within the social system.

This perspective allows us to reflect, at every moment, on the network society we are building.

REFERENCES

Backes, L., & Schlemmer, E. (2006). Aprendizagem em mundos virtuais: Espaço deconvivência na formação do educador. In Proceedings of VI Seminário de Pesquisa em Educação da Região Sul – ANPEDSul (pp. 1-6). Santa Maria, Brazil: ANPEDSul. Retrieved from http://www.portalanpedsul.com.br/admin/uploads/2006/Educacao,_Comunicacao_e_tecnologia/Painel/12_56_53_PA570.pdf

Backes, L. (2007). A formação do educador em mundos virtuais: Uma investigação sobre os processos de autonomia e de autoria. (Unpublished master's dissertation). Universidade do Vale do Rio dos Sinos, São Leopoldo, Brazil.

Backes, L. (2011). A configuração do espaço de convivência digital virtual: A cultura emergente no processo de formação do educador. (Unpublished doctoral thesis). Universidade do Vale do Rio dos Sinos, São Leopoldo, Brazil and Université Lumière Lyon 2, Lyon, France.

Backes, L. (2013). Espaço de convivência digital virtual (ECODI): O acoplamento estrutural no processo de interação. ETD - Educação Temática Digital, 15, 337-355.

Castells, M. (2003). *A sociedade em rede*. São Paulo, Brazil: Paz e Terra.

Costa, R. C. A. (2008). Interação em mundos digitais virtuais: uma investigação sobre a representação do emocionar na aprendizagem. (Unpublished master's dissertation). Universidade do Vale do Rio dos Sinos, São Leopoldo, Brazil.

Cuche, D. (1999). *A noção de cultura nas ciências sociais*. Bauru, Brazil: EDUSC.

Firmino, R. J., & Silva, F. D. A. (2010). Desterritorialização e mídia: Um ensaio. Fórum Patrimônio: Ambiente Construído e Patrimônio Sustentável (UFMG. Online), 3, 1-12. Retrieved from http://www.forumpatrimonio.com.br/view_full.php?articleID=158&modo=1

Lévy, P. (1996). O que é virtual? São Paulo, Brazil: Editora 34.

Lévy, P. (2010). Cibercultura. Rio de Janeiro, Brazil: Editora 34.

Maturana, H. R., & Varela, F. J. (2002). *A árvore do conhecimento: As bases biológicas da compreensão humana*. São Paulo, Brazil: Palas Athena.

Maturana, H. R. (1993). Uma nova concepção de aprendizagem. *Dois Pontos*, 2(15), 28–35.

Maturana, H. R. (1999). *Transformación en la convivência*. Santiago, Chile: Dólmen Ediciones.

Maturana, H. R. (2002). *A ontologia da realidade*. Belo Horizonte, Brazil: Ed. UFMG.

Maturana, H. R. (2005). *Emoções e linguagem na educação e na política*. Belo Horizonte, Brazil: Ed. UFMG.

Moraes, M. C. (2004). *O paradigma educacional emergente*. Campinas, Brazil: Papirus.

Negroponte, N. (2006). *A vida digital*. São Paulo, Brazil: Companhia das Letras.

Palloff, R. M., & Pratt, K. (2002). Construindo comunidades de aprendizagem no ciberespaço: Estratégias eficientes para a sala de aula on-line. Porto Alegre, Brazil. *The Art of Medication*.

Rabardel, P. (1995). *Les hommes e les technologies: approche cognitive des instruments contemporains*. Paris: Armand Colin Editeur.

Rabardel, P. (1999). Le language comme instrument? Eléments pour une théorie instrumentale élargie. In Y. Clot (Ed.), *Avec Vygotsky* (pp. 241–265). Paris: La Dispute.

Raleiras, M. (2007). Recensão da obra "A vida no écrã. A identidade na era da internet", de Sherry Turkle [1997]. Sísifo. *Revista de Ciências da Educação, 3,* 113–116.

Santos, M. (1980). *Por uma geografia nova: Da crítica da geografia a uma geografia crítica.* São Paulo, Brazil: Editora HUCITEC.

Santos, M. (2006). *A natureza do espaço: Técnica e tempo, razão e emoção.* São Paulo, Brazil: Editora da Universidade de São Paulo.

Santos, M. (2008). *Metarmofoses do espaço habitado: Fundamentos teóricos e metodológicos da geografia.* São Paulo, Brazil: Edusp.

Schlemmer, E. (2005). A aprendizagem com o uso das tecnologias digitais: Viver e conviver na virtualidade. *Série-Estudos, 0*(19), 103–126.

Schlemmer, E. (2008). ECODI - A criação de espaços de convivência digital virtual no contexto dos processos de ensino e aprendizagem em metaverso. *Cadernos IHU Idéias, 6,* 1–32.

Schlemmer, E. (2009). *Telepresença.* Curitiba, Brazil: IESDE Brasil S. A.

Schlemmer, E. (2010). Dos ambientes virtuais de aprendizagem aos espaços de convivência digitais virtuais – ECODIS: O que se mantêm? O que se modificou? In C. B. Valenti, & E. M. Sacramento (Eds.), Aprendizagem em ambientes virtuais: Compartilhando ideias e construindo cenários (pp. 145-191). Caxias do Sul, Brazil: Educs.

Schlemmer, E., et al. (2006). ECoDI: A criação de um espaço de convivências digital virtual. In Proceedings of XVII Simpósio Brasileiro de Informática na Educação (pp. 467–477). Brasília, Brazil: UNB/UCB; Retrieved from http://br-ie.org/pub/index.php/sbie/article/viewFile/507/493

Turkle, S. (1997). *A vida no écrã. A identidade na era da internet.* Lisboa: Relógio d'Água.

Turkle, S. (1999). Fronteiras do real e do virtual: Entrevista concedida a Federico Casalegno. Revista Famecos, (11), 117-123. Retrieved from http://revistaseletronicas.pucrs.br/ojs/index.php/revistafamecos/article/viewFile/3057/2335

KEY TERMS AND DEFINITIONS

Appropriate Conduct: For Maturana (2002), the appropriate conduct is effective when the observer or the one being observed recognizes the other's domain of action, meaning the expression of knowledge.

Digital Technological Hybridism: Consists in a coherent group (even when sometimes it seems contradicting) of possibilities of accomplishment by human action in a digital virtual space. Such integration takes effect when human beings take, create or mobilize the instruments (digital technology) in their interactions.

Digital Virtual Sharing Spaces: When configuring the digital virtual collaborating spaces, human beings represent their comprehension and definition, establishing each one's space within that living together. In such living together, it is through their disturbances and the comprehension of their disturbances that they define the suitable behavior for the group, configuring what is common, under the coexistence perspective, through the relations in which human beings are authors and coauthors.

Digital Virtual Sharing: Digital Virtual Collaborating happens when human beings, under the interaction and structural coupling in the digital virtual spaces, live and collaborate through dialogic relations, reflecting together about what they know, what they don't know and what they would like to know. These relations are effective in a heterarchical living of sharing representations in digital virtual spaces. Within this diversity of representations, human beings establish appropriate conduct for the social system, that become a common sense in living together up to the moment they are no longer desirable or they do not correspond to the group's needs. It is then that, through disturbance, common behavior is defined and redefined, because they are autopoietic social systems.

Digital Virtual Space: Under this perspective, for Backes (2011) digital virtual spaces are made only by hardware and software that enable *action* and the *interaction* process between human beings, as well as the *sharing* of representations and perceptions, or, when it is possible to configure a space of relationship between human beings through digital technology.

Instrumentalization: For Rabardel (1995) it consists in transforming the human being as he adapts, modifies, updates and creates new mental schemes for using the instrument.

Instrumentation: For Rabardel (1995) it consists in giving an instrument new property, functions and meaning, which were not foreseen in its creation.

Living Spaces: For Maturana and Varela (2002), the configuration of living spaces occurs in the flow of interactions between human beings and between human beings and the environment, that enables both human beings and the environment to transform, intertwined by emotions, perceptions, representations, disturbances and the comprehension of the disturbances. The configuration of the living space occurs throughout daily living and sharing.

ENDNOTES

[1] The concept of e-citizen, approached in Chapter 4 - Avatar: Building a "Digital Virtual Self," refers to the human beings, represented by the "digital virtual self", who establish an interaction process through: the construction of living rules with the other "selves", who emerge in the dynamic of relations of living in congruence with the digital virtual space – configuring a digital virtual living together; the comprehension of such living rules, considering the other as a legitimate "self" for the interaction processes, of using the digital virtual space to its full extent for the emancipation of the "self" and of those who live and share the digital virtual space.

[2] The concept of e-inhabitant, approached in Chapter 4 – Avatar: Building a "Digital Virtual Self," refers to human beings, represented by their avatars who carry out the interactions with other avatars through: text communication in the chat or IM; oral communication, through speech; gestural communication, or even by graphic and metaphoric communication.

[3] In the recursion, an operation is applied to the result of the operation previously carried out, different from the repetition, which consists of an operation always applied to the same factor.

[4] "… it is always an expression of the action of living beings in a domain of reciprocal structural coupling, and it will last as long as necessary" (Maturana, 1999, p.30).

[5] For Maturana 2002, suitable behavior is effective when the observer or the one being observed recognizes the other's domain of action, meaning the expression of knowledge.

Chapter 13
Digital Virtual Culture in Metaverse:
The Metaculture?

ABSTRACT

In this chapter, the authors approach Culture in Metaverse as Digital Virtual Cultures, or as the Metaculture of Metaculture. They present and discuss subtopics like "The Digital Virtual Culture," "Digital Virtual Culture in Metaverse," "Metaculture Formation in Virtual Digital Coexistence in Metaverse." They finish with a brief conclusion about the chapter's evidence that the essence of the living and collaborating, the eagerness of "being together," the sharing, the emoting, the underground power, the imagination, and the dynamics human beings create in their daily lives take part in the construction of all types of culture. They seek to understand "culture" the way it is.

INTRODUCTION

The human beings' way of living in congruence with the space has turned them into 'unique' and particular individuals, recognized as such by emerging paradigm-based theories. Within the dynamic relationship or collaborating between human beings, each group also starts acting in their own way; creating rites to represent emotions, establishing common values and rules for living together and expectancies of life, building culture through this. For Cuche (1999, p.11) "The use of the notion of culture leads directly to the symbolic order, referring to meaning, which is, the point on which it is most difficult to come to an agreement".

Therefore, within this complex interaction that constitutes culture, the relation between the individual (identity, identification) and the group (social, sociality) occurs under the same complex perspective (individual, difference, and group, similarity), complementary and systemic (the individual builds himself up through the group he constructs) and dynamics (in adapting, in recursion, in reconstruction and in creation). That is why, according to Cuche (1999) in an interactionist

DOI: 10.4018/978-1-4666-6351-0.ch013

approach, we can say that culture exists through human beings' interactive action, and that those actions are inserted within a context that needs to be taken into consideration. It is through research on digital virtual spaces developed by the Digital Education Research Group UNISINOS/CNPQ, that we make the distinction between interactions and interactivity, so, when we talk about the action we also mean the interaction between human beings.

Nowadays, with the ease of displacement, communication and interaction, human beings have broadened their knowledge and raised their awareness of different and varied existing contexts. Therefore, when considering the construction of culture through human beings' action in congruence with the environment, we also evidence diversity and difference in culture, at every change of the nature in the environment.

In this chapter we approach the concepts of identity and culture, constructed along history, in order to reach a reflection on "digital virtual culture" or its emergence, to be able to make some considerations about culture in Metaverses and, combining all these aspects, define the characteristics of Metaculture.

Identity and Culture in a Dialectic Perspective: Interactionist Grounds

In Chapter 4 - Avatar: building a "digital virtual self" we stated that the studies on identity and culture emerged at the same time. So, by the time humanity has developed through different cultures, the differences have made it possible to identify the particular characterizations of human beings belonging to a certain group, or, people's identity. From this perception, identity and culture are not comprehended in a dichotomous way, but in a dialectic one, meaning they are different units but intrinsically related. For Cuche (1999, p.15)

"'Culture' and 'identity' are concepts that lead to the same reality, seen from different angles".

Human beings construct their identity through identification, in transit and/or in belonging simultaneously to different groups. In this way, the feeling of belonging to a group and/or several ones, the eagerness to live together, results for Maffesoli (1998, 2007) in the underground centrality, meaning that all elements that make social life have a sense, a meaning and a growth.

Humanity constructs itself through modifications, including by its constant migratory processes that, with the advances of digital technology, and Metaverses above all, can be of another nature, such as a digital virtual one. So, they result in new disturbances about the construction of identity, identifications and the ways of relation and interaction in living and sharing. Therefore, as previously mentioned, migration is not only geographical, but also digital virtual. Human beings, when configuring their living and sharing of a digital virtual nature, characterize their group and, through the interaction process, reconstruct the digital virtual identity for themselves and for the group. According to what was discussed in Chapter 4 - Avatar: building a "digital virtual self", the different identities complement each other, and are congruent and make part of the 'self'.

When looking at the living, we perceive that there are many ways of collaborating, because for Maffesoli (1998, p.93) "Everyone takes part of the global 'us'". According to the author, we create a "collective soul" where there is an ephemeral individual and the reappropriation of the person, that is to say, the sociality – the set of practices that escape the rigid control, a being-together that does not depend on a goal to be reached, and therefore constructs culture.

According to Cuche (1999, p.140), cultural constructions occur in a mixed way, through processes of continuity between two cultures that are in contact and, in the same way through the temporary discontinuity. So, the notion of culture is understood,

as more or less a dynamic set. The elements compounding a culture are never integrated one to the other because they come from several sources in time and space. In other words, there is a 'game' in the system, especially because it is an extremely complex system. This game is in the interstitium in which the individual's and the group's freedom settles down to 'manipulate' culture.

In this sense, Freire (2008, p.43), having understood culture as a complex and systemic construction, creates the following concept:

Culture – being the opposite of nature, which is not created by man – is the contribution men make to what was given to them, or, to nature. Culture is all the result of human activity, from men's creating and recreating efforts, from their work on transforming and establishing relations of dialogue with other men.

So, from the perspective of a shared action between human beings towards the environment, in a tendency defined by sociology as interactionist, according to Péres Gómez (2001) culture is considered the result of social interaction and interchange among human beings, within a determined space and time. In this way it is possible to understand culture as a configuration of a living space of living and sharing in a flow of interactions, considering as natural, material, social and emotional conditions represented through values, icons, feelings, rites, customs that surround living and sharing. Living, in a certain culture, consists of interpreting, reproducing and/or changing it, which means that culture empowers and limits the development of human beings.

How do we think about cultural relations within such a diverse sphere? In order to better comprehend cultural relations in the action of hu-

man being, who constitute different livings, and in the action of human beings through living and sharing in the reconstruction of culture, Maturana and Yáñez (2009, p.216) state that "culture does not pre-determine the living that will be lived, but it does determine that the ones growing inside it are embodying it, and their corporality [embodiment] turns into, in a way that, unless in a disjunctive way, he or she reflects upon what they do, choose without choosing living, and that living implies culture". So, the maintenance of the existing culture, the transformation, the development and/or the recreation is related to the human beings' awareness level of themselves and of the other, in the social system they belong to. When we relate human's actions to the awareness level, how do we consider education within this scenario? Education, in the formal school space, when configured as an ecological space[1] of cultural crossing, can represent a space to promote autonomy and alterity[2], identification and reflexive criticism for the constitution of new generation.

Within this context and under this perspective, the school's role

is, precisely, offering the individual the possibility to detect and understand the value and the feeling of explicit or latent influxes, which they are receiving in their development, as a consequence of their participation in complex cultural life and their community. (Pérez Gómez, 2001, p.18)

However, what we see in the educational context are the determinations of a complex contemporaneous life 'running over' different cultures that meet at school, trying to "steer" the constitution of new generations in an "arbitrary" way. Complexity in contemporaneity consists of "…having a thought able to think the contradictory, of analyzing and synthesizing, of constructing, deconstructing and reconstructing something new" (Moraes, 2003, p.199).

Could we say that the educational system constructs its culture based on the relations established among students, mediated by the educator, assigning meanings that can reproduce or reconstruct an existent culture? What we have seen so far is that the paths to be followed are defined in the relation and intention of the human beings' group.

All education must have, as its constitutive base, the objective, the dynamization and recreation of its own culture, based on its roots and historical background in a dialogic relation with other cultures. Education is centered in the dynamization of the culture itself, it intentionally proposes the collective's identity self-awareness and its recreation and construction through the meeting with other cultures, new challenges to face in the present and in the future. (Peresson, 2006, p.88)

In this sense, it is relevant to state that culture is understood as having an important role in forming human beings' structure, as well as in the constitution of subjectivity, but without being deterministic. So,

school must be a place for learning and reconstructing culture, for learning how to think and collaborate. And the modus faciendi of learning culture is through the development of thinking processes which must be systematic, involving the capacity for investigating, thinking and concept construction and also dealing with them, and another capacity I call translation, which is knowing how to say with one's own words what the other is thinking. (Libâneo, 2003, p.42)

The construction of culture in education occurs in the human beings' living and collaborating, which are interacting within that environment (educational context), and considers, thus, the educator as the person legitimizing such living together. The educator's action within that environment is built through the formation of the group which constructs it own culture.

The teaching culture is specified in the methods that are used in the classroom, in the quality, in the sense and the orientation of interpersonal relations, in the definition of roles and functions they carry out, in the method of management, in the participating structures and the decision-making processes. (Pérez Gómez, 2001, p.164)

Despite the dialecticism in the construction of different levels of culture (social, educational and teaching) we have evidenced a paradoxical situation, as previously approached in Chapter 2 - Network Learning culture and the emerging paradigm. Social relations in contemporaneity are being more characterized by mobility, flexibility and uncertainty, mainly originating in digital technological complexity, cultural plurality and worldwide economic relations. The relation between educators, in turn, is constituted by routines, conventions and static and monopolistic customs, from an inflexible, blurred and bureaucratic scholar system. "Within this unavoidable tension, teachers are gradually more insecure and defenseless, feeling threatened by an accelerated evolution they cannot or do not know how to respond to" (Pérez Gómez, 2001, p.164).

Before that, cultural aspects drive and mediate, but do not determine the educator's action, and that can either facilitate or disconcert reflection processes and autonomy in pedagogical practices, influencing the quality of the educational process. The more reflective human beings are, in the sense of knowing what they don't know and knowing what they wish to know, the better they will understand the necessary actions to transform their situation.

So, considering the changes in the interaction processes linked to the use of digital technology previously stated, we have shown: the (re)signification of time and space concepts; quick access to information; the constitution of communication, interaction and relationship networks; the (re) signification of ways of relation and representation of sharing human beings' knowledge. This living is daily, and is the power to understand digital virtual culture. Nevertheless, technological advances can cause conflicts in the educational context, regarding the variety of information, their validity and use.

DIGITAL VIRTUAL CULTURE

When we consider culture as construction, in the relations established between human beings, in congruence with the environment, we are contemplating: dialectic between culture and nature; the character: creator, reproducer, recreator and transformer; its characterization as: dynamic, diversified and mixed; the construction of meanings, powers and limits. From these considerations we question ourselves: If the nature of the environment we live in changes, how does congruence happen? And consequently how does culture happen?

With the development of digital technology, collaborating also configures itself within a space (environment) of a digital virtual nature[3]. Collaborating between human beings, when configured in digital virtual spaces, allows us to have some particularities, such as: making "virtual friends", people we know, interact with, relate to exclusively mediated by digital technology, and these can be mingled among a network of relations, with 'physical face-to-face' friend – those we physically know in geographically located places. In this way we have shown other and new actions from human beings in the flow of interactions when configuring such living together. So we have articulated: space, culture and digital technology, some of the vocabulary currently presented, is immediately activated as: cyberspace and cyberculture.

For Lévy (2010b), cyberspace consists of a digital technology in which the center is all over and the circumference nowhere, meaning that it can be a hypertext computer, dispersed, living, simmering, unfinished. For Lemos (2007), cyberspace

also contemplates the interconnection between people making diversity emerge, communication, and social; in the same way that it contemplates viruses and hackers. In summary, it serves both the good and the bad.

We have demonstrated that generations are currently building up systems, under an ecological perspective, in which there is articulated knowledge, sociability, culture and digital technological spaces. This new system represents the central line that pervades the relations and transformations, creating new scenarios where our "digital virtual home" is constructed, through signs, where there is re(signification) between the significant and the signification. This "digital virtual home", for Lévy (2010a), is constructed in cyberspace, and it exists not only to spread content, but also to allow the flow of communication and interaction, contributing to the development of the daily living of autonomous subjects, as well as, from our perspective, of authors and co-authors. Therefore, we talk about *digital virtual space*, in reference to the previous chapter, when we configure living and daily sharing in cyberspace and so constructing a cognitive ecology. So, the configuration of a digital virtual space of living and collaborating broadens the concepts of cyberspace and cyberculture, because we approach living and daily sharing in their natural, cultural, historical, social and religious dimensions.

For Lévy (2010a) cognitive ecology consists of the study of technical and collective dimensions of cognition in different spaces, but directed beyond those spaces. In other words, from the learning processes developed and the grounding of education in cyberculture, it understands technologies from the perspective of contributing to the transformation of society in the same way as the society transforms technologies, through mixtures and imbrications, in the same way as in the perspective of Digital Virtual Sharing Space's[4]. So, "the thinking happens within a network were neurons, cognitive modules, humans, educational institutions, languages, written systems, books and computers interconnect, transform and translate the representation" (Lévy, 2010a, p.137).

For Lemos (2007, p.75) cultural constructions, originated from cyberspace, can be called cyberculture, so:

Cyberculture is the socio-technical configuration of the production of small catastrophes that feed fusion, impulse and contemporaneous symbiosis: the cyberculture interactive user is born from the elimination of social (Baudrillard) and the implosion of modern individualism.

With the development of our "digital virtual home", we perceive that the combination of different ways of interaction and expression is making the living web increasingly complex. The communication ways are revealing that our comprehension of reality is increasingly metaphoric, and that our metaphors create the content of our culture. As a result, "we are in the computer", "we become the history book", "we like friends' comments", "it clicked", among other examples. According to Lemos (2007), the man and the machine, within this process of interaction and communication we are living in, go through a symbiosis, in other words, through a technological coupling. We can then argue that digital virtual communities assume a disturbing character in modern society (hierarchized, supporting, classifying), because it differs from this logic. With the empowerment of communication by digital technology, we come across a paradoxical situation regarding our interaction processes: ease in communicating with everybody; as well as the weakness of such communication (excess of information and fragile information).

With culture being mediated and determined by communication, the cultures themselves, meaning, our system of beliefs and historically produced

codes, are transformed in a crucial way by the new technological system and will be even more so as time goes by. (Castells, 2003, p.414)

We often perceive, in the interactions and representations in digital virtual spaces, an ecological digital configuration within the space, with an educational culture sometimes traversed and sometimes (re)signified. As time goes by and with increasing familiarization with digital technology human beings are creating dynamics of relation, (re)signifying, transforming and constructing digital virtual spaces. Within this dynamic, human beings organize consensual behaviors suitable for living and collaborating, and begin to repeat them at every convenient moment. In this way, living is configured in digital virtual spaces and through the relational dynamic built in a living of digital virtual nature. Human beings construct, through this ecology, the emerging culture in digital virtual spaces, in other words, the *digital virtual culture*.

The use of digital technology has long triggered different discussions in several areas of knowledge, regarding its possibilities and limitations, setting up a complex situation. It is, however, a paradox, for we can see the porosity in the borders when we configure living and collaborating in digital virtual spaces, the discussions are still territorialized. The area of knowledge determines the positioning, which means that, for experts in Computer Science, their concern is to develop advanced digital technology. Experts in Communication are focused on the development of interfaces and the study of new ways of communication and interaction these means provide and experts in Sociology turn their studies to the construction of networks, the "being together" mediated by digital technology and in how we are organizing contemporaneous societies. Experts in Education, on the other hand, question everything regarding learning and teaching in the digital world, including the way in which courses are organized, the syllabus, methodologies, didactic pedagogical practices, pedagogical mediation, among others, in a context that involves differences between what is proposed in distance teaching, distance education, online education and so on. However, as we have previously said, the studies are territorialized, segmented, with little or no interaction with those areas.

Among the pros and cons and in search of dialectic in relations between the interests of different areas of knowledge working with digital technology, it is interesting to reflect on what Pérez Gómez (2001, p.106) tells us in his work, when referring to the electronic revolution, information and public opinion:

We need to recognize, therefore, the extraordinary potential for instruction and training that the electronic revolution offers, by allowing intercultural communication and trigger the decentralization of individuals and groups from their limited contexts.

Many things then become possible, including the broadening of spaces of movements and social manifestation, which start to occupy and to construct themselves from different digital technologies, mainly connected to social media. What happened in Brazil in the months of June and July 2013 is an example of movements and social protests that extended into physical spaces – and geographically located spaces, with protesters taking the streets all over Brazil, whilst simultaneously occupying digital virtual spaces in social media, in a hybrid multimodal movement. This shows us that geographically located spaces and digital virtual spaces are more and more permeable, imbricated and presenting them nowadays in the continuous living and collaborating lives of human beings.

Recognizing digital technology for the educational context nowadays is hardly questionable, and we can see an unquestioning adhesion or a groundless rejection. In this sense we have found

the use of softwares based on an empiric epistemological conception, or rather, the abandon of digital equipment in schools.

Therefore, the development of formative processes, mainly for the training of educators, needs a theoretical and practical maturity. There are several more pedagogical practices for teaching with the use of digital technology and distance teaching than pedagogical practices of education with digital technology and online education. The differences in the conception of formative processes, in the conception of teaching or in the conception of education will be decisive in the levels of signification, giving sense, by subject-educators, in different digital technologies within the educational context resulting in an awareness of reproduction or transformation.

Culture, in its different dimensions, constructs relationships, at the same time it is constructed by them. What we can observe are "… moments when culture emphasizes the sameness of experience whilst in others it underscores the multiplicity of experience" (Turkle, 1999, p.119).

At this time it is important to recall the subjectivist approach to identity, which "… has the merit of considering the variable character of identity, despite having the tendency of excessively emphasizing the ephemeral aspect of identity" (Cuche, 1999, p.181), as discussed in Chapter 4 - Avatar: building a "digital virtual self". Such duality of identity is intensified in contemporaneity because social context can be physical and/or digital virtual, constructed and defined by components (human beings), through suitable behaviors for each group, guiding forms of representation and each component's choices. In other words, the human being constructs behaviors that will guide their actions, in congruence with the nature of the environment, and will reformulate suitable behaviors as actions demand, so that they can identify with the groups to which they belong, thereby creating the uniformity and diversity.

Due to the complex characteristic of this emerging culture, it is outlined in the context of an emerging paradigm, mainly regarding the reflections on knowledge, developed by Sousa Santos (2004). According to the author we live between two paradoxical situations: the potentials of technological translation of accumulated knowledge make us believe in a threshold of a society of interactive communication free from the needs and insecurities that still nowadays are present among many of us; and opposed to that, a reflection that is gaining depth in terms of the limits scientific rigor with increasingly verisimilar dangers of the potential ecological catastrophe or nuclear war that make us fear the XXI century may be over before it has begun.

The crisis and impasses inherent to life cause tension in the relationship between human beings, causing transformations, creating the living of a certain time and space. Such transformations happen in different ways in different social segments, including when social relations are constituted in digital virtual spaces, through the space of flow in a timeless time, as defined by Castells (2003)[5].

Therefore, when relating the dominant paradigm and the emerging paradigm, according to Sousa Santos (2004) and Moraes (2004), there is the intention of constructing a digital virtual living and reflecting on the culture of immersion within this context, mainly when we deal with teaching and learning processes, as well as the training process of educators, articulated in a way that teaching and learning is constructed by educators who are constructed by certain ways of teaching and learning.

For Capra (2004), paradigmatic changes are also cultural transformation, for they trespass the scientific sphere in a way of transforming social relations as conceptions, values, perceptions and shared practices by a community.

However, before the ever-changing reality of the globalized world we live in and before new challenges that are presenting themselves little by little, the education, culturalization, transmitting and creation of a new culture, must be a project, a conscious and intentional act, that is active and proactive. (Peresson, 2006, p.89)

In context of training educators, Pérez Gómez (2001, p.164) points out that the teaching culture consists of "...the group of beliefs, values, habits and norms that determine what the social group considers valuable within their professional context, as well as the correct ways of thinking, feeling, acting and relating to each other."

This cultural construction is sustained by the dominant paradigm or constructed by the emerging paradigm that, in this case, contributes to the comprehension of the emerging culture of relations and interactions between human beings in digital virtual spaces. Culture is constituted as emergent because it is under construction and still does not take part in the living and sharing of different generations; it is a construction of that generation, dominated by research, such as that of Veen and Vrakking (2009, p.12), from Generation Homo Zappiens, that constructs and is constructed by the contemporaneous society:

"Homo zappiens" is the new generation that has learned to deal with new technologies, that has grown up using multiple technological resources since their childhood. Such resources have allowed them to take control of the flow of information, mingle virtual and real communities, communicate and collaborate in networks, according to their needs. The Homo zappiens is an active processor of information, solving problems with agility, using gaming strategy, and knowing very well how to communicate. Their relation with school has deeply changed... the Homo zappiens is digital and school is analogical. We emphasize that, in the same way we regard the term "digital native", the term "homo zappiens" has no biological connotation nor does it have to be used in the sense of classification, as seen in a dominant paradigm, but in the sense of comprehending the generation and cultural changes and transformations that are happening in order to enable the creation of generational bridges, hybrid cultures, in the perspective of complexity that it involves, which demonstrates the emerging paradigm.

Re-examining some of the reflections from Chapter 2 - Network Learning culture and the emerging paradigm, the dominant paradigm is characterized by its linearity, single truth and objectivity. This paradigm, according to Sousa Santos (2004), impelling and being impelled by natural sciences, works with the possibility of having only one way of true knowledge, this way constructing the distinction between scientific knowledge and common sense knowledge. Knowing means to quantify, divide and classify to afterwards determine systematic relations between the systems involved. These conceptions were constructed from the scientific revolution and have become models of rationality and were based on the domain of natural sciences, or, modern science.

However, through new ways of relation, interaction, reflection and social construction, this paradigm does not support the complexity in which we live. In the attempt to overcome a crisis, mankind, through relations of conjunction and/or disjunction, starts constructing a new group of master concepts that emerge in the living and sharing. This way the emerging paradigm, as the name suggests, does not configure a reality, but it announces many intentions, that have been already modifying the living, to overcome the impasses and the crisis.

Still considering the reflections in Chapter 2 - Network Learning culture and the emerging paradigm, knowing the emerging paradigm does not tend to be a dualist or dichotomous knowledge, therefore, a knowledge that is grounded in the overcoming of distinctions, so familiar and evident that until recently were considered irreplaceable.

Science is then constituted through constructed knowledge and social practices, knowledge starts being understood in its universal totality and so-

cial practices as projects of life in a certain social group. So, the constitution of science happens through themes that are found, interrelated and broadened as a big network. Under the emerging paradigm, scientific knowledge will make sense and be more valuable when transformed in common sense, because this way it will guide actions and transform life, because the same was understood and used.

The technological context in contemporaneity presents several faces: status, accessibility, power, democratization, socialization, deterritorialization, exclusion, among others. Such faces gain power and intensity according to the way human beings configure the ways of living and sharing, which influence current cultural constructions. For Maturana and Yàñez (2009) the cultural meeting of two or more cultures can constitute: a cultural disagreement, when only one culture is valued, while others are devalued or denied; or in the creative, dynamic and systemic meeting, when there is a reflection about cultural differences, adaptation and transformation, in a conversation triggering the emerging of a new culture.

In the context of the emerging paradigm we can find data for reflecting on the type of living we configure and how we configure it. The digital virtual living is the place where we can demonstrate which culture emerges, and if such culture contributes to the teaching and learning processes, in the formation of human beings able to produce themselves, in congruence with the environment. Consequently, by being aware of the world we have, we are able to change it into the world we want.

The emerging culture refers to the digital virtual living spaces, which coexist with other living spaces and are part of the human being's life. The living, in general, is constructed in the transformation of human beings and the environment. Such transformations, originating in living educational contexts, happen through teaching and learning processes.

When thinking about what we do in our daily living and sharing we understand how things we do are processed and how we turn actions into concepts, systematizing the processes we carry out. By systematizing what we do and turning it into concepts and theories, we are also defining actions for future generations who will build, through their reflective and conscious actions, a new systematization, thus broadening knowledge.

DIGITAL VIRTUAL CULTURE IN METAVERSE

When configuring this ontological, epistemological and methodological scenario, we can also think about a learning culture that develops itself in a complex, systemic and highly technologicized context.

Within this context culture can be understood as follows:

Cultures are closed conversation networks, meaning they are closed networks of recursive coordination of doing and feeling. Nevertheless, the configuration of emotions formed within the closed conversation network is what guides its members' individual behavior. (Maturana, 1999, p.51)

Technologies such as Metaverses, are shown in research developed within the educational context and corporative education, as digital virtual spaces that foster emotioning, for the digital virtual presence is immediately recognized by the participants due to its social, immersive and diversely communicational aspect. This way the participants can establish relations of legitimacy with the other and mutual respect, implied in emotional actions.

This continuous construction in network is effected through learning (mainly in recursion), that, in this context, involves aspects such as: familiarization with the new digital virtual spaces impacting on graphic, textual, oral and gestural representation, as well as on immersion; appropriating technological knowledge as in how to construct Digital-Virtual Worlds in 3D and an avatar, and what is done with this construction; using different possibilities to interact, through oral, textual, gestural and graphic communication, in 3D graphics environments; as well as articulating these different forms in order to identify when it is most appropriate to use one or another and what we are building out of each one of them.

This way, every avatar (e-inhabitant), in their living and sharing, should give a meaning to what they do towards themselves and what the other does for the social relation. This allows them to construct themselves as an autonomous subject and author of the world in which they live (of different natures), being aware of their choices and actions. We can then demonstrate that learning, in the Metaverse context, contributes to the development of the observation sense, when perceiving possibilities of the autonomous being and author of their learning process. It also implies exploring, experimenting, living, experiencing, getting into relationships, letting one be provoked by the environment, acting and interacting with other e-inhabitants, in congruence with the Digital-Virtual Worlds in 3D, getting close and distant in order for signification and (re)signification. It is in this conjoined and disjoined action between e-inhabitants, that where we build up networks:

Every community exists as a network of processes, acts, meetings, behavior, technical emotion, ... configuring a system of collaborating relations which penetrates all aspects in children's lives until they become adults, affecting all dimensions in their doing and acting. (Maturana, 1999, p.10)

The network configuration is particular to each group, for it is maintained, it organizes itself and self-organizes through the autopoiesis of human beings. The group takes the shape of the participants who create it, the same way the participants start acting according to the way created by the group. The configuration of the network defines suitable and unsuitable behavior of its members, considered as legitimacy; therefore, the relations are not submissive, but they are productive, re-productive, adaptable, transforming and creative.

Revisiting the focus of this chapter, emerging culture refers to the digital virtual living spaces that coexist with other living spaces in the human body's daily life, still from the perspective of coexisting. Collaborating or "being together", in general, is characterized by the transformation of human beings and the environment, in congruence with one another.

Thinking about a learning culture in network implies thinking about the configuration of spaces where there is affective (emotional) involvement between human beings, for the construction of rules that contemplate reciprocity and recur-sion. In this sense, it is possible to establish relations, in order to elaborate new opinions, in which human beings are able to self-produce in a continuous movement of living, knowing, and which is often supplied by conflicts, differences and contradictions.

We argue that, one of the keys for consider-ing something communitarian is the absence of transition, that is to say the permanence and adaptation, linked to the underground power of participants. It is then possible to share a history, a memory. With continuity comes the possibility of constructing social norms, rites, sense.

We learn, little by little, as an online culture is established, with common experiences, to trust each other. But again, I want to highlight that the best possibilities for the development of communi-ties are found in places where they cross virtual experiences and the rest of their lives. (Trukle, 1999, p.120)

In this way, the construction of a digital virtual identity makes sense (through the representation of an avatar), in the human being's immersion in 3D Digital-Virtual Worlds where he can: act and interact with other e-inhabitants (other avatars present in 3D Digital-Virtual Worlds); construct digital virtual living networks; create virtual communities; structure habits and attitudes and define suitable behavior for the living and sharing among e-citizens, building up a certain group. We have to call our attention, though, to the fact that in immersion in Digital-Virtual Worlds in 3D, the human being takes with him 'the rest of life'.

We also expect that this digital virtual identity is constructed by relations of responsibility and in a free way, when considering the legitimacy of the other as a core characteristic. We consider that the construction of the digital virtual identity occurs towards dialectics with the construction of a digital virtual culture.

For this, the construction of the digital virtual identity and the digital virtual culture happens in a recursive way, in the possibility of getting in touch with the other (in an expanded view, the other represents the different individuals of a certain society or group) in a daily living and sharing, and why not, through social differences, or alterity? In this way, the existence of an avatar (another representation of the body, a technologi-cized version of the same human being), happens in the interaction between avatars, in this other avatar's view, in co-presence[6], allowing the com-prehension of the Digital Virtual Worlds in 3D from a different regard, relating different points of view and enabling the decentralization of the "self avatar". In this sense, we demonstrate that the avatars' actions in Digital-Virtual Worlds in 3D value the potentialities of digital technology and the comprehension of congruence between the Digital Virtual Worlds in 3D, the avatar and the human being (who also live in different geo-graphically located spaces).

Therefore, in reference to Chapter 4 - Avatar: building a "Digital Virtual self", the individual dialectic relation and the social cause a stronger feeling of presentiality, of vivacity, triggered by this "digital virtual social presence" (forged in the relation with the other), which brings human beings together, who, from their "digital virtual selves" (avatars) can have the feeling of "being there", "being together" in the same digital virtual environment in a more intense and significant way.

As a result, there is often a feeling of being distant and absent in digital virtual relations due to the physical distance and the representation of perception in a less diverse way, this is overcome when we live and share in a digital virtual way, acting and interacting in different Digital-Virtual Worlds in 3D, through the "digital virtual self", making it possible for the construction of cognitive structures that transform the human being in an autopoietic way.

Moving away from stereotypes, which are also created by the media, we face a deterritorialized self, who deals with global values at the same time as carrying their own ones. The person who would settle in the global village has looked himself in the mirror and seen himself as multicultural pieces. (Silva & Firmino, 2009, p.6)

With deterritorialization, the broadening of space beyond the geographically located one, we are given an infinite number of possibilities. Consequently, the differences, diversity and multiplicity become characteristics of the digital virtual culture.

What we have to observe is that every type of intellectual technology we live with, either oral, written or informational places a particular emphasis in certain cognitive dimensions and in certain values, which will lead to specific cultural manifestation. (Moraes, 2004, p.123)

In this sense, we recursively alter humanity's ways of doing and thinking.

The human mind, or, the individual's cognitive equipment, is influenced by culture, by collectiveness providing the language, by classification systems, by concepts and analogies, by metaphors

and images [the same way it is influenced]. Therefore, any changes in storing techniques, changes in transmitting representation of information and knowledge, trigger changes in the ecological environment where representations are spread, causing cultural changes and changes in knowledge. (Moraes, 2004, p.124)

Culture constructed in the digital virtual spaces emerges when there is living and collaborating among human beings who are autonomous, autopoietic and the author of their actions, who accept each other in an interaction process and mutual respect, thus constituting autopoietic social systems in digital virtual spaces. The emerging culture is constituted in the digital virtual living and collaborating, where human beings' digital virtual identity and the autopoietic social systems regulate the level of interference of culture in education, training processes, for the construction of an emerging culture.

We have identified many common aspects in different formative processes developed within the context of our researches: Backes (2007 and 2011), Moretti (2010) and Machado (2012), which are related to culture in education, in different countries. Nevertheless different ways of acting were identified regarding common aspects, which characterize the capacity of transforming human beings in congruence with the environment. This way, culture in education, in different moments, is represented by e-inhabitants, but it is in the dynamics of the relation that it is reproduced, (re)signified, or transformed, which implies in e-inhabitants' responsibility. "Responsibility has to do with people's desire to realize that, the consequences of their acts, are desirable" (Maturana, 2002, p.45).

The dynamic in the relationship between human beings and their capacity for transformation allow us to comprehend the construction of the emerging culture, either implying or being implied, in the movement between the configuration of the digital virtual space of living and the digital virtual living. This fluidity makes the emerging culture in these spaces not to be determining nor determined, but signified at every moment that the dynamic in the relation between human beings is constructed.

So, it relies on us – who are placed in several realities and cultural contexts – to think in innovative educational methodologies, which can problematize realities and propose reflection. There is a need to using digital technologies that are challenging for each context, improving teaching and learning processes, and that are capable of enabling heterarchical interaction flows, from a perspective of democratization. The combination of innovative methodologies and digital technology can make the development of men and women possible for human promotion. We believe then, that we can think of a digital emancipation. For Backes and Schlemmer (2010, p.14), emancipation is possible through pedagogical practice, so, "Within this dynamic two previous moments are highlighted: the incitement and the promotion. Thus the emancipation pedagogy consists of raising awareness and empowering human beings to have autonomy in the search for transformation".

However it is important to highlight that digital technologies are only potentialities, and human beings, the e-inhabitants in the digital virtual spaces are the ones able to concretize such potentiality. So, when we configure the living and sharing of a digital virtual nature for human emancipation, men and women are able to transform, aiming for the common good, from a perspective of human emancipation. In this living and collaborating is where the training of the educators we want is effective, within the context of digital technological hybridism. A transformation in which we can make a new culture emerge, when configuring digital virtual living, and we hope that this emerging culture is in the perspective of a freeing culture.

a freeing culture relies on the real conditions of people who are making and remaking their society, in a way that their daily curriculum

cannot be invented by someone else, at distance, and delivered or imposed on them. On the other hand, we can take as a reference our own learning process, our own teaching body and reflect upon what they suggest. (Freire & Shor, 1992, p.100)

In this sense the construction of the digital virtual culture in Metaverse is carried out in a complex way, by human beings, by the construction of a digital virtual identity, in a daily living and sharing, in congruence with the environment.

CONCLUSION: METACULTURE FORMATION IN VIRTUAL DIGITAL COEXISTENCE IN METAVERSE

When we understand culture as a construction happening in human beings' living and sharing, in their congruence with the environment, involving factors such as history, society, politics, religion, time and space, in a complex way, we reflect about the possibilities we find in the contemporaneity towards the environment with which we are in congruence. With technological advances, we can easily modify the nature of the environment where we have settled our daily living.

Through this, we establish some considerations about digital virtual culture, being it mainly characterized by the porosity of its edges and deterritorialization. We emphasize that the digital virtual culture implies protests of the collective conscience, in a (re)signification of the significant and the signification of new signs constructed in the daily living together, striving for being together, in learning through network communication. For Malizia (2012, p.27)

It is a fact that, more than being a means of communication, the network seems to be truly its own 'territory' detached from concrete relations, absolutely (more than any other media) free from space (or not specialized), where 'social' is 'virtual'; in a kind of autonomous reality that creates flows (sometimes ephemeral, others constant) of communication per se, without necessarily a univocal connection communication/comprehension, without interaction, not even 'almost'.

The network dimensions, or beyond them, become complex with the development of emerging technologies, as in the case of Metaverses. So we begin to discuss all this complexity through digital virtual culture in Metaverses, where daily life occurs through the diversity of communication and representation of perception, empowering the immersion process, in the avatar's digital virtual presence. We can than talk about 'metaculture'.

Metaculture could be approached under two dimensions: metaculture being the nomenclature used to defined digital virtual culture in metaverse; metaculture in the etymological sense of the word, which means beyond culture, or thinking about culture through culture itself.

Our reflection follows the second tendency - thinking metaculture beyond culture. Thus, when understanding digital virtual culture as one that goes beyond the territorial to deterriorial, where borders are porous and all elements are in interaction, in a complex way, it would be, in a certain way, paradoxical to keep classifying and characterizing every cultural movement that we see in contemporaneity.

We do not deny any congruence with the environment, nor any transformation evidenced in the communication, interaction and representation processes from digital technology, and mainly in the emerging ones. Nevertheless, we show that the essence of living and collaborating, the eagerness of 'being together', sharing, emotioning, the underground power, imagination and the dynamic human beings create in their daily lives, take part in the construction of all types of culture that can possibly be identified. In this way we hope to understand 'culture' and that is all.

REFERENCES

Backes, L. (2007). *A formação do educador em mundos virtuais: Uma investigação sobre os processos de autonomia e de autoria.* (Unpublished master's dissertation). Universidade do Vale do Rio dos Sinos, São Leopoldo, Brazil.

Backes, L. (2011). *A configuração do espaço de convivência digital virtual: A cultura emergente no processo de formação do educador.* (Unpublished doctoral thesis). Universidade do Vale do Rio dos Sinos, São Leopoldo, Brazil and Université Lumière Lyon 2, Lyon, France.

Backes, L., & Schlemmer, E. (2010). As Aprendizagens nos processos de formação de educadores em metaversos para emancipação digital. In *Proceedings of XXIX International Congress of the Latin American Studies Association* (pp. 1-18). Toronto, Canada: Associação de Estudos Latino-Americanos – LASA.

Capra, F. (2004). A teia da vida: Uma nova compreensão científica dos sistemas vivos. São Paulo, Brazil: Editora Cultrix.

Castells, M. (2003). A sociedade em rede. São Paulo, Brazil: Paz e Terra.

Chuche, D. (1999). A noção de cultura nas ciências sociais. Bauru, Brazil: EDUSC.

Freire, P. (2008). Conscientização: Teoria e prática da libertação: Uma introdução ao pensamento de Paulo Freire. São Paulo, Brazil: Centauro.

Freire, P., & Shor, I. (1992). Medo e ousadia: Cotidiano do professor. Rio de Janeiro, Brazil: Paz e Terra.

Lemos, A. (2007). Cibercultura: Tecnologia e vida social na cultura contemporânea. Porto Alegre, Brazil: Sulina.

Lévy, P. (2010a). As tecnologias da inteligência: O futuro do pensamento na era da informática. Rio de Janeiro, Brazil: Editora 34.

Lévy, P. (2010b). Cibercultura. Rio de Janeiro, Brazil: Editora 34.

Libâneo, J. C. (2003). A escola com que sonhamos é aquela que assegura a todos a formação cultural e científica para a vida pessoal, profissional e cidadã. In M. V. Costa (Ed.), A escola tem future (pp. 23-52). Rio de Janeiro, Brazil: DP&A.

Machado, L. (2012). *Mundos virtuais tridimensionais como ambiente para o desenvolvimento de competência intercultural.* (Unpublished master's dissertation). Universidade do Vale do Rio dos Sinos, São Leopoldo, Brazil.

Maffesoli, M. (1998). O tempo das tribos: O declínio do individualismo nas sociedades de massa. Rio de Janeiro, Brazil: Forense Universitária.

Maffesoli, M. (2007). Tribalismo pós-moderno: Da identidade às identificações. *Ciências Sociais UNISINOS, 43*(1), 97–102.

Malizia, P. (2012). Comunidades virtuais de aprendizagem e de prática. In E. Schlemmer et al. (Eds.), Comunidades de aprendizagem e de prática em metaverso (pp. 25-60). São Paulo, Brazil: Editora Cortez.

Maturana, H. R. (1999). *Transformación em la convivência.* Santiado, Chile: Dólmen Ediciones.

Maturana, H. R. (2002). A ontologia da realidade. Belo Horizonte, Brazil: Ed. UFMG.

Maturana, H. R., & Yáñez, X. D. (2009). Habitar humano em seis ensaios de biologia-cultural. São Paulo, Brazil: Palas Athena.

Moraes, M. C. (2003). Educar na biologia do amor e da solidariedade. Petrópolis, Brazil: Vozes.

Moraes, M. C. (2004). O paradigma educacional emergente. Campinas, Brazil: Papirus.

Moretti, G. (2010). *La simulazione come strumento di produzione di conescenza: Comunità di apprendimento e di pratica nei mondi virtuali.* (Unpublished doctoral thesis). Libera Università Maria Ss. Assunta, Roma, Italy.

Peresson, M. L. (2006). Pedagogias e culturas. In C.C. S. Scarlatelle, D. R. Streck, & J. I. Follmann (Eds.), Religião, cultura e educação (pp. 57-107). São Leopoldo, Brazil: Ed. Unisinos.

Pérez Gómez, A. I. (2001). A cultura escolar na sociedade neoliberal. Porto Alegre, Brazil: ARTMED. Editora.

Silva, F. D. A., & Firmino, R. J. (2009). Desterritorialização e mídia: Um ensaio. In *Forum patrimônio: Ambiente, construção e patrimônio, sustentabilidade* (pp. 1-17). Belo Horizonte, Brazil: Instituto Brasileiro de Desenvolvimento Sustentável. Retrieved from http://forumpatrimonio.com.br/seer/index.php/forum_patrimonio/article/view/22/21

Souza Santos, B. (2004). Um discurso sobre as ciências. São Paulo, Brazil: Cortez.

Turkle, S. (1999). Fronteiras do real e do virtual: Entrevista concedida a federico casalegno. *Revista Famecos*, (11), 117-123. Retrieved from http://revistaseletronicas.pucrs.br/ojs/index.php/revistafamecos/article/viewFile/3057/2335

Veen, W., & Vrakking, B. (2009). *Homo zappiens: Educando na era digital.* Porto Alegre, Brazil: *The Art of Medication.*

KEY TERMS AND DEFINITIONS

Alterity: From Latin alteritas, from alter 'other'. For Maffesoli (2006, p.278) "we only exist because the other, my neighbor, or the other, the social, we give our existence. The reason I am the way I am is because others know me like this."

Culture: It is more or less a dynamic set. The elements that compound a culture are never integrated, one to the other, because they come from several sources in time and space. In other words, there is a 'game' in the system, especially because it is an extremely complex system. This game is in the interstitium in which the individual's and the group's freedom settles to 'manipulate' culture (Cuche, 1999, p.140).

Cyberculture: "Is the socio-technical configuration of the production of small catastrophes that feed fusion, impulse and contemporaneous symbiosis: the cyberculture interactive user is born from the elimination of social (Baudrillard) and the implosion of modern individualism" (Lemos, 2007, p.75).

Cyberspace: For Lévy (2010) cyberspace consists in a digital technology in which the center is all over and the circumference nowhere, which means that it can be a hypertext computer, disperse, living, boiling, unfinished. For Lemos (2007) cyberspace also contemplates the interconnection between people that makes emerge diversity, communication, and social; in the same way it contemplates virus, hackers. In summary, for the good and for the bad.

Digital Virtual Culture: Its living is configured in digital virtual spaces and through the relational dynamic, built in the living of digital virtual nature. Human beings construct, through this ecology, the emerging culture in digital virtual spaces, in other words, the digital virtual culture.

Ecological Space: Pérez Gomez (2001) understands as ecological space "... the school's possibilities as a living center of culture recreation, using critical culture to tease the reconstruction of student's personal experimental culture" (p. 273).

Metaculture: We think metaculture and being beyond culture. Thus, we understand metaculture as one that trespasses territoriality towards deterrioriality, where borders are porous and all elements are in interaction.

Sociality: For Maffesoli (1998) Set of practices that escape the rigid control, the being-together that does not depend on a goal to be reached, and therefore construct culture.

ENDNOTES

[1] Pérez Góméz (2001) understands ecological space as "... the school's possibilities as a living center of cultural recreation, using critical culture to tease the reconstruction of student's personal experimental culture" (p.273).

[2] Concept approached in Chapter 12 - Digital Virtual Sharing Spaces.

[3] According to what was said in Chapter 12 - Digital Virtual Sharing Spaces.

[4] Digital virtual sharing spaces is a concept-technology defined in Chapter 12- Digital Virtual Sharing Spaces.

[5] The concepts of flow and atemporal time are developed in Chapter 14- Nomadic Hybridism.

[6] Concept approached in Chapter 12 - Digital Virtual Sharing Spaces.

Chapter 14
Nomadic Hybridism

ABSTRACT

In this chapter, the authors approach the perspective of Nomadic Hybridism that appears from the interaction of subject-avatars as digital technologies, mainly with the Metaverse technology, in a space of flow. They present and discuss subtopics like "Space of Flow, Nomadism, and Interculturalism," "Digital Virtual Nomadism or Metanomadism." The conclusion about the chapter is that hybridism and nomadism, even being different elements, are mutually empowering. In other words, the hybrid context makes evident the difference and triggers mobility of other differences. The possibility of being anywhere and/ or everywhere contributes to the capacity of articulating, relating, and consequently, mingling.

INTRODUCTION

We currently find ourselves in a highly connected and paradoxical scenario, being anywhere without leaving home, fluid frontiers, permeable boarders, plural places and presences. We are becoming very intimate with digital technology and we are developing the capacity to "think with" and "from" the use of such technologies, constructing 3D digital virtual worlds, which are also the worlds in which we live.

Therefore, we configure ways of living, particular and singular, for several reasons. Firstly, because we are thinking and building relationships within a digital virtual environment[1]. Secondly, because coexisting starts being timeless and space is understood as flow, according to Castells (2003)[2]. Thirdly, because this configuration of living contributes to the future generations developing more

dialectic, systemic, complex, hybrid and nomadic perspectives[3]. In the dynamic described above, we have seen complex movements in the sense of highlighting hybridism, in different domains, empowering the nomadic instinct, between human beings.

We deal with the nomadic instinct, according to Maffesoli (2012), designer of the postmodern nomadic relating it to the Greeks' daemon (evil and good creatures, who presented several faces). As a result, when we think of digital technology in synergy with archaism (formation of tribes), we have the action of this critical and sensual spirit, in other words, the daemon. With the advances of techniques, and scientific development and the totalitarian rationalization of life, we can see a species of "unveiling the world", individualized, dichotomy, lonely, human beings. However, with postmodern technology, which has linked the

DOI: 10.4018/978-1-4666-6351-0.ch014

logia (Greek work meaning study) to the *teckné* (Greek word meaning technique, art or work) under the action of this daemon, the opposite seems to happen, "becoming enchanted with the world", collectivized human beings, plural in a "being together" and in all spaces, which configure themselves as hybrid.

Hybridism consists, in its common sense, of the crossing of two distinct elements, to make up another element, so, hybridism is the action of mingling elements or objects. According to Backes (2013), the origin of the hybridism concept comes from biology (Canclini, 2006), meaning mingling different species, for Franck (2012). In this domain, according to Santaella (2008, p.20), hybridism characterizes: "instabilities, interstice, sliding and constant reorganizations of cultural scenarios, the interactions and reintegration of levels, genres and ways of culture, identity crossing, culture transnationalization, fast growth of technologies and communicational media, expansion of cultural markets and emergence of new habits of consuming".

We therefore configure spaces in the context of digital technological hybridism[4]. The concept of Digital technological hybridism, developed in the context of the Research Group GPe-dU – UNISINOS/CNPq, is in a process of construction, reflection, maturing and systematization.

The word hybridism combined with the adjectives technological and digital, according to Backes (2011), results in digital technological hybridism, in other words, a coherent conjunction (which in the crossing can be different and contradictory) of accomplishment possibilities of human action in a space of digital virtual nature, through digital technology. Therefore, digital technological hybridism happens in the crossing of different technological resources, that normally complement each other (under a more technical and physical perspective); and in the contradictory crossing of usually consolidated logic, as in the case of metaphorical representations and graphic

of knowledge in pedagogical practices (under a more philosophical and conceptual perspective). So, the crossing, integration and articulation between digital technology happens as human beings appropriate, elaborate or mobilize instruments (digital technology) in their actions and interactions under the coexistence perspective.

Therefore, as already approached in Chapter 8 - Cognition and Socio-Cognition in Metaverse, we evidence what is hybrid in the analogical sense, in the digital sense, and in the analogical-digital sense. Then, when we consider dynamicity, it is possible to attribute to digital technology the condition, also form a place, or sometimes territories of digital virtual nature, which means, a space of immersion, action, interaction, construction, communication and socialization. Spaces where human beings transit, live and share, by the desire of "being together", empowered by the feeling of belonging. Digital technology, mainly Metaverses – 3D Digital Virtual Worlds – contribute to the configuration of a new living for presenting in its structure characteristics as: immersion through avatars, graphic representation in 3D, dynamic spaces constructed online through human interaction and the breaking of the linearity of knowledge, making it possible to construct innovation in the practices of the educational system.

Hybrid spaces (hybridism in the digital virtual context), such as Digital Virtual Living Space, are spaces which empower nomadism. According to the Sociologist and Anthropologist Latour (1994), the concept of "hybrid" sustains that the modern behavior could be characterized by a senseless search for purity, consubstantiated in the obsession of separating nature and culture. According to these instances, they do not exist separately, in its purity. In this context, we can use the example of the hole in the ozone layer. The hole is natural, the rays affecting it are physical, but it is simultaneously cultural, because the pollution is the consequence of cultural practices. This way, there are no dichotomies, they are different and distinct elements, but interdependent, articulated, mingled. The same reflection was made throughout the research developed by Backes (2011), during the construction of the 3D digital virtual world in classes held in the university. In few moments, the French students interacted only in the virtual digital world through their avatars as if they were in the same place (the classroom). At other times, they brought metaphorical examples to the discussions in the classroom, as they did when in a digital virtual world in 3D. At the end of the research, it was not possible to distinguish the actions provoked by interactions between students in the digital virtual space, from actions in the geographically located space.

According to the author, we live surrounded by hybrids, such as the social and the individual and not pure forms in these instances. Therefore, for Latour (1994), hybrids emerge as intermediary between heterogeneous elements – objective and subjective, individual and collective. They are forms that "connect at the same time to the nature of things and the social context, without reducing one thing or the other" (Latour, 1999, p.11). This intermediation is possible, according to the author, because such elements are not firm.

We have noticed, in the research developed at the *Digital Education Research Group* UNISINOS/CNPq, that when we configure living and sharing in digital virtual spaces we find a crossing of different digital virtual spaces that start being understood as a single space, also crossed with geographically located spaces. It means for Maffesoli (2012, p.75), "in all areas, the frontiers are fluid".

In this fluidity, we develop the nomadic instinct and the transnationalities in the porosity of the edges, whose relations of those who "e-inhabit" are constituted from a hybridism of identities, thoughts, ideas, languages, knowledge and practices. In the common sense of the word, nomadic is the human being who has no fixed residence, who changes places constantly. For Maffesoli

(2010), the nomadic instinct is the constant search for infinite time, a patchwork of opinions, and/or, a professional turn over. "In fact, several lives in one" (p.73). The author also highlights that we are not talking about anarchy that is ephemeral, but renovation and dynamicity.

Therefore, nomadic hybridism implies mingling, crossing, changing, ignoring frontiers, plural presences, respecting and keeping the other, returning to the "point beyond the beginning", constant change (in the sense of always being) and constantly interacting (in the sense of being frequent). In this sense, reality is:

... The conflictual conjunction of contradicting elements. A harmony that relies on the maintenance of tension and not on its resolution. Polytheism of values, policulturalism and absolute relativism that was in the base of great cultures, and whose actuality is very difficult to deny. (Maffesoli, 2012, p.73)

In the reality of nomadic hybridism, what pulses is the possibility of dialogue in its etymological sense, which means, in the crossing of the words "dia" and "logos". "Dia" means "through" and "Logos" has been translated to Latin as "ratio" or "reason". In this way, dialogue happens from a perspective of establishing and strengthening bonds, of linking and gathering, to identify, make explicit and understand the assumptions that impair the perception in relations. The idea consists of getting through different rationalities under the perspective of coexistence, in the complexity paradigm, according to Morin (2011) facilitating the meeting between the "old" and the "new".

In order to establish dialogue in the nomadic hybridism context we revisit the concept of spaces of flow, approaching the aspects of nomadism and the interculturality, to advance towards the digital virtual nomadism or metanomadism and systematize some reflections around the theme.

SPACE OF FLOW, NOMADISM, AND INTERCULTURALISM

According to Castells (2003), society's organization in networks causes changes in the comprehension of space and time. The localities are (re) signified regarding their cultural, historical and geographical sense, which replaces the geographically located space. This way, the past, present and future interact within themselves in the same message. The space of flows and the timeless time are essential bases of a new culture that transcends and includes, in a dynamic and complex way, the diversity of historically transmitted representation systems: the real virtuality culture.

Also for Castells (1999, apud Schlemmer, 2002), the space of flows has as key element the "innovation means", a specific group of production and management relations based on a social organization that, in general, shares a culture of work and instrumental goals, aiming for the generation of new knowledge, processes and products. The capacity of synergy that is established in the flow, is what defines the specificity of innovation in the environment, in other words, the added value resulting not from cumulative effects of the elements present in the environment, but in their interaction. Therefore, the new space is organized around information flows. The emphasis on interactivity between places breaks spatial behavior patterns in a fluid network of interchanges that forms the basis for spaces of flow to arise.

Therefore, revisiting the concept of space, for Castells (2003) it is society's expression, meaning, the society itself. Therefore, as society passes through structural changes, there are new ways and spatial processes, as the new society is grounded in knowledge, organized in networks and formed by flows. In this way, the support material of dominant processes in our society will be the group of elements that sustain these flows and enable the material possibility of their articulation in simultaneous time, in the articulation of space and time. Indeed, the space of flows is a new spatial characteristic in social practices that dominate and mold the network society. This way, the space of flow consists of the organization of social practices that happen in the interchange and interactions between social actors in an intentional, repetitive and programmable way, in a shared time.

Time, according to Castells (2003) seems to be specific to a certain context, regarding both nature and society, in other words, time is local. Considering that we have an emerging social structure, the author says, "the actual mind is the mind that denies time", and that this new "timeless system" is related to the development of communication technologies. So, the linear, irreversible, measurable and predictable time is (re)signified, in the same way as space in the network society.

Castells (2003), in discussing the concept of non-temporal space says that "... our society's dominant lack of temporality occurs when the characteristics of a given context, or the informational paradigm and the network society, cause systemic confusion in the sequential order of phenomena occurred within that context". Therefore, the order of the significant events loses its chronological internal rhythm and remains organized in temporal sequences conditioned to the social context of its use. It is, at the same time, the eternal and ephemerons culture. The new culture's eternal/ephemerons time goes beyond any specific sequence and adapts to the dynamic of the network society, enabling individual interactions and collective representations forming a timeless mental panorama.

It is in this context of space of flow and timeless time that we approach nomadism. The concept of nomadism has been studied by different theorists, who state that contemporary society is immersed in several types of nomadism, and this denomination is attributed to the movement of nomadic peoples.

As mentioned in the introduction, the term "nomadic" is commonly used to refer to persons or people who are constantly changing places, not inhabiting a fixed territory. According to Pinheiro and Silva (2008), the nomadic transits through different points because of the path they have chosen. However, for Deleuze and Guattari (1980, apud Pinheiro & Silva 2008) the nomadic takes over the whole space, making it wrong to define the nomadic by movement. The nomadic is the absolute deterritorialized and for Deleuze and Guattari (1980) "The nomand, under no circumstance, is a migrant... the nomaidic path... distributes men in an open, indefinite and non-communicable space" (pp.472-473).

Turning to Maffesoli (1997, 2012), when abandoning the nomadic instinct, we highlight that we understand it as nomadic processes, for we create displacement of bodies and information, fragment the individual identity in multiple identifications, in the daily living and sharing that happens in the historic course. Within this context, we could talk about a nomadism hybridism, understanding human beings as avatars, characters, props, a "login", a 2D image and/or, a physical body.

Can we also say that in the context of Meta-verses technologies, where the human being, represented by an avatar or character – in Massively Multiplayer Online Role-Playing Games – (which enables him to simultaneously interact in two or more worlds, which can also be of different natures), displaces in a space of flow between several 3D digital virtual worlds, is living nomadic processes in the digital virtual context? Would this "nomadic hybridism" be unveiling intercultural processes?

To understand interculturalism, we return to our reflection on the concept of culture and broaden it to a comprehension of multiculturalism. In Chapter 13 - Digital Virtual Culture in Metaverse: the Metaculture?, culture is considered a set of meanings, expectations and appropriate behaviors defined in coexistence. These combined actions are partitioned and shared in the social group, which encourages and/or limits the everyday living of men and women who constitute the social group that occupies a space at a given time, regardless of the nature of space and time.

The research of Machado (2012), inserted in this intercultural context, demonstrates the development of competencies in the use of Metaverse. Machado et al. (2013), highlight: the communication abilities; the construction of specific cultural knowledge; the comprehension of the view of the world of other participants; the ability to analyze; assess and have relationship; the ability to listen; observe and interpret; as well as respect, openness, tolerance and ambiguities, among others. These competencies are related to the social interchanges.

Therefore, culture is a social construction that gives a certain time and space and propagates along times and spaces, affecting the lives of human beings and communities. According to Chapter 13 - Digital Virtual Culture in Metaverse: the Metaculture? culture is constructed by human beings in the same amount that it is constructed.

To understand this recursivity between the human being and culture, regarding the constructor, the construction and the constructed, we take the ways of living and sharing in society through digital virtual spaces. Initially, these ways of living and sharing in society marked the geographically located spaces, but, with: migratory processes; the development of the means of transportation and, mainly, the technological development, the human being begins to recognize the living in other spaces, also of different natures.

The human being of a certain space lives and shares with another human being of another space, this way forming different cultures occupying the same space. In this sense, we have a cultural crossing that generates movements of aculturality, multiculturality and interculturality, indicating the coexistence of several cultural groups within the same society, sometimes pointing to living and sharing.

According to Cuche (1999), the prefix "a" in acculturation does not mean privation; its etymological origin comes from Latin *ad*, meaning proximity. Therefore, acculturation implies changing, understanding and propagating, when two or more cultures meet. Therefore, "acculturation does not necessarily eliminate the culture it is receiving, nor does it modify its internal logic that can remain dominant (p.118). As a result, acculturation cannot be mistaken for deculturation, which consists of eradicating one of the cultures, when there is a cultural crossing.

Multiculturalism, according to Cogo (2006, p.21) "is understood as the recognition that in the same territory there are different cultures, interculturality, which in turn, makes reference to a perspective of intervention before this reality that tends to give emphasis to the relation between cultures."

Interculturality indicates groups of sharing proposals, for Maturana (2002); human beings live and share as they are structurally coupled in congruence with the environment, among different cultures, searching for their integration without impairing their diversity. The interculturality issue comes in the context of globalized processes, mainly regarding the economy. The creation of a worldwide market, where exchanges of material goods are made, communication and the increase of immigration have fostered the increase of flows and interactions, and consequently, diminished the frontiers.

In this dynamic movement of living and sharing many significant changes, happen in different instances constituting society. An education that positively responds to the a/multi/interculturality contributes to reflecting on the specificities of these cultures at the same time as having no intention for the individuals to become "immersed" and closed within their cultures, thus constructing a space for an "emmerse" attitude (Camilleri & Falk, 1992).

Therefore, intercultural education conceived as an intentional intervention in this multicultural reality empowers the cultural elements that constantly metamorphose. Interculturality (or an intercultural education) contemplates this intervention in a broad way in social cultural reality,

and congregates in his interior, by the construction of the concept, the interchange between theses hybrid ways of cultural manifestations, the mutual enrichment by the permanent changes occurred in the routines, in combating xenophobia, to the discriminatory and ghettoizer processes.

All these movements gain speed with the development of digital technology that broaden the communication possibilities, relation and interaction between people, also provoking a higher contact between the different cultures. The digital media is today a powerful technology of intelligence, according to Lévy (2010), for accessing data and incentivizing intra and intercultural processes of communication.

Interculturality carries the relations between human beings from different cultures and the processes that, in the meeting/confronting, enabled by the interchange, do not separate or ghettoize, but put human beings in relation, stimulating the changes and interchanges, making it possible for other cultural forms to become visible. From this process, which is not recent but historical, new ways of cultural expression are configured. Therefore, within this scenario, school and the educational system legitimate the human beings' living and sharing, coming from multiple cultures and that may have constructed an intercultural history. Therefore, school in particular, and the educational system, in general, are cross-cultural spaces, and have responsibility for the reflexive mediation of cultural flows and inflows in the constitution of new generation. For Pérez Goméz (2001),

Both personal interchanges and institutional relations need to be mediated by the complex network that interrelate within this artificial space, and that constitute a rich and thick web of meanings and expectations where every subject transits in their formation, precisely in the most active period in the construction of their meanings and their identity. (p.18)

For Medina and Dominguez (2005), the formation of teachers implies a differentiated formation, which manages creative intercultural practices and the construction of the discourse between cultures. The formation of teachers, from this perspective, consists of an interactive situation and synthesis, overcoming values; the concept of transforming practices, implying all cultures in a process of solidarity and responsible equality.

Therefore, we understand digital media as a fecund source for the intercultural studies approached from the perspective of mediatic reception. It is a way where different data transit, available for people with different interests, and where they affirm and recreate identities and identifications, since their use is related to the processes of collective and subjective signification.

Therefore, we are not talking about a space where different cultures meet, or about a space where there is a synthesis of these different cultures. We are talking about a space, in congruence with human beings who, by interacting, enable the configuration of other ways of living and sharing, and from this living and sharing another particular and singular culture emerges, mainly because the environment is neither territorialized nor geographically located.

DIGITAL VIRTUAL NOMADISM OR METANOMADISM

In the reflections proposed we can perceive that the nomadism concept is bigger (in the sense of new spaces of other nature), acquires new perspectives (in the form of mobility) and is (re)signified (different spaces become the only space) with the development of digital technology. Consequently, we need to take into account now only the physical space, but also the digital virtual one, which configures itself in cyberspace. The digital virtual spaces empower the nomadic concept, in the creation of Digital Virtual Nomadic, and consequently, of all the movement coming from the digital virtual nomadism.

Like the nomad, the digital virtual nomadic move themselves in cyberspace in the search for information, interaction, etc. that satisfies their needs as human beings. Digital virtual nomads inhabit digital virtual communities of learning, relationships, practices, blogs, photo logs, web chats, forums, etc. and from their interactions; they construct a movement, a network with indefinite paths, present in a space of flows (Castells, 2003) that do not have linearity. However, the nomad and digital virtual nomad frequently meet in their dynamic movements, in the same way that a nomad can also be a digital virtual nomad.

For Santaella (2008), within this dynamic context between the hybrid and the nomadic, cyberspace and cyberculture are (re)signified when acquiring a hybrid nature in the constitution of spaces, and in this sense, the concept of interstitial emerges.

Interstitial spaces refer to the edges between physical and digital spaces, compounding connected spaces, which break the traditional distinction between physical spaces, on one hand, and digital on the other. Therefore, an interstitial or hybrid space happens when there is no need to "get out" of the physical space to get in touch with digital environments. This way, the edges between digital and physical spaces become diffuse and not completely distinguishable. (Santaella, 2008, p.21)

Then, through hybrid spaces (in the analogical, digital and digital-analogical sense), we can see a nomadism that is effective in the same way, especially because human beings are in congruence with the spaces, establishing a daily life sharing. So, how do we think about nomadism with digital virtual technological hybridism?

We consider that we configure a digital virtual space of sharing and constitute a living and sharing of a digital virtual nature, using the term Digital Virtual Living and Sharing Space[5]. The Digital Virtual Sharing Space represents the synthesis of the theoretical constructions and the establishment of relations and articulations carried on from the result of different research developed in the latest 10 years, in the GP e-du UNISINOS/CNPq. According to Schlemmer et al. (2006) and Schlemmer (2008, 2009), a Digital Virtual Sharing Space has different integrated Digital Technologies such as Virtual Environments of Learning, Metaverses that enable the creation of 3D Digital Virtual Worlds (in which the interaction happens between the subjects represented by avatars, "virtual humans" of bots), communicative agents (created and programmed by the interaction), among other digital technologies, that together favor different ways of communication (written language – text, imagistic language – images, gestural language – movement and oral language – speech, sound), gathering all these languages in a single interaction space; the communication and interaction flow between subjects that are present within this space and, the interaction flow between the subjects and the environment, which means, the technological space itself.

As already detailed in Chapter 12 - Digital Virtual Sharing Spaces, are hybrid spaces, of different nature, specific to this digital virtual environment, with properties, possibilities and differentiated rules that can be constructed during the living and sharing by their e-inhabitants, e-residents and/or e-citizens. For Schlemmer (2009), Digital Virtual Living Spaces need to be lived, understood and appropriated by those involved in the educational process in order to be able to construct an educational innovation. In cases where there is no human action in congruence with hybrid spaces, we are merely speaking of a novelty and not an innovation. These new digital virtual spaces need to be understood not as replacement of the existing ones, but as differentiated spaces, complementary, in a way they can coexist.

"Human creativity is the limit", are we before a digital virtual space of living and sharing or a living and sharing of a digital virtual nature? In the first, to put it briefly, we understand the digital virtual space as "one more" space for living and represent that we perceive and live in a similar way as in we do in the physical real world. In the second, we understand that living in a digital virtual nature presents itself as another nature, specific to the environment, related to this real virtuality. Therefore, following Backes (2011), the constitution of a sharing of digital virtual nature comes from the interactions made in the digital technological context, through the particularities and dynamics built by a certain group. Merely territorial issues, being, within this dimension, cultural, historical and linguistic, do not place the particularities and dynamics attributed to each group in a specific way. "But also by human beings that transform themselves by the time of the interaction, thus producing recurrent transformations in the dynamic of relations of the social system they belong to, called autopoietic social systems" (p.233).

For Backes (2011), the reflection on digital virtual sharing implies rethinking education and training processes using hybrid digital virtual technological spaces, as the relations promoted within these spaces are mediated by cultural networks that are constituted in this digital virtual sharing. Mediation is the characterization of pedagogical mediation, consisting of a

…communicational, conversational, co-construction of meanings process, whose objective is to open and facilitate the dialogue and develop a significant negotiation of processes and contents to be worked in educational environments, as well

as encourage the construction of a relational, contextual knowledge, generated in the interaction teacher/student. (Moraes, 2003, p.210)

Thus, when we think about the human formation in the sense of constructing sharing of a digital virtual nature, we can certainly understand the complexity empowered in the combination of the digital technological hybridism and the pedagogical proposal. Digital technological hybridism represents a disturbing element, mainly when this hybridism has technologies in Metaverse and its use is through a pedagogical proposal based in the epistemological interacting/constructivist/ systemic conception. Human beings when disturbed and problematized in living and sharing are pushed forward by their transformative nature.

The digital technological hybrid space, mingling different digital technologies that articulate among themselves, will only result from the action and interaction of the human beings e-inhabitants.

In this logic, we understand that the hybrid spaces can empower nomadism, for the avatars, the text and/or the voice of human beings transit through the different spaces they integrate, occupying all its space. In Figure 1 we can observe different digital virtual spaces, used in Backes's (2011) research: Metaverse (Eduverse) and *blog* (Analyse du travail et polyvalence).

In the hybrid context, seen in Figure 1, there are two digital, integrated, different technologies, but which can be complementary. To the left of Figure 1 the Metaverse with the possibility of graphical representation, the representation of immersion for avatar and a dynamic logic operation (different dimensions and teleportation). To the right of Figure 1 a blog post with the possibility of textual representation links to other web sites and a linear logic operation (temporal sequence of posts and comments).

Therefore, human beings, through telepresence and digital virtual presence[6], interact in the blog

Figure 1. AWSINOS Interface and "Analyse du travail et Polyvalence" blog
Source: Authors

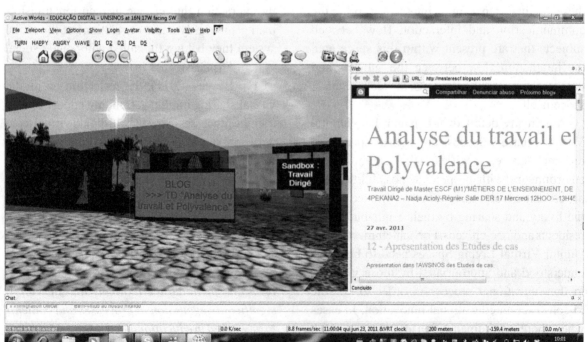

that is coupled to the Metaverse, through texts in post and/or comments, as well as represent part of the records in the blog, through their avatars, building metaphors in graphic representation in 3D Digital Virtual Worlds. These actions can be seen in the following figures:

In Figure 2, the French students, who worked with the teaching methodology of case study, discuss the possibility of making the most significant metaphorical representation from interactions with other travel groups. The group discussed the case study that involves the "École Primaire" in France, highlighting issues such as lying, punishment, prejudice and discipline. In Figure 3, we can see that the metaphor was complemented by establishing a relationship with the story of Pinocchio (the mast represented to the right of Figure 3), to discuss the matter of lying.

In this way, human beings move from one point to another, considering their "home" being configured from other digital virtual spaces through which they transit. The possibility of being constantly connected when moving through different spaces constituting a Digital Virtual Living Space, for example, enables different ways of interaction (textual, oral, graphic and gestural language simultaneously), and modifies the human being's experience of space, both referring to social interactions and the connections with the different spaces of information representation. In this way, we talk about digital virtual hybridism when we refer to the Digital Virtual Living Space technology, which constitutes the nomadic hybridism.

According to Hayles (1999), "the context is unfolding itself, in a way that there is no more homogeneous context for a certain spatial area, but pockets of different implied contexts, or imbricated within themselves". For example, someone talking on the cell phone is part of the context of individuals who share the same spatial area, but it is also part of a distant context, for he is speaking

Figure 2. Image of blog interaction
Source: Authors

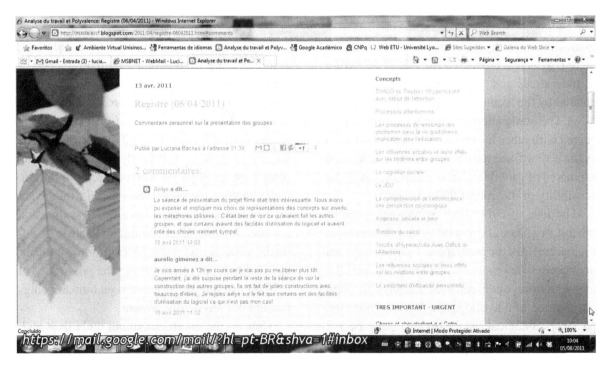

Figure 3. Image of the graphic representation in Metaverse
Source: Authors

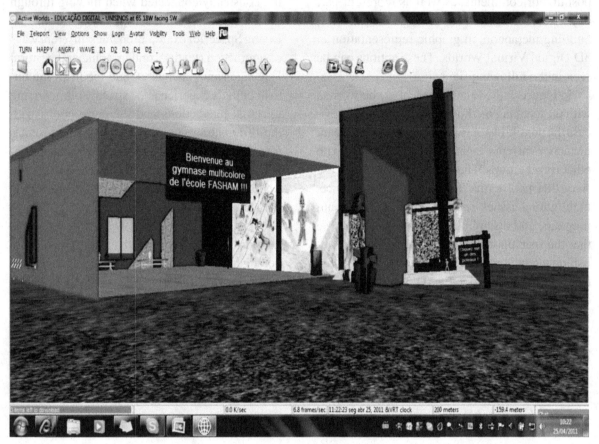

to someone spatially remote to his area. Therefore, there is a context created by the spatial proximity of individuals and, within him, another context created by the technology (the cell phone in this case). The implication of contexts can also be perceived with other means of communication such as the TV or fixed telephones, but the difference promoted by mobile technologies is precisely the possibility of movement through space.

The idea of cyberspace as another space to inhabit, or a place understood by human beings, as a replacement of the geographically located spaces does not exist anymore. So, the focus becomes the interaction ways between human beings, through the creation of a hybrid space that combines the physical-analogical and the digital, the voice and the Internet, written and image.

Digital technological hybridism enables and empowers the reinvention of urban spaces as multiuser spaces. So, cities which have already transformed into places and processes, are now introduced as hybrid spaces of different natures (geographically located and digital virtual). The sociality that happened firstly in geographically placed spaces in an era when the pace of the trip and/or mobility was relatively low, with the advent of the Internet has started in a timeless time and a space of flow. After the intensification of nomadic movements, multiuser environments occur in hybrid spaces, representing the possibility of relation and interrelation between human beings that are not physically present.

Hybrid spaces are part of our daily lives and, therefore, needed for human communication and interaction. The notion of hybrid space simultaneously broadens the world (creating a new type of reality made "at the same time" from physical and digital) and condenses the world (minimizing the perception of physical distances and giving the connection between human beings from different places). Since the end of the last decade, it has become increasingly clear that the physical-analogical and the digital are strongly interconnected. The digital virtual space is no longer used in an isolated way, but mingled with the geographically located space, as for example happens in the development of an experience with Mixed Reality and Augmented Reality.

In fact, the concept of "cyberspace" is outmoded, as it originally meant an information world that existed apart from the material space. This hybrid reality becomes real, partially due to the change in the way we connect to digital spaces: from the imaginary neural implants and static interfaces to mobile technologies. When the digital space becomes a continuation to the physical space, the issue "should it simulate reality?" does not matter anymore, because both spaces are mingled in the same environment.

The nomadic movements in hybrid spaces have also changed our concept of "presence". Presence has always been an important concept in virtual environments, as the creation of an avatar was required to represent a body in the digital world. The avatar is the interface of an absent physical body. Gergen (apud Katz & Aakhus, 2002) exemplifies other types of technology that also have the power to exclude us from an environment where we are physically, such as the *Walkman*, books, computer screens and telephones. For him, such technologies are responsible for the creation of an absent presence, because when we talk on the telephone, for example "one is physically absorbed by a world of the beyond technologically mediated". This statement is partially true, especially regarding fixed telephones, but it is also important to consider two additional topics.

Firstly, the fact of being absently present within this context may mean that one is presently absent in another context. For Mantovani and Mouras (2012) "the ambiguous dimension of presence/absence in space also means the re-structuring of the sense of belonging to a place". Secondly, the feeling of belonging to someone's communicative network does not depend on a specific place or the physical presence anymore, but the space and exchange of messages. Curiously, the researcher Mizuko Ito (apud Rheingold, 2002, p.6) has observed that the "thumb tribes" from Tokyo consider themselves "present" in a meeting when they are in contact via SMS. "By the time the colleagues took part in the communication shared by the group, it seems that the others were considered to be present". This distributed presence makes it possible for users to physically take part in a social event, while they communicate with others in another social event, creating a double sociability network, and the capacity of being "present" in both places.

CONCLUSION

From context presented in this chapter, we can reflect on the following questions: is hybridism only spatial (enclosing all natures)? Is humanity becoming "hybrid nomadic"? Alternatively, could spaces also be hybrid nomadic?

When we take human beings as a reference, we could think of Hybrid in the sense of having an identity of a geographically placed nature (with its different dimensions) and a digital virtual identity (also in its different dimensions); a physical existence (physical body) and a digital virtual existence (technologicized - avatar body); and also a living and sharing simultaneously in a physical world and in a digital virtual world, considering this existence in function from the other and for the other.

When taking space as a reference, we could think of Nomadic as the possibility of accessing and being everywhere or in any specific place. For this, you only need a connection to the world network, where the person is, and it can also displace the digital virtual space and establish living relations and interrelations. All this makes more sense if we think about wireless technologies. Therefore, the spaces are constantly changing, ignoring frontiers, in order to search new relations and interactions to feed the flow.

However, when we consider all problematization and reflections provided in this chapter, we believe that hybridism and nomadism, even being different elements, mutually empower. In other words, the hybrid context makes evident the difference and so, triggers mobility of living other differences. The possibility of being anywhere and/or everywhere, contributes to the capacity to articulate the different places, to relate, and therefore to mingle, both for human beings, (autopoietic machines), and for digital technologies (alopoietic machines).

REFERENCES

Backes, L. (2011). *A configuração do espaço de convivência digital virtual: A cultura emergente no processo de formação do educador.* (Unpublished doctoral thesis). Universidade do Vale do Rio dos Sinos, São Leopoldo, Brazil and Université Lumière Lyon 2, Lyon, France.

Backes, L. (2013). Hibridismo tecnológico digital: Configuração dos espaços digitais virtuais de convivência. In Proceedings of III Colóqui Luso-Brasileiro de Educação a Distância e E-Learning (pp. 1–18). Lisboa: Universidade Aberta.

Camilleri, J. A., & Falk, J. (1992). *The end of sovereignty. The politics of a shrinking and fragmenting world.* Aldershot, UK: Edward Elgar.

Canclini, N. G. (2006). Culturas híbridas. São Paulo, Brazil: Edusp.

Castells, M. (2003). A sociedade em rede. São Paulo, Brazil: Paz e Terra.

Cogo, D. M. (2006). Mídia, interculturalidade e migrações contemporâneas. Rio de Janeiro, Brazil: E-papers Serviços Editoriais Ltda.

Cuche, D. (1999). A noção de cultura nas ciências sociais. Bauru, Brazil: EDUSC.

Deleuze, G., & Guattari, F. (1980). *Capitalisme et schizophrénie 2: Mille plateaux.* Paris: Les Editions de Minuit.

Frank, C. O. (2012). *Aprendizagem da língua espanhola por meio das tecnologias digitais.* (Unpublished master's dissertation). Centro Universitário La Salle, Canoas, Brazil.

Hayles, N. K. (1999). Simulando narrativas: Que criaturas virtuais podem nos ensinar. *Investigação Crítica, 26* (1), 1-26.

Kenneth, J. G. (2002). The challenge of absent presence. In J. E. Katz, & M. Aakhus (Eds.), Perpetual contact: Mobile communication, private talk, public performance (pp. 227-241). New York, NY: Cambridge University Press.

Latour, B. (1994). Jamais fomos modernos. São Paulo, Brazil: Editora 34.

Latour, B. (1999). On recalling ANT. In J. Law & J. Hassard (Eds.), *Actor-network theory and after* (pp. 15–25). Oxford, UK: Blakcwell Publishers.

Lévy, P. (2010). As tecnologias da inteligência: O futuro do pensamento na era da informática. Rio de Janeiro, Brazil: Editora 34.

Machado, L. (2012). *Mundos virtuais tridimensionais como ambiente para o desenvolvimento de competência intercultural.* (Unpublished master's dissertation). Universidade do Vale do Rio dos Sinos, São Leopoldo, Brazil.

Machado, L., et al. (2013). O uso de mundos virtuais tridimensionais para o desenvolvimento de competência intercultural: Uma experiência entre Brasil e Portugal. In *Proceedings of XII Simpósio Brasileiro de Jogos e Entretenimento Digital* (pp. 38-49). São Paulo, Brazil: Industry Track. Retrieved from http://www.sbgames.org/sbgames2013/proceedings/industria/05-full-paper-indtrack.pdf

Maffesoli, M. (1997). *Du nomadisme: Vagabondages initiatiques*. Paris: Livres de Poche.

Maffesoli, M. (2012). O tempo retorno: Formas elementares da pós-modernidade. Rio de Janeiro, Brazil: Editora Forense Universitária.

Mantovani, C., & Moura, M. A. (2012). Informação, interação e mobilidade. *Informação & Informação, 17*(2), 55-76. Retrieved from http://www.uel.br/revistas/uel/index.php/informacao/article/view/13764

Maturana, H. R. (2002). Ontologia da realidade. Belo Horizonte, Brazil: Ed. UFMG.

Medina, A. R., & Domínguez, C. D. (2005). La formación del Profesorado ante los nuevos retos de La interculturalidad. In A. R. Medina et al. (Eds.), *Interculturalidad: Formación del profesorado y educación*. Madrid: Pearson.

Moraes, M. C. (2003). Educar na biologia do amor e da solidariedade. Petrópolis, Brazil: Vozes.

Morin, E. (2011). Introdução ao pensamento complexo. Porto Alegre, Brazil: Sulina.

Pérez Goméz, A. I. (2001). A cultura escolar na sociedade neoliberal. Porto Alegre, Brazil: ARTMED Editora.

Pinheiro, L. V., & Silva, E. L. (2008). As redes cognitivas na ciência da informação brasileira: Um estudo nos artigos científicos publicados nos periódicos da área. *Ci. Inf., 37*(3), 38–50. doi:10.1590/S0100-19652008000300003

Rheingold, H. (2002). *Smart mobs: The next social revolution*. Cambridge, MA: Perseus Publishing.

Santaella, L. (2008). A ecologia pluralista das mídias locativas. *Revista Famecos*, (37), 20-24. Retrieved from http://revistaseletronicas.pucrs.br/ojs/index.php/revistafamecos/article/view/4795

Schlemmer, E. (2002). *AVA: Um ambiente de convivência interacionista sistêmico para comunidades virtuais na cultura da aprendizagem.* (Unpublished doctoral thesis). Universidade Federal do Rio Grande do Sul, Porto Alegre, Brazil.

Schlemmer, E. (2008). ECODI - A criação de espaços de convivência digital virtual no contexto dos processos de ensino e aprendizagem em metaverso. *Cadernos IHU Idéias, 6*, 1–32.

Schlemmer, E. (2009). *Telepresença*. Curitiba, Brazil: IESDE Brazil S. A.

Schlemmer, E., et al. (2006). ECoDI: A criação de um espaço de convivências digital virtual. In *Proceedings of XVII Simpósio Brasileiro de Informática na Educação* (pp. 467-477). Brasília, Brazil: UNB/UCB. Retrieved from http://br-ie.org/pub/index.php/sbie/article/viewFile/507/493

KEY TERMS AND DEFINITIONS

Acculturation: Implies in changing, understanding and propagating, when two or more cultures meet. Therefore, "the acculturation does not necessarily eliminates the culture received, nor modifies its internal logic that can remain dominant (Cuche, 1999, p. 118). That way, acculturation cannot be mistaken with deculturation, which consists in eradicating one of the cultures, when there is a cultural crossing.

Hybridism: For Santaella (2008, p. 20), hybridism characterizes as: "instabilities, interstice, sliding and constant reorganizations of cultural scenarios, the interactions and reintegration of levels, genres and ways of culture, identity crossing, culture transnationalization, fast growth of technologies and communicational media, expansion of cultural markets and emergency of new habits of consume."

Identity: Is an instrument that allows thinking about the articulation of the psychological and social elements in a subject. It expresses the result of the several interactions between the subject and his social environment, either close or distant. The subject's social identity is characterized by the grouping of his links within a social system: links with a social class, age, nation, etc. The identity allows the subject to find his place within a social system and be socially located (Cuche, 1999, p.177).

Interculturality: Indicates groups of sharing proposals, for Maturana (2002) human beings live and share as they are structurally coupled in congruence with the environment, among different cultures, searching for their integration without impairing their diversity. The interculturality issue comes in the context of globalized processes, mainly regarding the economy. The creation of a worldwide market, where exchanges of material goods are made, communication and the increase of immigration has fostered the increase of flows and interactions, and consequently, diminished the frontiers.

Multiculturalism: "is understood as the recognition that in the same territory there are different culture, the interculturality, which in turn, makes reference to a perspective of intervention before this reality that tents do give emphasis to the relation between cultures" (Cogo, 2006, p. 21).

Nomadic: According to Maffesoli (2012), the design of the post modern nomadic is related to the Greeks' daïmon (evil and good creatures, who presented several faces). That way, when we think of digital technology in synergy with archaism (constitution of tribes), we act in such critical and sensual way, in other words, being a daïmon. With the advances of techniques, and scientific development and the totalitarian rationalization of life, we evidenced a species of "unveiling the world", individualized, dichotomy, lonely, human beings.

Nomadic Hybridism: Conflictual conjunction of contradicting elements. Harmony that relies on the maintenance of tension and not on its resolution. Polytheism of values, policulturalism and absolute relativism that were in the base of great cultures and whose actuality is very difficult to deny (Maffesoli, 2012, p. 73).

ENDNOTES

[1] According to what was discussed in Chapter 4 - Avatar: Building a "Digital Virtual Self".

[2] Theme approached in Chapter 12 - Digital Virtual Sharing Spaces.

[3] Theme approached in Chapter 13 - Digital Virtual Culture in Metaverse: The Metaculture?

[4] Concept detailed in Chapter 12 - Digital Virtual Sharing Spaces.

[5] As previously discussed in Chapter 12 - Digital Virtual Sharing Spaces.

[6] Concepts dealt with in Chapter 5 – Immersion, Telepresence, and Digital Virtual Presence in Metaverses.

Chapter 15
Brazilian Experiences in Metaverse

ABSTRACT

This chapter presents and discusses some experiences linked to the research in the context of the Digital Education Research Group UNISINOS/CNPq, which was developed in Brazil from the use of different technologies in metaverses. The following subtopics are approached: "AWSINOS: A World of Learning" (performed in metaverses Eduverse), "UNISINOS Island," and "RICESU Island" (Second Life and Open Wonderland). As the main conclusion of chapter, learning in metaverse is understood as human beings' effective action within metaverses, present in the history of the structural coupling emerging in an inseparable world, in its way of life, showing there is also a cultural issue. In this process, the authors try to build elements to allow the development of innovative pedagogical practices, proper for this historic time and social space.

INTRODUCTION

The research developed with Metaverse technologies, in both educational and organizational contexts is a recent. Some of the surveys are the isolated actions of researchers, working directly in the field of Education, while others are already institutionalized, covering universities as a whole. Thus, some educational institutions and organizations in different continents have ventured into these "new worlds".

The areas of expertise are diverse. Many have used this technology to develop social simulation, to investigate social relationships, or explore different areas of knowledge such as history, architecture, pedagogy, regarding those theories, practices of representation issues related to learning in general, also including people with disabilities, among others.

In the Brazilian context, the first research experiments in Education developed with Metaverse technology[1] were carried out in 1999 at the Federal University of Rio Grande Sul, coordinated by Dr. Liane Margarida Rockenbach Tarouco[2] and, in the same year, at the Universidade do Vale do Rio dos Sinos, coordinated by Dr Eliane Schlem-

DOI: 10.4018/978-1-4666-6351-0.ch015

mer. Many other higher education institutions have developed and are still developing research involving Metaverses in the Brazilian context.

Other initiatives emerge and research in Metaverse has been gaining ground. In this chapter we present some of these experiments, performed in Metaverses Eduverse, Second Life and Open Wonderland, in the context of the Digital Education Research Group UNISINOS/CNPq.

AWSINOS: A WORLD OF LEARNING

In 2000, the Universidade do Vale do Rio dos Sinos, through a research project entitled "The construction of virtual worlds for distance education", coordinated by Dr. Eliane Schlemmer and sent to the company ActiveWorlds, Inc, got a "Galaxy" in Metaverse Eduverse (educational version of Active Worlds software), and so began the development of digital virtual world in 3D AWSINOS.

Upon entering AWSINOS, the subject is shown the Teleporters Center that gives access to both the Central Square as well as the different "villages" created at AWSINOS (Figure 1), including village GPe-dU (Grupo de Pesquisa em Educação Digital GPe-dU UNISINOS/CNPq) - a graphical representation of the Research Group (Figure 2). In practice, the operation is as follows: to find the Teleporters Center (Figure 1) the user clicks the plate corresponding to the "place", like 'GPe-dU *boroughs*', for example, where he or she wants to be, to be instantly teleported, as shown in Figure 2.

After this initial organization of the AWSINOS World, the research Project has developed, from a general objective, which resulted in the creation of 3D digital virtual worlds and in the study of socio-cognitive mechanisms, expressed in the trainee teachers' behavior towards de use of technology. The exploratory research aims to carry out a case study in which subjects construct a 3D virtual world.

Amongst the research's main findings is the creation of the 3D digital virtual world called AWSINOS – in which the teachers being trained in the use of technologies have constructed a World of Tales (Mundo de Contos). During the creation process of the World of Tales it was possible to understand how socio-cognitive mechanisms

Figure 1. Central Square: Teleport center to AWSINOS for different "villages"
Source: Authors

Figure 2. Research group GPe-dU boroughs
Source: Authors

originating in the interaction process among subject-participants happen, being the strongest evidenced cooperation mechanism, and being related to mutual respect, internal solidarity and constructed rules. The trainee educator perceived that, for learning and knowledge construction his action is crucial. Regarding conceptualization, it happened through previous awareness. However, from a certain level on, it influences action. Conceptualization empowers coordination, immanent in action.

We also demonstrated that during the construction process, people learned the necessary technological resources for the construction of 3D digital virtual worlds. Therefore, learning happens according to needs, in other words, new information became meaningful due to context and established relations. The research has evidenced that the teacher's training process has to take place during the teaching action and not in a separate way, demanding technological knowledge as prerequisite. Being trained in action enables the trainee educator to be followed up, making it easy to understand the theory behind the situations presented throughout the teaching practice.

We consider it important that the educator being trained in digital virtual tools have the possibility of "being the subject of the world's construction", of displacing oneself and virtually interacting within the world, so as to better understand the potential of those learning spaces based on the development of humanistic values.

Figure 3 presents the different boroughs created in the World of Tales (Mundo de Contos) where it is possible to be teleported to from Figure 1 Teleport Center to AWSINOS.

In AWSINOS several projects were developed, in the context of undergraduate and postgraduate courses, as continuing education, involving boroughs (Figure 4) and villages (Figure 5) of digital games and languages club, among others.

Among the research projects developed we highlight: "Teacher formation in interaction with Virtual Learning Environments in a virtual world: perceptions and representations". The research project was developed with the general objective of integrating the communicative agent Mariá, UNISINOS Virtual Learning Environment and 3D digital virtual worlds AWSINOS, in order to understand how subjects move and interact in

Figure 3. Mundo de Contos (World of Tales) in AWSINOS
Source: Authors

Figure 4. Horror Borough: AWSINOS
Source: Authors

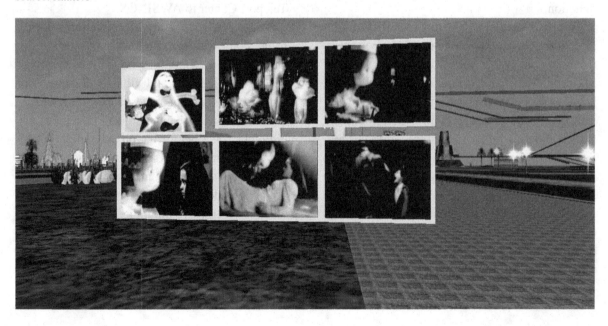

Figure 5. Languages Club: Village of Virtual Worlds Learning
Source: Authors

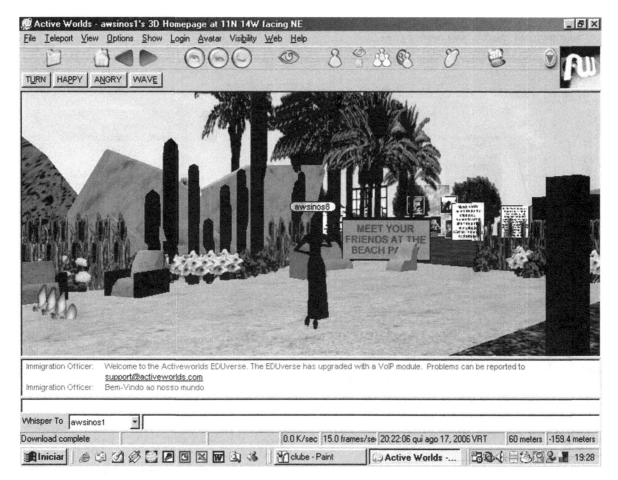

an integrated environment, especially regarding the perception of space and space representation, in the educator's formation. The exploratory research involves both qualitative and quantitative data analysis, and is developing a case study, in which subjects being trained had the opportunity to interact with the AVA, with Mariá and with AWSINOS, making both synchronous and asynchronous exchanges, trying out telepresence and digital virtual presence through an avatar.

The research resulted in the integration of three digital technologies within the same environment (Virtual Learning Environment, Communicative Agent and 3D Digital Virtual Worlds), and in the creation of the Digital Virtual Collaborating Space, triggering the development of theories based on the data collected and the analysis made. This is the main result obtained from the research, showing both theoretical and experimental advances of the practical application, regarding the creation of the technology-concept – Digital Virtual Collaborating Space[3] (Figure 6).

A Digital Virtual Collaborating Space basically presupposes a kind of interaction, giving the subject 'e-inhabiting' the space (considering his interaction background) the opportunity to

Figure 6. Digital virtual collaborating space
Source: Authors

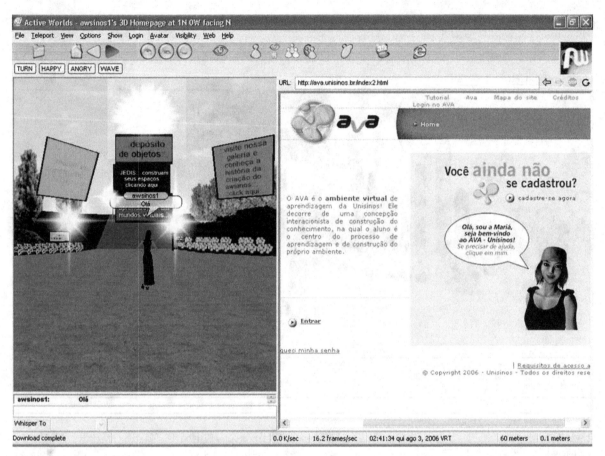

configure this space both in collaborative and co-operative ways, in his own way, meaning, through his own living and collaborating.

Also linked to this research Backes (2007) wrote her dissertation in Education, "Virtual Worlds in the Educator's Education: an investigation into the processes of autonomy and authorship". This research was grounded in theoretical study, especially in the Theory of Biology of Cognition, of Maturana and Varela, connected to living and socializing in the training of educators in the 3D digital virtual world. The research was developed with the objective of "searching for evidence to help the reflection on and better comprehension of formative process in the university", through the "case study" research methodology.

So two Enrichment Activities were developed: Learning in Virtual Worlds and Pedagogical Practice in Virtual Worlds, for students of different degree courses at the Universidade of Vale do Rio dos Sinos - UNISINOS and Learning in the Virtual Worlds Village (Figure 7).

In Figure 5 we visualize the constructions carried out by the research students, resulting in metaphoric representation of knowledge constructed in problem-based learning projects[4].

The main focus of the research was to study how to develop autonomy and authorship in the teacher education process, through the construction of Virtual Worlds, whose pedagogical proposal is based on an interactional/systemic constructivist conception. The evidence from this

Figure 7. Learning in Virtual Worlds Village
Source: Authors

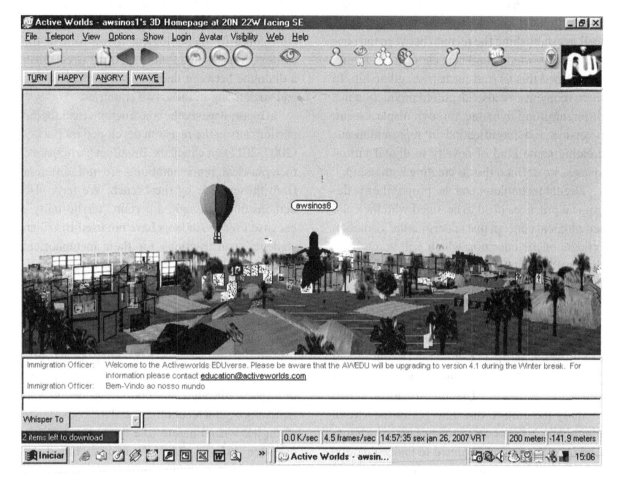

research shows that the constructions of graphic representation of knowledge in a Virtual World extend the autonomy and develop authorship of the educator being trained.

Three moments were identified in the autonomy process: individual autonomy, autopoiesis and social autonomy. Individual autonomy we understand as the living being's own action, making his own rules for the action. It is then possible to demonstrate that action leads to reflection, and that the living being produces itself in the action and knowledge, making autopoiesis. In this sense, we also identified autonomy in the group's action, in which the action transforms the network, in a social autonomy. It is essential for the educator

being trained to build himself through these three moments of autonomy, in order to produce his actions within the educational context. He needs to produce himself in actions for the construction of new knowledgement and transform his actions for his students and other educators.

In the construction of the virtual world, as well as in the interactions carried out in other digital virtual spaces, it was possible to identify the development of three levels of the trainee educator's authorship. In the training process, pre-authorship may be the unchaining point for other authorship processes, because it is not a copy, it is the intention of representing the living being's subjectivity. In situations in which trainee educators' critical positioning regarding the construction of the 3D Digital Virtual World and theoretical knowledge were approached, as well as establishing the relation between the constructed knowledge and new elements of living, we defined this as transformative authorship. In these moments we also identified production in a different group dynamic, through displacement, inversion and modification in representations, creating some kind of novelty in digital virtual spaces, we defined this as creating authorship.

Digital technology and the proposal of pedagogical practices need to be tuned with the epistemological concept that underpins the formation process of the educator, which will be outlined during the living experience of the educator's training. The Virtual World is a possibility of setting the virtual digital living space.

Continuing with her research, Backes (2011) developed the thesis in Education and Sciences of Education entitled "Setting the Digital Living Virtual Space: The emerging culture in the teacher education process". The investigation aimed to study the culture that emerges in the virtual digital space in processes of teacher education. The observations made aimed to understand the constitution of the coexistence of a digital virtual nature, identifying the aspects of this coexistence that can contribute to building a "new culture" and learning which elements of the educational process and teaching practice imply the emerging digital culture in virtual spaces. The research methodology was based on a scientific explanation described by Maturana and Varela (2002), and the data analysis came from content analysis.

The understanding of this issue is constructed on a theoretical basis, which includes: "Biology of Cognition", by Maturana and Varela, the "Biology of Love", by Maturana and "Biology-Cultural", by Maturana and Yáñez. This foundation is complemented by contemporary theorists that address issues related to virtual digital technology, especially digital virtual 3D worlds, and processes

of teaching and learning spaces in virtual digital nature. The empirical results from the development of formative processes in digital spaces were configured by technological hybridism, in the context of Brazil and France, in order to establish a dialogue between theories and students living and socializing in these two countries.

In Figure 8 we see the constructions made by the participants in the research developed by Backes (2007, 2011), in which the Brazilian participants' metaphorical representations are not different from those made by the French. We have also demonstrated, though, a certain "territoriality", because French students have not used Brazilian students' constructions for their metaphorical representations.

Data analysis enabled us to identify, in the processes of interaction, structural couplings: structural coupling, technological structural coupling and structural coupling of a digital virtual nature. It is also possible to identify the dialectic between the configuration of virtual digital living space (through autonomy, authorship and matching digital technology) and the coexistence of digital virtual nature (the thrill, through disturbance and recursion), the construction of an emerging culture (mutual respect, legitimacy and the other elements of culture in education), and students in the educational process. Considering the dialectical aspect in the construction of the emerging culture we conclude the training process must be effective in teaching practices that address the problematic and contextualization of knowledge through dialogical relations, where all are teaching and learning. The humans, the e-inhabitants in this formative process, are aware of their actions and are authors of their choices.

The process of approaching the subject with AWSINOS leads us to discuss some aspects that emerged during the research developed in the Digital Education Research Group UNISINOS/CNPq, namely: sensations experienced when interacting in 3D digital virtual worlds; relations

Figure 8. Final construction of the Learning Village in Virtual Worlds
Source: Authors

established in this interaction, learning afforded in the world construction, skills and competencies needed to interact in the 3D digital virtual world and used in teaching and pedagogical practices.

In the construction of AWSINOS we realized that through active participation subjects experience the learning process (live experiences), make exchanges and also experience telepresence and virtual digital presence via an avatar, allowing them to act and cooperate in building theoretical and technical inputs to understand how this technology can be used in different contexts. Construction happens in a playful way, it can be an adventure, playing, a 'make-believe' in which adults construct learning to "virtualize" a world of its intentions and implications, constructing and reconstructing knowledge, interacting and cooperating.

UNISINOS ISLAND

With the institutionalization in 2004 of the Digital Education Research Group UNISINOS/CNPq, currently affiliated to the Research Line of Education, Development and Technology of Universidade do Vale do Rio dos Sinos Post Education, the first experiments with Metaverse Second Life began. In 2006, the GPE-dU, through research, acquired an Island in Second Life and started building the UNISINOS Island (Figure 9) along with the space for the Digital Education Research Group UNISINOS/CNPq (Figure 10). The main objective was to create a digital virtual information space; communication and interaction for the academic community of Universidade do Vale do Rio dos Sinos, so that teacher-researchers and students could explore, experiment and ex-

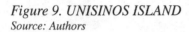

Figure 9. UNISINOS ISLAND
Source: Authors

perience this new space within Online Education while potentiating the processes of teaching and learning.

Other development and research projects were developed within this context. Among the development projects we can name: "Digital Virtual Collaborating Space - UNISINOS VIRTUAL" (2007-2009), which aimed to create a Digital Virtual Collaborating Space to offer Online Education within UNISINOS context. Through its 3D representation and with the possibilities it might offer, this space should reflect a methodological proposal capable of promoting educational processes based in an epistemological interactionist/constructivist/systemic concept, in order to effectively create a collaborating space to trigger

learning. Within this context, some common use spaces were created in UNISINOS VIRTUAL, such as the Administrative Headquarters (Figure 11); Teaching and learning spaces, including study rooms, meeting rooms, group work rooms, a digital virtual library (virtual library, multimedia library), auditory, laboratories, gathering areas (café, pub, reading room, etc.) (Figure 12). Also present were online academic activities such as the Learning Program of Teaching and Learning in the Digital World (Figure 13 and 14), Degree in Pedagogy, and the subject of Physics of the Earth System (Figure 15 and 16), from the Degree in Physics.

Dissertations associated with these projects were developed, and among them: "Interaction in Virtual Digital 3D Worlds: an investigation

Figure 10. Digital education research group UNISINOS/CNPq
Source: Authors

into the representation of emotion in learning" - Masters degree in Education Ceconi (2008). This dissertation aimed to understand how adolescents represent 'Emotioning', when interacting in 3D digital virtual worlds, such as Second Life, and how this environment triggers learning, in a way that allow the development of innovative pedagogical practices. Evidence from this investigation has shown that the possibility of the avatar's presence in a tridimensional environment intensifies social exchanges, an essential condition for learning, and also, for being considered as a provoking space for learning due to the countless possibilities of simulation of concrete situations. 'Emotioning' is represented in living and collaborating, happening in a natural and spontaneous way, because almost all communication and interaction ways possible

for the human being in the physical world are also possible in 3D digital virtual worlds, allowing more familiar and intuitive interactions. Living and collaborating imply human action (both physical and mental), and the reflection about such action, happening in a certain environment, and regarding other humans. We can then infer, based on the results of research, that the use of 3D digital virtual worlds in education opens perspectives for innovative and differentiated practices, capable of giving teaching and learning processes a new meaning.

Another dissertation developed was: "The Construction of Social Networks in the Case of Teacher Training in Metaverse, in the context of Program Loyola" - Masters Degree in Education, by Locatelli (2010). This dissertation starts with

Figure 11. UNISINOS virtual administrative headquarters
Source: Authors

the following problem: How are the processes of continuous formation, in the net, configured and empowered, in the constitution of Digital Virtual Collaborating Spaces, based on the Ignatian Pedagogical Paradigm (Context-Experience-Reflection-Action-Assessment), in Jesuit Schools, through the Loyola Program? The research identified that teachers and professors, who had taken the course, have a satisfactory understanding of the Ignatian Pedagogy, and therefore are capable of working on the theme in Digital Virtual Collaborating Spaces, establishing relations between the themes. Also, after learning how to use Metaverse, they feel very comfortable working in groups, regardless of geographical distances. In addition, one of their main objectives, in doing the course,

is to find new ways of teaching and learning to work with the homo zapiens generation.

Another piece of research conducted in the context of UNISINOS Island is entitled "Digital Virtual Living Space in Post-Graduate Programs (stricto sensu) - PPG - ECODI UNISINOS: a proposal in researchers training" (2009-2013), which is focused on creating a Virtual Digital Collaborating Space – 'Espaço de Convivência Digital Virtual' - to develop pedagogical practices and processes of teacher-researchers from the Post-Graduate Stricto Sensu (SS), Universidade do Vale do Rio dos Sinos which is in the process of completion. The main objective is to create an information space, interaction and research for the development of educational practices and

Figure 12. Teaching and learning spaces with study rooms, meeting rooms, group work rooms, library, auditory, laboratory, gathering area
Source: Authors

processes of teacher-researchers in the context of post-graduate studies at the University, using the concept technology of Digital Virtual Collaborating Space, (Figure 17). Regarding the main findings, the research showed:

- There are isolated initiatives focused on the use of digital technology in the stricto sensu, risking the prospect of Blended-Learning, but without compromising the physical classroom mode, since Brazilian law does not contemplate offering stricto sensu in online mode.

- That digital technology can contribute significantly to the training of teacher-researchers, particularly if they can experience their didactic-pedagogic use while learning subjects, which helps to expand the process of meaning about limits and possibilities of different digital technology for pedagogical practices. In particular, in the Master's and Doctorate in Education, since these professionals will be trainers of new generations of teachers.

- That most coordinators of Postgraduate Stricto Sensu Programmes (Humanities at

Figure 13. Initial space of the Learning Program of Teaching and Learning in the Digital World
Source: Authors

Figure 14. Constructions made by the students in the Learning Program of Teaching and Learning in the Digital World
Source: Authors

Figure 15. Space of the subject Physics of the Earth System
Source: Authors

Universidade do Vale do Rio dos Sinos) understand the importance of using digital technology in teacher-researchers training, even though this understanding is not followed up with a more consistent reflection from the theoretical- epistemological point of view in relation to the limits and potential of digital technology. Regarding Distance Education mode in teacher-researcher training, most coordinators understand that this is a possible route, considering the level of autonomy and authorship of the audience. Some understand the need of this kind can be experienced in the training process of the teacher-researcher. However, doubts and issues related to distance education are many, which, in a way, reflect the lack of knowledge and experience in this modality.

- There was a theoretical-methodological advance in experiments using digital technol-

ogy in the strict sense in online mode, since several experiments were carried out in the context of Post-Graduate in Education and Post-Graduate in Management at Universidade do Vale do Rio dos Sinos, which allowed us to theorize the results.
- There is an expanding, deepening and consolidation of the concept-technology - Digital Virtual Collaborating Space, especially regarding digital technology and hybrid multimodality. This result was published in journals, book chapters and events and is being used in research carried out by Master's and doctorate students, and as theoretical background in proposing new research.
- The broadening of insights about possibilities and limits of using the Digital Virtual Collaborating Space as an environment for the training of teachers-researchers in online mode;

Figure 16. Tsunami simulation in the subject of Physics of the Earth System
Source: Authors

- Advances in studies on the contribution of education to new technological creations, which can be observed in various environments created in different research projects.

- An advance in reflections on the nature of media-specific characteristics, especially with regards to Immersive Learning, enabled by the social presence of the subject-avatar (virtual digital identity), that inhabit and co-inhabit these spaces, which enables them to have access to information and mechanisms of action and interaction (through the combined textual, oral, gestural and graphic language) for the expansion of knowledge as well as their relationship with the methods, based on a systemic-constructivist-interactionist epistemological concept, possible by means of problem-solving teaching and pedagogical practices. It is important to mention that this epistemological-methodological perspective, linked to the potentialities of the concept technology of the Digital Virtual Collaborating Space, brought the need to expand research in the field of Gamefication.

- Advances in the debate on the concepts of time, space, distance, novelty and innovation, these being reframed, and depth in the context of the concept-technology of Digital Virtual Collaborating Spaces.

Figure 17. Digital virtual living space in post-graduate programs (stricto sensu)
Source: Authors

This research aims to gain a better understanding of how these integrated digital technologies can be used to enlarge the area of training for teacher-researchers.

It is worth noting that theorization about concept technology is being used in *Libera Università Maria Ss. Assunta*, in the Group of International Research Project "Postbureaucratics Organizations", through the research developed by Moretti (2010), and at the Sorbonne - *L' université Paris Descartes - Paris V*, the *Centre d' Etudes sur l' Actuel et le Quotidien*, in the postdoctoral research entitled "The Constitution of Tribes in Digital Technology Hybridism: The possibility of re-enchanting the worlds" of Backes (2013-2014), under the guidance of Dr. Michel Meffesoli. The aim of the research is: 'To reflect on how tribes, in the contemporary context, are formed, where the borders between what is real and what is virtual

are permeable, and also if such formation enables the re-enchantment of worlds', using 'case study' and 'content analysis' methodologies.

We also emphasize that research regarding the point of view of digital technology contributed to create Digital Virtual Collaborating Space-PPGs UNISINOS, which represents a significant advance in understanding the development of learning environments through the Web that also includes virtual reality technology.

Also, regarding the clarification and socialization of the knowledge built in the research context, these occurred at the level of:

- Undergraduate, in activities performed in the Learning Programme Teaching and Learning in the Digital World, at the School of Education and also in supporting the development of final projects.

- In continuing education, by offering extension courses for the educational communities.
- In Post-Graduate curricular seminars and also in supporting the development of doctoral theses and dissertations.
- In Scientific Initiation, through scholarships, where the student participates actively in the research process.

Tutorials on the Second Life Metaverse, as well as videos about the research Project were developed, and learning materials that can be used in future training processes.

Thus, it is possible to observe that, from an even broader perspective, the research results also helped to subsidize the development of Digital Virtual Collaborating Spaces applications in other areas and sectors. In this sense the possibilities of this technology for learning processes (and digital emancipation) are promising.

It is important to emphasize that the main purpose and expected outcome of the research was to create an information space, for interaction and research in the development of educational practices and processes of teacher-researchers in the context of post-graduate studies in the University, using the concept of technology Digital Virtual Collaborating Space. This goal, which also translates into a result, was achieved in the context of the Post-Graduate in Education and Management of the Universidade do Vale do Rio dos Sinos. The Post-Graduate in Philosophy, started the process, though, did not proceed with it. Other Post-Graduate subjects such as History, Social Sciences, Applied Linguistics and Communication showed interest but due to limited knowledge of the technology and not having trained human resources for the creation of their spaces, they have yet to conduct their presence in the Metaverse.

Linked to the research "Digital Virtual Living Space in Post-Graduate Programs (stricto sensu) - PPG - ECODI UNISINOS: a proposal in researcher training" (2009-2013), the research "METARIO - Research Network and Teacher Training in Metaverses: Skills Development for Management Teachers" (2010-2014), was developed, funded by the Coordenação de Aperfeiçoamento de Pessoal de Nível Superior, also in the process of completion. The research objective was to create METARIO Network – Research Network and Teacher Education in Metaverses - a network of academic cooperation, of interinstitutional and interdisciplinary nature, with the participation of the Post-Graduate Program in Management of the Pontifícia Universidade Católica of Rio de Janeiro and the Post-Graduate Programs of Management and Education of the Universidade do Vale do Rio dos Sinos to develop environments and teacher training programs in Management, including methodologies that translate into educational practices and processes of mediation in the context of the online mode, using the technology of Metaverse and mobile and wireless technologies providing access both by personal computer or by mobile devices (Mobile Learning). This way, the project aims to contribute to generating knowledge and practices that significantly contribute to the improvement of teaching and learning processes in Administration.

Within the research context, 80 masters students of various strictu sensu courses from the Universidade do Vale do Rio dos Sinos were trained, (including in Management, Accounting, Law, Engineering, Social Sciences). The students participated in a class called Higher Education Methodololy in Management, now called "Teaching and Learning in Management with the use of ICT (Information and Communication Technologies)". In this discipline the knowledge generated was systematically shared through the METARIO Project, and the discipline was also the space of concrete experience of technology and methodology developed by the project, such as the realization of an interchange among students of the Masters in Management from Universidade do Vale do Rio dos Sinos and Instituto Superior de Economia e Gestão, Portugal, using a whole environment of intercultural exchange developed within the Second Life Metaverse. In 2013 the proposal of the discipline evolved further and was developed based on the methodology of learning projects in higher education proposed by Schlemmer (1999), in view of the concept of hybridism digital technology and multimodality.

Despite being offered in classroom mode some meetings were held using web conferencing (Adobe Connect) technology and also mobile technologies. During the semester students used different digital technologies (blogs, Prezi, Google tools, YouTube, Facebook, etc.) for the development of learning projects. Our goal from that proposal was that students could experience a pedagogical practice immersed in a context of multimodality and digital technological hybridism in order to assign senses to give meaning to what constitutes learning and teaching from the perspective of digital culture.

The teacher training, from this perspective, had repercussions at undergraduate level, mainly linked to the processes of teaching and learning with practical experiences of using metaverses for courses like Management of Human Resources and Management for Innovation and Leadership.

One result of the research involves the methods developed for teaching and learning in Metaverse, especially regarding the development of skills for teamwork and leadership (at undergraduate level) and intercultural skills at masters level) in both modalities - totally online, as well as in blended learning (part online, part classroom). Each method has its own design according to the targeted competence to be trained, but basically work with starting the development of skills of self-assessment of the current level of competence with the targeted learners, which are held after experiential learning activities (applied, based in solving problems of work) and finally, review the development process of the target jurisdiction, which includes self-assessment, assessment by the facilitator and/or peer review. All three

methods were developed and evaluated according to the methodology of Design Research, allowing generating both tangible artifacts (methods of teaching and learning that can be replicated) and knowledge about the use of Metaverses for teaching in management and skills development.

Figure 18 presents some of the environments created in the context of the Metario Project, when activities were taking place.

Just at UNISINOS, three dissertations were written based on this research, all of which were in the context of Post-Graduate Management:

"The Development of Competence for Distance Teamwork using the Second Life Metaverse" - Masters degree in Management by Gomes (2012). The objective of this dissertation was to identify if and how the use of Metaverse technology can contribute to the development of teamwork skills in distance education, in Human Resources Management. The artifact developed is a training method for the development of individual skills of team work in distance education using Metaverse technology. The results have indicated that participants might find the following possibilities in Metaverse technology for the development of individual skills in team work: construction of a context for skill development; simulation of situations to make people plan, act and interact; enabling application of management techniques and practical activities; enabling the development of interpersonal relationship aspects; complementing face-to-face activities, especially those related to education; promotion of group activities, even at a distance. Regarding the artifact developed, the key aspects for improvement identified were improper meeting times and little time for interaction. Regarding the technology used, there were also unsatisfactory aspects, such as difficulties associated to the technological resources used by the participants (Internet connection and hardware), and the instability of the Second Life platform (software).

"The Development of Leadership Skills in Digital Virtual Worlds in 3D: The Case of the

Figure 18. Project METARIO
Source: Authors

Second Life Metaverse" - Masters degree in Management, by Freitas Jr. (2012). The objective here was to identify how Metaverse can be used as an environment for the development of leadership skills in Higher Education in Administration. The results have identified some affordances in the use of the Second Life Metaverse, indicated in the literature, such as interaction and communication, in all meetings. As for Leadership, the most approached aspects were planning and systemic view, decision-making skills, relationships, communication and resilience. On the other hand, the least approached aspect was the ability to encourage staff. The use of Metaverse has positively contributed to the development of

leadership skills by enabling: 1) the simulation of a real work situation, in which a particular skill could be developed; 2) the simulation of working conditions not possible in physical face-to-face education context or in other digital virtual distance education platforms, like the simulation of real problems; 3) a digital virtual 3D environment with rich resources for interaction between leaders and followers (for example, personification with the use of avatars, environments with 3D resources and objects, etc.). The Metaverse affordances favored the development of activities.

Machado (2012) defended the Masters degree "Three-Dimensional Virtual Worlds as an Environment for the Development of Intercultural

Competence" - Masters degree in Management. The objective of the dissertation was to identify if, and how, 3D digital virtual worlds can be used as an environment for the development of intercultural abilities in the Post-Graduate stricto sensu program. The subjects in this research were the students from Instituto Superior de Economia e Gestão da Universidade Técnica de Lisboa - ISEG, from Portugal, and students from Universidade do Vale do Rio do Sinos - UNISINOS, do Brasil, enrolled in different Masters Degree courses, who took part in a capacitating activity carried out at distance. For this dissertation an artifact was created in the format of a capacitating method for the development of intercultural ability, consisting of a set of activities to encourage Virtual Intercultural Interchange in Second Life 3D Digital Virtual Worlds.

The artifact (method) developed had diagnosis instruments, environments shaped in Second Life 3D Digital Virtual Worlds, training for the use of 3D Digital Virtual Worlds, interchange activities (interchange opening, general meeting, group meetings, talks and general meeting for closing interchange activities), and final assessment. The artifact proposed to have the Brazilian student (individually or in pairs) as the facilitator of his respective Portuguese group, in the process of developing a work in the format of a scientific paper, being one of the assignments of the course taking place in Portugal, where every student would take part with their own avatar in the virtual experience. In order to assess the process of developing the intercultural ability in the 3D Digital Virtual World, the 'Technique of Critical Incidents' was adopted, to select from direct behavior observation, incidents or situations from the virtual environment during subjects' collaborating and interchange. It was then possible to identify evidence of opportunities for the development of intercultural abilities in the researched context. We also highlight that the contribution 3D Digital Virtual Worlds gave

to the development of intercultural abilities was connected to the educational affordances, which were, in general, perceived by students.

RICESU ISLAND

In 2007, also under Second Life Metaverse, the Digital Education Research Group UNISINOS/CNPQ created RICESU[5] Island. In this context the project developed from development and training on "Space of Virtual Digital Living - ECODI RICESU" (2008-2009). The project consisted of specifically creating a digital virtual space of information, communication and interaction for the development of virtual communities of learning and practice in the context of Network Catholic Institutions of Higher Learning and process development training for the construction of 3D spaces in the Second Life Metaverse, offered for Catholic Higher Education Institutions that integrate Catholic Network of Higher Education Institutions in the context of the Digital Education Work Group. This project included two steps, as follows:

The first step of the project consisted of the acquisition of an Island in the Metaverse Second Life for the creation of RICESU Island, which took shape from the creation of different Digital 3D Virtual Spaces for shared use by the Catholic Network of Higher Education Institutions such as the virtual "headquarters" of the Catholic Network of Higher Education Institutions, with the representation of a center of coexistence and shared projects in the Network, as well as areas for collaborative/cooperative work spaces for meetings, discussions, lectures, among others, created with the objective of providing configuration for the Digital Virtual Collaborating Space, to enable the development of Virtual Community of Learning and Practice in the context of Digital Education, and more specifically of Online Education in

Metaverse. Thus, the virtual "headquarters" of the digital Catholic Network of Higher Education Institutions created spaces for each Catholic Higher Education Institution participating in the network, so they could develop their specific projects.

The second step was to offer two training processes (totaling 80 hours) for teachers/researchers/ Catholic Higher Education Institutions professionals, members of the Catholic Network of Higher Education Institutions. The aim of the Digital Education Research Group UNISINOS/CNPq was for each Catholic Higher Education Institution to appoint one teacher from the area of pedagogy, one from the area of technological-3D design and programming, and one from the area of architecture, so that these three professionals could be the basis of what might become a subgroup of development and research in the Metaverse technology in their Catholic Higher Education Institution. Each Catholic Higher Education Institution member of the Catholic Network of Higher Education Institutions, indicated three participants to represent them in both formative processes, aiming to create 'us' institutional capacities for developing educational proposals in Metaverse, thus contributing to the development of both local and network actions, constituting a micro-network (micro-community) that enabled the creation of a new Work Group, the ECODI RICESU Work Group.

In this way, 13 teams, from different Catholic Higher Education Institutions, were formed, totaling 39 physically distant participants, who acted together in virtual digital classroom, in the context of RICESU Island in Second Life-3D digital virtual worlds. In addition to teachers-counselors, responsible for the training processes, three teams were constituted with members of the Digital Education Research Group UNISINOS/CNPq. Each team was composed of a Masters student and a student of scientific research, responsible for the follow-up. These teams had the primary task of monitoring the learning process of the participants, guiding them.

The methodology and materials (texts, tutorials, videos, challenges, etc.), used in both formative processes, were built by the Digital Education Research Group UNISINOS/CNPq, which caused the need to create specific objects in space for the training process, as the panel integrator. Participants also used as a space for the development of training processes, the "Chest" of its Catholic Higher Education Institutions (where they put the results of the challenges and also developed the designs of problem-based learning space for the Catholic Higher Education Institutions. These spaces can be seen in the following figures. During the training process, in addition to the Second Life Metaverse, many kinds of technologies were used, such as: blog, discussion forums, YouTube, etc.).

Currently the main activities developed in the context of ECODI-RICESU refer to meetings of the Management Committee, meetings of working groups and organization and development of virtual events, created in Second Life. In the context of the spaces that integrate the different Catholic Higher Education Institutions, ECODI - RICESU can perceive different levels of development as well as activities with distinct objectives. So, when visiting the island you can see that each Catholic Higher Education Institution develops some kind of activity in these spaces created.

Next, Figure 19 shows different spaces constructed within the context of Digital Virtual Collaborating Spaces in the Catholic Network of Higher Education Institutions, involving both steps mentioned above.

Linked to this project, the dissertation entitled "Online Education in Metaverse: the mediation through telepresence and virtual presence via digital avatar in Digital Virtual Worlds in 3 Dimensions" was written by Trein (2010). The dissertation had as its main theoretical basis 'The Biology of Learning' by Humberto Maturana and Francisco Varela, when living and collaborating in the Second Life Metaverse, both from the subjects taking part in the research sample and the researcher herself. Notes were taken in the context

Figure 19. Space of virtual digital living: ECODI RICESU
Source: Authors

of two training processes developed by the Digital Education Research Group UNISINOS/CNPq and the Catholic Network of Higher Institutions; and a training process developed in the Learning Program 'Teaching and Learning in the Digital World', part of the syllabus of the Pedagogy course from UNISINOS, where a complementary activity called 'Online Education in 3D Digital Virtual Worlds: possibility or reality?' was developed. Besides this, questionnaires and interviews were carried out with subjects from different investigative domains.

The main objective of the investigation was to understand in what way the (re)creation of digital virtual identities interacting in 3D Digital Virtual Worlds can contribute to overcoming paradigms associated with the teacher's 'lack of physical presence' in Online Education, and with other more responsible processes of pedagogical mediation. The scientific method developed by Humberto Maturana was the methodological approach that helped structure this research, as well as the articulation of data collected with the theory, in the development of analysis. The data collected came from observation, questionnaires and interviews developed in different physical and digital virtual spaces (UNISINOS Informatics Lab, Metaverso Second Life, MSN, Google Talk), as well as from images collected in Metaverso-SL. The evidence obtained from this investigation has shown that the possibility of creating digital virtual identities, through avatars, increases the subjects' feeling of

'presence' and 'belonging', in the teaching and learning processes in Metaverses, through telepresence and digital virtual presence, contributing to overcoming the paradigm of 'lack of physical presence' in Online Education. The increase in the commitment of both telepresent and digital virtually present subjects through their avatars, has contributed to the development of more responsible Pedagogical Mediation processes.

Still connected to RICESU Island, the research "Anatomy in Metaverse Second Life: a proposal for i-Learning" (2011-2013) was developed and funded by FAPERGS, finalized in June 2013. The research linked to the discipline of Anatomy was developed in the context of the Network of Catholic Institutions of Higher Education by a interinstitutional group (Universidade do Vale do Rio dos Sinos, Centro Universitário La Salle and Universidade Católica de Pelotas) and interdisciplinary group (teaching team - teachers of anatomy, didactic-pedagogic staff and technical team). The research problem was to "understand how the processes of teaching and learning concepts of anatomy, and the development of immersive learning experience (i-Learning) can be developed using the technology of Metaverse". The main findings demonstrated that the 3D shaped systems facilitated giving meaning to concepts and processes connected to different systems, mainly when there was the possibility of avatar entering the system being studied. This immersion, when associated to challenges/problematization, gives the students a bigger involvement in the concepts. We have identified that i-Learning experiences may enrich learning contexts in Anatomy, compounding hybrid environments, from the multimodality perspective.

The use of Metaverse technology was initially understood as a simple novelty in teaching and learning processes, evidenced in the transposition of representations (human anatomy laboratory), material (images present in the anatomy atlas), methodologies and practices present in the analogical environment to the digital media. Throughout the research, through interdisciplinary and interinstitutional interactions, the development of technical-didactic-pedagogical competences was possible and was observed within the different teams (although different from subject to subject), providing some level of innovation, thought for the different teaching and learning processes.

In Figure 20, for instance, the participants in the research have built a transparent human body that, as systems were molded, they became visible and sensitive, making it possible for the student, repre-

sented by his avatar, to enter in the molded system and experience virtual reality and real virtuality. The innovation only emerged when teaching and learning processes were thought in congruence with the Metaverse technology (possible due to a higher familiarization with technology and the specialized analysis about limits and possibilities for the pedagogical-didactic practice, from nature and environment's specificity).

Innovation was perceived by students, as well as by some teachers, as they were assessing the experienced lived, mainly related to understanding the perspective of Immersive Learning and Gamification Learning, originated in the data collecting developed with students, during the pilot-project. Immersive Learning is possible through the avatar's immersion into an environment moulded with gamification elements, present in learning situations along the process (clues and challenges). Such questions were perceived and stated by students and educators at the time data was being collected.

Figure 20. Anatomy laboratory
Source: Authors

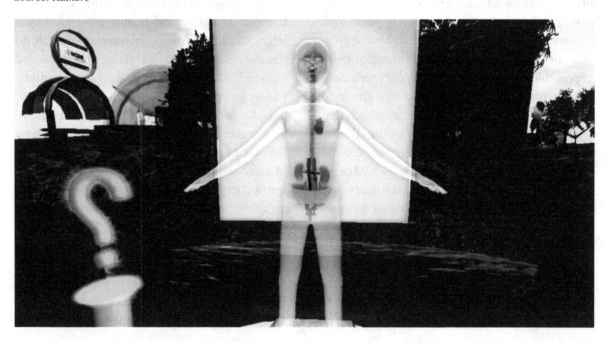

In addition, regarding Innovating in undergraduate teaching and learning processes, an experiment using UNITY technology was developed, associated with the SDK technology from Kinect (Figure 21). The experience created allows more interaction between the student and the 3D moulded system, allowing his action in the physical world to affect the digital virtual world. This technology was used with the objective of testing an interface that could be more natural and intuitive, using one's own body movements to select organs and visualize them in 3D.

This research allowed teachers to expand their skills in a technical and didactic-pedagogic framework and created the conditions for expanding institutional and interdisciplinary skills in order to contribute to the development of actions (projects) and local network, allowing the constitution of a microweb and technical-didactic-pedagogic innovation networks. It is believed that the "we" of institutional and interdisciplinary skills was built, so they can provide new training and capacitating building programs in their home institutions, to contribute to the development of actions (projects) as well as a local network, providing in the micro-network (micro-communities) technical-didactic-pedagogic innovation.

CONCLUSION

Both, 3D digital virtual worlds (AWSINOS, UNISINOS and RICESU Island) and developed projects are open to the entire community, and the main activity currently being carried out in the context of UNISINOS Island refers to research in the area of Digital Education. The research involves creating spaces for the exploration, experimentation and experience of these spaces for students and teachers. At UNISINOS Island,

Figure 21. Modeling of the circulatory system
Source: Authors

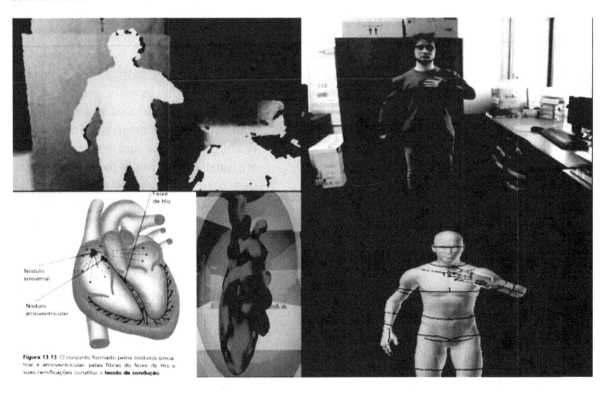

there is general information about the University, interaction spaces for digital virtual coexistence, as well as dissertation presentations, talks in virtual meetings of research groups, exhibitions, events, and others.

However, we are aware of the difficulties of changing a paradigm, predominantly connected to the use of Virtual Learning Environment and 2D Environments, to a Web 3D paradigm, and moreover, one that proposes digital-technological hybridism and multimodality, mainly when talking about Formal Education. Within this context, we do not refer only to the financial costs associated, which depend on an institution's technological options, (in the case of property Metaverses like Second Life, for instance, and other open source ones, like Open Simulator, Open Wonderland, among others), nor the difficulties related to machine resources (processors, graphic board) and internet speed, but basically to the cultural 'costs' needed to trigger such changes.

Amongst the main difficulties implied within this *cultural 'cost'* are:

- The ingrained teaching culture within our institutions, which needs to open up a space for a learning culture, under a hybrid and multimodal perspective to emerge.
- Massive and standardized Distance Education models, which need to evolve to different designs and educational proposals constructed from:
  ◦ An analysis of the formative process by the target public;
  ◦ Analysis of specificities from the knowledge area in question;
  ◦ Theoretical-epistemological conception about what teaching and learning processes will be developed; not excluding; and
  ◦ Modality, methodologies, practices and pedagogical mediation processes that can be developed regarding an analytical process about limits and

potentialities of different technologies, in an imbrication between analogical and digital.

- Management needs to be aligned with the paradigm emerging from such hybridism and multimodality, and, therefore must consider the three laws or principles that ground the current cultural process: According to Lemos (2002), they are: '(1) liberation of the emission pole, (2) network connection, and (3) socio-cultural reconfiguration, based on new productive and recombination practices' (p.39). The first principle refers to the 'post-massive culture', in which subjects have the opportunity to produce and publicize real time data, 'under different format and modulations, adding and collaborating with others in the network, reconfiguring the cultural industry ('massive')' (p.38). The second one refers to the possibility of emitting in the network, of getting connected to other people, 'generating synergy, exchanging pieces of information, circulating, distributing'. (p.40). The third principle derives from the first two, because emission and connection generate 'the reconfiguration (of practices and institutions) from the massive cultural industry and sociability networks of the industrial society' (p.41).
- Linked to management is infrastructure, teaching processes and operation, which are usually rigid. But in the new paradigm they need to give space to the dynamicity of a network society interconnected by ever-changing and updating technologies, unpredictability, what is emerging. Structures and processes need to flow, necessarily implying in giving up an exaggerated 'control' over those who teach and those who learn, having trust as a core principle. Related to this problematic is also the following:

○ Teachers' lack of technical-didactic-pedagogical appropriation. To make it happen, firstly Educational Institutions, teachers and professors need to understand what Digital Culture means, again implying considering the three laws or principles that are the basis of the current cultural process, presented by Lemos (2002), outlined above.

We understand that the three laws or principles forming the base of the current cultural process, presented by Lemos (2002), can contribute to our reflection on the way an educational institution changes its way of teaching, from an emerging paradigm that contemplates hybridism and multimodality.

Let us consider the following: when thinking about the pedagogical political project, are syllabus organization, methodologies, practices and processes of pedagogical mediation, principles of emission pole liberation and network connection present? According to Lopes and Schlemmer (2012), the emission movement, production and connection, imply a growing process of reorganization of social relations mediated by digital technologies, affecting, to a certain degree, all aspects of human action, within a movement of reconfiguration of practices and institutions.

So, based on Lévy (1999) and Lemos (2002), we can say that cyberculture is not a particular subculture, from certain 'tribes', but a new way of culture, that is evolving into Hybridism and Multimodality Culture. For Maffesoli (1998), new ways of culture emerging in tribes are related to common sense knowledge, the underground power found in emotional communities, being-together in a dynamic rooting perspective of a collectiveness that establishes relations through alterity. In this way, aspects of daily life emerge, such as: aesthetics, religion, myth, nomadism, and saturation. It is in this hybrid culture that most of the learning subjects are located.

In order to get the student involved in a different way there must be such a reconfiguration of pedagogical practices, because otherwise, we will continue using digital technologies only as a novelty in Education, reproducing the same pedagogical practices we used in the dominant paradigm, repressing the disturbing element present in digital technologies, or furthermore, in a hybrid and multimodal process, capable of triggering reflection on what teaching and learning in a culture of hybridism and multimodality really mean.

Regarding the financial 'cost', our experience at Universidade do Vale do Rio dos Sinos involved:

- **Property Metaverse:** Eduverse-Active World - AWSINOS maintenance, costing around U$ 400.00 a year; acquisition of UNISINOS Island, costing around U$ 900.00 (for being an Island for educational purpose) and annual maintenance costing around U$ 880.00.
- **Open Source Metaverse:** Server acquisition, costing around U$ 5,000.00, in which two Open source Metaverse softwares were installed: Open Simulator and Open Worldland.

The use of this technology by students and educators does not imply additional costs, they only need a computer with a good processing capacity, graphic board and internet connection. To create avatars, and to use property Metaverses, there is no related cost. There is only the cost of building spaces, objects, etc., but in this case, because the institution has acquired an Island, only e-residents have permission to build inside it.

As Education Research, all financial cost involved is paid for by resources from research developed by the Digital Education Research Group UNISINOS/CNPq, coming from public notices for research published from Brazilian research-promotion agencies, such as Coordenação de Aperfeiçoamento de Pessoal de Nível

Superior, Conselho Nacional de Desenvolvimento Científico e Tecnológico, and the Fundação de Amparo à Pesquisa do Estado do Rio Grande do Sul, to whom the group the group's projects are submitted and supported. This includes property Metaverses, the acquisition of UNISINOS Island and annual maintenance fees, both for UNISINOS Island and AWSINOS, and in the case of open sources Metaverses, the acquisition of the server, with maintenance carried out by the members of the Digital Education Research Group UNISINO/CNPq.

In this way, the Digital Education Research Group UNISINOS/CNPq has managed to maintain research and the development of Learning areas in Metaverses, as well as, more recently, in the hybridism and multimodality context.

It is important to say that, the objective of the research developed by the Digital Education Research Group UNISINOS/CNPq, is not to compare effectiveness of digital technologies, regarding learning, because there is no way to affirm that certain learning was possible exclusively because of a specific digital technology, once subjects are immersed in a hybrid world of interaction with different technologies, and therefore there is no way to control such variable. Learning is a continuous, systemic process that happens in living and collaborating, through a network of interconnected elements capable of structural changes along a continuous history. Therefore, the objective of the research we are carrying out consists of understanding who the current learning subject is, and how he constructs meanings, in other words, how he learns in the imbrication with different digital technologies, under the hybridism and multimodality perspective. We aim to evolve, from a perspective that transcends a deterministic polarized thinking, to a thinking in which subject and world are mutually defined, correlated and codetermining.

Based on Varela (2005), we understand that living and collaborating in Metaverses comes from the coupling between autopoietic machines,

mediated by alopoietic machines (digital virtual structural coupling), and between autopoietic machines and alopoietic machine (technological structural coupling). During coupling, both autopoietic and alopoietic machines are co-determined in the interaction, in such a way that many coupling stories have resulted in a world that is inseparable from its way of life, pointing out an issue that is also cultural. Learning in the Metaverse is the effective action of human beings, and with Metaverses coming into the history of the structural coupling that makes a world emerge. In this process we try to build elements to allow the development of innovative pedagogical practices, proper for this historical time and social space.

We comprehend, then, that the technological presence in Metaverse, or in any other teaching and learning process, does not aim to reinforce teaching, but to broaden its spaces, to foster interaction processes between the subject and the environment, in order to enable the construction of knowledge in a collaborative and cooperative way, providing learning. We understand that different technologies coexist within the universe of human relations, and therefore, learning. The idea is not to exclude but to give them meaning in the educational process, according to the context and one's own objectives.

In the development of this research, we, as researchers/professors belonging to the Digital Education Research Group – GPe-dU UNISINOS/CNPq, have learned a lot, and this can improve our comprehension of learning in Metaverses. Some of the points we have identified are:

- Adopting a new technology, such as Metaverse technology, is not a simple process. It implies facing difficulties, previously related to cultural 'cost'.
- Metaverses represent another digital technological possibility, presenting the potential to significantly contribute to teaching and learning processes, thus, they are not unique. It is not about replacing other tech-

nologies by this one, but in the creation of different educational design, but the coexistence of different digital technologies.

- The use of an emerging digital technology establishes disturbances regarding teaching and learning processes, because it modifies the collaborating dynamic for both educators and students. This way, new methodologies, practices and pedagogical mediation processes emerge. However, this does not mean we have changed everything, or that what we have done in the past is no longer valid. Sometimes, according to Maffesoli (2012), we retake ways of living from our human origin (the archaic) and, in synergy with technologies (the future), we create a new meaning. As, for instance, in the case of emotional relations, which are strongly present in our primitive relations, in which the legitimacy of living together has constituted collaborating, and is empowered with the presence of different digital technologies. Teaching and learning processes are, this way, given new meaning, based on the dialogue between: The education developed within geographically located spaces, digital education, different learning theories, digital technologies, paradigms.

We understand that from 1999 until today, the number of Metaverses linked to research, MDV3D has grown significantly, especially in the last 10 years. However they are still incipient in terms of understanding the potential of its use in teaching and learning, for developing methodologies and pedagogical mediation processes, which could lead to paradigm shift regarding teaching and learning, promoting the rise of innovation.

The development of research reveals a trend regarding hybridization and multimodality in order to create a learning environment that is different from integrated digital technologies (mainly web 2.0 web and 3D), also used from phones and tablets, in connection with analog spaces, thus referring to the coexistence and the need for overlapping of physical and digital worlds. Nevertheless, from the perspective of complexity, the systemic thinking and the self-eco-organizing conception, we go beyond our research. We believe that other issues need and deserve to be on the agenda of researchers and educators. Among those issues we highlight two: the presence of adult content in digital technologies, as well as ways of developing the students' critical thinking towards this reality; the broad dimension of ubiquity in digital virtual spaces, with 3D digital virtual worlds interface with mobile and wireless technologies.

On our agenda, as future research (already underway), we are making further investigations into learning in the contexts of hybridism and multimodality, connected to the perspective of games and gamification, including Mixed Reality and Augmented Reality (also supported by mobile and wireless devices), as well as the incorporation of technologies like Kinect (started in the research 'Anatomy in Metaverse Second Life: a proposal for i-Learning' (2001-2013), finished in June 2013), Leap Motion[6] and Rift glasses[7]. In this process we are trying to better know the Actor-Network Theory, and Cartography of Controversies, both proposed by the Sociologist Bruno Latour, in order to have both theoretical and methodological elements to help broaden our comprehension of the subjects' effective action in and with such different digital technologies, to understand how structural coupling makes a world emerge. In this process we continue the search for elements that make innovative pedagogical practices possible, for subjects of this historical social time. Also, under the hybridism perspective (geographically located spaces and digital virtual spaces), through interdisciplinary education processes, we want to investigate the permeability of different frontiers: cultural and geographical, and the domains and degrees of knowledge. This way we can better understand how co-presence takes place in hybrid spaces, from the perspective of post-modernity.

REFERENCES

Backes, L. (2007). *A formação do educador em mundos virtuais: Uma investigação sobre os processos de autonomia e de autoria.* (Unipublished master's dissertation). Universidade do Vale do Rio dos Sinos, São Leopoldo, Brazil.

Backes, L. (2011). *A configuração do espaço de convivência digital virtual: A cultura emergente no processo de formação do educador.* (Unipublished doctoral thesis). Universidade do Vale do Rio dos Sinos, São Leopoldo, Brazil and Université Lumière Lyon 2, Lyon, France.

Ceconi, R. (2008). *A interação em mundos virtuais digital 3D: Uma investigação sobre a representação da emoção no aprendizado.* (Unipublished master's dissertation). Universidade do Vale do Rio dos Sinos, São Leopoldo, Brazil.

Freitas, J. J. C. (2012). *O desenvolvimento de habilidades de liderança em mundos virtuais tridimensionais: O Caso do metaverso Second Life.* (Unpublished master's dissertation). Universidade do Vale do Rio dos Sinos, São Leopoldo, Brazil.

Gomes, A. C. (2012). *O desenvolvimento de competências para o trabalho em equipe distância usando metaverso Second Life.* (Unipublished master's dissertation). Universidade do Vale do Rio dos Sinos, São Leopoldo, Brazil.

Lemos, A. (2002). Cibercultura: Tecnologia e vida social na cultura contemporânea. Porto Alegre, Brazil: Sulina.

Lévy, P. (1999). Cibercultura. Rio de Janeiro, Brazil: Editora 34.

Locatelli, E. L. (2010). *A construção de redes sociais no processo de formação docente em metaverso, no contexto do programa loyola.* (Unipublished master's dissertation). Universidade do Vale do Rio dos Sinos, São Leopoldo, Brazil.

Machado, L. (2012). *Mundos virtuais tridimensionais como ambiente para o desenvolvimento de competência intercultura.* (Unpublished master's dissertation). Universidade do Vale do Rio dos Sinos, São Leopoldo, Brazil.

Maffesoli, M. (1998). O tempo das tribos: O declínio do individualismo nas sociedades de massa. Rio de Janeiro, Brazil: Forense Universitária.

Maffesoli, M. (2012). O tempo retorna: Formas elementares da pós-modernidade. Rio de Janeiro, Brazil: Forense Universitária.

Maturana, H. R., & Varela, F. J. (2002). A árvore do conhecimento: As bases biológicas da compreensão humana. São Paulo, Brazil: Palas Athena.

Moretti, G. (2010). *La simulazione come strumento di produzione di conoscenza: comunitã di apprendimento e di pratica nei mondi virtuali.* (Unipublished doctoral thesis). Universidade de Lumsa, Roma, Italy.

Schlemmer, E. (1999). CAVI - Criando ambientes virtuais interativos. *Informática na Educação, Porto Alegre, 2*(2), 87–97.

Schlemmer, E., & Lopes, D. Q. (2012). Redes sociais digitais, socialidade e MDV3D: Uma perspectiva da tecnologia-conceito ECODI para a educação online. In P. L. Torres, & P. R. Wagner (Eds.), Redes sociais e educação: Desafios contemporâneos (pp. 1-15). Porto Alegre, Brazil: EDIPUCRS.

Trein, D. (2010). *Educação online em metaverso: A mediação pedagógica por meio da telepresença e da presença digital virtual via avatar em mundos digitais virtuais em 3 dimensões.* (Unpublished master's dissertation). Universidade do Vale do Rio dos Sinos, São Leopoldo, Brazil.

Varela, F. J. (2005). Conocer: Las ciencias cognitivas: Tendencias y perspectivas: Cartografia de las ideas actuales. Barcelona: Gedisa Editorial.

KEY TERMS AND DEFINITIONS

Culture of Real Virtuality: According Castells (2003) the cultures consist of processes and communication that, once being based communication signals, no more separation between 'reality' and symbolic representation. It is important to highlight that human relations, increasingly, are given in a multimedia environment, whose impacts are still being studied.

Digital Education Research Group UNISINOS/CNPq: The Digital Education Research Group - GPE-dU UNISINOS / CNPq - is linked to the research line "Education, Development and Technology" of the Post-Graduate Education UNISINOS. The primary subject field of research developed by GPE-dU is the Digital Culture and Education, both in school and non-school contexts. Conducts research in the field of training / human capacity in relation to the cognitive and socio-cognitive; and research in the field of socio-cultural development and the processes of schooling in the context of emerging digital culture.

Digital Virtual Collaborating Spaces: Digital Virtual Collaborating Spaces comprise: 1) different digital technologies integrated such as virtual learning environments, 3D Digital Virtual Worlds, Web 2.0 technologies, conversational agents (created and programmed for interaction), among others, to encourage different forms of communication (textual, oral, graphical and gestural); 2) flow of communication and interaction among individuals in this space, and 3) flow of interaction between individuals and the environment, i.e. the technological space. A Digital Virtual Collaborating Space assumes fundamentally a type of interaction that enables "e-inhabitants" (according to their ontogeny) of this space, set it collaboratively and cooperatively, through its "living and coexisting" (Schlemmer, 2010, p. 14).

Formation: For Maturana and Rezepka (2008) is the development of men and women as persons capable of being co-creator (with others) in a desirable human space of social life.

Gamification: it is the use of elements from game design in contexts different from games. In other words, gamification analyzes the fun elements present in a game design to adapt for applications usually not considered games.

Hybrid and Multimedia Collaborating Spaces: they are the imbrication of Digital Virtual Collaborating Spaces with perspective of games, gamification, Mixed Reality, Augmented Reality, and the inclusion of technologies like Kinect, Leap Motion, Rift glasses, among others. Considering multimediality (mobile learning, ubiquitous learning, immersive Learning, gamification learning e physical face-to-face modality).

Immersive Learning: The social presence of the subject-avatar (virtual digital identity), and that inhabit and co-inhabit these spaces, which enables them to have access to information and mechanisms of action and interaction (through the combined textual, oral, gestural and graphic language) for the expansion of knowledge as well as their relationship with the methods, based on a systemic-constructivist-interactionist epistemological concept, possible by means of problem-solving teaching and pedagogical practices.

ENDNOTES

1   As mentioned in Chapter 3: Metaverse, 3D Digital Virtual Worlds

2   The research "Ambiente de Realidade Virtual Cooperativo de Aprendizagem - ARCA" (Cooperative Virtual Reality Learning Environment), (1999-2002), developed by Universidade Federal do Rio Grande do Sul, Universidade Luterana do Brasil and

Universidade Católica de Pelotas, aimed to develop a learning and teaching environment capable of helping with a differentiated pedagogical practice, giving conditions for meaningful learning in a cooperative Virtual Reality environment. Metaverso Eduverse was the one chosen for that purpose. The results achieved showed that: the 3D virtual environment, either immersive or not, can provide more meaningful learning, making the approach of complex themes easy, and assuring empowerment of social relations with the use of avatars and other graphic objects. However, in order to build up such learning environments both interdisciplinary knowledge and praxis are needed. (Project Arca, 2002, available at http://www.pgie. ufrgs.br/projetos/arca/).

[3] Concept-technology is approached in detail in Chapter 12 - Digital Virtual Sharing Space

[4] The pedagogical practice of learning projects based in problems is defined in Chapter 9 - Online Education in Metaverse: novelty or innovation?

[5] RICESU http://www.ricesu.com.br is a Catholic Network of Higher Education Institutions that groups together 14 Catholic Higher Education Institutions all over Brazil.

[6] Leap Motion is a motion detector device that allows one to interact with a computer through gestures.

[7] Rift glasses are glasses for virtual reality, with a head-mounted display system with built-in motion detectors and LCD screen. It presents 3D images that move as the user's head turns.

Compilation of References

Almeida, M. E. B. (2009). Gestão de tecnologias, mídias e recursos na escola: O compartilhar de significados. *Em Aberto, 22*, 75–89.

Argyris, C., & Schön, D. (1996). *A aprendizagem organizacional II: Teoria, método e prática*. Reading, MA: Addison-Wesley.

Backes, L. (2007). *A formação do educador em mundos virtuais: Uma investigação sobre os processos de autonomia e de autoria*. (Unipublished master's dissertation). Universidade do Vale do Rio dos Sinos, São Leopoldo, Brazil.

Backes, L. (2010). A cultura emergente na convivência em MDV3D. *Conjectura: Filosofia e Educação (UCS), 15*, 99-117.

Backes, L. (2011). *A configuração do espaço de convivência digital virtual: A cultura emergente no processo de formação do educador*. (Unipublished doctoral thesis). Universidade do Vale do Rio dos Sinos, São Leopoldo, Brazil and Université Lumière Lyon 2, Lyon, France.

Backes, L. (2012) Metodologias, práticas e mediação pedagógica em metaverso. In E. Schlemmer, P. Malizia, L. Backes, & G. Moretti (Eds.), Comunidades de aprendizagem e de prática em metaverso (pp. 179-202). São Paulo, Brazil: Editora Cortez.

Backes, L. (2013). Espaço de convivência digital virtual (ECODI): O acoplamento estrutural no processo de interação. ETD - Educação Temática Digital, 15, 337-355.

Backes, L. (2013). Hibridismo tecnológico digital: Configuração dos espaços digitais virtuais de convivência. In Proceedings of III Colóqui Luso-Brasileiro de Educação a Distância e E-Learning (pp. 1–18). Lisboa: Universidade Aberta.

Backes, L., & Schlemmer, E. (2006). Aprendizagem em mundos virtuais: Espaço deconvivência na formação do educador. In *Proceedings of VI Seminário de Pesquisa em Educação da Região Sul – ANPEDSul* (pp. 1-6). Santa Maria, Brazil: ANPEDSul. Retrieved from http://www.portalanpedsul.com.br/admin/uploads/2006/Educacao,_Comunicacao_e_tecnologia/Painel/12_56_53_PA570.pdf

Backes, L., & Schlemmer, E. (2008). A configuração do espaço digital virtual de convivência na formação do educador em mundos virtuais. In Proceedings of 14° Congresso Internacional ABED de Educação a Distância (vol. 1, pp. 1-11). São Paulo, Brazil: ABED.

Backes, L., & Schlemmer, E. (2010). As Aprendizagens nos processos de formação de educadores em metaversos para emancipação digital. In *Proceedings of XXIX International Congress of the Latin American Studies Association* (pp. 1-18). Toronto, Canada: Associação de Estudos Latino-Americanos – LASA.

Backes, L. et al. (2006). As relações dialéticas numa Comunidade Virtual de Aprendizagem. *UNIrevista, 1*, 1–12.

Becker, F. (2008). Aprendizagem – concepções contraditórias. *Schème: Revista Eletrônica de Psicologia e Epistemologia Genéticas, 1* (1), 53-73. Retrieved from http://www2.marilia.unesp.br/revistas/index.php/scheme/article/view/552

Becker, F. (2003). *A origem do conhecimento e a aprendizagem escolar*. Porto Alegre, Brazil: *The Art of Medication*.

Belloni, M. L. (2009). Educação a distância. Campinas, Brazil: Autores Associados.

Benford, S., et al. (1993). From rooms to cyberspace: models of interaction in large virtual computer spaces. Nottingham, UK: University Park Nottingham.

Brown, E., & Cairns, P. (2004). A grounded investigation of game immersion. In Proceedings of CHI 2004 (pp. 1279–1300). New York, NY: ACM Press.

Camilleri, J. A., & Falk, J. (1992). *The end of sovereignty. The politics of a shrinking and fragmenting world.* Aldershot, UK: Edward Elgar.

Canclini, N. G. (2006). Culturas híbridas. São Paulo, Brazil: Edusp.

Cantoni, R. C. A. (2001). *Realidade virtual: Uma história de imersão interativa.* (Unpublished master's dissertation). Pontifícia Universidade Católica de São Paulo, São Paulo, Brazil.

Capra, F. (2002). As conexões ocultas: Ciência para uma vida sustentável. São Paulo, Brazil: Cultrix.

Capra, F. (2004). A teia da vida: Uma nova compreensão científica dos sistemas vivos. São Paulo, Brazil: Cultrix.

Castells, M. (1999). A sociedade em rede. São Paulo, Brazil: Paz e Terra.

Castells, M. (2003). A galáxia da internet: Reflexões sobre a internet, os negócios e a sociedade. Rio de Janeiro, Brazil: Zahar.

Castells, M. (2003). A sociedade em rede. São Paulo, Brazil: Paz e Terra.

Castells, M. (2013). Redes de indignação e esperança: Movimentos sociais na era da internet. Rio de Janeiro, Brazil: Zahar.

Castronova, E. (2005). *Synthetic worlds.* Chicago, IL: University of Chicago Press.

Ceconi, R. (2008). *A interação em mundos virtuais digital 3D: Uma investigação sobre a representação da emoção no aprendizado.* (Unipublished master's dissertation). Universidade do Vale do Rio dos Sinos, São Leopoldo, Brazil.

Chuche, D. (1999). A noção de cultura nas ciências sociais. Bauru, Brazil: EDUSC.

Cogo, D. M. (2006). Mídia, interculturalidade e migrações contemporâneas. Rio de Janeiro, Brazil: E-papers Serviços Editoriais Ltda.

Corrêa, E. S. (2009). Cibercultura: Um novo saber ou uma nova vivência? In E. Trivinho, & E. Cazeloto (Eds.), *A cibercultura e seu espelho [recurso eletrônico]: Campo de conhecimento emergente e nova vivência humana na era da imersão interativa* (pp. 47-51). São Paulo, Brazil: ABCiber; Instituto Itaú Cultural. Retrieved from http://abciber.com/publicacoes/livro1/a_cibercultura_e_seu_espelho.pdf

Costa, R. C. A. (2008). Interação em mundos digitais virtuais: uma investigação sobre a representação do emocionar na aprendizagem. (Unpublished master's dissertation). Universidade do Vale do Rio dos Sinos, São Leopoldo, Brazil.

Csíkszentmihályi, M. (1990). *Flow: The psychology of optimal experience.* New York, NY: Harper Perennial.

Cuche, D. (1999). A noção de cultura nas ciências sociais. Bauru, Brazil: EDUSC.

Daniel, B., Schwier, R. A., & Mccalla, G. (2003). Social capital in virtual learning communities and distributed communities of practice. *Canadian Journal of Learning and Technology, 29*(3), 113–139.

De Marchi, A. C. B., & Costa, A. C. da R. (2006). CVmuzar – Um ambiente de suporte a comunidades virtuais para apoio à aprendizagem em museus. *Revista Brasileira de Informática na Educação, 14*(3), 9–26.

Deleuze, G., & Guattari, F. (1980). *Capitalisme et schizophrénie 2: Mille plateaux.* Paris: Les Editions de Minuit.

Dias, P. (2001). Comunidades de Aprendizagem na Web. *INOVAÇÃO, 14*(3), 27–44.

Domingues, D. (2003). Arte, vida, ciência e criatividade com as tecnologias numéricas. In D. Domingues (Ed.), *Arte e vida no século XXI: Tecnologia, ciência e criatividade* (pp. 11-14). São Paulo, Brazil: Editora UNESP. Retrieved April 20, 2007, from http://artecno.ucs.br/livros_textos/textos_site_artecno/3_capitulo_livros/diana2003_artevidaxxi_cap.rtf

Durkheim, E. (1895). *The rules of sociological method.* New York: The Free Press.

Fagundes, L. da C., Sato, L. S., & Maçada, D. L. (1999). Projeto? O que é? Como se faz? In L. da C. Fagundes (Ed.), *Aprendizes do futuro: As inovações começaram!* (pp. 15-26). Brasília, Brazil: MEC. Retrieved from http://www.dominiopublico.gov.br/download/texto/me003153.pdf

Fichtner, B. (2010). *Introdução na abordagem histórico-cultural de Vygotsky e seus Colaboradores.* São Paulo, Brazil: USP. Retrieved from http://www3.fe.usp.br/secoes/inst/novo/agenda_eventos/docente / PDF_SWF/226Reader%20Vygotskij.pdf

Figueiredo, A. D., & Afonso, A. P. (2006). *Managing Learning in Virtual Settings: The role of context.* Coimbra: Universidade de Coimbra.

Firmino, R. J., & Silva, F. D. A. (2010). Desterritorialização e mídia: Um ensaio. Fórum Patrimônio: Ambiente Construído e Patrimônio Sustentável (UFMG. Online), 3, 1-12. Retrieved from http://www.forumpatrimonio.com.br/view_full.php?articleID=158&modo=1

Franco, S. R. K. (1999). Piaget e a dialética. In F. Becker, & S. R. K. Franco (Eds.), Revisitando Piaget (pp. 9-20). Porto Alegre, Brazil: Mediação.

Frank, C. O. (2012). *Aprendizagem da língua espanhola por meio das tecnologias digitais.* (Unpublished master's dissertation). Centro Universitário La Salle, Canoas, Brazil.

Freire, P. (1996). Pedagogia da autonomia: Saberes necessários à prática educativa. São Paulo, Brazil: Paz e Terra.

Freire, P. (2007). Educação e mudança. Rio de Janeiro, Brazil: Paz e Terra.

Freire, P. (2008). Conscientização: Teoria e prática da libertação: Uma introdução ao pensamento de Paulo Freire. São Paulo, Brazil: Centauro.

Freire, P., & Shor, I. (1992). *Medo e ousadia: Cotidiano do professor.* Rio de Janeiro, Brazil: Paz e Terra.

Freitas, J. J. C. (2012). *O desenvolvimento de habilidades de liderança em mundos virtuais tridimensionais: O Caso do metaverso Second Life.* (Unpublished master's dissertation). Universidade do Vale do Rio dos Sinos, São Leopoldo, Brazil.

Galimberti, C., Ignazi, S., Vercesi, P., & Riva, G. (2001). Communication and cooperation in Networked environments: An experimental analysis. *Cyberpsychology & Behavior, 4*(1), 131–146. doi:10.1089/10949310151088514 PMID:11709902

Gibson, W. (1984). Neuromancer. New York, NY: Ace.

Giddens, A. (1991). As conseqüências da modernidade. São Paulo, Brazil: Unesp.

Gomes, A. C. (2012). *O desenvolvimento de competências para o trabalho em equipe distância usando metaverso Second Life.* (Unipublished master's dissertation). Universidade do Vale do Rio dos Sinos, São Leopoldo, Brazil.

Gonseth, F. (1948). Les conceptions mathématiques et le réel. In *Proceedings of Symposium de l'Institut International des Sciences théoriques.* Bruxelles: Les sciences et leréel.

Hayles, N. K. (1999). Simulando narrativas: Que criaturas virtuais podem nos ensinar. *Investigação Crítica, 26* (1), 1-26.

Hegel, G. W. (1955). *Lectures on the history of philosophy.* Humanities.

Howe, N., & Strauss, W. (2000). *Millennials Rising: The Next Great Generation.* New York, NY: Vintage Books.

Hu, O. R. Tsan. (2006). *Contribuições ao desenvolvimento de um sistema de telepresença por meio da aquisição, transmissão e projeção em ambientes imersivos de vídeos panorâmicos.* (Unpublished doctoral thesis). Universidade de São Paulo, São Paulo, Brazil. Retrieved from http://www.teses.usp.br/teses/disponiveis/3/3142/tde-19092006-134926/

Kadirire, J. (2009). Mobile learning demystified. In *R. Guy (Ed.), The evolution of mobile teaching and learning* (pp. 103–118). Santa Rosa, CA: Informing Science Press.

Kant, I. (1983). Crítica da razão pura: Os pensadores. São Paulo, Brazil: Abril Cultural.

Kenneth, J. G. (2002). The challenge of absent presence. In J. E. Katz, & M. Aakhus (Eds.), Perpetual contact: Mobile communication, private talk, public performance (pp. 227-241). New York, NY: Cambridge University Press.

Klastrup, L. (2003). A poetics of virtual worlds. In *Proceedings of Melbourne DAC2003* (pp. 100-109). Melbourne, Australia: DIAC. Retrieved from http://hypertext.rmit.edu.au/dac/papers/

Koenig, S. (1967). Elementos de sociologia. Rio de Janeiro, Brazil: Zahar.

Latour, B. (1994). Jamais fomos modernos. São Paulo, Brazil: Editora 34.

Latour, B. (1999). On recalling ANT. In J. Law & J. Hassard (Eds.), *Actor-network theory and after* (pp. 15–25). Oxford, UK: Blakcwell Publishers.

Laux, L. C. P. D., & Schlemmer, E. (2011). Anatomia no metaverso Second Life: Colaboração e cooperação interdisciplinar e interinstituicional. In *Proceedings of VII Congresso Internacional de Educação* (pp. 1-13). São Leopoldo, Brazil: Casa Leiria.

Lemos, A. (1997). Anjos interativos e retribalização do mundo: sobre interatividade e interfaces digitais. In *Proceedings of Lisboa: Tendências XXI* (pp. 19-29). Lisboa: Associação Portuguesa para o Desenvolvimento das Comunicações. Retrieved from http://www.facom.ufba.br/ciberpesquisa/lemos/interativo.pdf

Lemos, A. (2002). Cibercultura: Tecnologia e vida social na cultura contemporânea. Porto Alegre, Brazil: Sulina.

Lemos, A. (2007). Cidade digital: Portais, inclusão e redes no Brasil. Salvador, Brazil: Edufba.

Lévy, P. (1993). As tecnologias da inteligência: O futuro do pensamento na era da informática. Rio de Janeiro, Brazil: Editora 34.

Lévy, P. (1996). O que é virtual?. São Paulo, Brazil: Editora 34.

Lévy, P. (1999). Cibercultura. Rio de Janeiro, Brazil: Editora 34.

Lévy, P. (1999). Cibercultura. São Paulo, Brazil: Editora 34.

Lévy, P. (2010). A inteligência coletiva: para uma antropologia do ciberespaço. Rio de Janeiro, Brazil: Editora 34.

Lévy, P. (2010). As tecnologias da inteligência: O futuro do pensamento na era da informática. Rio de Janeiro, Brazil: Editora 34.

Lévy, P. (2010). Cibercultura. Rio de Janeiro, Brazil: Editora 34.

Lévy, P. (2010a). As tecnologias da inteligência: O futuro do pensamento na era da informática. Rio de Janeiro, Brazil: Editora 34.

Lévy, P. (2010b). Cibercultura. Rio de Janeiro, Brazil: Editora 34.

Libâneo, J. C. (2003). A escola com que sonhamos é aquela que assegura a todos a formação cultural e científica para a vida pessoal, profissional e cidadã. In M. V. Costa (Ed.), A escola tem future (pp. 23-52). Rio de Janeiro, Brazil: DP&A.

Locatelli, E. L. (2010). *A construção de redes sociais no processo de formação docente em metaverso, no contexto do programa loyola*. (Unipublished master's dissertation). Universidade do Vale do Rio dos Sinos, São Leopoldo, Brazil.

Lombard, M., & Ditton, T. (1997). At the heart of it all: The concept of presence. *Journal of Computer Mediated-Communication, 3* (2). Retrieved from http://www.ascusc.org/jcmc/vol3/issue2/lombard.html

Machado, L. (2012). *Mundos virtuais tridimensionais como ambiente para o desenvolvimento de competência intercultura*. (Unpublished master's dissertation). Universidade do Vale do Rio dos Sinos, São Leopoldo, Brazil.

Machado, L., et al. (2013). O uso de mundos virtuais tridimensionais para o desenvolvimento de competência intercultural: Uma experiência entre Brasil e Portugal. In *Proceedings of XII Simpósio Brasileiro de Jogos e Entretenimento Digital* (pp. 38-49). São Paulo, Brazil: Industry Track. Retrieved from http://www.sbgames.org/sbgames2013/proceedings/industria/05-full-paper-indtrack.pdf

Maffesoli, M. (1998). O tempo das tribos: O declínio do individualismo nas sociedades de massa. Rio de Janeiro, Brazil: Forense Universitária.

Maffesoli, M. (2012). O tempo retorna: Formas elementares da pós-modernidade. Rio de Jenairo, Brazil: Forense Universitária.

Maffesoli, M. (1997). *Du nomadisme: Vagabondages initiatiques*. Paris: Livres de Poche.

Maffesoli, M. (2007). Tribalismo pós-moderno: Da identidade às identificações. *Ciências Sociais UNISINOS*, *43*(1), 97–102.

Maia, C., & Mattar, J. (2007). ABC da EaD. São Paulo, Brazil: Pearson Prentice.

Malizia, P. (2006). Comunic-a-zioni. Roma, Italy: Franco Angeli.

Malizia, P. (2012). Comunidades virtuais de aprendizagem e de prática. In E. Schlemmer et al. (Eds.), Comunidades de aprendizagem e de prática em metaverso (pp. 25-60). São Paulo, Brazil: Editora Cortez.

Mantovani, C., & Moura, M. A. (2012). Informação, interação e mobilidade. *Informação & Informação, 17*(2), 55-76. Retrieved from http://www.uel.br/revistas/uel/index.php/informacao/article/view/13764

Mattar, J. (2008). O uso do Second Life como ambiente virtual de aprendizagem. *Revista Fonte, 5*(8), 88-95. Retrieved from http://www.prodemge.gov.br/images/stories/volumes/volume8/ucp_joaomattar.pdf

Mattar, J. (2012). Tutoria e interação em educação a distância. São Paulo, Brazil: Cengage Learning.

Maturana, H. R. (1993). As bases biológicas do aprendizado. Belo Horizonte, Brazil: Ed. Primavera.

Maturana, H. R. (1997). A ontologia da realidade. Belo Horizonte, Brazil: Ed. UFMG.

Maturana, H. R. (1999). *Transformación em la convivência*. Santiado, Chile: Dólmen Ediciones.

Maturana, H. R. (2001). Cognição, ciência e vida cotidiana. Belo Horizonte, Brazil: Ed. UFMG.

Maturana, H. R. (2002). A ontologia da realidade. Belo Horizonte, Brazil: Ed. UFMG.

Maturana, H. R. (2004). Amar e brincar: Fundamentos esquecidos do humano. São Paulo, Brazil: Palas Athena.

Maturana, H. R. (2005). Emoções e linguagem na educação e na política. Belo Horizonte, Brazil: Ed. UFMG.

Maturana, H. R., & Dávia, X. Y. (2009). Habitar humano em seis ensaios de biologia-cultural. São Paulo, Brazil: Palas Athena.

Maturana, H. R., & de Rezepka, S. N. (2000). Formação humana e capacitação. Petrópolis, Brazil: Vozes.

Maturana, H. R., & Varela, F. J. (1997). De máquina e seres vivos: Autopoiese - a organização do vivo. Porto Alegre, Brazil: Artes Médicas.

Maturana, H. R., & Varela, F. J. (2001). A árvore do conhecimento: As bases biológicas da compreensão humana. São Paulo, Brazil: Palas Athena.

Maturana, H. R., & Verden-Zöller, G. (2008). A origem do humano. In H. R. Maturana, & S. N. Rezepka (Eds.), Formação humana e capacitação (pp. 59-75). Petrópolis, Brazil: Vozes.

Maturana, H. R., & Yáñez, X. D. (2009). Habitar humano em seis ensaios de biologia-cultural. São Paulo, Brazil: Palas Athena.

Maturana, R. M., & Verden-Zöller, G. (2004). Amar e brincar – Fundamentos esquecidos do humano. São Paulo, Brazil: Palas Athena.

Maturana, H. R. (1980). *Autopoiesi and cognition - The realization of the living*. Boston: D. Reidel Publishing Company. doi:10.1007/978-94-009-8947-4

Maturana, H. R. (1992). Conhecer o conhecer. *Ciência Hoje, 14*(184), 44–49.

Maturana, H. R. (1993a). Uma nova concepção de aprendizagem. *Dois Pontos, 2*(15), 28–35.

Medina, A. R., & Domínguez, C. D. (2005). La formación del Profesorado ante los nuevos retos de La interculturalidad. In A. R. Medina et al. (Eds.), *Interculturalidad: Formación del profesorado y educación*. Madrid: Pearson.

Menegoto, D. B. (2006). *Práticas pedagógicas on line: Os processos de ensinar e de aprender utilizando o ava-unisinos*. (Unpublished master's dissertation). Universidade do Vale do Rio dos Sinos, São Leopoldo, Brazil.

Minsky, M. (1980, June). Telepresence. *Omni*, 45-51.

Moraes, M. C. (2003). Educar na biologia do amor e da solidariedade. Petrópolis, Brazil: Vozes.

Moraes, M. C. (2004). O paradigma educacional emergente. Campinas, Brazil: Papirus.

Moretti, G. (2009). Mundos digitais virtuais em 3D e aprendizagem organizacional: uma relação possível e produtiva. In *Proceedings of IV Congreso de La CiberSociedad*. Espanha: Crisis Analógica, Futuro Digital. Retrieved from http://www.cibersociedadnet/congres2009/es/coms/mundos-digitais-virtuais-em-3d-e-aprendizagem-organizacional-uma-relasao-possivel-e-produtiva/644

Moretti, G. (2009). Sistema i impresa. Roma, Italy: Polimata.

Moretti, G. (2010). *La simulazione come strumento di produzione di conescenza: Comunità di apprendimento e di pratica nei mondi virtuali*. (Unpublished doctoral thesis). Libera Università Maria Ss. Assunta, Roma, Italy.

Moretti, G. (2010). *La simulazione come strumento di produzione di conoscenza: Comunità di apprendimento e di pratica nei mondi virtuali*. (Unpublished doctoral thesis). Universidade de LUMSA, Roma, Italy.

Moretti, G. (2012). Comunidades virtuais de aprendizagem e de prática em metaverso. In E. Schlemmer et al. (Eds.), Comunidades de aprendizagem e de prática em metaverso (pp. 127-178). São Paulo, Brazil: Editora Cortez.

Morin, E. (2011). Introdução ao pensamento complexo. Porto Alegre, Brazil: Sulina.

Murray, J. H. (2003). Hamlet no holodeck. São Paulo, Brazil: Itaú Cultural.

Murray, J. (1997). *Hamlet on the holodeck: The future of narrative in cyberspace*. Cambridge, MA: The MIT Press.

Negroponte, N. (2006). A vida digital. São Paulo, Brazil: Companhia das Letras.

Nonaka, I. T. (1998). The knowledge creating company: Creare le dinamiche dell'innovazione. Milano, Italy: Guerini e Associati. doi:10.1016/B978-0-7506-7009-8.50016-1

Okada, A. (2004). A mediação pedagógica e tecnologias de comunicação e informação: um caminho para a inclusão digital? *Revista da FAEEBA - Educação e Novas Tecnologias, 22*(13), 327-341. Retrieved from http://people.kmi.open.ac.uk/ale/journals/r03faeba2004.pdf

Okada, A., & Okada, S. (2007). Novos paradigmas na educação online com a aprendizagem aberta. In *Proceedings of V Conferência Internacional de Tecnologias de Informação e Comunicação na Educação - Challenges* (pp. 1-12). Braga, Portugal: Universidade do Minho. Retrieved from http://people.kmi.open.ac.uk/ale/papers/a10challenges2007.pdf

Ondrejka, C. (2008). Education unleashed: Participatory culture, education, and innovation in Second Life. In K. Salen (Ed.), *The ecology of games: Connecting youth, games, and learning* (pp. 229–252). Cambridge, MA: MIT Press.

Palloff, R. M., & Pratt, K. (2002). Construindo comunidades de aprendizagem no ciberespaço: Estratégias eficientes para a sala de aula on-line. Porto Alegre, Brazil. *The Art of Medication*.

Paloff, R. M., & Pratt, K. (1999). *Building learning communities in cyberspace – Effective strategies for the online classroom*. São Francisco, CA: Jossey-Bass Publishers.

Papert, S. (1988). Logo: Computador e educação. São Paulo, Brazil: Editora Brasiliense S.A.

Parrat, S., & Tryphon, A. (1998). Jean Piaget: Sobre a pedagogia: Textos inéditos. São Paulo, Brazil: Casa do Psicólogo.

Peresson, M. L. (2006). Pedagogias e culturas. In C.C. S. Scarlatelle, D. R. Streck, & J. I. Follmann (Eds.), Religião, cultura e educação (pp. 57-107). São Leopoldo, Brazil: Ed. Unisinos.

Pérez Goméz, A. I. (2001). A cultura escolar na sociedade neoliberal. Porto Alegre, Brazil: ARTMED Editora.

Piaget, J. (1973). Estudos sociológicos. Rio de Janeiro, Brazil: Companhia Editora Forense.

Piaget, J. (1978). Fazer e compreender. São Paulo, Brazil: Melhoramentos.

Piaget, J. (1987). O nascimento da inteligência na criança (4th ed.). Rio de Janeiro, Brazil: Guanabara.

Piaget, J. (1995). Abstração reflexionante: Relações lógico-aritméticas e ordem das relações espaciais. Porto Alegre, Brazil: Artes Médicas.

Piaget, J., & Inhelder, B. (1993). A psicologia da criança. Rio de Janeiro, Brazil: Ed. Bertrand Brasil.

Piaget, J., & Inhelder, B. (1993). A representação do espaço na criança. Porto Alegre, Brazil: Artes Médicas.

Piaget, J. (1972). Development and learning. In C. S. Lavatelly & F. Stendler (Eds.), *Reading in child behavior and development* (pp. 7–20). New York, NY: Hartcourt Brace Janovich.

Piaget, J., & Garcia, R. (1998). *Psicogênese e história das ciências*. Lisboa: Publicações Dom Quixote.

Pinheiro, L. V., & Silva, E. L. (2008). As redes cognitivas na ciência da informação brasileira: Um estudo nos artigos científicos publicados nos periódicos da área. *Ci. Inf.*, *37*(3), 38–50. doi:10.1590/S0100-19652008000300003

Prensky, M. (2001). Digital Natives, Digital Immigrants. *Horizon*, *9*(5), 1–6. doi:10.1108/10748120110424816

Primo, A. (2000). Uma análise sistêmica da interação mediada por computador. Informática na Educação: Teoria & Prática/Programa de Pós-Graduação em Informática na Educação, 3(1), 73-84.

Primo, A. F. T. (1998). Interação mútua e interação reativa: Uma proposta de estudo. In *Proceedings of Intercom 1998 - XXI Congresso Brasileiro de Ciências da Comunicação*. Rio de Janeiro, Brazil: Anais.

Primo, A. F. T. (1999). Interfaces potencial e virtual. *Revista da Famecos*, (10), 94-103. Retrieved from http://usr.psico.ufrgs.br/~aprimo/pb/interfa2.htm

Primo, A. F. T. (2000). Interação mútua e reativa: Uma proposta de estudo. Revista da Famecos, (12), 81-92.

Primo, A. F. T. (2005). Enfoques e desfoques no estudo da interação mediada por computador. In *Proceedings of Intercom 2003 - XXVI Congresso Brasileiro de Ciências da Comunicação*. Retrieved from http://www.facom.ufba.br/ciberpesquisa/404nOtF0und/404_45.htm

Primo, A. F. T. (2005). Seria a multimídia realmente interativa? *Revista da Famecos,* (6), 92-95.

Primo, A. F. T., & Cassol, M. B. F. (1999). Explorando o conceito de interatividade: Definições e taxonomias. *Informática na Educação: Teoria e Prática*, *2*(2), 65–80.

Quéau, P. (1993). O tempo do virtual. In A. Parente (Ed.), Imagem máquina (pp. 91-99). Rio de Janeiro, Brazil: Editora 34.

Rabardel, P. (1995). *Les hommes e les technologies: approche cognitive des instruments contemporains*. Paris: Armand Colin Editeur.

Rabardel, P. (1999). Le language comme instrument? Eléments pour une théorie instrumentale élargie. In Y. Clot (Ed.), *Avec Vygotsky* (pp. 241–265). Paris: La Dispute.

Raleiras, M. (2007). Recensão da obra "A vida no écrã. A identidade na era da internet", de Sherry Turkle [1997]. Sísifo. *Revista de Ciências da Educação*, *3*, 113–116.

Rheingold, H. (1993). *The virtual community: Homesteading at the electronic frontier*. Cambridge, MA: Addison-Wesley Publishing Company. Retrieved from http://www.rheingold.com/vc/book

Rheingold, H. (2002). *Smart mobs: The next social revolution*. Cambridge, MA: Perseus Publishing.

Rios, T. A. (2002). Competência ou competências – O novo e o original na formação de professores. In D. E. Rosa, V. C. Sousa, & D. Feldman (Eds.), Didáticas e práticas de ensino: Interfaces com diferentes saberes e lugares formatives (pp. 154-172). Rio de Janeiro, Brazil: DP&A.

Rymaszewski, M., et al. (2007). Second Life: O guia oficial. Rio de Janeiro, Brazil: Ediouro.

Saccol, A. Z., Schlemmer, E., & Barbosa, J. L. V. (2010). M-learning e u-learning: Novas perspectivas da aprendizagem móvel e ubíqua. São Paulo, Brazil: Pearson Education.

Santaella, L. (2008). A ecologia pluralista das mídias locativas. *Revista Famecos*, (37), 20-24. Retrieved from http://revistaseletronicas.pucrs.br/ojs/index.php/revista-famecos/article/view/4795

Santos, M. (1980). Por uma geografia nova: da crítica da geografia a uma geografia crítica. São Paulo, Brazil: Editora HUCITEC.

Santos, M. (2008). Metarmofoses do espaço habitado: Fundamentos teóricos e metodológicos da geografia. São Paulo, Brazil: Edusp.

Santos, M. (2006). *A natureza do espaço: Técnica e tempo, razão e emoção.* São Paulo, Brazil: Editora da Universidade de São Paulo.

Santos, M. (2008). *Metarmofoses do espaço habitado: Fundamentos teóricos e metodológicos da geografia.* São Paulo, Brazil: Edusp.

Schlemmer, E. (1998). *A representação do espaço cibernético pela criança, na utilização de um ambiente virtual.* (Unpublished master's dissertation). Universidade Federal do Rio Grande do Sul, Porto Alegre, Brazil.

Schlemmer, E. (2001). Projetos de aprendizagem baseados em problemas: Uma metodologia interacionista/construtivista para formação de comunidades em ambientes virtuais de aprendizagem. *Colabor@, 1*(2), 10-19. Retrieved from http://pead.ucpel.tche.br/revistas/index.php/colabora/article/viewFile/17/15

Schlemmer, E. (2002). *AVA: Um ambiente de convivência interacionista sistêmico para comunidades virtuais na cultura da aprendizagem.* (Unpublished doctoral thesis). Universidade Federal do Rio Grande do Sul, Porto Alegre, Brazil.

Schlemmer, E. (2004). Sócio-cognição em ambientes virtuais de aprendizagem. In Proceedings of XII ENDIPE: Conhecimento local e conhecimento universal. Curitiba, Brazil: Anais.

Schlemmer, E. (2005). Metodologias para educação a distância no contexto da formação de comunidades virtuais de aprendizagem. In R. M. Barbosa (Ed.), Ambientes virtuais de aprendizagem (pp. 29-50). Porto Alegre, Brazil: Artmed Editora.

Schlemmer, E. (2008). ECODI - A criação de espaços de convivência digital virtual no contexto dos processos de ensino e aprendizagem em metaverso. *Caderno IHU Idéias, 6*(103), 1-31.

Schlemmer, E. (2009). *Espaço de convivência digital virtual – ECODI RICESU* (Research Report). São Leopoldo: Universidade do Vale do Rio dos Sinos.

Schlemmer, E. (2010). Dos ambientes virtuais de aprendizagem aos espaços de convivência digitais virtuais – ECODIS: O que se mantém? O que se modificou? In C. B. Valenti, & E. M. Sacramento (Eds.), Aprendizagem em ambientes virtuais: Compartilhando ideias e construindo cenários (pp. 145-191). Caxias do Sul, Brazil: Educs.

Schlemmer, E. (2010). ECODI-RICESU formação/capacitação/ação pedagógica em rede utilizando a tecnologia de metaverso. In Proceedings of XV ENDIPE Encontro Nacional de Didática e Prática de Ensino (pp. 1-13). Belo Horizonte, Brazil: Editora da Universidade Federal de Minas Gerais.

Schlemmer, E. (2012). A aprendizagem por meio de comunidades virtuais na prática. In F. M. Litto, & M. Formiga (Eds.), Educação a distância: O estado da arte (pp. 265-279). São Paulo, Brazil: Pearson Educational do Brasil.

Schlemmer, E. (2013). O trabalho do professor e as novas tecnologias. In M. J. Fuhr (Ed.), Sob a espada de dâmocles: Relação dos professores com a docência e ambiente de trabalho no ensino privado (pp. 98-115). Porto Alegre, Brazil: Carta Editora.

Schlemmer, E. (2013a). *Espaço de convivência digital virtual nos programas de pós-graduação (stricto sensu) ecodi-ppgs unisinos: Uma proposta para a formação de pesquisadores* (Research Report). São Leopoldo: Universidade do Vale do Rio dos Sinos.

Schlemmer, E. (2013b). *Anatomia no metaverso Second Life: Uma proposta em i-Learning* (Research Report). São Leopoldo: Universidade do Vale do Rio dos Sinos.

Schlemmer, E., & Backes, L. (2008). Metaversos: Novos espaços para construção do conhecimento. *Revista Diálogo Educacional (PUCPR), 8,* 519-532.

Schlemmer, E., & Lopes, D. de Q. (2012b). A tecnologia-conceito ECODI: Uma perspectiva de inovação para as práticas pedagógicas e a formação universitária. In *Proceedings of VII Congresso Iberoamericano de Docência Universitária: Vol 1: Ensino Superior: Inovação e qualidade na docência* (pp. 304-318). Porto: CIIE Centro de Investigação e Intervenção Educativas.

Schlemmer, E., & Lopes, D. de Q. (2013). *Educação e cultura digital.* São Leopoldo, Brazil: Editora UNISINOS.

Schlemmer, E., & Lopes, D. de Q. (in press). Ambientes 3D e educação In Tecnologias e mídias na educação presencial e a distância. Rio de Janeiro, Brazil: Editora LTC.

Schlemmer, E., & Lopes, D. Q. (2012). Redes sociais digitais, socialidade e MDV3D: Uma perspectiva da tecnologia-conceito ECODI para a educação online. In P. L. Torres, & P. R. Wagner (Eds.), Redes sociais e educação: Desafios contemporâneos (pp. 1-15). Porto Alegre, Brazil: EDIPUCRS.

Schlemmer, E., & Marson, F. P. (2013). Immersive learning: Metaversos e jogos digitais na educação. In Proceedings of 8ª Conferência Ibérica de Sistemas e Tecnologias de Informação. Lisboa: Anais.

Schlemmer, E., & Trein, D. (2008). Criação de identidades digitais virtuais para interação em mundos digitais virtuais em 3D. In *Proceedings of Congresso Internacional de EaD–ABED* (pp. 1-11). Retrieved from http://www.abed.org.br/congresso2008/tc/515200815252PM.pdf

Schlemmer, E., & Trein, D. (2009). Espaço de convivência digital virtual (ECODI) ricesu: Uma experiência em rede com a tecnologia de metaverso Second Life. In Proceedings of 15° Congresso Internacional ABED de Educação a Distância (pp. 1-12). Fortaleza, Brazil: Anais.

Schlemmer, E., & Trein, D. (2009). Web 2.0-context learning projects: Possibilities for the teaching practice. In *Proceedings of World Conference on Educational Multimedia, Hypermedia & Telecommunications.* Honolulu, HI: EDMEDIA. Retrieved from https://www.aace.org/conf/edmedia

Schlemmer, E., et al. (2002). Princípios e pressupostos norteados para a construção de uma nova graduação. São Leopoldo, Brazil: Universidade do Vale do Rio dos Sinos – UNISINOS.

Schlemmer, E., et al. (2004). AWSINOS: Construção de um mundo virtual. In *Proceedings ofVIII Congresso Ibero-Americano de Gráfica Digital: SIGRADI* (pp. 110-113). São Leopoldo, Brazil: Anais.

Schlemmer, E., et al. (2006). ECoDI: A criação de um espaço de convivências digital virtual. In *Proceedings of XVII Simpósio Brasileiro de Informática na Educação* (pp. 467-477). Brasília, Brazil: UNB/UCB. Retrieved from http://br-ie.org/pub/index.php/sbie/article/viewFile/507/493

Schlemmer, E., Malizia, P., Backes, L., & Moretti, G. (2012). Comunidades de aprendizagem e de prática em metaverso. São Paulo, Brazil: Cortez.

Schlemmer, E., Mallmann, M. T., & Daudt, S. I. D. (2000). Virtual learning environment: An interdisciplinary experience. In *Proceedings of WEBNET 2000 World Conference on the WWW and Internet* (pp. 134-201). San Antônio, TX: Webnet Journal Internet Tecnologies, Applications & Issues.

Schlemmer, E., Menegotto, D. B., & Backes, L. (2005). Uma nova forma de pensamento na utilização e na construção de mundos virtuais para uma educação on line autônoma e cooperativa. In *Proceedings ofIV Congresso Internacional de Educação: A Educação nas Fronteiras do Humano.* São Leopoldo, Brazil: Anais.

Schlemmer, E., Saccol, A. Z., Barbosa, J., & Reinhard, N. (2007). M-learning ou aprendizagem com mobilidade: Casos no contexto brasileiro. In Proceedings of 13o. Congresso Internacional da ABED (pp. 1-10). São Paulo, Brazil: ABED.

Schlemmer, E., Trein, D., & Oliveira, C. (2008). Metaverso: A telepresença em mundos digitais virtuais 3D por meio do uso de avatares. In Proceedings of SBIE (pp. 441 - 450). Fortaleza, Brazil: Anais.

Schlemmer, E. (1999). CAVI - Criando ambientes virtuais interativos. *Informática na Educação, Porto Alegre, 2*(2), 87–97.

Schlemmer, E. (2001). Projetos de aprendizagem baseados em problemas: Uma metodologia interacionista/construtivista para formação de comunidades em ambientes virtuais de aprendizagem. *Colabor, 1*(2), 1–10.

Schlemmer, E. (2005). A aprendizagem com o uso das tecnologias digitais: Viver e conviver na virtualidade. *Série-Estudos, 0*(19), 103–126.

Schlemmer, E. (2006). O trabalho do professor e as novas tecnologias. *Textual, 1*(8), 33–42.

Schlemmer, E. (2009). *Telepresença*. Curitiba, Brazil: IESDE Brasil S.A.

Schlemmer, E. (2010). Formação de professores na modalidade online: Experiências e reflexões sobre a criação de Espaços de Convivência Digitais Virtuais ECODIs. *Em Aberto, 23*, 99–122.

Schlemmer, E., & Backes, L. (2008). Metaversos: Novos espaços para construção do conhecimento. *Revista Diálogo Educacional, 8*, 519–532.

Silva, F. D. A., & Firmino, R. J. (2009). Desterritorialização e mídia: Um ensaio. In *Forum patrimônio: Ambiente, construção e patrimônio, sustentabilidade* (pp. 1-17). Belo Horizonte, Brazil: Instituto Brasileiro de Desenvolvimento Sustentável. Retrieved from http://forumpatrimonio.com.br/seer/index.php/forum_patrimonio/article/view/22/21

Silva, M. (2001). Sala de aula interativa: A educação presencial e a distância em sintonia com a era digital e com a cidadania. *Boletim Técnico do Senac, 27*(2), 1-20. Retrieved from http://www.senac.br/informativo/BTS/272e.htm

Small, G., & Vorgan, G. (2008). iBrain: Surviving the technological alteration of the modern mind. New York, NY: HarperCollins Publishers.

Soares, L. H. (2010). *Complexidade e autopoiese no metaverso - Estratégias e cenários cognitivos* (Unpublished master's dissertation). Universidade Católica de Brasília, Brasília, Brazil.

Sousa Santos, B. (2004). Um discurso sobre as ciências. São Paulo, Brazil: Cortez.

Souza, R. R. (2000). *Aprendizagem colaborativa em comunidades virtuais*. (Unpublished master's dissertation). Universidade Federal de Santa Catarina, Florianópolis, Brazil.

Starobinski, J. (2002). Ação e reação: Vida e aventuras de um casal. Rio de Janeiro, Brazil: Civilização Brasileira.

Stephenson, N. (1992). *Snow crash*. New York: Bantam.

Steuer, J. (1992). Defining virtual reality: Dimensions determining telepresence. *Journal of Communication, 42*(4), 73–93. doi:10.1111/j.1460-2466.1992.tb00812.x

Tapley, R. (2008). Construindo o seu Second Life. Rio de Janeiro, Brazil: Alta Books.

Tönnies, F. (1995). Comunidade e sociedade. In F. Tönnies, & O. Miranda (Eds.), Para ler ferdinand tönnies. São Paulo, Brazil: Edusp.

Torres, F. C., & Vivas, G. P. M. (2009). Mitos, realidades y preguntas de investigación sobre los 'nativos digitales': Una revision. *Universitas Psychologica, 8* (2), 323-338. Retrieved from http://revistas.javeriana.edu.co/index.php/revPsycho/article/view/476/355

Trein, D. (2010). *Educação online em metaverso: A mediação pedagógica por meio da telepresença e da presença digital virtual via avatar em mundos digitais virtuais em 3 dimensões.* (Unpublished master's dissertation). Universidade do Vale do Rio dos Sinos, São Leopoldo, Brazil.

Trein, D., & Backes, L. (2009). A biologia do amor para uma educação sem distância. In Proceedings of 15º Congresso Internacional ABED de Educação a Distância (pp. 1-10). Fortaleza, Brazil: ABED.

Trein, D., & Schlemmer, E. (2009). Projetos de aprendizagem no contexto da web 2.0: Possibilidades para a prática pedagógica. *Revista E-Curriculum, 4*(2), 1-20. Retrieved from http://revistas.pucsp.br/index.php/curriculum/article/viewFile/3225/2147

Trivinho, E. (1996). Epistemologia em ruínas: A implosão da teoria da comunicação na experiência do cyberspace. *Revista da Famecos, (6)*, 73-81. Retrieved from http://www.pucrs.br/famecos/producao_cientifica/publicacoes_online/revistafamecos/fam5/epistemologia.html

Turkle, S. (1999). Fronteiras do real e do virtual: Entrevista concedida a federico casalegno. *Revista Famecos, (11)*, 117-123. Retrieved from http://revistaseletronicas.pucrs.br/ojs/index.php/revistafamecos/article/viewFile/3057/2335

Turkle, S. (1997). *A vida no écrã. A identidade na era da internet*. Lisboa: Relógio d'Água.

Valente, C., & Mattar, J. (2007). Second life e web 2.0 na educação: O potencial revolucionário das novas tecnologias. São Paulo, Brazil: Novatec Editora.

Varela, F. J. (1997). Prefácio de Francisco J. García Varela. In H. R. Maturana, & F. J. Varela (Eds.), De máquinas e seres vivos: Autopoiese - a organização do vivo. Porto Alegre, Brazil: Artes Médicas.

Varela, F. J. (2005). Conocer: Las ciencias cognitivas: Tendencias y perspectivas: Cartografia de las ideas actuales. Barcelona: Gedisa Editorial.

Varela, F. J. (1989). *Autonomie et connaissance - essai sur le vivant.* Paris: Éditions du Seuil.

Vaz, N. M. (2008). O linguagear é o modo de vida que nos tornou humanos. *Ciencia e Cultura, 60,* 62–67. Retrieved from http://cienciaecultura.bvs.br/pdf/cic/v60nspe1/a1160ns1.pdf

Veen, W., & Vrakking, B. (2009). *Homo zappiens: Educando na era digital.* Porto Alegre, Brazil: *The Art of Medication.*

Wagner, E. D. (1994). In support of a function definition of interaction. *American Journal of Distance Education, 8*(2), 6–29. doi:10.1080/08923649409526852

Wenger, E. (2006). Comunità di pratica: Apprendimento, significato, identità. Milano, Italy: Raffaello Cortina.

Wenger, E. (2009). *Communities of practice: A brief introduction.* Portland, OR: CPsquare. Retrieved from http://www.ewenger.com/theory/index.htm

Wenger, E., Mcdermott, R., & Snyder, W. (2007). Coltivare comunità di pratica. Milano, Italy: Guerini e Associati.

Yin, R. K. (2005). *Estudo de caso: Planejamento e métodos.* Porto Alegre, Brazil: *The Bookman.*

About the Authors

Eliane Schlemmer, Violet Ladybird (avatar), is a Scholar in Productivity in Research from CNPq. She is a Doctor in Informatics and Education and Master in Psychology granted by the Universidade Federal do Rio Grande do Sul – UFRGS. She graduated in Informatics from the Universidade do Vale do Rio dos Sinos – UNISINOS. She is currently a Researcher Professor in the Pos Graduation Program in Education at UNISINOS (ranked 7 by CAPES), in the Pedagogy Course and Digital Games Course. She is the leader of the Digital Education Research Group – GPe-dU UNISINOS/CNPq (www.unisinos. br/pesquisa/educacao-digital), since its creation in 2004 and a member of the Committee Board of the Catholic Higher Education Institutions Network (*Comitê Gestor da Rede de Instituições Católicas de Ensino Superior*) - RICESU. She is a concept maker and developer of software and educational digital virtual environments,such as: Virtual Learning Environment – AVA-UNISINOS, 3D Digital Virtual World AWSINOS (Eduverse Metaverse), UNISINOS Island and RICESU Island (Second Life), Communicative Agent MARIÁ – (developed together with the Pos Graduation Program in Applied Computing), and Virtual Learning Environment for mobile devices – COMTEXT® (Competencies in Context – developed in partnership with the Pos Graduation Program in Administration and with the Pos Graduation Program in Applied Computing). She is also a concept maker of the concept-technology Digital Virtual Space of Living and Sharing – ECODI and Hybrid and Multimodal Space of Living and Sharing - ECOHIM. The main areas she works in are research, development, teaching, advisement and consultancy in the Educational area: Digital Education, New modalities in Education (online Education and its derivations: e-learning, b-learning, m-learning, p-learning, u-learning), Virtual Learning Environments, Metaverses (Digital Virtual Worlds in 3 dimensions – Immersive Learning), Gamification, Digital Virtual Communities of Learning, and Project Methodology. She has been working, since 1989, in the area with experience in Children's Education, Elementary Education, High School, and Graduate Studies including Pos Graduation – in the specialization levels master's and doctorate and in advisement and consultancy in capacitating. Several of her articles have been published in journals and events throughout Brazil and abroad, besides being the author of books and chapters in books published in Brazil, Latin America, United States and Europe. She is the author of the books, *m-learning and u-learning: novas perspectivas da aprendizagem móvel e ubíqua*, edited by Pearson Prentice Hall, in 2011 and *Comunidades de Aprendizagem e de Prática em Metaversos*, edited by Cortez in 2012.

Luciana Backes, Luci Bebb (avatar), is a Scholar in the Post Doctoral State Abroad from CAPES at l'Université Paris Descartes – Paris V – Sorbonne, in the context of the Centre d'Études sur l'Actuel et le Quotidien (CEAQ). She is a Doctor in Education received from the Universidade do Vale do Rio dos Sinos (UNISINOS) and in Sciences de l'Éducation by Université Lumière Lyon 2. She received a Masters in Education from UNISINOS and Specialist in Informatics in Distance Education from the Universidade Federal do Rio Grande do Sul (UFRGS). She graduated in Pedagogy also from UNISINOS. She is currently a Researcher Professor in the Pos Graduation Program in Education from the Centro Universitário La Salle (UNILASSALE), in the Computing Course. She is a member of the Research Group in Digital Education – GPe-dU UNISINOS/CNPq, the Research Group of Contemporanea Culture, socialbilities and educational practices – UNILASALLE/CNPq, and the Groupe de Recherche sur la Technique et le Quotidien – GRETECH/Sorbonne. Through different groups, he develops research projects and theorization about Education, Educator's Formation, Pedagogical Practices, Digital Technologies, Emerging Digital Technologies (mainly in metaverses – 3D Digital Virtual World– in the context of digital technological Hybridism), Virtual Communities of Learning, Tribes, Structural Coupling in different domains, Configuring of Digital Virtual Spaces, Constitution of Co-existing of Digital Virtual Nature, and Emerging Culture in Digital Virtual Spaces. She has been working, since 1989, in the area with experience in Children Education, Elementary Education, High School, Professionalizing Education, and Graduate Studies including Pos Graduation – in the specialization levels of master's and doctorate. She has also worked in human resources in the capacitating and development processes. Several of her articles have been published in journals and events in Brazil and abroad, besides being the author of books and chapters in books published in Brazil. She is one of the authors of the book *Comunidades de Aprendizagem e de Prática em Metaversos*, edited by Cortez in 2012.

Index

A

Accommodation 14-15, 166, 181
Acculturation 298-299, 307
Adaptation 14-15, 39, 55, 85, 129, 137, 152-153,
    158, 160, 166, 172, 181, 202, 265, 286, 288
Alopoietic Machines 85, 138-139, 145-147, 150-
    151, 156, 158-161, 168, 306, 336
Alterity 187, 280, 288, 292, 335
Appropriate Conduct 276-277
Assimilation 10, 14, 24, 31, 166-167, 169-170, 181
Autopoiesis 10, 12, 43, 51, 85, 93, 145, 148-151,
    154, 156, 160-161, 171, 178, 265, 274, 287,
    315
Autopoietic Machines 85, 138-139, 145-147, 149-
    151, 159-162, 306, 336

C

Communities 1, 7, 13, 15-17, 21, 42, 48, 50, 59,
    61, 65, 68, 71, 83-84, 94, 96, 100, 113, 134,
    215-232, 234-235, 239, 250-251, 255, 259-260,
    270, 273, 283, 285, 288, 298, 300, 329, 335
Community of Practice 223-226, 229, 234
Cooperation 6-7, 17, 22, 41, 44, 57, 59, 129, 132,
    157, 162, 164-165, 175-178, 181, 186-187,
    189, 195, 211, 216, 218-219, 222, 225-227,
    232, 234, 239-240, 311, 326
Culture of Real Virtuality 4, 220, 236-237, 247-249,
    339
Cyberculture 93, 282-283, 293, 300, 335
Cyberspace 50, 55-56, 60, 68, 83, 86-87, 96, 107,
    142, 168, 186, 219, 250, 258, 282-283, 293,
    300, 304-305

D

Dialogical relationship 1, 19-20
Digital Education Research Group UNISINOS 185,
    188, 191, 270, 272, 274, 279, 296, 309-310,
    316-317, 319, 329-331, 335-336, 339
Digitally Naturalized 1, 18-20, 24
Digital Technological Hybridism 250, 254, 268-270,
    272, 274, 276, 290, 295, 302, 304, 327
Digital Virtual Collaborating Spaces 229, 274, 276,
    320, 326, 330, 339
Digital Virtual Communities 215-216, 218-223,
    225, 227-232, 234, 259-260, 283, 300
Digital Virtual Communities of Learning and Prac-
    tice 215-216, 225, 227-232, 234
Digital Virtual Communities of Practice 223, 225,
    228-229, 234
Digital Virtual Culture 136, 278-279, 282-283, 287-
    291, 293, 298
Digital Virtual Identity 49, 64, 70, 82-83, 92, 94, 97,
    100, 110, 115-117, 120, 124, 273, 279, 288-
    290, 305
Digital virtual learning and practice communities
    215
Digital Virtual Learning Communities 215, 220-
    222, 225, 229, 235
Digital Virtual Presence 50, 65, 69-70, 74-75, 83,
    86, 94, 102-104, 106-114, 116, 119-122, 124,
    127, 135, 139, 158, 187, 191, 216, 219-220,
    225, 229, 235, 240, 259, 287, 291, 302, 313,
    331
Digital Virtual Self 8, 48, 64, 82-83, 94, 96-97, 100,
    110, 116-117, 124, 238, 241, 279, 284, 288-289